# Ranma 1/2

2

# Ranma 1/2
## 2-in-1 Edition
## Vol. 1

STORY AND ART BY
# RUMIKO TAKAHASHI

RANMA 1/2 Vol. 1, 2
by Rumiko TAKAHASHI
© 1988 Rumiko TAKAHASHI
All rights reserved.
Original Japanese edition published by SHOGAKUKAN.
English translation rights in the United States of America,
Canada, the United Kingdom and Ireland arranged with
SHOGAKUKAN.

English Adaptation/Gerard Jones, Matt Thorn
Touch-up Art & Lettering/Deron Bennett
Design/Yukiko Whitley
Editors/(First Edition) Satoru Fujii, Trish Ledoux; (Second Edition)
Julie Davis; (2-in-1 Edition) Hope Donovan

Printed in the U.S.A.

Published by VIZ Media, LLC
P.O. Box 77010
San Francisco, CA 94107

10 9 8 7 6 5 4 3 2 1
First printing, March 2014

www.viz.com

WWW.SHONENSUNDAY.COM

# Ranma 1/2

## 1·2

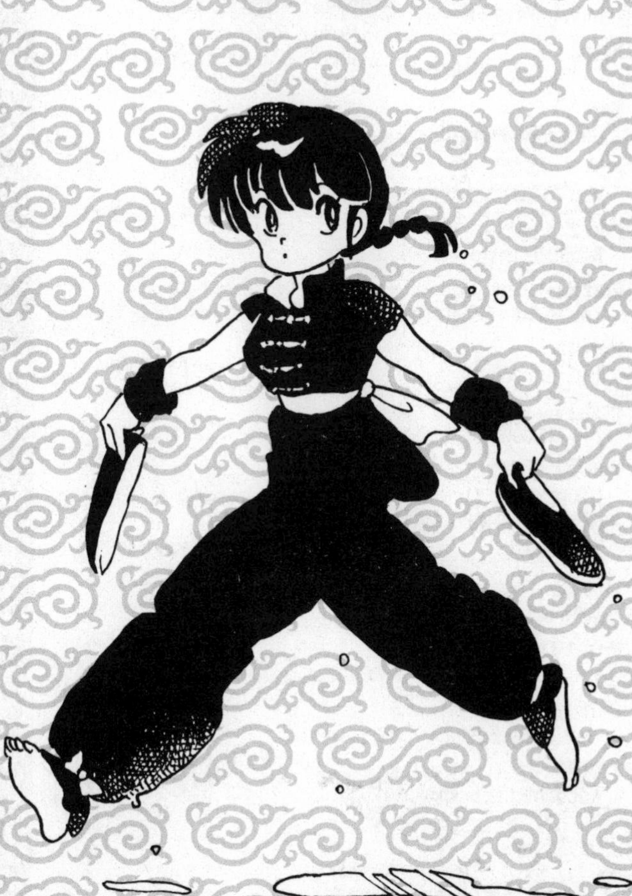

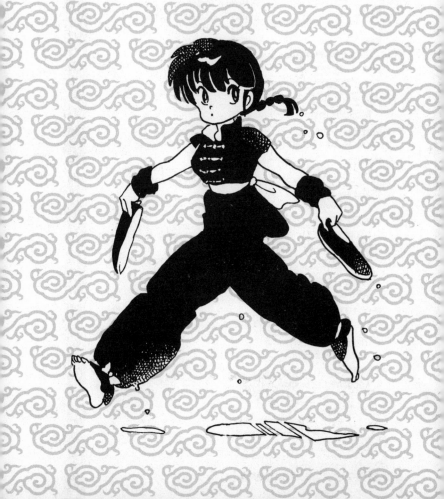

# Contents

**Part 1**
Here's Ranma ............................................. 5

**Part 2**
Ranma's Secret ..................................... 35

**Part 3**
I Hate Men! ............................................. 59

**Part 4**
Never, Never, Never.................................... 79

**Part 5**
To the Tree-Borne Kettle-Girl ...................... 99

**Part 6**
Body and Soul.......................................... 119

**Part 7**
You'll Understand Soon Enough ............... 139

**Part 8**
Because There's a Girl He Likes ............... 159

**Part 9**
You're Cute When You Smile .................... 181

**Part 10**
The Hunter ............................................. 201

**Part 11**
Bread Feud ........................................... 221

**Part 12**
Showdown................................................ 241

**Part 13**
A Bad Cut............................................... 261

**Part 14**
Who Says You're Cute?!.......................... 281

**Part 15**
The Transformation of Ryoga.................... 301

**Part 16**
He's Got a Beef ...................................... 321

**Part 17**
Kodachi, the Black Rose.......................... 341

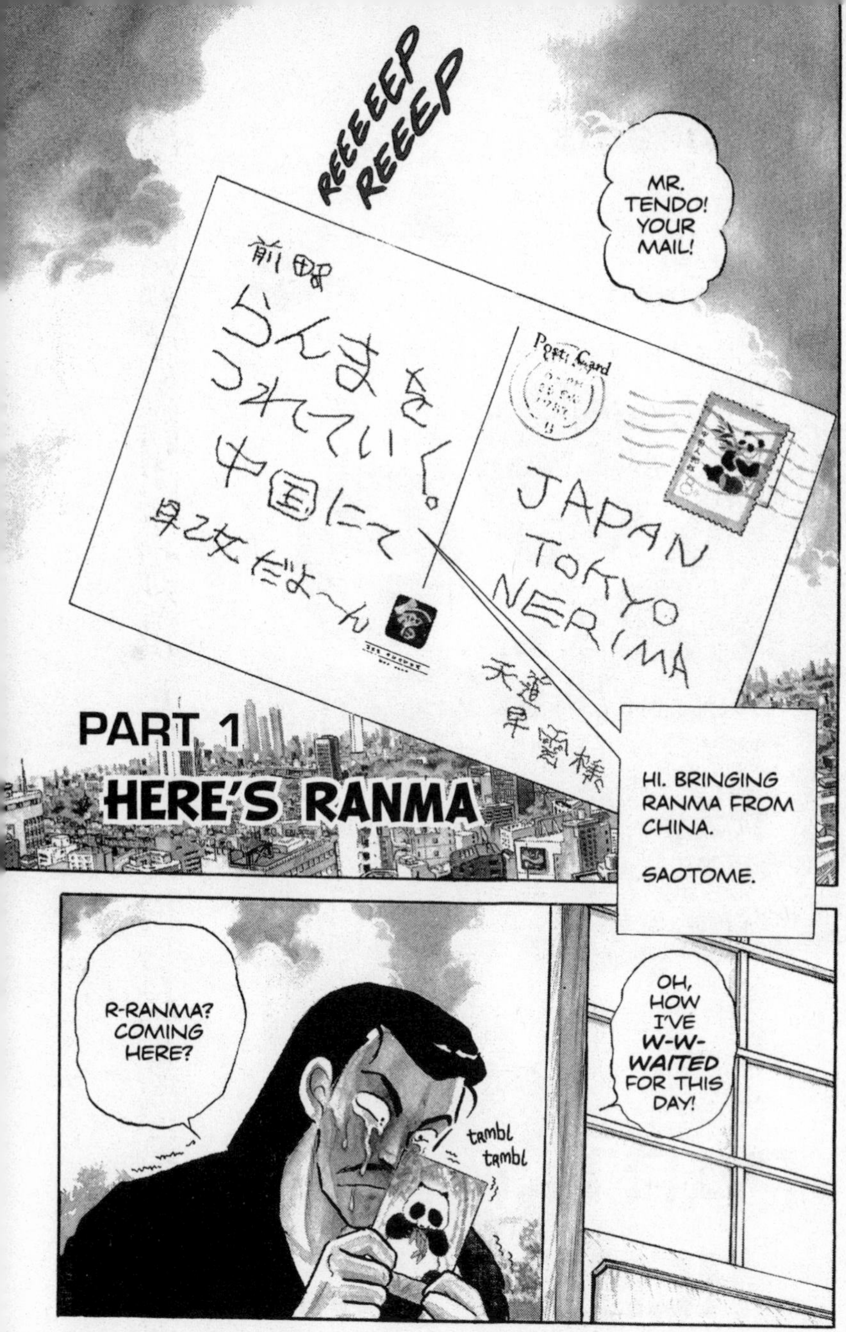
REEEEEP REEEEP
MR. TENDO! YOUR MAIL!
前略
らんまをつれていく。
中国にて
早乙女だよ〜ん
Post Card
JAPAN TOKYO NERIMA
天道早雲様
PART 1
HERE'S RANMA
HI. BRINGING RANMA FROM CHINA.
SAOTOME.
OH, HOW I'VE W-W-WAITED FOR THIS DAY!
R-RANMA? COMING HERE?
trmbl trmbl

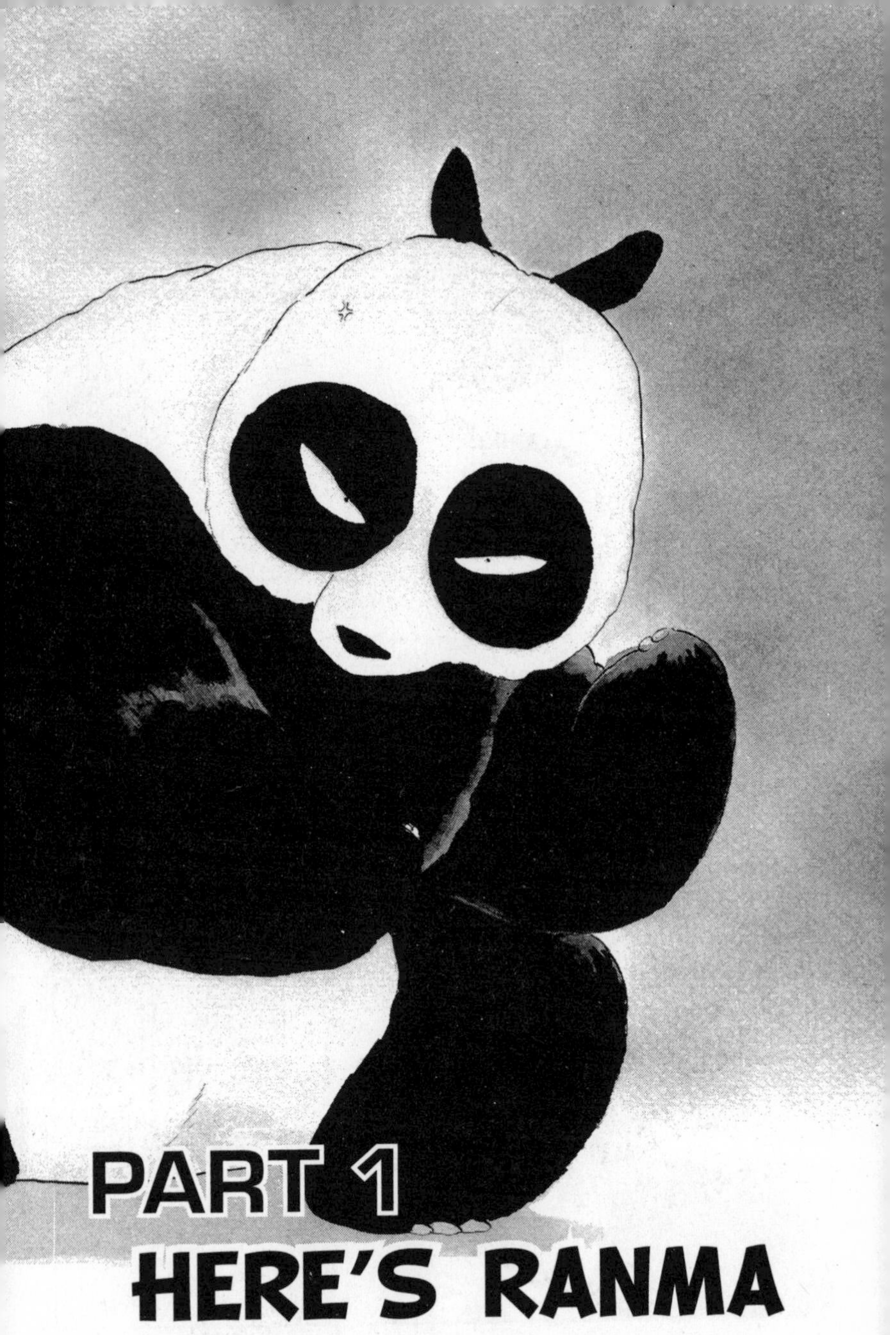

# PART 1
# HERE'S RANMA

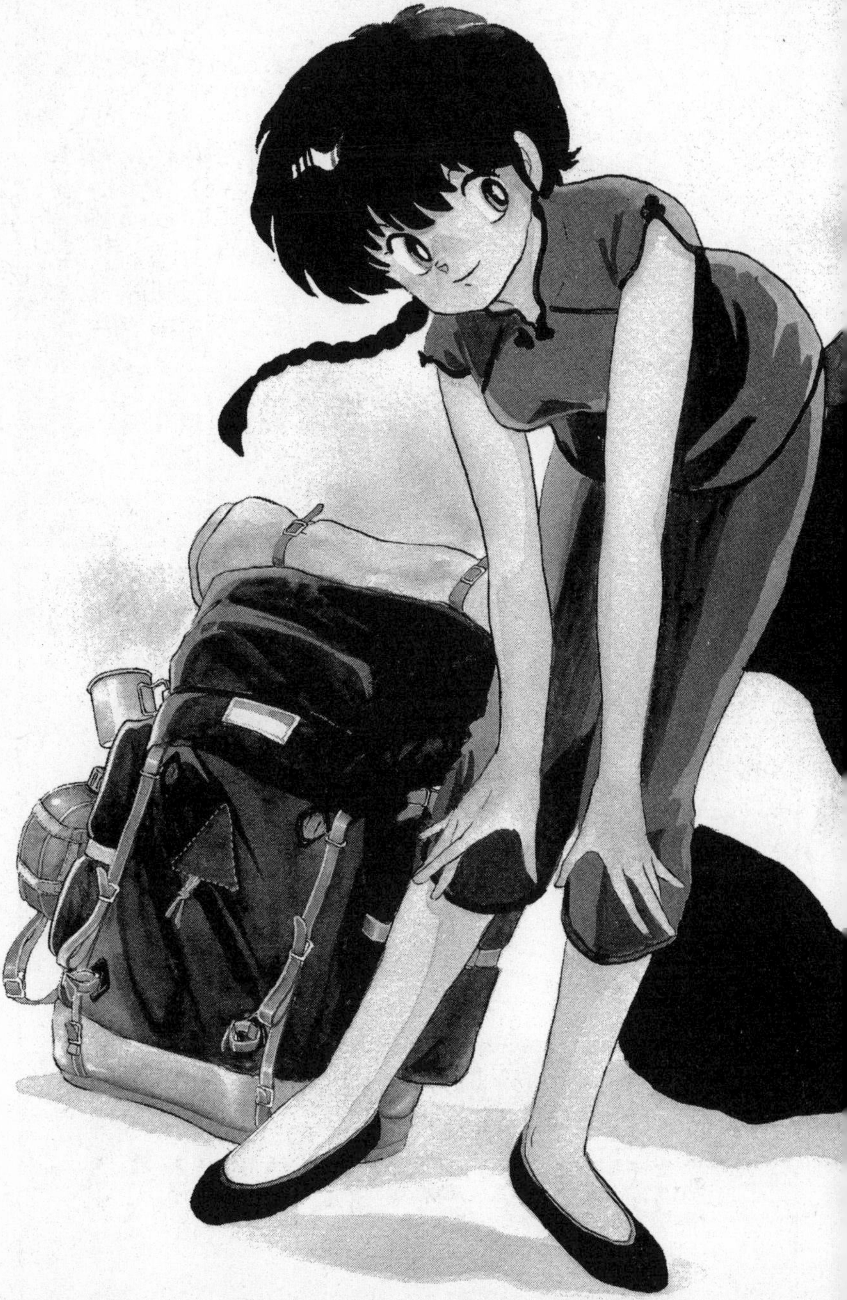

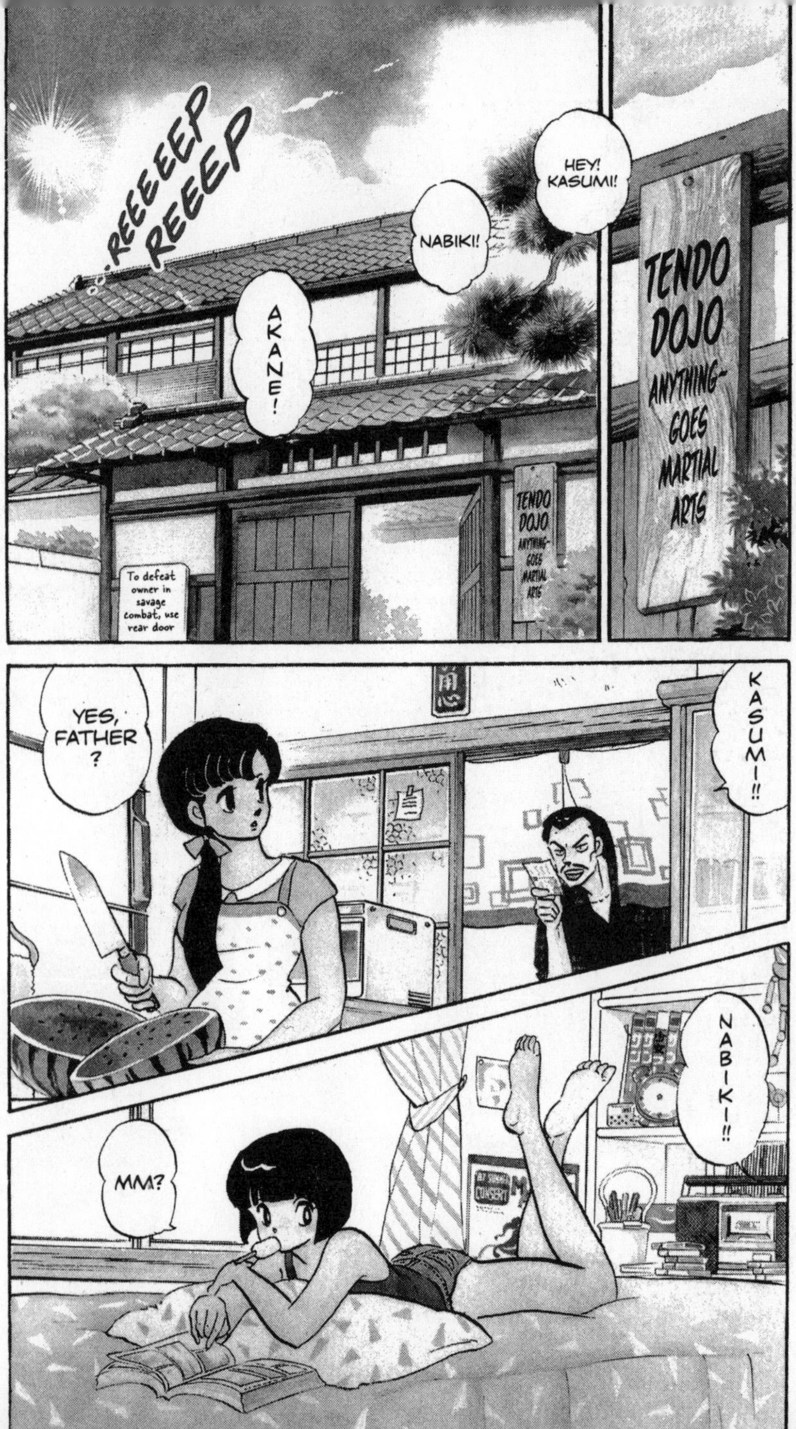
TENDO DOJO ANYTHING-GOES MARTIAL ARTS
REEEEEP REEEP
HEY! KASUMI!
NABIKI!
AKANE!
TENDO DOJO ANYTHING-GOES MARTIAL ARTS
To defeat owner in savage combat, use rear door
KASUMI!!
YES, FATHER?
NABIKI!!
MM?

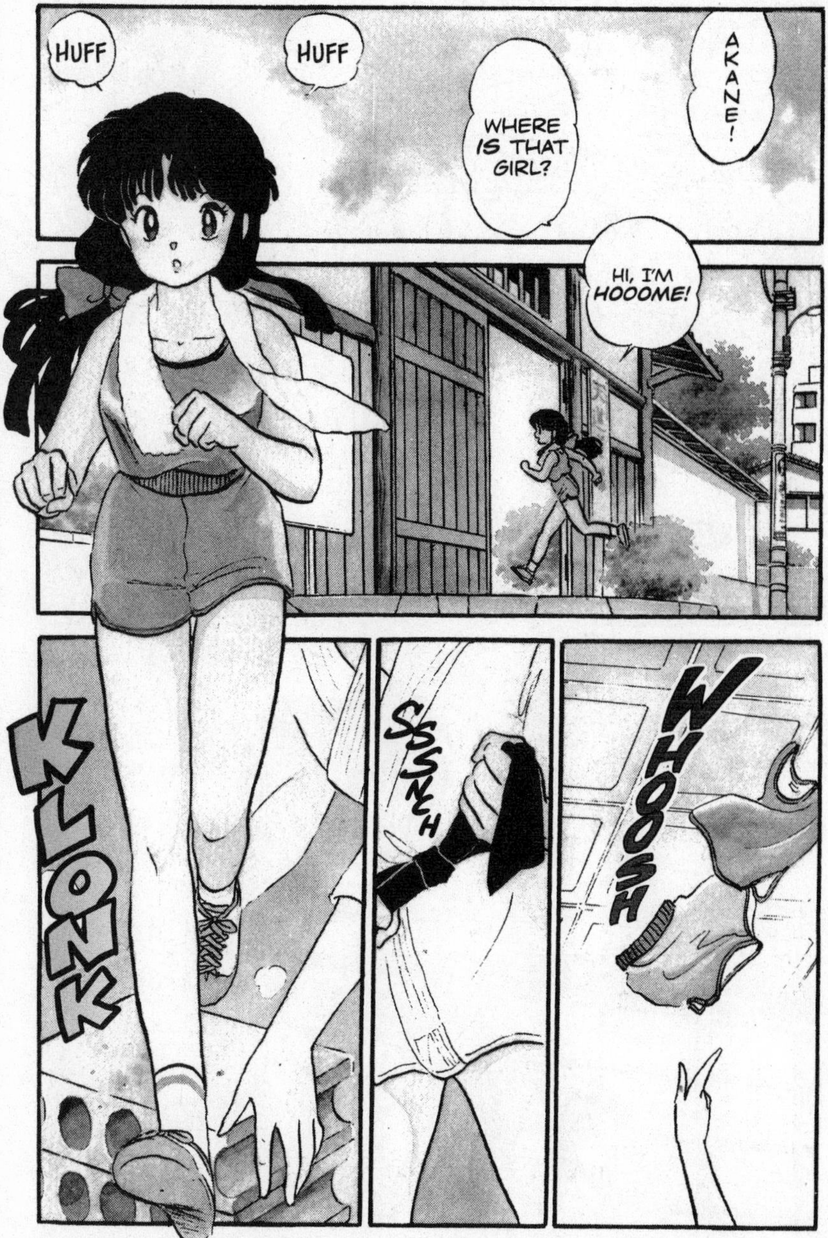
AKANE!
WHERE IS THAT GIRL?
HUFF
HUFF
HI, I'M HOOOME!
WHOOSH
SSSNCH
KLONK

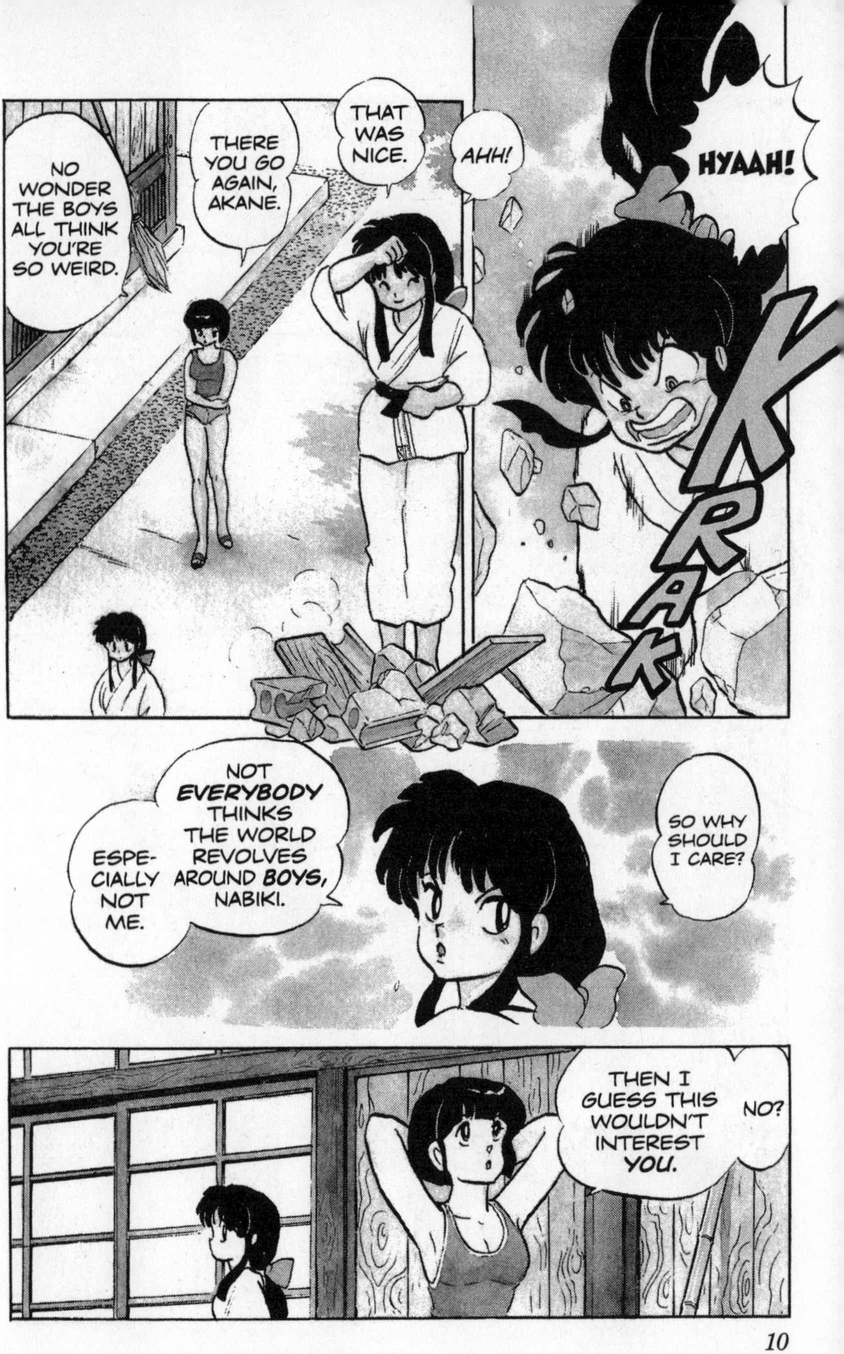
HYAAH!
KRAK
AHH!
THAT WAS NICE.
THERE YOU GO AGAIN, AKANE.
NO WONDER THE BOYS ALL THINK YOU'RE SO WEIRD.
SO WHY SHOULD I CARE?
NOT **EVERYBODY** THINKS THE WORLD REVOLVES AROUND **BOYS**, NABIKI.
ESPE-CIALLY NOT ME.
THEN I GUESS THIS WOULDN'T INTEREST **YOU**.
NO?

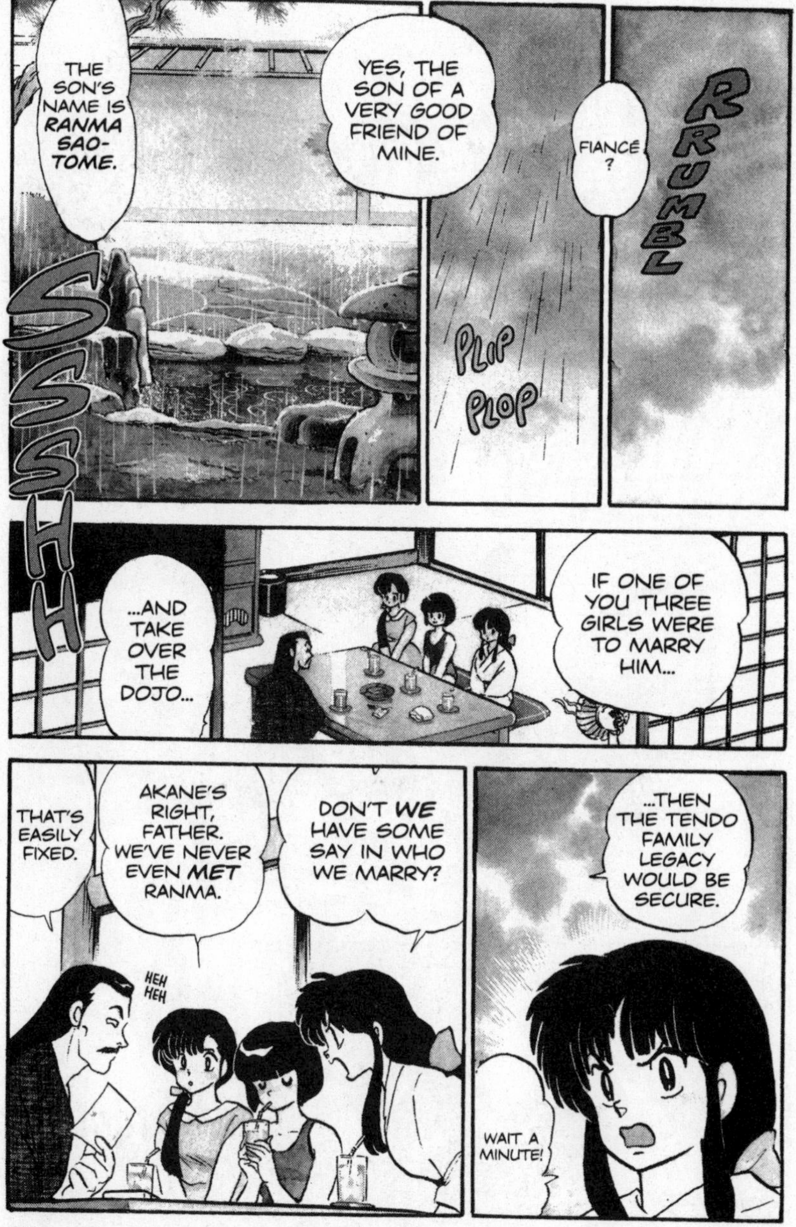
RRUMBL
FIANCÉ?
PLIP PLOP
YES, THE SON OF A VERY GOOD FRIEND OF MINE.
THE SON'S NAME IS RANMA SAOTOME.
SSSSHHH
IF ONE OF YOU THREE GIRLS WERE TO MARRY HIM...
...AND TAKE OVER THE DOJO...
...THEN THE TENDO FAMILY LEGACY WOULD BE SECURE.
WAIT A MINUTE!
DON'T WE HAVE SOME SAY IN WHO WE MARRY?
AKANE'S RIGHT, FATHER. WE'VE NEVER EVEN MET RANMA.
THAT'S EASILY FIXED.
HEH HEH

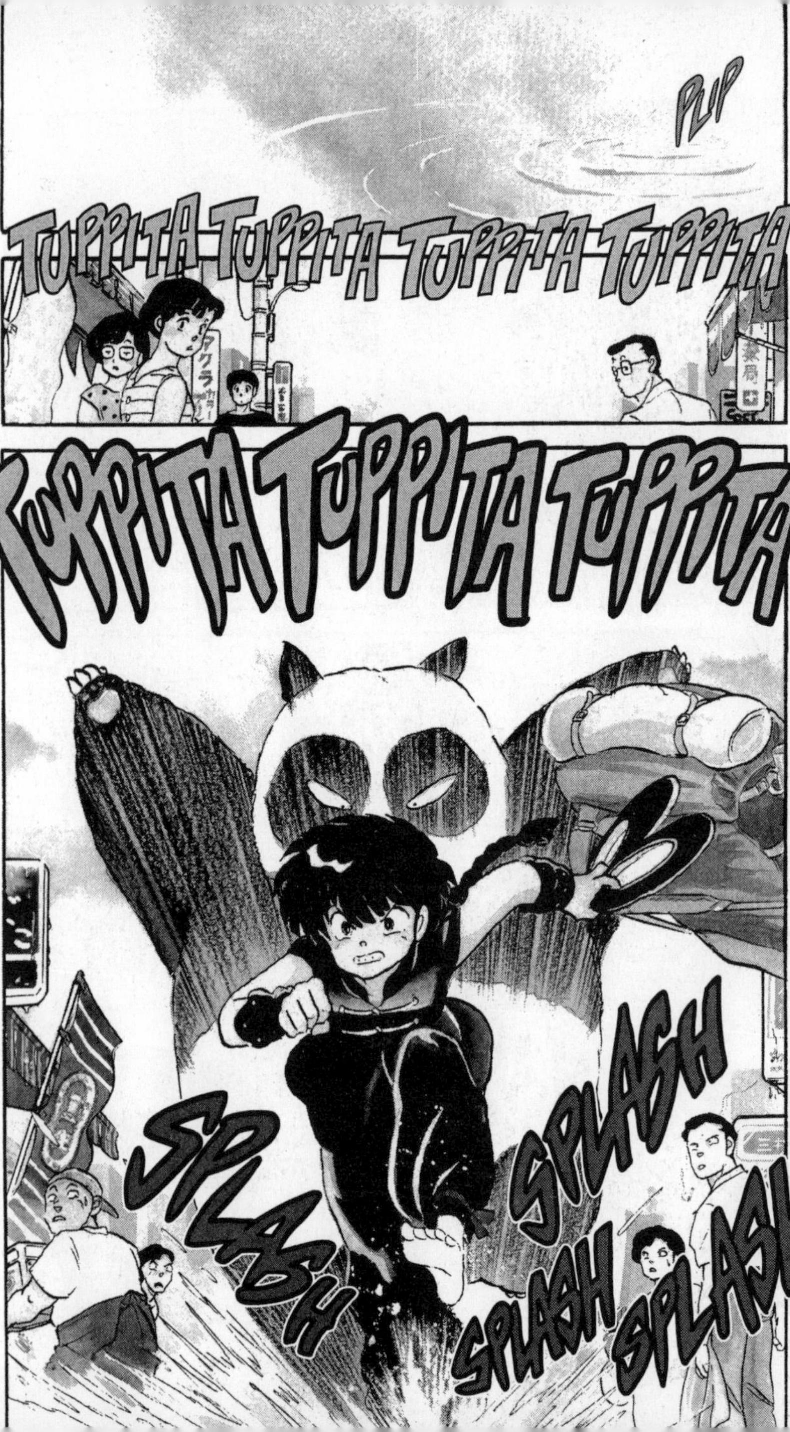
PLIP
TUPPITA TUPPITA TUPPITA TUPPITA
TUPPITA TUPPITA TUPPITA
SPLASH
SPLASH
SPLASH
SPLASH
SPLASH

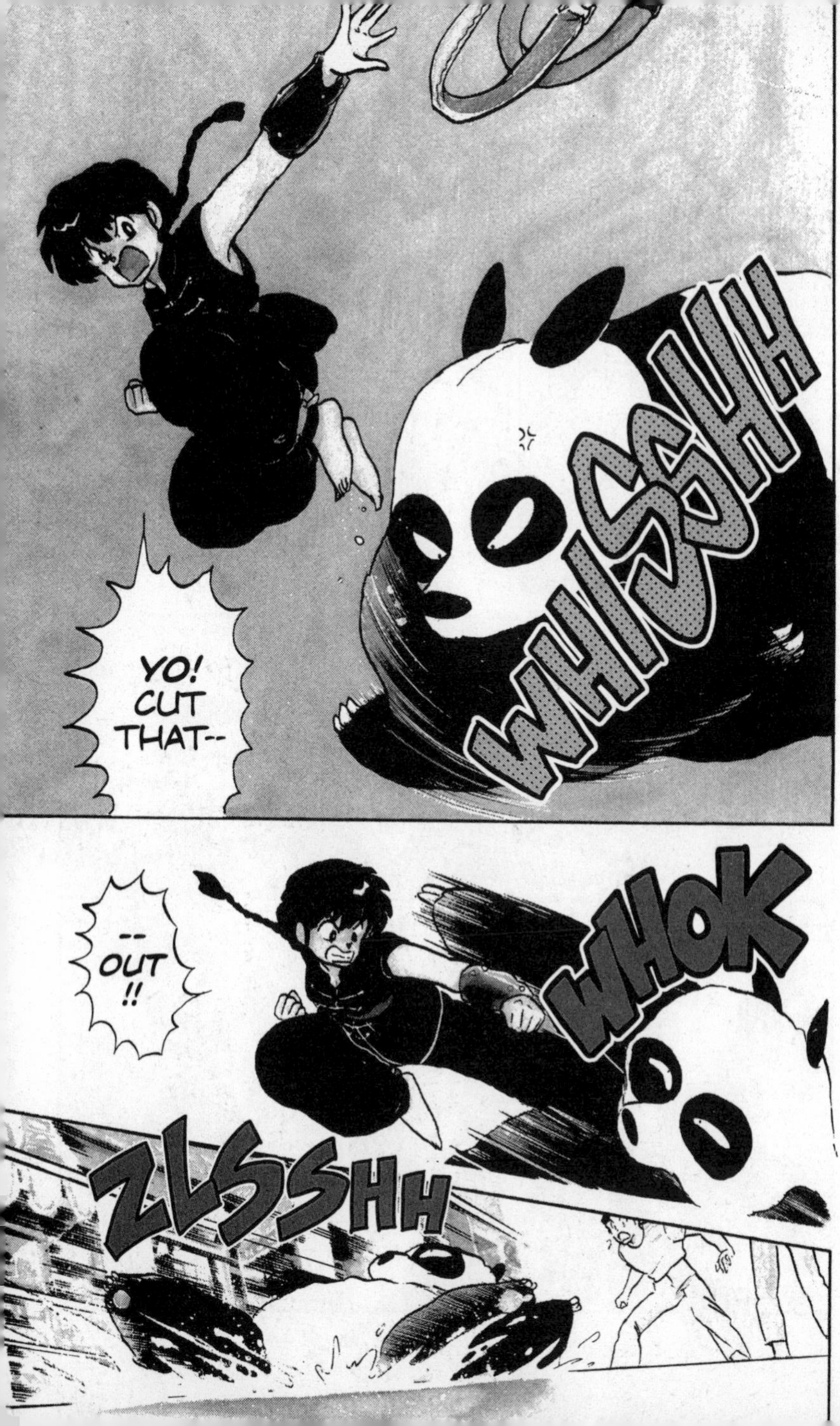
WHISSHH
YO! CUT THAT--
WHOK
--OUT!!
ZLSSHH

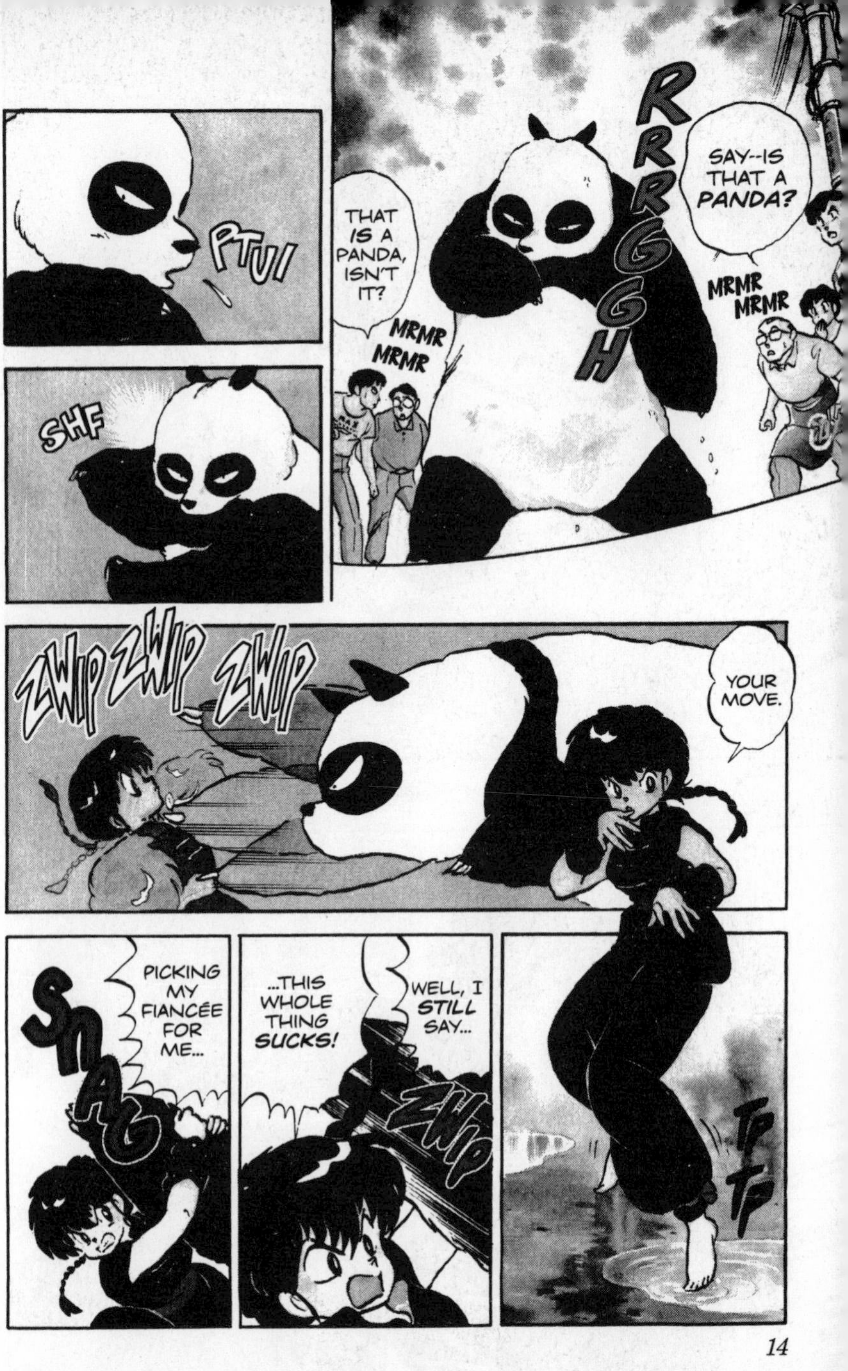
SAY--IS THAT A PANDA?
MRMR MRMR
RRRGGH
THAT IS A PANDA, ISN'T IT?
MRMR MRMR
PTUI
SHF
YOUR MOVE.
ZWIP ZWIP ZWIP
TP TP
WELL, I STILL SAY...
...THIS WHOLE THING SUCKS!
ZWIP
PICKING MY FIANCÉE FOR ME...
SNAG

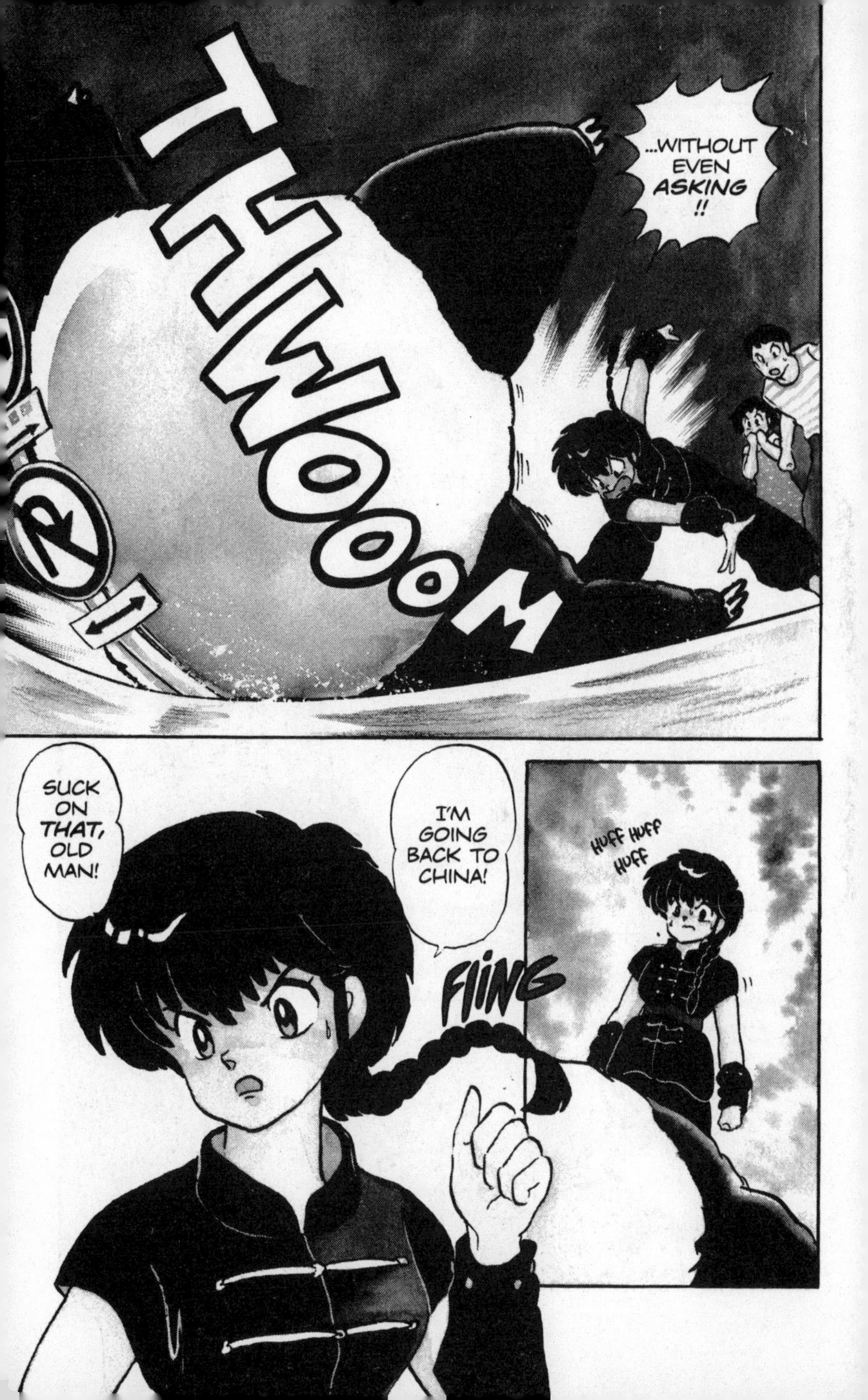
...WITHOUT EVEN ASKING !!
THWOOOOM
I'M GOING BACK TO CHINA!
HUFF HUFF HUFF
SUCK ON THAT, OLD MAN!
FLING

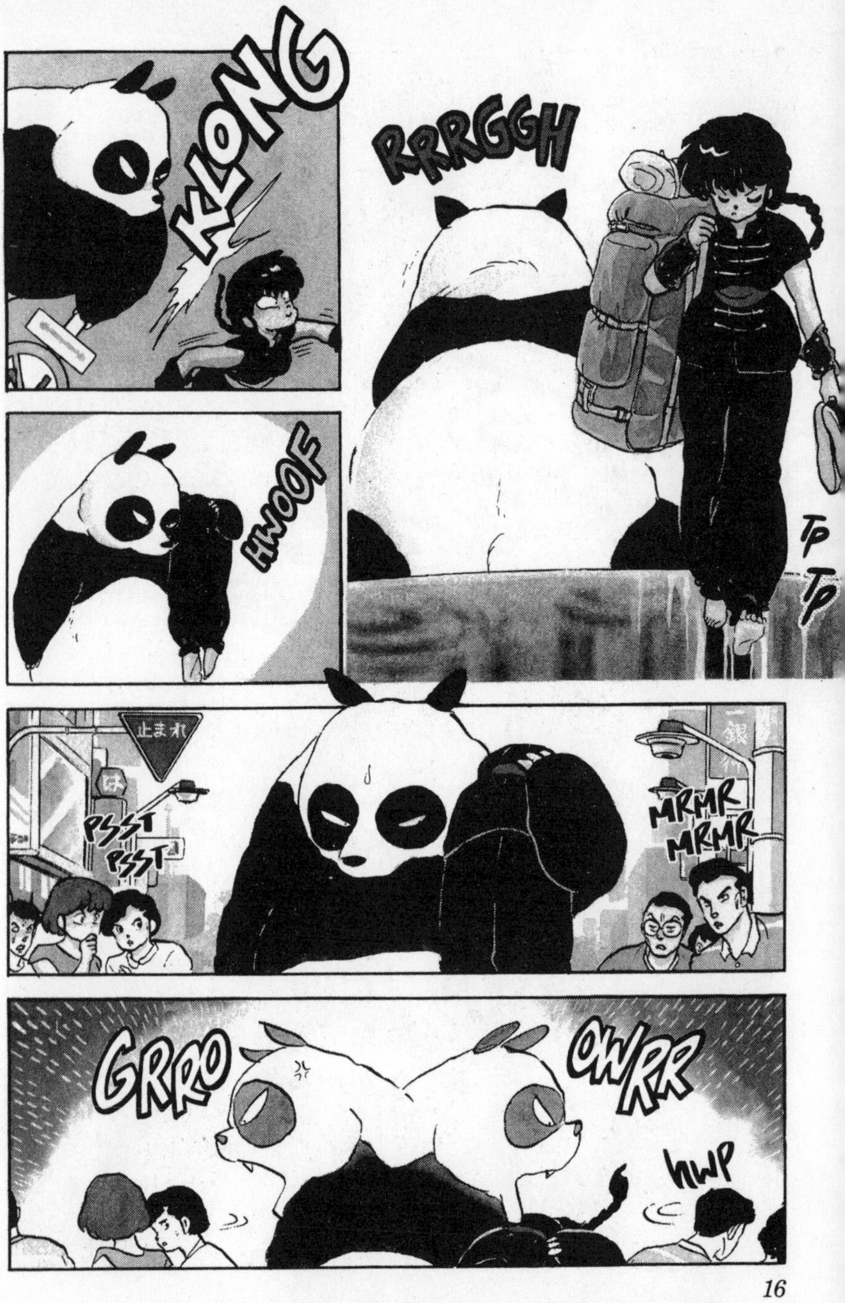
RRRGGH
Tp Tp
KLONG
HWOOF
MRMR MRMR
止まれ
PSSST PSSST
GRRO OWRR
HWP

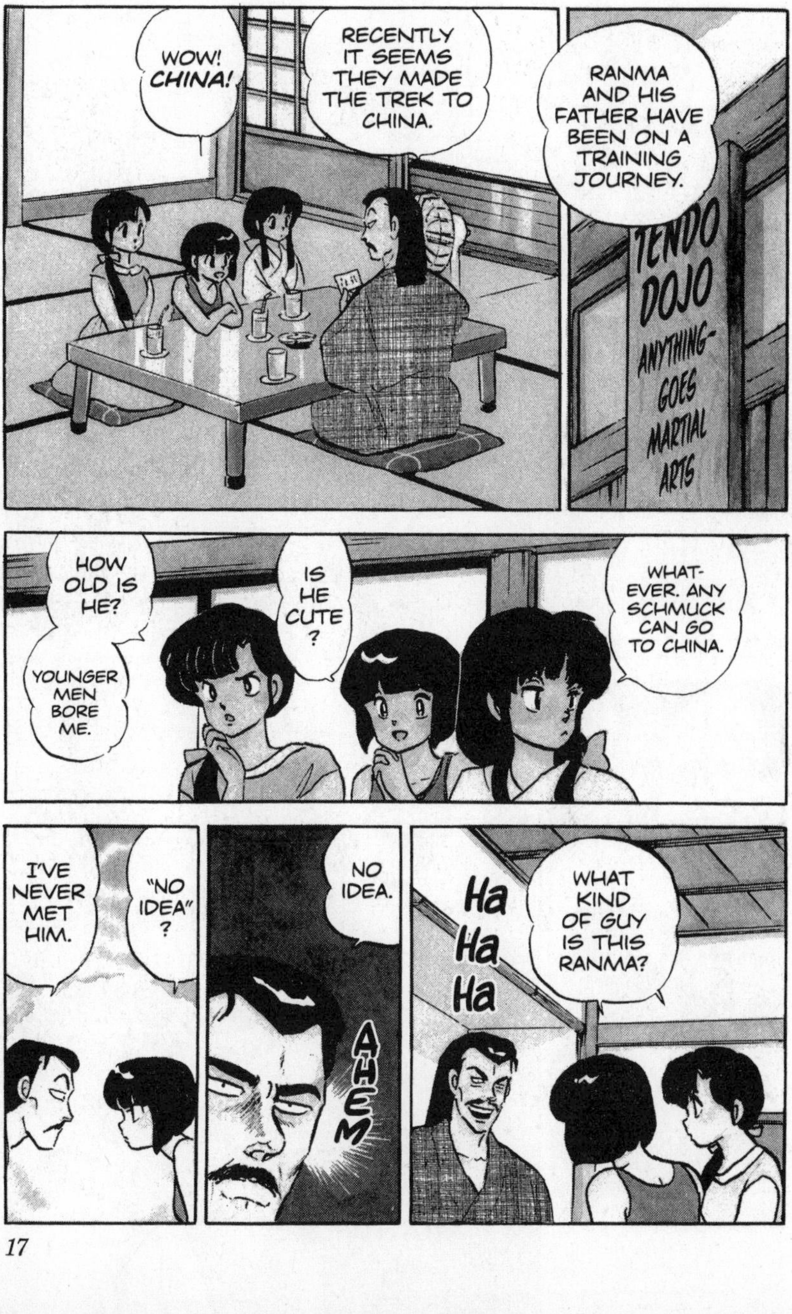
RANMA AND HIS FATHER HAVE BEEN ON A TRAINING JOURNEY.
TENDO DOJO
ANYTHING-GOES MARTIAL ARTS
RECENTLY IT SEEMS THEY MADE THE TREK TO CHINA.
WOW! CHINA!
WHAT-EVER. ANY SCHMUCK CAN GO TO CHINA.
IS HE CUTE?
HOW OLD IS HE?
YOUNGER MEN BORE ME.
WHAT KIND OF GUY IS THIS RANMA?
Ha Ha Ha
NO IDEA.
AHEM
"NO IDEA"?
I'VE NEVER MET HIM.

SAOTOME, MY FRIEND! WE'VE BEEN EXPECTING YOU!

TUMP TUMP TUMP

OOOH! IT MUST BE RANMA!

WE HAVE VISITORS!

HM?

LEGGO, YOU OLD FOOL!

POW BOP

HOW DEPRESSING. BOYS!

OH, I HOPE HE'S OLDER!

Tp Tp

TOPITA TOPITA

YOU'RE SCARING 'EM SPITLESS!

HEY! YO!

TOPITA TOPITA

THOOM THOOM

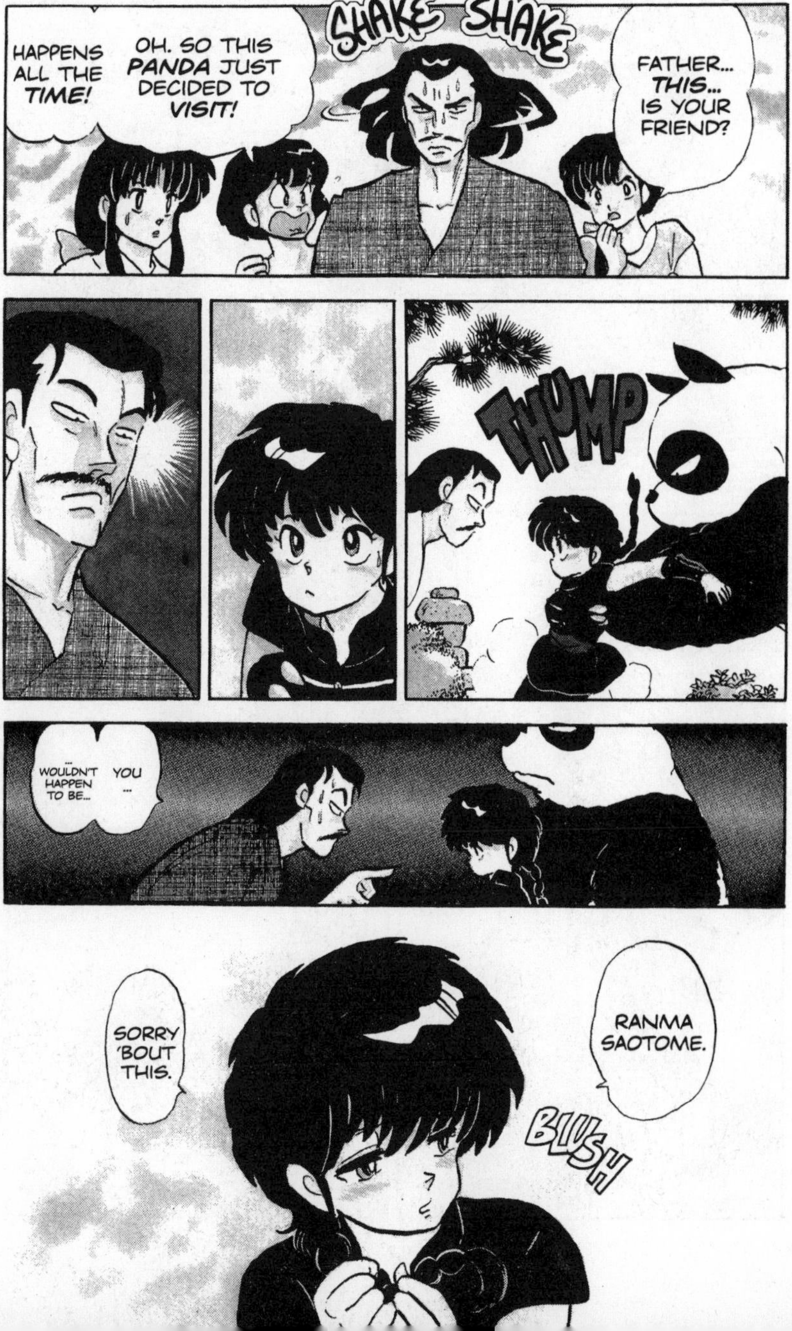
FATHER... THIS... IS YOUR FRIEND?
SHAKE SHAKE
OH. SO THIS PANDA JUST DECIDED TO VISIT!
HAPPENS ALL THE TIME!
THUMP
YOU ... ...WOULDN'T HAPPEN TO BE...
RANMA SAOTOME.
BLUSH
SORRY 'BOUT THIS.

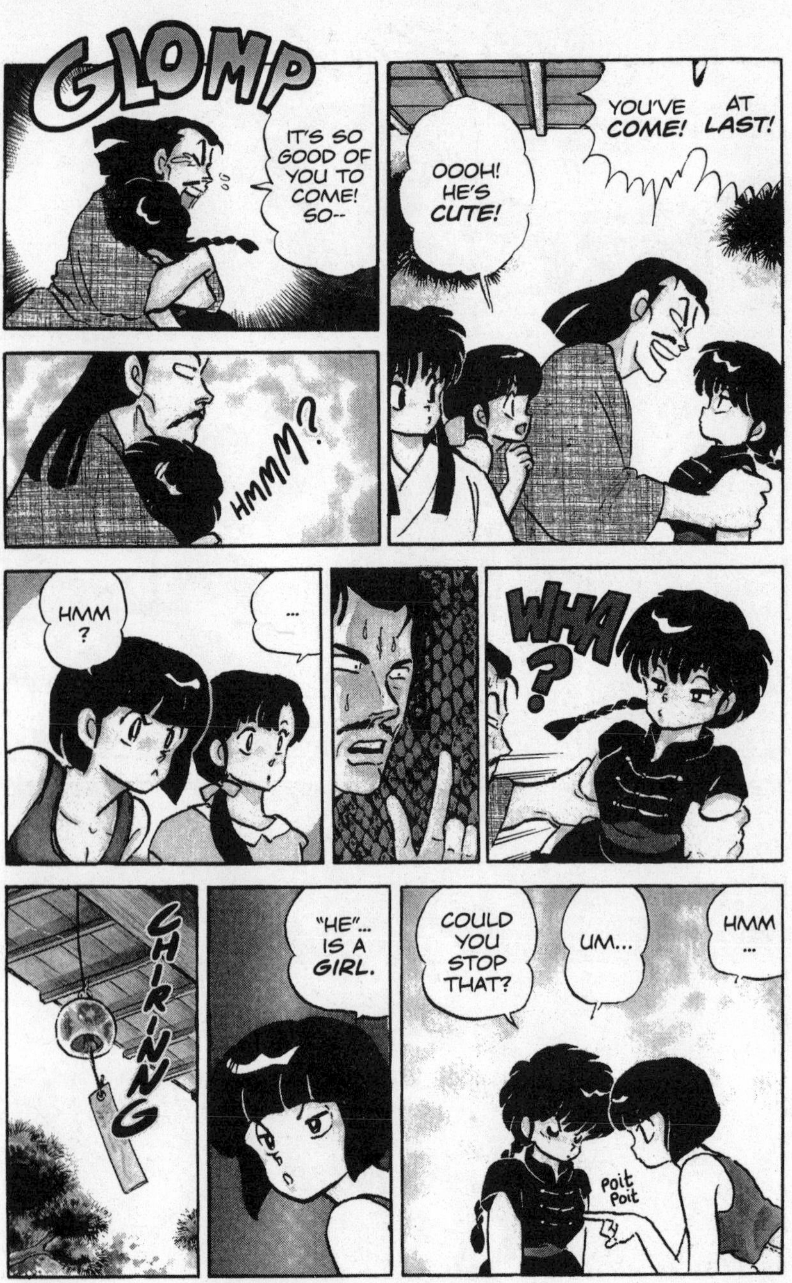
YOU'VE COME! AT LAST!
OOOH! HE'S CUTE!
GLOMP
IT'S SO GOOD OF YOU TO COME! SO--
HMMM?
WHA?
...
HMM ?
HMM ...
UM...
COULD YOU STOP THAT?
Poit Poit
"HE"... IS A GIRL.
CHIRINNG

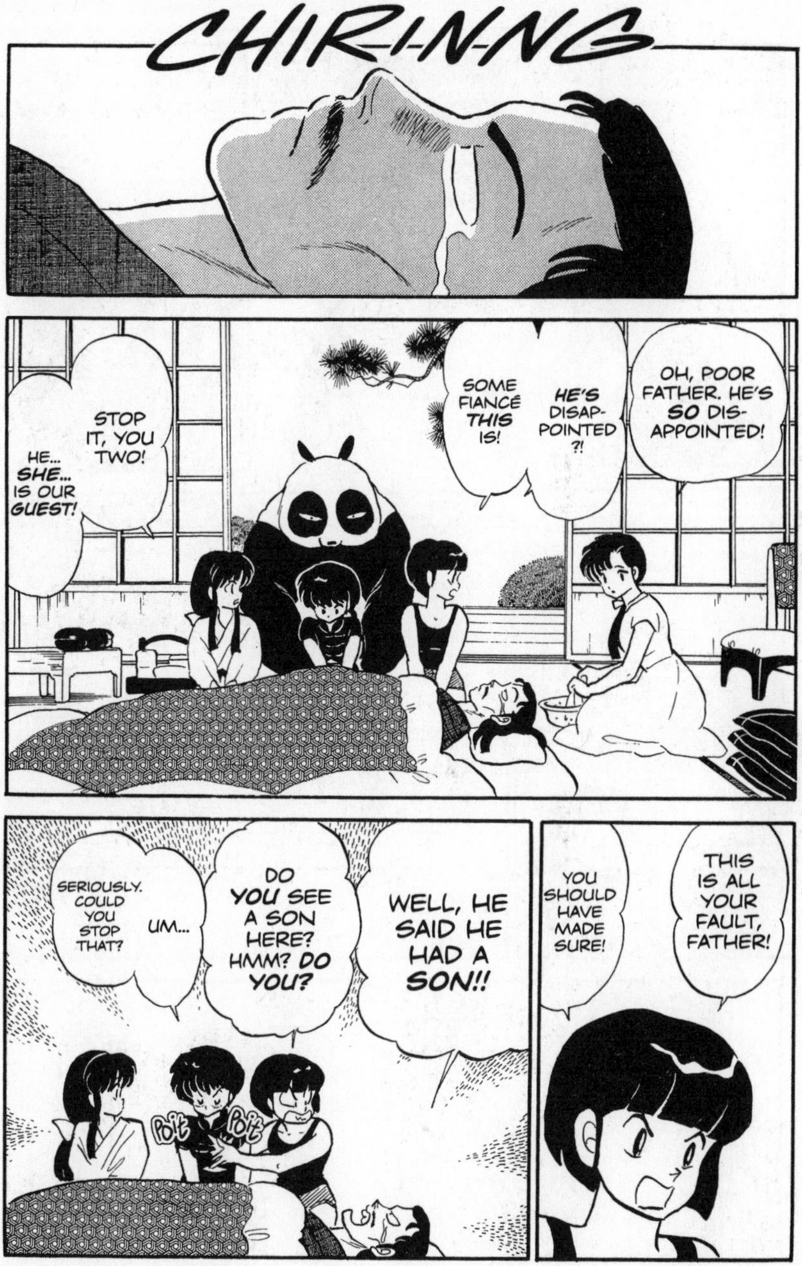
CHIRINNG
OH, POOR FATHER. HE'S SO DISAPPOINTED!
HE'S DISAPPOINTED?!
SOME FIANCÉ THIS IS!
STOP IT, YOU TWO!
HE... SHE... IS OUR GUEST!
THIS IS ALL YOUR FAULT, FATHER!
YOU SHOULD HAVE MADE SURE!
WELL, HE SAID HE HAD A SON!!
DO YOU SEE A SON HERE? HMM? DO YOU?
UM...
SERIOUSLY. COULD YOU STOP THAT?
Poit
Poit

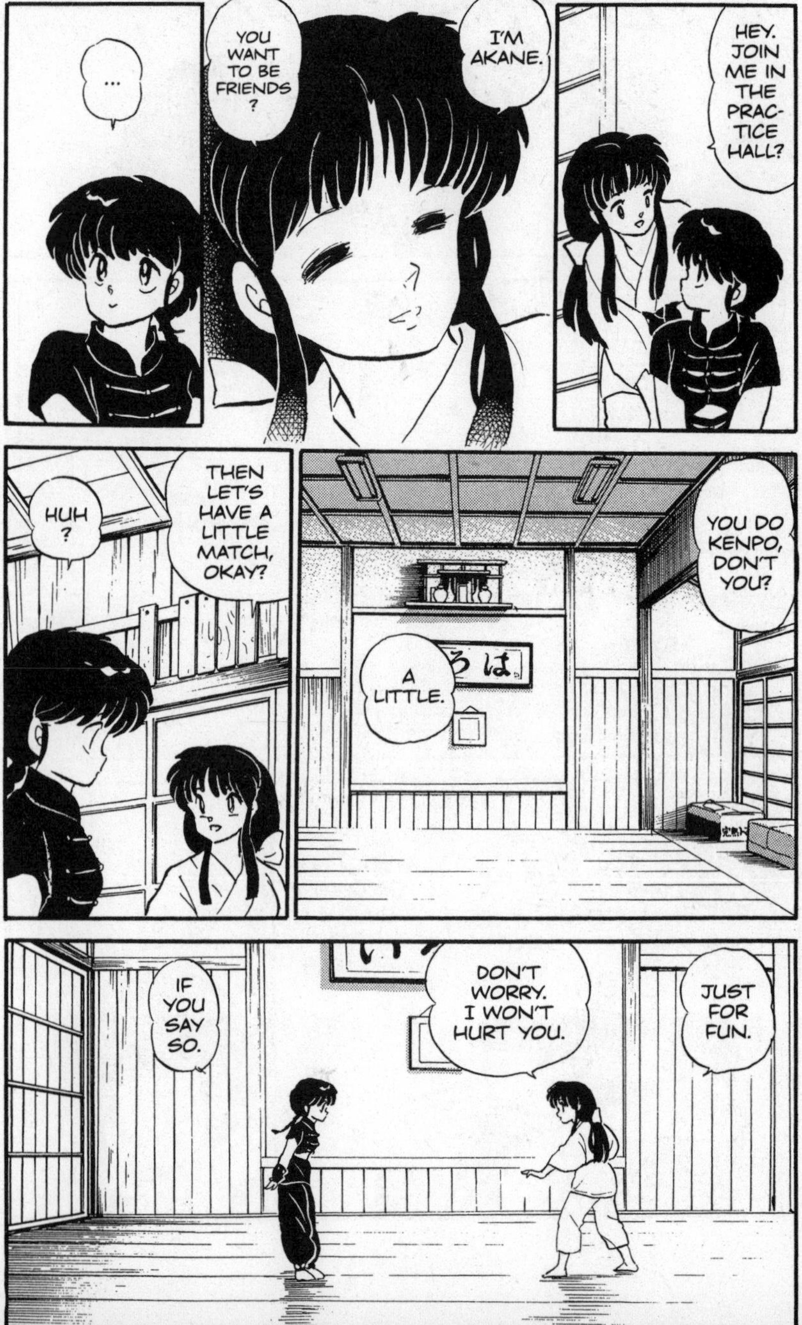
HEY. JOIN ME IN THE PRAC-TICE HALL?
I'M AKANE.
YOU WANT TO BE FRIENDS?
...
YOU DO KENPO, DON'T YOU?
A LITTLE.
THEN LET'S HAVE A LITTLE MATCH, OKAY?
HUH?
JUST FOR FUN.
DON'T WORRY. I WON'T HURT YOU.
IF YOU SAY SO.

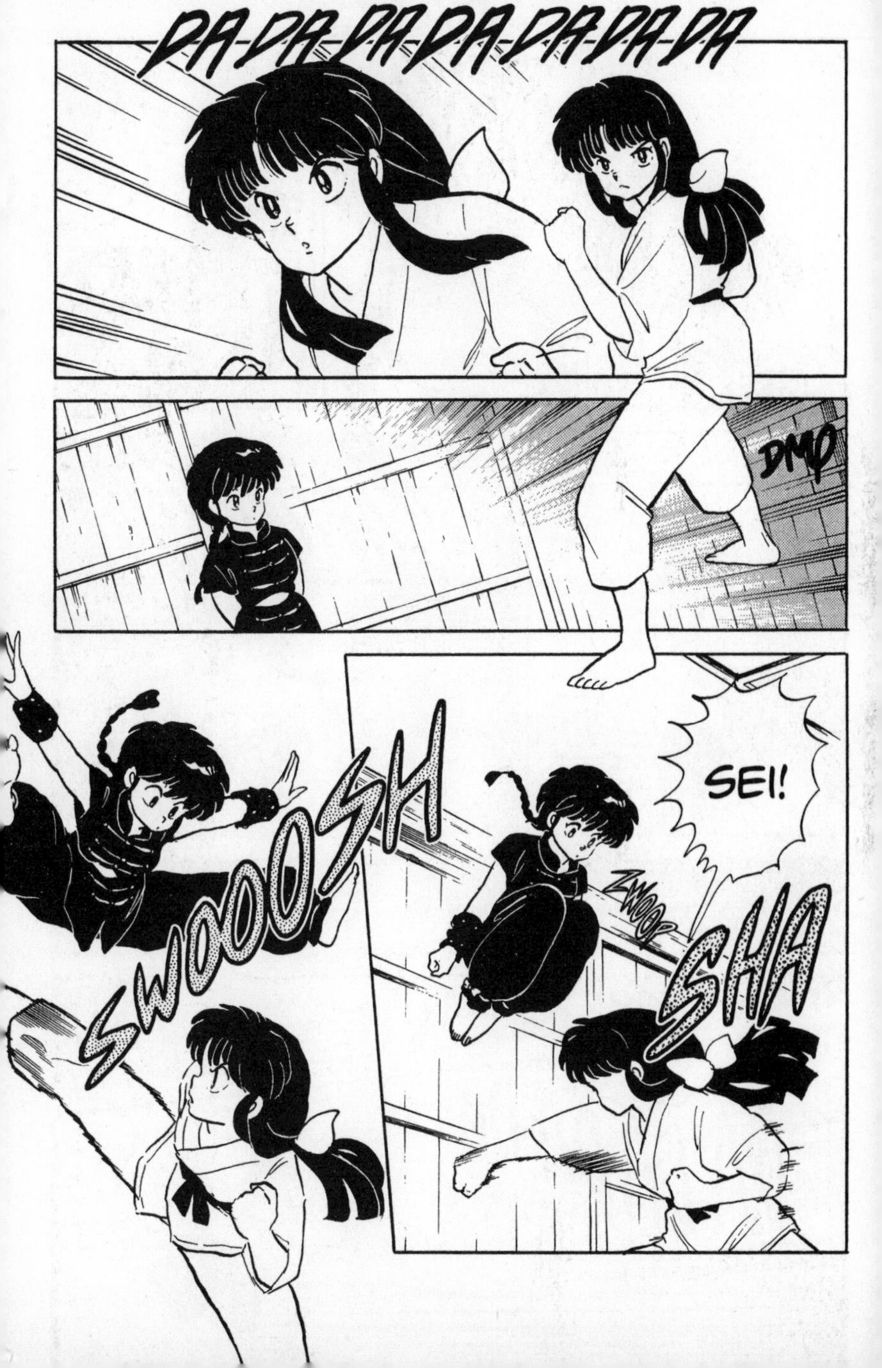
DA-DA-DA-DA-DA-DA-DA-DA
DMP
SEI!
ZWOOP
SHA
SWOOOSH

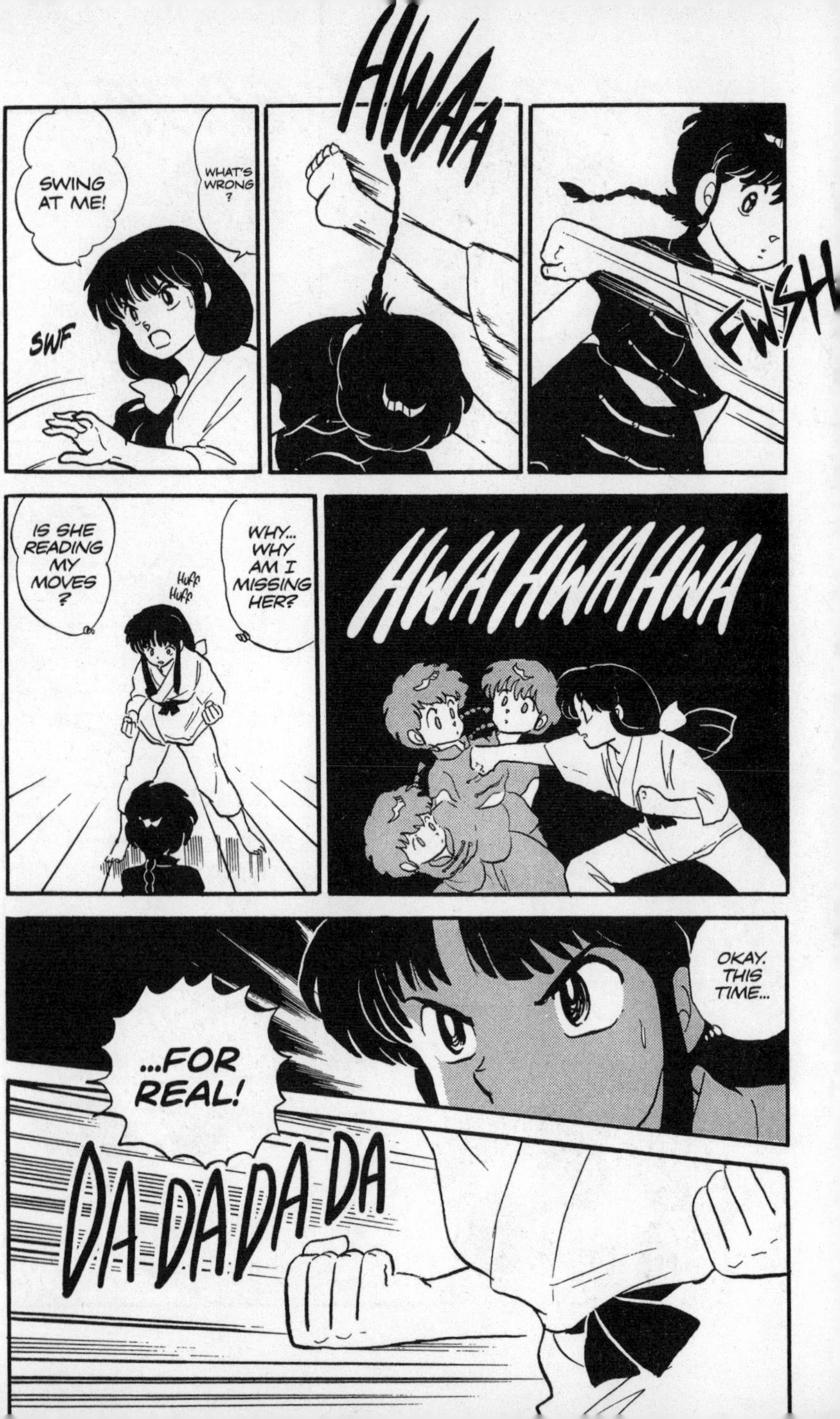
FWSH
HWAA
WHAT'S WRONG?
SWING AT ME!
SWF
HWA HWA HWA HWA
WHY... WHY AM I MISSING HER?
Huff Huff
IS SHE READING MY MOVES?
OKAY. THIS TIME...
...FOR REAL!
DA DA DA DA DA

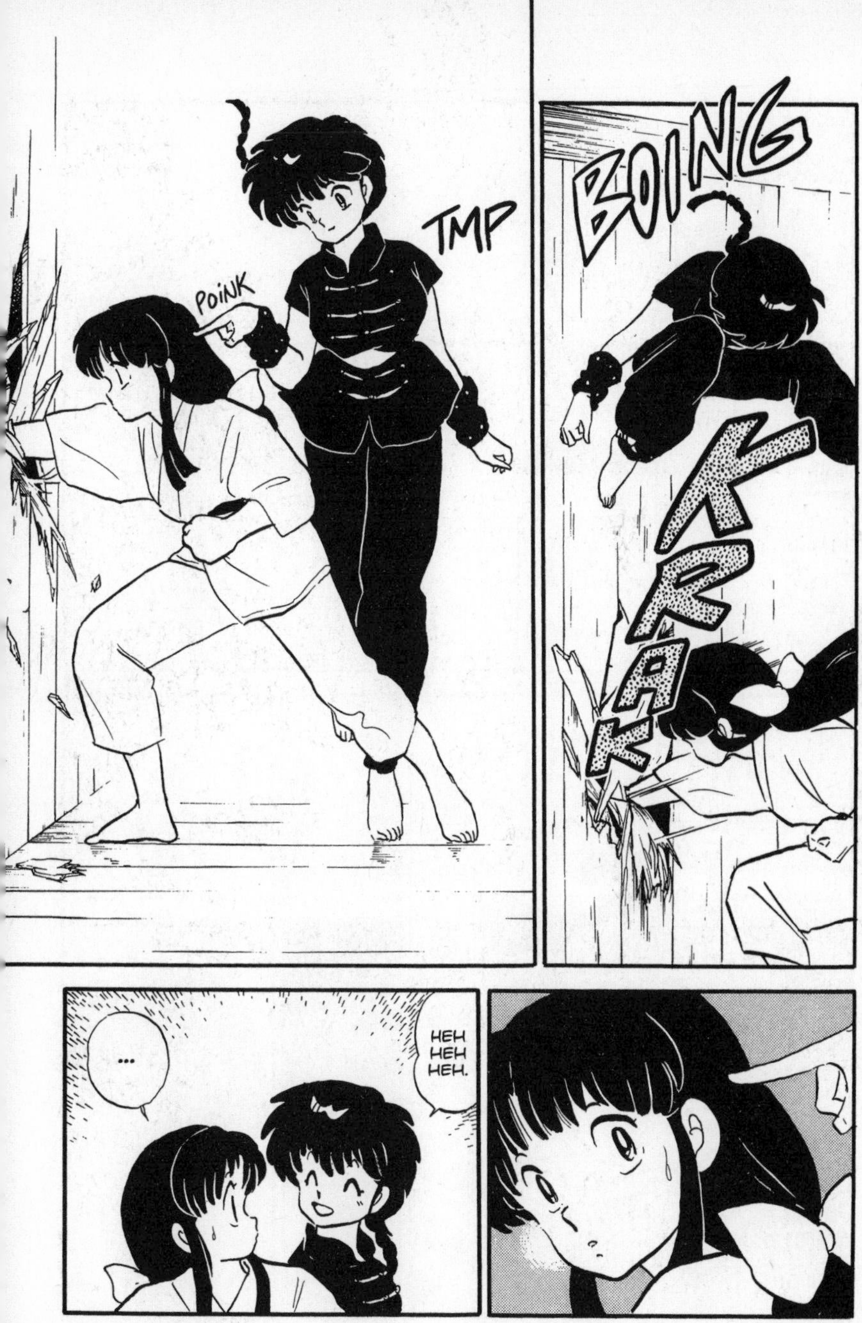
BOING
KRAK
TMP
POINK
HEH HEH HEH.
...

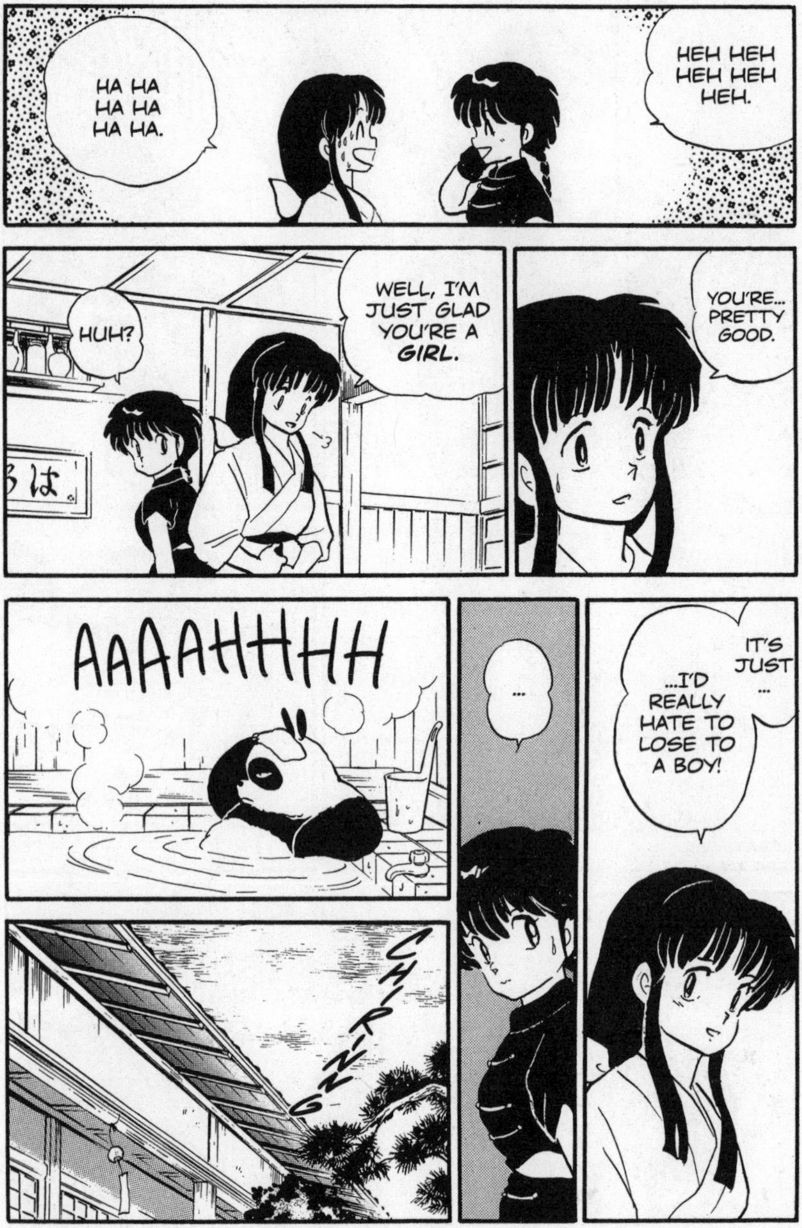
HEH HEH HEH HEH HEH.
HA HA HA HA HA HA.
YOU'RE... PRETTY GOOD.
WELL, I'M JUST GLAD YOU'RE A GIRL.
HUH?
IT'S JUST ...
...I'D REALLY HATE TO LOSE TO A BOY!
...
AAAAHHHH
CHI-R-I-N-N-G

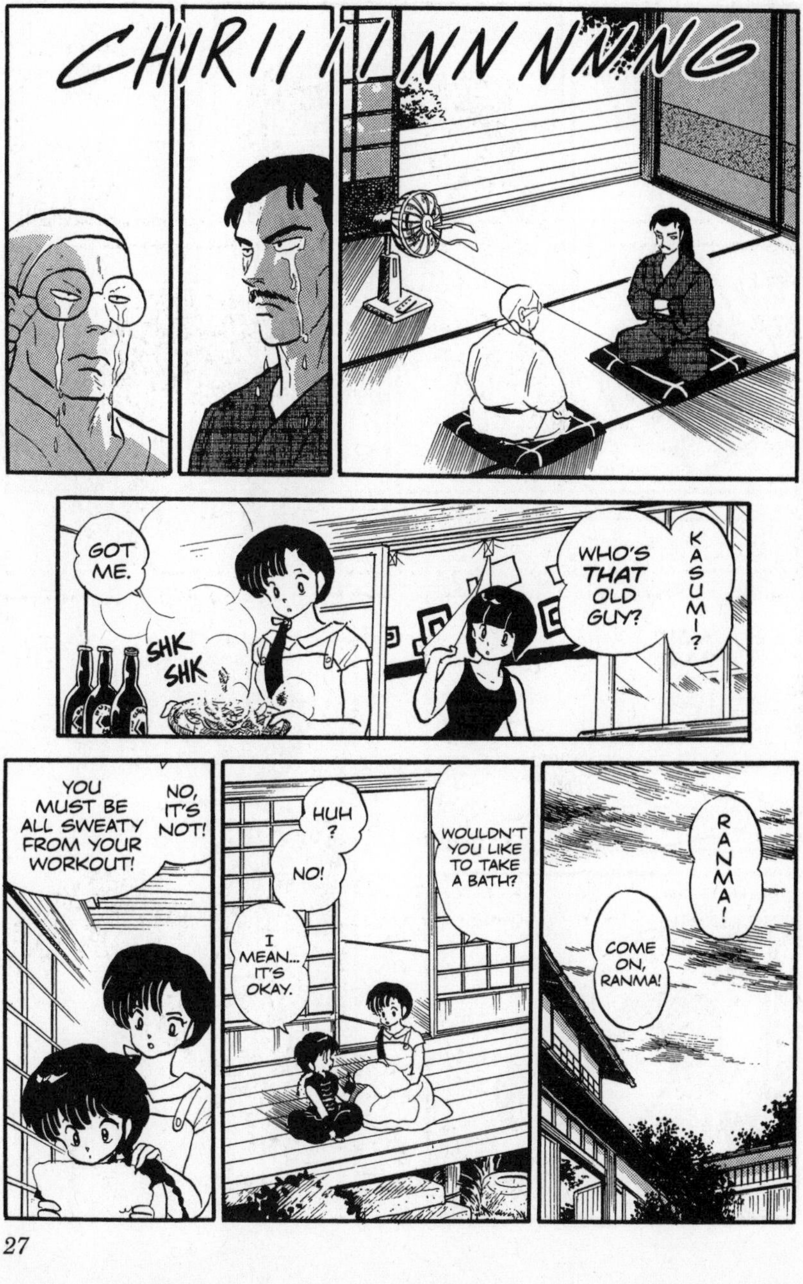
CHIRIIIINNNNNG
KASUMI-?
WHO'S THAT OLD GUY?
GOT ME.
SHK SHK
RANMA!
COME ON, RANMA!
WOULDN'T YOU LIKE TO TAKE A BATH?
HUH?
NO!
I MEAN... IT'S OKAY.
NO, IT'S NOT!
YOU MUST BE ALL SWEATY FROM YOUR WORKOUT!

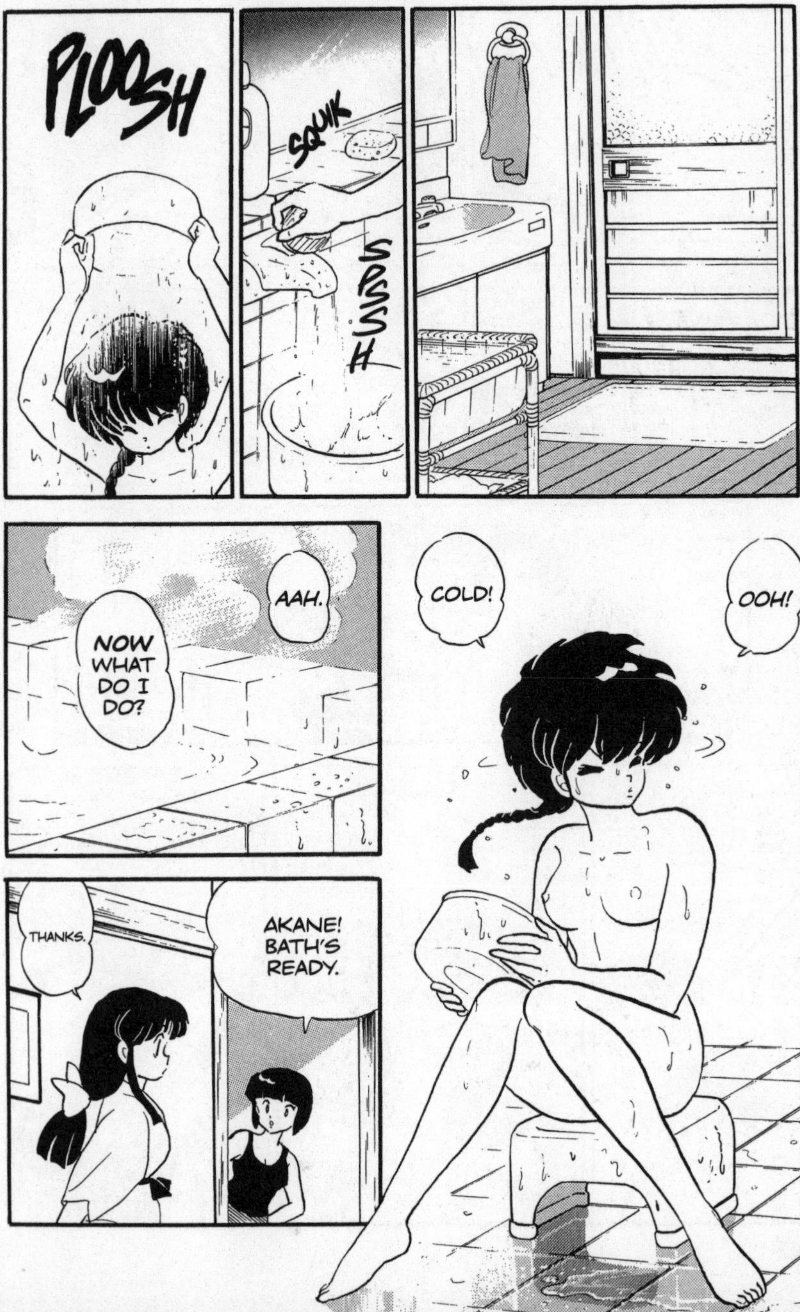
SQUIK
SPSSH
PLOOSH
OOH!
COLD!
AAH.
NOW WHAT DO I DO?
AKANE! BATH'S READY.
THANKS.

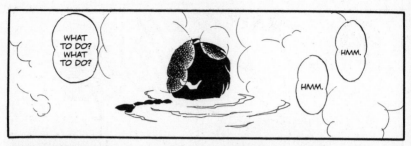

HMM.
HMM.
WHAT TO DO? WHAT TO DO?
KLIK
VIP
WELL, THEY'LL FIND OUT ANY-WAY.
SOONER OR LATER.
SHF
ZHFF
TP TP TP
MAY AS WELL JUST GO OUT AS I AM.
PLISH

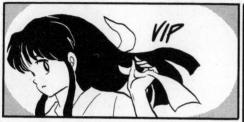

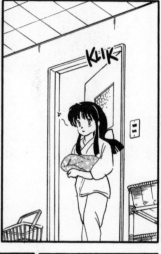

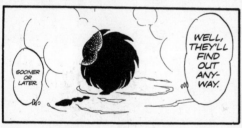

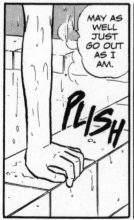

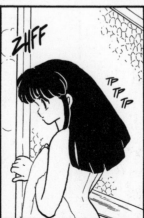

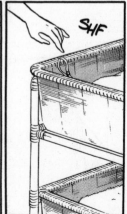

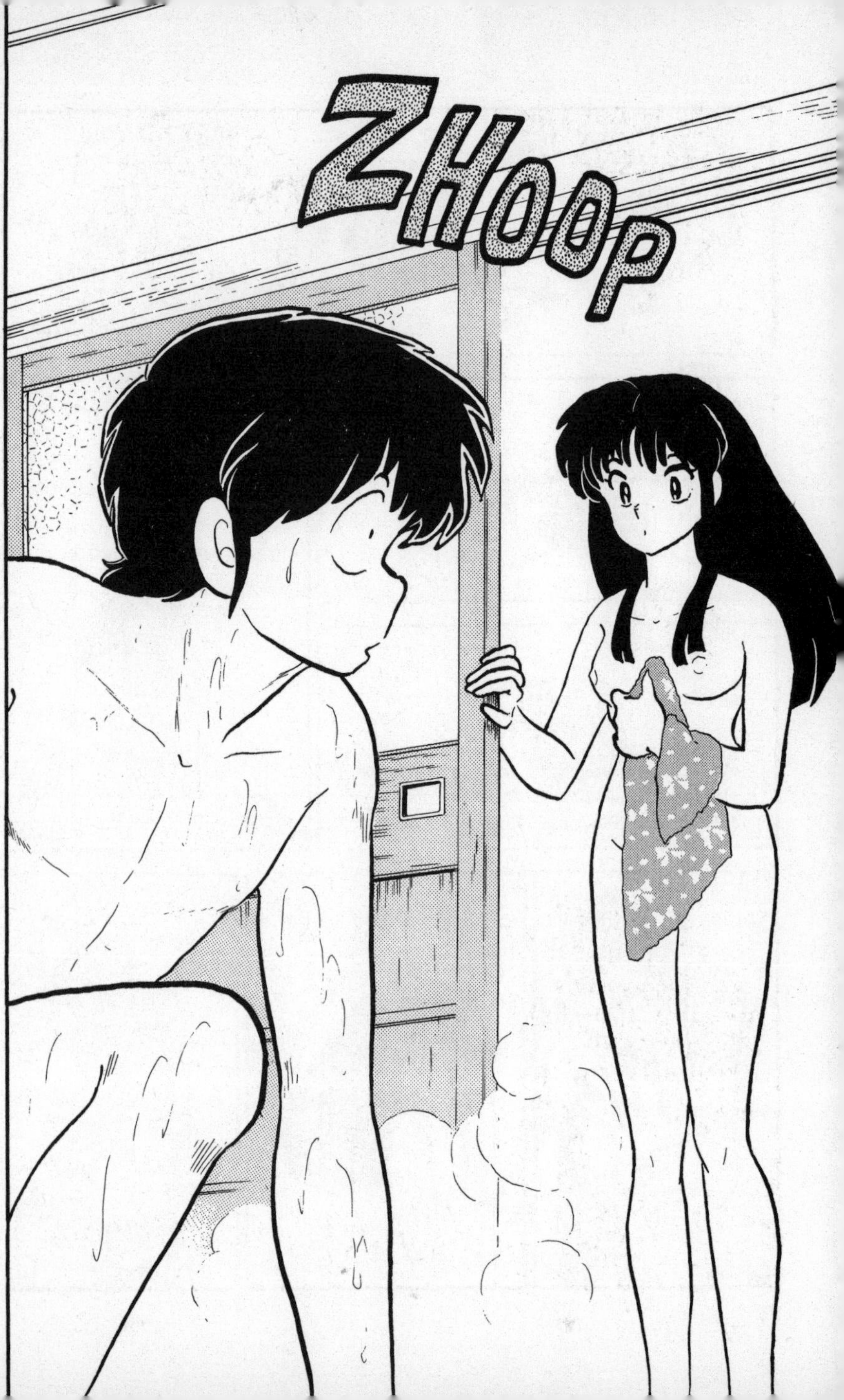
ZHOOP

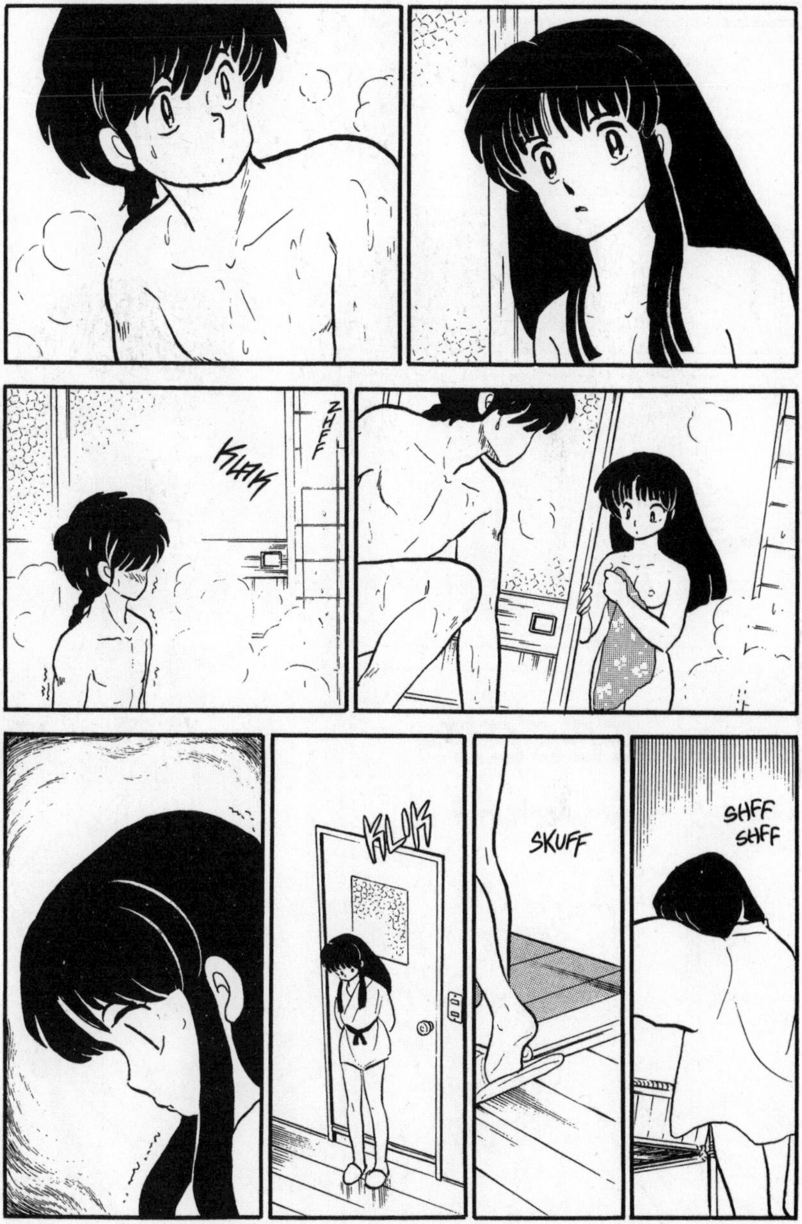
ZHFF
KLAK
SHFF SHFF
SKUFF
KLIK

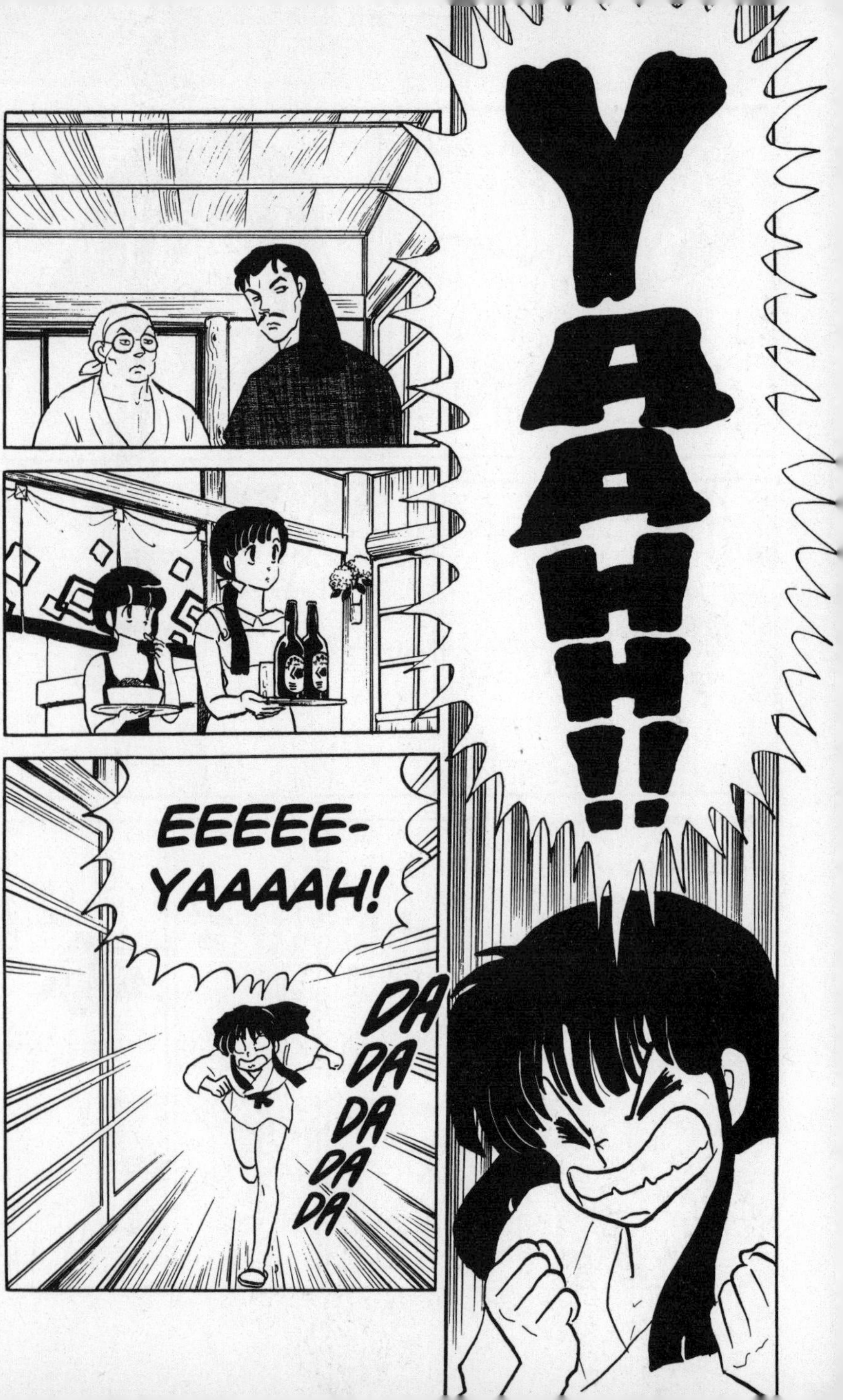
YAAHHH!!
EEEEE-YAAAAH!
DA DA DA DA DA DA DA

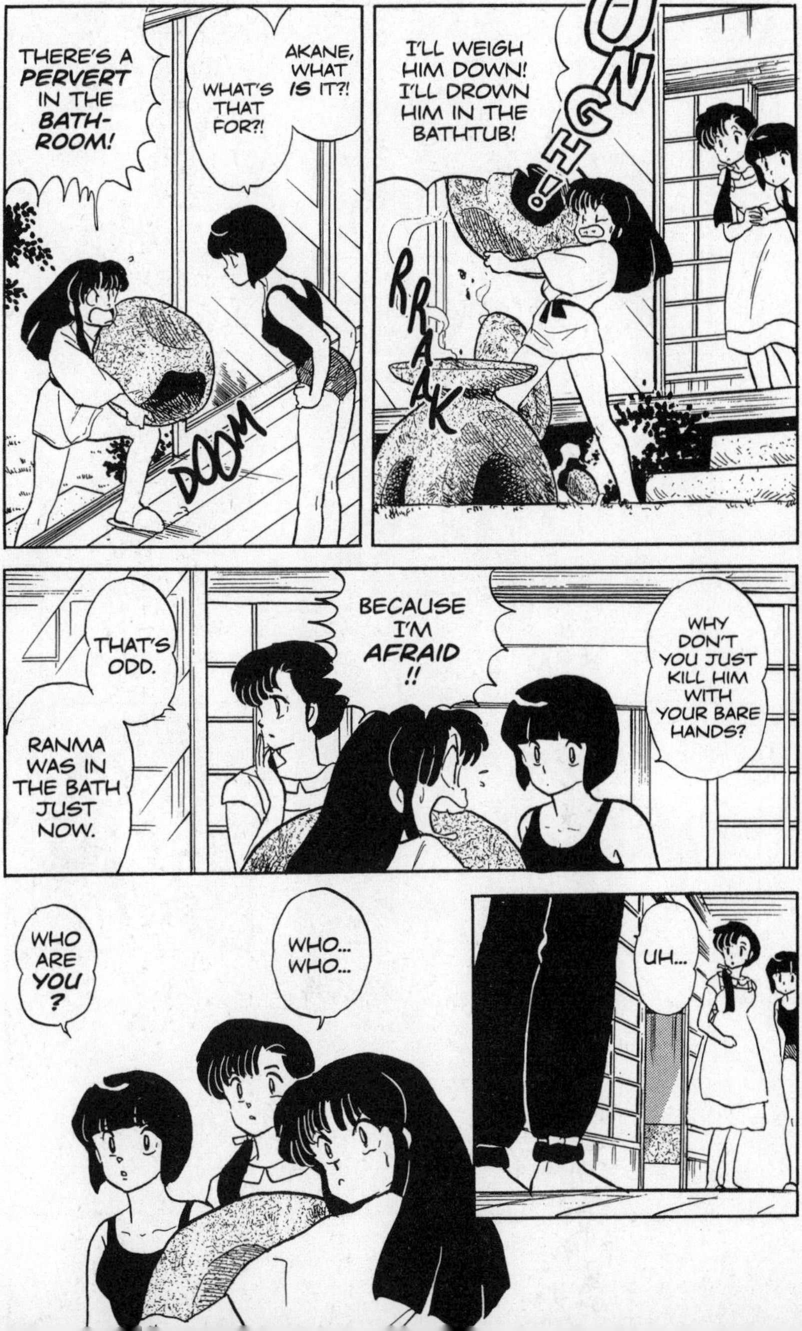
UNGH!
I'LL WEIGH HIM DOWN! I'LL DROWN HIM IN THE BATHTUB!
RRAAK
AKANE, WHAT IS IT?!
WHAT'S THAT FOR?!
THERE'S A PERVERT IN THE BATH-ROOM!
DOOM
WHY DON'T YOU JUST KILL HIM WITH YOUR BARE HANDS?
BECAUSE I'M AFRAID !!
THAT'S ODD.
RANMA WAS IN THE BATH JUST NOW.
UH...
WHO... WHO...
WHO ARE YOU ?

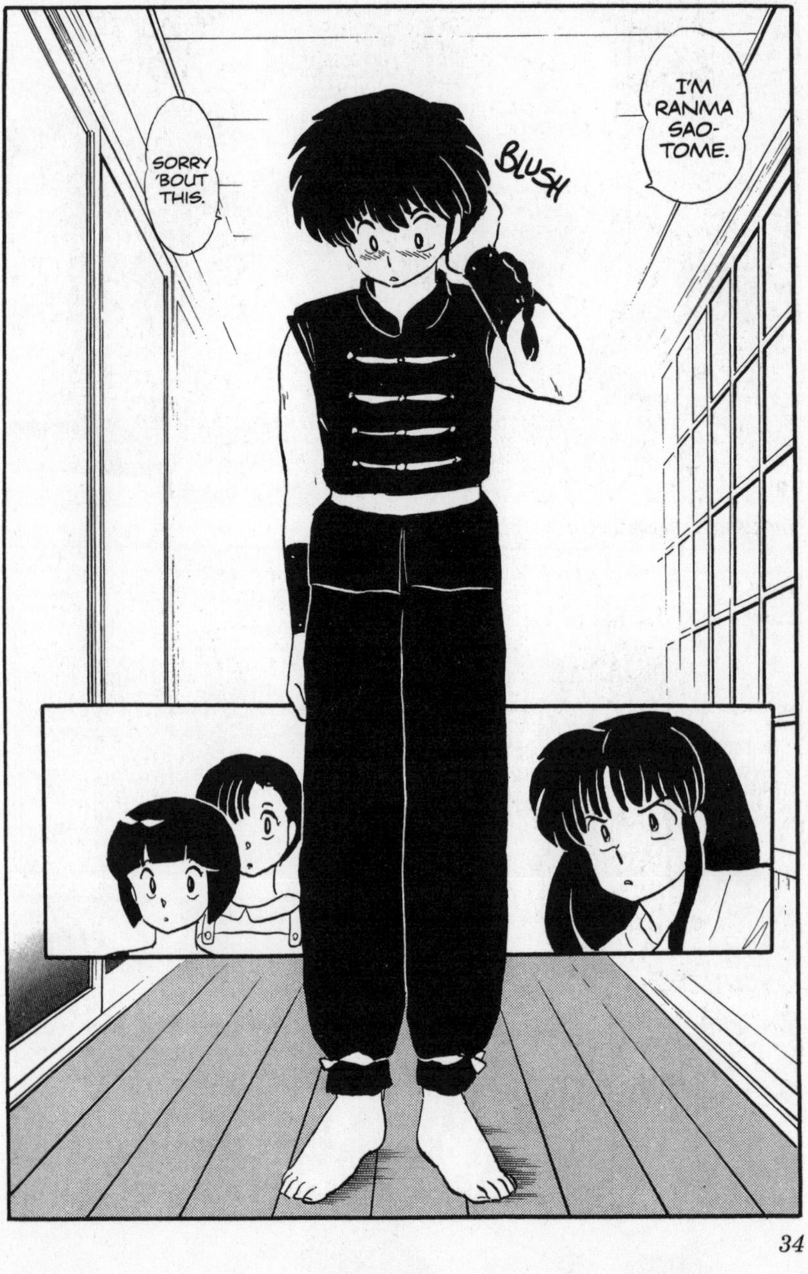
I'M RANMA SAO-TOME.
BLUSH
SORRY 'BOUT THIS.

# PART 2 RANMA'S SECRET

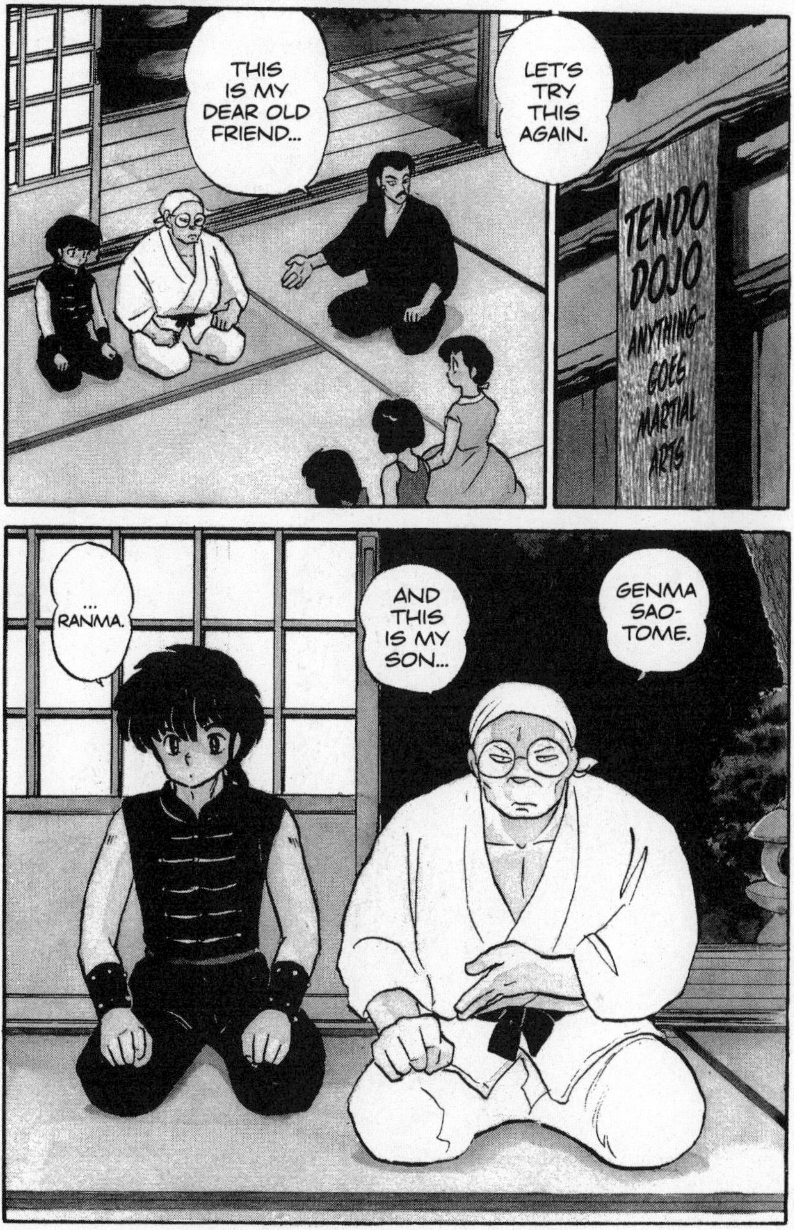
TENDO DOJO ANYTHING-GOES MARTIAL ARTS
LET'S TRY THIS AGAIN.
THIS IS MY DEAR OLD FRIEND...
GENMA SAO-TOME.
AND THIS IS MY SON...
... RANMA.

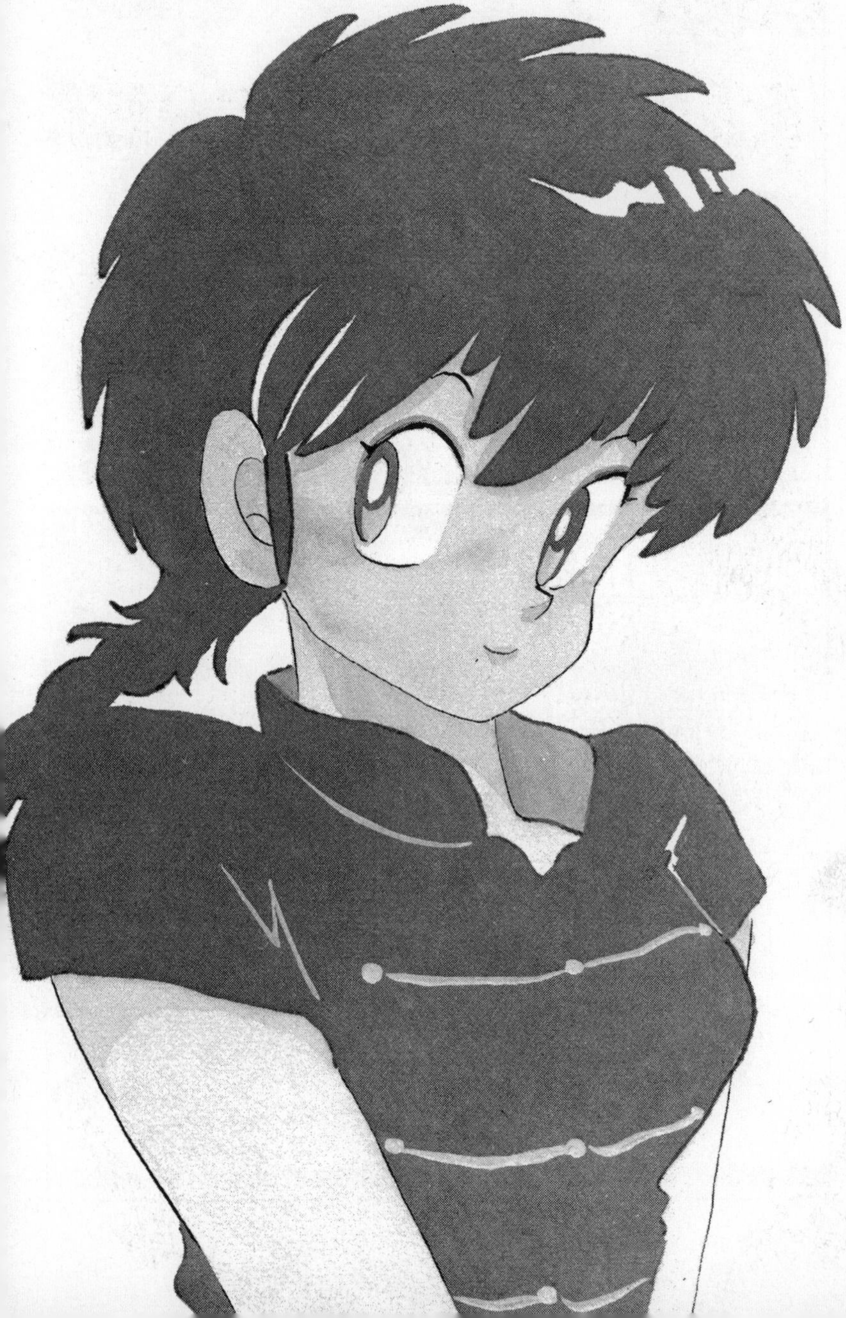

# PART 2
# RANMA'S SECRET

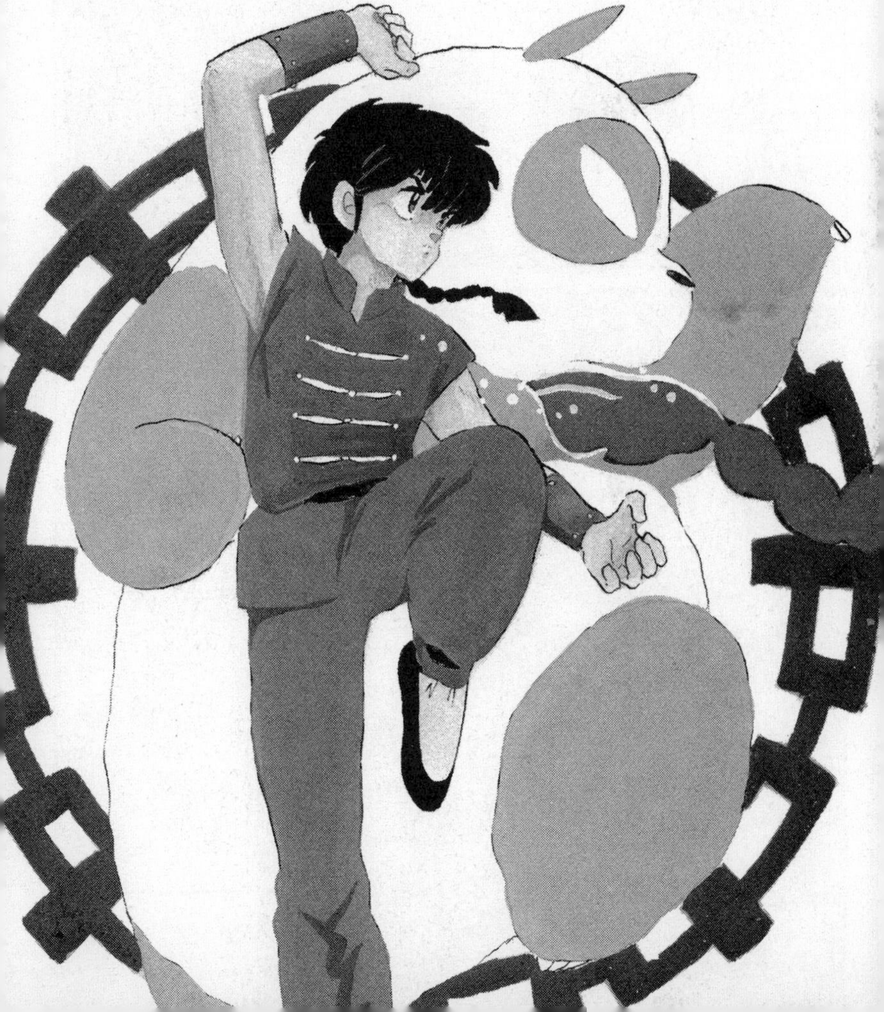

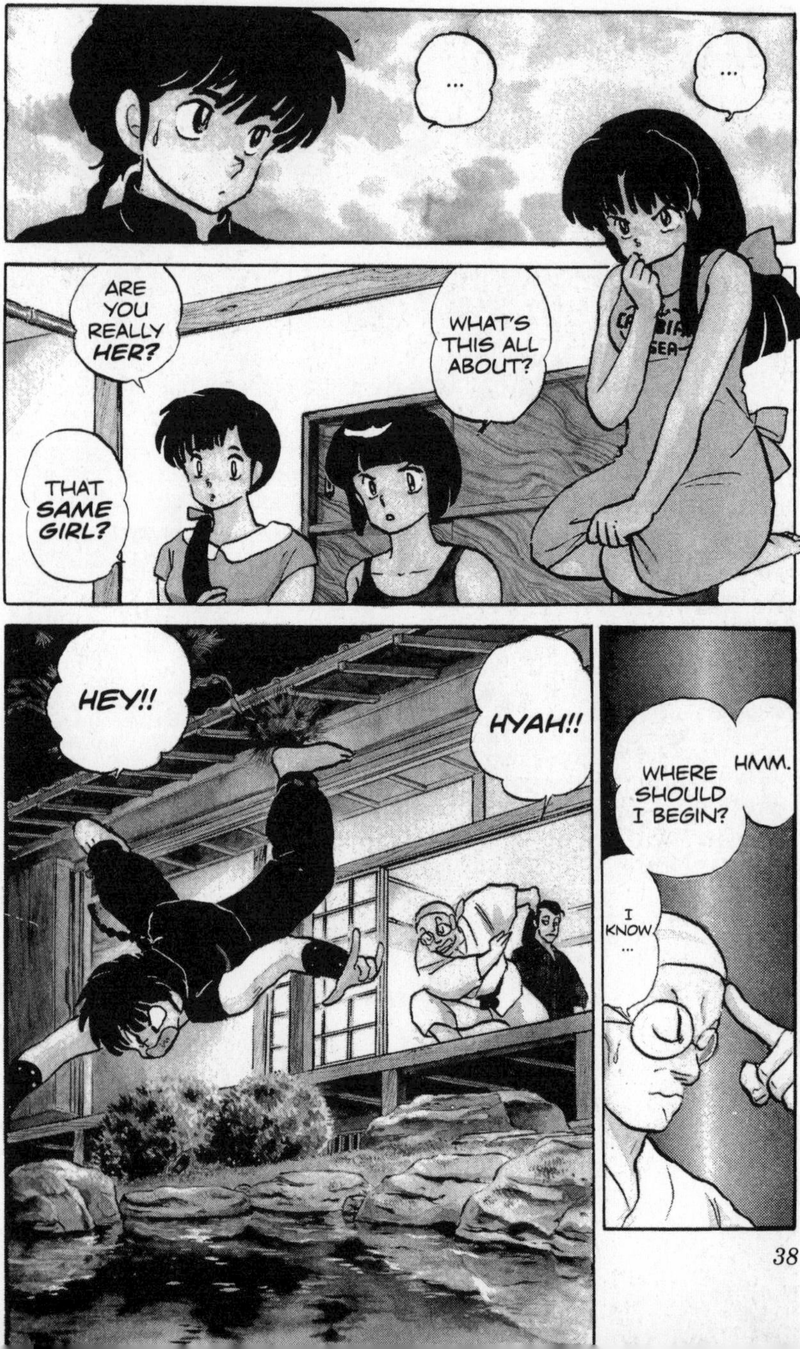
...
...
WHAT'S THIS ALL ABOUT?
ARE YOU REALLY HER?
THAT SAME GIRL?
HMM.
WHERE SHOULD I BEGIN?
I KNOW ...
HYAH!!
HEY!!

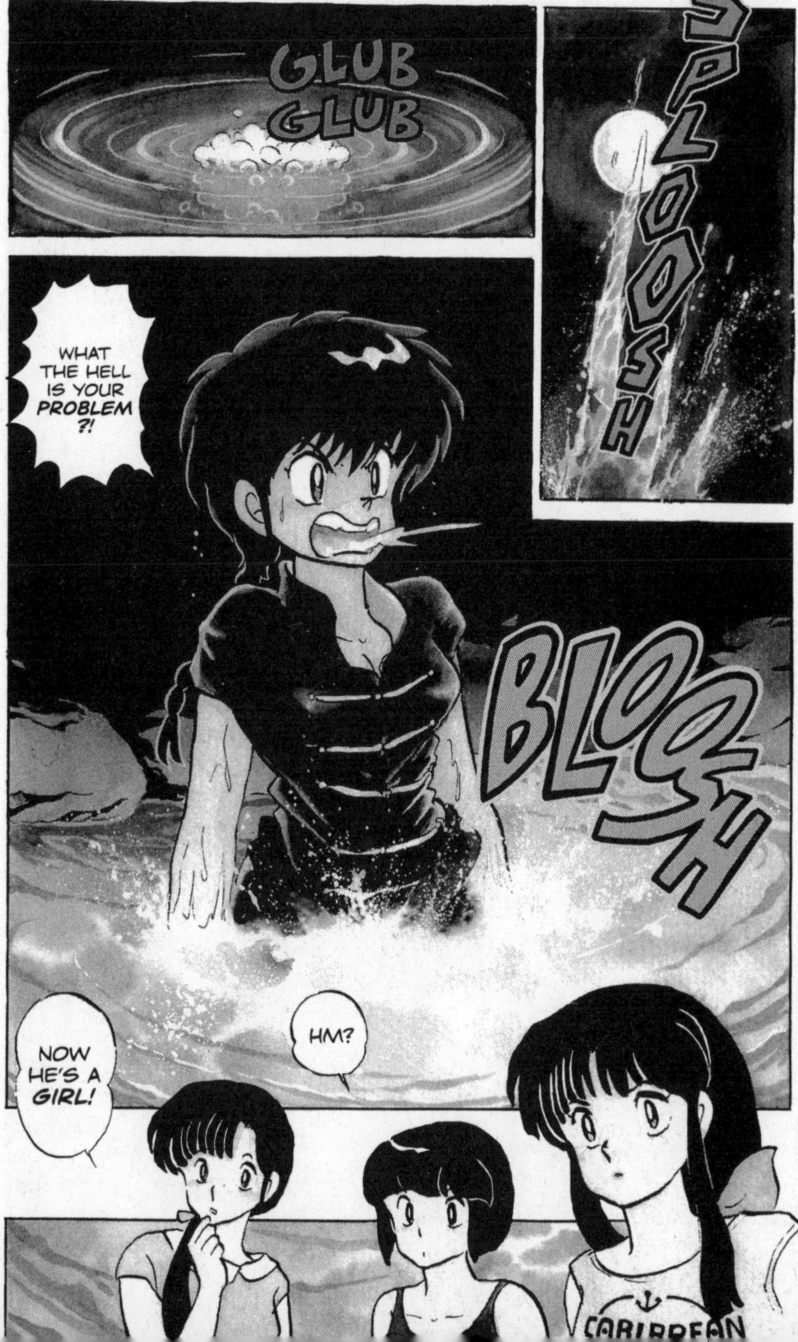
SPLOOSH
GLUB GLUB
WHAT THE HELL IS YOUR PROBLEM ?!
BLOOSH
HM?
NOW HE'S A GIRL!

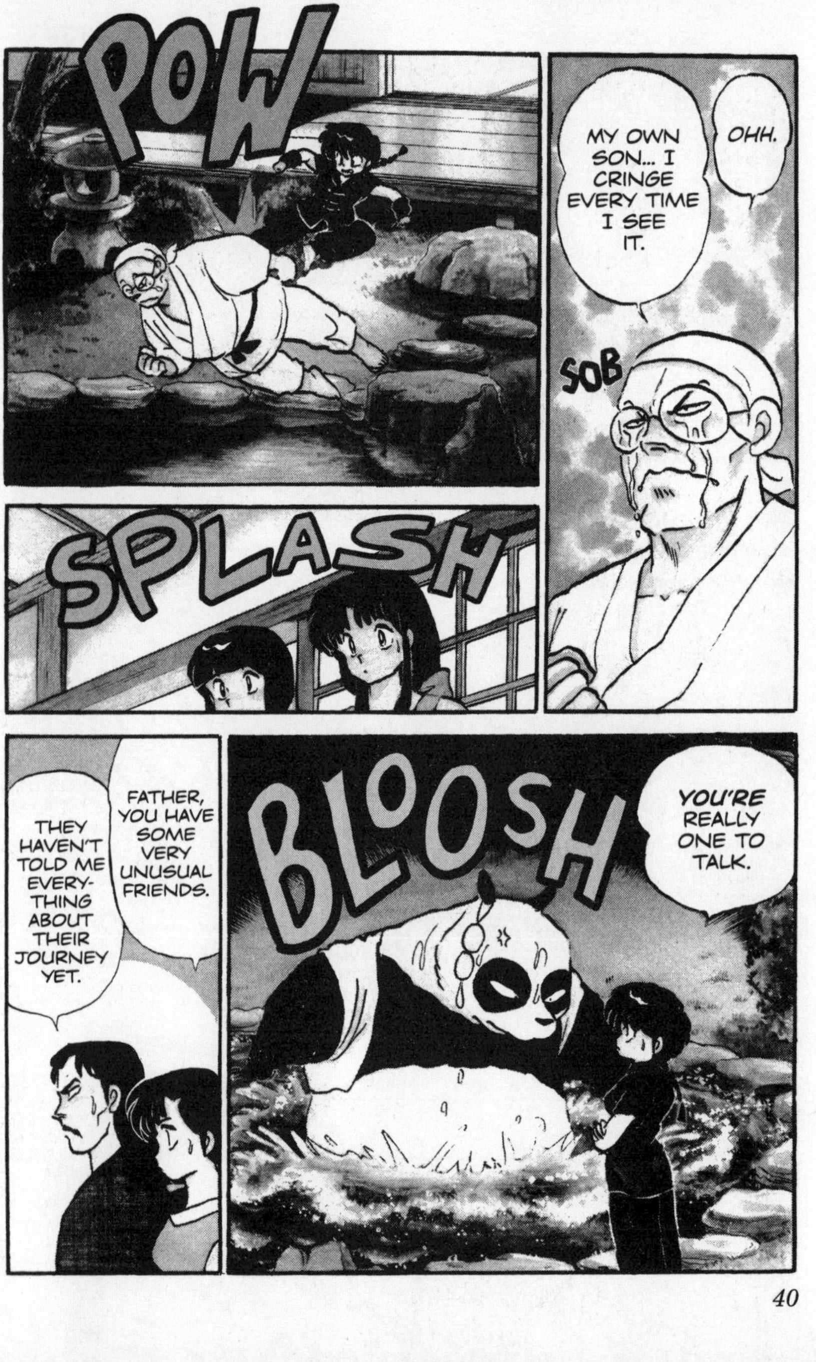
OHH.
MY OWN SON... I CRINGE EVERY TIME I SEE IT.
SOB
POW
SPLASH
YOU'RE REALLY ONE TO TALK.
BLOOSH
FATHER, YOU HAVE SOME VERY UNUSUAL FRIENDS.
THEY HAVEN'T TOLD ME EVERYTHING ABOUT THEIR JOURNEY YET.

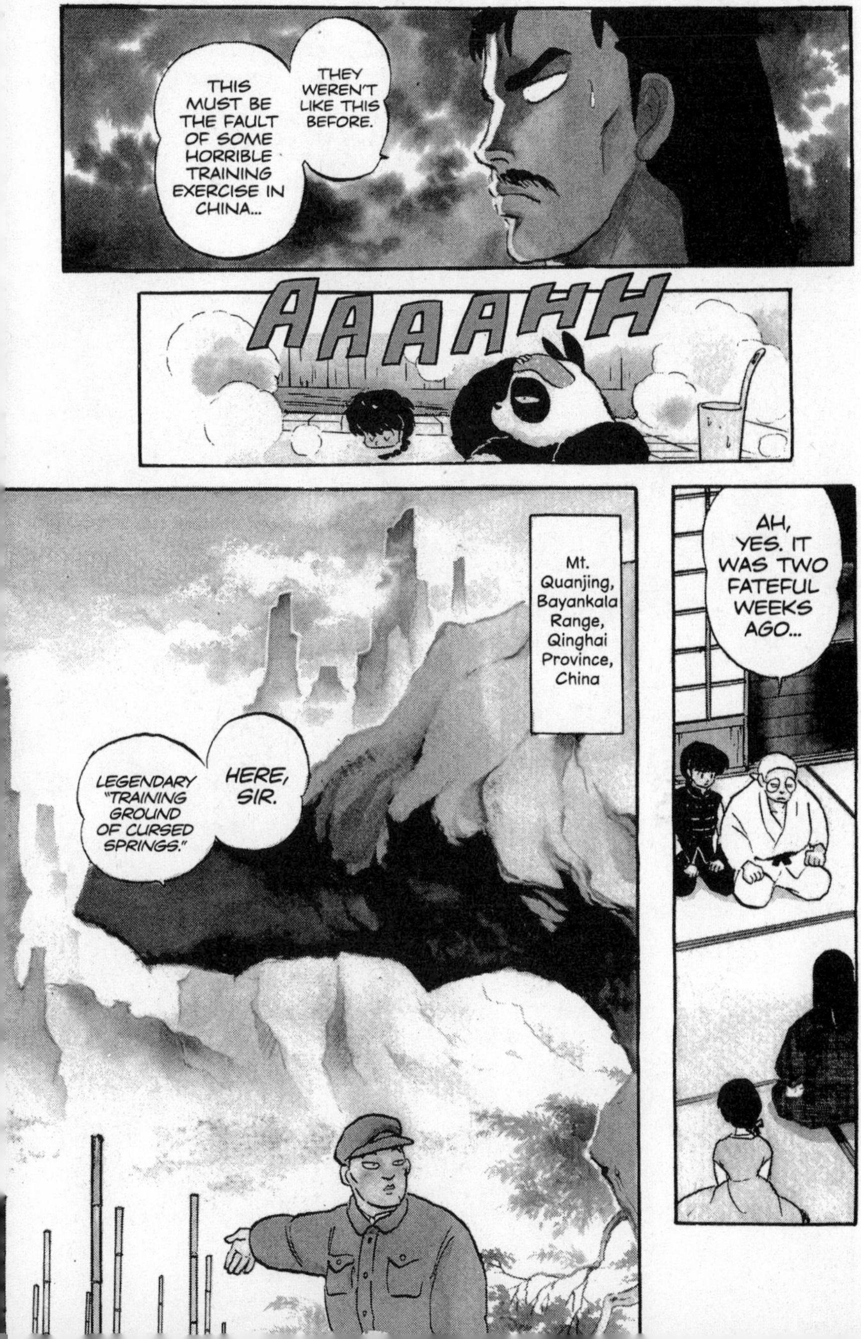
THEY WEREN'T LIKE THIS BEFORE.
THIS MUST BE THE FAULT OF SOME HORRIBLE TRAINING EXERCISE IN CHINA...
AAAAHH
AH, YES. IT WAS TWO FATEFUL WEEKS AGO...
Mt. Quanjing, Bayankala Range, Qinghai Province, China
HERE, SIR.
LEGENDARY "TRAINING GROUND OF CURSED SPRINGS."

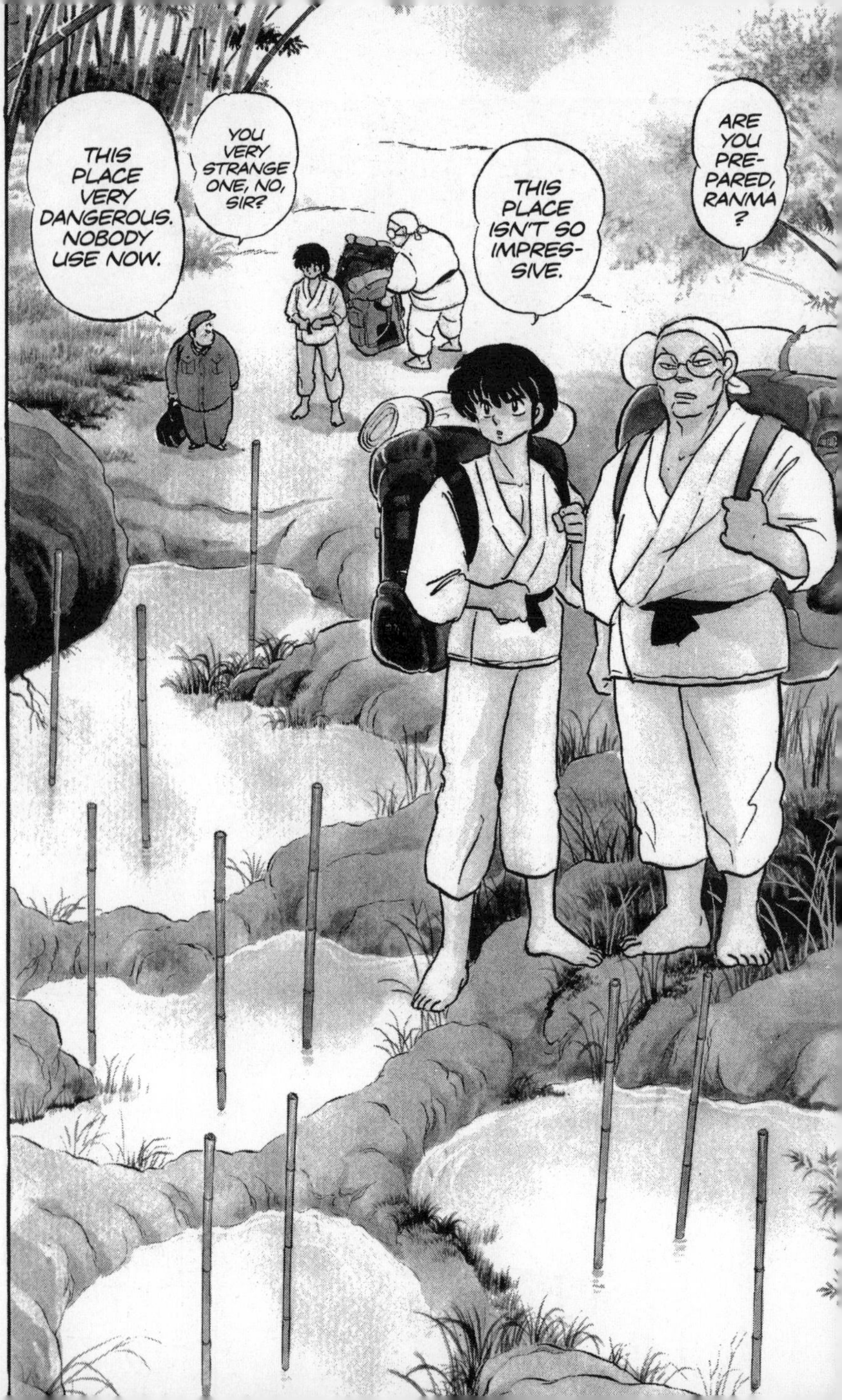
ARE YOU PRE-PARED, RANMA?
THIS PLACE ISN'T SO IMPRES-SIVE.
YOU VERY STRANGE ONE, NO, SIR?
THIS PLACE VERY DANGEROUS. NOBODY USE NOW.

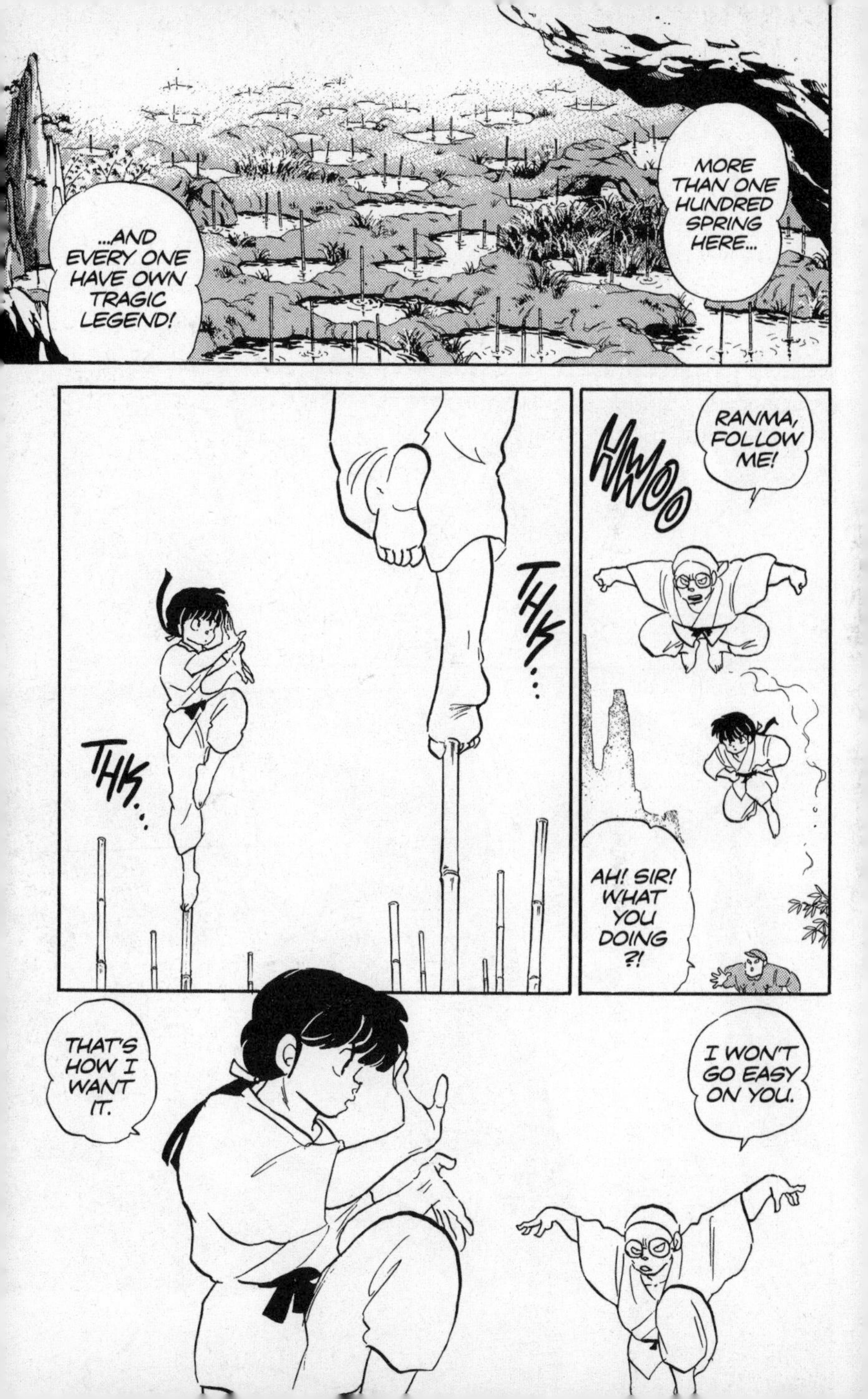
MORE THAN ONE HUNDRED SPRING HERE...
...AND EVERY ONE HAVE OWN TRAGIC LEGEND!
RANMA, FOLLOW ME!
HWOO
AH! SIR! WHAT YOU DOING ?!
THK...
THK...
I WON'T GO EASY ON YOU.
THAT'S HOW I WANT IT.

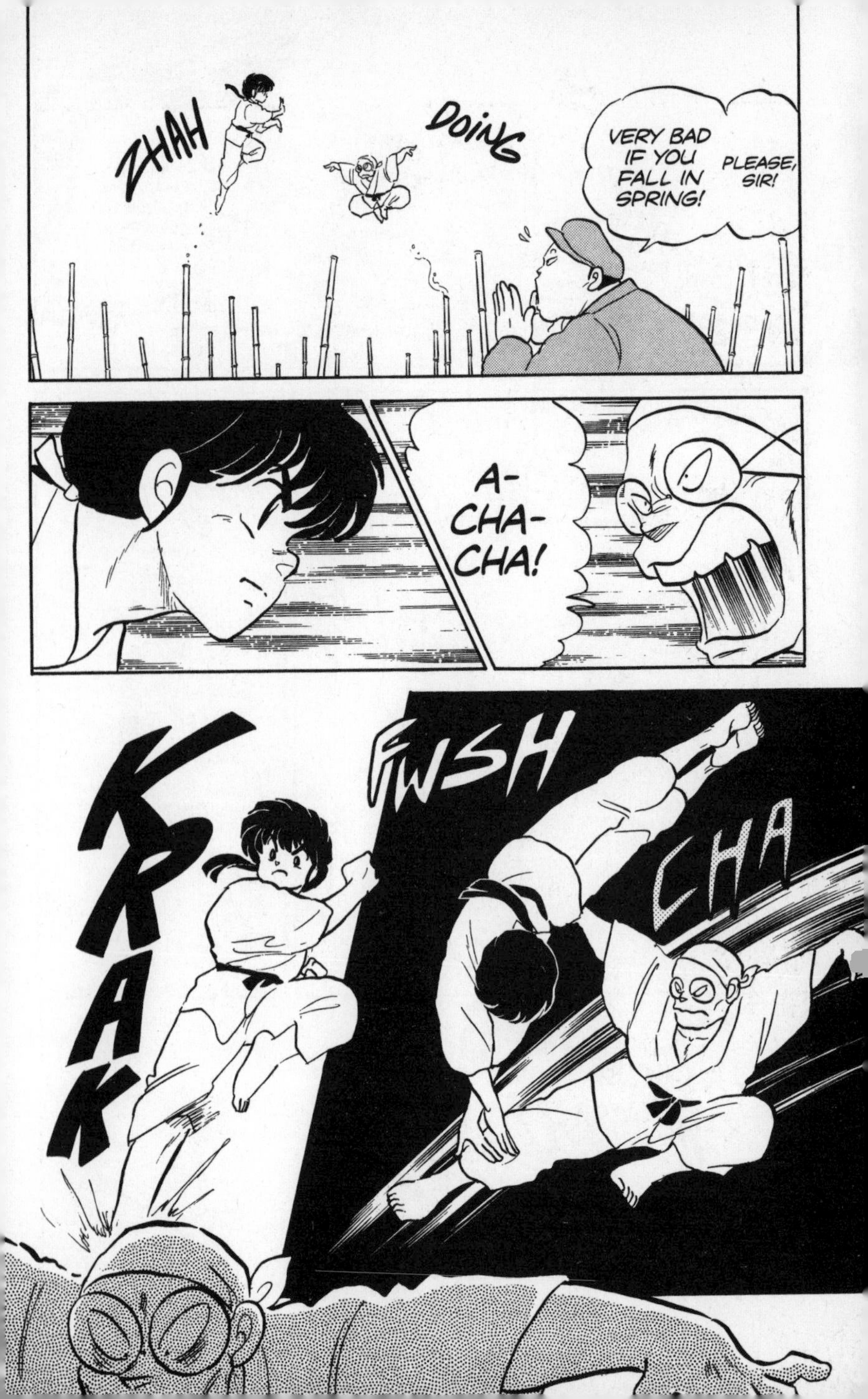
PLEASE, SIR!
VERY BAD IF YOU FALL IN SPRING!
DOING
ZHAH
A-CHA-CHA!
CHA
FWSH
KRAAK

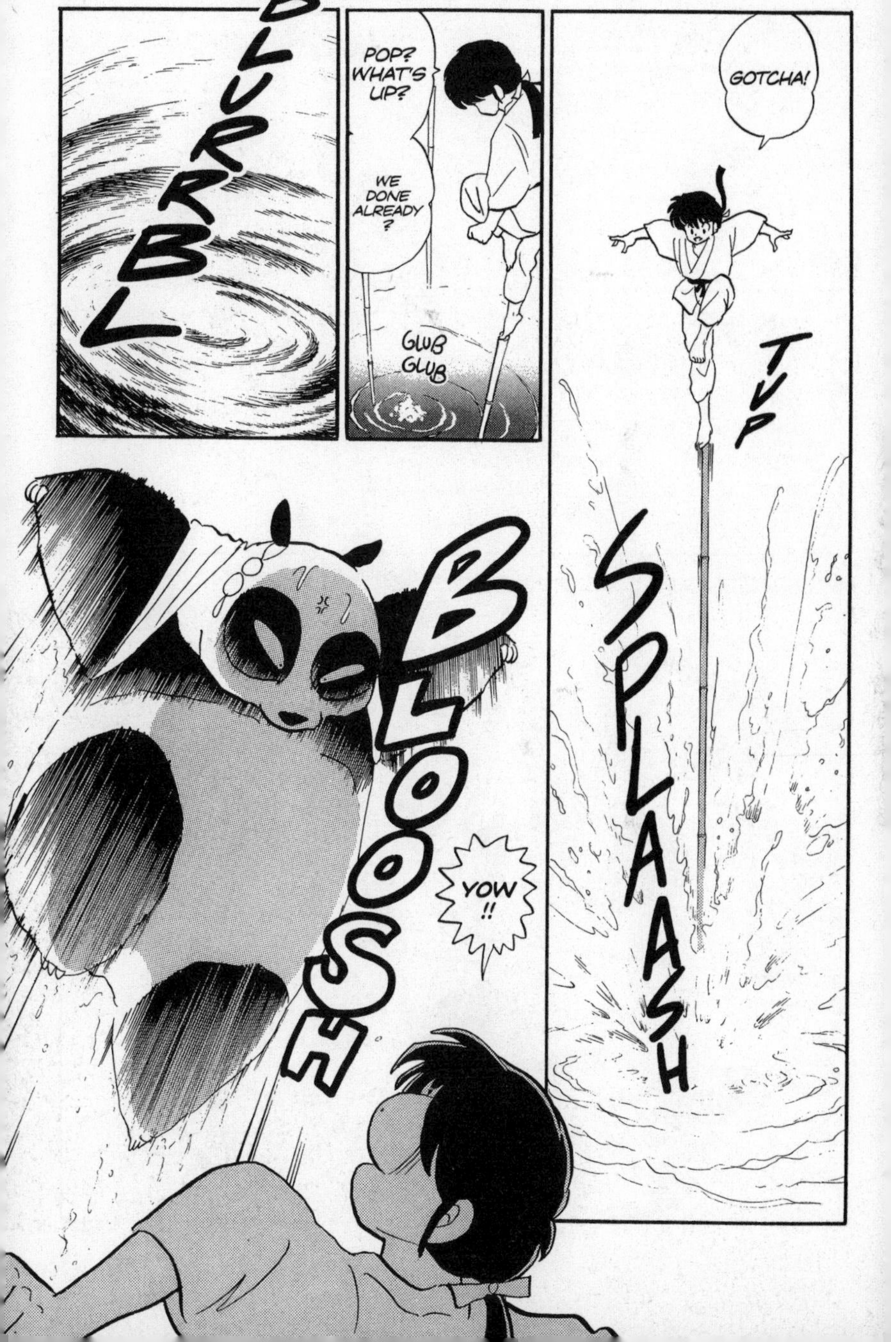
GOTCHA!
TUP
SPLAASH
POP? WHAT'S UP?
WE DONE ALREADY ?
GLUB GLUB
BLURRBL
BLOOSH
YOW !!

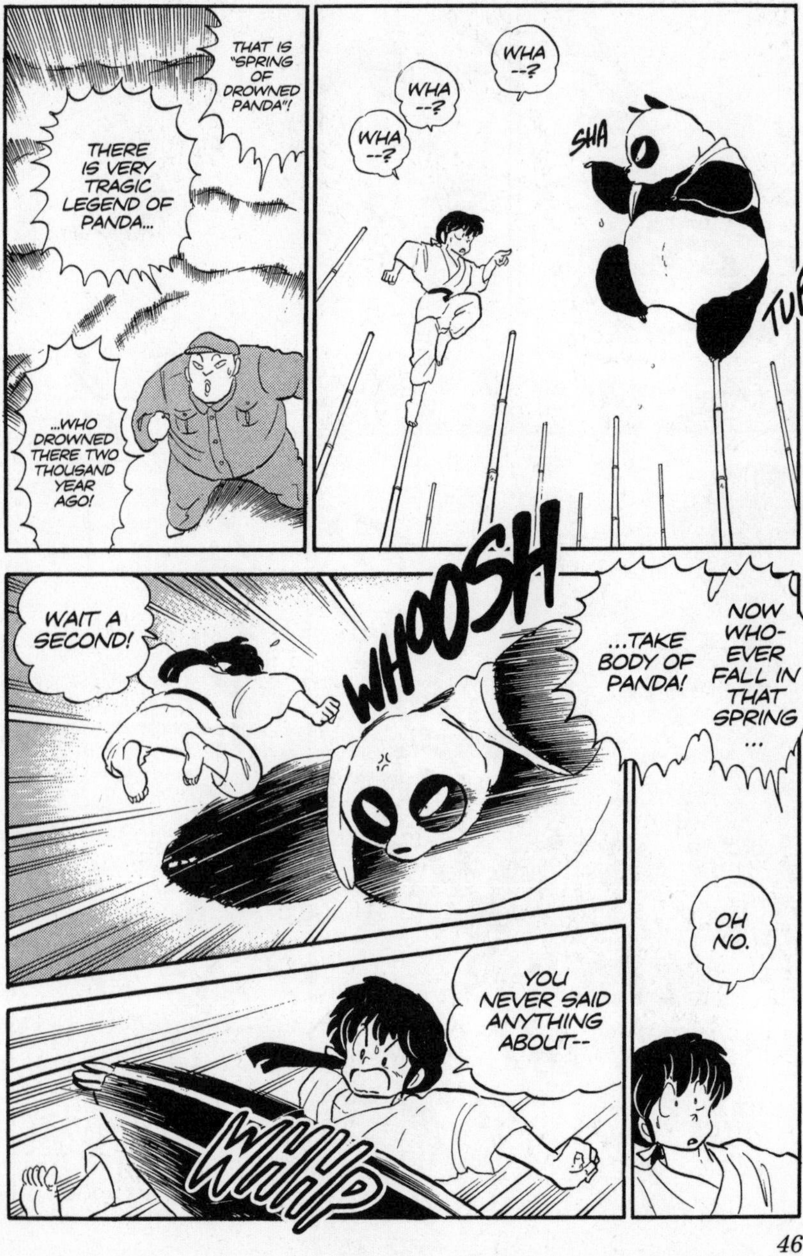
WHA --?
WHA --?
WHA --?
SHA
TUP
THAT IS "SPRING OF DROWNED PANDA"!
THERE IS VERY TRAGIC LEGEND OF PANDA...
...WHO DROWNED THERE TWO THOUSAND YEAR AGO!
NOW WHO-EVER FALL IN THAT SPRING...
...TAKE BODY OF PANDA!
WHOOSH
WAIT A SECOND!
OH NO.
YOU NEVER SAID ANYTHING ABOUT--
WHIP

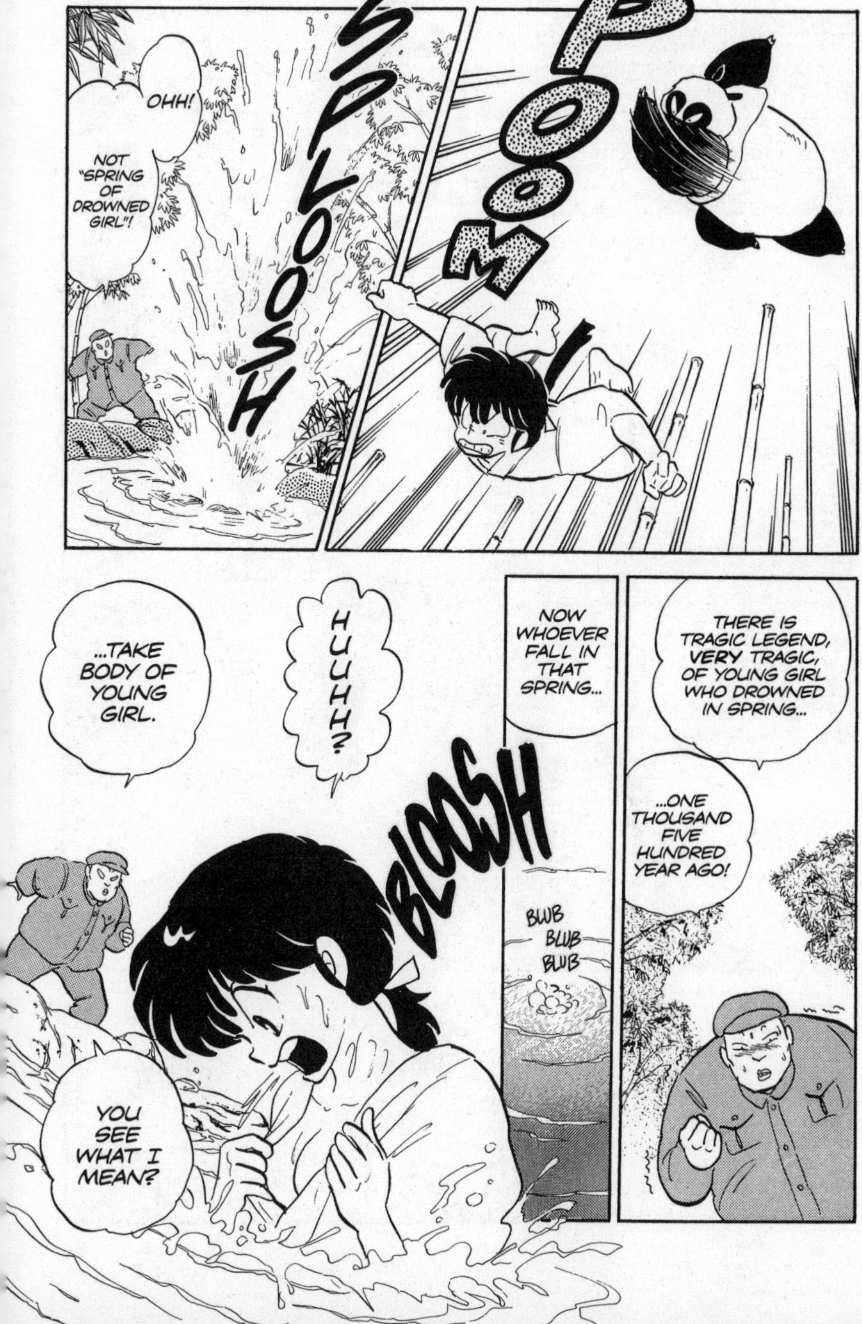
POOOM
SPLOOSH
OHH!
NOT "SPRING OF DROWNED GIRL"!
THERE IS TRAGIC LEGEND, VERY TRAGIC, OF YOUNG GIRL WHO DROWNED IN SPRING...
...ONE THOUSAND FIVE HUNDRED YEAR AGO!
NOW WHOEVER FALL IN THAT SPRING...
BLUB BLUB BLUB
BLOOSH
HUUHH?
...TAKE BODY OF YOUNG GIRL.
YOU SEE WHAT I MEAN?

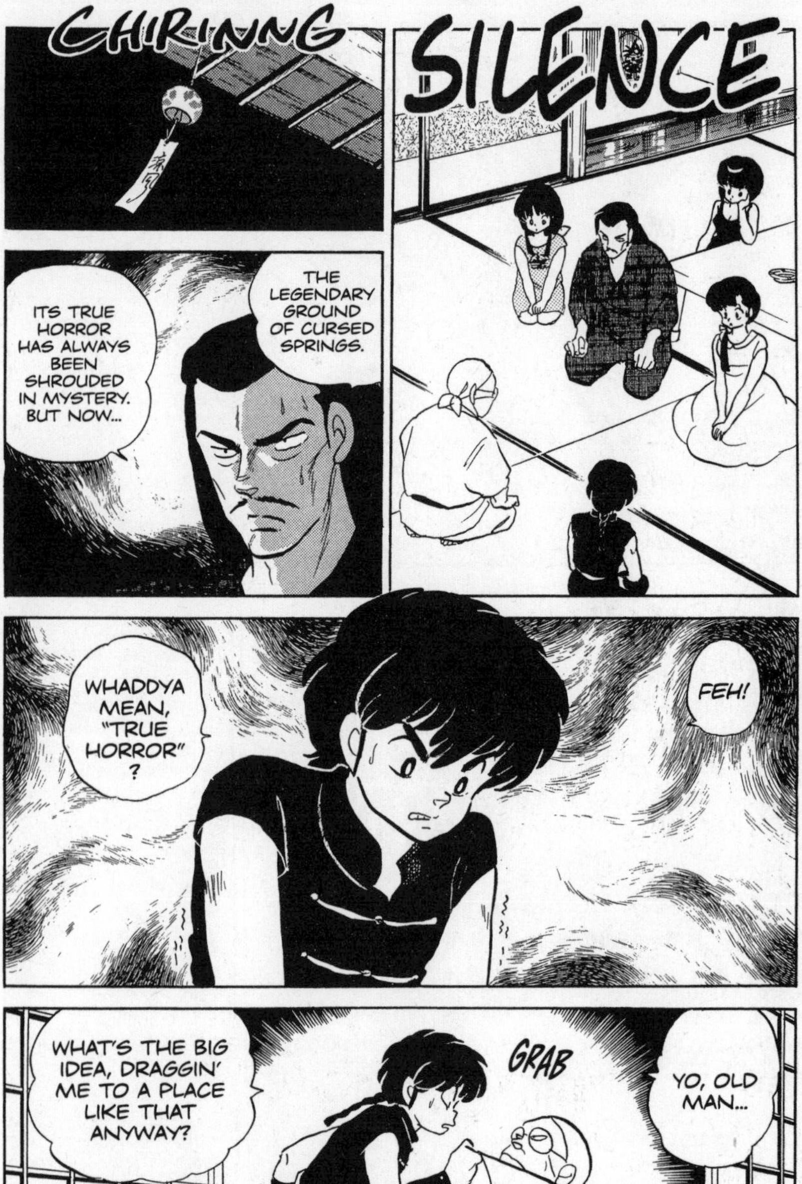
SILENCE
CHIRINNG
THE LEGENDARY GROUND OF CURSED SPRINGS.
ITS TRUE HORROR HAS ALWAYS BEEN SHROUDED IN MYSTERY. BUT NOW...
FEH!
WHADDYA MEAN, "TRUE HORROR"?
YO, OLD MAN...
GRAB
WHAT'S THE BIG IDEA, DRAGGIN' ME TO A PLACE LIKE THAT ANYWAY?

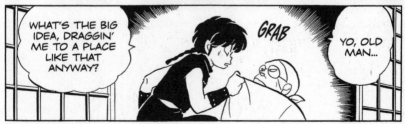

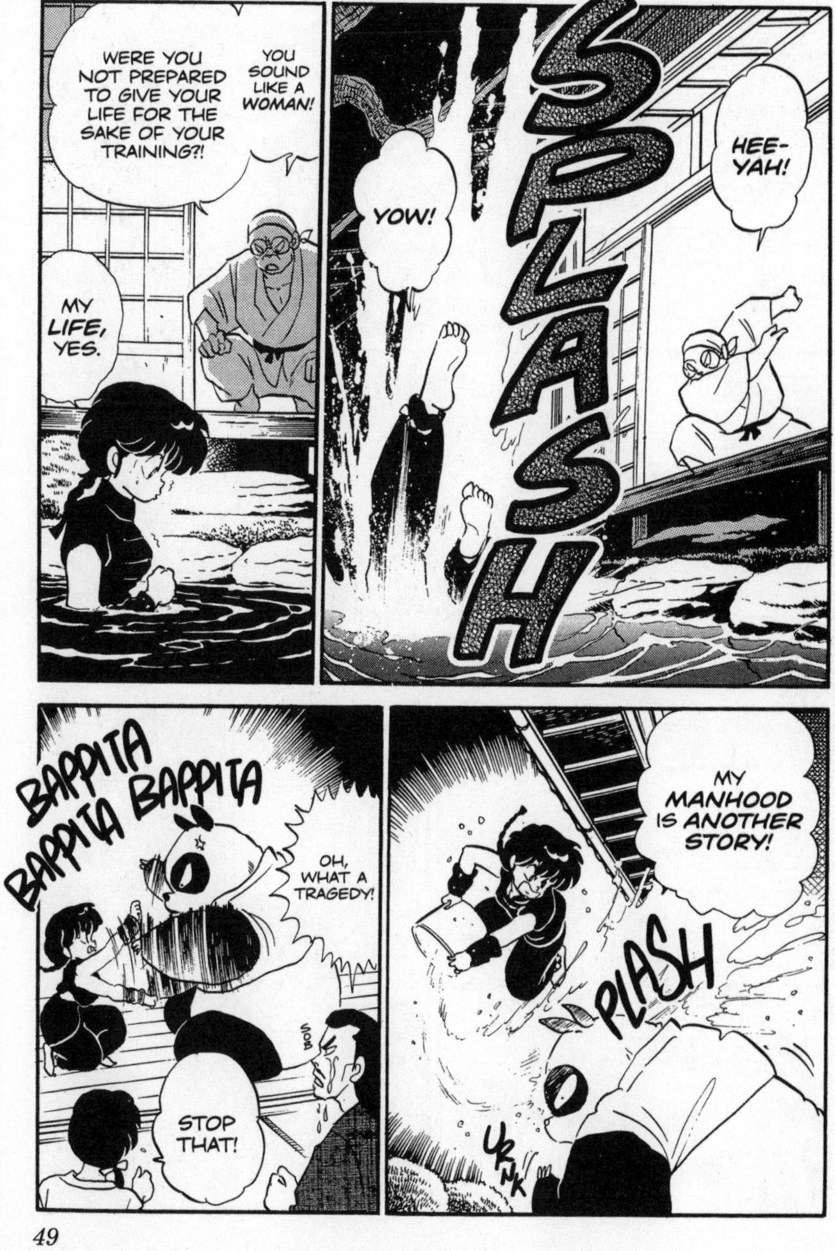
HEE-YAH!
SPLASH
YOW!
YOU SOUND LIKE A WOMAN!
WERE YOU NOT PREPARED TO GIVE YOUR LIFE FOR THE SAKE OF YOUR TRAINING?!
MY LIFE, YES.
MY MANHOOD IS ANOTHER STORY!
PLASH
URNK
BAPPITA BAPPITA BAPPITA
OH, WHAT A TRAGEDY!
SOB
STOP THAT!

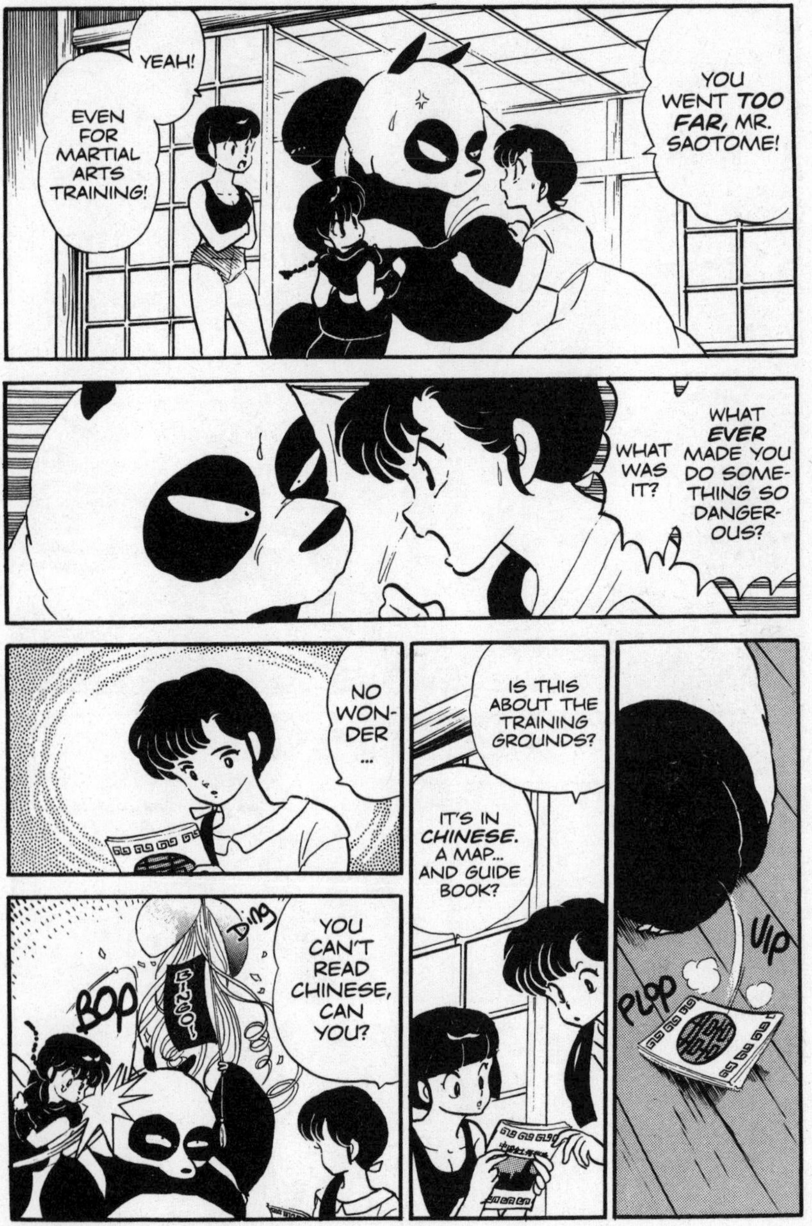
YOU WENT TOO FAR, MR. SAOTOME!
YEAH!
EVEN FOR MARTIAL ARTS TRAINING!
WHAT EVER MADE YOU DO SOME-THING SO DANGER-OUS?
WHAT WAS IT?
UIP
PLOP
IS THIS ABOUT THE TRAINING GROUNDS?
IT'S IN CHINESE. A MAP... AND GUIDE BOOK?
NO WON-DER ...
YOU CAN'T READ CHINESE, CAN YOU?
Ding
BINGO!
BOP

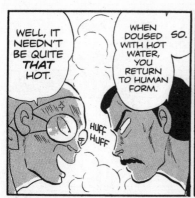

....
PSSHHH
SO.
WHEN DOUSED WITH HOT WATER, YOU RETURN TO HUMAN FORM.
WELL, IT NEEDN'T BE QUITE THAT HOT.
HUFF HUFF
WHEN DOUSED WITH COLD WATER, YOU BECOME A GIRL...
...BUT HOT WATER TURNS YOU BACK INTO A BOY!
PSSHHH
HOT WATER! NOT BOILING!
NO SWEAT.
YOUR PROBLEM ISN'T SO TERRIBLE AFTER ALL!
PAT
PAT
HUH?

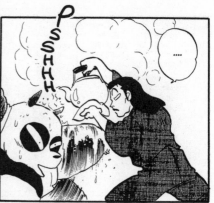

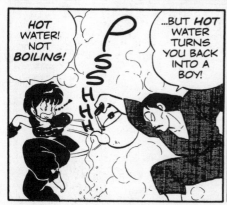

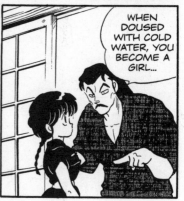

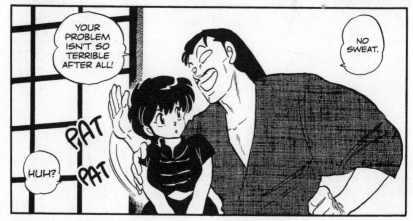

MY DAUGHTER KASUMI. NINETEEN.
AND NABIKI. SEVENTEEN.
AND AKANE. SIXTEEN.
PICK THE ONE YOU WANT.
SHE'S YOUR FIANCÉE.
OH, HE WANTS AKANE!
HUH?
OH, DEFINITELY!
YOU MUST BE JOKING!
WHY WOULD I BE...
WELL ...
YOU HATE **BOYS**, DON'T YOU?
SO, YOU'RE IN LUCK! HE'S **HALF-GIRL!**
ME? MARRY THAT PERVERT?! NEVER!
GRR

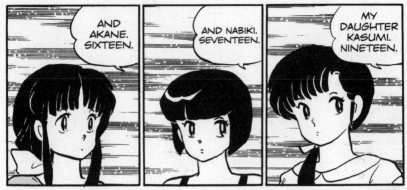

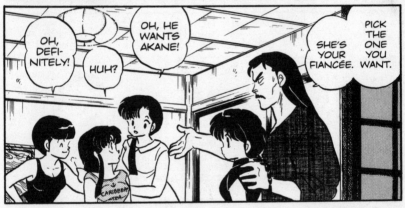

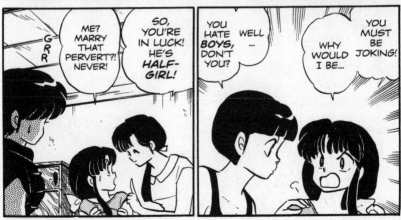

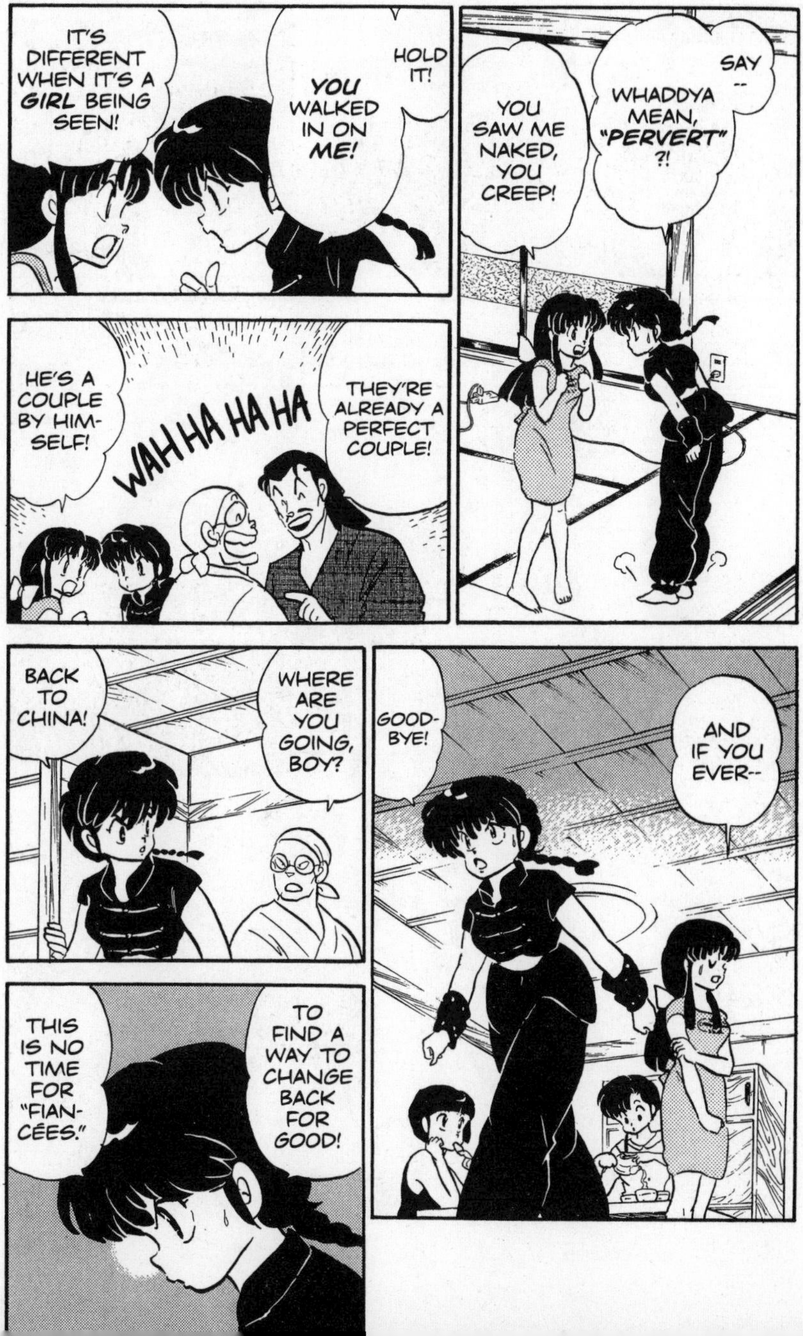
SAY -- WHADDYA MEAN, "PERVERT"?!
YOU SAW ME NAKED, YOU CREEP!
HOLD IT! YOU WALKED IN ON ME!
IT'S DIFFERENT WHEN IT'S A GIRL BEING SEEN!
THEY'RE ALREADY A PERFECT COUPLE!
WAH HA HA HA
HE'S A COUPLE BY HIMSELF!
AND IF YOU EVER--
GOOD-BYE!
WHERE ARE YOU GOING, BOY?
BACK TO CHINA!
TO FIND A WAY TO CHANGE BACK FOR GOOD!
THIS IS NO TIME FOR "FIANCÉES."

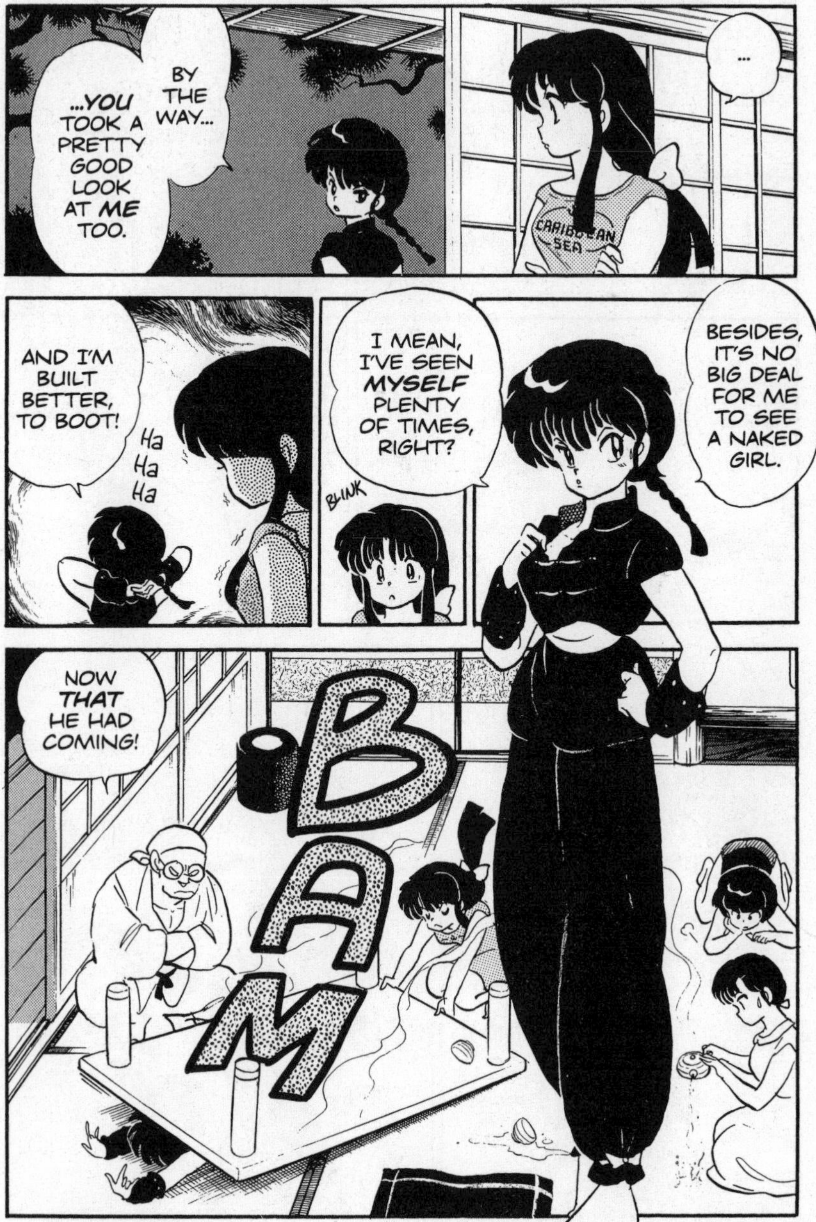
...
BY THE WAY...
...YOU TOOK A PRETTY GOOD LOOK AT ME TOO.
BESIDES, IT'S NO BIG DEAL FOR ME TO SEE A NAKED GIRL.
I MEAN, I'VE SEEN MYSELF PLENTY OF TIMES, RIGHT?
BLINK
AND I'M BUILT BETTER, TO BOOT!
Ha Ha Ha
BAM
NOW THAT HE HAD COMING!

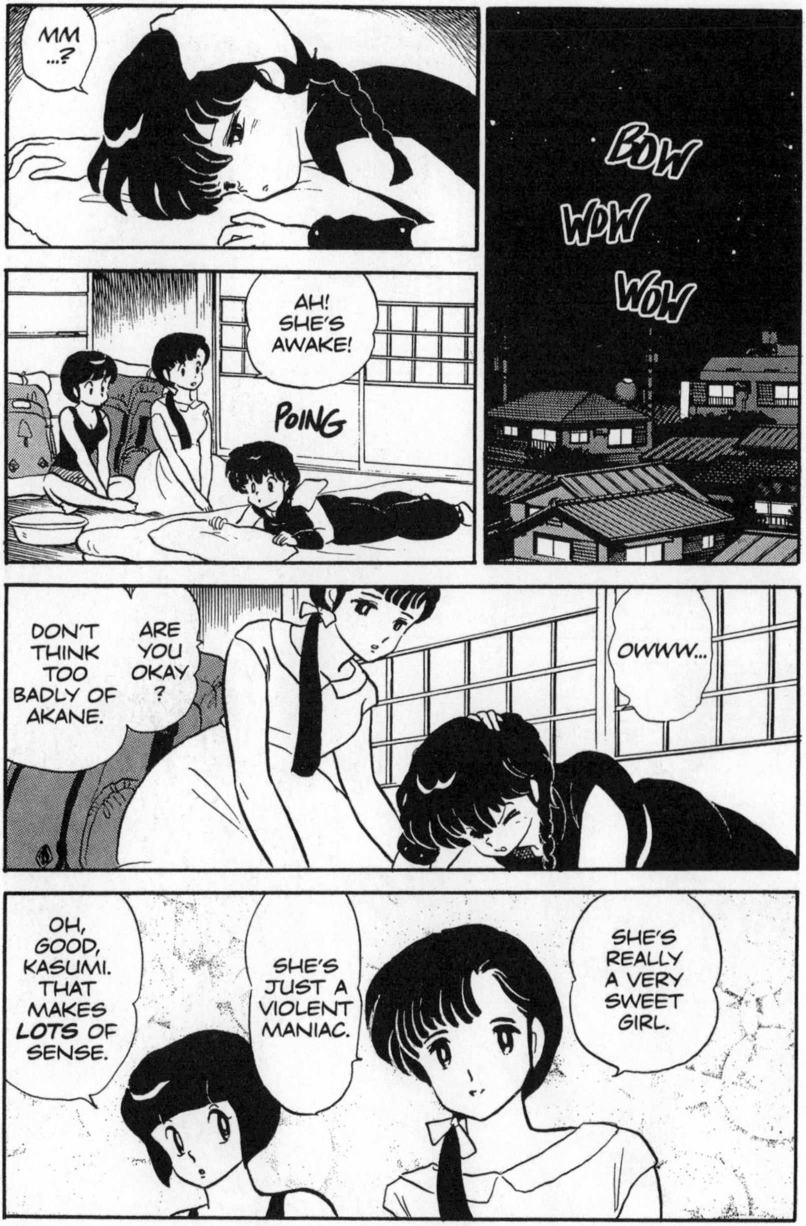
BOW
WOW
WOW
MM ...?
AH! SHE'S AWAKE!
POING
OWWW...
ARE YOU OKAY?
DON'T THINK TOO BADLY OF AKANE.
SHE'S REALLY A VERY SWEET GIRL.
SHE'S JUST A VIOLENT MANIAC.
OH, GOOD, KASUMI. THAT MAKES **LOTS** OF SENSE.

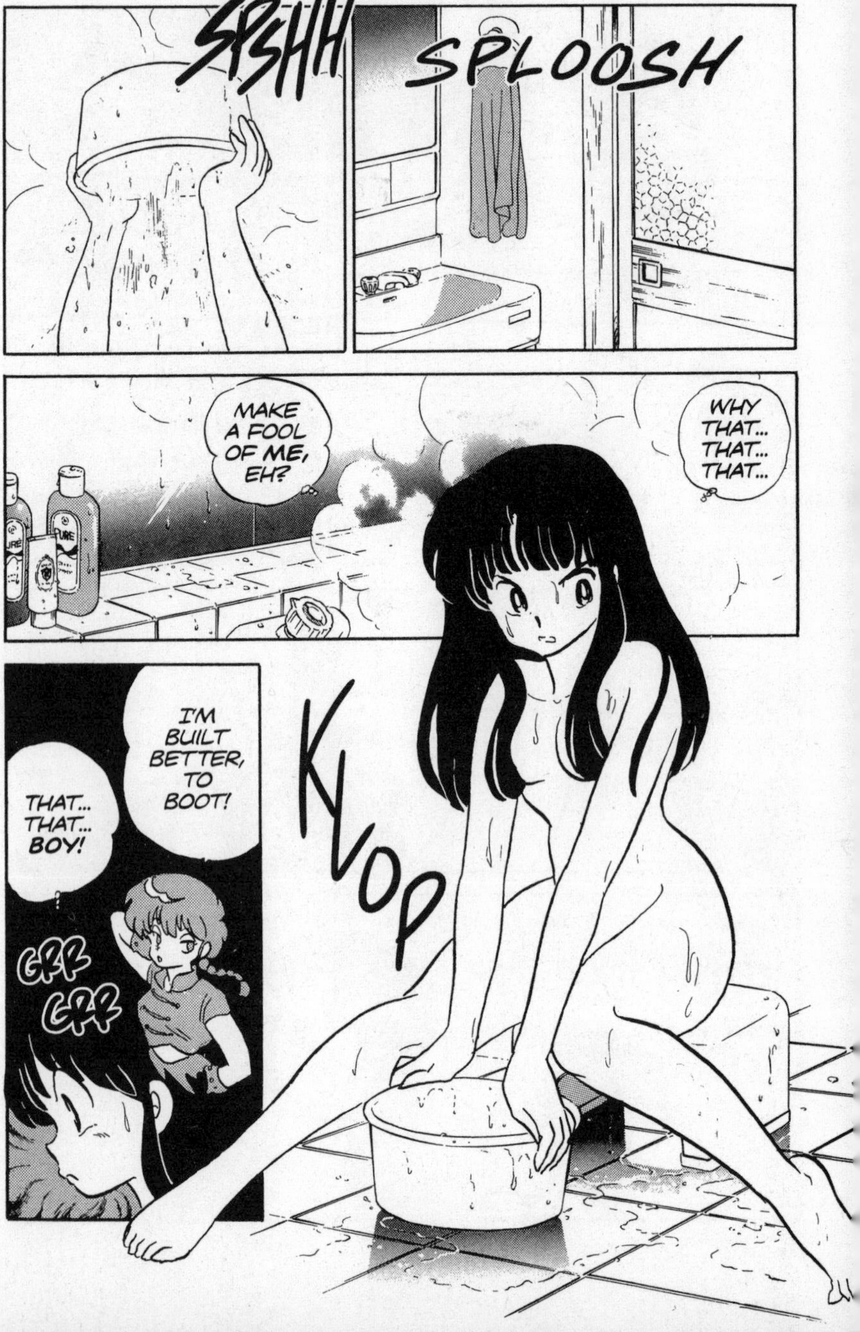
SPLOOSH
SPSHH
WHY THAT... THAT... THAT...
MAKE A FOOL OF ME, EH?
KLOP
I'M BUILT BETTER, TO BOOT!
THAT... THAT... BOY!
GRR GRR

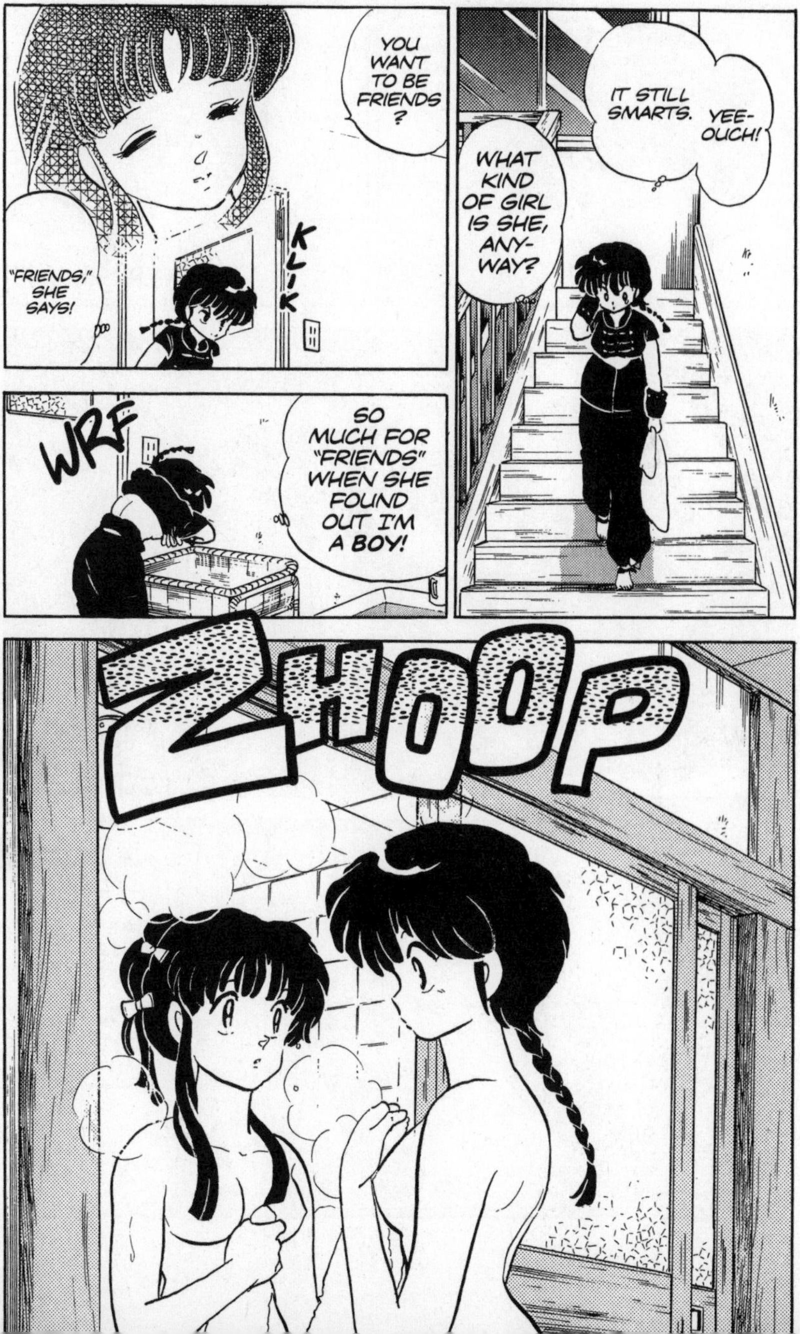
YEE-OUCH!
IT STILL SMARTS.
WHAT KIND OF GIRL IS SHE, ANYWAY?
YOU WANT TO BE FRIENDS?
KLIK
"FRIENDS," SHE SAYS!
SO MUCH FOR "FRIENDS" WHEN SHE FOUND OUT I'M A BOY!
WRF
ZHOOP

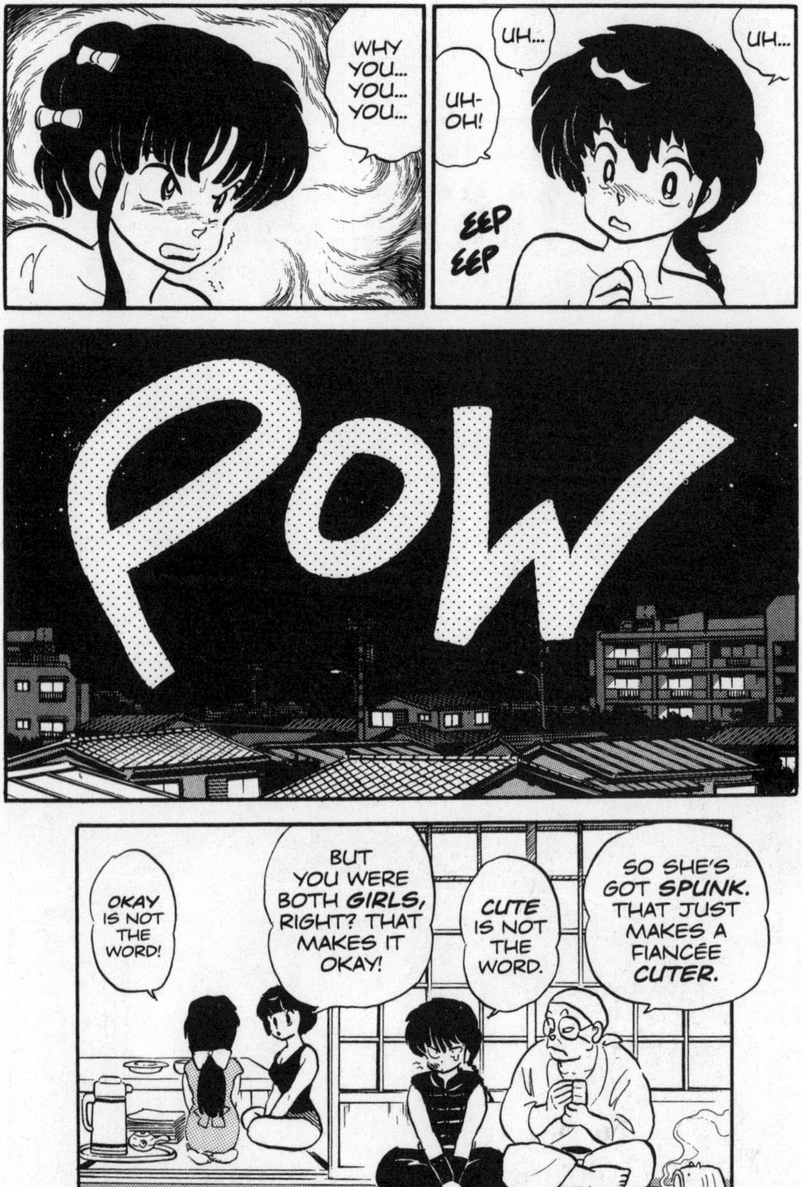
UH...
UH...
UH-OH!
EEP EEP
WHY YOU... YOU... YOU...
POW
SO SHE'S GOT SPUNK. THAT JUST MAKES A FIANCÉE CUTER.
CUTE IS NOT THE WORD.
BUT YOU WERE BOTH GIRLS, RIGHT? THAT MAKES IT OKAY!
OKAY IS NOT THE WORD!

# PART 3
# I HATE MEN!

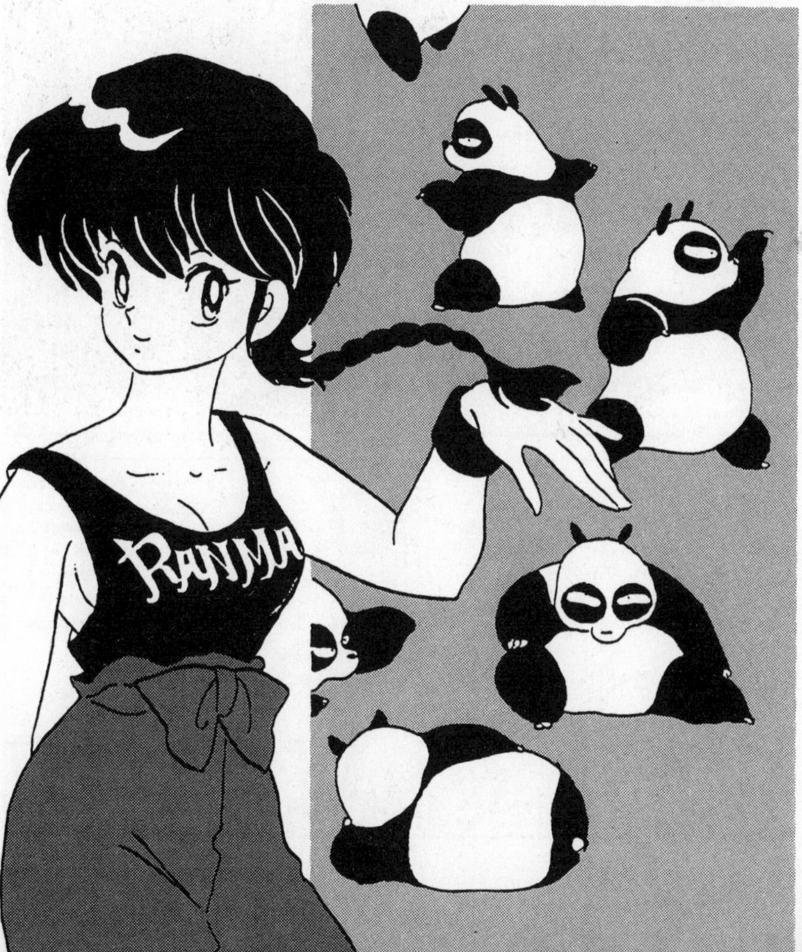
RANMA

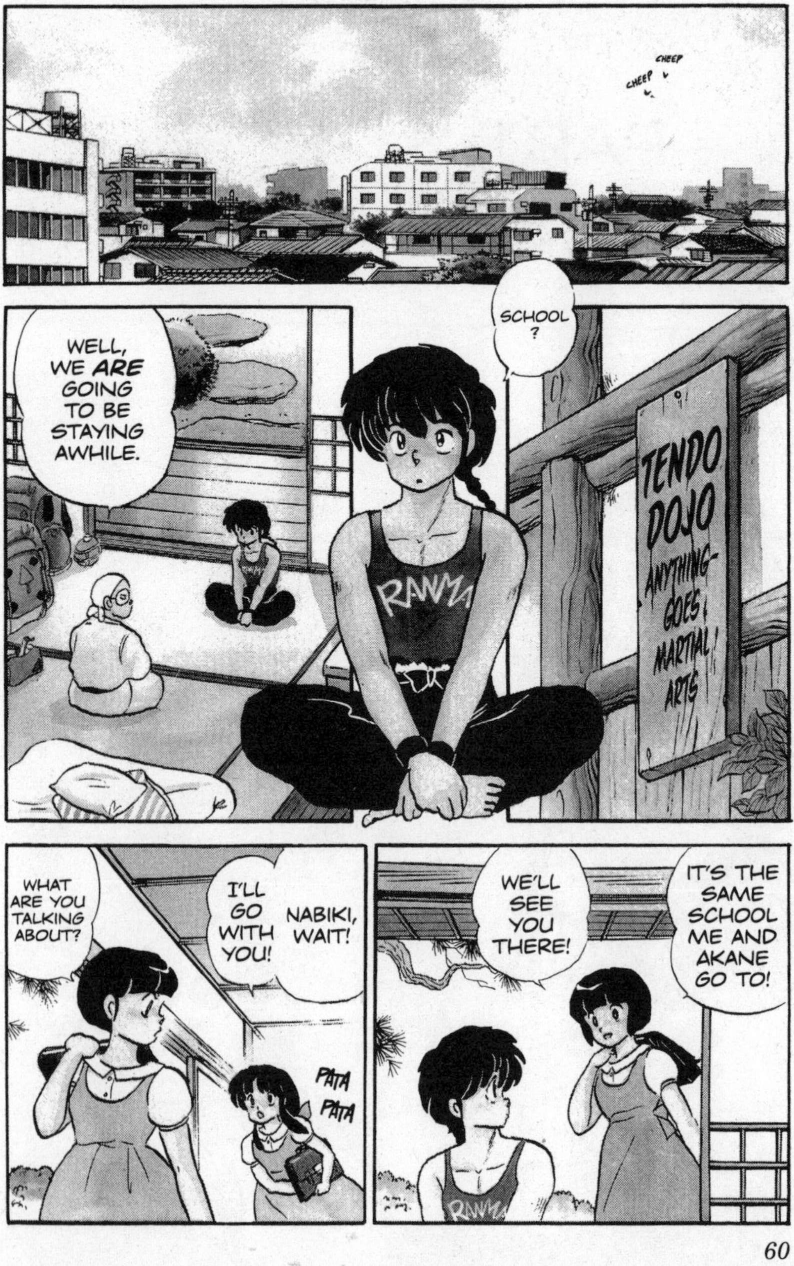
CHEEP
CHEEP
SCHOOL ?
WELL, WE ARE GOING TO BE STAYING AWHILE.
TENDO DOJO ANYTHING-GOES MARTIAL ARTS
IT'S THE SAME SCHOOL ME AND AKANE GO TO!
WE'LL SEE YOU THERE!
NABIKI, WAIT!
I'LL GO WITH YOU!
WHAT ARE YOU TALKING ABOUT?
PATA PATA

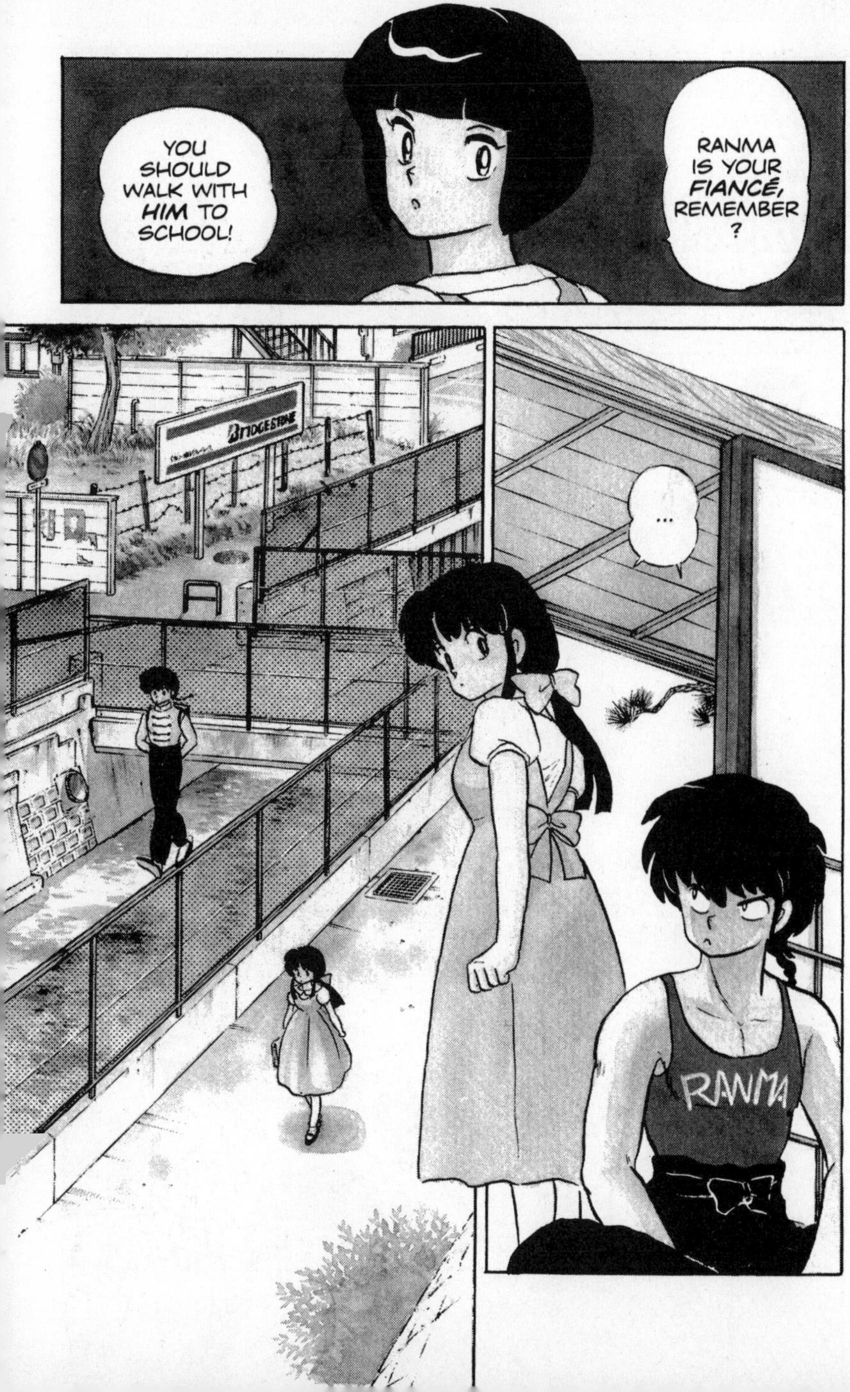
RANMA IS YOUR FIANCÉ, REMEMBER?
YOU SHOULD WALK WITH HIM TO SCHOOL!
...
RANMA
BRIDGESTONE

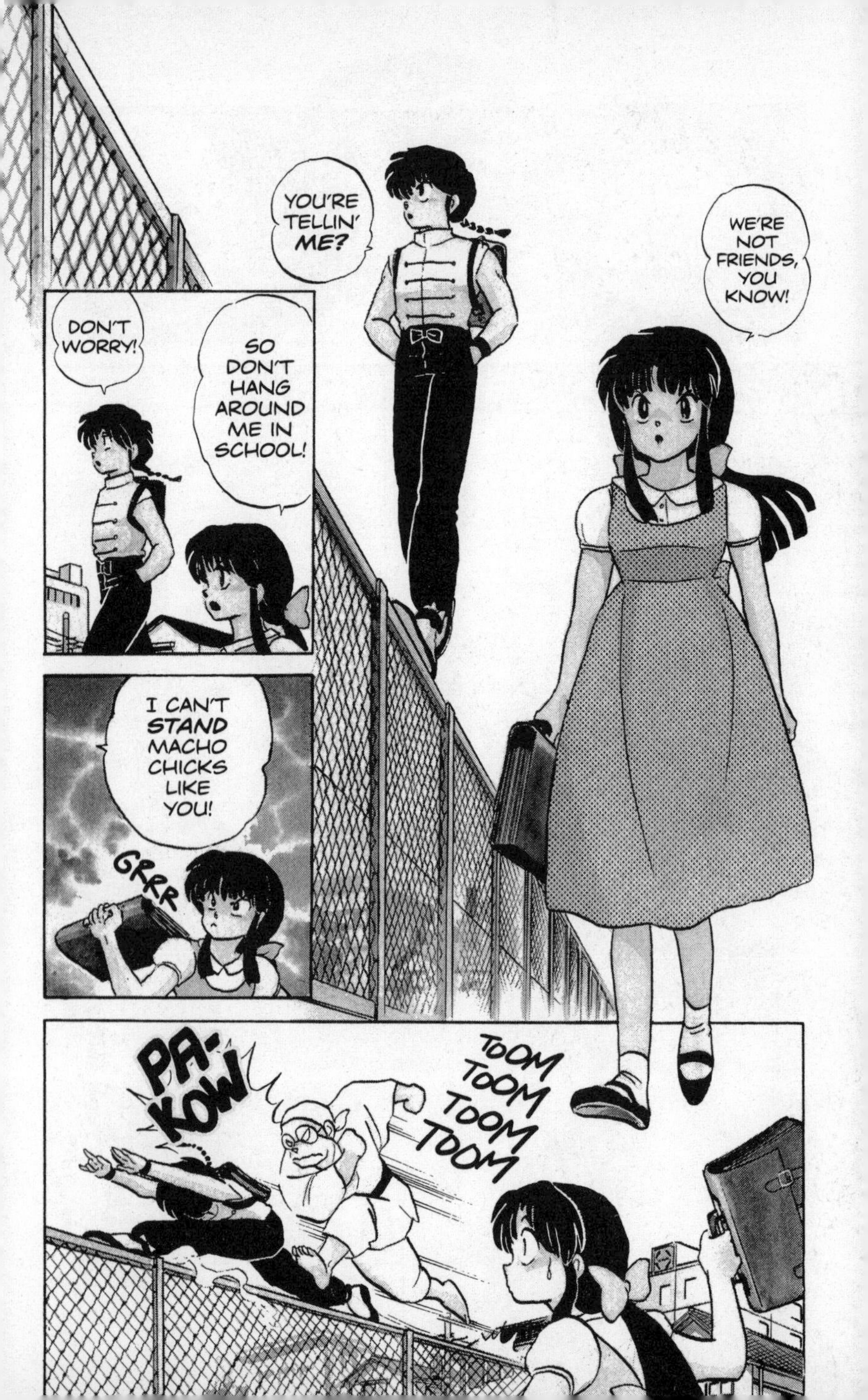

WE'RE NOT FRIENDS, YOU KNOW!
YOU'RE TELLIN' ME?
SO DON'T HANG AROUND ME IN SCHOOL!
DON'T WORRY!
I CAN'T STAND MACHO CHICKS LIKE YOU!
GRRR
TOOM TOOM TOOM TOOM
PA-KOW

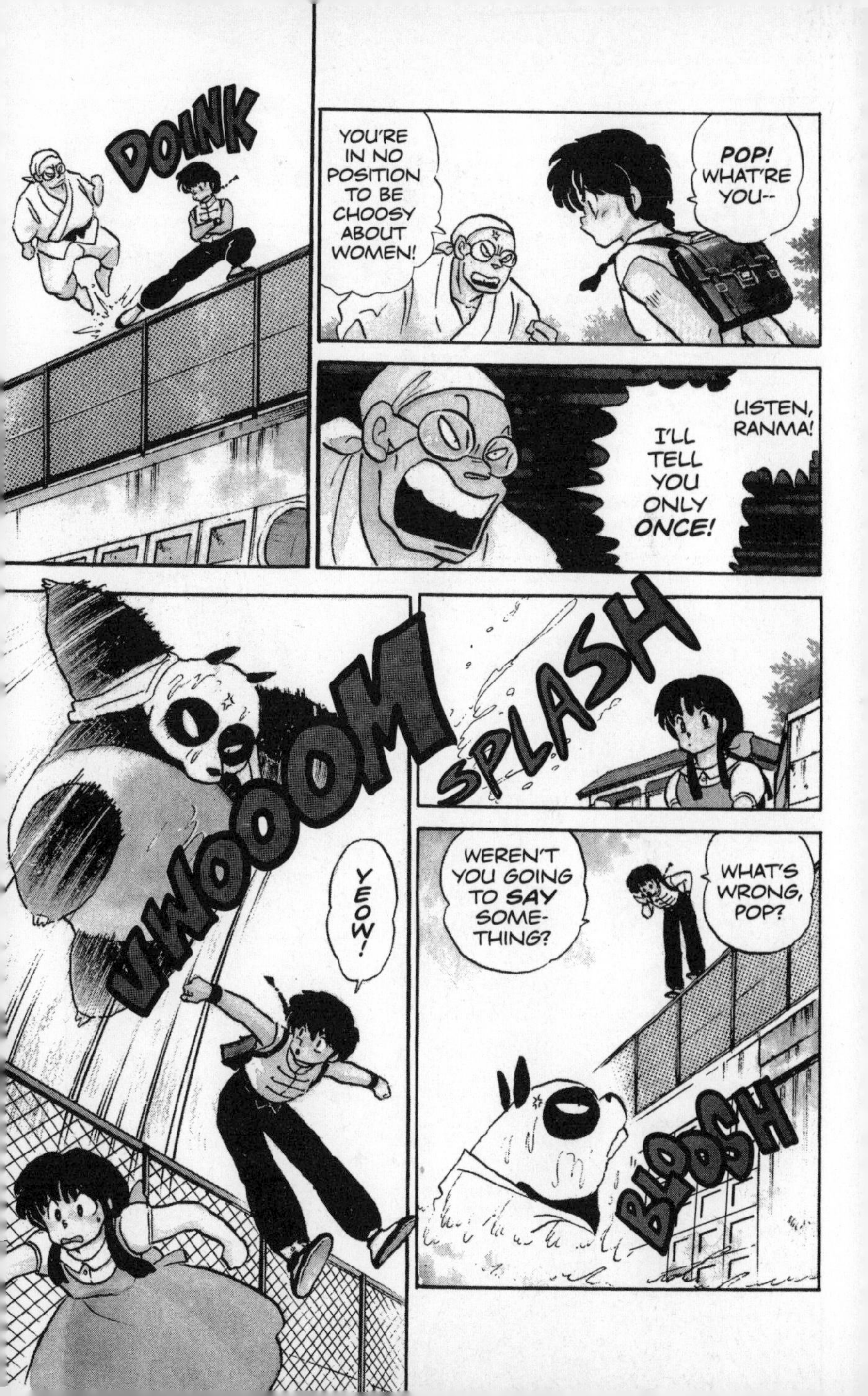
POP! WHAT'RE YOU--
YOU'RE IN NO POSITION TO BE CHOOSY ABOUT WOMEN!
LISTEN, RANMA!
I'LL TELL YOU ONLY ONCE!
DOINK
SPLASH
WHAT'S WRONG, POP?
WEREN'T YOU GOING TO SAY SOME-THING?
BLOOSH
VWOOOOM
YEOW!

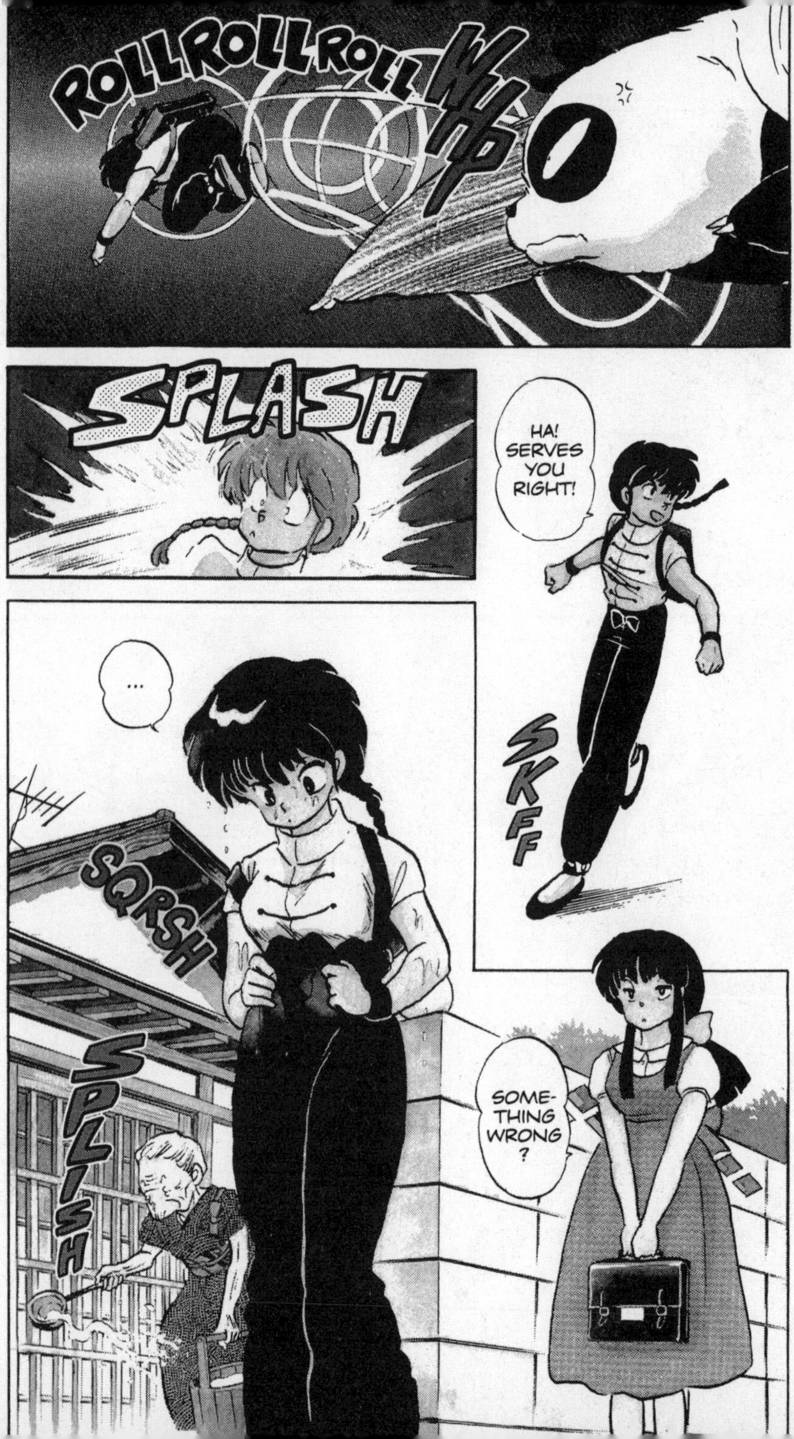
WHAP
ROLL ROLL ROLL
HA! SERVES YOU RIGHT!
SKFF
SPLASH
...
SQRSH
SPLISH
SOME-THING WRONG?

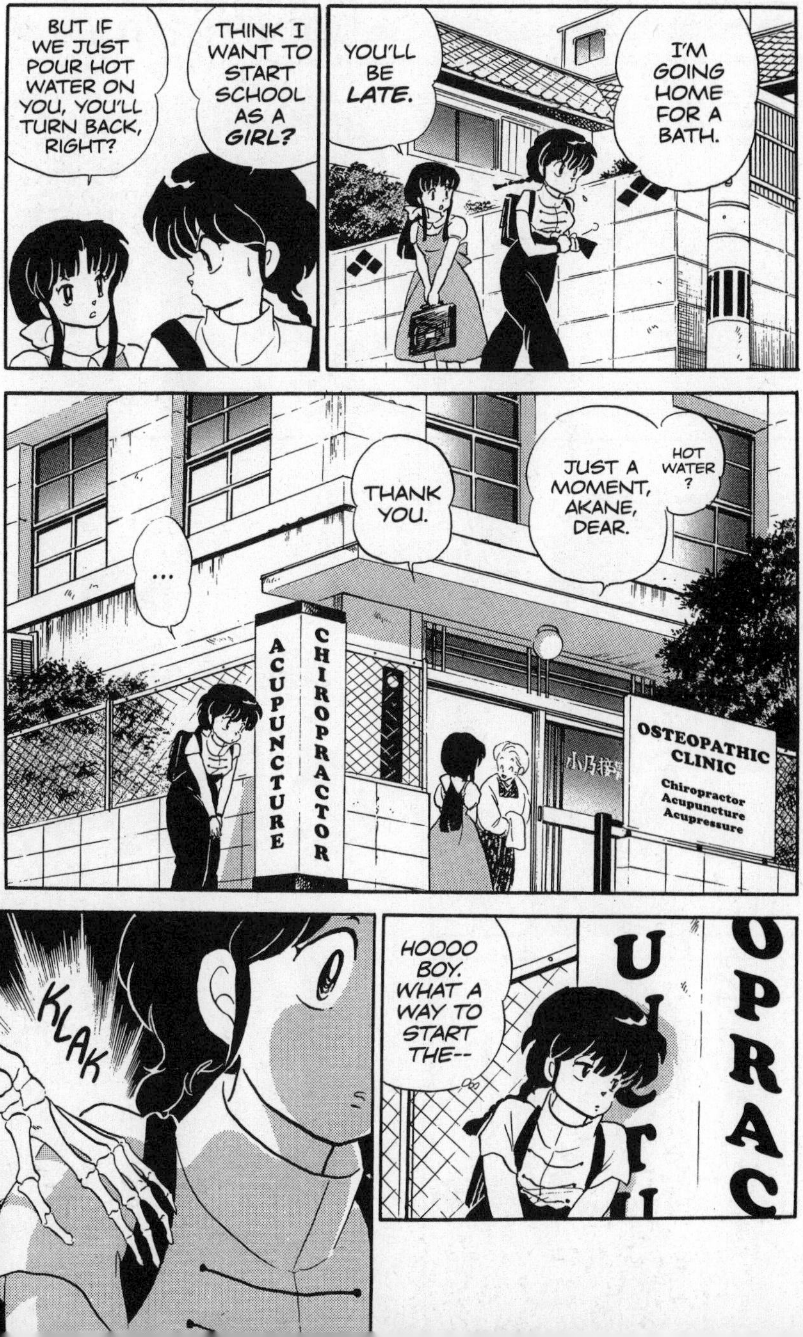
I'M GOING HOME FOR A BATH.
YOU'LL BE *LATE.*
THINK I WANT TO START SCHOOL AS A *GIRL?*
BUT IF WE JUST POUR HOT WATER ON YOU, YOU'LL TURN BACK, RIGHT?
HOT WATER?
JUST A MOMENT, AKANE, DEAR.
THANK YOU.
...
CHIROPRACTOR
ACUPUNCTURE
OSTEOPATHIC CLINIC
Chiropractor
Acupuncture
Acupressure
HOOOO BOY. WHAT A WAY TO START THE--
KLAK

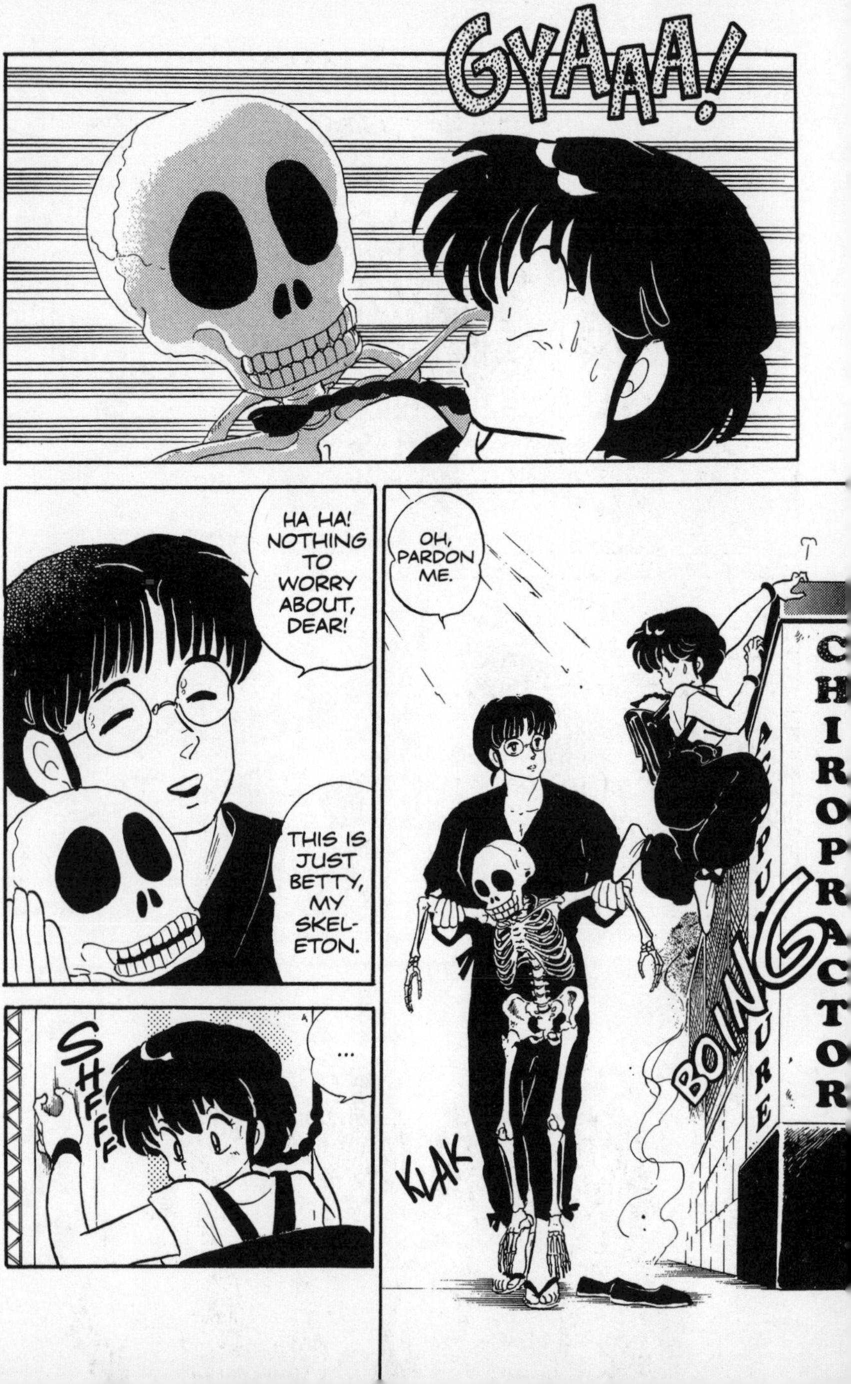
GYAAA!
OH, PARDON ME.
CHIROPRACTOR
ACUPUNCTURE
BOING
KLAK
HA HA! NOTHING TO WORRY ABOUT, DEAR!
THIS IS JUST BETTY, MY SKELETON.
SHFFF
...

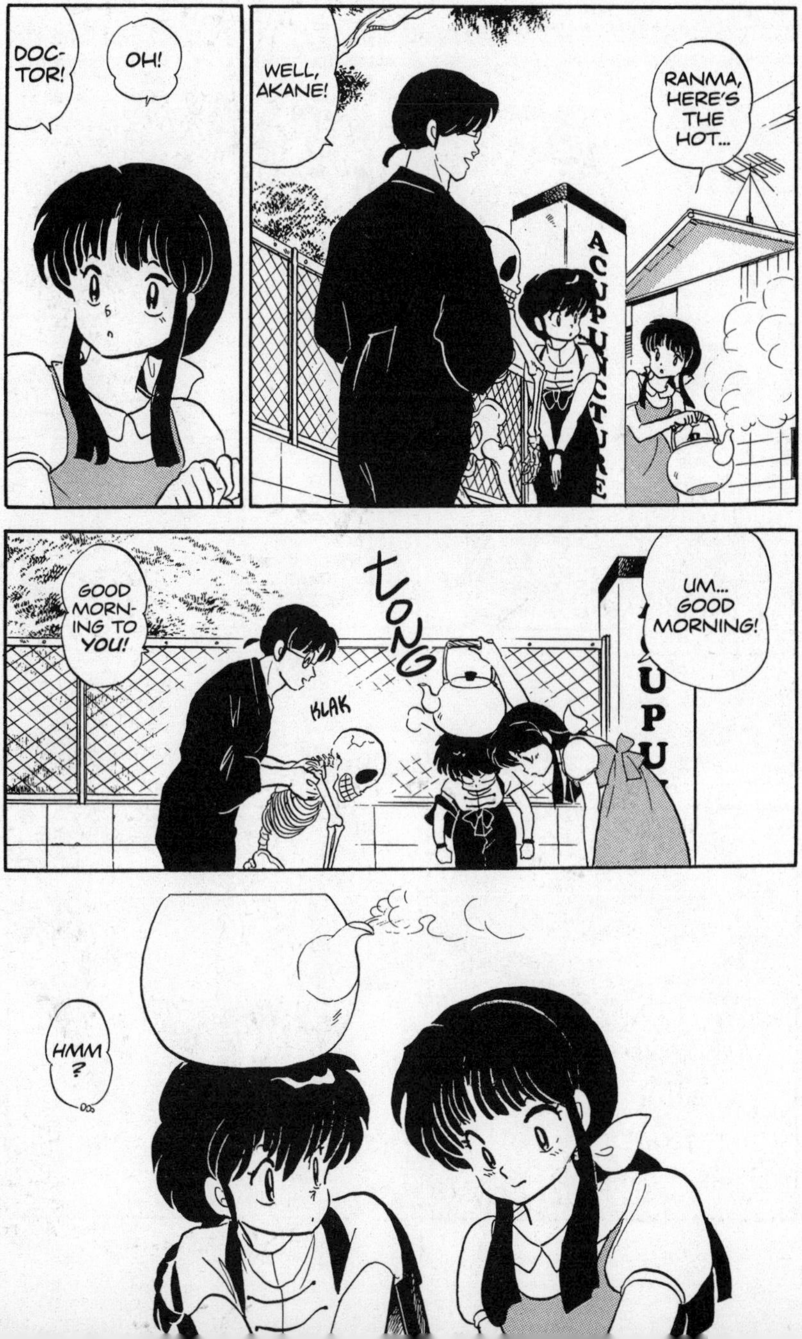
RANMA, HERE'S THE HOT...
ACUPUNCTURE
WELL, AKANE!
OH!
DOC-TOR!
UM... GOOD MORNING!
TONG
KLAK
GOOD MORNING TO YOU!
HMM ?

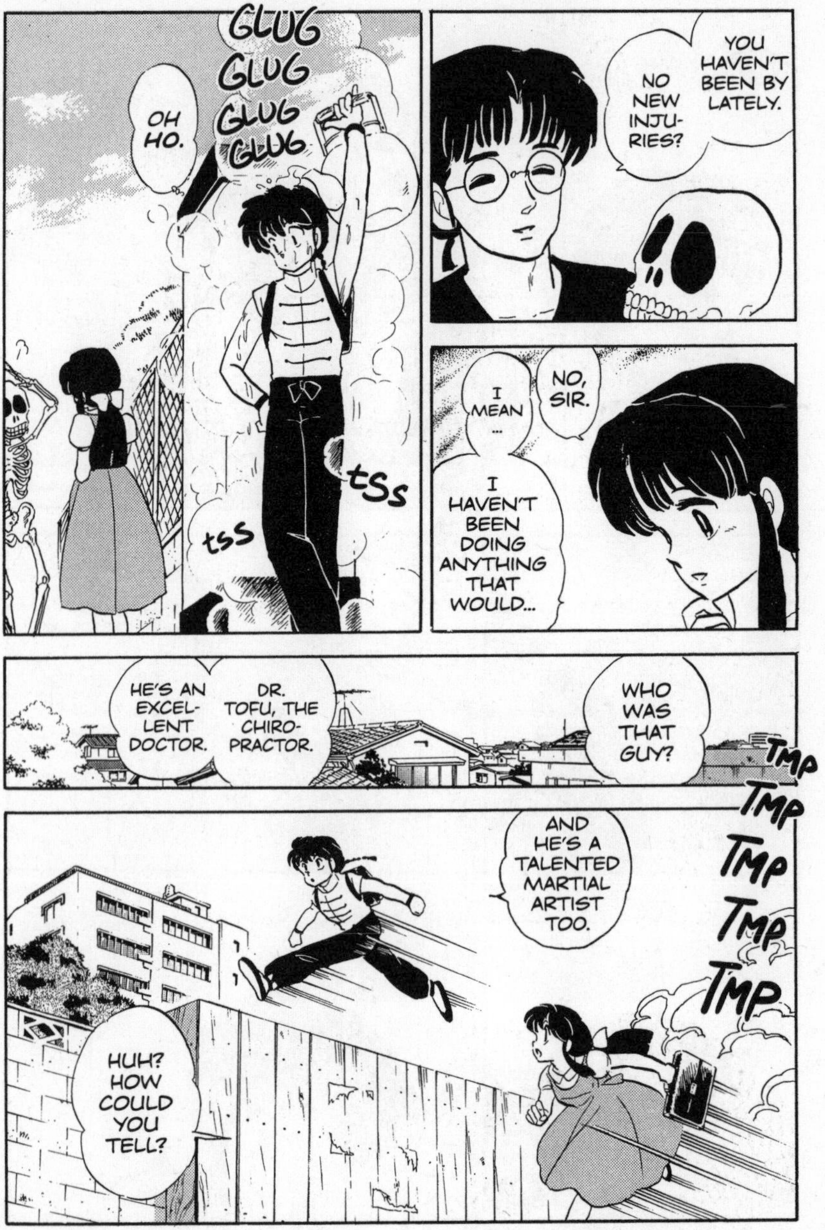
YOU HAVEN'T BEEN BY LATELY.
NO NEW INJURIES?
NO, SIR.
I MEAN ...
I HAVEN'T BEEN DOING ANYTHING THAT WOULD...
GLUG GLUG GLUG GLUG
OH HO.
tSs
tss
WHO WAS THAT GUY?
DR. TOFU, THE CHIROPRACTOR.
HE'S AN EXCELLENT DOCTOR.
TMP TMP TMP TMP TMP
AND HE'S A TALENTED MARTIAL ARTIST TOO.
HUH? HOW COULD YOU TELL?

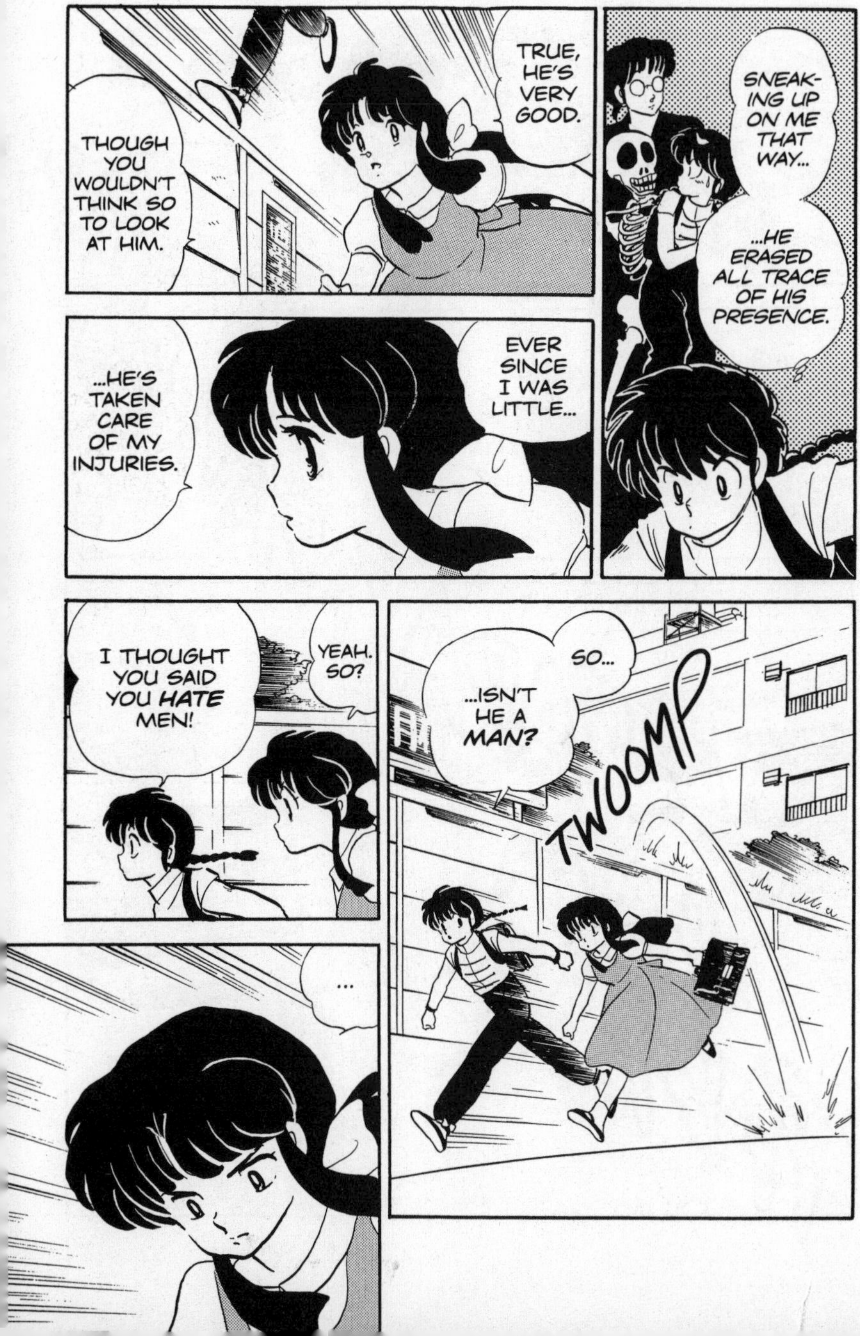
SNEAKING UP ON ME THAT WAY...
...HE ERASED ALL TRACE OF HIS PRESENCE.
TRUE, HE'S VERY GOOD.
THOUGH YOU WOULDN'T THINK SO TO LOOK AT HIM.
EVER SINCE I WAS LITTLE...
...HE'S TAKEN CARE OF MY INJURIES.
I THOUGHT YOU SAID YOU HATE MEN!
YEAH. SO?
SO...
...ISN'T HE A MAN?
TWOOMP
...

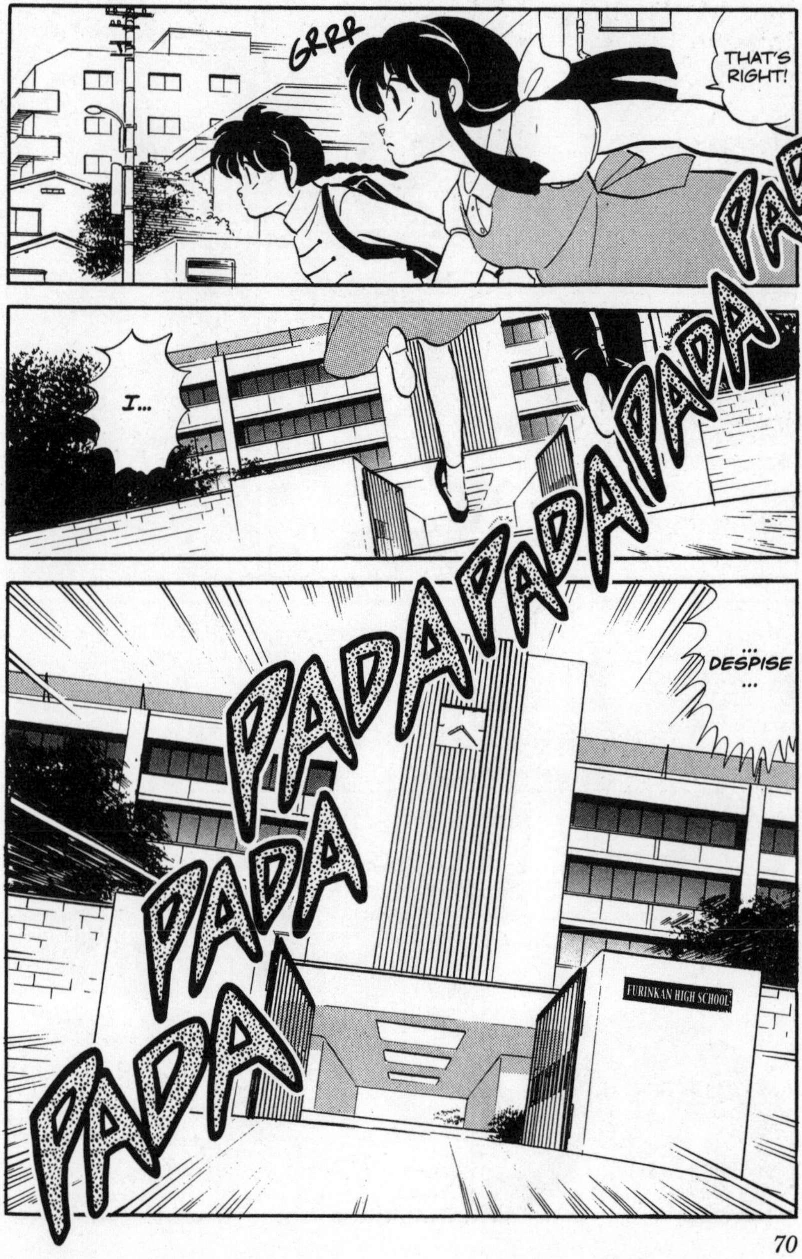
THAT'S RIGHT!
GRRR
I...
... DESPISE ...
PADA PADA PADA PADA PADA PADA PADA PADA
FURINKAN HIGH SCHOOL

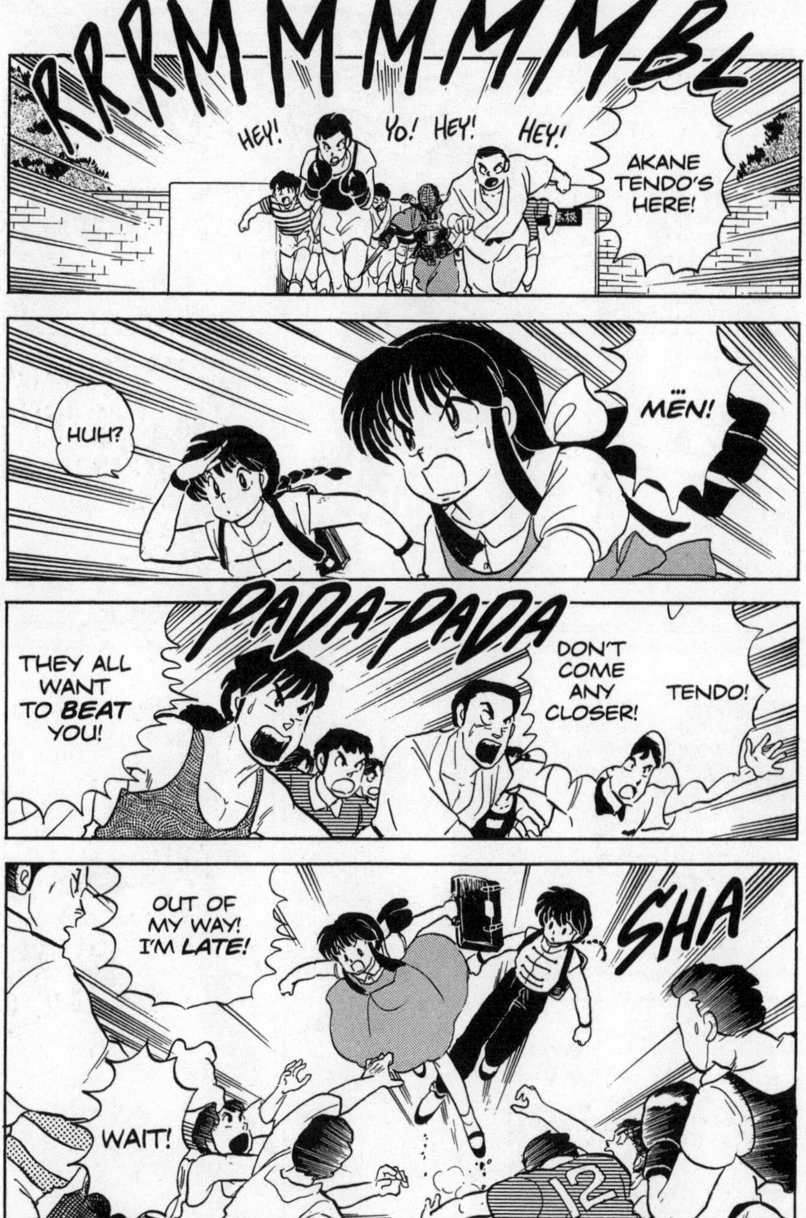
RRRMMMMMMBL
AKANE TENDO'S HERE!
HEY!
YO! HEY!
HEY!
...MËN!
HUH?
PADA PADA
TENDO!
DON'T COME ANY CLOSER!
THEY ALL WANT TO BEAT YOU!
SHA
OUT OF MY WAY! I'M LATE!
WAIT!

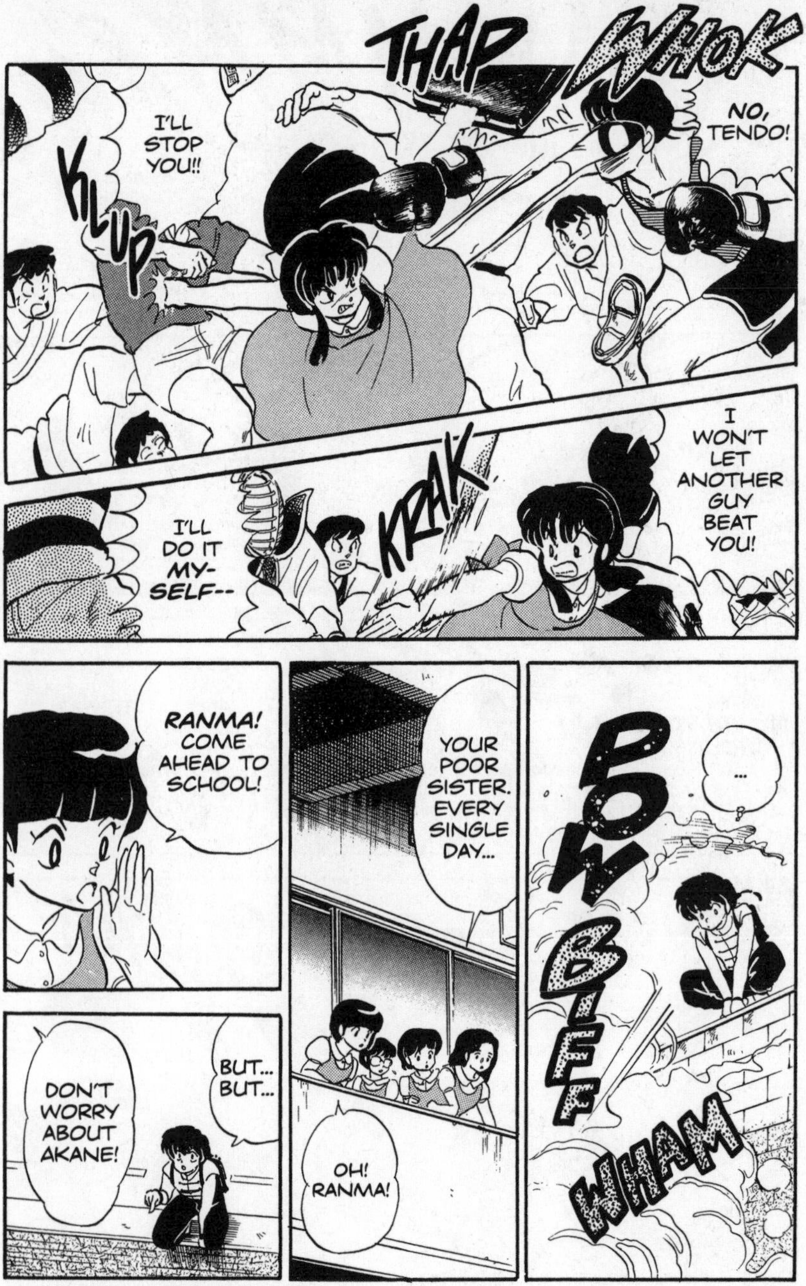
WHOK
NO, TENDO!
THAP
I'LL STOP YOU!!
KLUP
I WON'T LET ANOTHER GUY BEAT YOU!
KRAK
I'LL DO IT MY-SELF--
...
POW
BIFF
WHAM
YOUR POOR SISTER. EVERY SINGLE DAY...
OH! RANMA!
RANMA! COME AHEAD TO SCHOOL!
BUT... BUT...
DON'T WORRY ABOUT AKANE!

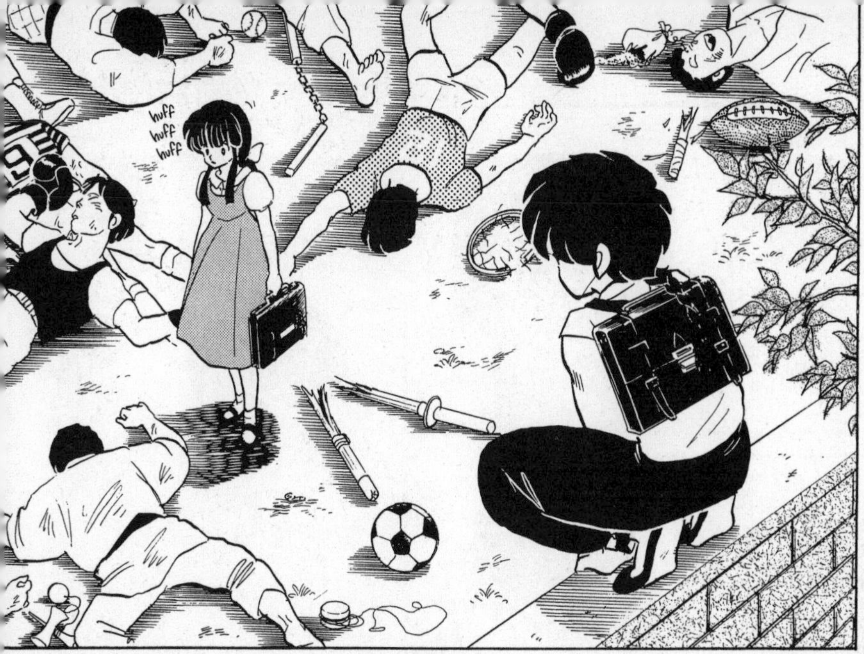
huff
huff
huff

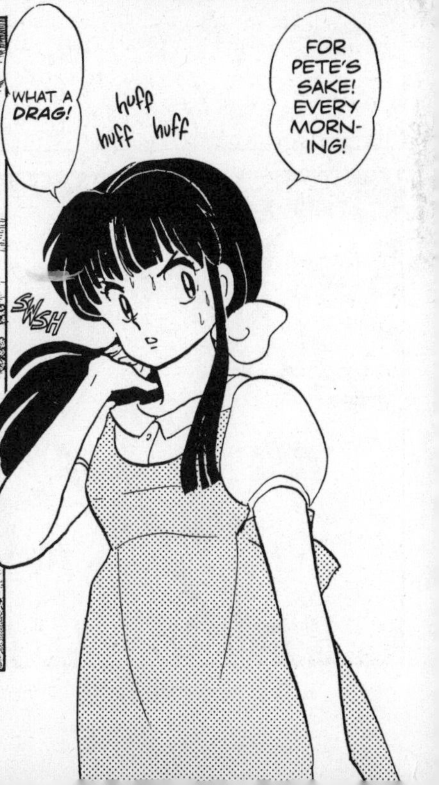
FOR PETE'S SAKE! EVERY MORNING!
huff huff huff
WHAT A DRAG!
SWSH

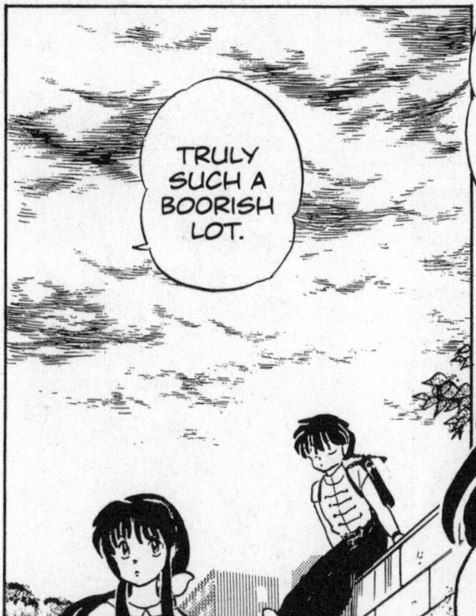
TRULY SUCH A BOORISH LOT.

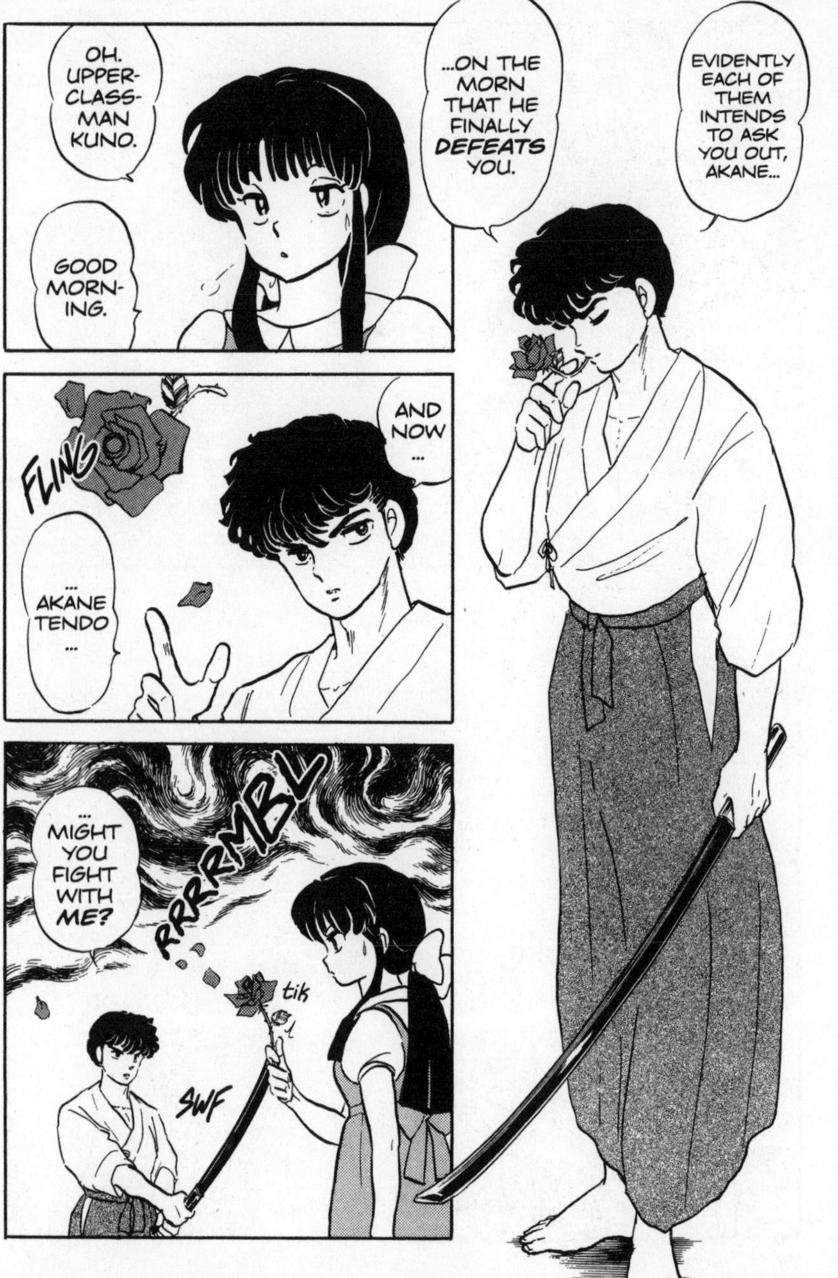
EVIDENTLY EACH OF THEM INTENDS TO ASK YOU OUT, AKANE...
...ON THE MORN THAT HE FINALLY **DEFEATS** YOU.
OH. UPPER-CLASS-MAN KUNO.
GOOD MORN-ING.
AND NOW ...
FLING
... AKANE TENDO ...
RRRRMBL
... MIGHT YOU FIGHT WITH **ME?**
tik
SWF

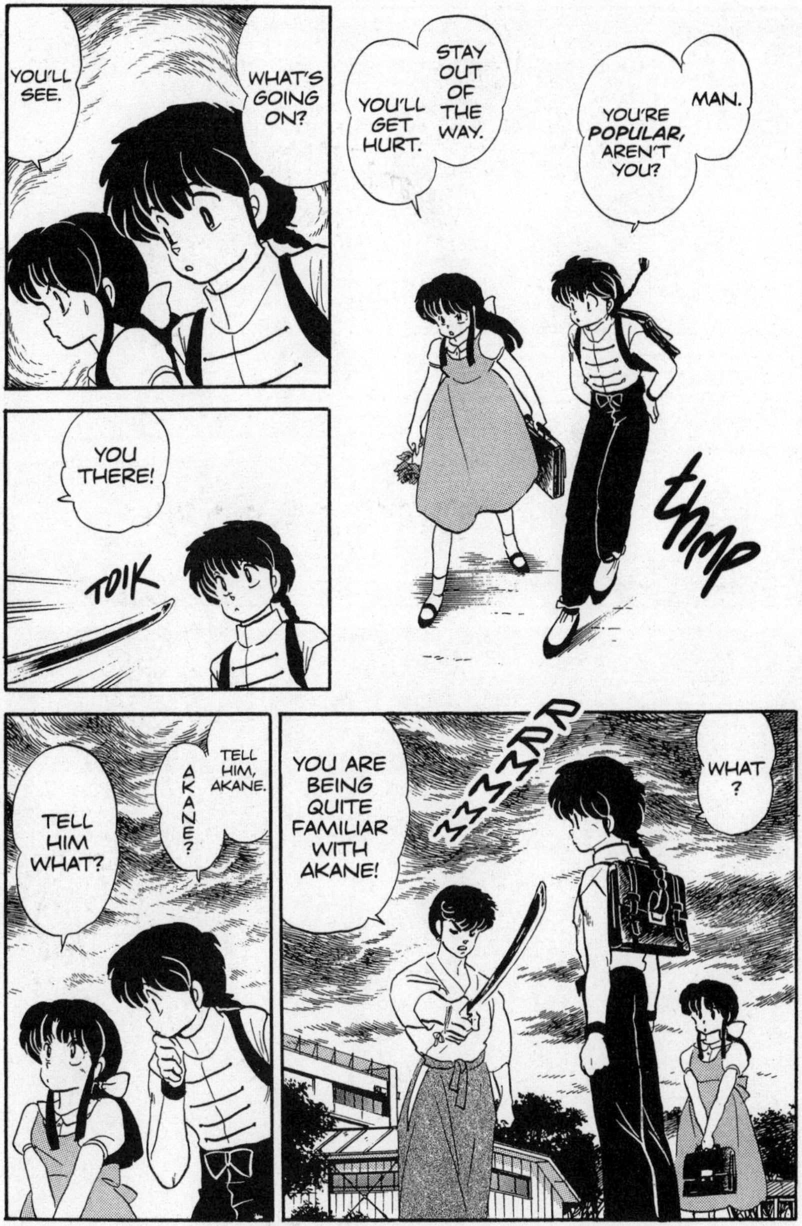
MAN. YOU'RE POPULAR, AREN'T YOU?
STAY OUT OF THE WAY. YOU'LL GET HURT.
thmp
WHAT'S GOING ON?
YOU'LL SEE.
YOU THERE!
TOIK
WHAT?
RRRMMMMMM
YOU ARE BEING QUITE FAMILIAR WITH AKANE!
TELL HIM, AKANE.
AKANE?
TELL HIM WHAT?

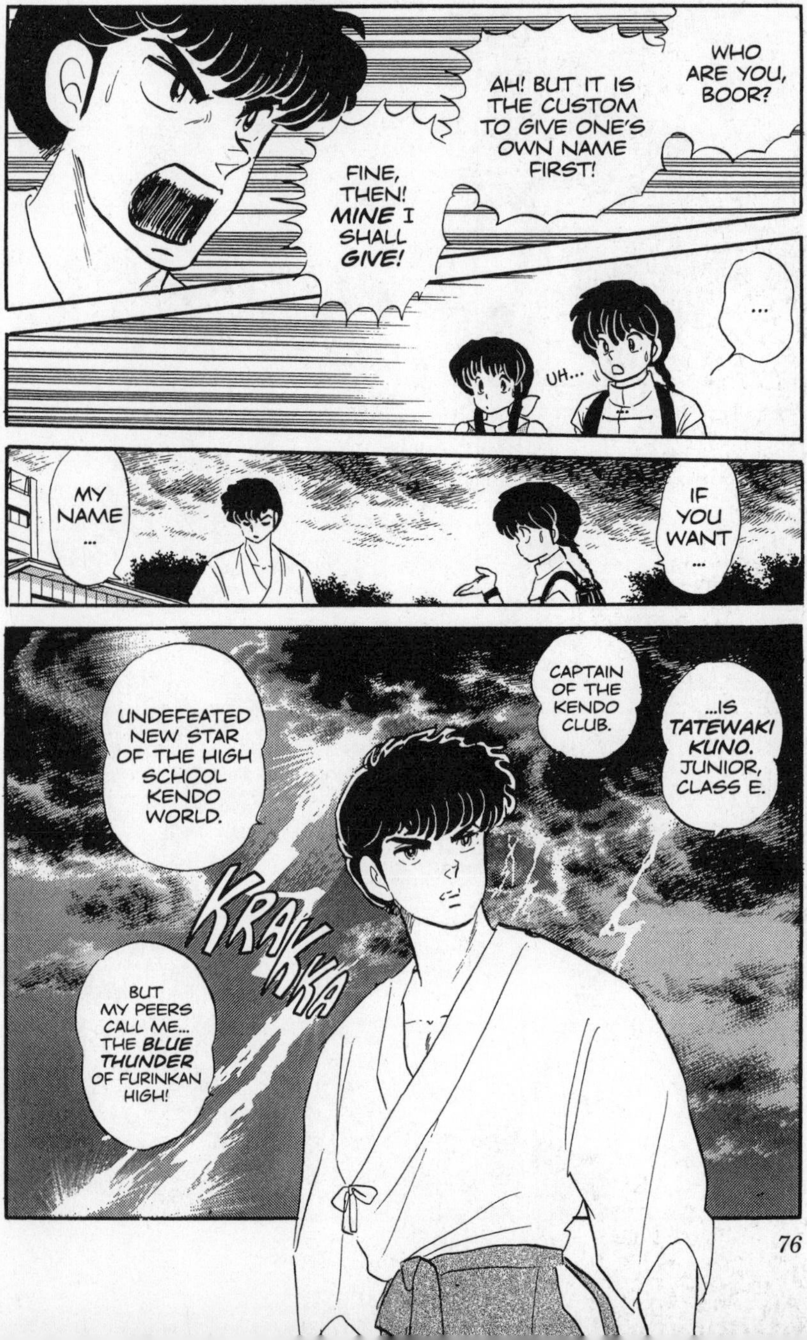
WHO ARE YOU, BOOR?
AH! BUT IT IS THE CUSTOM TO GIVE ONE'S OWN NAME FIRST!
FINE, THEN! **MINE** I SHALL **GIVE!**
...
UH...
IF YOU WANT ...
MY NAME ...
...IS **TATEWAKI KUNO.** JUNIOR, CLASS E.
CAPTAIN OF THE KENDO CLUB.
UNDEFEATED NEW STAR OF THE HIGH SCHOOL KENDO WORLD.
KRAKKA
BUT MY PEERS CALL ME... THE ***BLUE THUNDER*** OF FURINKAN HIGH!

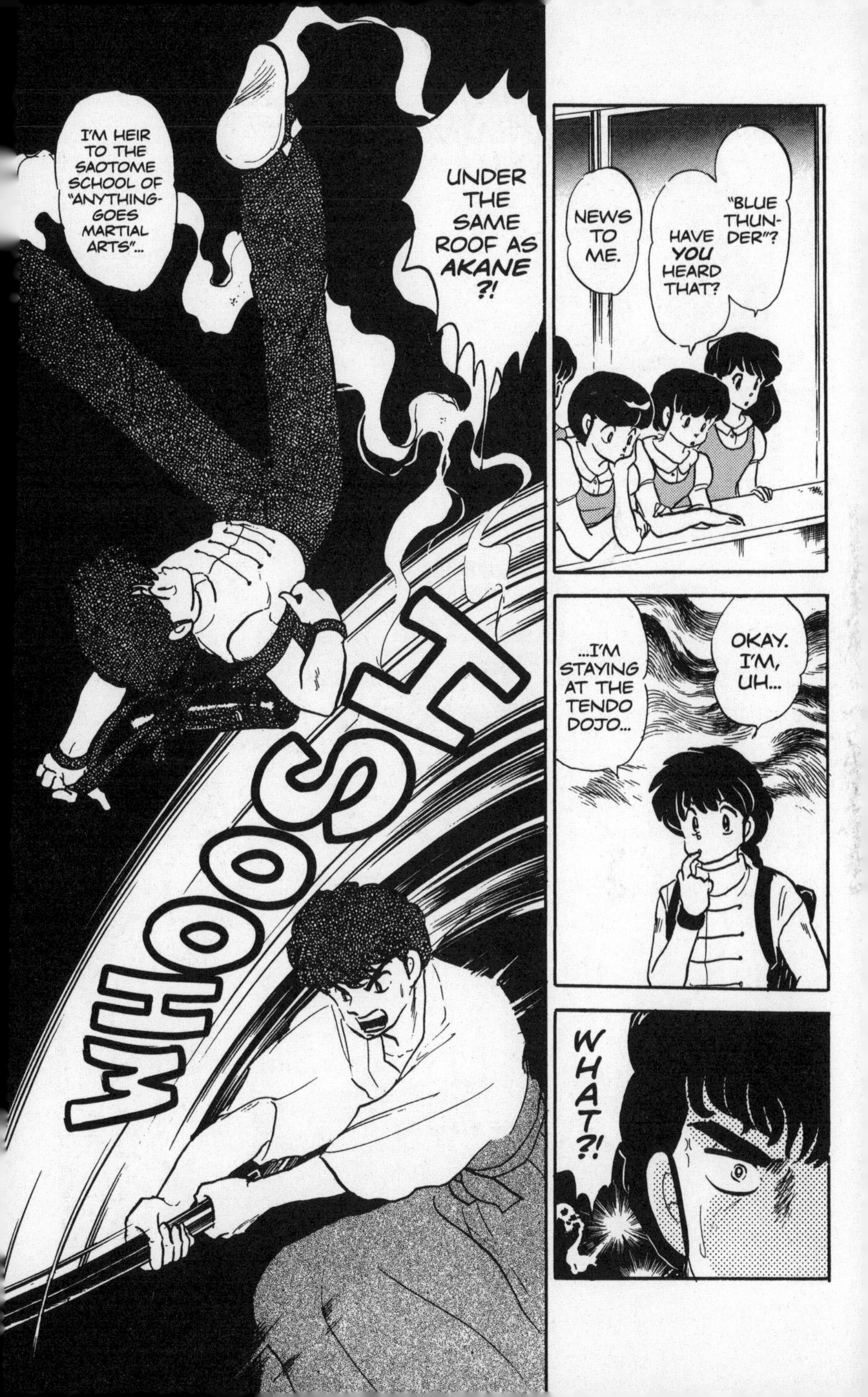
"BLUE THUNDER"?
HAVE YOU HEARD THAT?
NEWS TO ME.
OKAY. I'M, UH...
...I'M STAYING AT THE TENDO DOJO...
WHAT?!
UNDER THE SAME ROOF AS AKANE?!
I'M HEIR TO THE SAOTOME SCHOOL OF "ANYTHING-GOES MARTIAL ARTS"...
WHOOSH

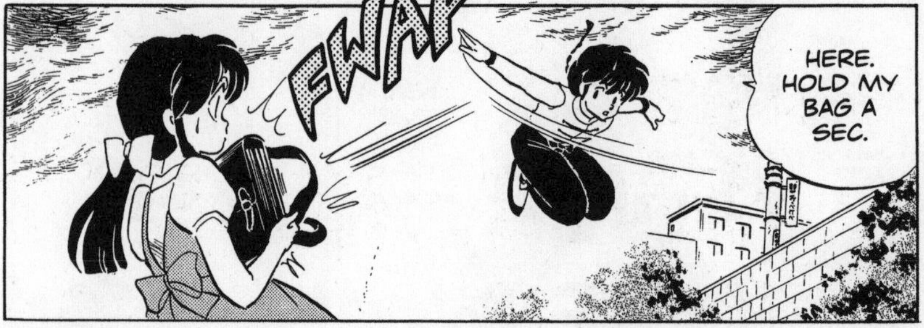
HERE. HOLD MY BAG A SEC.
FWAP

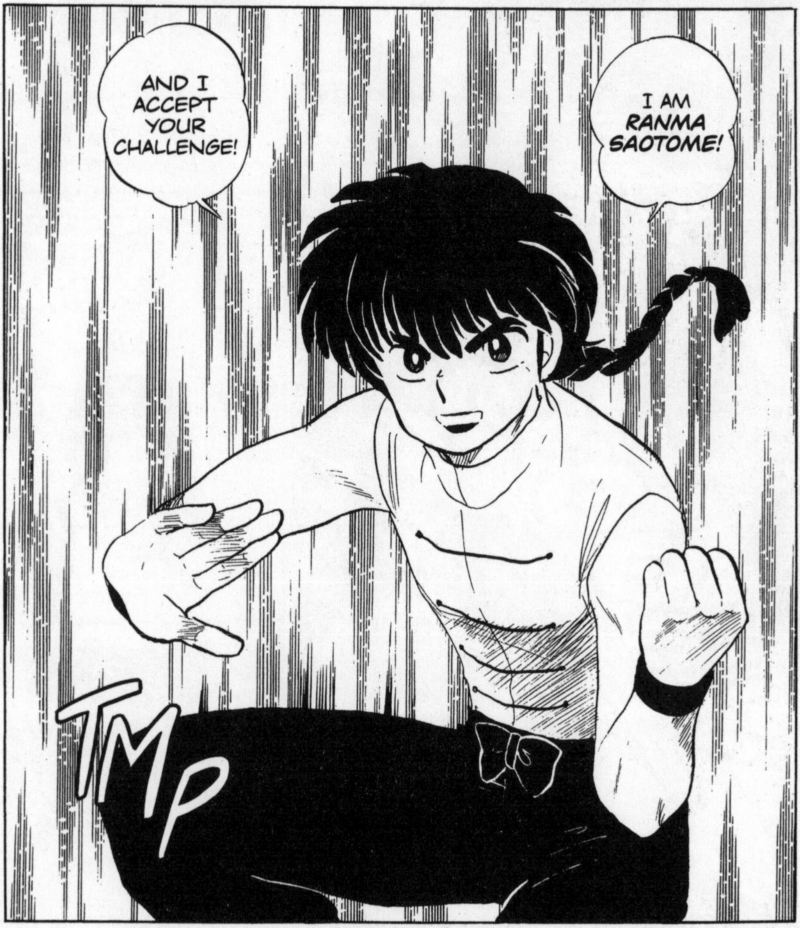
I AM *RANMA SAOTOME!*
AND I ACCEPT YOUR CHALLENGE!
TMP

## PART 4

# NEVER, NEVER, NEVER

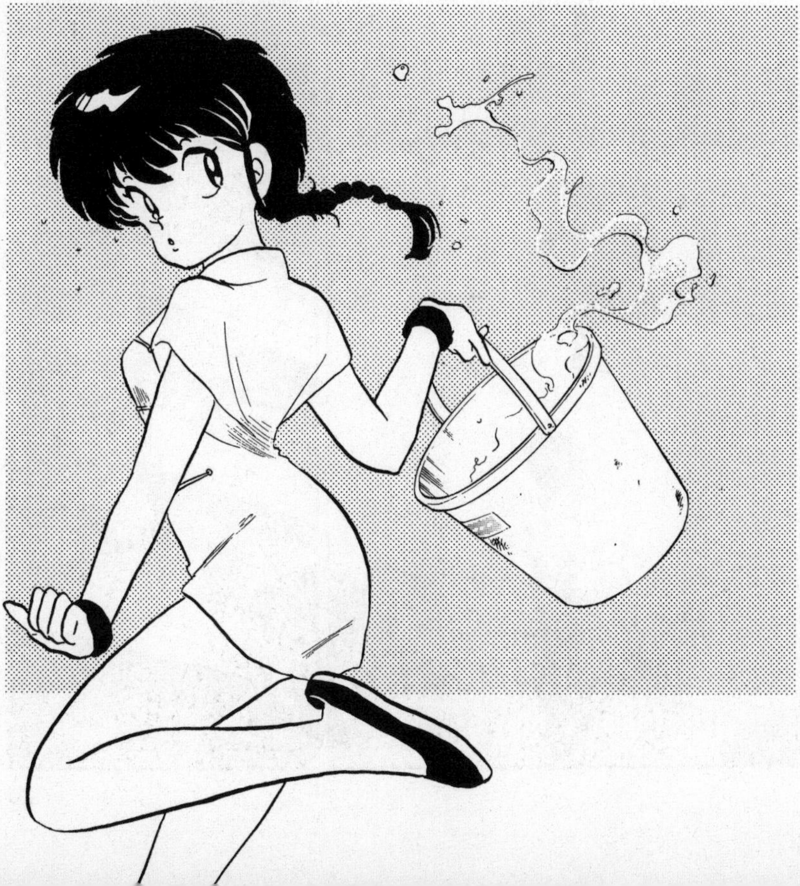

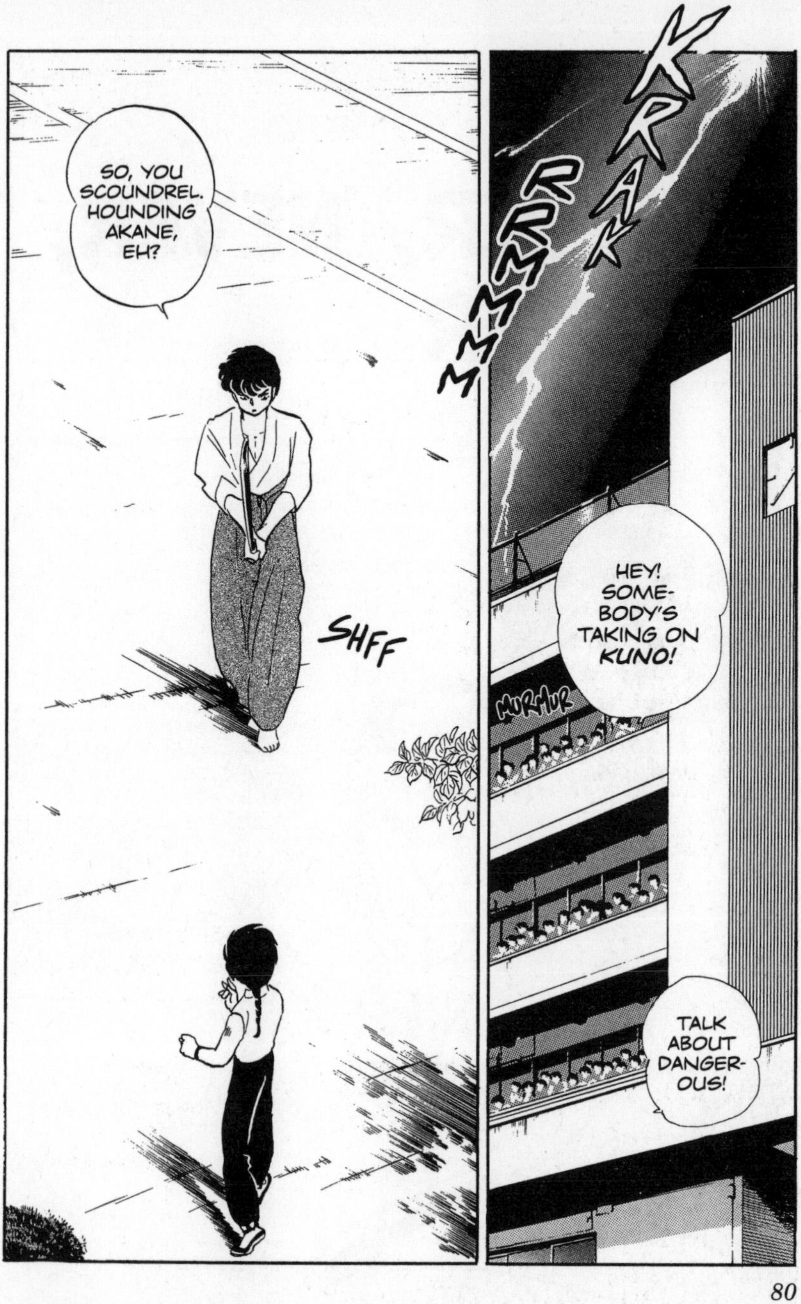
KRAK
RRMMMMM
HEY! SOME-BODY'S TAKING ON KUNO!
MURMUR
TALK ABOUT DANGER-OUS!
SO, YOU SCOUNDREL. HOUNDING AKANE, EH?
SHFF

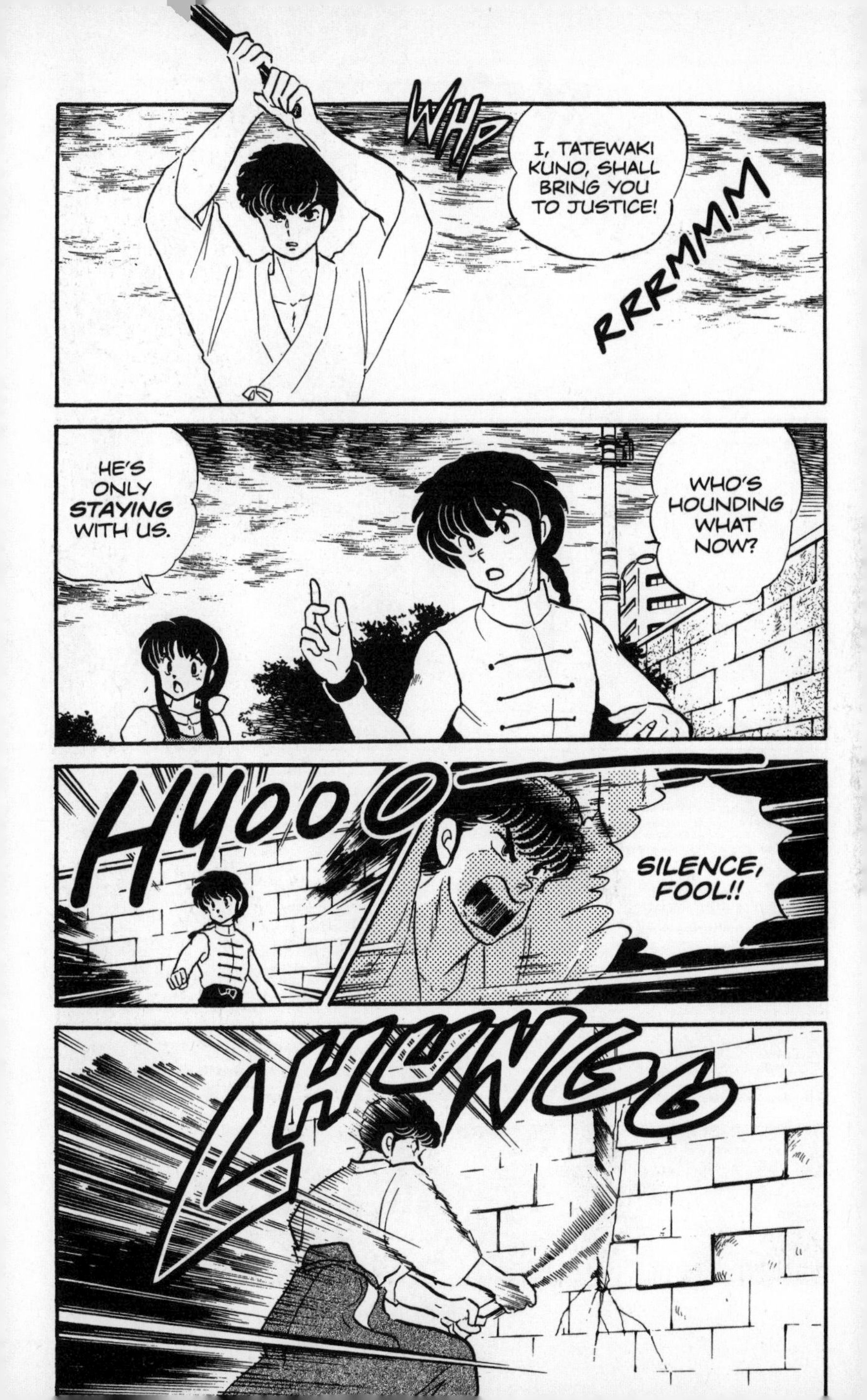
I, TATEWAKI KUNO, SHALL BRING YOU TO JUSTICE!
WHP
RRRMMM
WHO'S HOUNDING WHAT NOW?
HE'S ONLY STAYING WITH US.
SILENCE, FOOL!!
HYOOO
ZHONGG

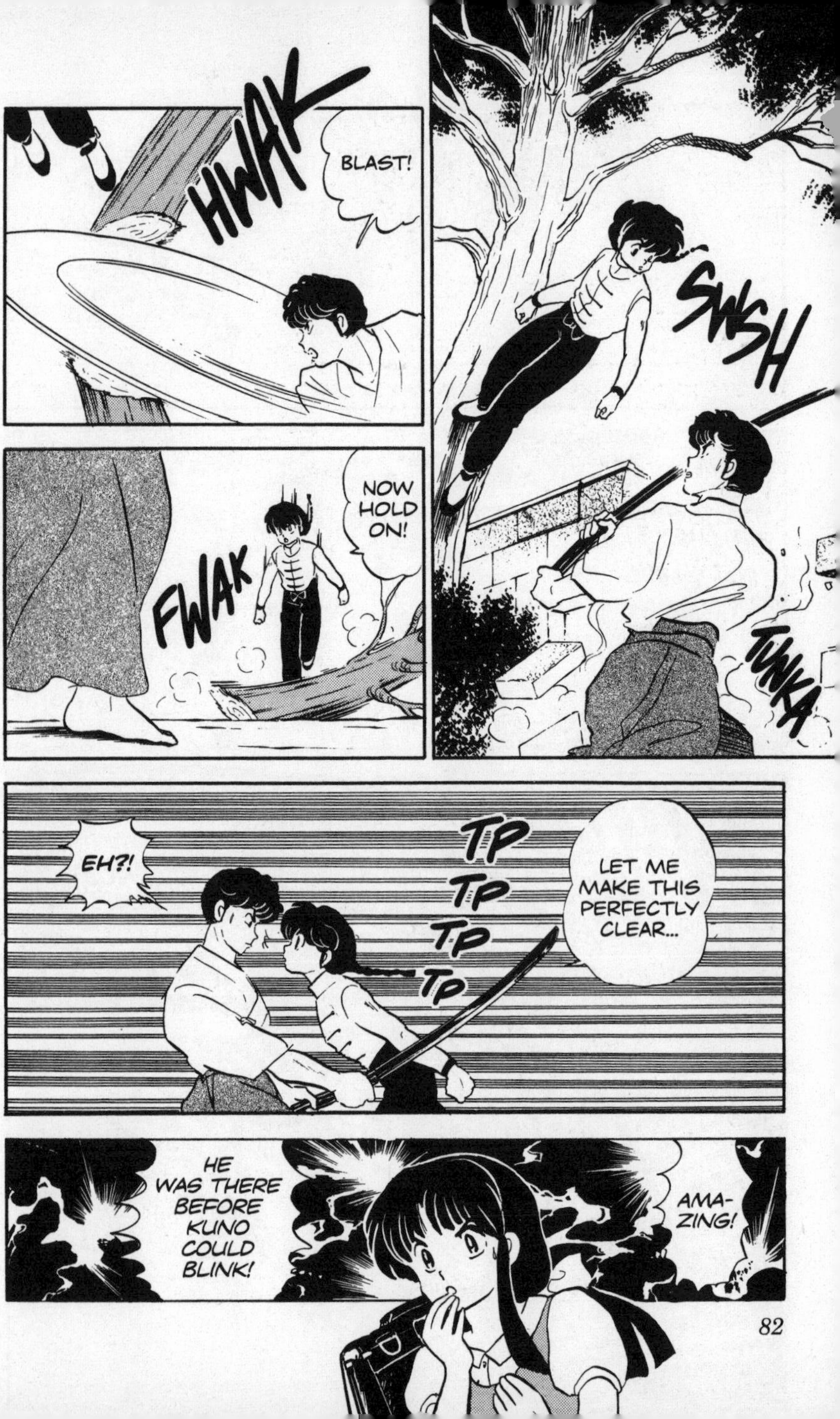
SWSH
TUNKA
HWAK
BLAST!
FWAK
NOW HOLD ON!
LET ME MAKE THIS PERFECTLY CLEAR...
TP TP TP TP
EH?!
AMA-ZING!
HE WAS THERE BEFORE KUNO COULD BLINK!

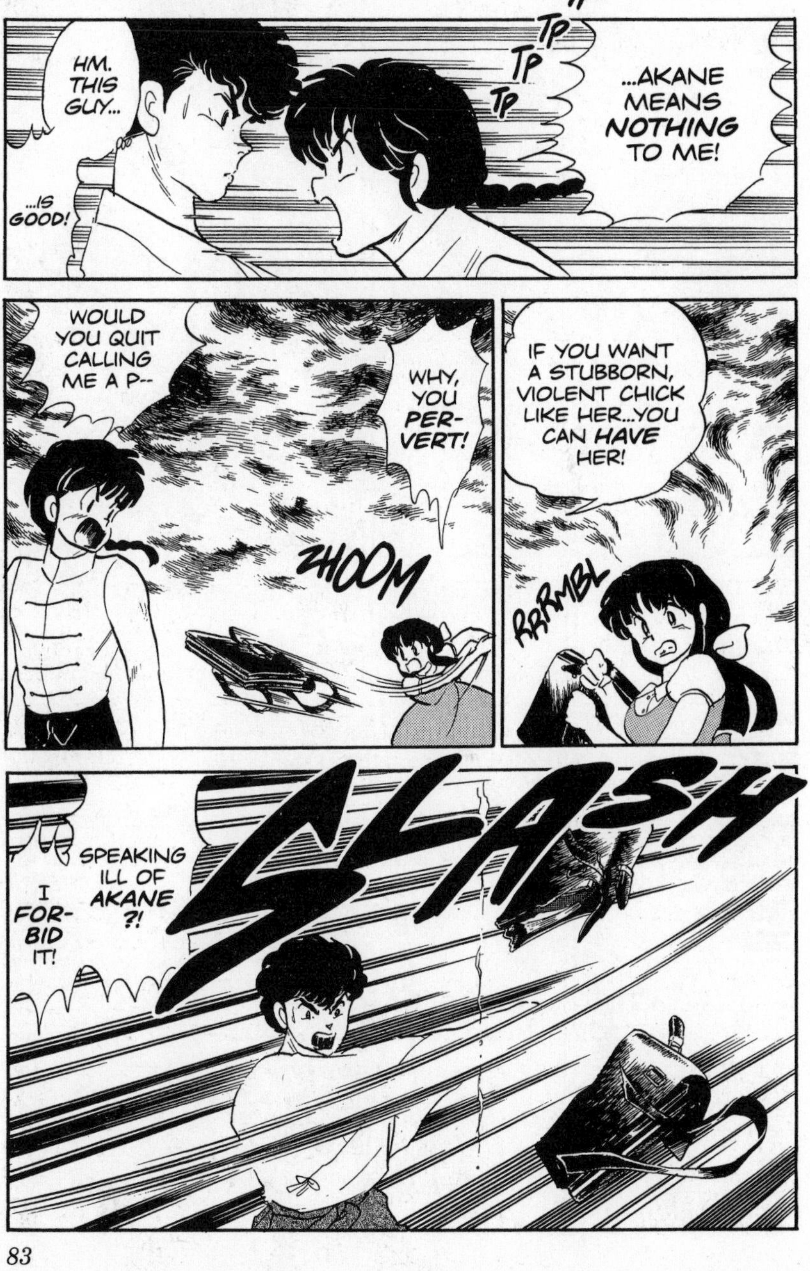
TP TP TP TP
...AKANE MEANS NOTHING TO ME!
HM. THIS GUY...
...IS GOOD!
IF YOU WANT A STUBBORN, VIOLENT CHICK LIKE HER...YOU CAN HAVE HER!
RRRMBL
WHY, YOU PER-VERT!
WOULD YOU QUIT CALLING ME A P--
ZHOOM
SLASH
SPEAKING ILL OF AKANE ?!
I FOR-BID IT!

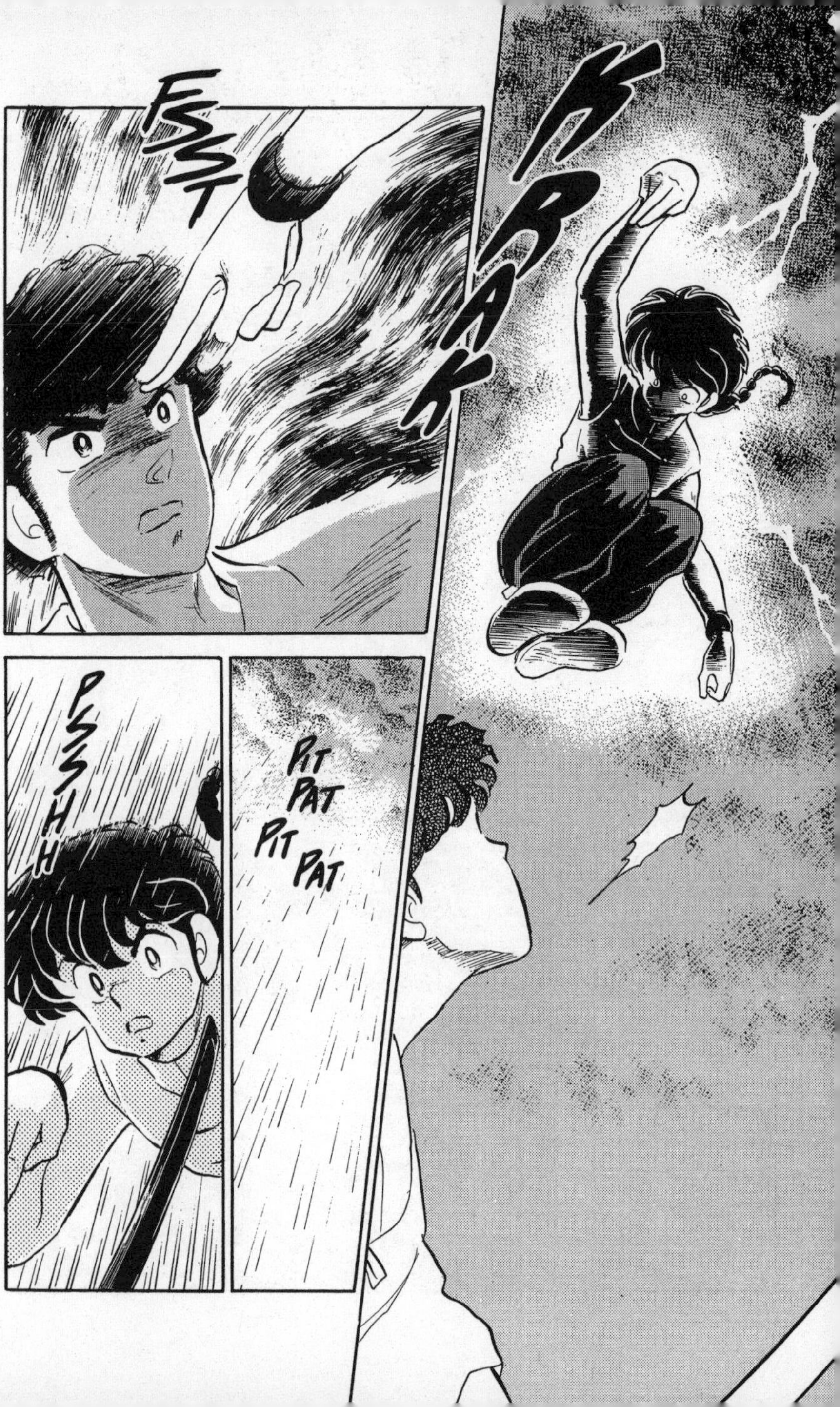
KRAAK
FSST
PIT
PAT
PIT
PAT
PSSHH

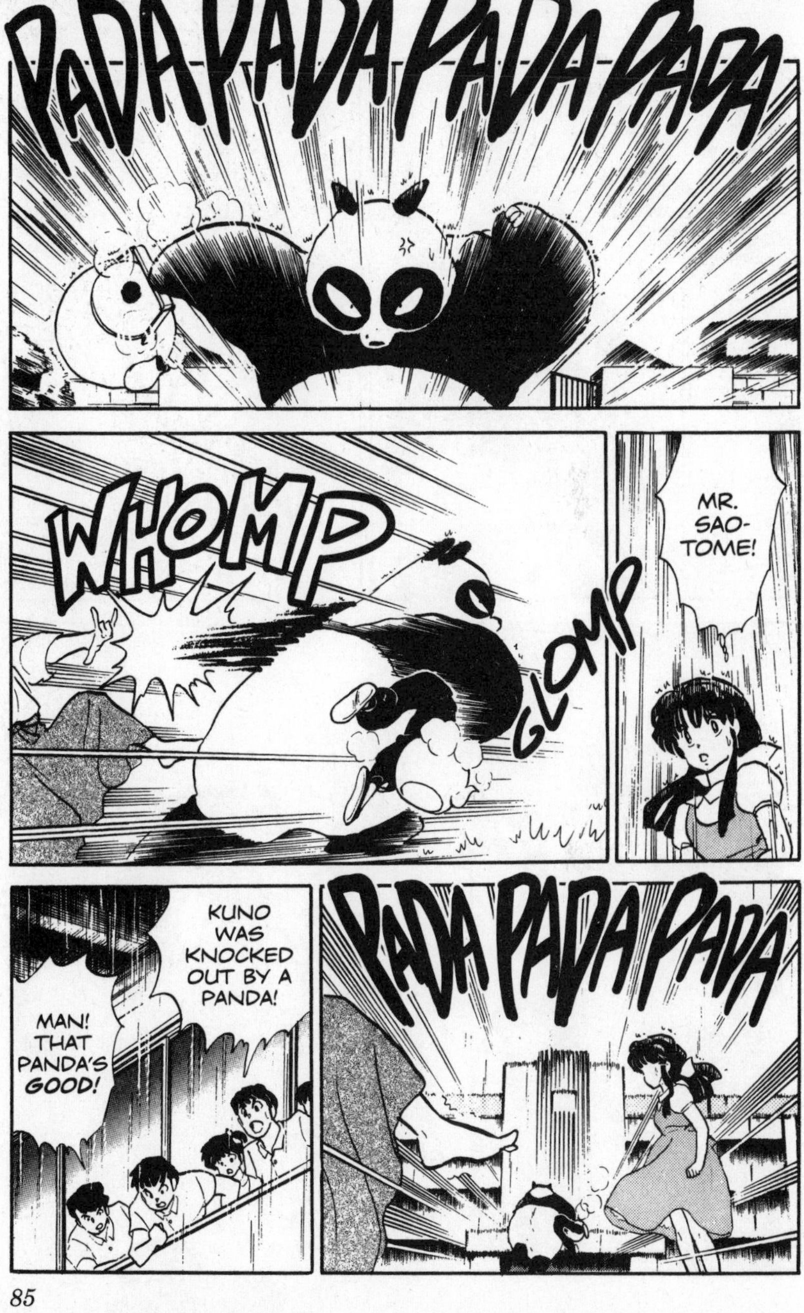
PADA PADA PADA PADA PADA
MR. SAO-TOME!
WHOMP
GLOMP
PADA PADA PADA
KUNO WAS KNOCKED OUT BY A PANDA!
MAN! THAT PANDA'S GOOD!

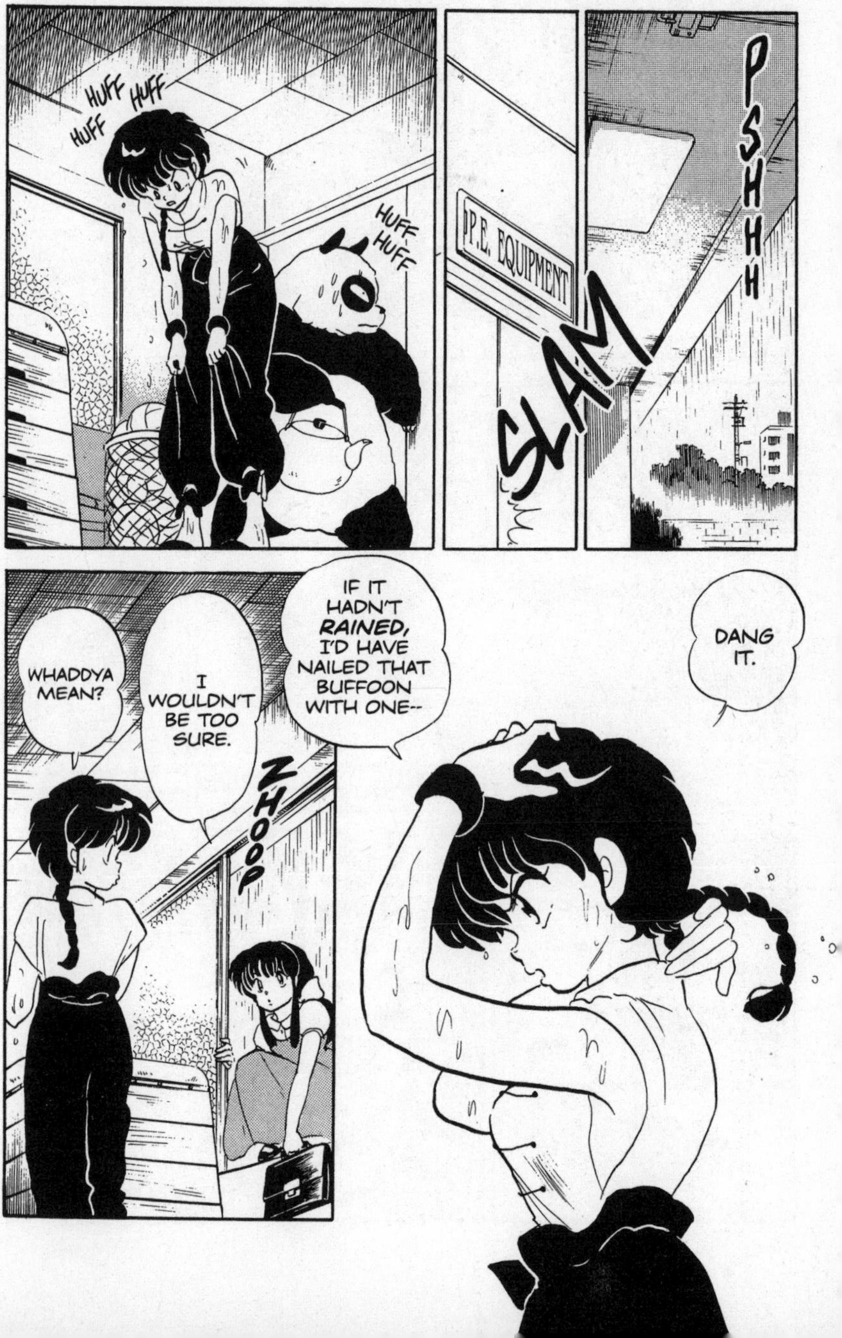
PSHHH
P.E. EQUIPMENT
SLAM
HUFF HUFF
HUFF HUFF HUFF
DANG IT.
IF IT HADN'T *RAINED,* I'D HAVE NAILED THAT BUFFOON WITH ONE--
I WOULDN'T BE TOO SURE.
WHADDYA MEAN?
ZHOOP

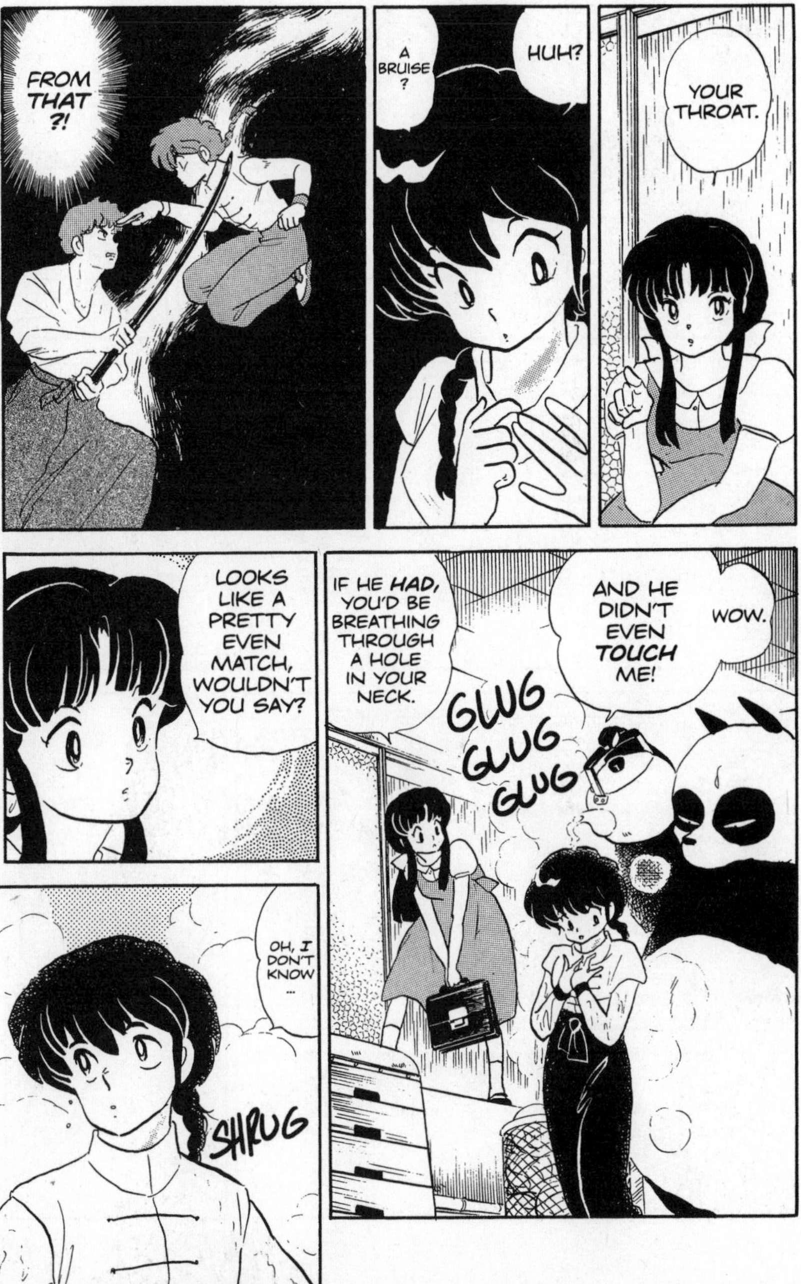
YOUR THROAT.
HUH?
A BRUISE ?
FROM THAT ?!
WOW.
AND HE DIDN'T EVEN TOUCH ME!
IF HE HAD, YOU'D BE BREATHING THROUGH A HOLE IN YOUR NECK.
GLUG GLUG GLUG
LOOKS LIKE A PRETTY EVEN MATCH, WOULDN'T YOU SAY?
OH, I DON'T KNOW ...
SHRUG

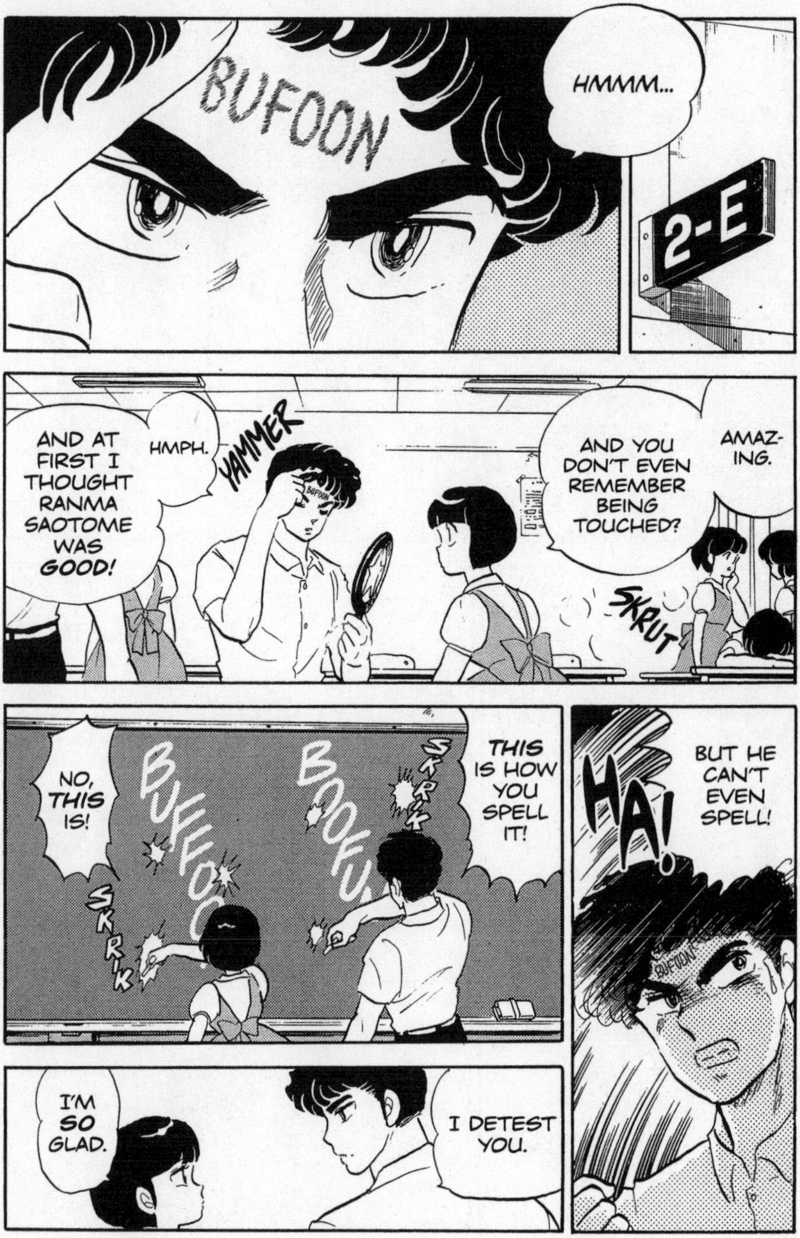
2-E
BUFOON
HMMM...
AMAZ-ING.
AND YOU DON'T EVEN REMEMBER BEING TOUCHED?
SKRUT
BUFOON
YAMMER
HMPH.
AND AT FIRST I THOUGHT RANMA SAOTOME WAS **GOOD**!
HA!
BUT HE CAN'T EVEN SPELL!
BUFOON
**THIS** IS HOW YOU SPELL IT!
SKRIK
BOOFU
BUFFOO
NO, **THIS** IS!
SKRIK
I DETEST YOU.
I'M **SO** GLAD.

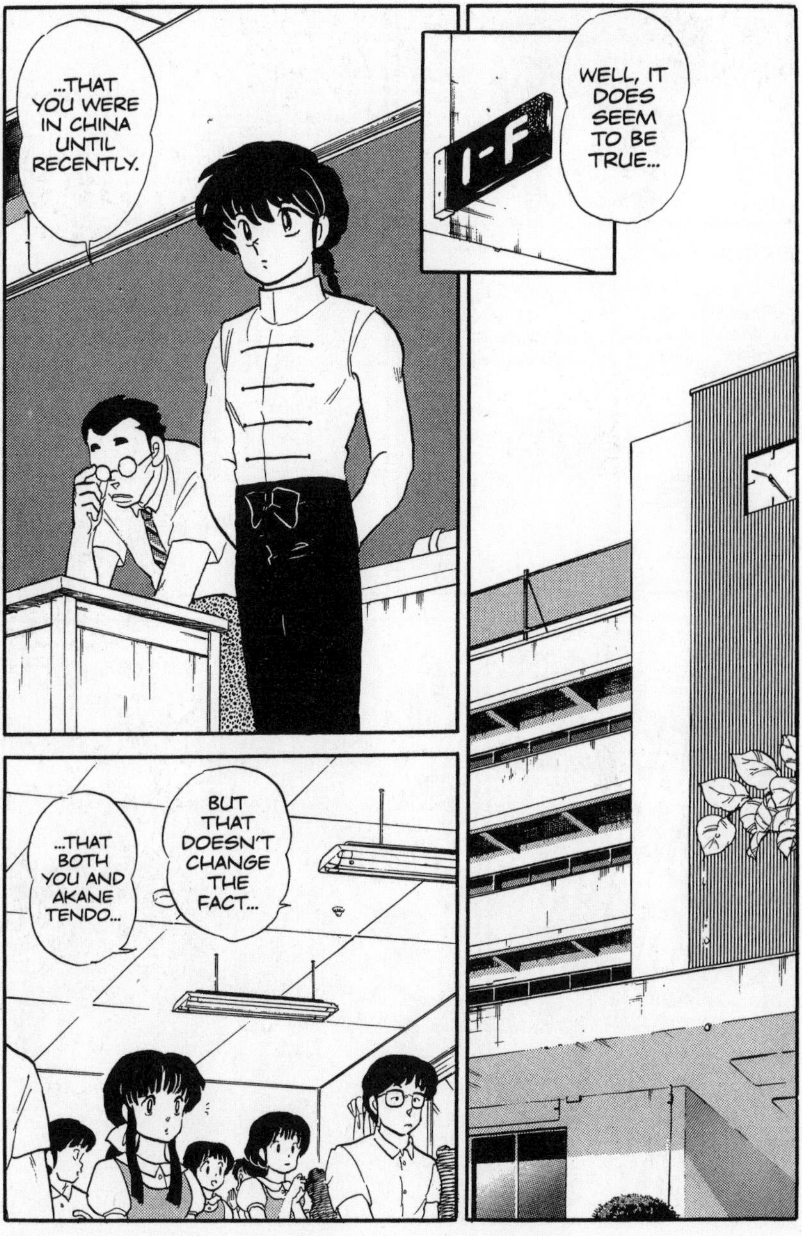
1-F
WELL, IT DOES SEEM TO BE TRUE...
...THAT YOU WERE IN CHINA UNTIL RECENTLY.
BUT THAT DOESN'T CHANGE THE FACT...
...THAT BOTH YOU AND AKANE TENDO...

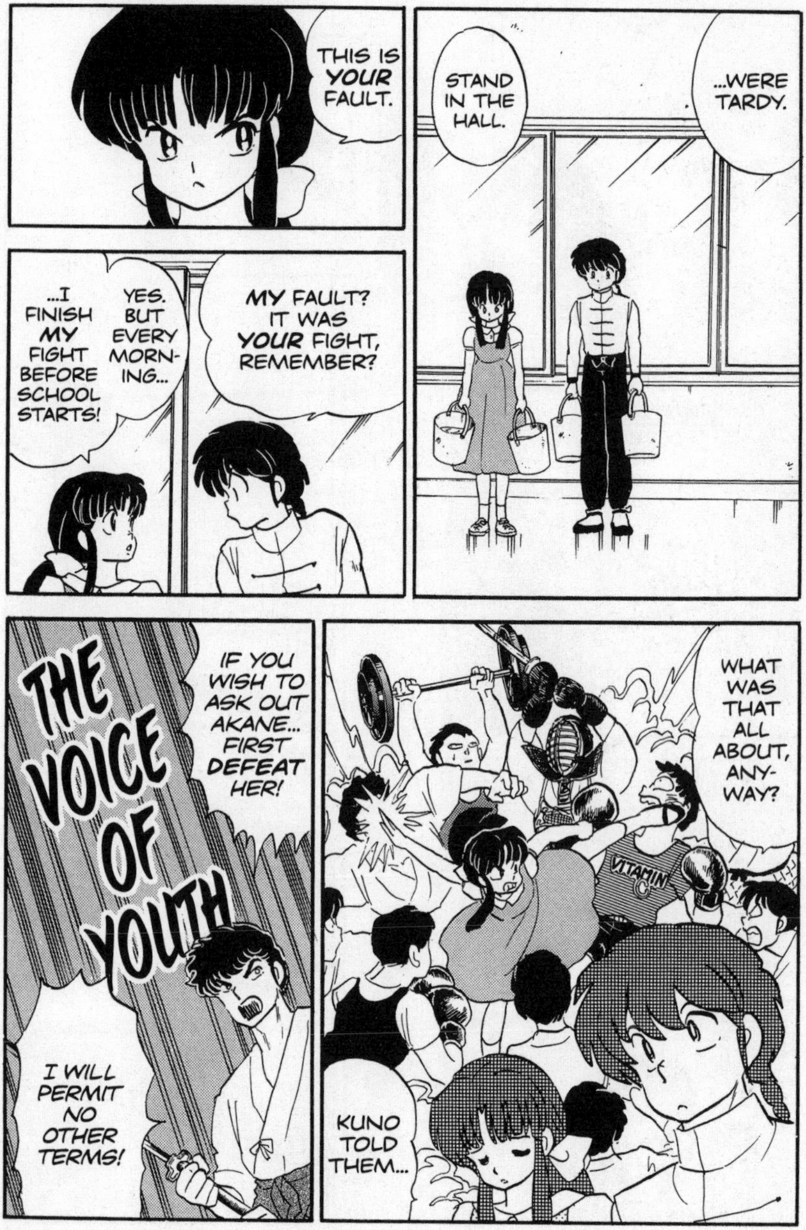

...WERE TARDY.
STAND IN THE HALL.
THIS IS YOUR FAULT.
MY FAULT? IT WAS YOUR FIGHT, REMEMBER?
YES. BUT EVERY MORNING...
...I FINISH MY FIGHT BEFORE SCHOOL STARTS!
WHAT WAS THAT ALL ABOUT, ANYWAY?
KUNO TOLD THEM...
IF YOU WISH TO ASK OUT AKANE... FIRST DEFEAT HER!
THE VOICE OF YOUTH
I WILL PERMIT NO OTHER TERMS!

WHAT ?!
WHAM
"FIANCÉ" ?!
UH HUH!
MY DAD AND HIS DAD DECIDED. AKANE'S GOING TO MARRY RANMA.
RANMA SAOTOME--!
WHP WHP WHP
KUNO.
STAND IN THE HALL.
I FORBID IT!
SLOSH SLOSH SLOSH SLOSH
YOU MEAN YOU FIGHT KUNO EVERY MORNING ?!
AND FOR SOME REASON I ALWAYS WIN!

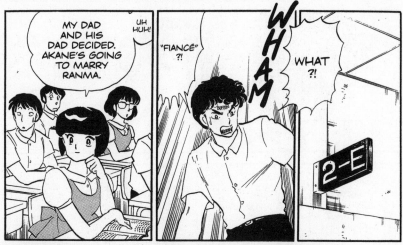

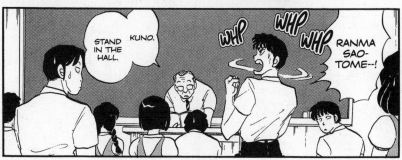

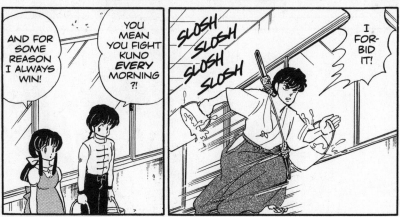

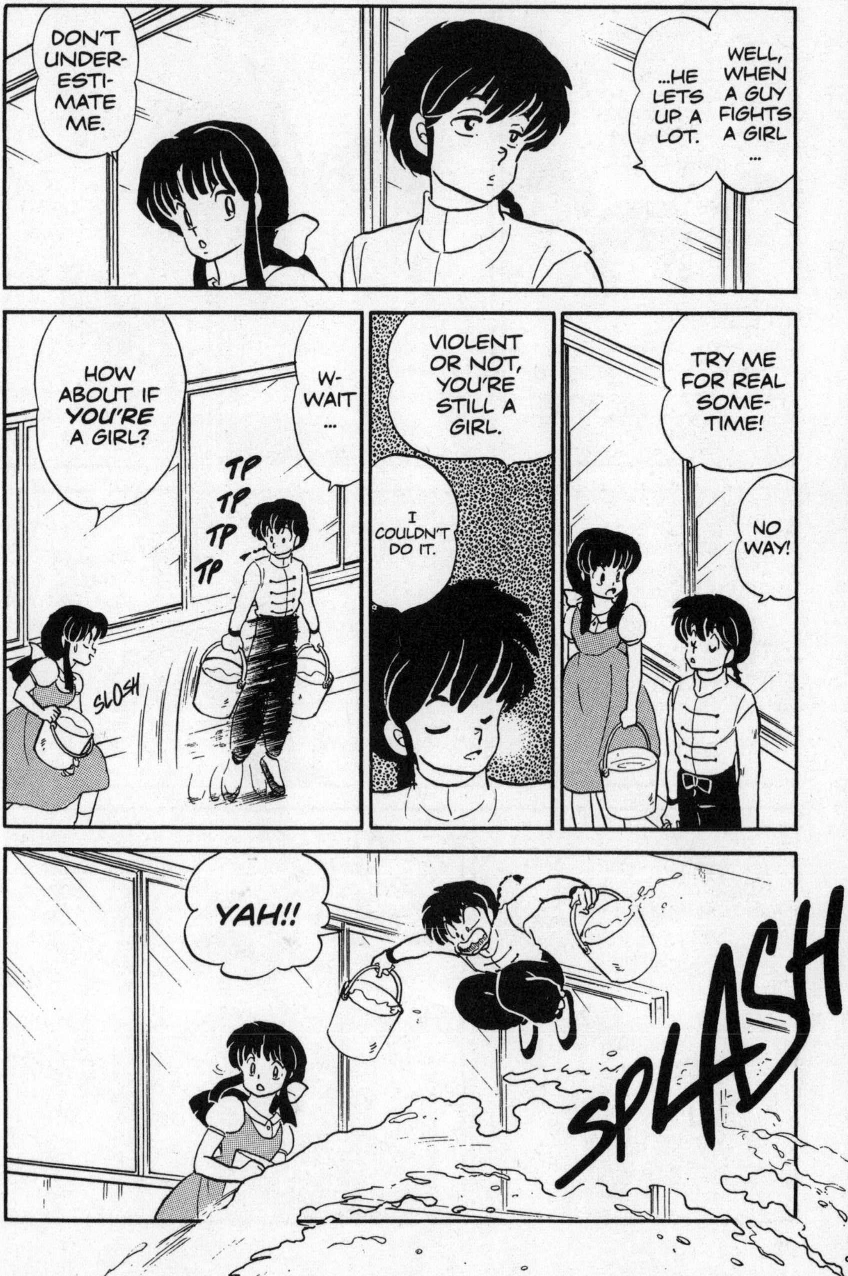
WELL, WHEN A GUY FIGHTS A GIRL ...
...HE LETS UP A LOT.
DON'T UNDER-ESTI-MATE ME.
TRY ME FOR REAL SOME-TIME!
NO WAY!
VIOLENT OR NOT, YOU'RE STILL A GIRL.
I COULDN'T DO IT.
W-WAIT ...
HOW ABOUT IF *YOU'RE* A GIRL?
TP TP TP TP
SLOSH
YAH!!
SPLASH

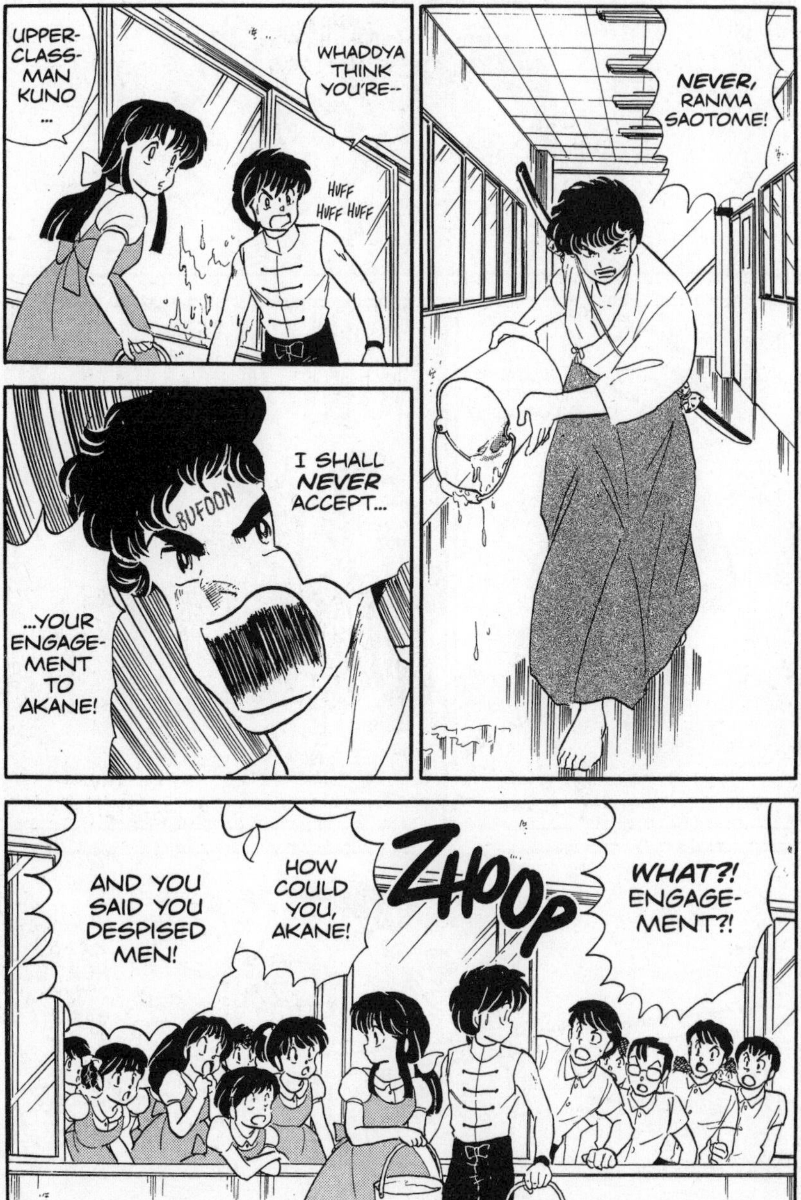
NEVER, RANMA SAOTOME!
WHADDYA THINK YOU'RE--
UPPER-CLASS-MAN KUNO ...
HUFF HUFF HUFF
I SHALL NEVER ACCEPT...
BUFOON
...YOUR ENGAGE-MENT TO AKANE!
WHAT?! ENGAGE-MENT?!
ZHOOP
HOW COULD YOU, AKANE!
AND YOU SAID YOU DESPISED MEN!

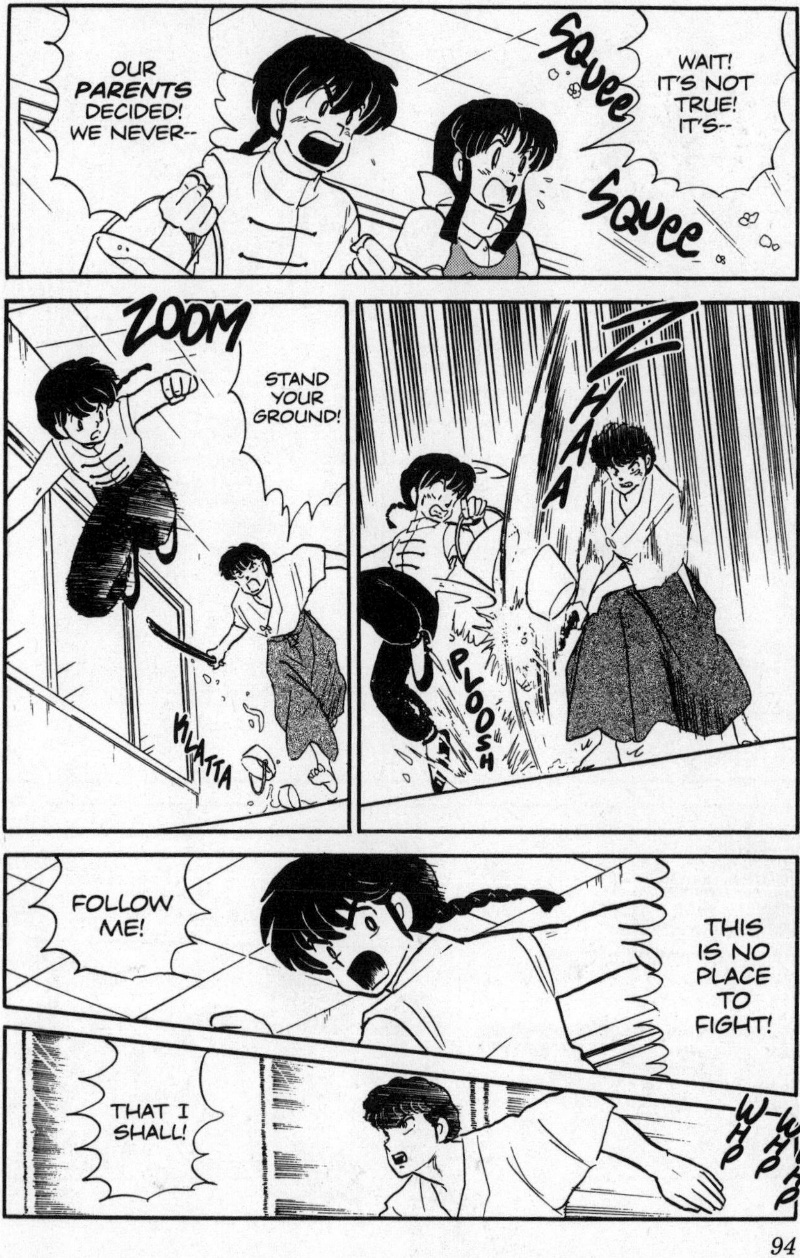
SQUEE
WAIT! IT'S NOT TRUE! IT'S--
SQUEE
OUR PARENTS DECIDED! WE NEVER--
ZHAAA
PLOOSH
ZOOM
STAND YOUR GROUND!
KLATTA
THIS IS NO PLACE TO FIGHT!
FOLLOW ME!
WHP WHP WHP
THAT I SHALL!

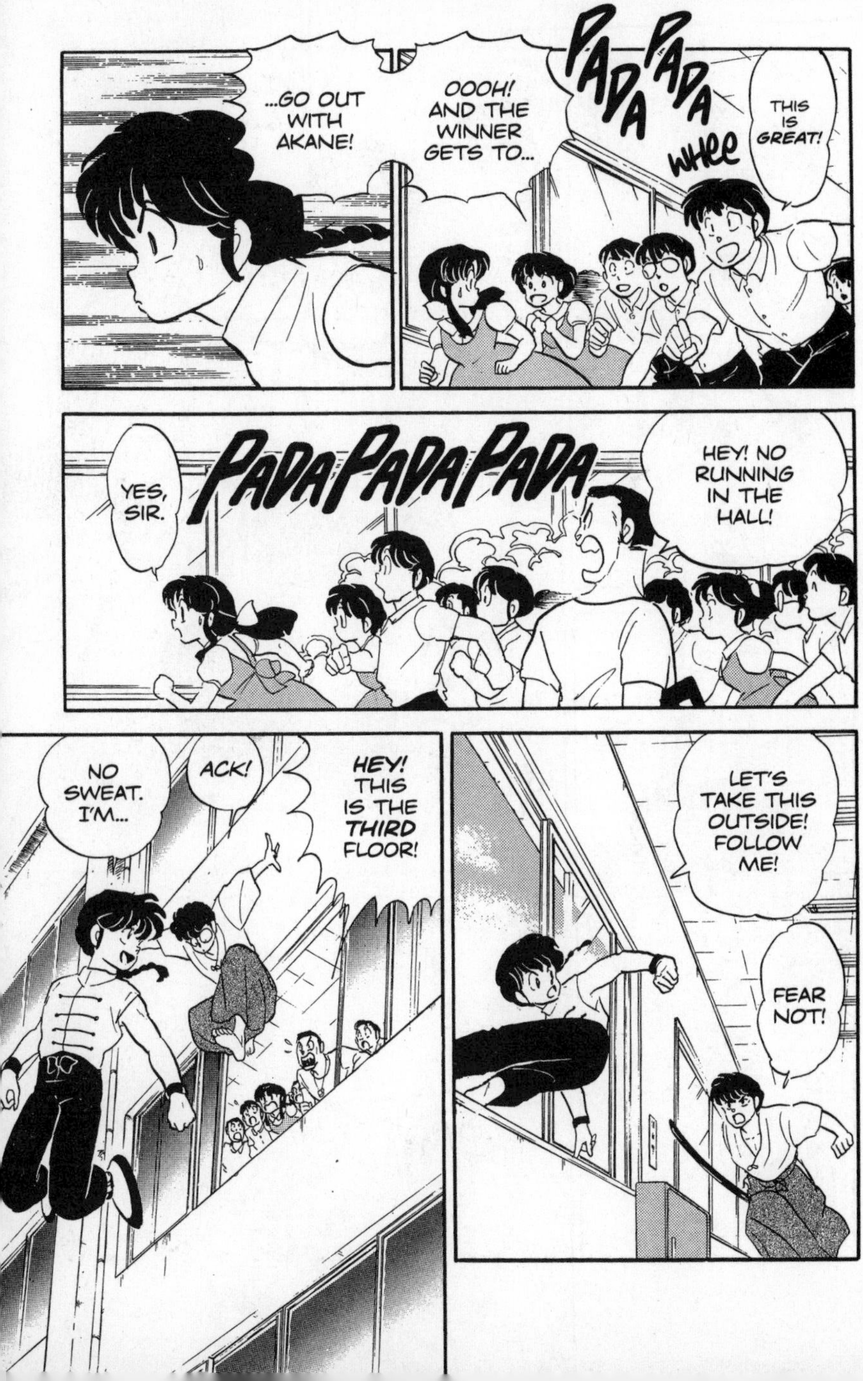
THIS IS GREAT!
PADA PADA
whee
OOOH! AND THE WINNER GETS TO...
...GO OUT WITH AKANE!
HEY! NO RUNNING IN THE HALL!
PADAPADAPADA
YES, SIR.
LET'S TAKE THIS OUTSIDE! FOLLOW ME!
FEAR NOT!
HEY! THIS IS THE THIRD FLOOR!
ACK!
NO SWEAT. I'M...

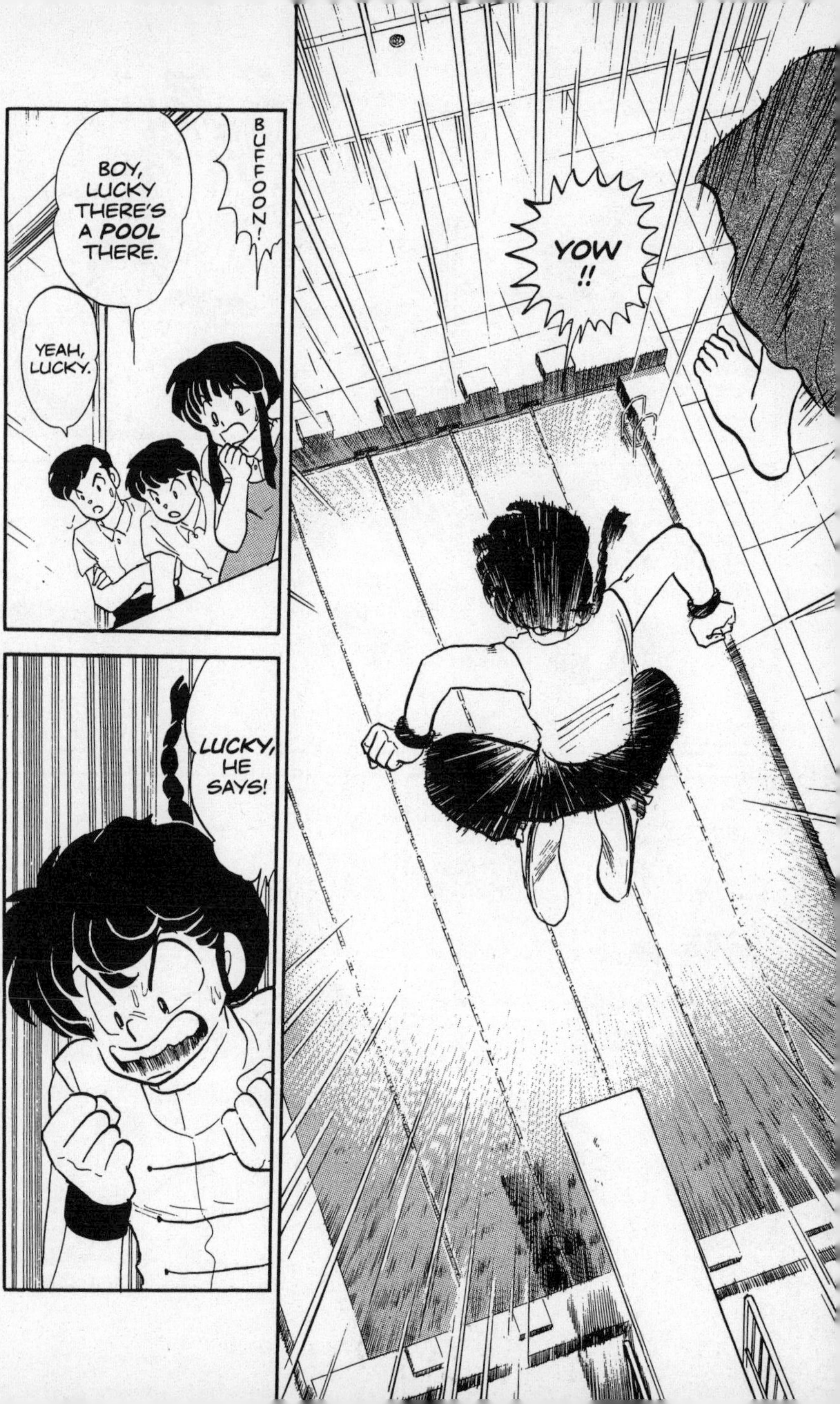
YOW !!
BUFFOON!
BOY, LUCKY THERE'S A POOL THERE.
YEAH, LUCKY.
LUCKY, HE SAYS!

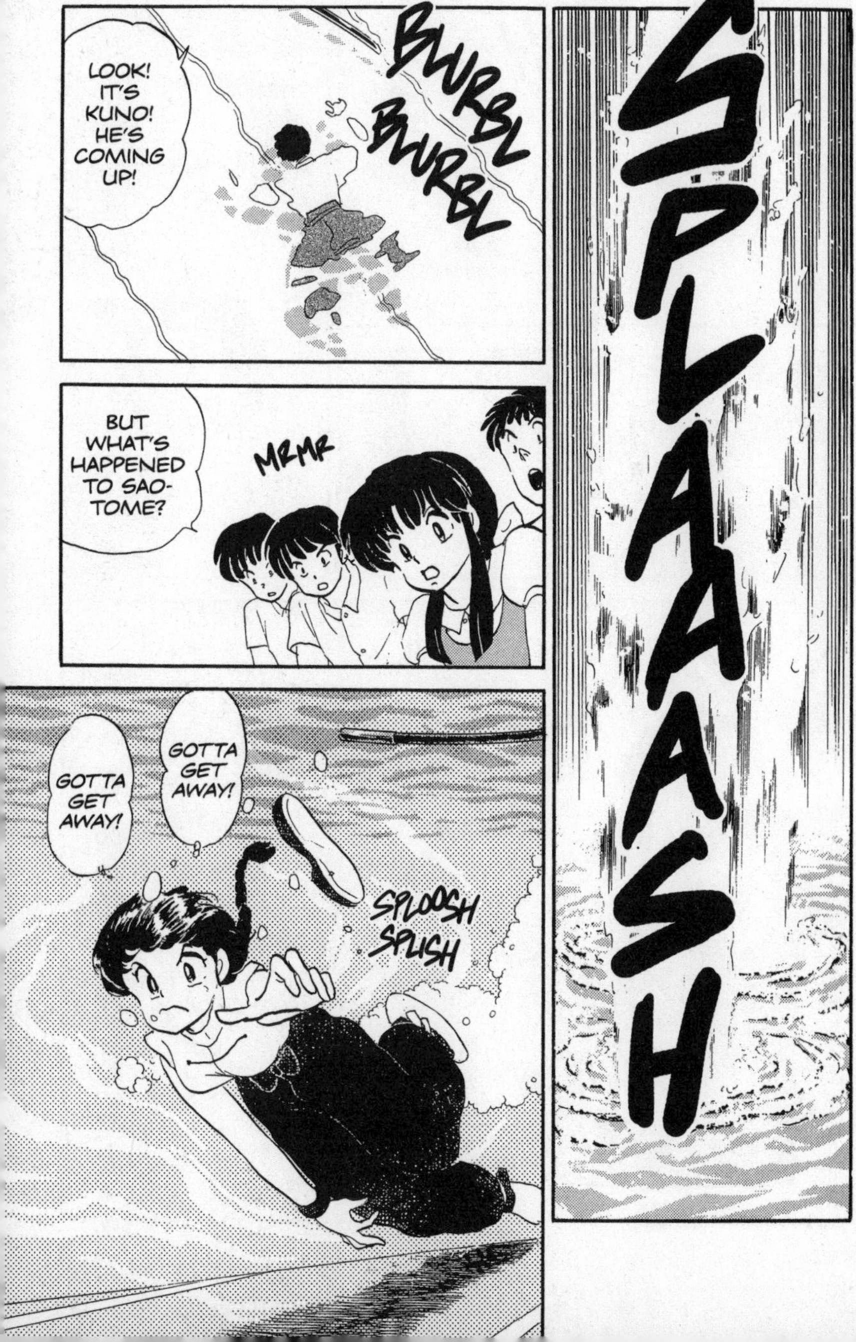
SPLAAAASH
BLURBL BLURBL
LOOK! IT'S KUNO! HE'S COMING UP!
MRMR
BUT WHAT'S HAPPENED TO SAO-TOME?
GOTTA GET AWAY!
GOTTA GET AWAY!
SPLOOSH SPLISH

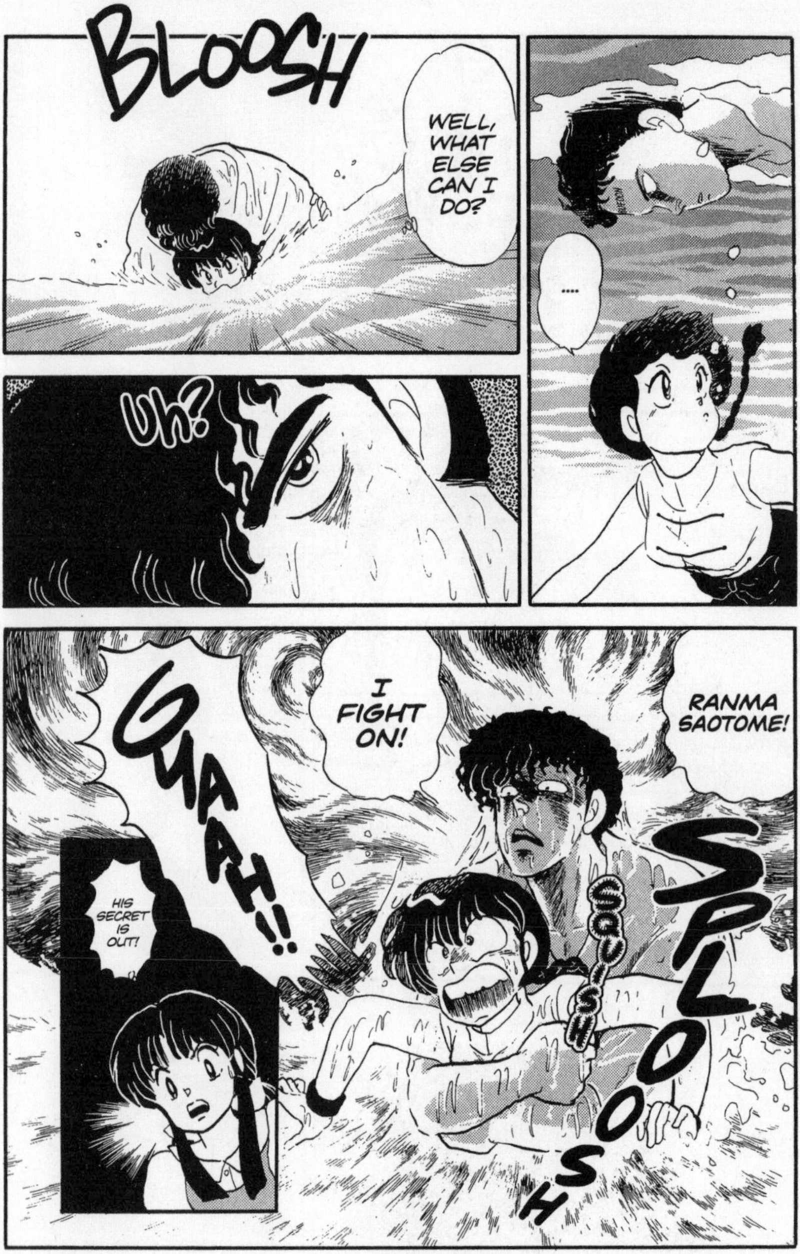
.....
BLOOSH
WELL, WHAT ELSE CAN I DO?
Uh?
RANMA SAOTOME!
I FIGHT ON!
SPLOOOOSH
SQUISH
GUAAH!!
HIS SECRET IS OUT!

# PART 5
# TO THE TREE-BORNE KETTLE-GIRL

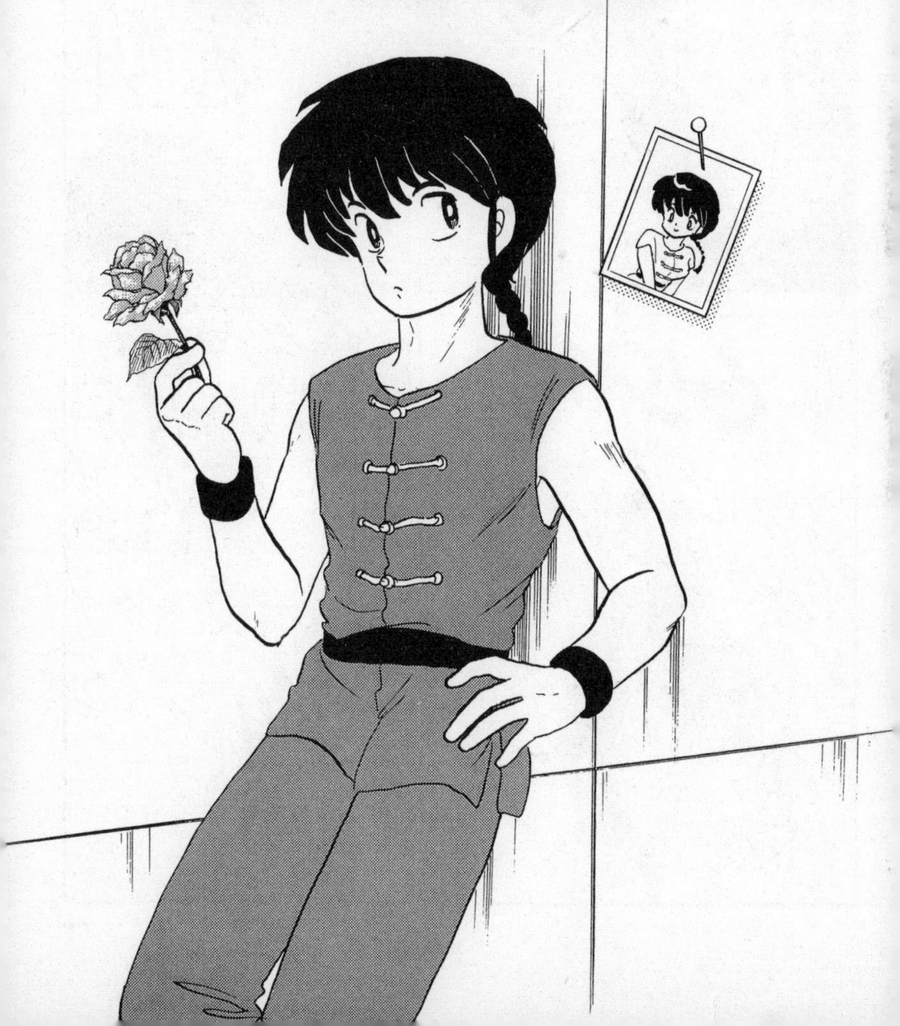

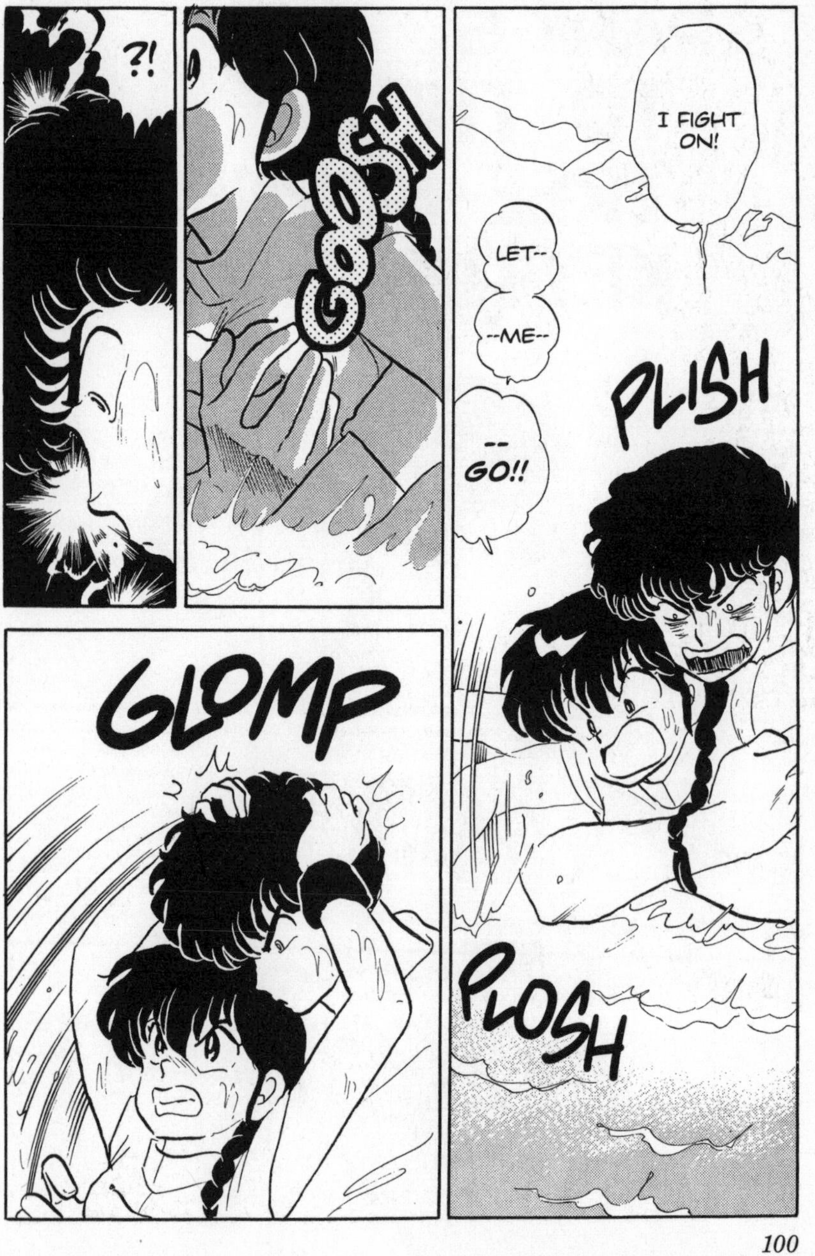
I FIGHT ON!
LET--
--ME--
--GO!!
PLISH
PLOSH
GOOSH
?!
GLOMP

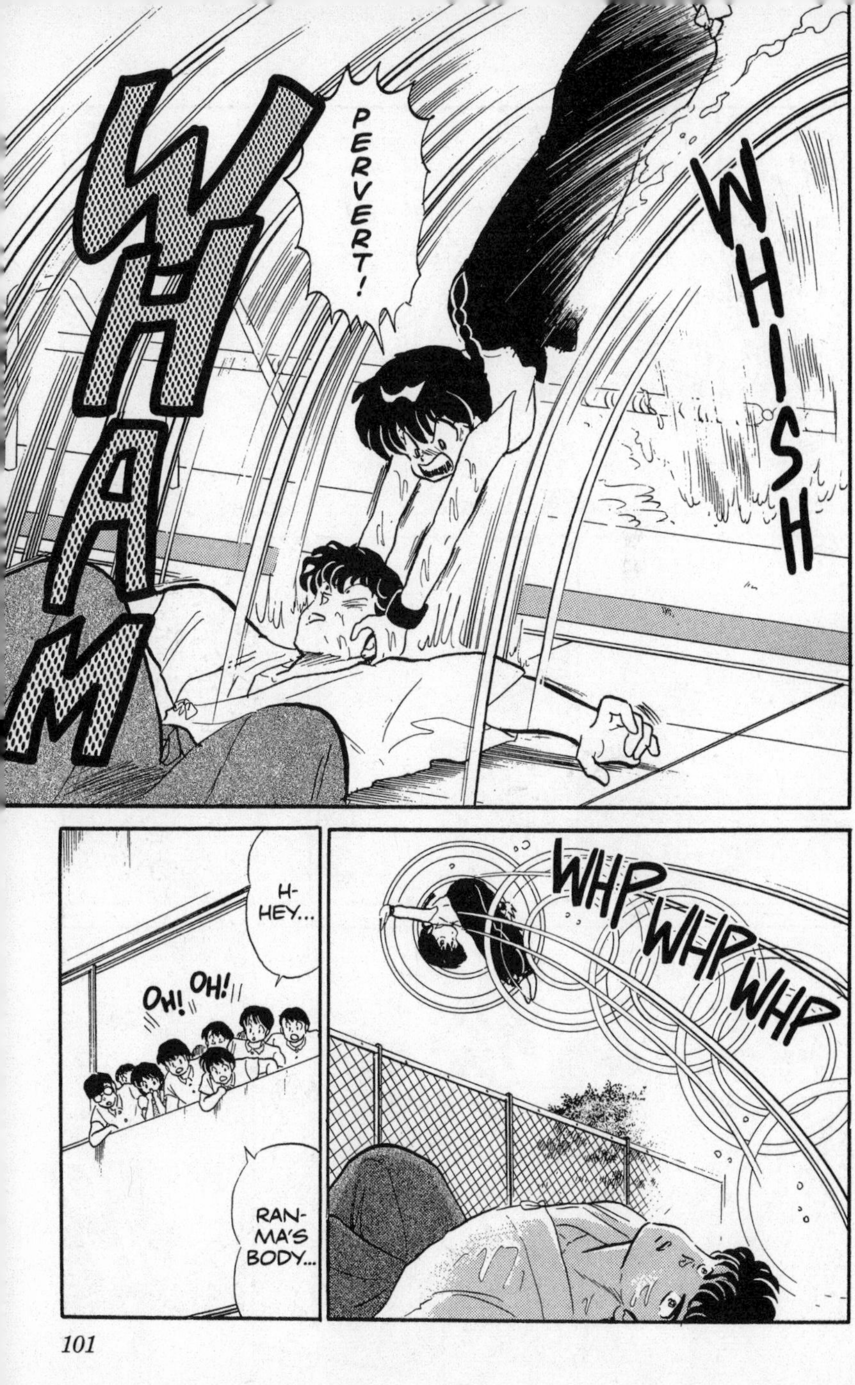
WHAM
PERVERT!
WHISH
WHP WHP WHP
H-HEY...
OH! OH!
RAN-MA'S BODY...

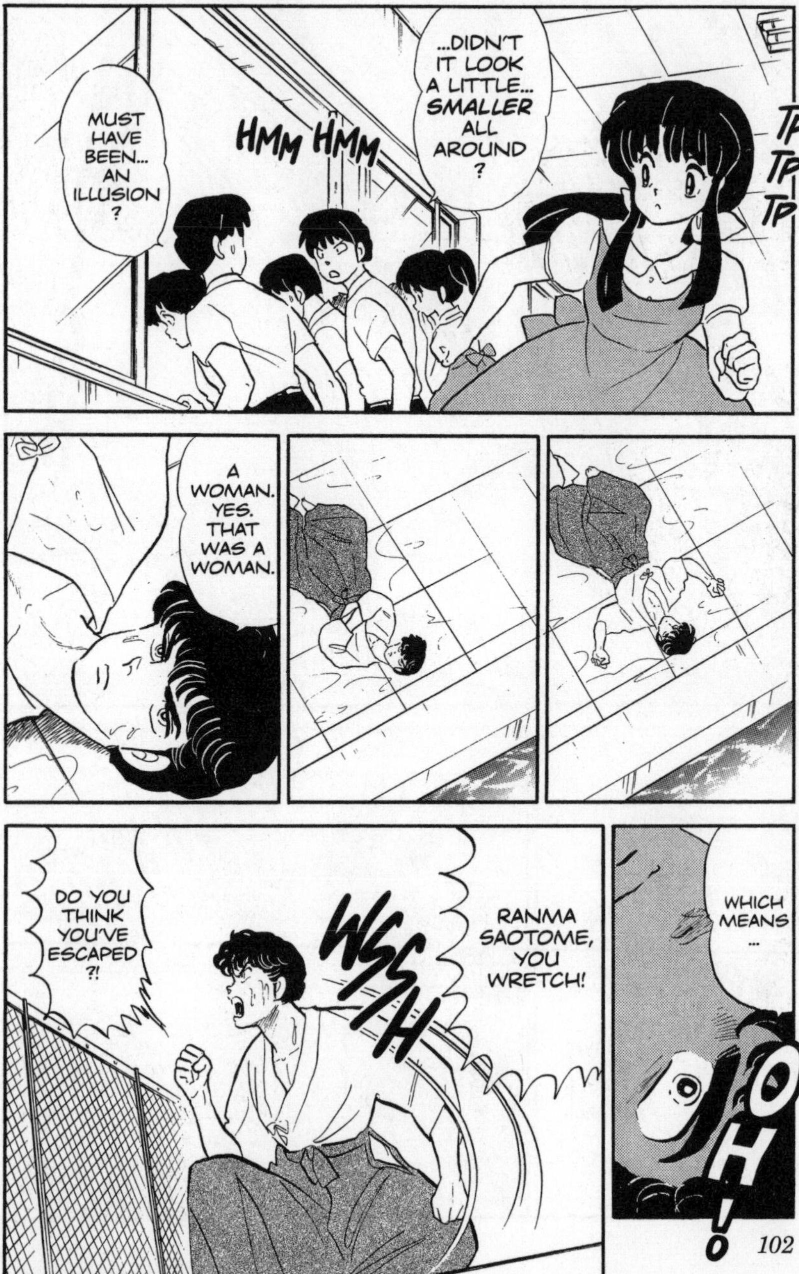
TP TP TP
...DIDN'T IT LOOK A LITTLE... SMALLER ALL AROUND?
HMM HMM
MUST HAVE BEEN... AN ILLUSION?
A WOMAN. YES. THAT WAS A WOMAN.
WHICH MEANS...
OHO
RANMA SAOTOME, YOU WRETCH!
WSSH
DO YOU THINK YOU'VE ESCAPED?!

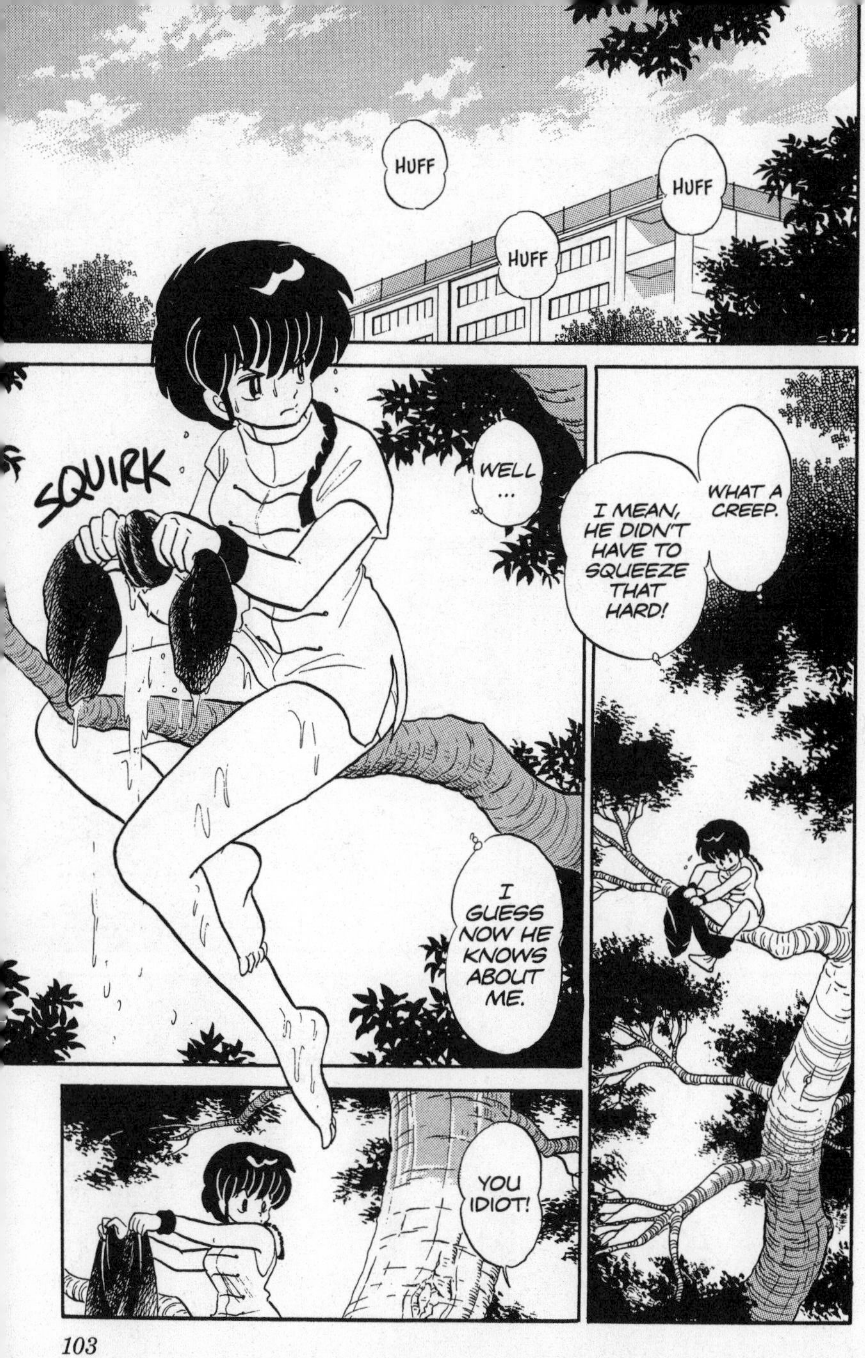
HUFF
HUFF
HUFF
WHAT A CREEP.
I MEAN, HE DIDN'T HAVE TO SQUEEZE THAT HARD!
WELL ...
SQUIRK
I GUESS NOW HE KNOWS ABOUT ME.
YOU IDIOT!

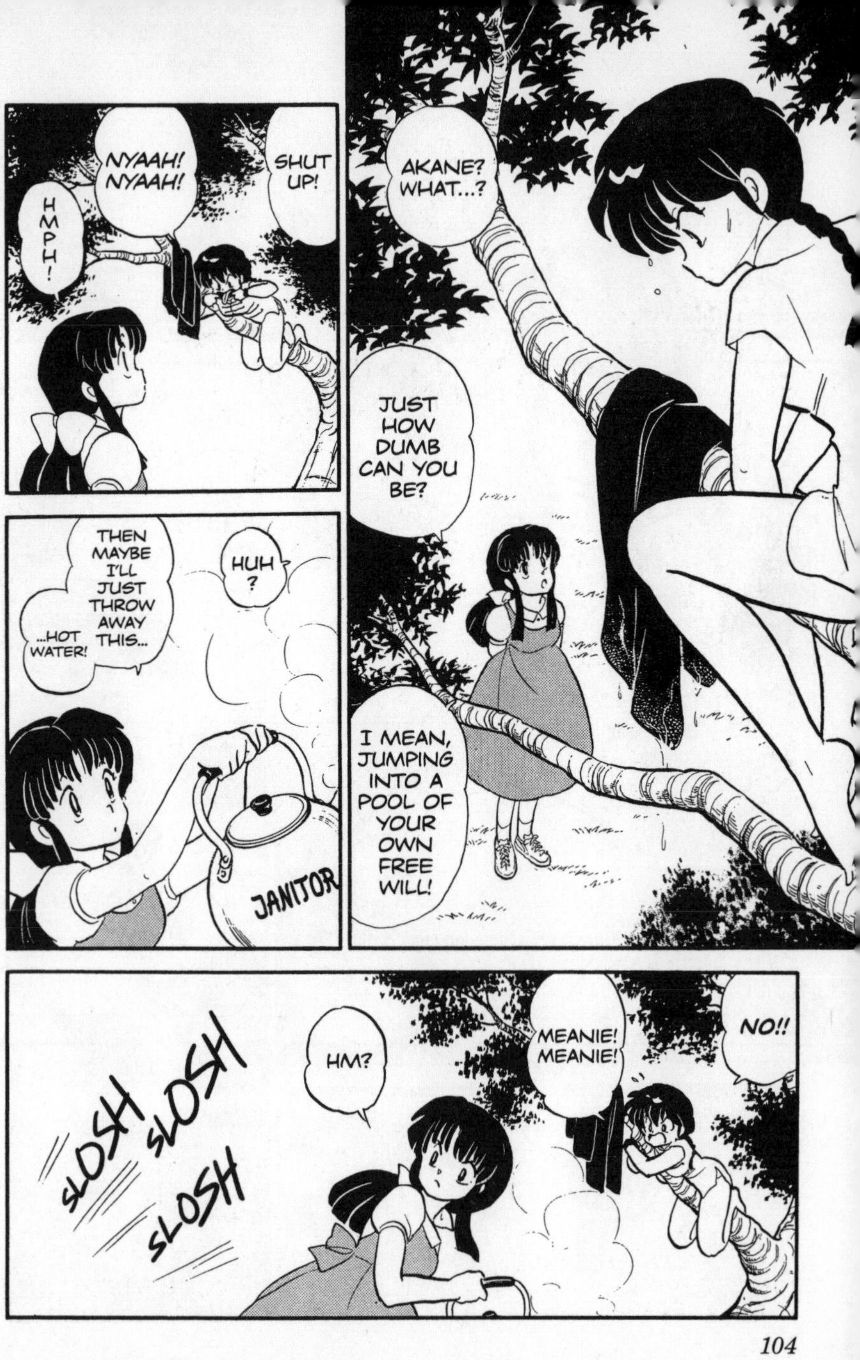
AKANE? WHAT...?
JUST HOW DUMB CAN YOU BE?
I MEAN, JUMPING INTO A POOL OF YOUR OWN FREE WILL!
SHUT UP!
NYAAH! NYAAH!
HMPH!
HUH?
THEN MAYBE I'LL JUST THROW AWAY THIS...
...HOT WATER!
JANITOR
NO!!
MEANIE! MEANIE!
HM?
SLOSH SLOSH
SLOSH
SLOSH

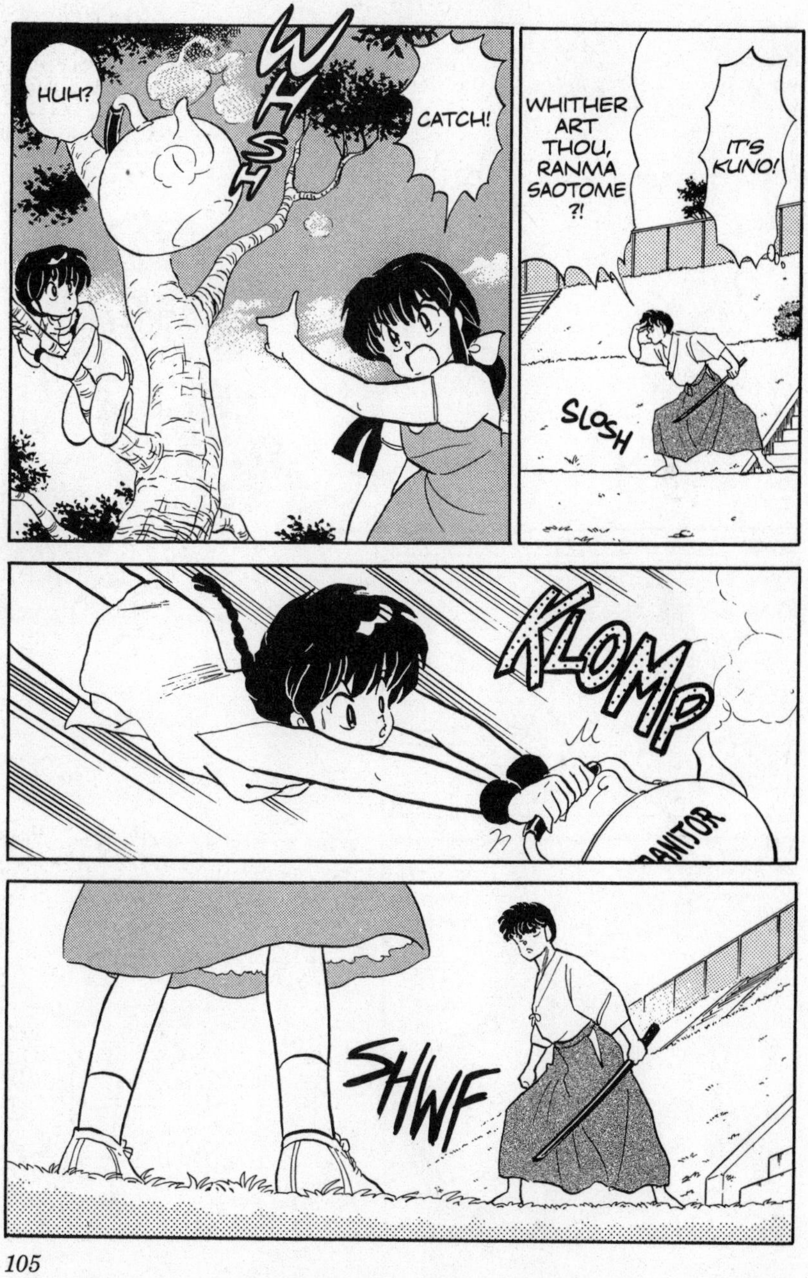
IT'S KUNO!
WHITHER ART THOU, RANMA SAOTOME ?!
SLOSH
CATCH!
WHSH
HUH?
KLOMP
ANITOR
SHWF

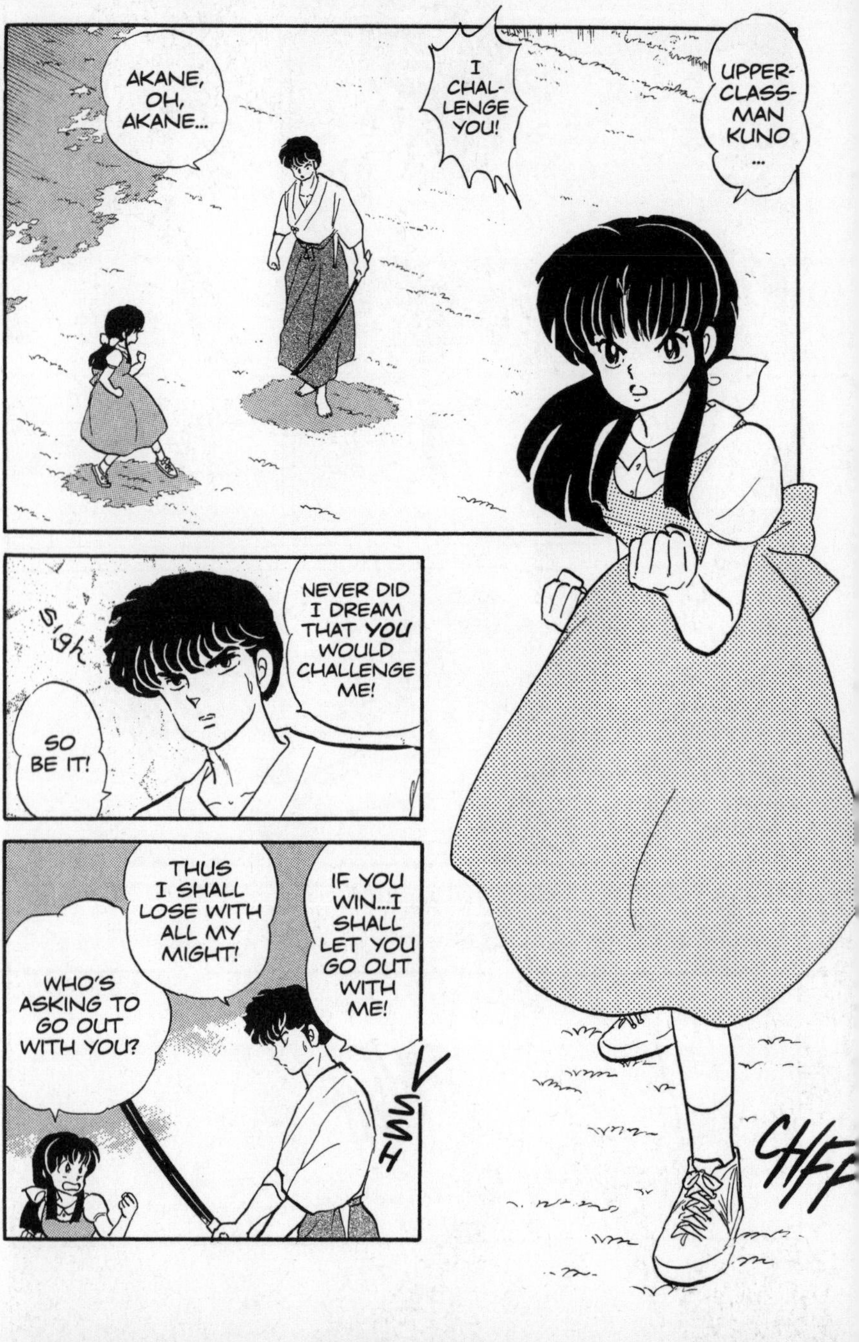
UPPER-CLASSMAN KUNO ...
I CHALLENGE YOU!
AKANE, OH, AKANE...
CHFF
NEVER DID I DREAM THAT YOU WOULD CHALLENGE ME!
sigh
SO BE IT!
IF YOU WIN...I SHALL LET YOU GO OUT WITH ME!
THUS I SHALL LOSE WITH ALL MY MIGHT!
WHO'S ASKING TO GO OUT WITH YOU?
SHUN

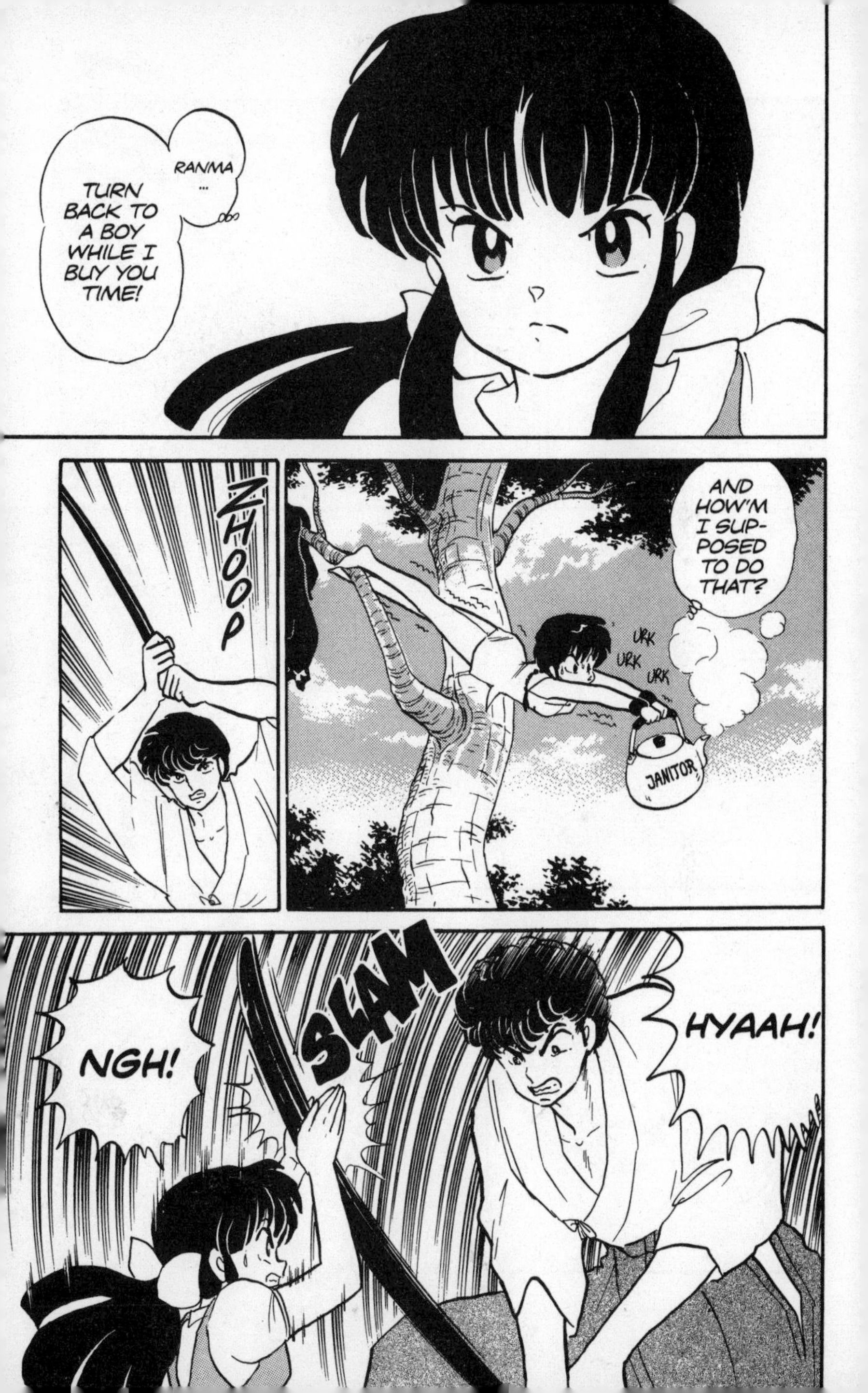

RANMA ... TURN BACK TO A BOY WHILE I BUY YOU TIME!
AND HOW'M I SUP-POSED TO DO THAT?
URK
URK
URK
JANITOR
ZHOOOP
HYAAH!
SLAM
NGH!

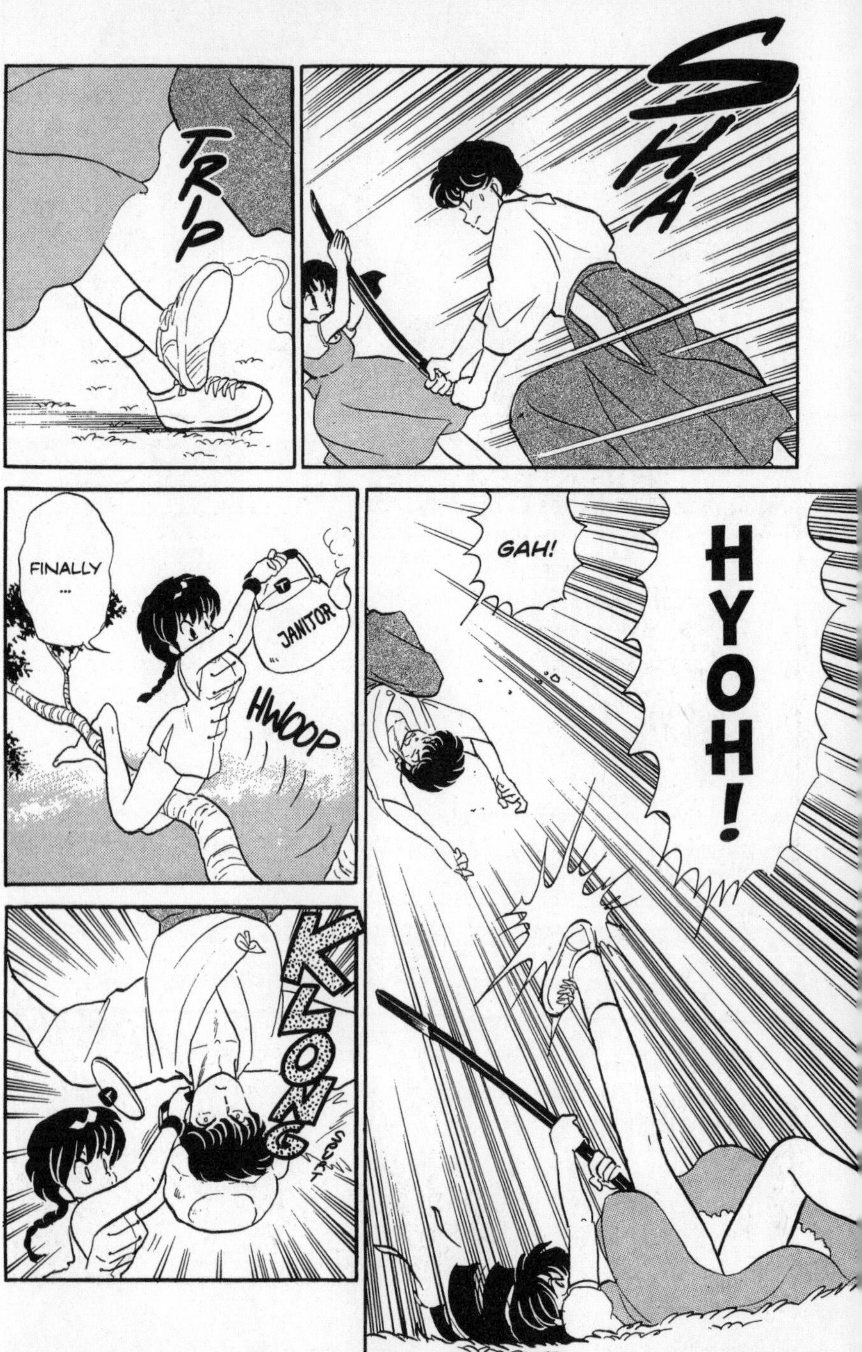
SHA
TRIP
GAH!
HYOH!
FINALLY ...
JANITOR
HWOOP
KWONG

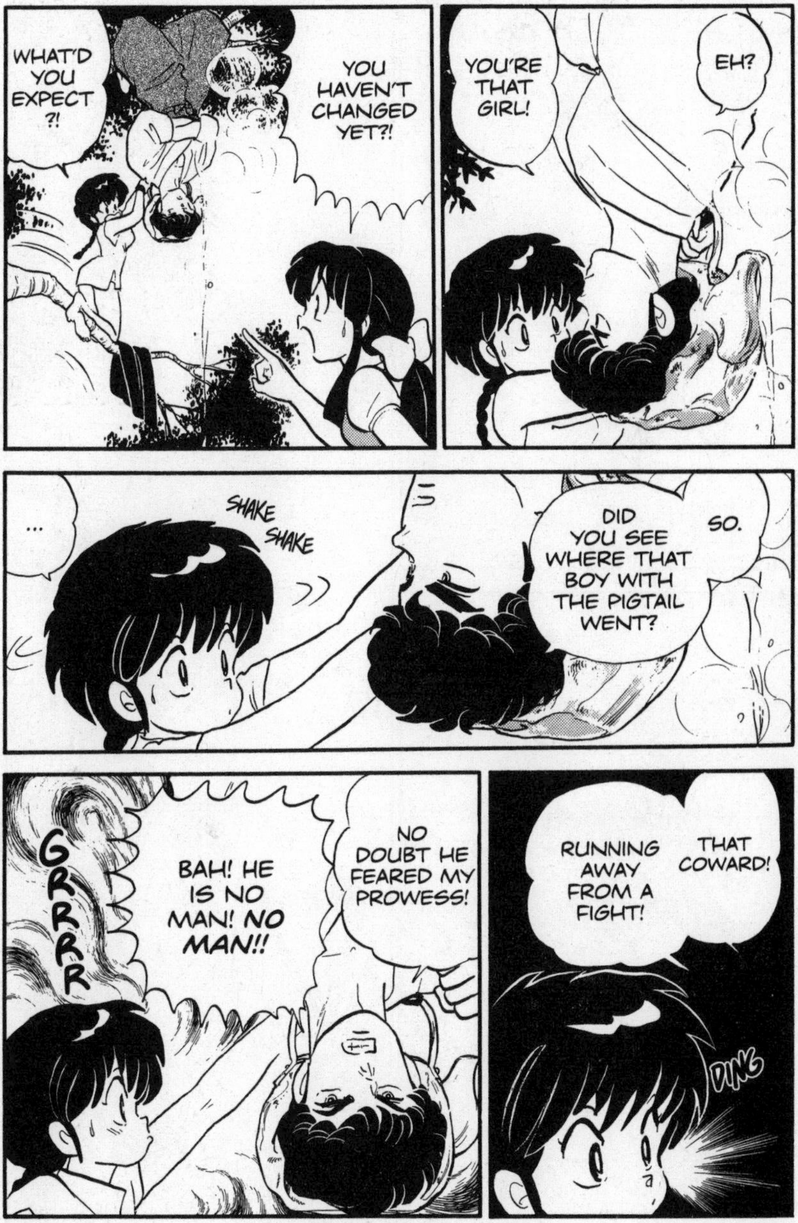
EH?
YOU'RE THAT GIRL!
YOU HAVEN'T CHANGED YET?!
WHAT'D YOU EXPECT ?!
SO.
DID YOU SEE WHERE THAT BOY WITH THE PIGTAIL WENT?
SHAKE SHAKE
...
THAT COWARD!
RUNNING AWAY FROM A FIGHT!
DING
NO DOUBT HE FEARED MY PROWESS!
BAH! HE IS NO MAN! NO MAN!!
GRRRR

VOOP
BONK
THAT HURT, YOU KNOW.
I'M NOT GONNA HANG THERE AND TAKE THIS!
DOINK
TP
I CAN TAKE YOU ANY TIME!
COME ON!
ZAAH

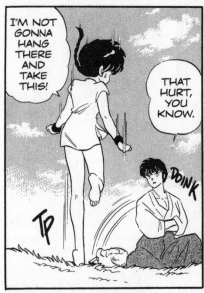

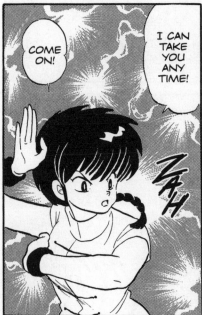

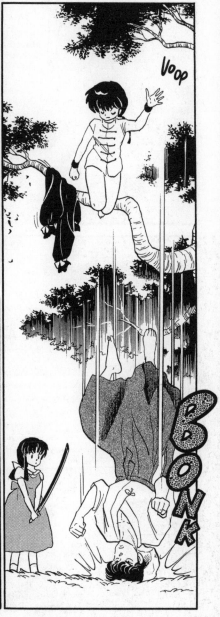

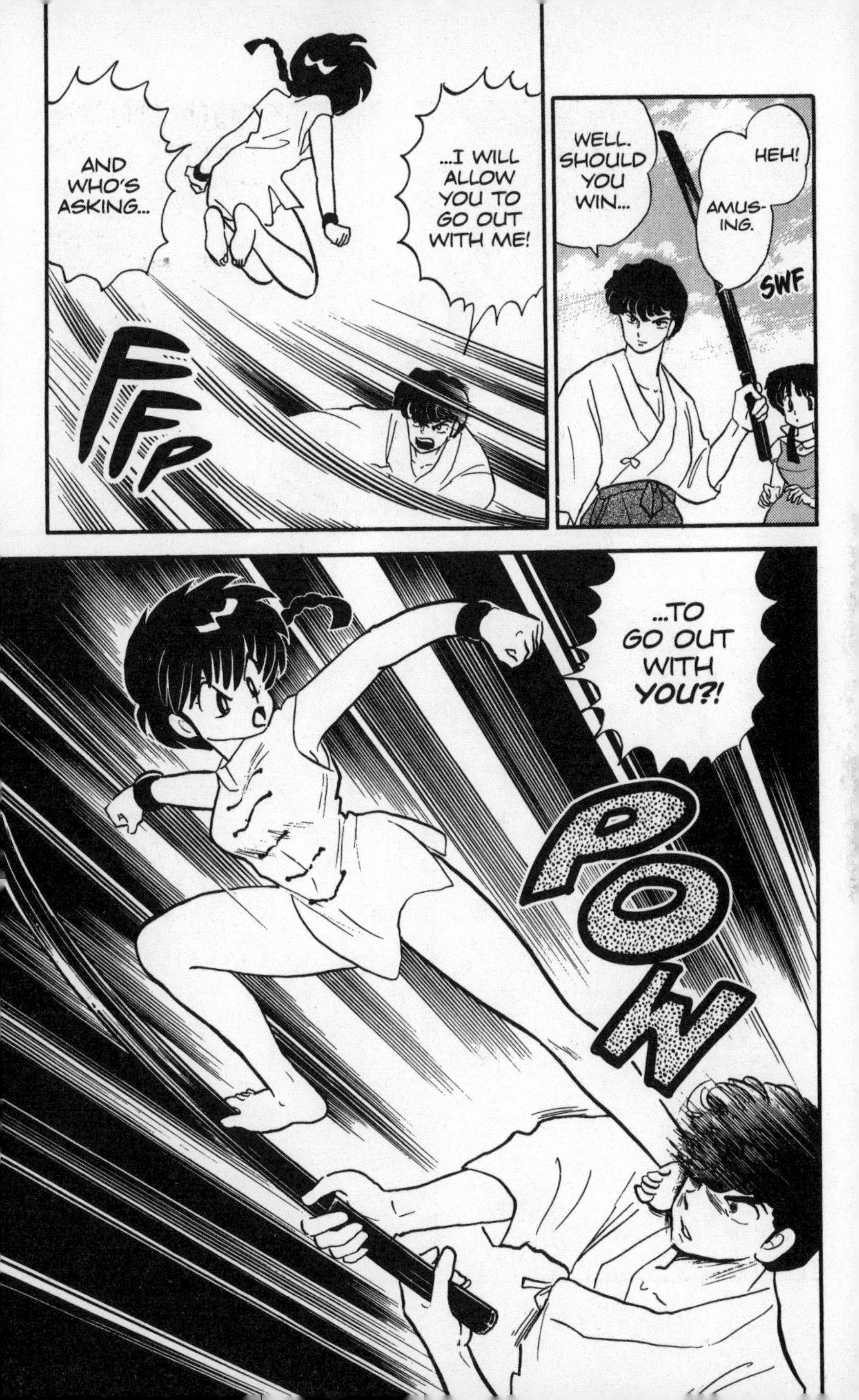
HEH!
AMUSING.
WELL. SHOULD YOU WIN...
SWF
...I WILL ALLOW YOU TO GO OUT WITH ME!
AND WHO'S ASKING...
FFP
...TO GO OUT WITH YOU?!
POW

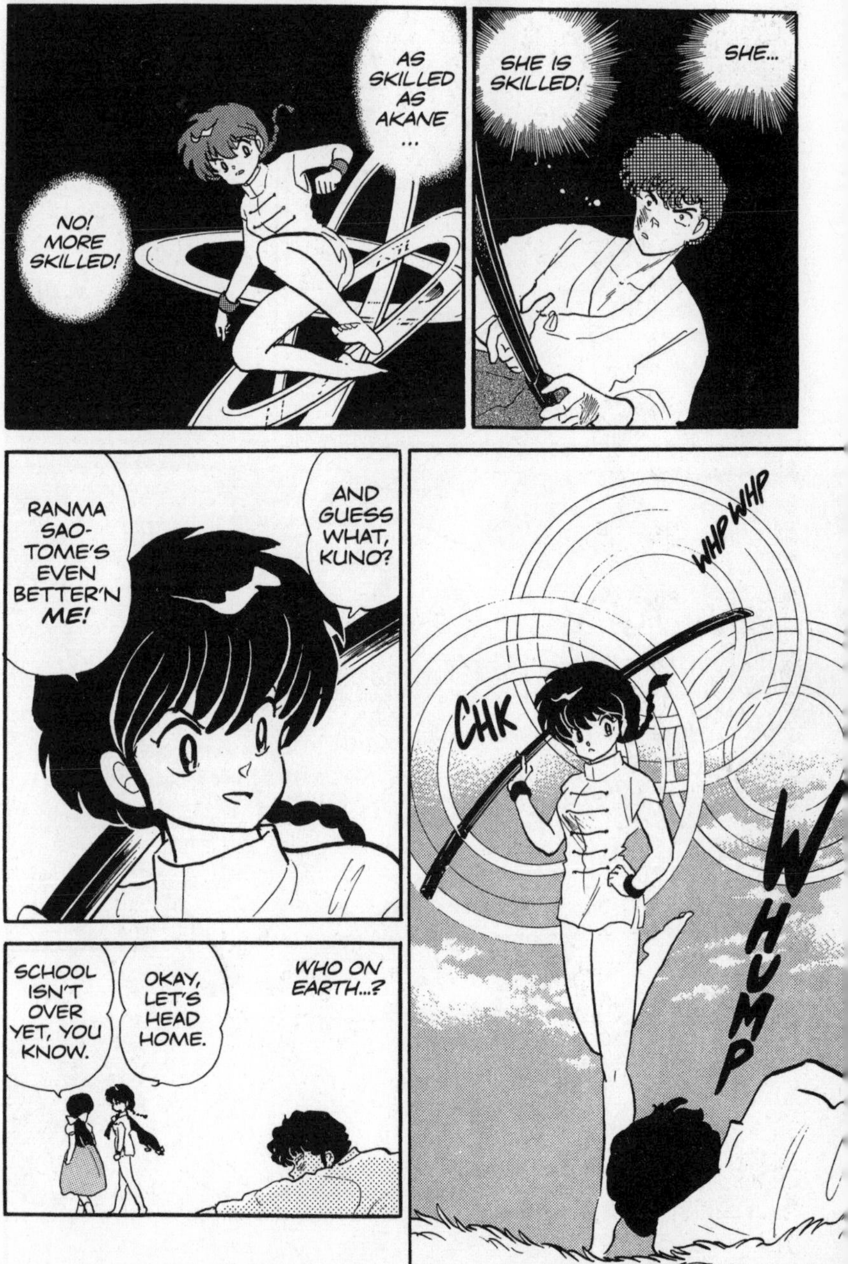
SHE...
SHE IS SKILLED!
AS SKILLED AS AKANE ...
NO! MORE SKILLED!
WHP WHP
CHK
WHUMP
AND GUESS WHAT, KUNO?
RANMA SAO-TOME'S EVEN BETTER'N ME!
WHO ON EARTH...?
OKAY, LET'S HEAD HOME.
SCHOOL ISN'T OVER YET, YOU KNOW.

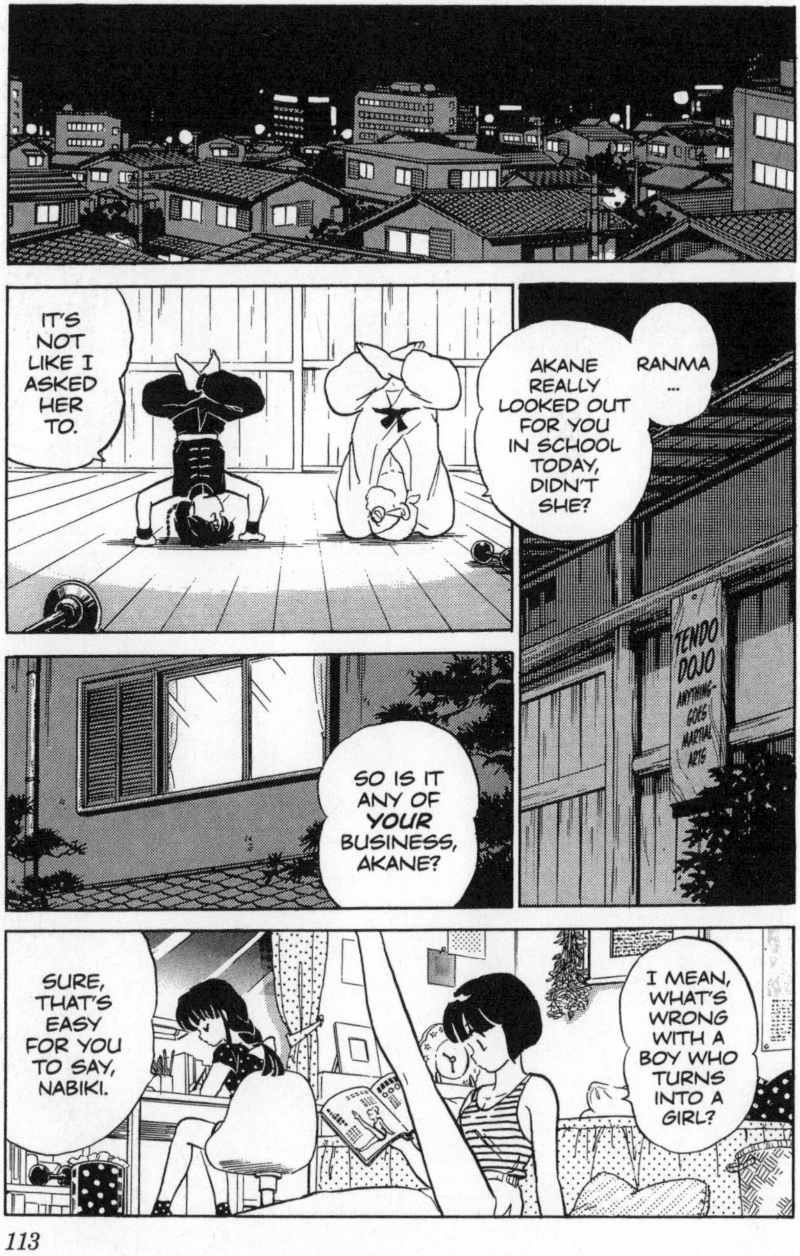
RANMA ...
AKANE REALLY LOOKED OUT FOR YOU IN SCHOOL TODAY, DIDN'T SHE?
TENDO DOJO ANYTHING-GOES MARTIAL ARTS
IT'S NOT LIKE I ASKED HER TO.
SO IS IT ANY OF *YOUR* BUSINESS, AKANE?
I MEAN, WHAT'S WRONG WITH A BOY WHO TURNS INTO A GIRL?
SURE, THAT'S EASY FOR YOU TO SAY, NABIKI.

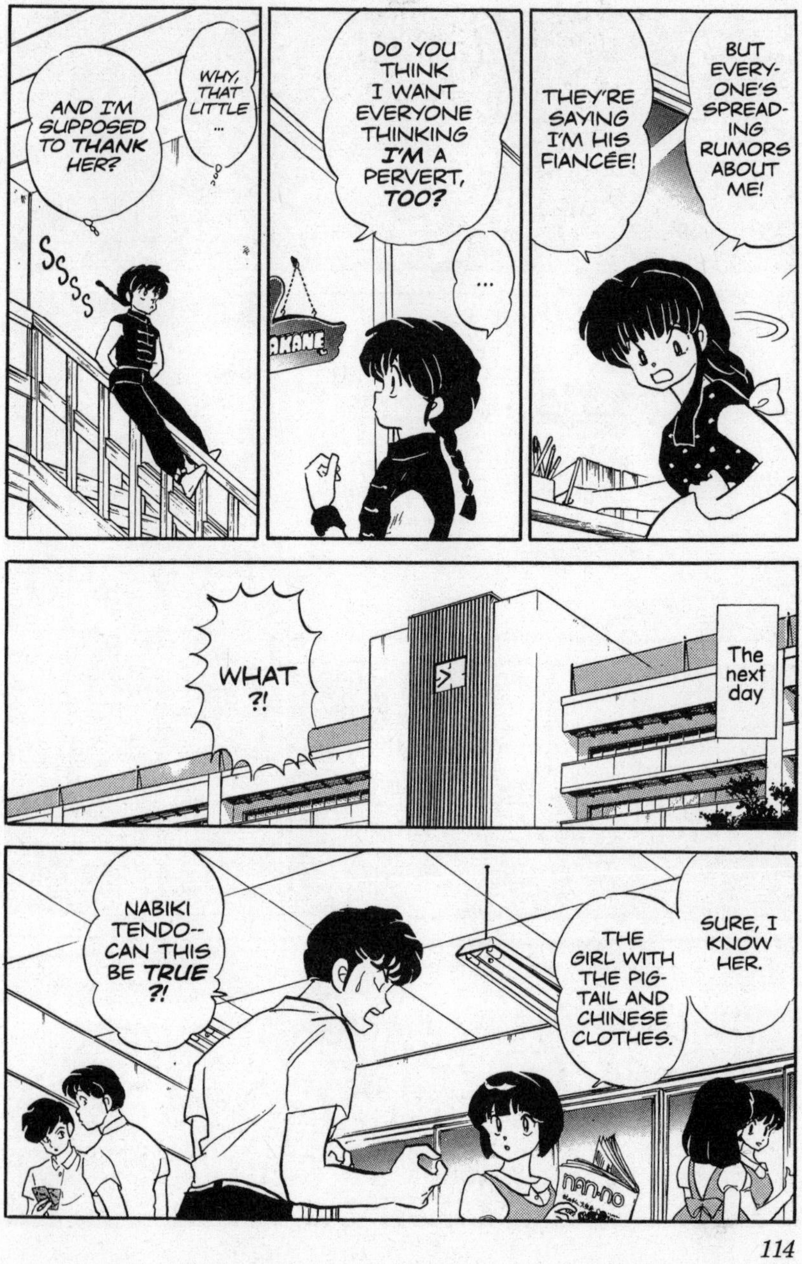
BUT EVERYONE'S SPREADING RUMORS ABOUT ME!
THEY'RE SAYING I'M HIS FIANCÉE!
DO YOU THINK I WANT EVERYONE THINKING I'M A PERVERT, TOO?
...
AKANE
WHY, THAT LITTLE ...
AND I'M SUPPOSED TO THANK HER?
SSSS
The next day
WHAT ?!
SURE, I KNOW HER.
THE GIRL WITH THE PIG-TAIL AND CHINESE CLOTHES.
NABIKI TENDO-- CAN THIS BE TRUE ?!
nan-no

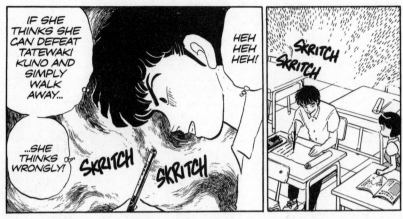

SKRITCH
SKRITCH
HEH HEH HEH!
IF SHE THINKS SHE CAN DEFEAT TATEWAKI KUNO AND SIMPLY WALK AWAY...
...SHE THINKS WRONGLY!
SKRITCH
SKRITCH
HERE.
TO THE TREE-BORNE KETTLE-GIRL
THIS IS TO ME?
TO THE GIRL SIDE.
I DON'T THINK HE BELIEVES YOU'RE THE SAME PERSON.
"ON SUNDAY, IN THE TENTH HOUR...
...MEET ME ON THE SECOND FIELD OF FURINKAN HIGH SCHOOL."
SOUNDS LIKE A DUEL, HUH?
KUNO JUST HATES TO LOSE!
HE WANTS REVENGE?

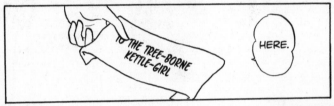

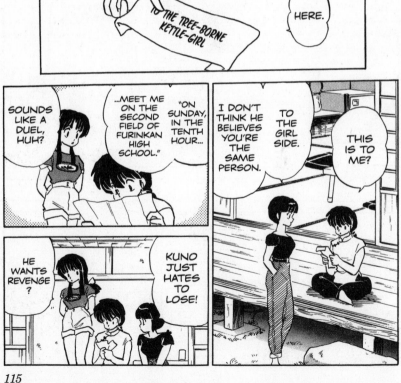

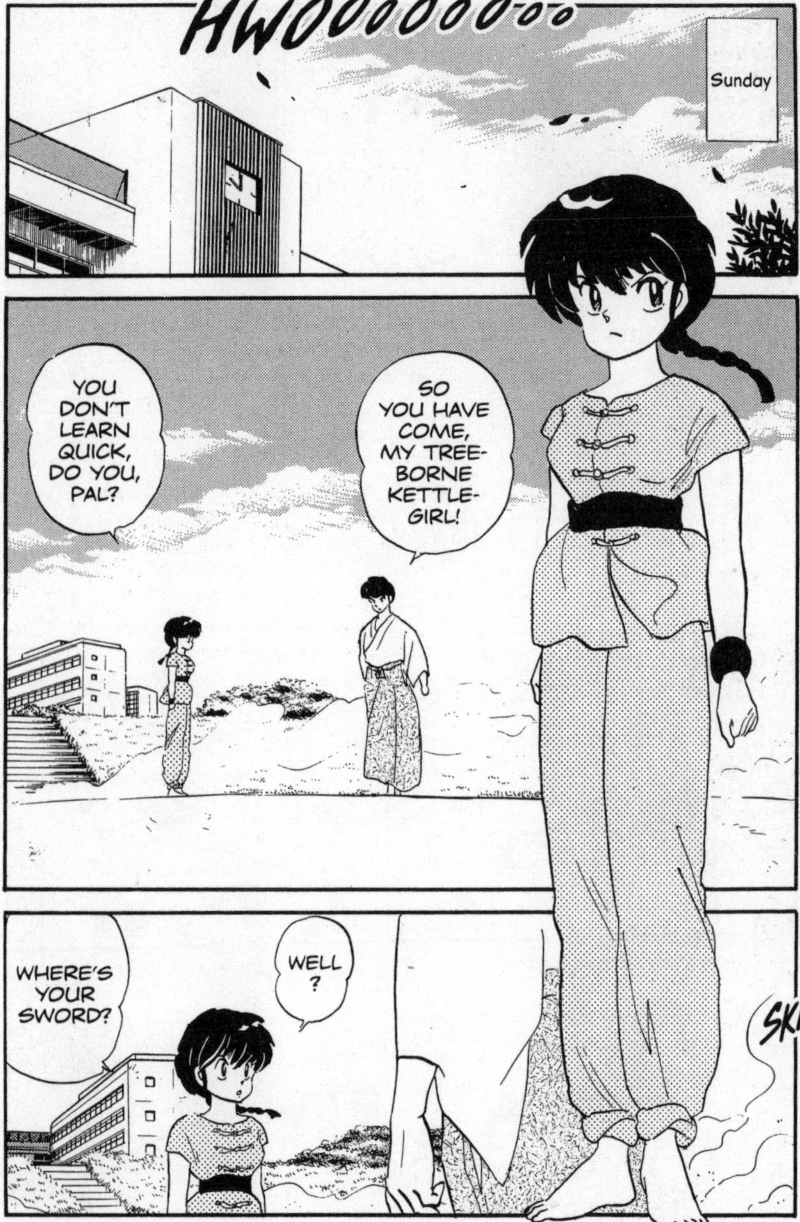
Sunday
HWOOOOOOOoo
SO YOU HAVE COME, MY TREE-BORNE KETTLE-GIRL!
YOU DON'T LEARN QUICK, DO YOU, PAL?
SKFF
WELL ?
WHERE'S YOUR SWORD?

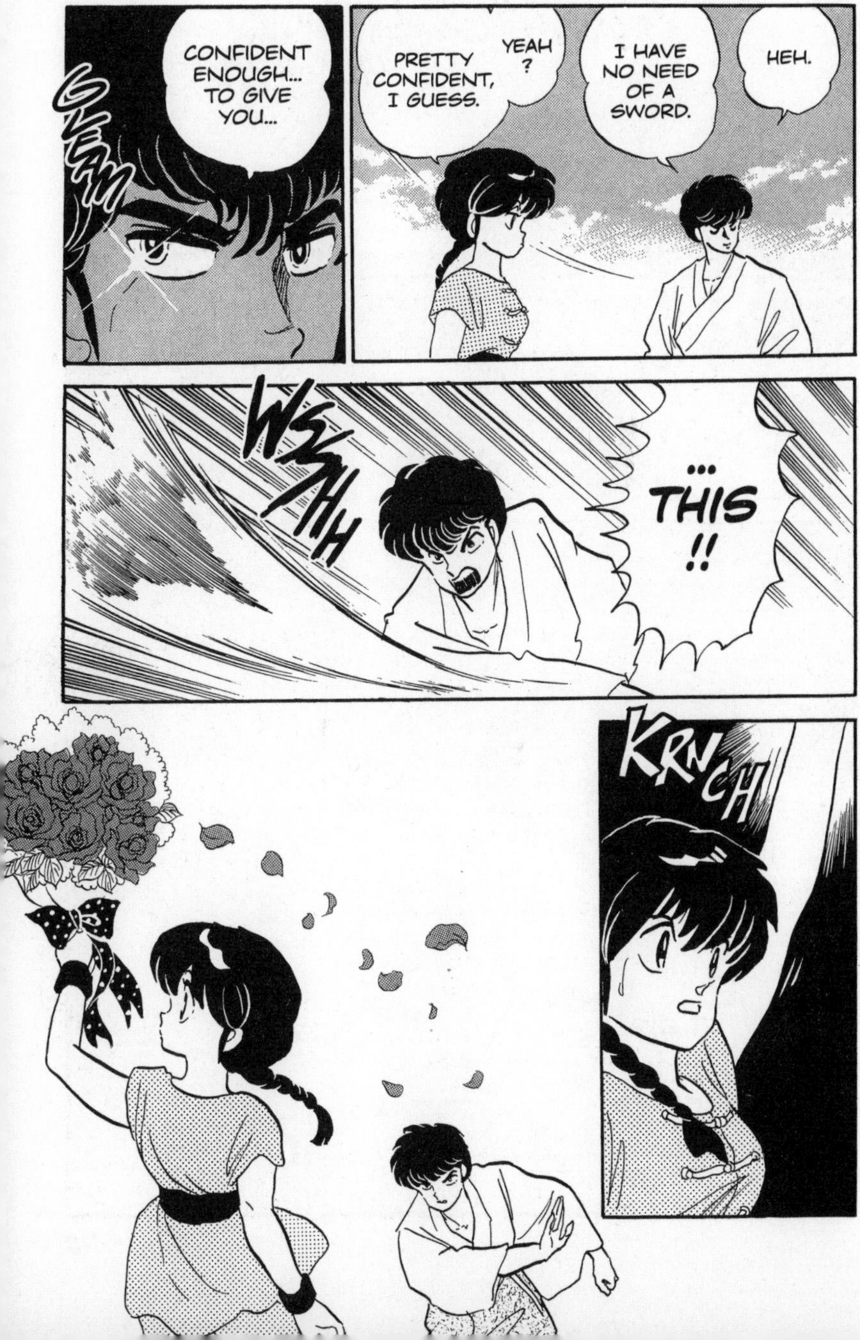
HEH.
I HAVE NO NEED OF A SWORD.
YEAH?
PRETTY CONFIDENT, I GUESS.
CONFIDENT ENOUGH... TO GIVE YOU...
GLEAM
...THIS!!
WSSHHH
KRNCH

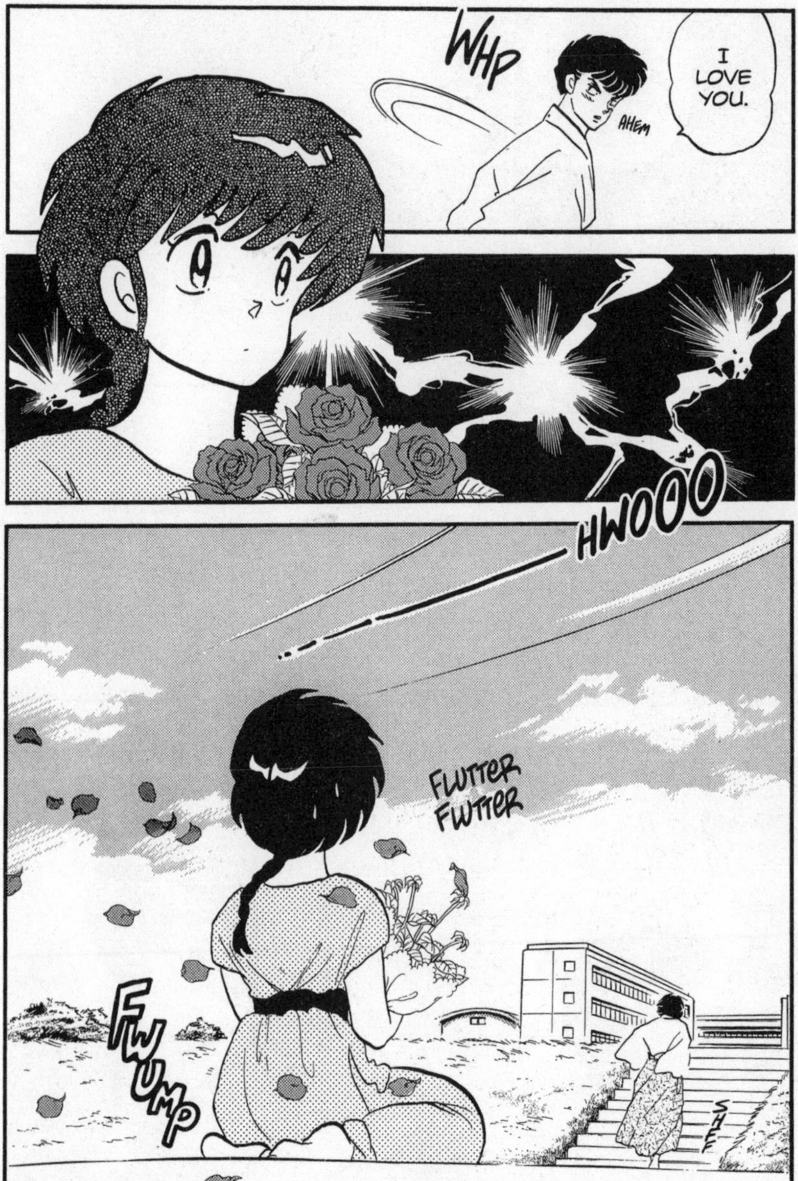
I LOVE YOU.
AHEM
WHP
HWOOO
FLUTTER FLUTTER
SHFF
FWUMP

# PART 6
# BODY AND SOUL

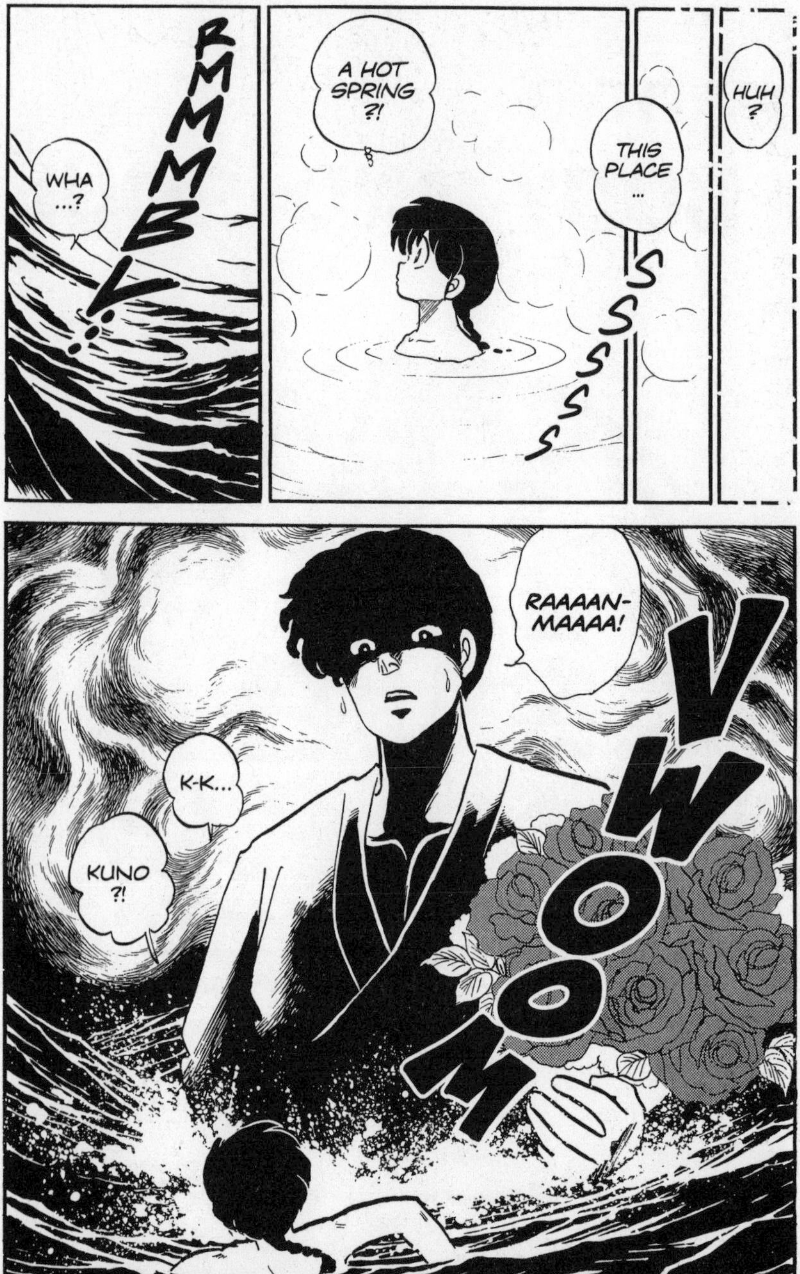
HUH ?
THIS PLACE ...
SSSSSS
A HOT SPRING ?!
RMMMBV!!
WHA ...?
RAAAAN-MAAAA!
VWOOOM
K-K...
KUNO ?!

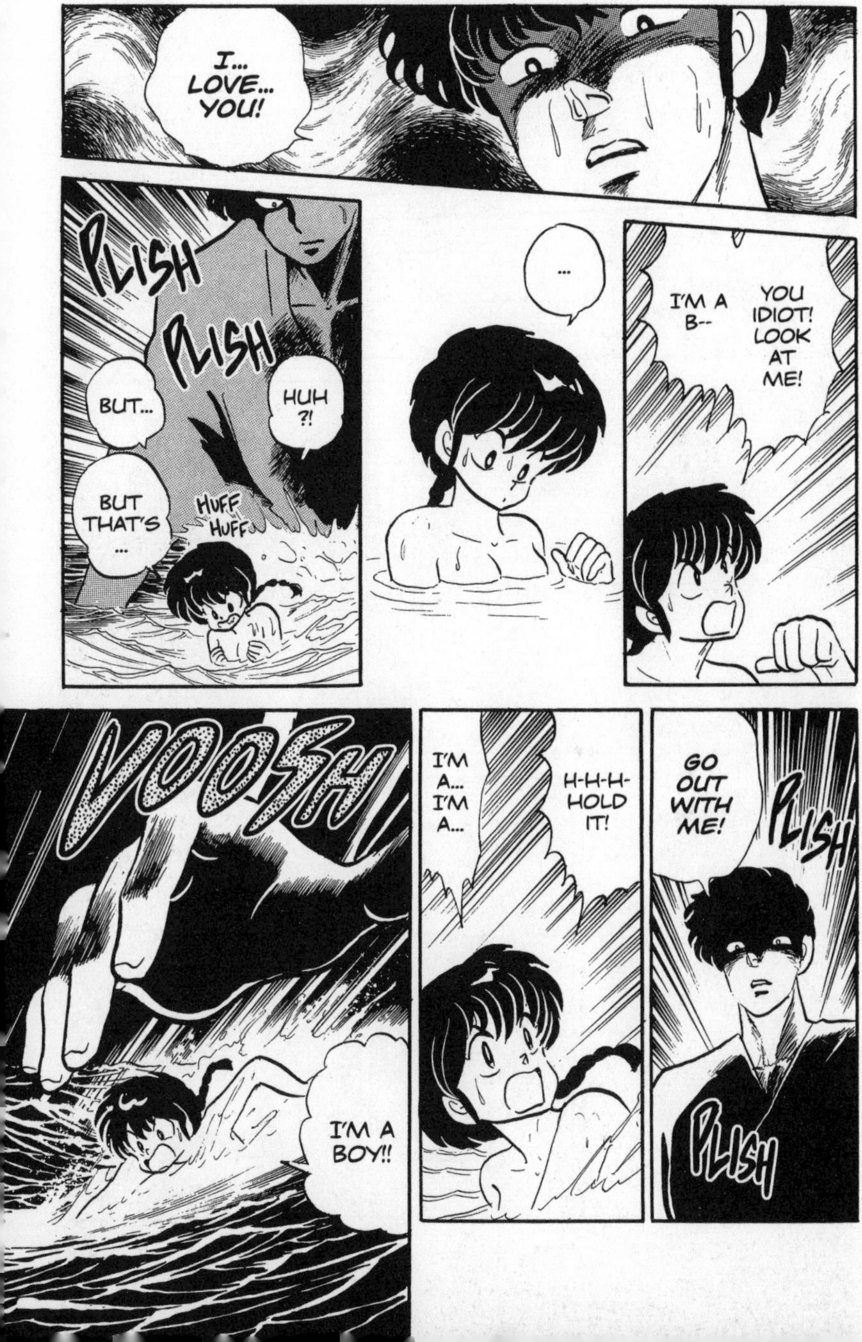
I... LOVE... YOU!
YOU IDIOT! LOOK AT ME!
I'M A B--
...
PLISH
PLISH
HUH ?!
BUT...
BUT THAT'S ...
HUFF HUFF
GO OUT WITH ME!
PLISH
PLISH
H-H-H-HOLD IT!
I'M A... I'M A...
VOOSH
I'M A BOY!!

I... LOVE... YOU!
WAAAAA--
AAH!
JOLT
TWEET TWEET
A...A DREAM?
WEEN WEEN
I LOVE YOU.
BLUSH
SHUDDER
RIP

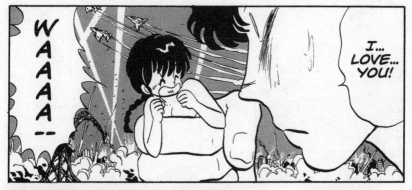

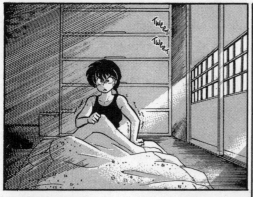

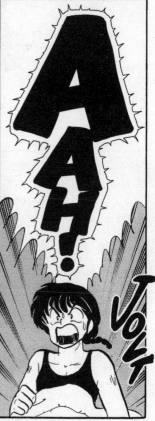

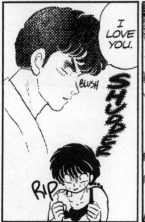

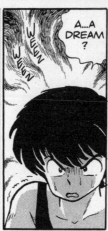

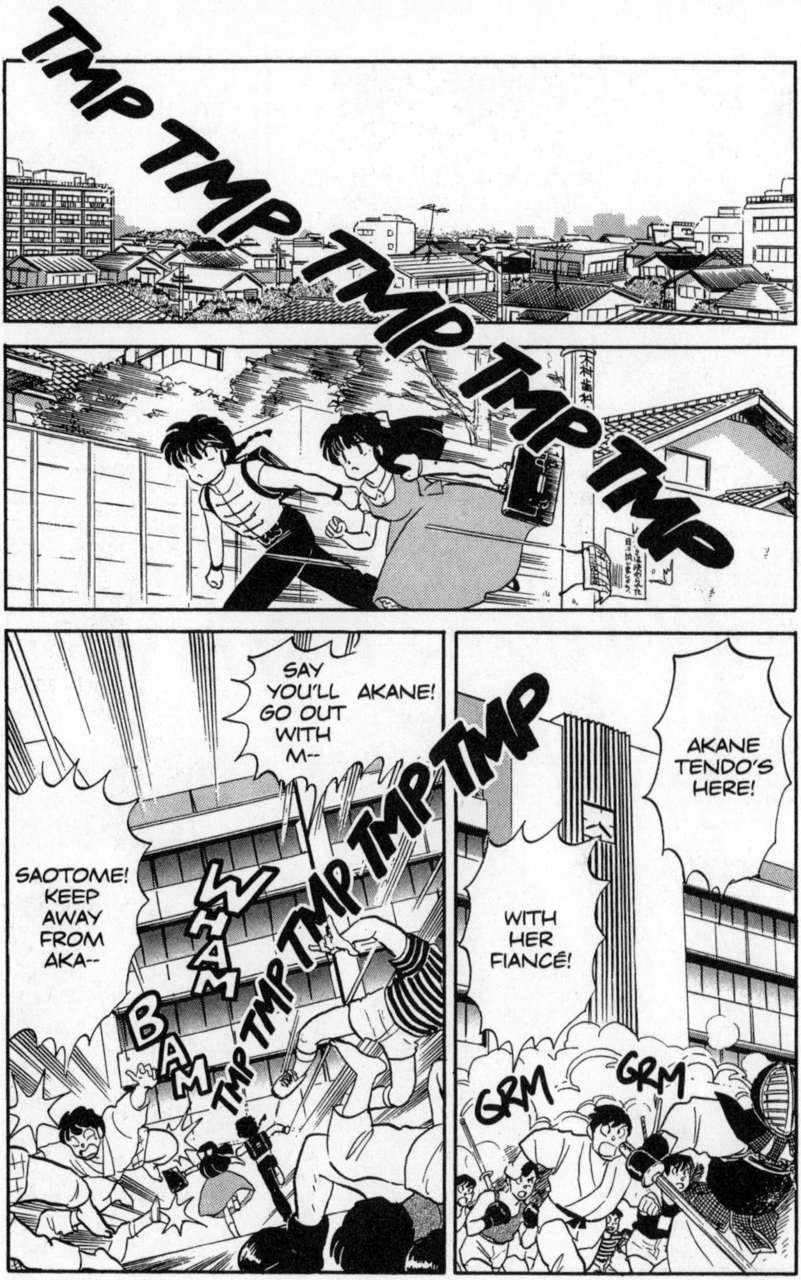
TMP TMP TMP TMP TMP TMP
AKANE TENDO'S HERE!
WITH HER FIANCÉ!
GRM GRM
SAY YOU'LL GO OUT WITH M-- AKANE!
SAOTOME! KEEP AWAY FROM AKA--
WHAM
BAM
TMP TMP TMP TMP TMP TMP

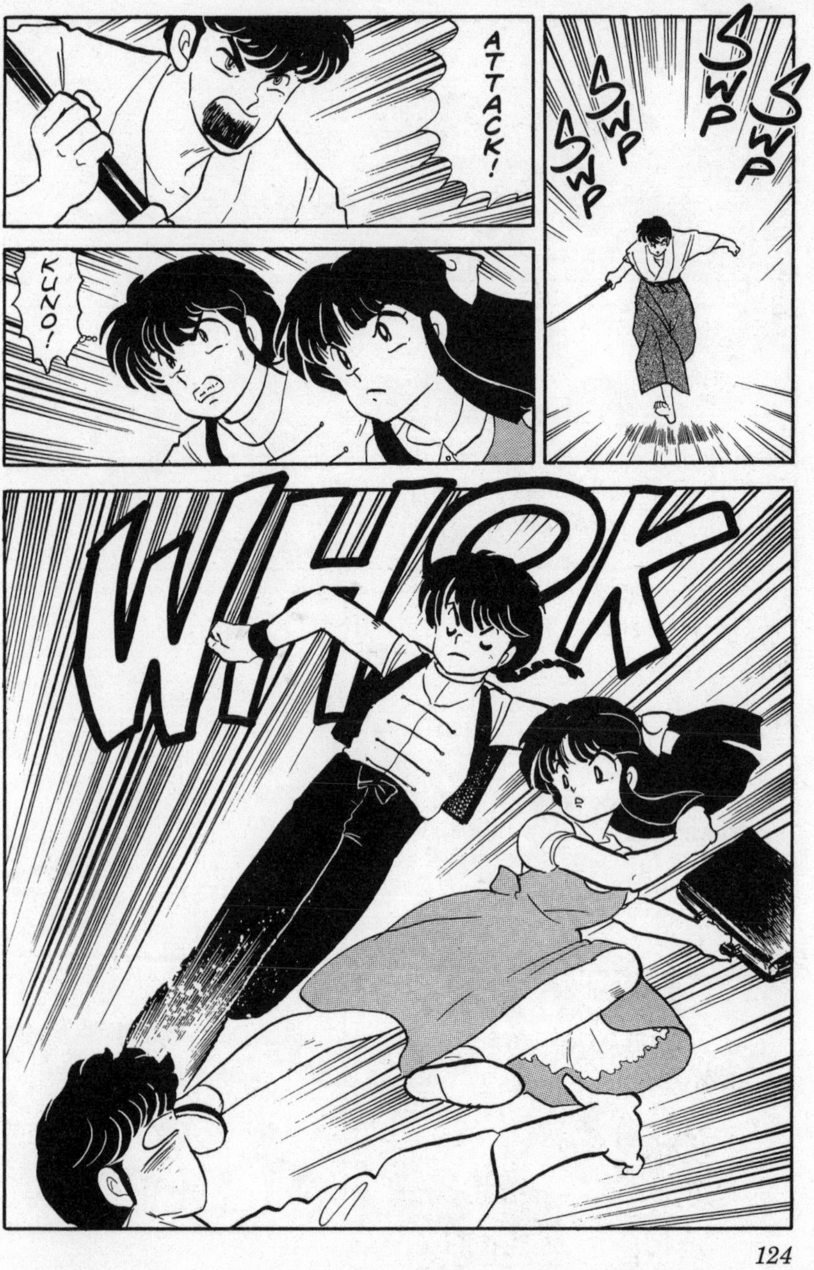
SWP
SWP
SWP
SWP
ATTACK!
KUNO!
WHOK

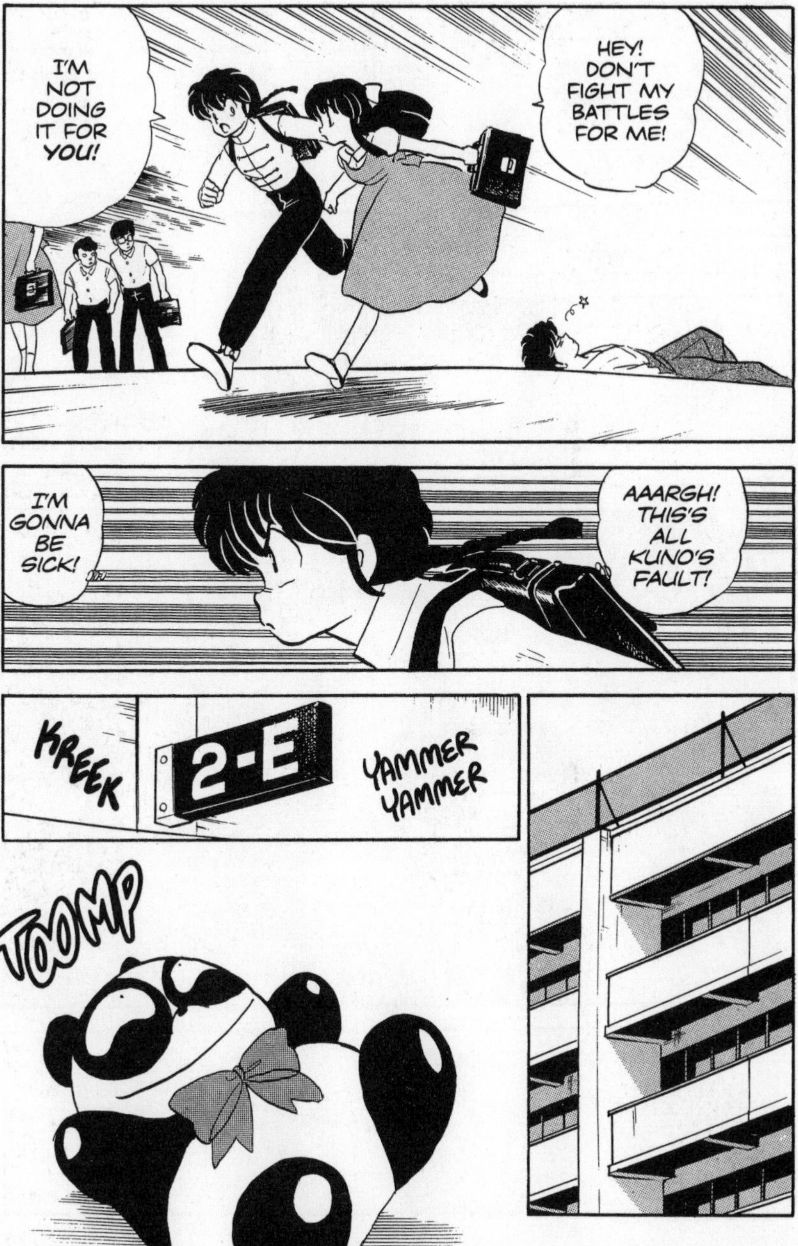
HEY! DON'T FIGHT MY BATTLES FOR ME!
I'M NOT DOING IT FOR YOU!
AAARGH! THIS'S ALL KUNO'S FAULT!
I'M GONNA BE SICK!
YAMMER YAMMER
2-E
KREEK
TOOMP

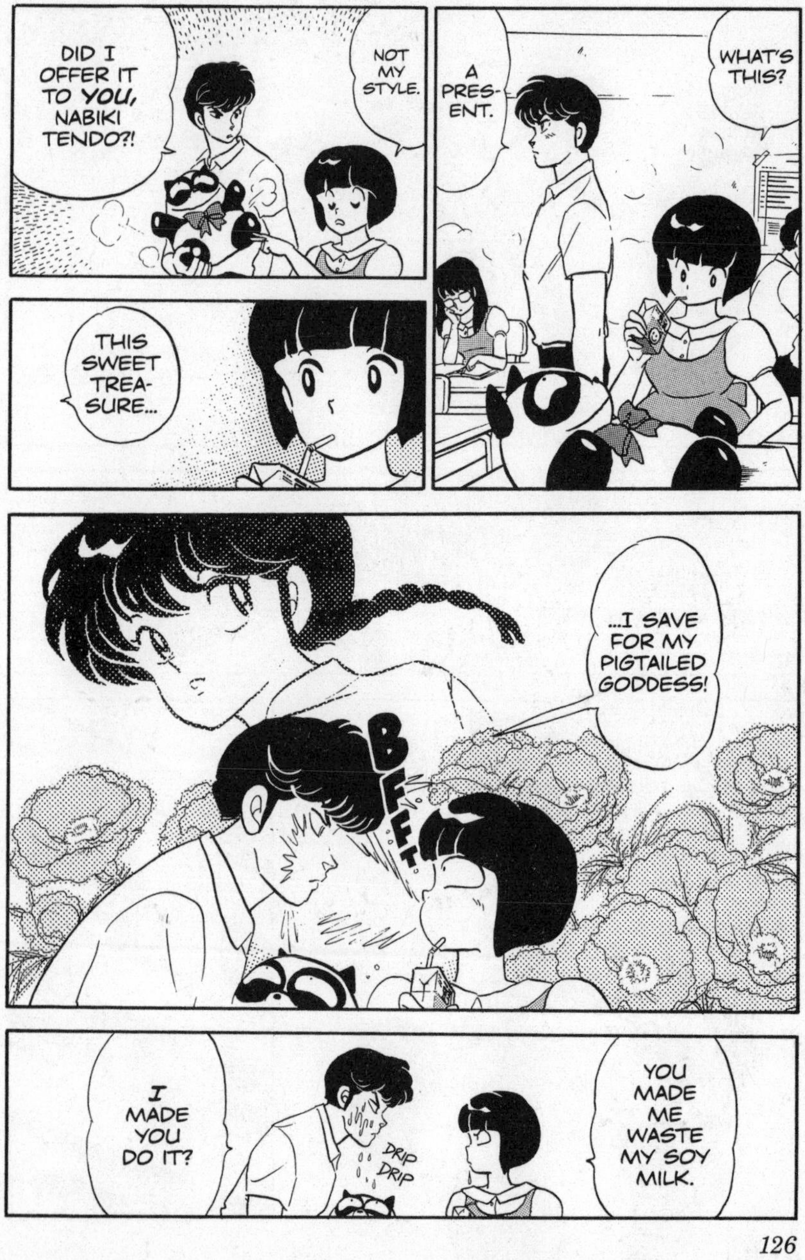
WHAT'S THIS?
A PRESENT.
NOT MY STYLE.
DID I OFFER IT TO YOU, NABIKI TENDO?!
THIS SWEET TREASURE...
...I SAVE FOR MY PIGTAILED GODDESS!
BFFT
YOU MADE ME WASTE MY SOY MILK.
DRIP DRIP
I MADE YOU DO IT?

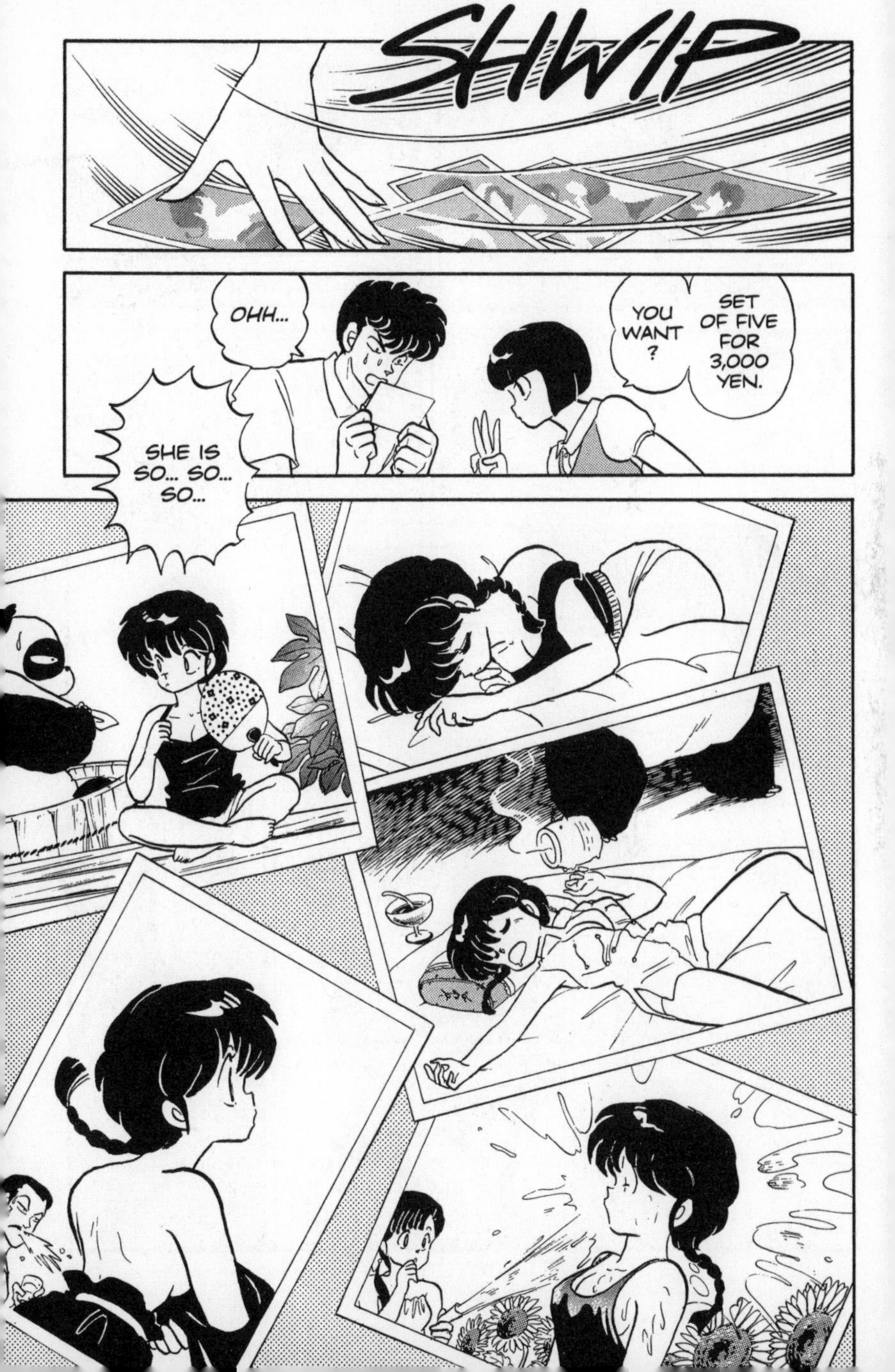
SHWIP
SET OF FIVE FOR 3,000 YEN.
YOU WANT?
OHH...
SHE IS SO... SO... SO...

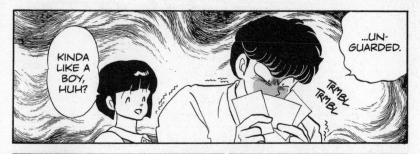

...UN-GUARDED.
TRMBL TRMBL
KINDA LIKE A BOY, HUH?
YOU'RE REALLY SOMETHING, YOU KNOW?
I MEAN, DROPPING AKANE JUST LIKE THAT?
DROPPING HER?
YOU'RE **NOT** GOING TO TWO-TIME HER!
GRRR
HMPH.
DON'T BE VULGAR.
AKANE, SO PURE AND TIDY.
THE PIG-TAILED GIRL, BURSTING WITH HEALTHY BEAUTY!

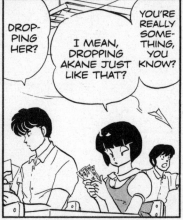

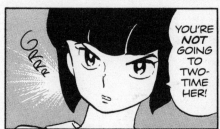

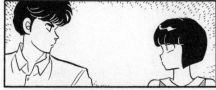

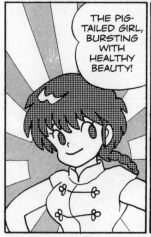

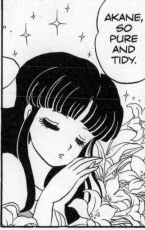

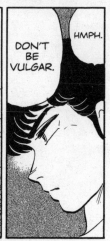

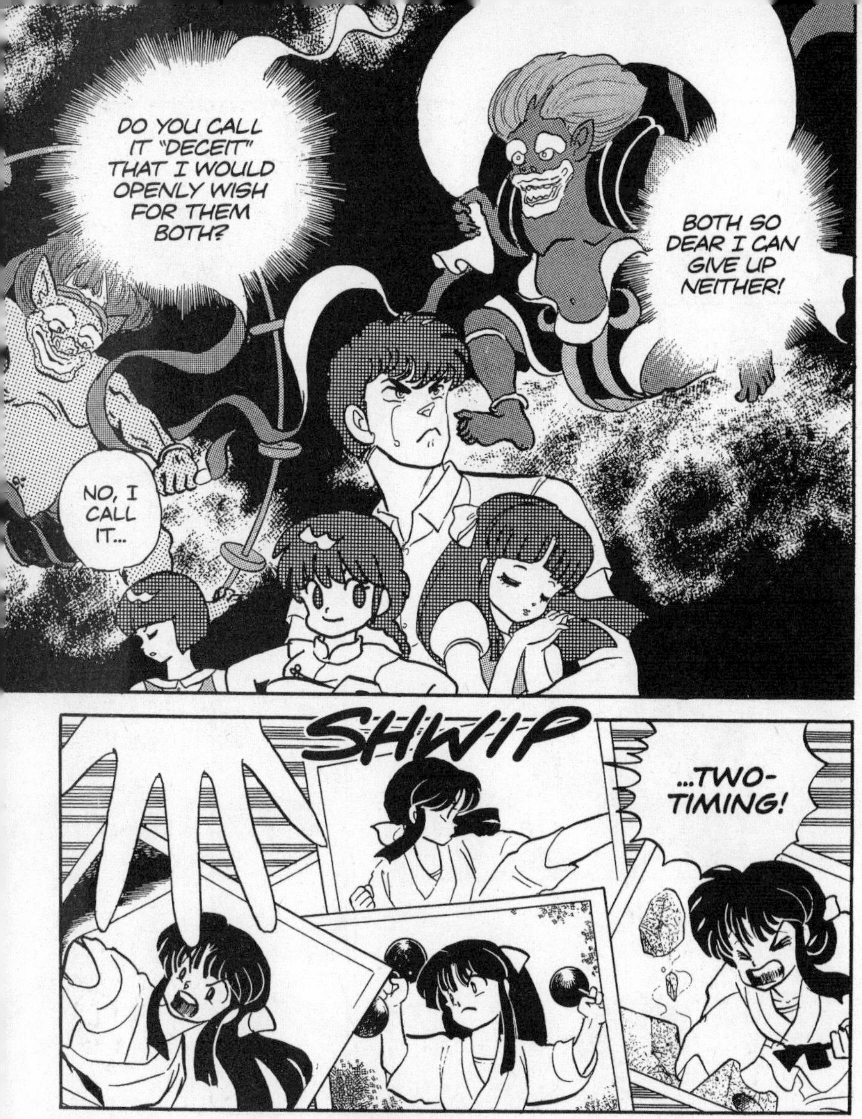
DO YOU CALL IT "DECEIT" THAT I WOULD OPENLY WISH FOR THEM BOTH?
BOTH SO DEAR I CAN GIVE UP NEITHER!
NO, I CALL IT...
SHWIP
...TWO-TIMING!
SET OF FIVE FOR 3,000 YEN.
SUCH... SUCH... FEROCITY!
SOLD.

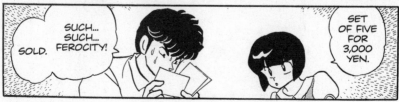

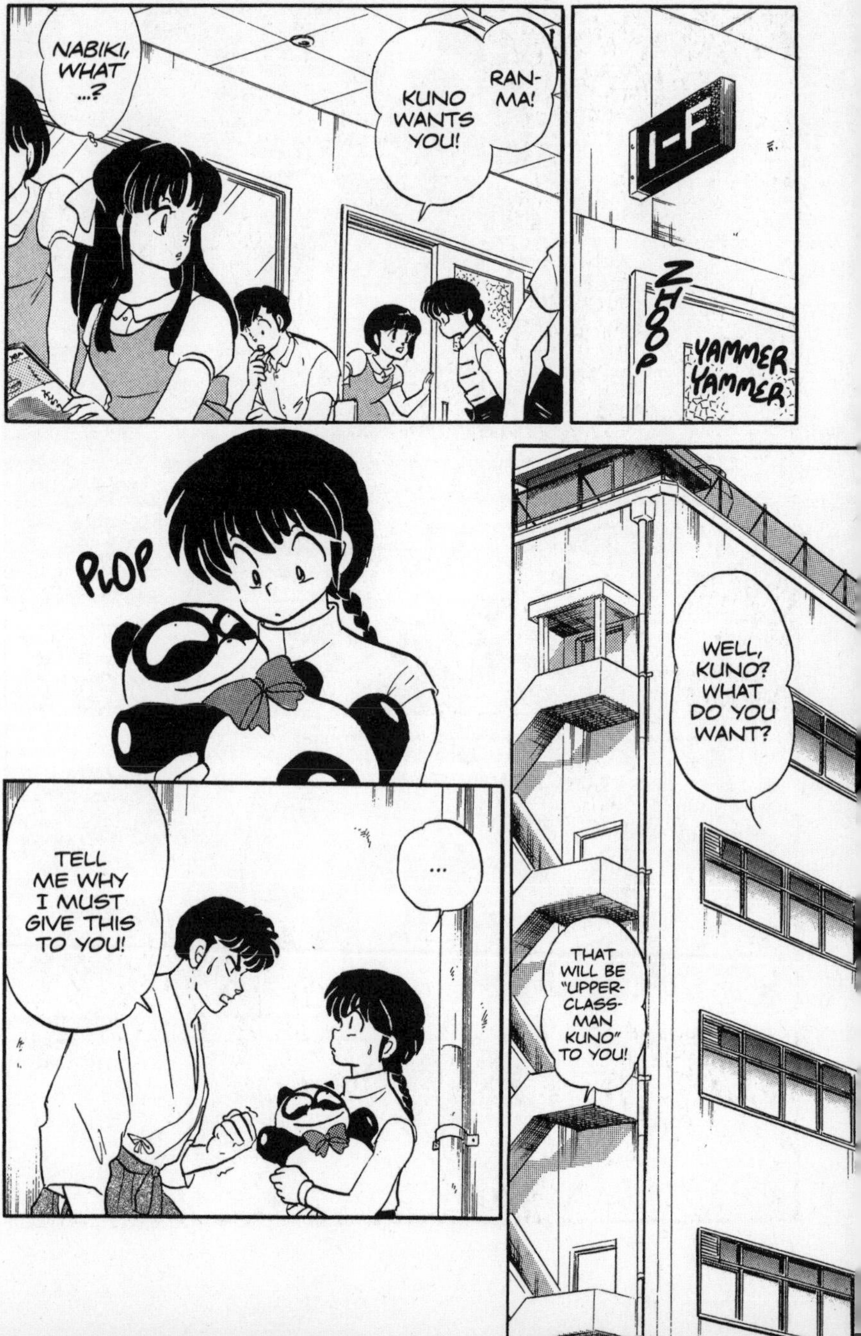
I-F
ZHOOP
YAMMER YAMMER
RAN-MA! KUNO WANTS YOU!
NABIKI, WHAT ...?
WELL, KUNO? WHAT DO YOU WANT?
THAT WILL BE "UPPER-CLASS-MAN KUNO" TO YOU!
PLOP
...
TELL ME WHY I MUST GIVE THIS TO YOU!

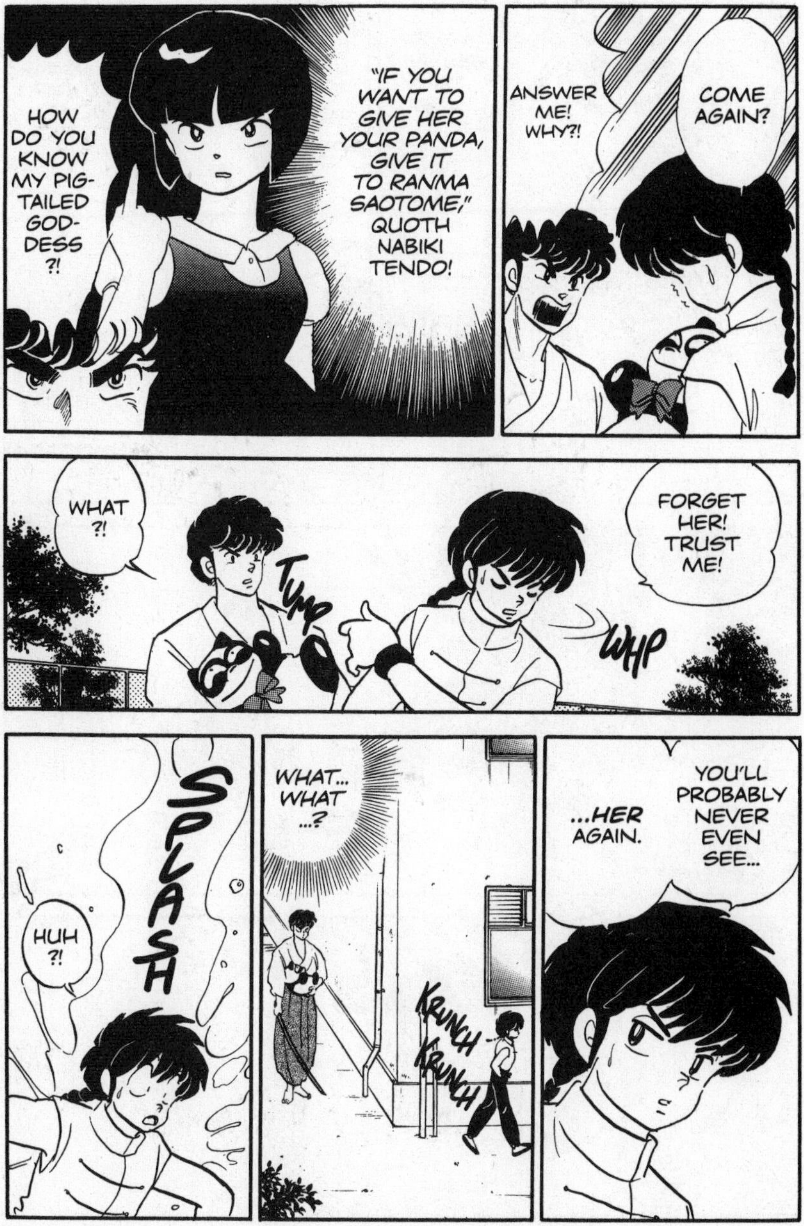
COME AGAIN?
ANSWER ME! WHY?!
"IF YOU WANT TO GIVE HER YOUR PANDA, GIVE IT TO RANMA SAOTOME," QUOTH NABIKI TENDO!
HOW DO YOU KNOW MY PIG-TAILED GODDESS ?!
FORGET HER! TRUST ME!
WHP
TUMP
WHAT ?!
YOU'LL PROBABLY NEVER EVEN SEE...
...HER AGAIN.
WHAT... WHAT ...?
KRUNCH
KRUNCH
SPLASH
HUH ?!

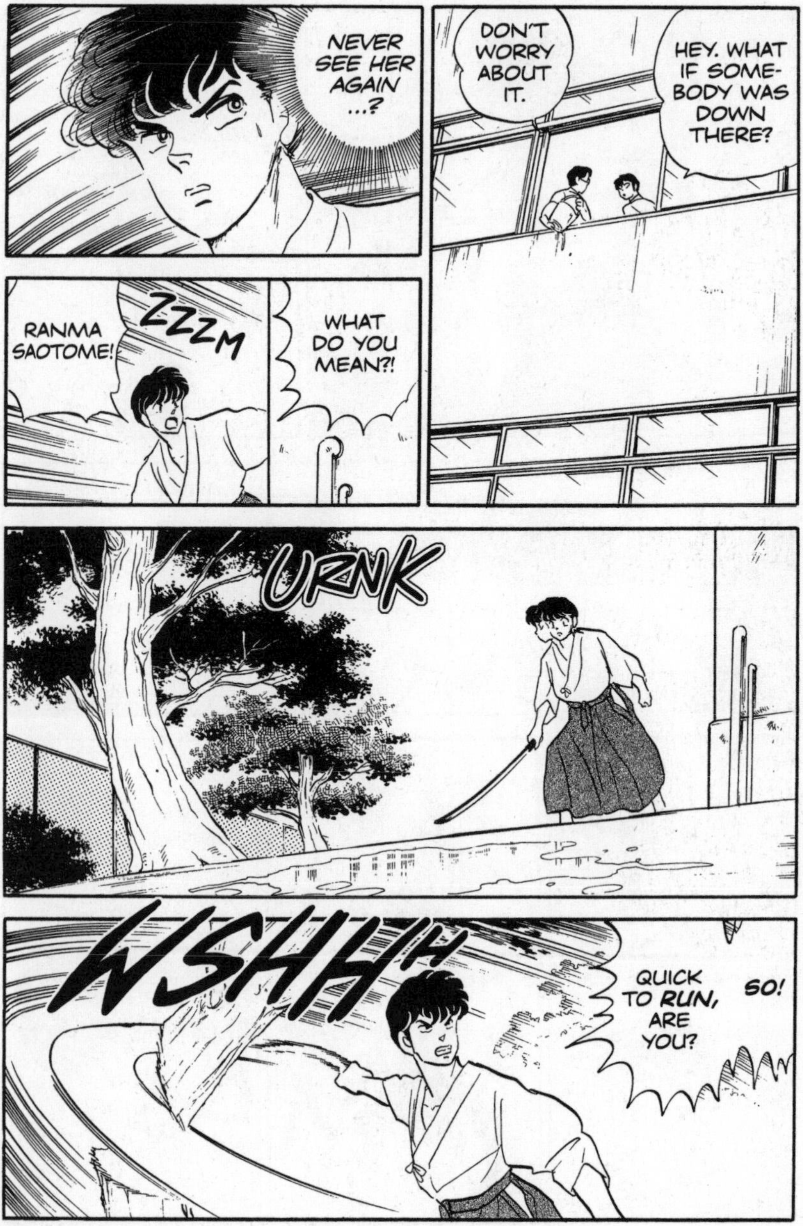
HEY. WHAT IF SOME-BODY WAS DOWN THERE?
DON'T WORRY ABOUT IT.
NEVER SEE HER AGAIN ...?
WHAT DO YOU MEAN?!
ZZZM
RANMA SAOTOME!
URNK
SO!
QUICK TO RUN, ARE YOU?
WSHHH

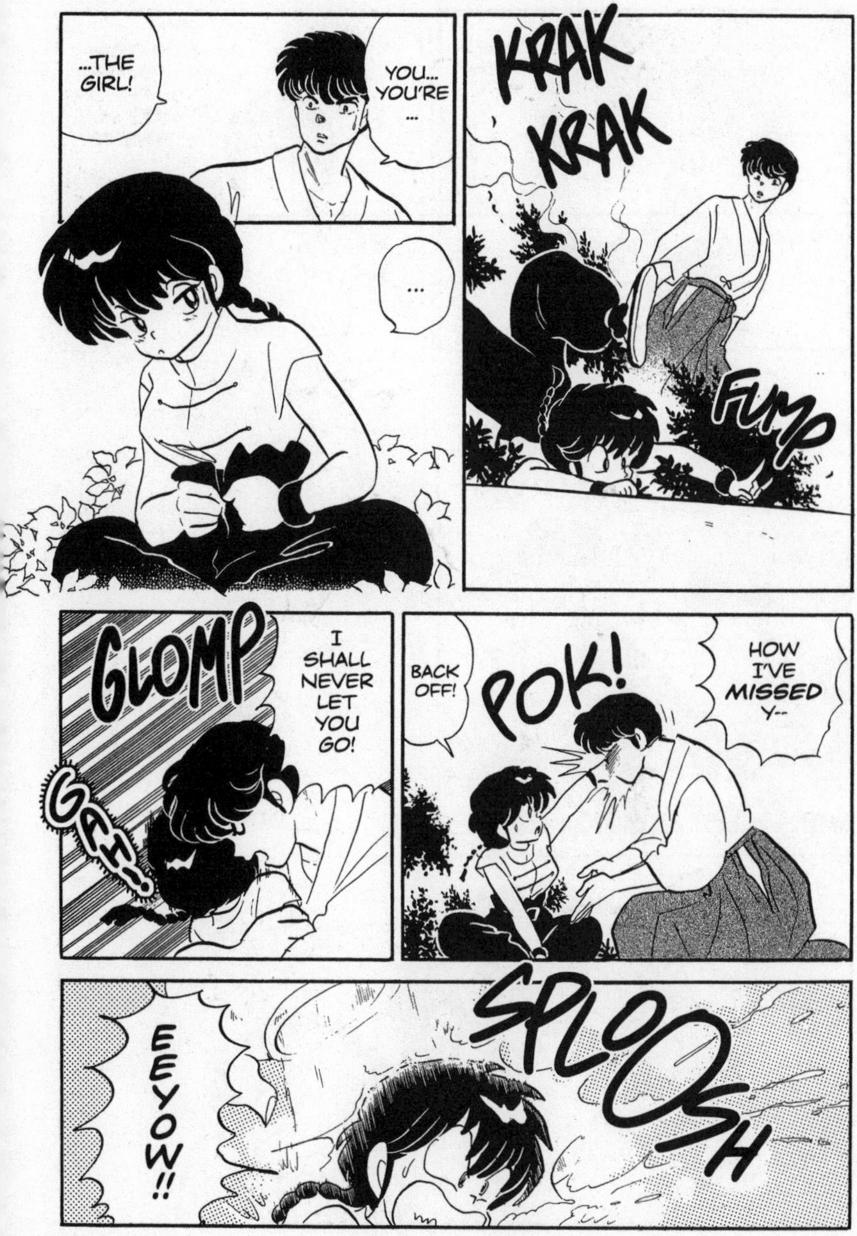
KRAK
KRAK
FUMP
YOU... YOU'RE ...
...THE GIRL!
...
HOW I'VE MISSED Y--
POK!
BACK OFF!
I SHALL NEVER LET YOU GO!
GLOMP
GAH!!
SPLOOSH
EEYOW!!

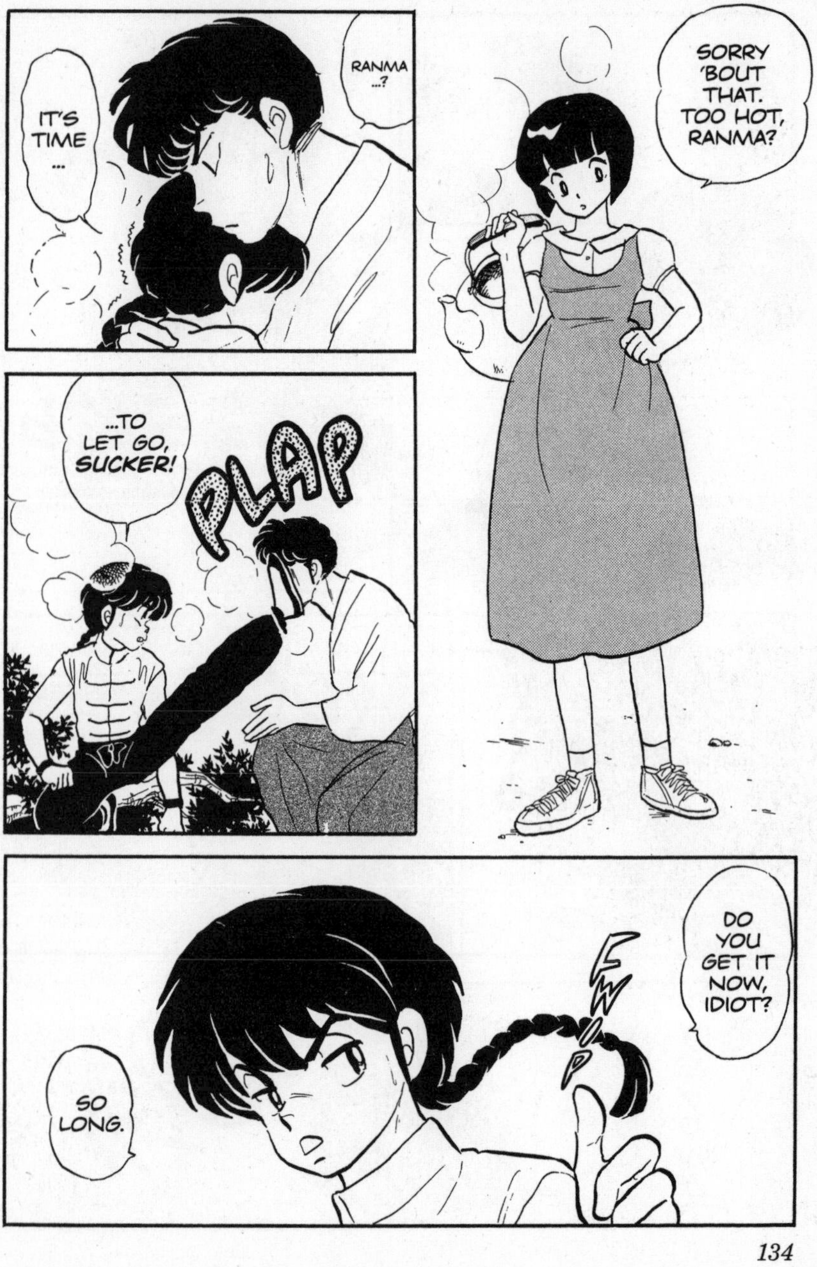
SORRY 'BOUT THAT. TOO HOT, RANMA?
RANMA ...?
IT'S TIME ...
...TO LET GO, SUCKER!
PLAP
DO YOU GET IT NOW, IDIOT?
FWOOP
SO LONG.

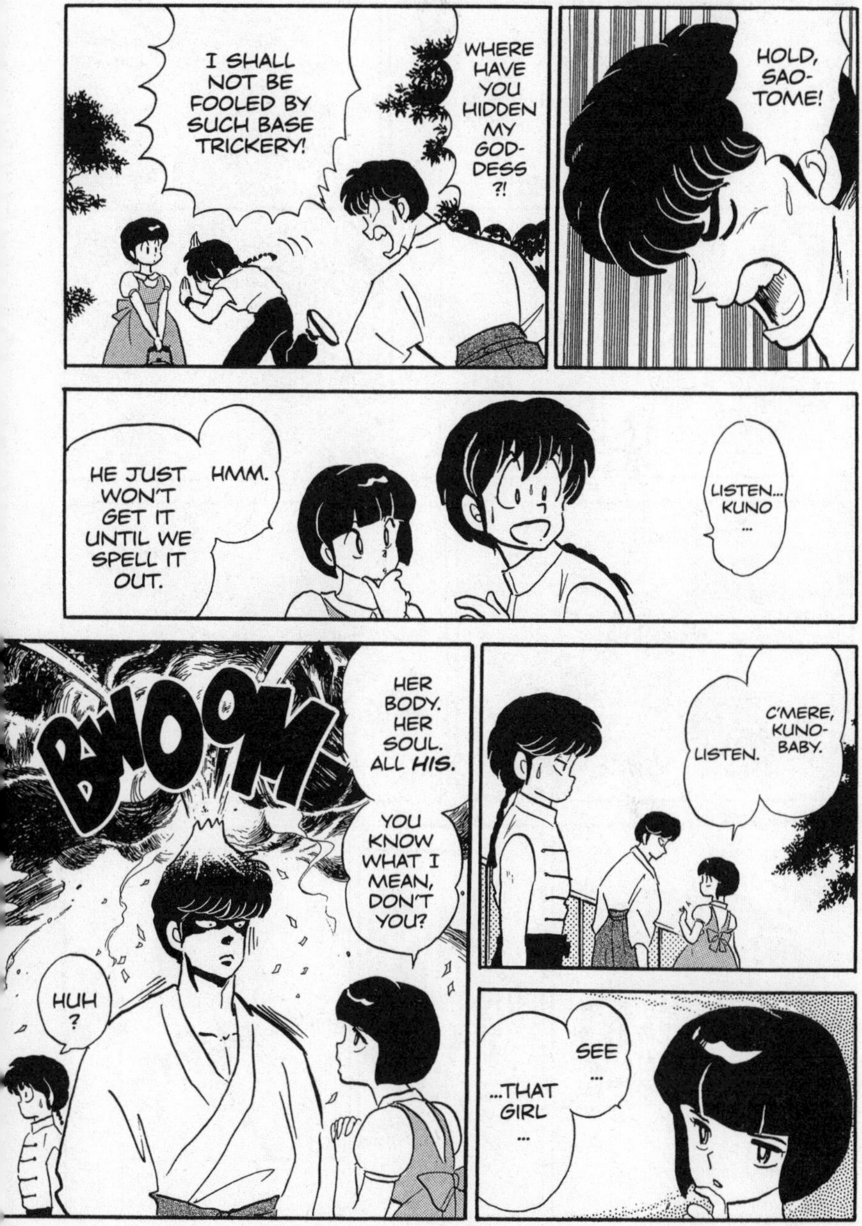
HOLD, SAO-TOME!
WHERE HAVE YOU HIDDEN MY GOD-DESS ?!
I SHALL NOT BE FOOLED BY SUCH BASE TRICKERY!
LISTEN... KUNO ...
HMM.
HE JUST WON'T GET IT UNTIL WE SPELL IT OUT.
C'MERE, KUNO-BABY.
LISTEN.
SEE ...
...THAT GIRL ...
HER BODY. HER SOUL. ALL HIS.
YOU KNOW WHAT I MEAN, DON'T YOU?
BWOOM
HUH ?

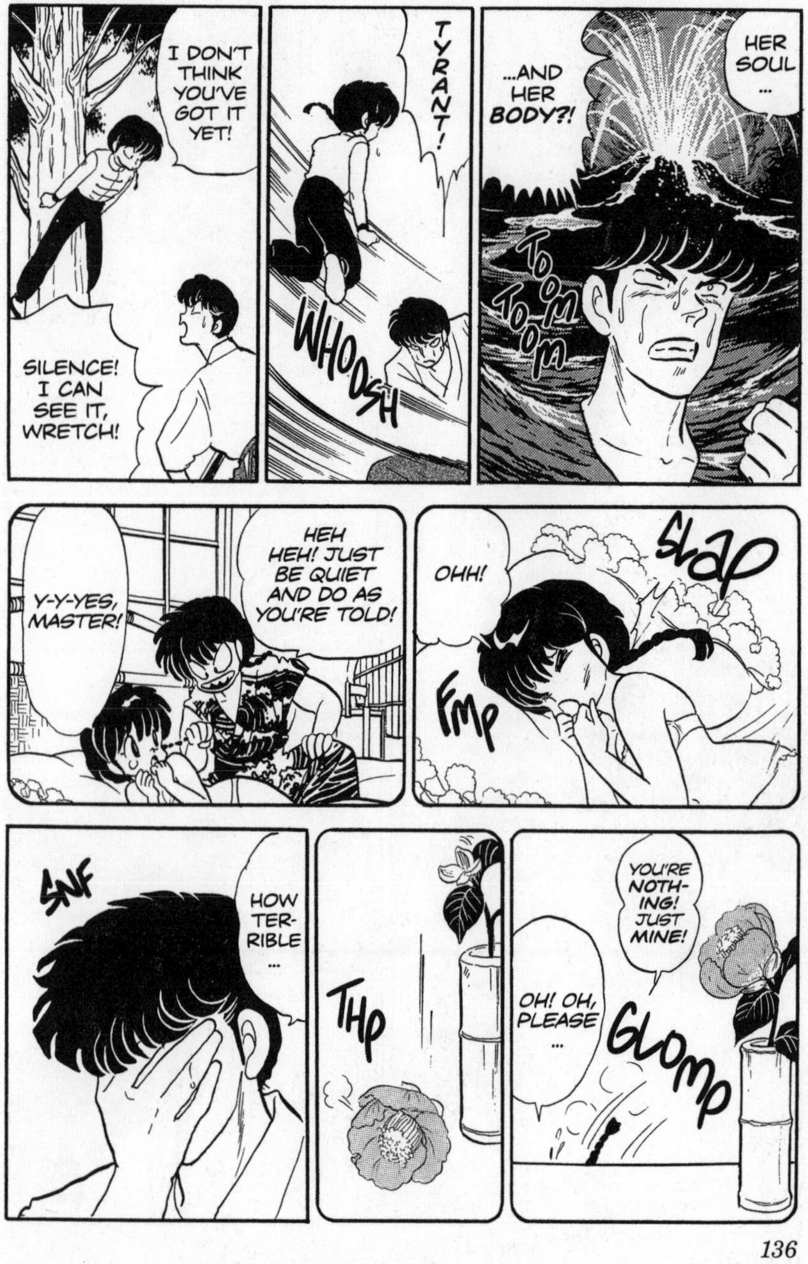
HER SOUL ...
...AND HER BODY?!
TOOM TOOM
TYRANT!
WHOOSH
I DON'T THINK YOU'VE GOT IT YET!
SILENCE! I CAN SEE IT, WRETCH!
SLAP
OHH!
FMP
HEH HEH! JUST BE QUIET AND DO AS YOU'RE TOLD!
Y-Y-YES, MASTER!
YOU'RE NOTHING! JUST MINE!
OH! OH, PLEASE ...
GLOMP
THP
HOW TERRIBLE ...
SNF

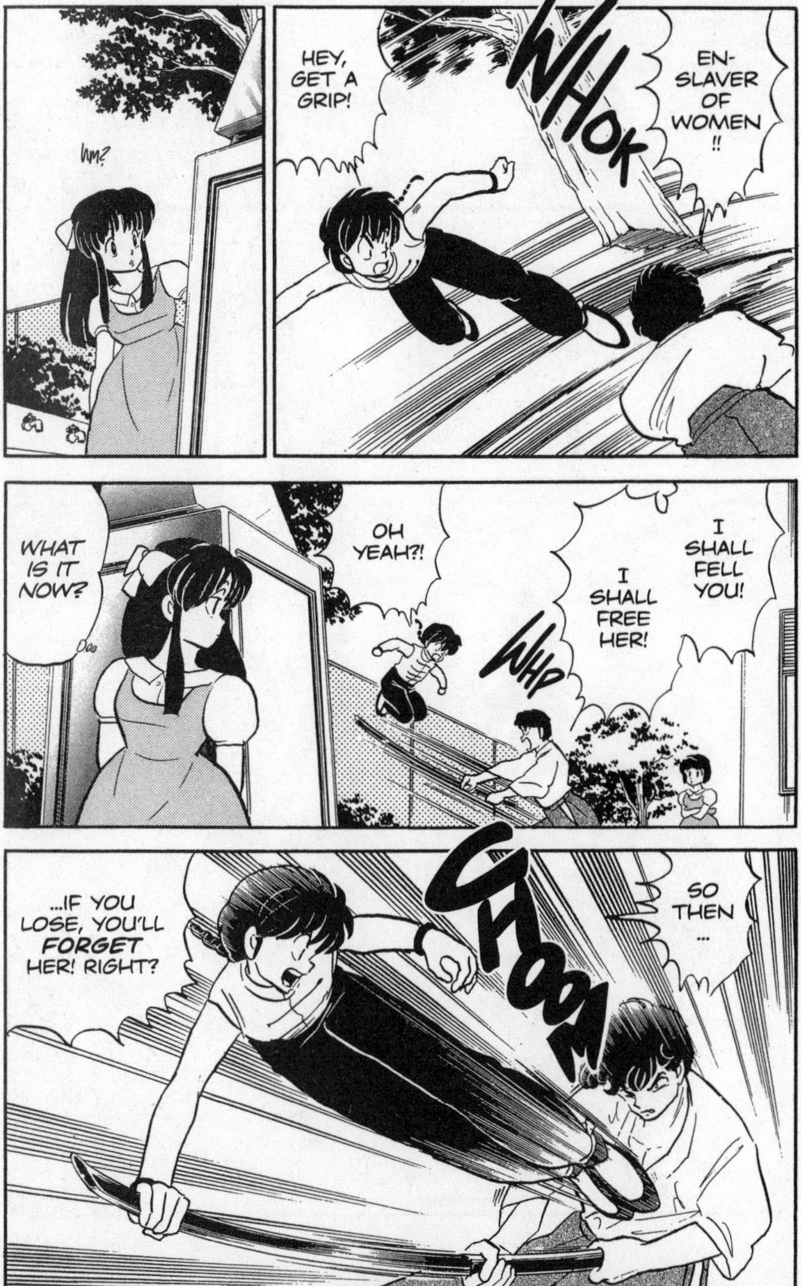
EN-SLAVER OF WOMEN!!
WHOK
HEY, GET A GRIP!
HM?
I SHALL FELL YOU!
I SHALL FREE HER!
WHP
OH YEAH?!
WHAT IS IT NOW?
SO THEN...
CHOOM
...IF YOU LOSE, YOU'LL **FORGET** HER! RIGHT?

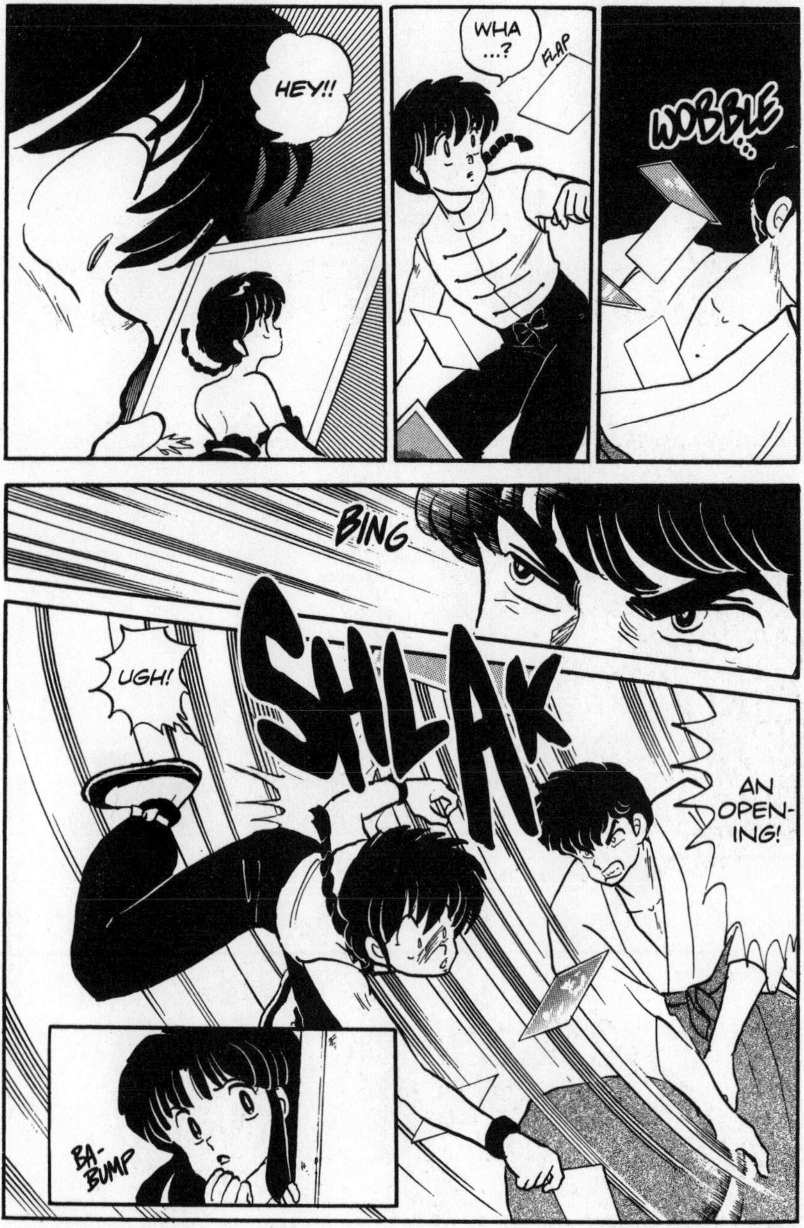
WOBBLE...
WHA ...?
FLAP
HEY!!
BING
AN OPEN-ING!
SHLAK
UGH!
BA-BUMP

# PART 7

# YOU'LL UNDERSTAND SOON ENOUGH

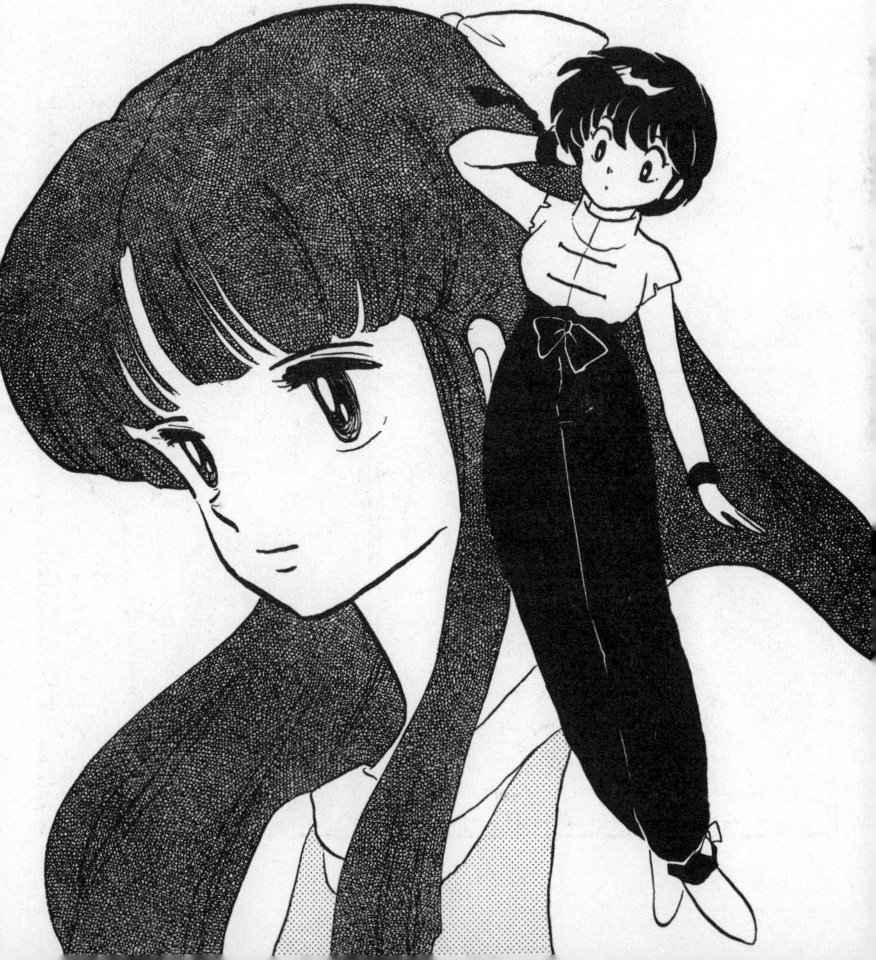

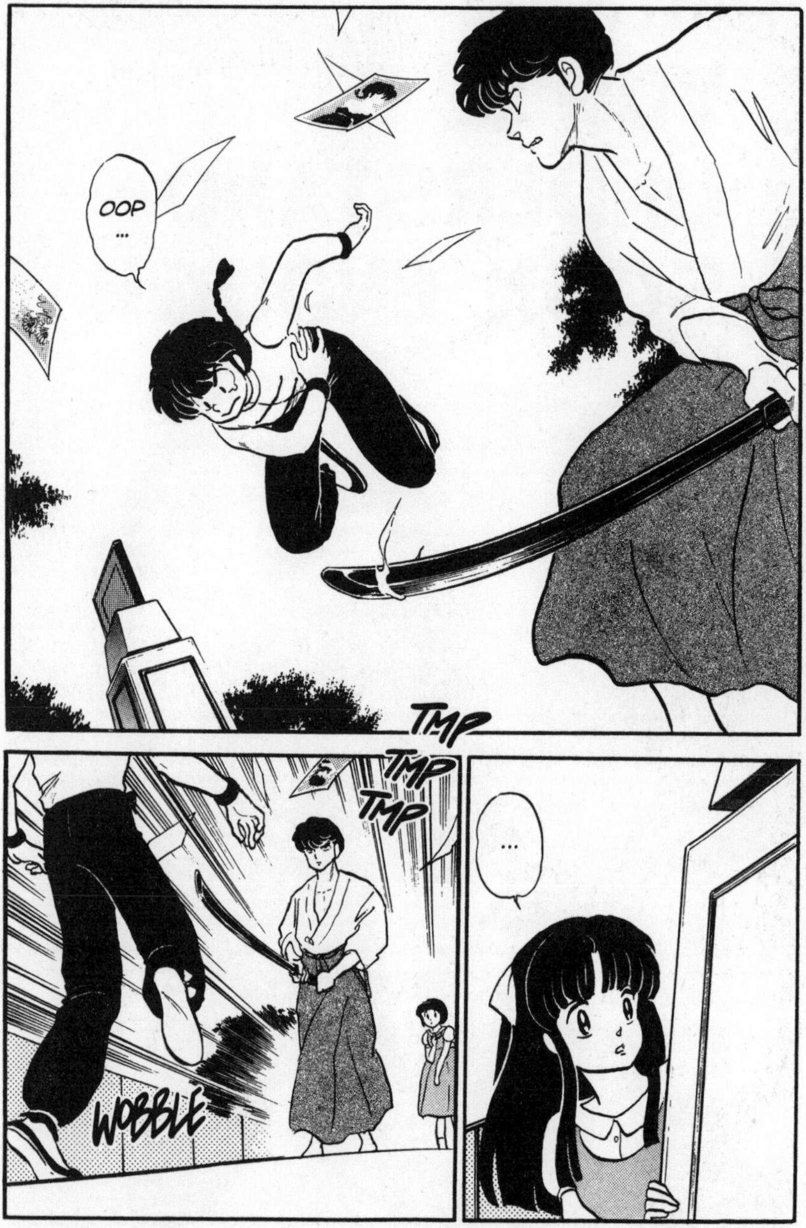
OOP ...
TMP TMP TMP
...
WOBBLE

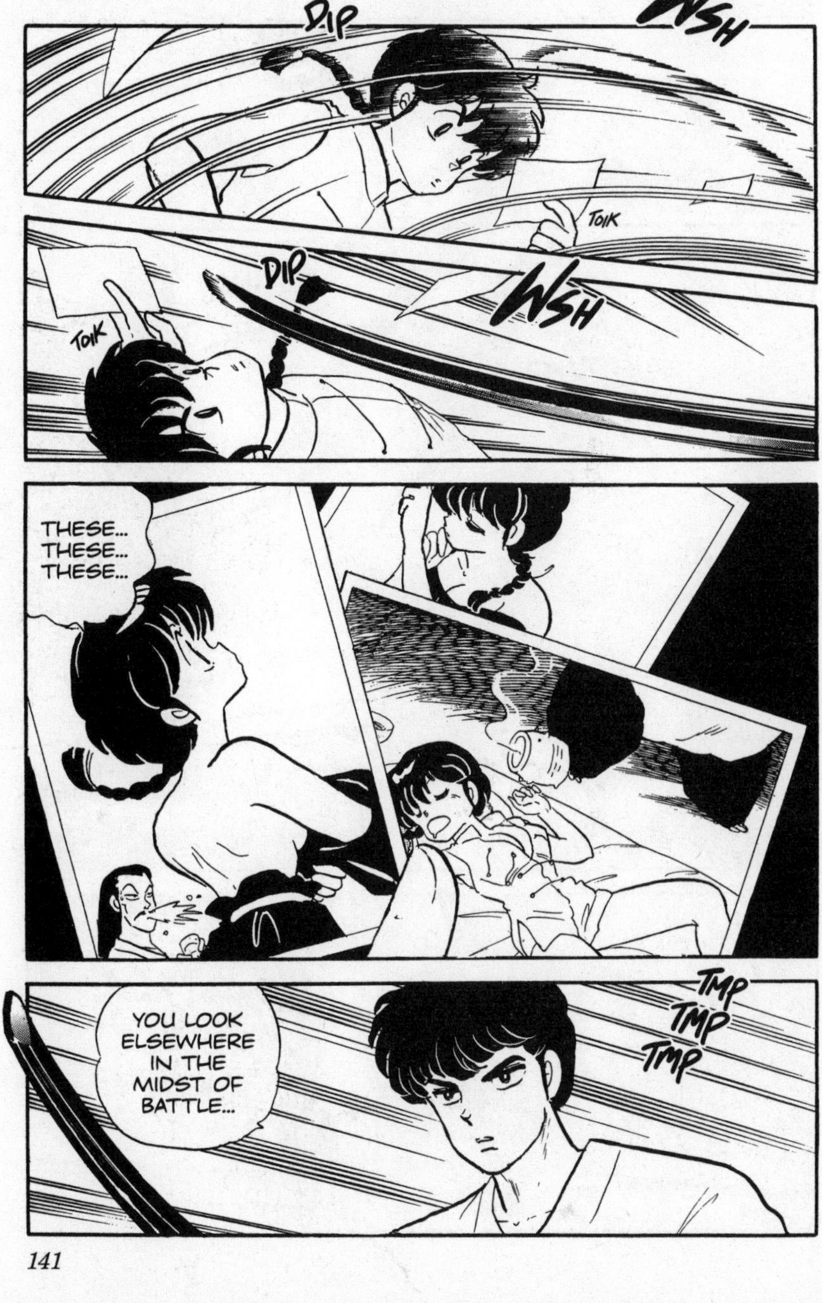
WSH
DIP
TOIK
WSH
DIP
TOIK
THESE... THESE... THESE...
TMP TMP TMP
YOU LOOK ELSEWHERE IN THE MIDST OF BATTLE...

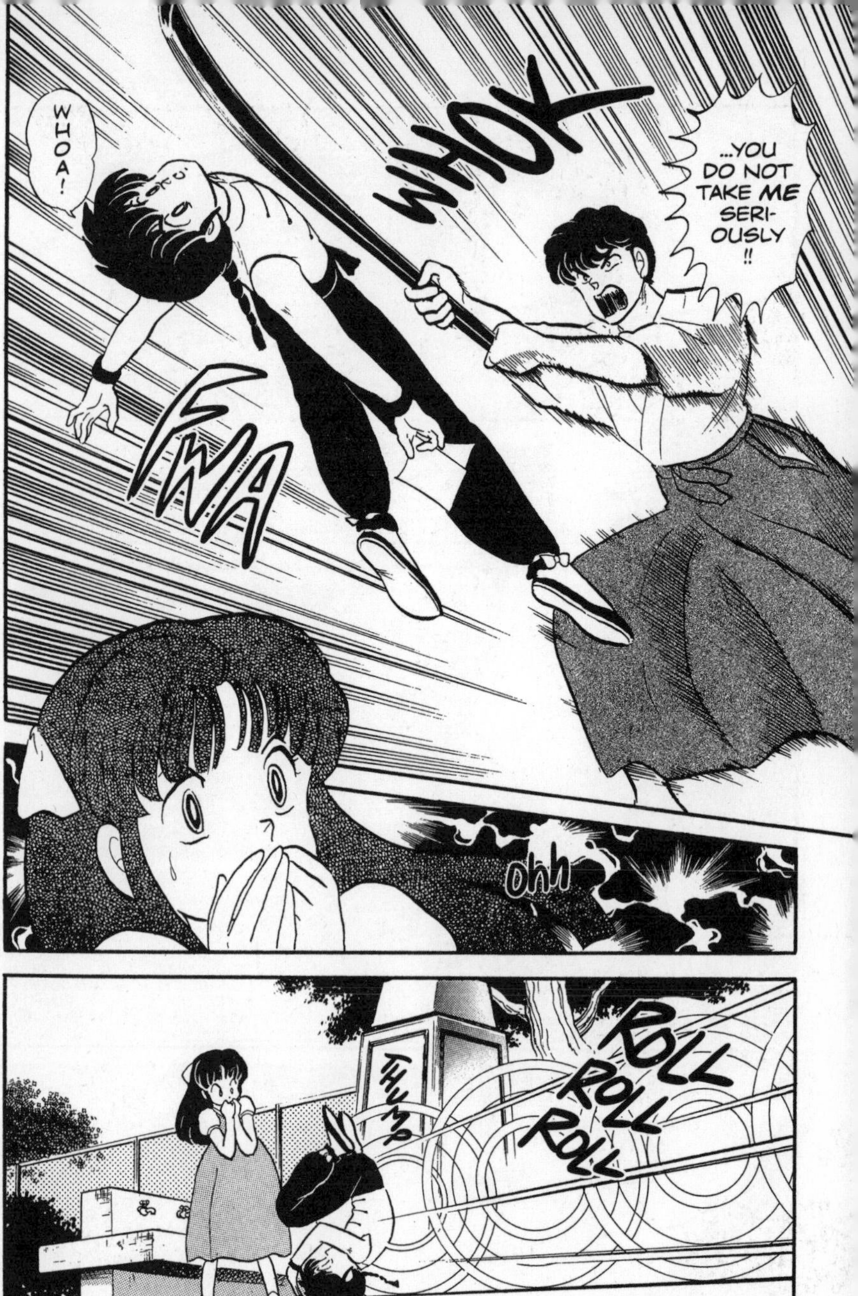
...YOU DO NOT TAKE ME SERIOUSLY!!
WHOK
WHOA!
FWA
ohh
ROLL ROLL ROLL
THUMP

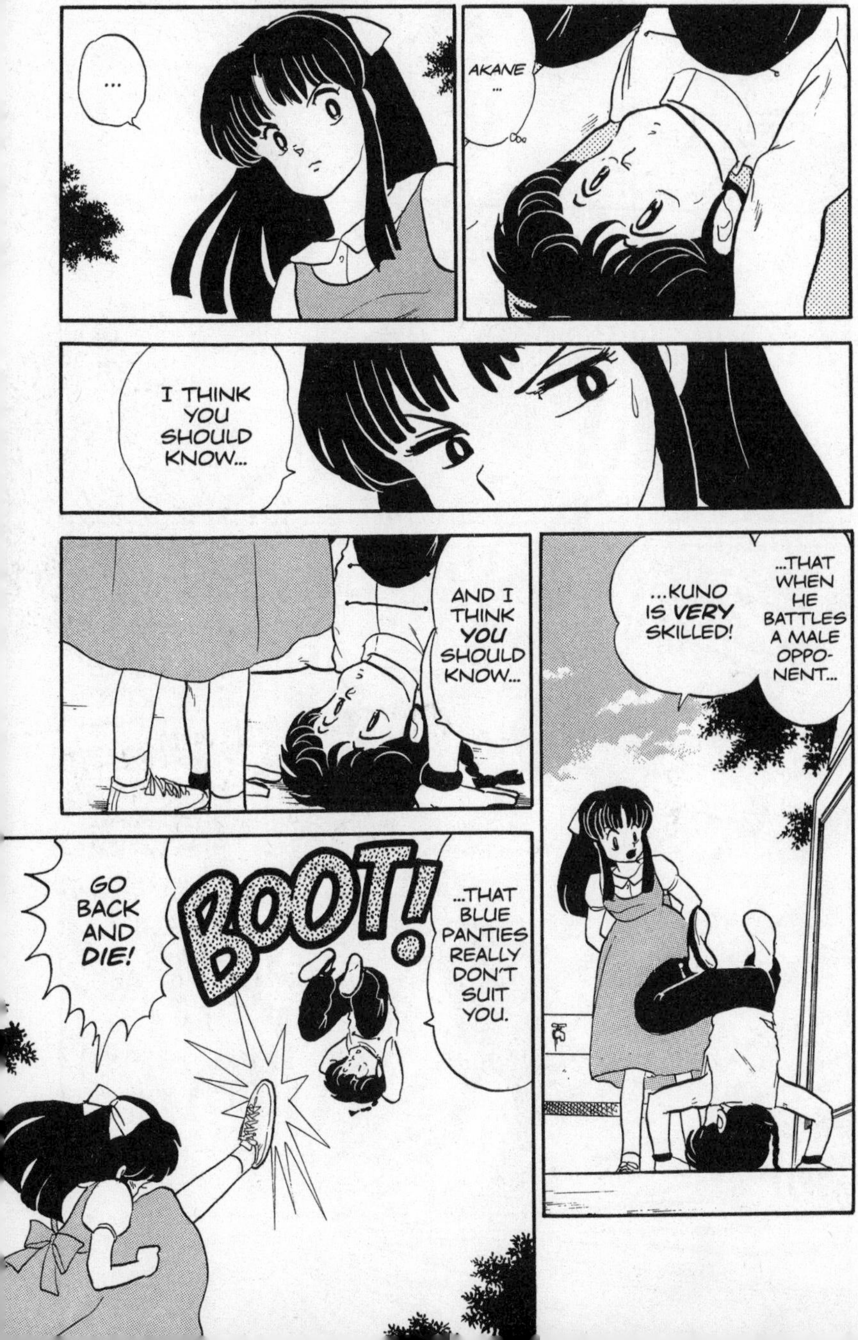
AKANE ...
...
I THINK YOU SHOULD KNOW...
...THAT WHEN HE BATTLES A MALE OPPONENT...
...KUNO IS **VERY** SKILLED!
AND I THINK ***YOU*** SHOULD KNOW...
...THAT BLUE PANTIES REALLY DON'T SUIT YOU.
BOOT!
GO BACK AND ***DIE!***

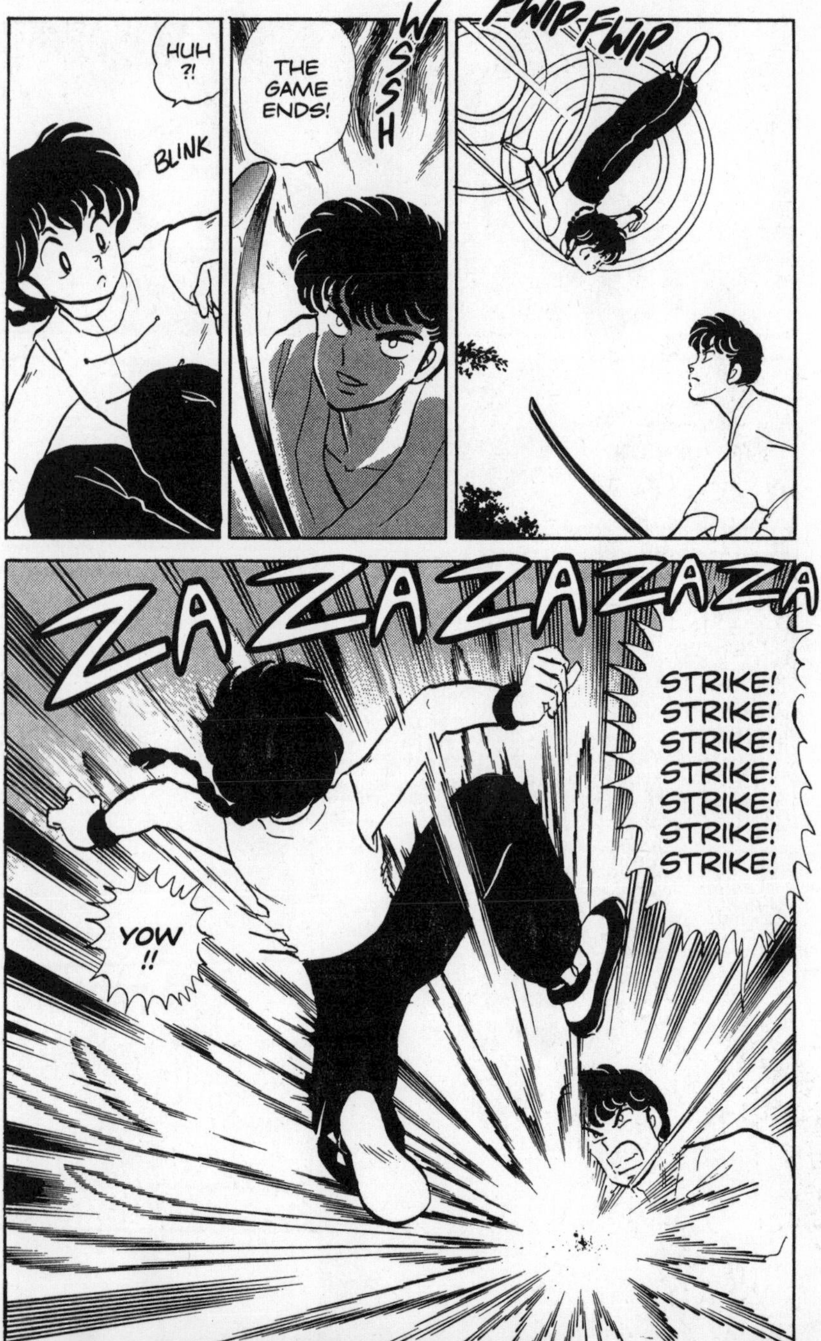
FWIP FWIP
WSSH
THE GAME ENDS!
HUH ?!
BLINK
ZAZAZAZAZA
STRIKE! STRIKE! STRIKE! STRIKE! STRIKE! STRIKE! STRIKE!
YOW !!

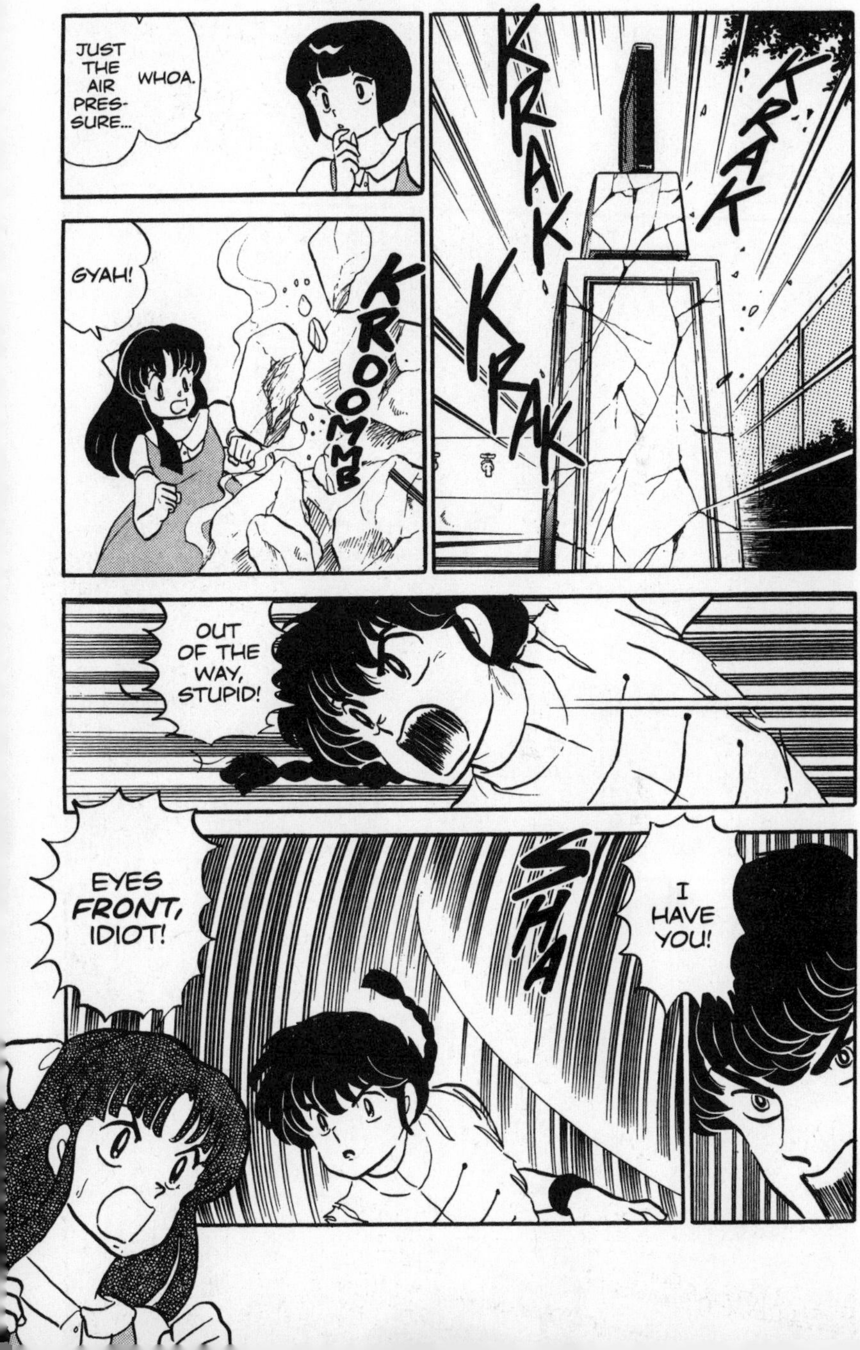

KRAK KRAK
KRAK KRAK
WHOA.
JUST THE AIR PRESSURE...
KROOMMB
GYAH!
OUT OF THE WAY, STUPID!
I HAVE YOU!
SHA
EYES FRONT, IDIOT!

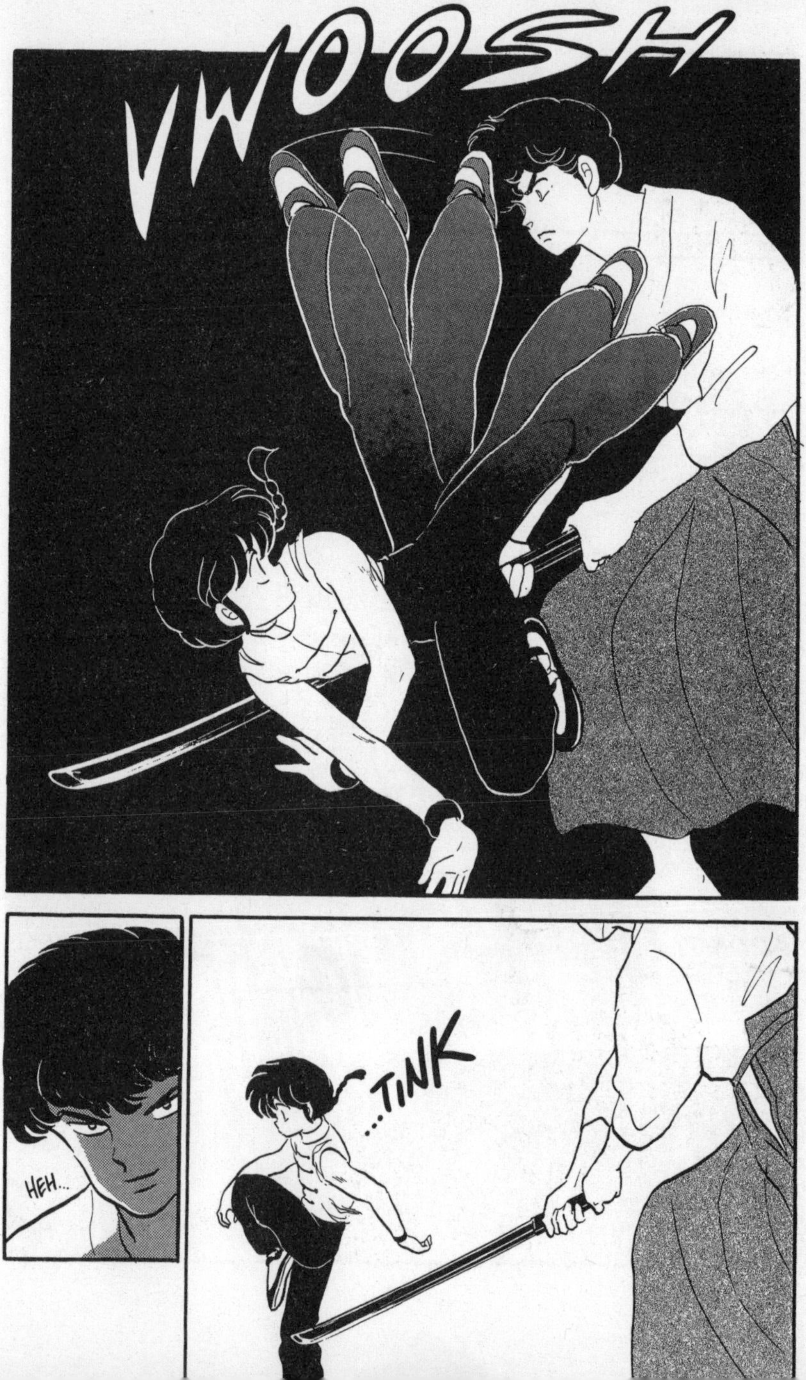
VWOOSH
...TINK
HEH...

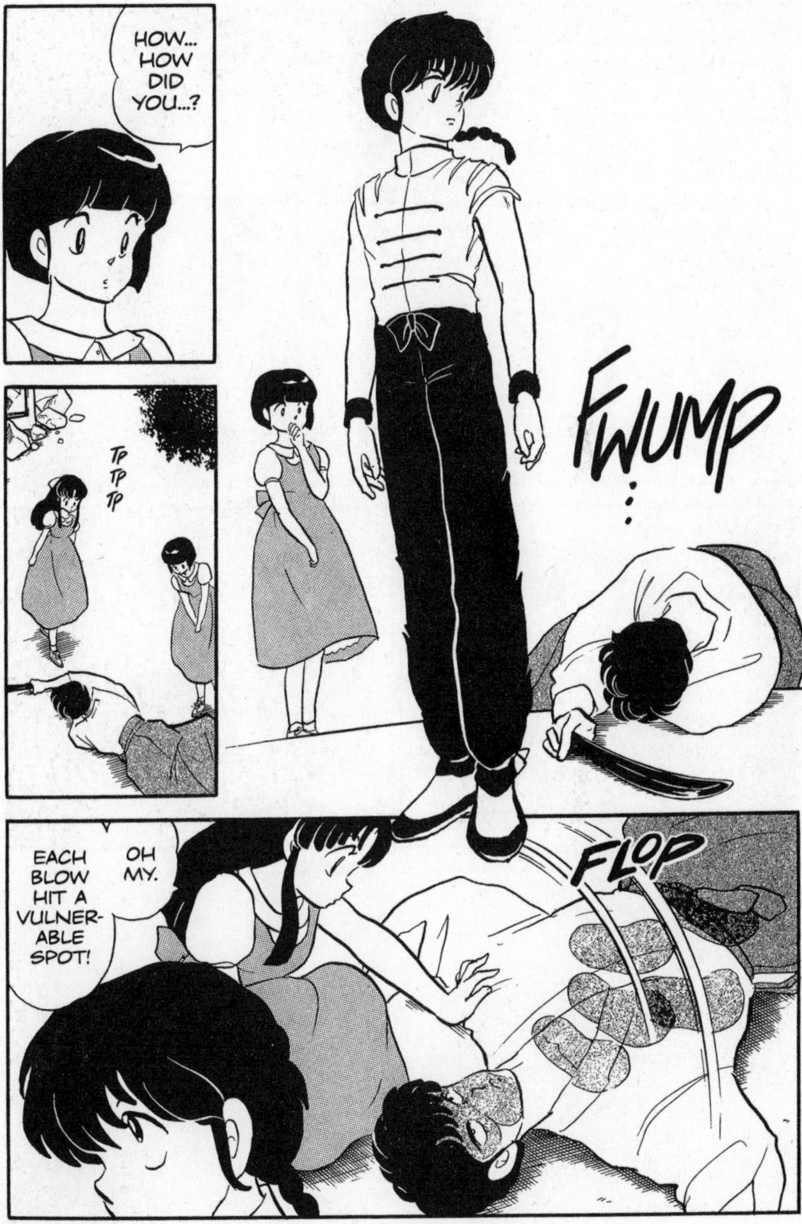
FWUMP
HOW... HOW DID YOU...?
TP TP TP
FLOP
OH MY.
EACH BLOW HIT A VULNER-ABLE SPOT!

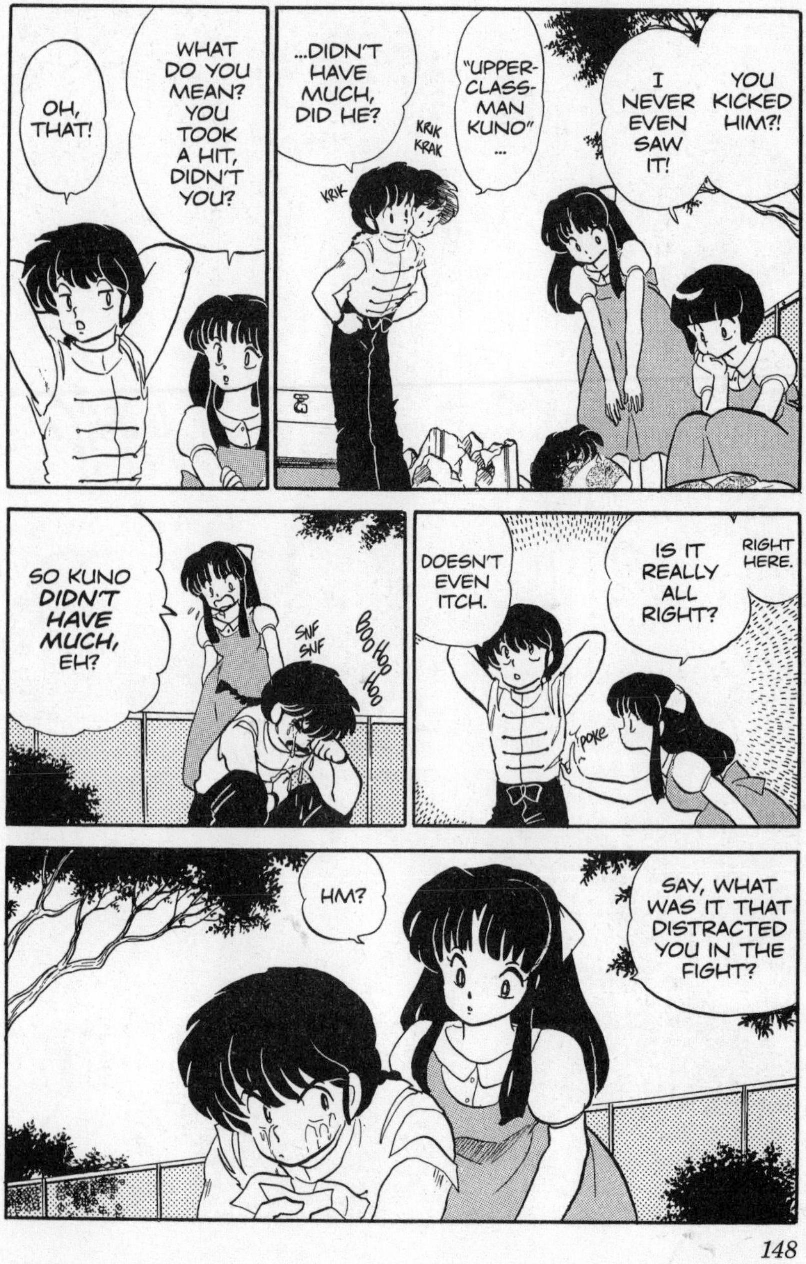
YOU KICKED HIM?!
I NEVER EVEN SAW IT!
"UPPER-CLASSMAN KUNO" ...
KRIK KRAK
...DIDN'T HAVE MUCH, DID HE?
KRIK
WHAT DO YOU MEAN? YOU TOOK A HIT, DIDN'T YOU?
OH, THAT!
RIGHT HERE.
IS IT REALLY ALL RIGHT?
DOESN'T EVEN ITCH.
POKE
BOO HOO HOO
SNF SNF
SO KUNO DIDN'T HAVE MUCH, EH?
SAY, WHAT WAS IT THAT DISTRACTED YOU IN THE FIGHT?
HM?

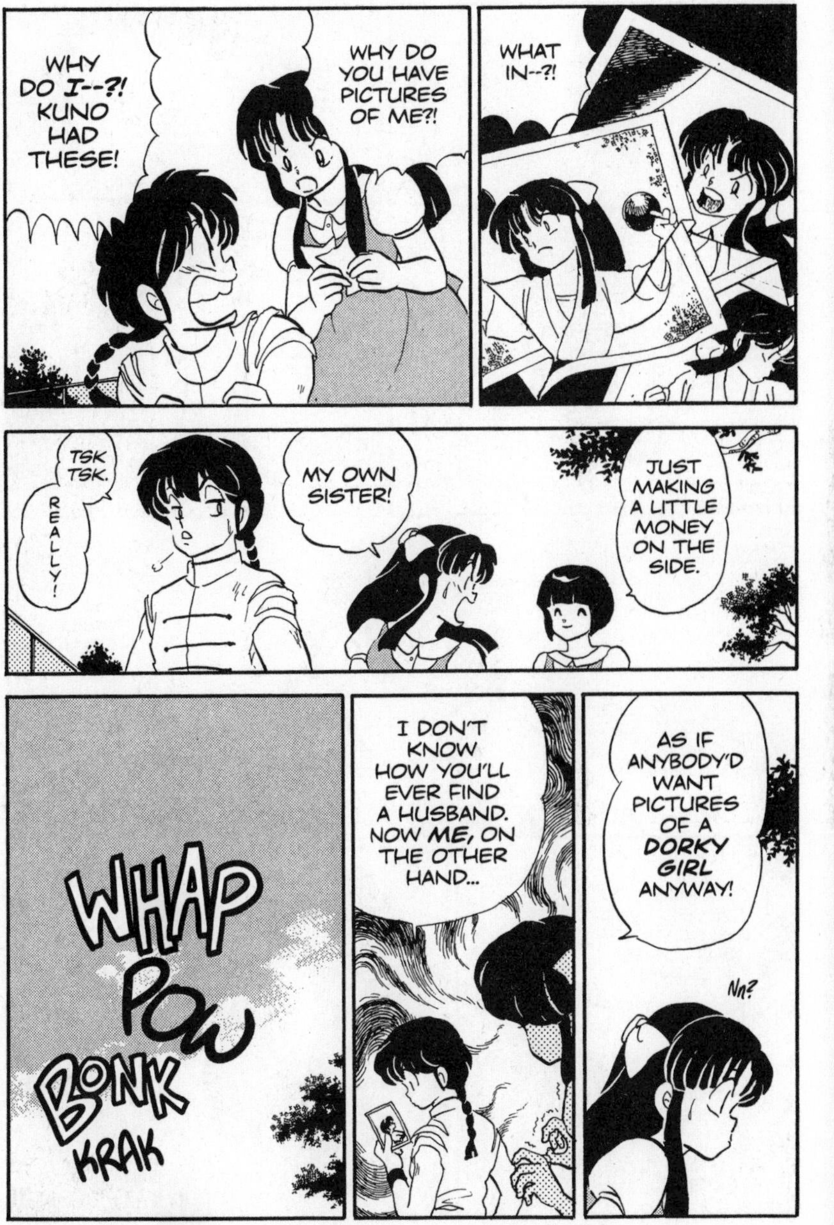
WHAT IN--?!
WHY DO YOU HAVE PICTURES OF ME?!
WHY DO I--?! KUNO HAD THESE!
JUST MAKING A LITTLE MONEY ON THE SIDE.
MY OWN SISTER!
TSK TSK.
REALLY!
AS IF ANYBODY'D WANT PICTURES OF A DORKY GIRL ANYWAY!
Nn?
I DON'T KNOW HOW YOU'LL EVER FIND A HUSBAND. NOW ME, ON THE OTHER HAND...
WHAP
POW
BONK
KRAK

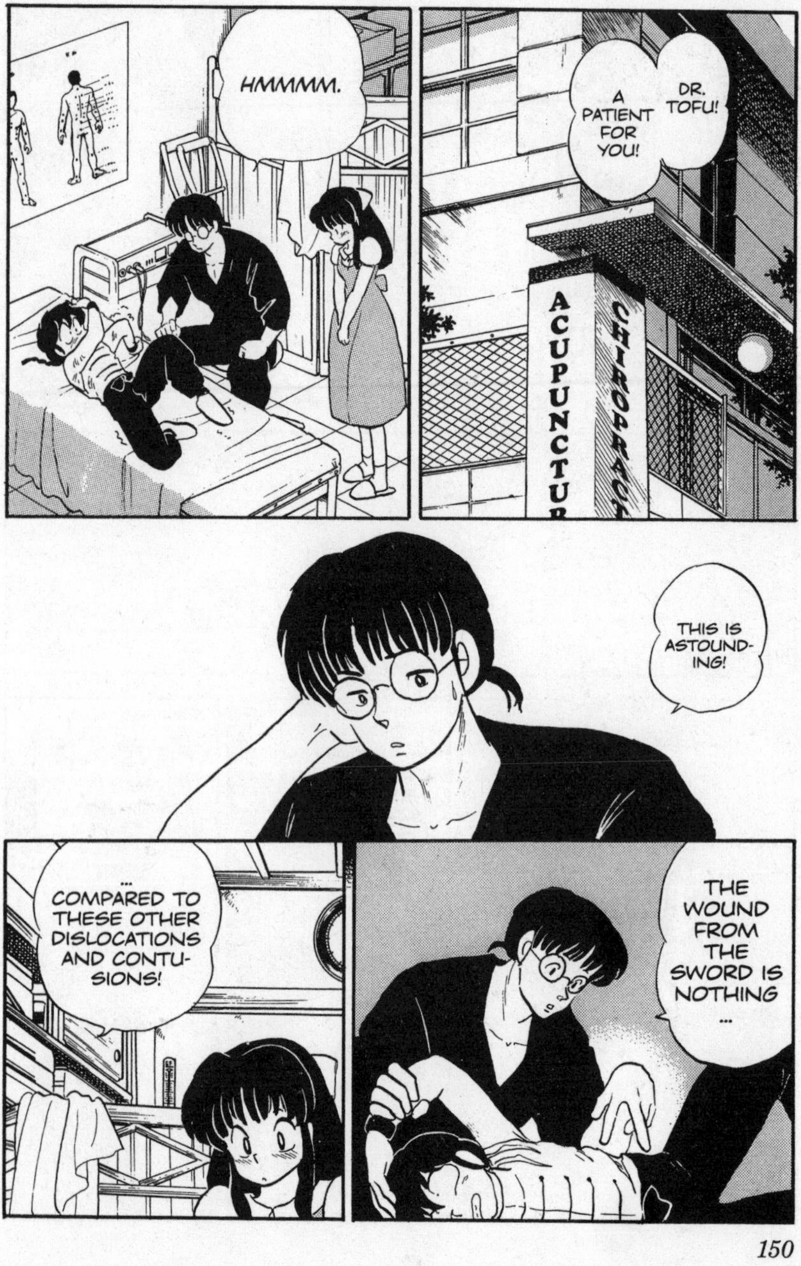
DR. TOFU! A PATIENT FOR YOU!
ACUPUNCTUR
CHIROPRACT
HMMMM.
THIS IS ASTOUND-ING!
THE WOUND FROM THE SWORD IS NOTHING ...
... COMPARED TO THESE OTHER DISLOCATIONS AND CONTU-SIONS!

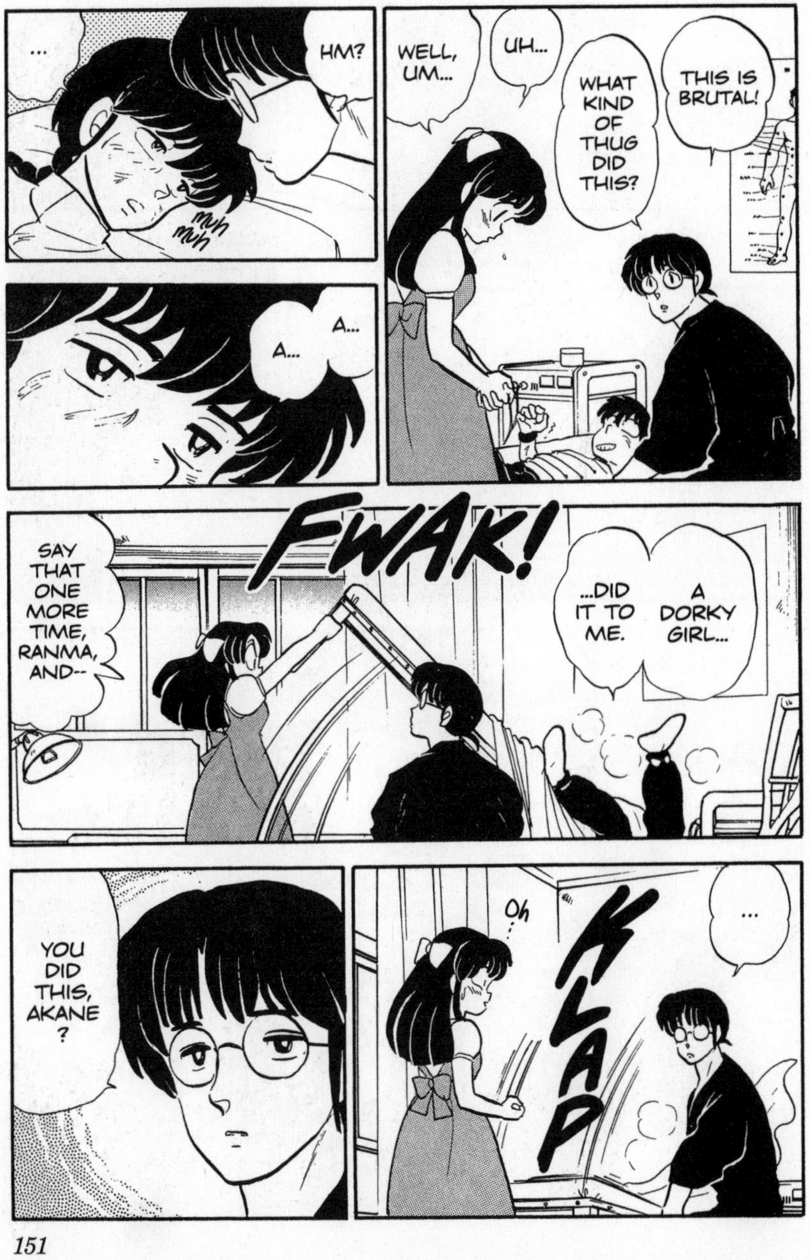
THIS IS BRUTAL!
WHAT KIND OF THUG DID THIS?
UH...
WELL, UM...
HM?
...
muh muh
A...
A...
A DORKY GIRL...
...DID IT TO ME.
FWAK!
SAY THAT ONE MORE TIME, RANMA, AND--
...
KLAP
Oh...
YOU DID THIS, AKANE?

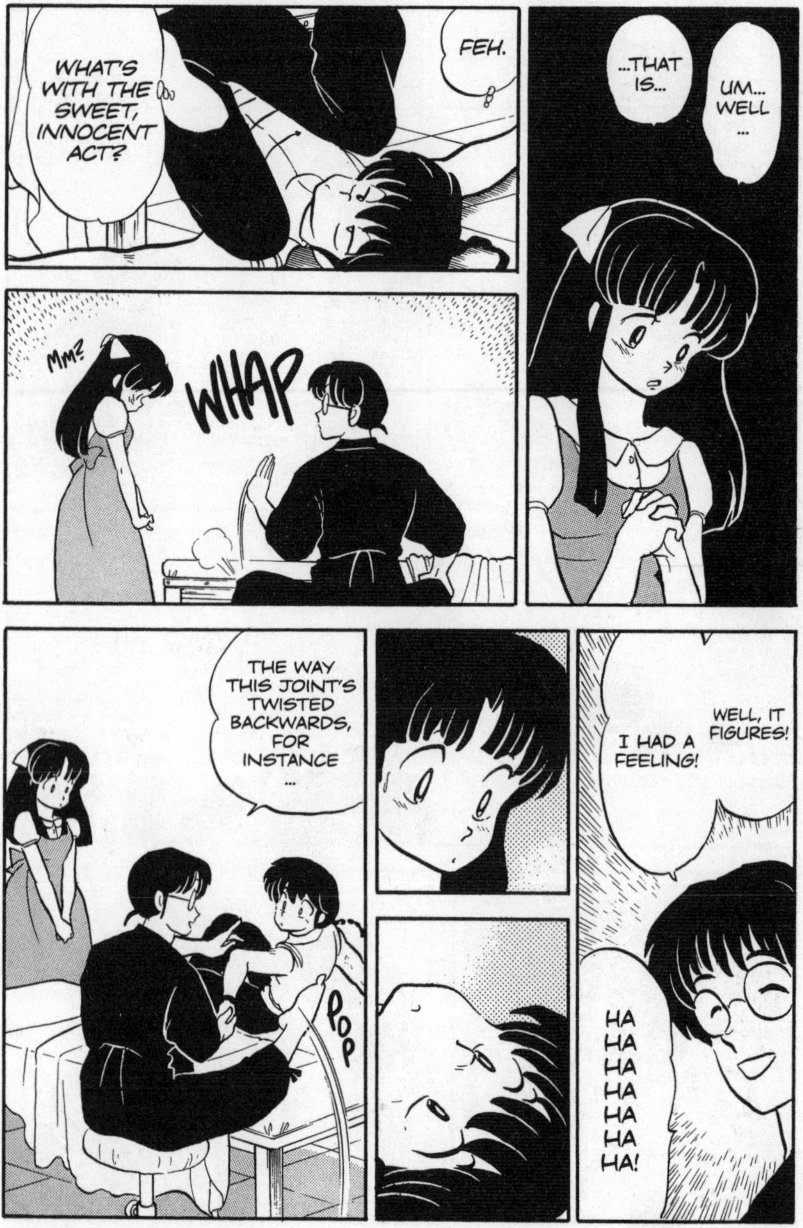
UM... WELL ...
...THAT IS...
FEH.
WHAT'S WITH THE SWEET, INNOCENT ACT?
WHAP
Mm?
WELL, IT FIGURES!
I HAD A FEELING!
HA HA HA HA HA HA HA HA!
THE WAY THIS JOINT'S TWISTED BACKWARDS, FOR INSTANCE ...
POP

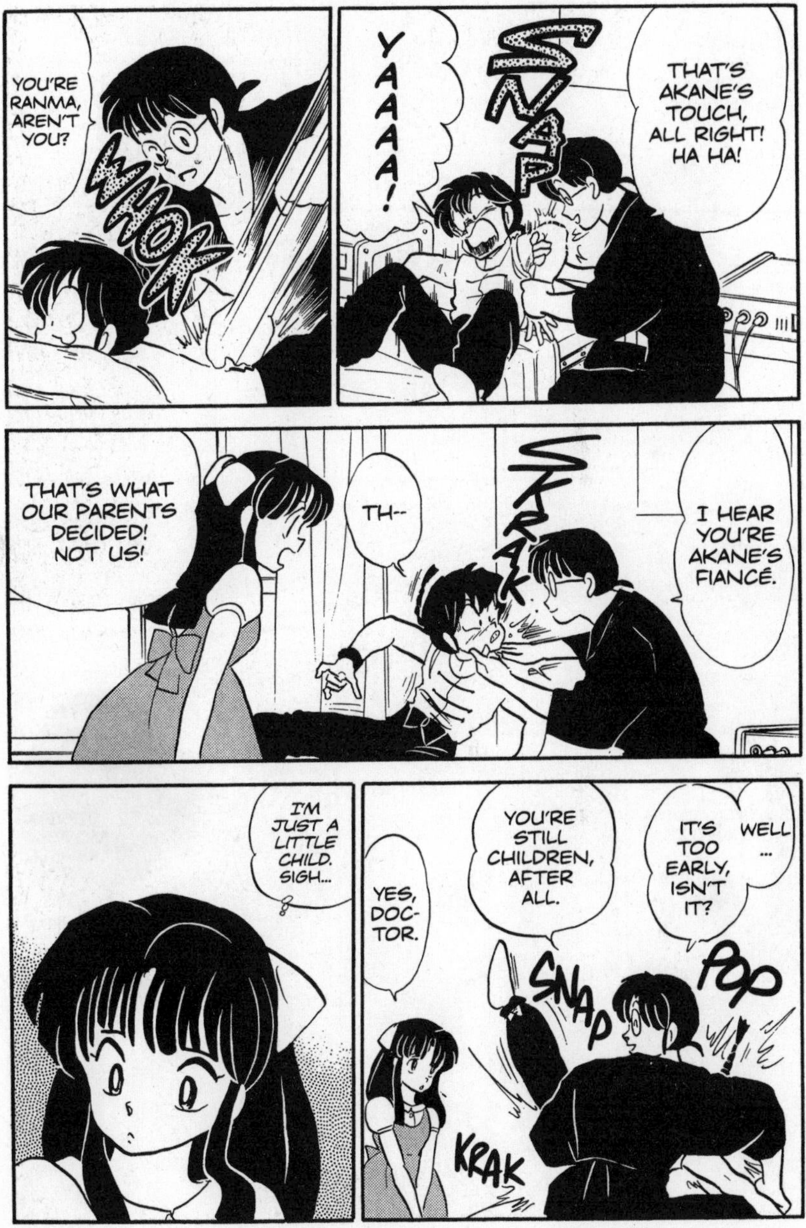
THAT'S AKANE'S TOUCH, ALL RIGHT! HA HA!
SNAP
YAAAAA!
YOU'RE RANMA, AREN'T YOU?
WHOK
I HEAR YOU'RE AKANE'S FIANCÉ.
SKRAK
TH--
THAT'S WHAT OUR PARENTS DECIDED! NOT US!
WELL ...
IT'S TOO EARLY, ISN'T IT?
POP
YOU'RE STILL CHILDREN, AFTER ALL.
SNAP
YES, DOCTOR.
KRAK
I'M JUST A LITTLE CHILD. SIGH...

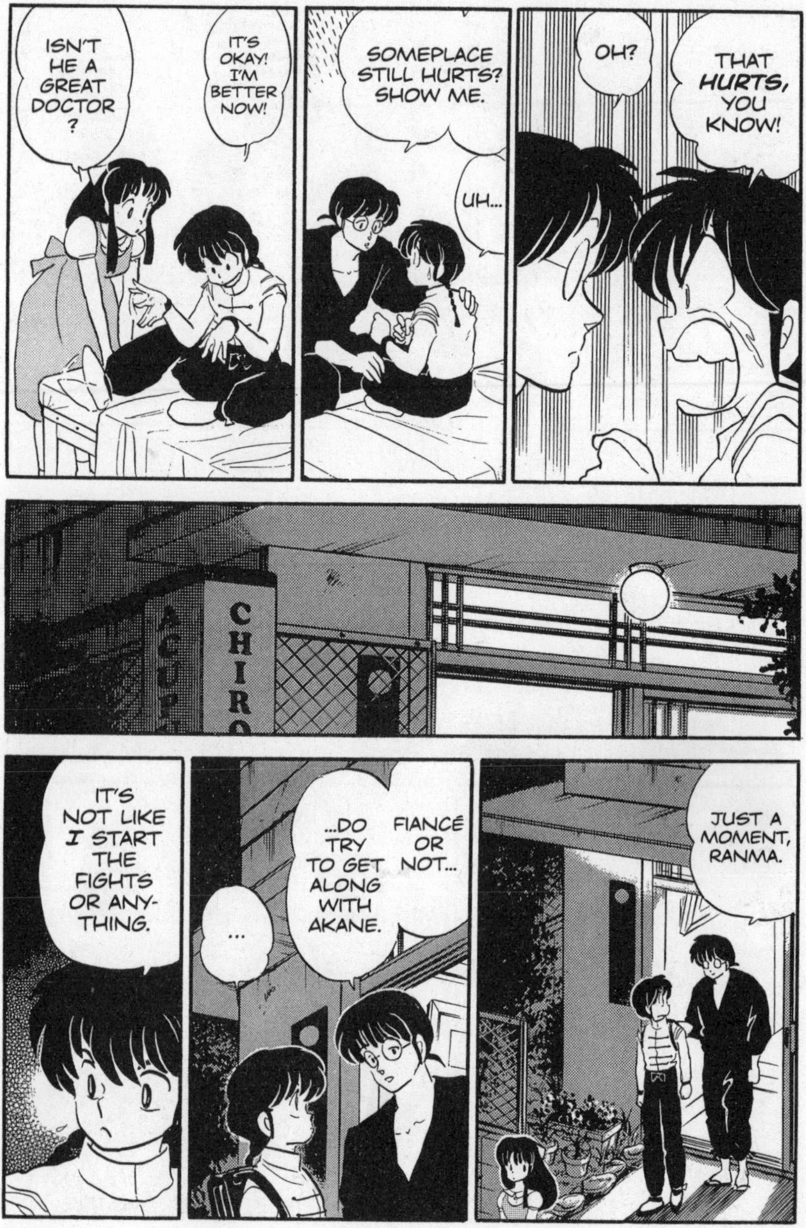
THAT HURTS, YOU KNOW!
OH?
SOMEPLACE STILL HURTS? SHOW ME.
UH...
IT'S OKAY! I'M BETTER NOW!
ISN'T HE A GREAT DOCTOR?
CHIRO
JUST A MOMENT, RANMA.
FIANCÉ OR NOT...
...DO TRY TO GET ALONG WITH AKANE.
...
IT'S NOT LIKE I START THE FIGHTS OR ANYTHING.

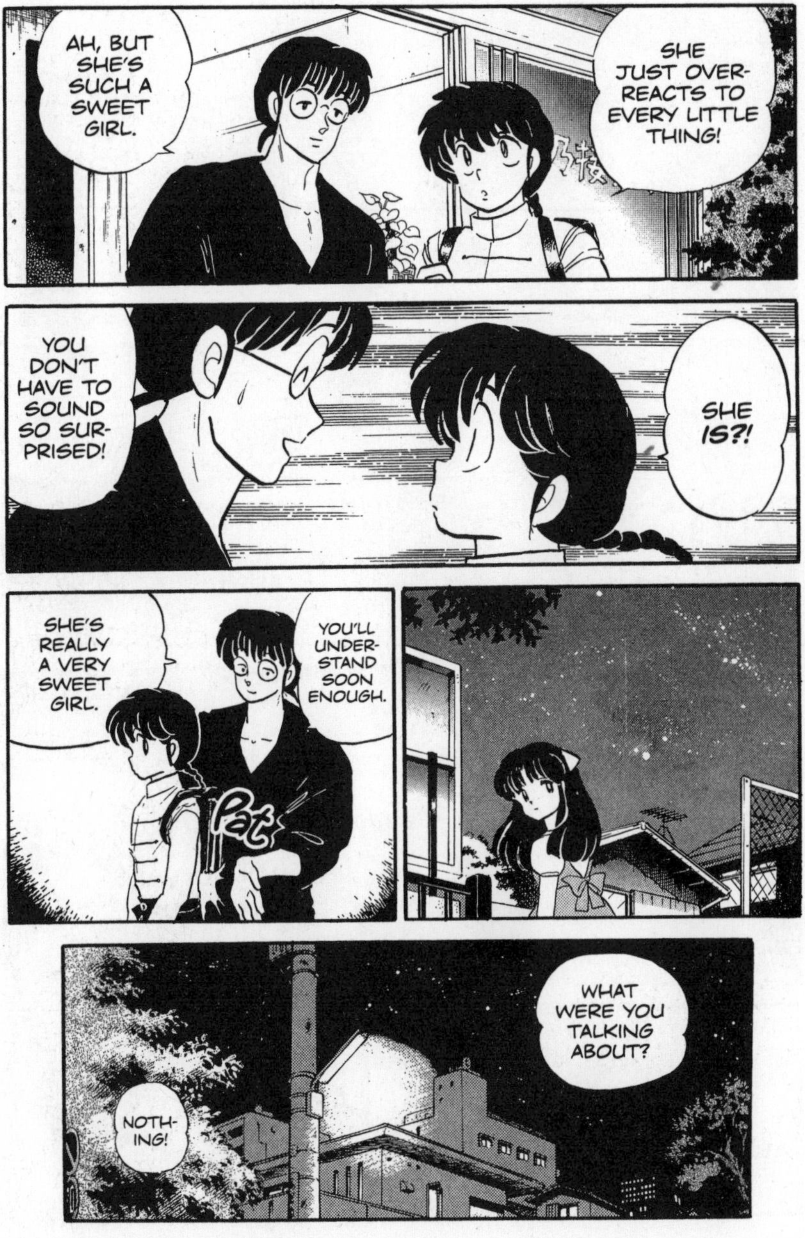
SHE JUST OVER-REACTS TO EVERY LITTLE THING!
AH, BUT SHE'S SUCH A SWEET GIRL.
SHE IS?!
YOU DON'T HAVE TO SOUND SO SUR-PRISED!
YOU'LL UNDER-STAND SOON ENOUGH.
SHE'S REALLY A VERY SWEET GIRL.
Pat
WHAT WERE YOU TALKING ABOUT?
NOTH-ING!

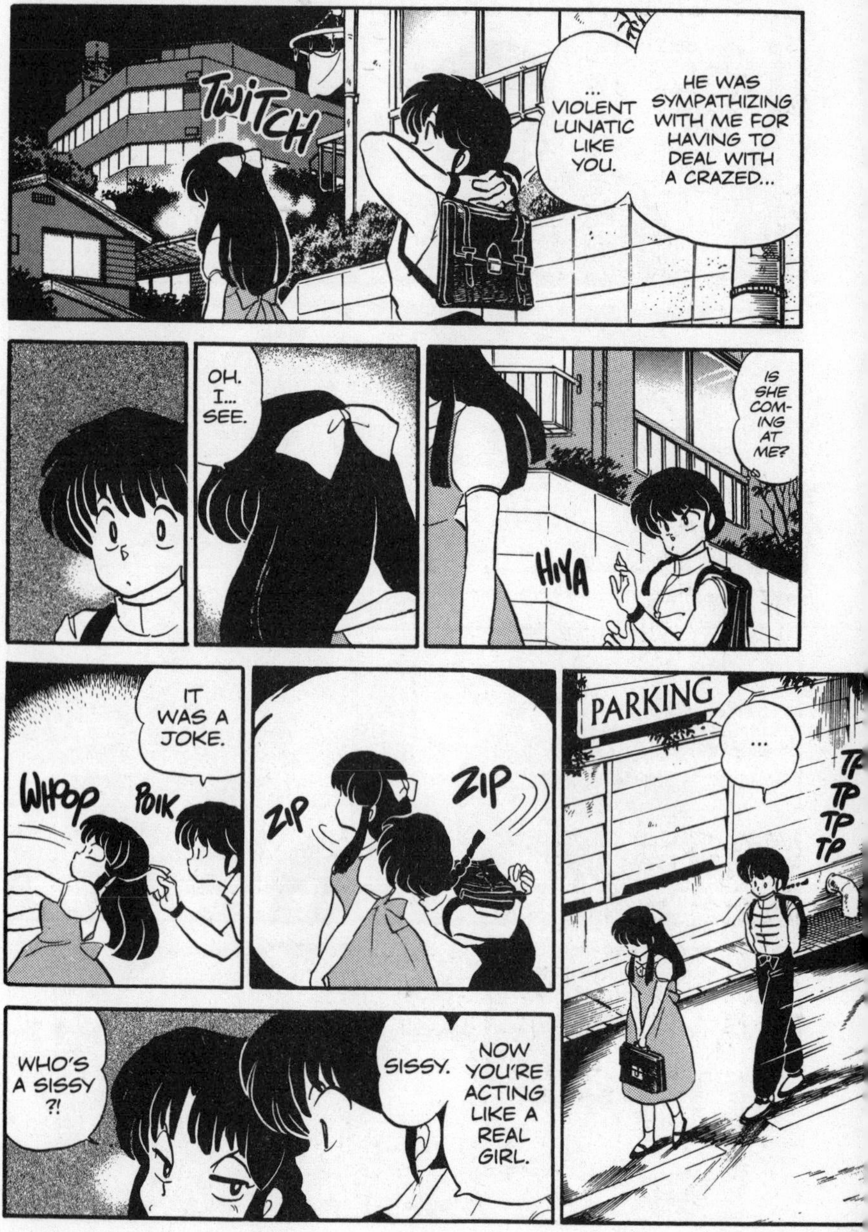
HE WAS SYMPATHIZING WITH ME FOR HAVING TO DEAL WITH A CRAZED...
... VIOLENT LUNATIC LIKE YOU.
TWITCH
IS SHE COMING AT ME?
HIYA
OH. I... SEE.
PARKING
...
TP TP TP TP
ZIP
ZIP
IT WAS A JOKE.
POIK
WHOOP
NOW YOU'RE ACTING LIKE A REAL GIRL.
SISSY.
WHO'S A SISSY ?!

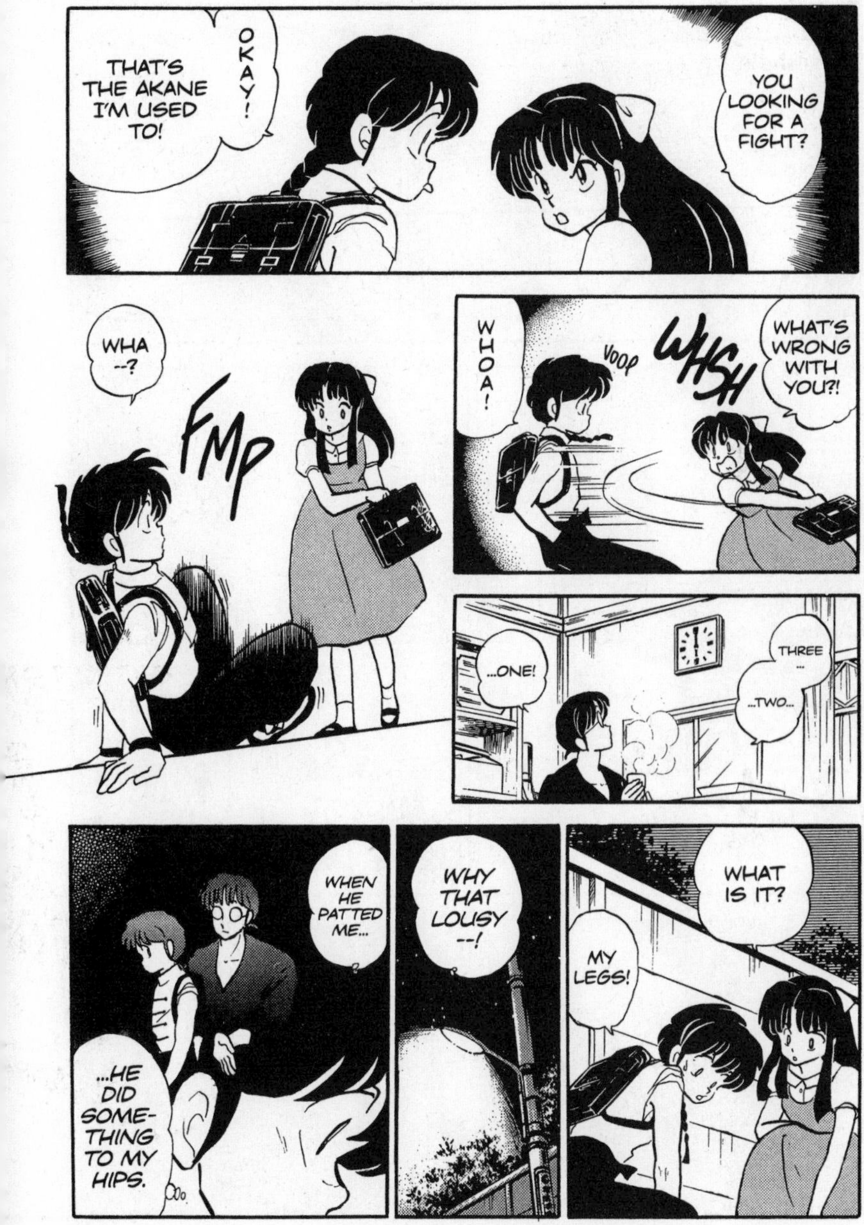
YOU LOOKING FOR A FIGHT?
OKAY!
THAT'S THE AKANE I'M USED TO!
WHAT'S WRONG WITH YOU?!
WHSH
VOOP
WHOA!
THREE...
...TWO...
...ONE!
WHA--?
FMP
WHAT IS IT?
MY LEGS!
WHY THAT LOUSY--!
WHEN HE PATTED ME...
...HE DID SOMETHING TO MY HIPS.

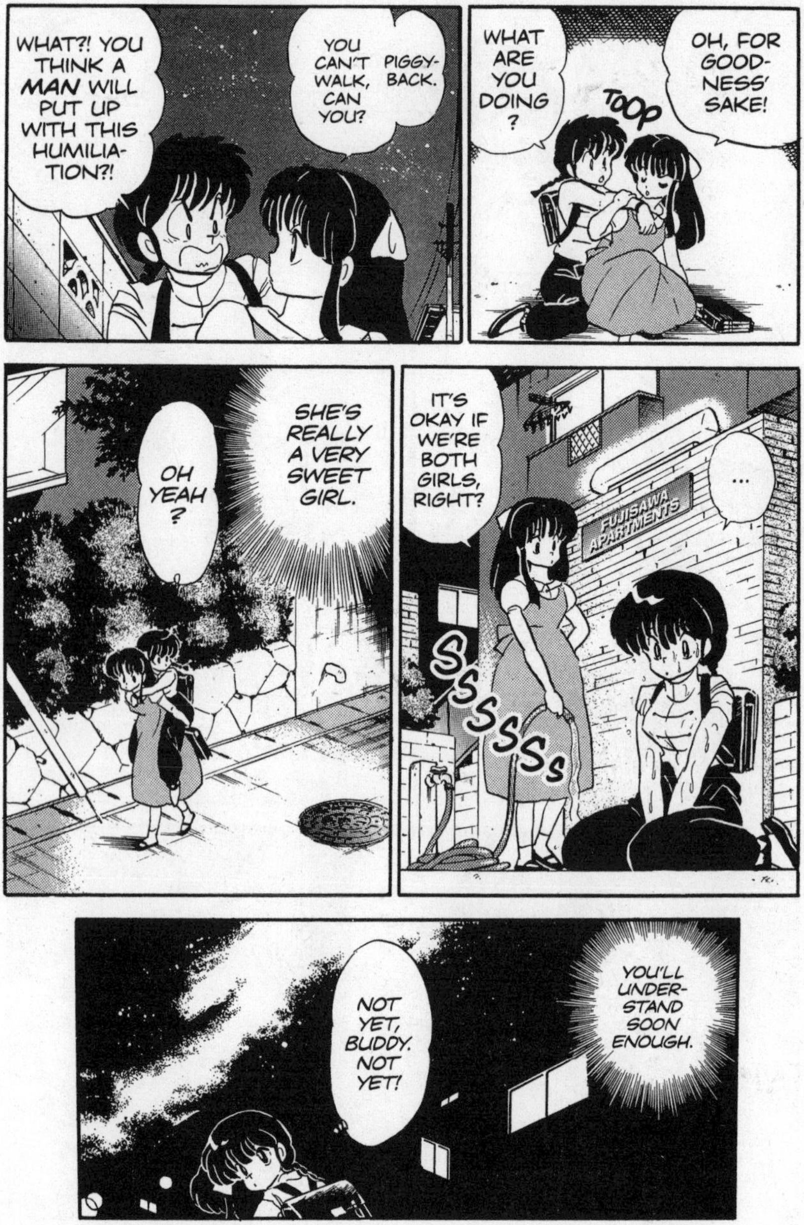
OH, FOR GOODNESS' SAKE!
TOOP
WHAT ARE YOU DOING?
PIGGY-BACK.
YOU CAN'T WALK, CAN YOU?
WHAT?! YOU THINK A *MAN* WILL PUT UP WITH THIS HUMILIATION?!
...
IT'S OKAY IF WE'RE BOTH GIRLS, RIGHT?
FUJISAWA APARTMENTS
SSSSSSs
SHE'S REALLY A VERY SWEET GIRL.
OH YEAH?
YOU'LL UNDERSTAND SOON ENOUGH.
NOT YET, BUDDY. NOT YET!

# PART 8
# BECAUSE THERE'S A GIRL HE LIKES

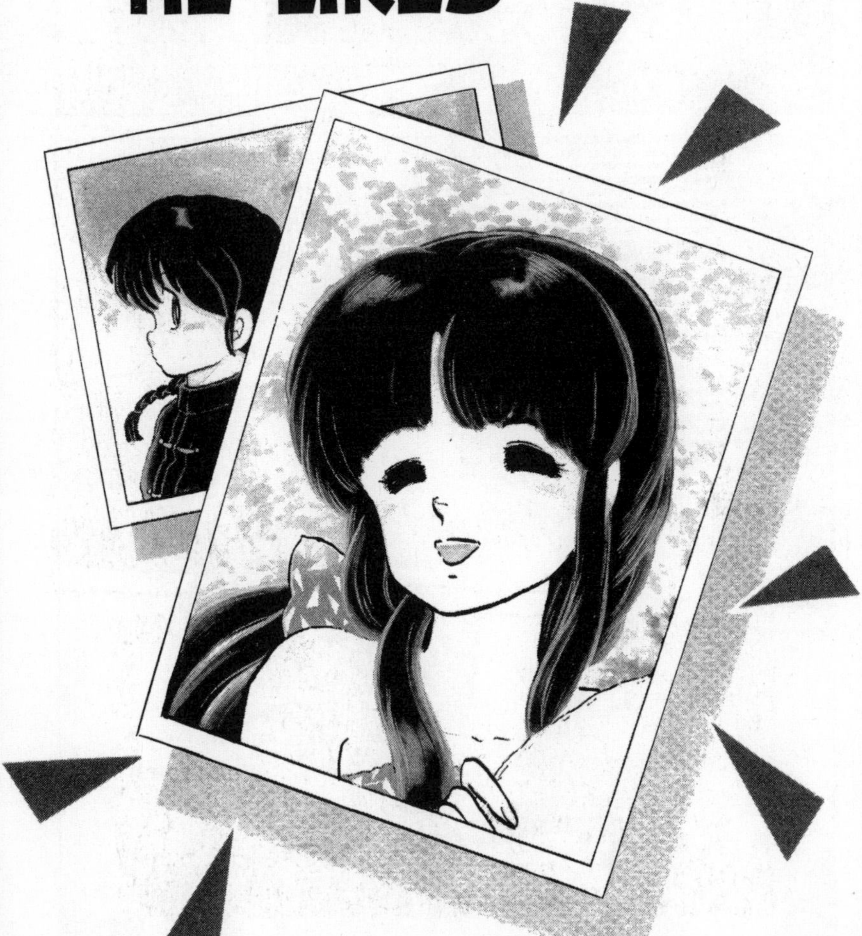

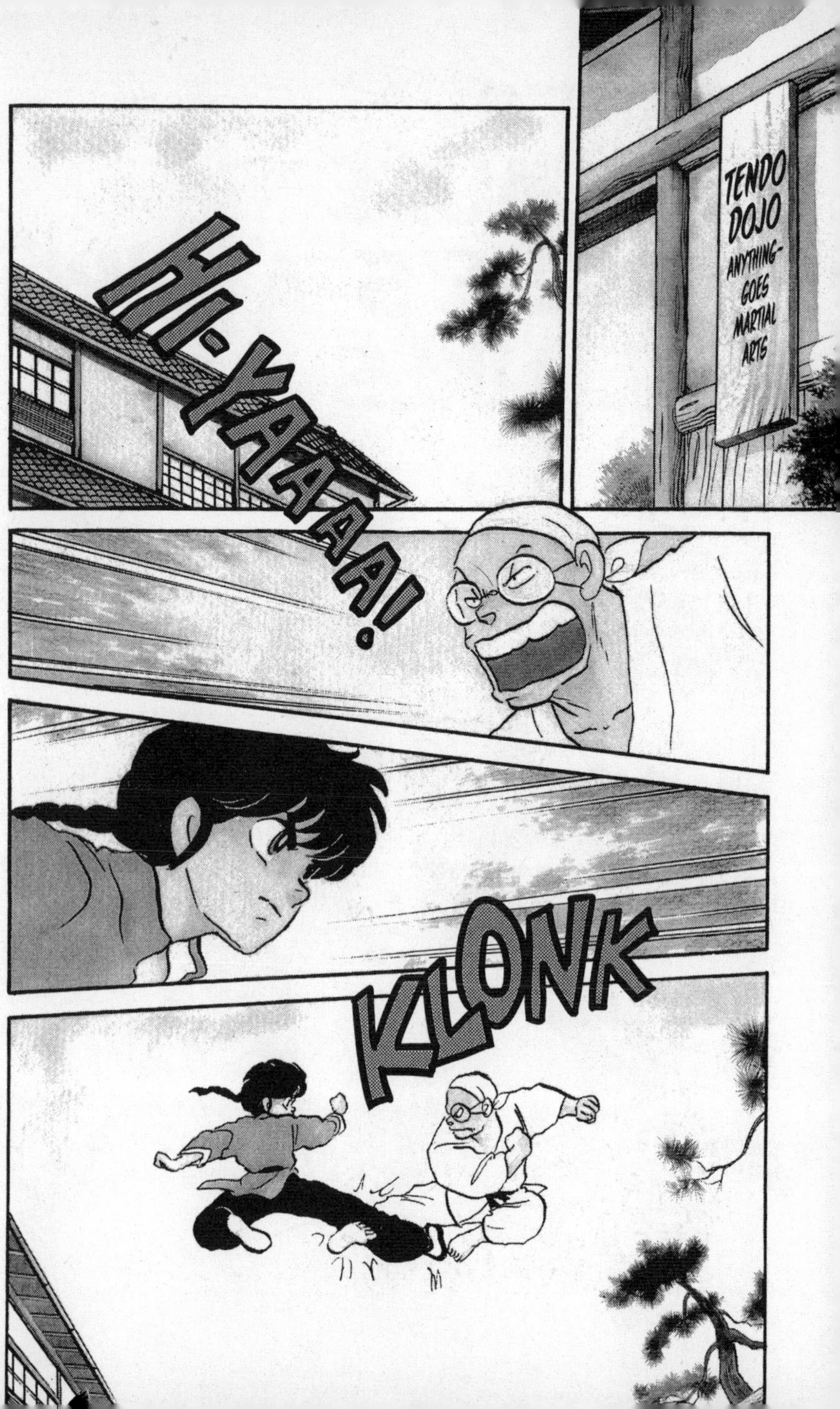
TENDO DOJO ANYTHING-GOES MARTIAL ARTS
HI-YAAAAI!
KLONK

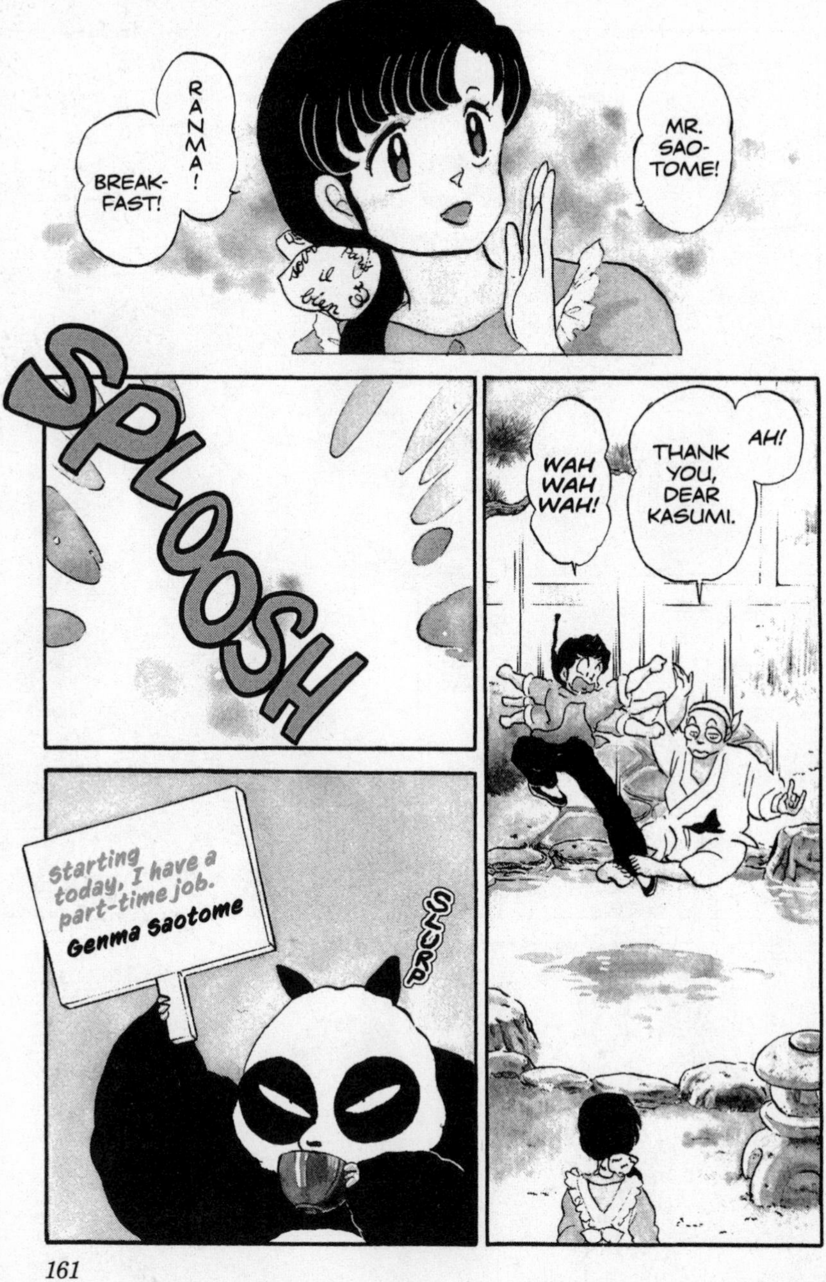

MR. SAO-TOME!
RANMA!
BREAK-FAST!
AH!
THANK YOU, DEAR KASUMI.
WAH WAH WAH!
SPLOOSH
Starting today, I have a part-time job.
Genma Saotome
SLURP

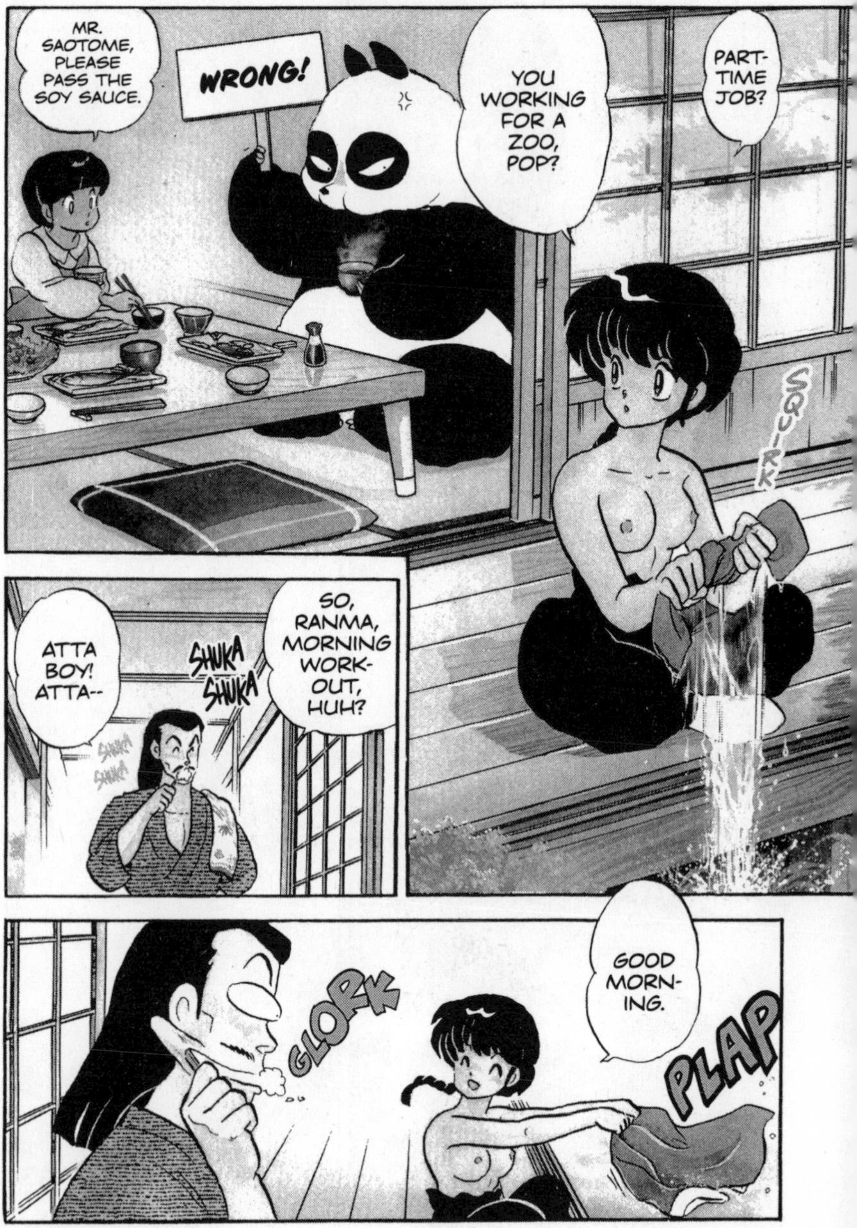
PART-TIME JOB?
YOU WORKING FOR A ZOO, POP?
WRONG!
MR. SAOTOME, PLEASE PASS THE SOY SAUCE.
SQUIRK
SO, RANMA, MORNING WORK-OUT, HUH?
SHUKA SHUKA
ATTA BOY! ATTA--
SHUKA SHUKA
GOOD MORN-ING.
PLAP
GLORK

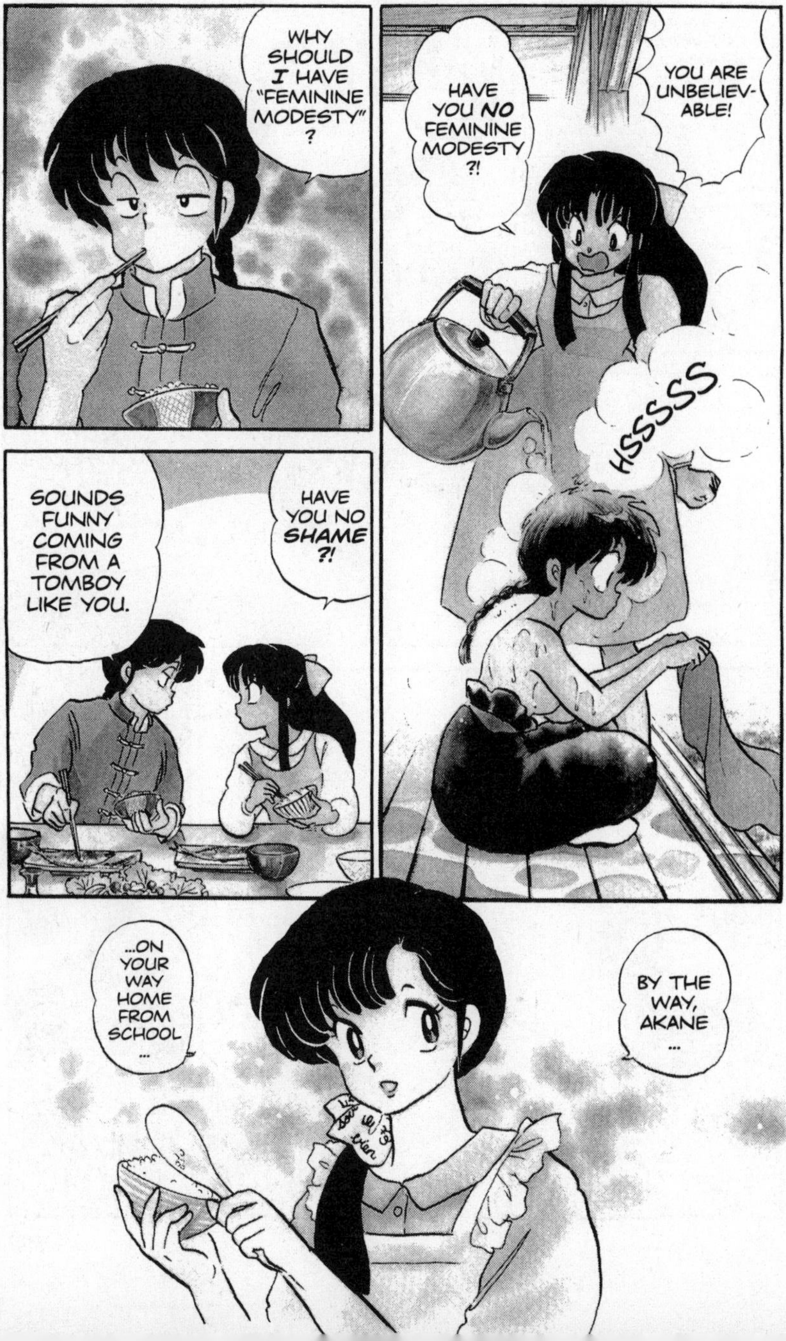
YOU ARE UNBELIEVABLE!
HAVE YOU NO FEMININE MODESTY?!
HSSSSS
WHY SHOULD I HAVE "FEMININE MODESTY"?
HAVE YOU NO SHAME?!
SOUNDS FUNNY COMING FROM A TOMBOY LIKE YOU.
BY THE WAY, AKANE...
...ON YOUR WAY HOME FROM SCHOOL...

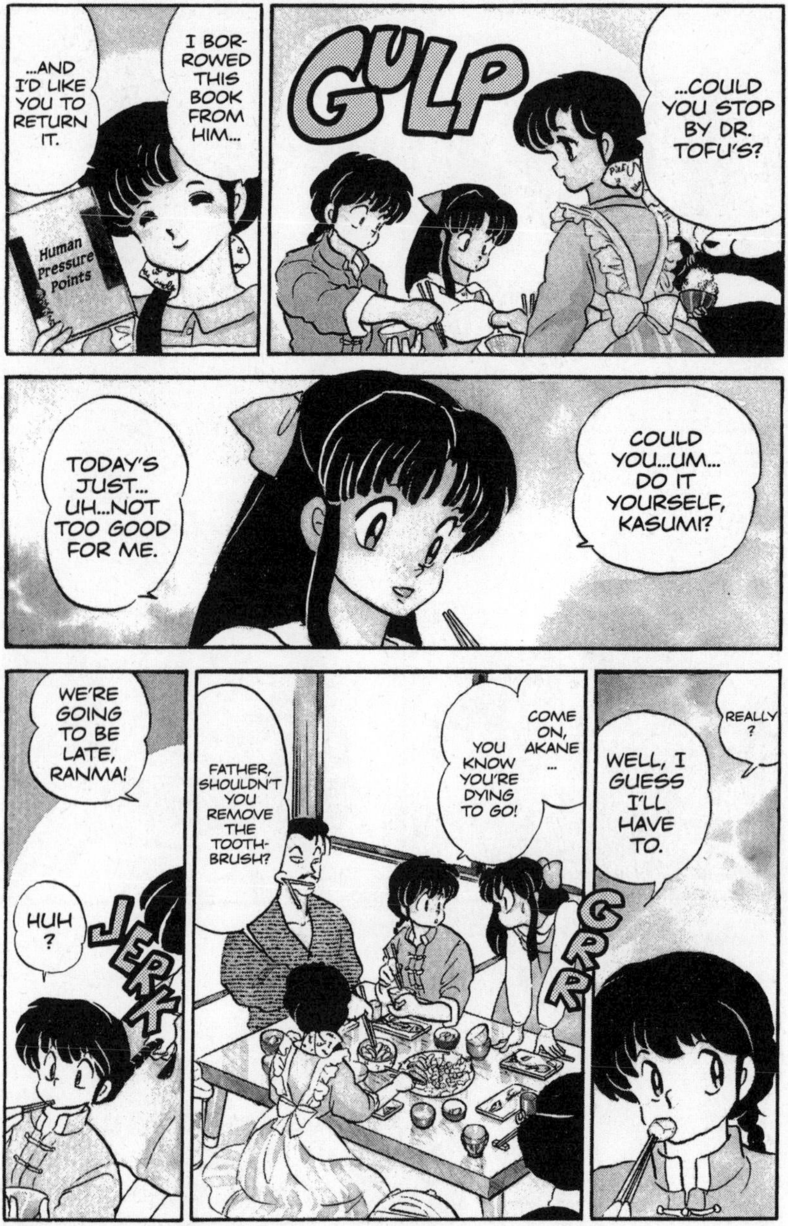
...COULD YOU STOP BY DR. TOFU'S?
GULP
I BOR-ROWED THIS BOOK FROM HIM...
...AND I'D LIKE YOU TO RETURN IT.
Human Pressure Points
COULD YOU...UM... DO IT YOURSELF, KASUMI?
TODAY'S JUST... UH...NOT TOO GOOD FOR ME.
REALLY?
WELL, I GUESS I'LL HAVE TO.
GRRR
COME ON, AKANE...
YOU KNOW YOU'RE DYING TO GO!
FATHER, SHOULDN'T YOU REMOVE THE TOOTH-BRUSH?
WE'RE GOING TO BE LATE, RANMA!
HUH?
JERK

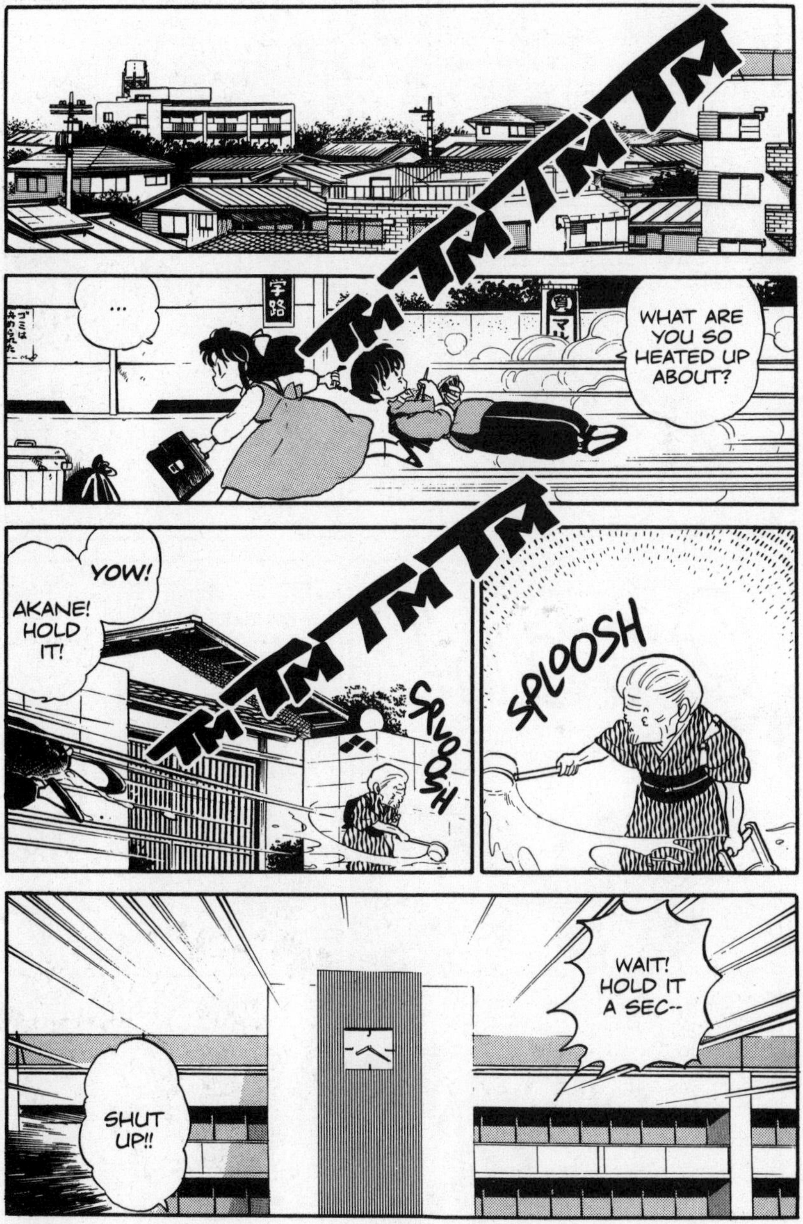
TM TM TM TM TM
WHAT ARE YOU SO HEATED UP ABOUT?
...
SPLOOSH
YOW!
AKANE! HOLD IT!
SPLOOSH
TM TM TM TM
WAIT! HOLD IT A SEC--
SHUT UP!!

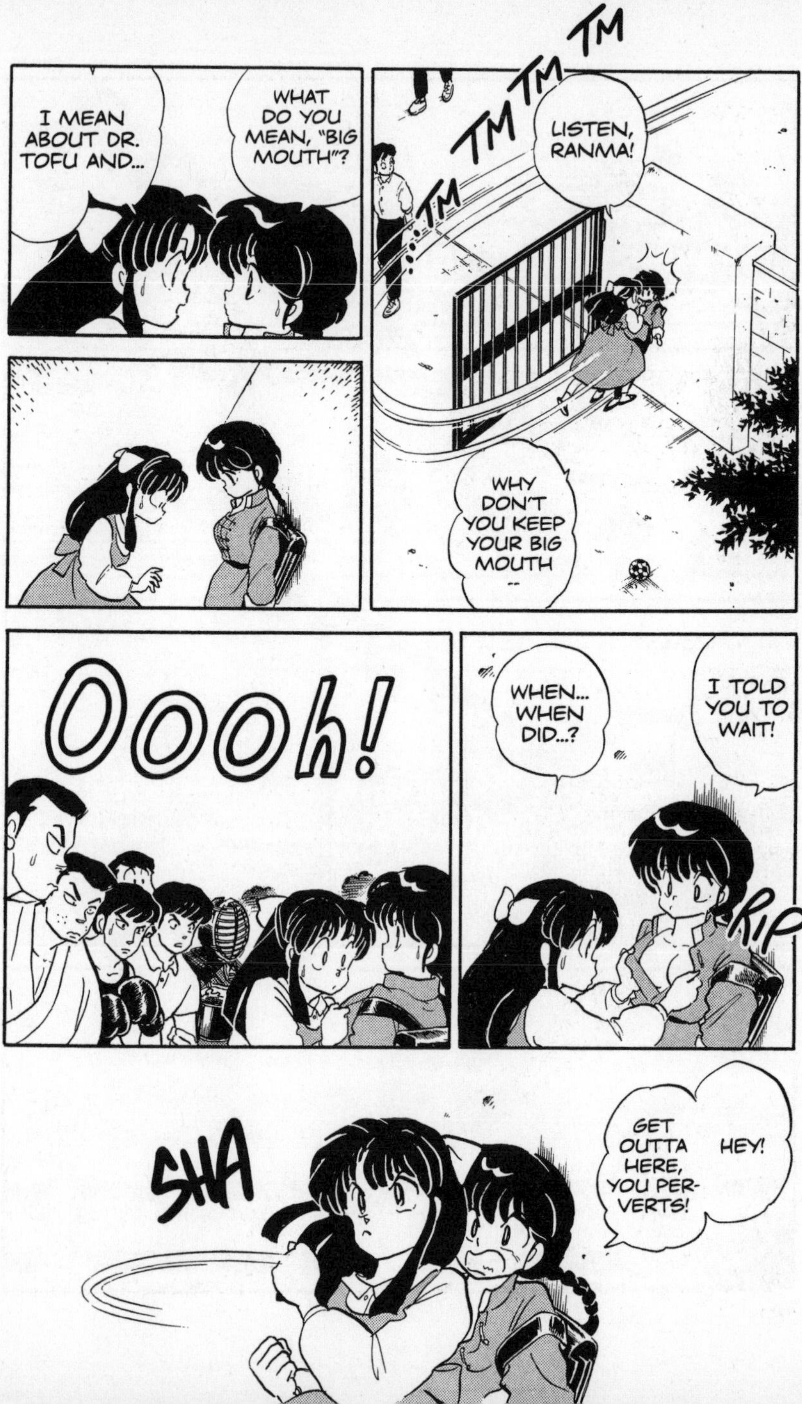
TM TM TM TM
LISTEN, RANMA!
WHY DON'T YOU KEEP YOUR BIG MOUTH --
WHAT DO YOU MEAN, "BIG MOUTH"?
I MEAN ABOUT DR. TOFU AND...
I TOLD YOU TO WAIT!
WHEN... WHEN DID...?
RIP
Oooh!
HEY!
GET OUTTA HERE, YOU PERVERTS!
SHA

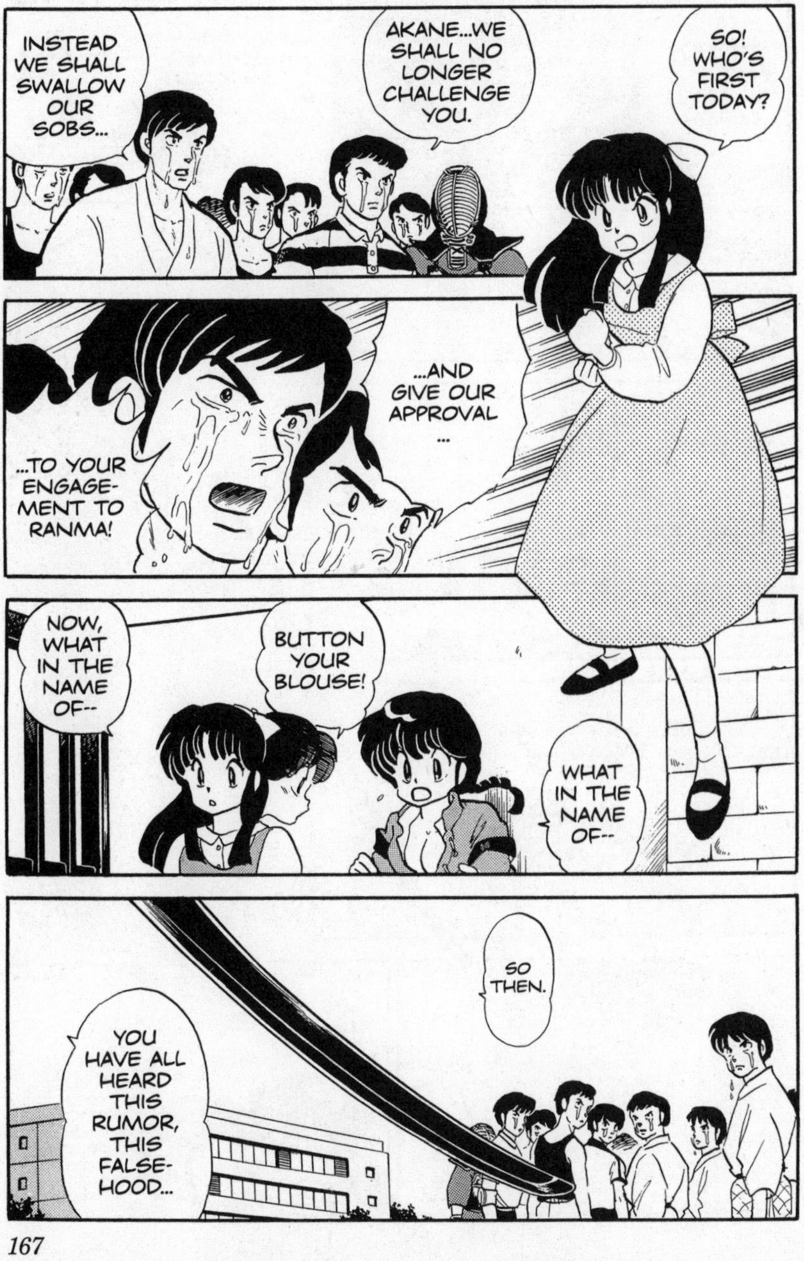
SO! WHO'S FIRST TODAY?
AKANE...WE SHALL NO LONGER CHALLENGE YOU.
INSTEAD WE SHALL SWALLOW OUR SOBS...
...AND GIVE OUR APPROVAL ...
...TO YOUR ENGAGEMENT TO RANMA!
WHAT IN THE NAME OF--
BUTTON YOUR BLOUSE!
NOW, WHAT IN THE NAME OF--
SO THEN.
YOU HAVE ALL HEARD THIS RUMOR, THIS FALSEHOOD...

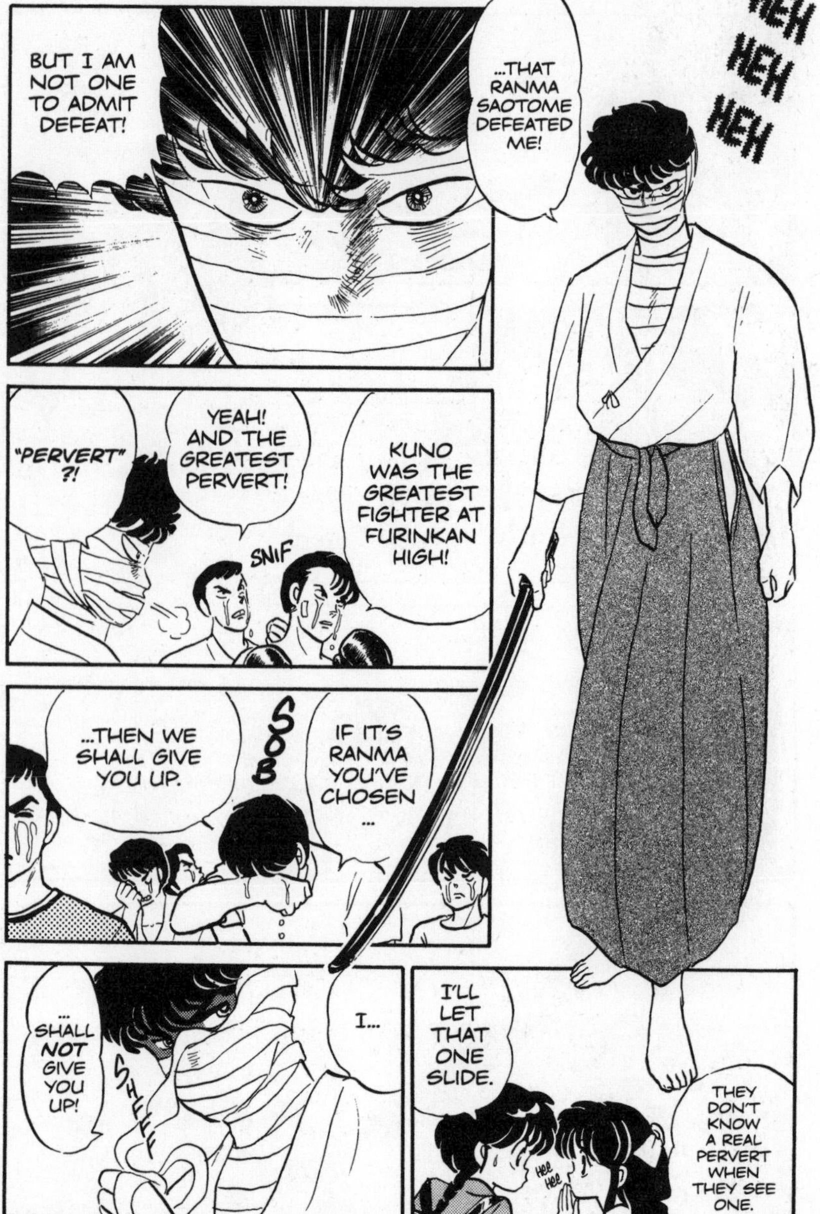
BUT I AM NOT ONE TO ADMIT DEFEAT!
HEH HEH HEH
...THAT RANMA SAOTOME DEFEATED ME!
KUNO WAS THE GREATEST FIGHTER AT FURINKAN HIGH!
SNIF
YEAH! AND THE GREATEST PERVERT!
"PERVERT" ?!
IF IT'S RANMA YOU'VE CHOSEN ...
SOB
...THEN WE SHALL GIVE YOU UP.
I'LL LET THAT ONE SLIDE.
HEE HEE
THEY DON'T KNOW A REAL PERVERT WHEN THEY SEE ONE.
I...
... SHALL NOT GIVE YOU UP!
SHFFFF

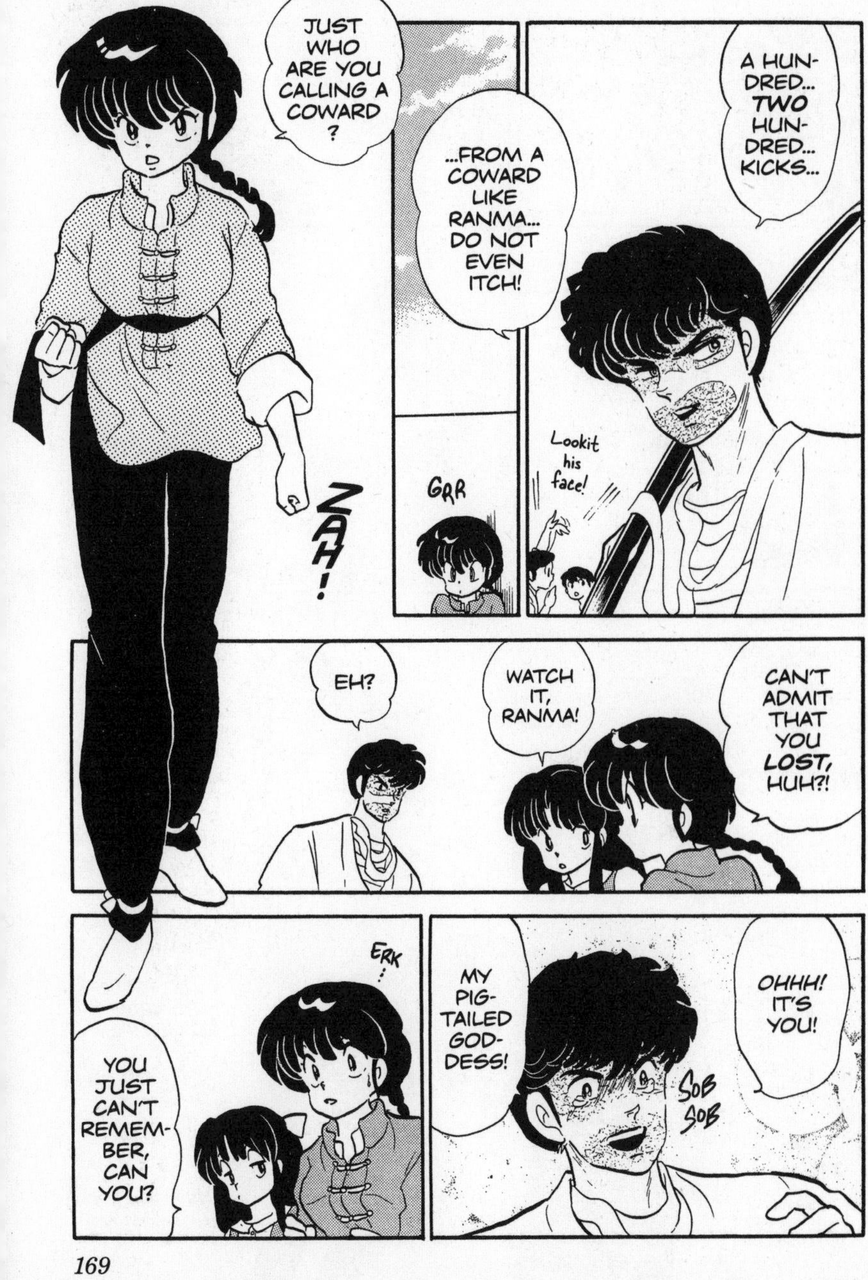
A HUNDRED... TWO HUNDRED... KICKS...
Lookit his face!
...FROM A COWARD LIKE RANMA... DO NOT EVEN ITCH!
GRR
JUST WHO ARE YOU CALLING A COWARD?
ZAAH!
CAN'T ADMIT THAT YOU LOST, HUH?!
WATCH IT, RANMA!
EH?
OHHH! IT'S YOU!
MY PIG-TAILED GODDESS!
SOB SOB
ERK...
YOU JUST CAN'T REMEMBER, CAN YOU?

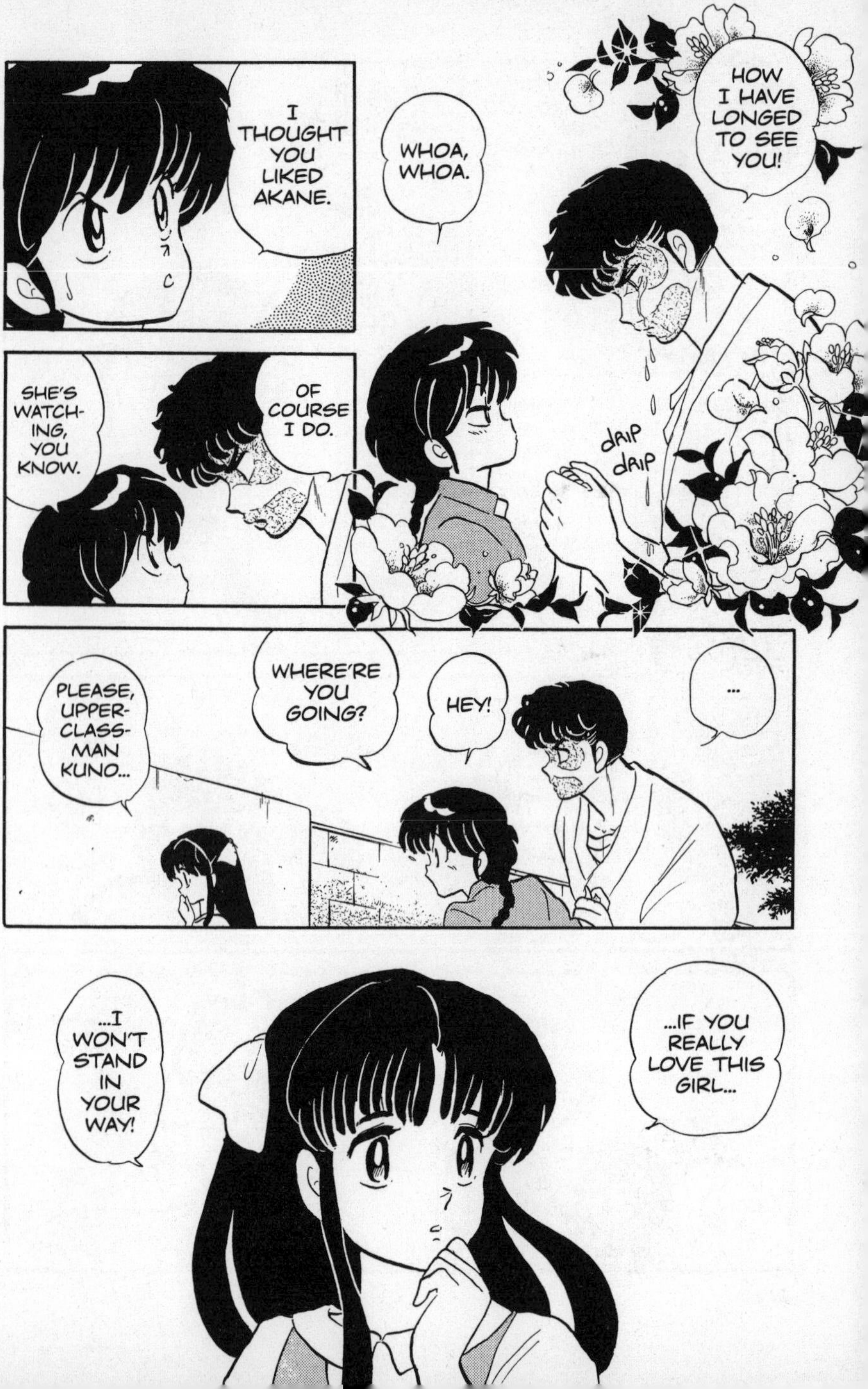
HOW I HAVE LONGED TO SEE YOU!
drip drip
WHOA, WHOA.
I THOUGHT YOU LIKED AKANE.
OF COURSE I DO.
SHE'S WATCHING, YOU KNOW.
...
HEY!
WHERE'RE YOU GOING?
PLEASE, UPPERCLASSMAN KUNO...
...IF YOU REALLY LOVE THIS GIRL...
...I WON'T STAND IN YOUR WAY!

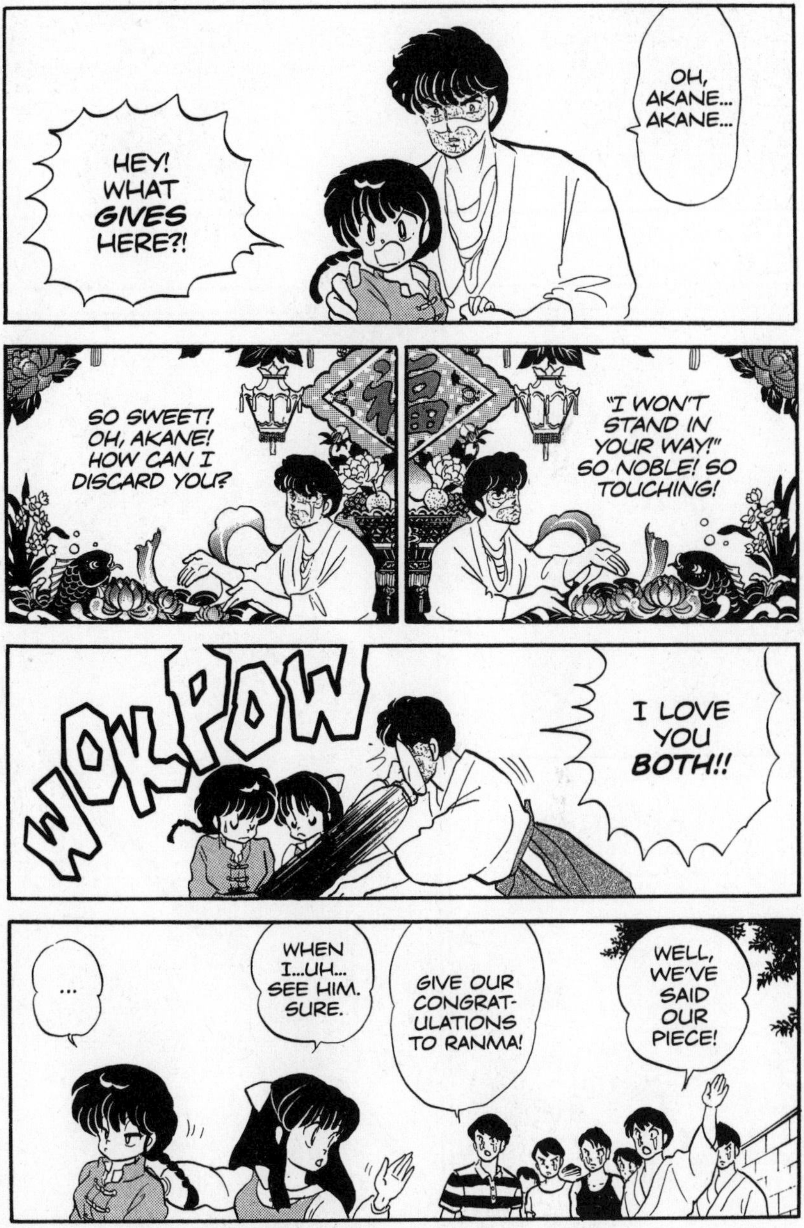
OH, AKANE... AKANE...
HEY! WHAT GIVES HERE?!
"I WON'T STAND IN YOUR WAY!" SO NOBLE! SO TOUCHING!
SO SWEET! OH, AKANE! HOW CAN I DISCARD YOU?
I LOVE YOU BOTH!!
WOKPOW
WELL, WE'VE SAID OUR PIECE!
GIVE OUR CONGRAT-ULATIONS TO RANMA!
WHEN I...UH... SEE HIM. SURE.
...

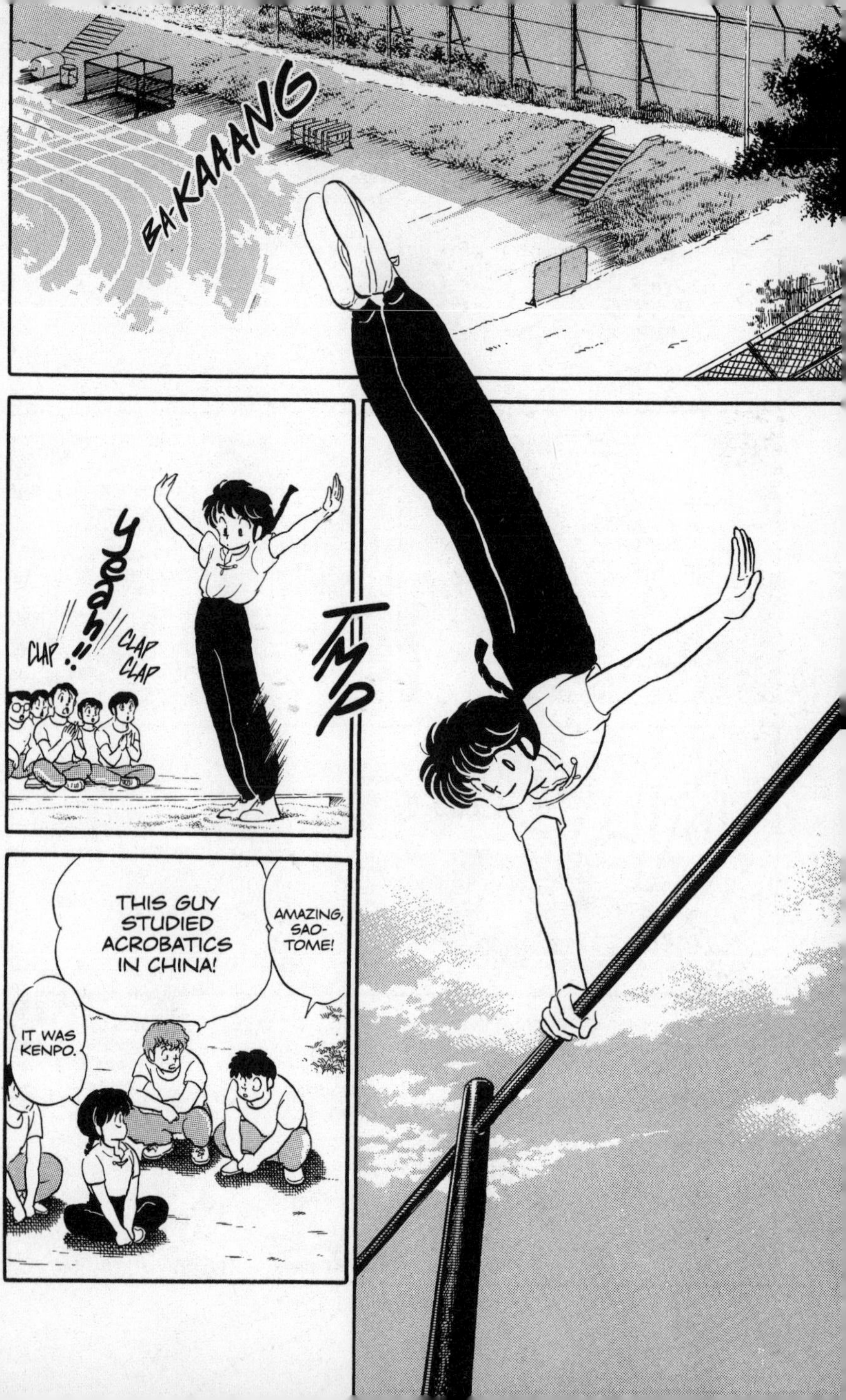
BA-KAAANG
TMP
CLAP CLAP
Yeah!!
CLAP
AMAZING, SAO-TOME!
THIS GUY STUDIED ACROBATICS IN CHINA!
IT WAS KENPO.

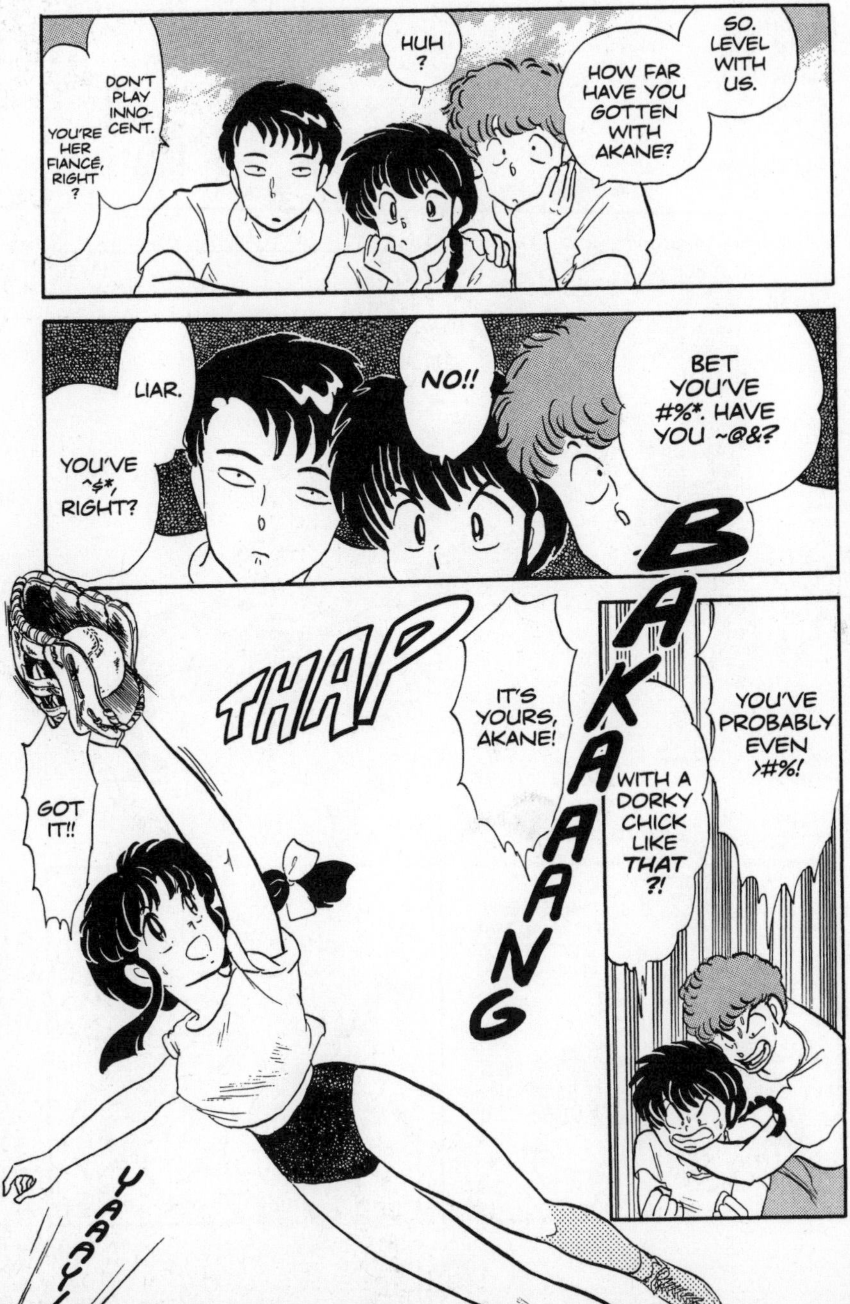
SO. LEVEL WITH US.
HOW FAR HAVE YOU GOTTEN WITH AKANE?
HUH?
DON'T PLAY INNO-CENT.
YOU'RE HER FIANCÉ, RIGHT?
BET YOU'VE #%*. HAVE YOU ~@&?
NO!!
LIAR.
YOU'VE ^$*, RIGHT?
YOU'VE PROBABLY EVEN >#%!
WITH A DORKY CHICK LIKE THAT?!
BAKAAAANG
IT'S YOURS, AKANE!
THAP
GOT IT!!
YAAAAY!

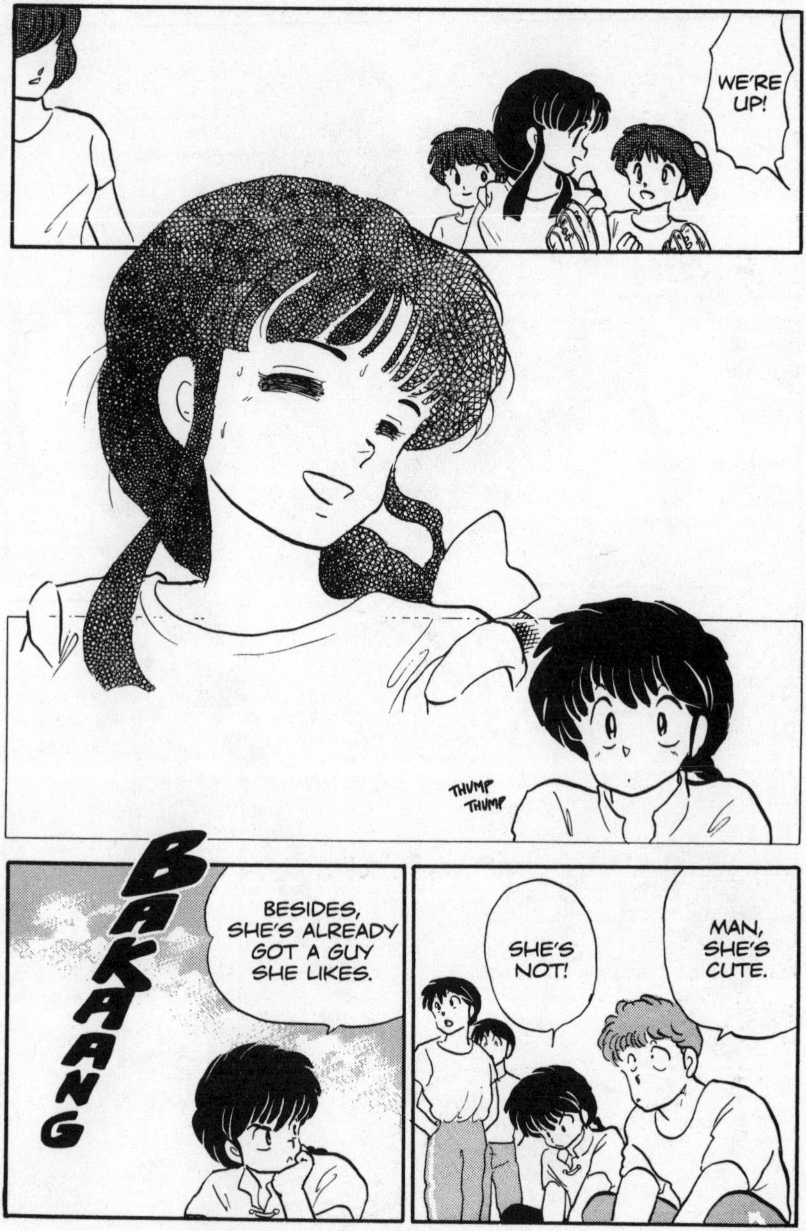
WE'RE UP!
THUMP THUMP
MAN, SHE'S CUTE.
SHE'S NOT!
BESIDES, SHE'S ALREADY GOT A GUY SHE LIKES.
BAKAANG

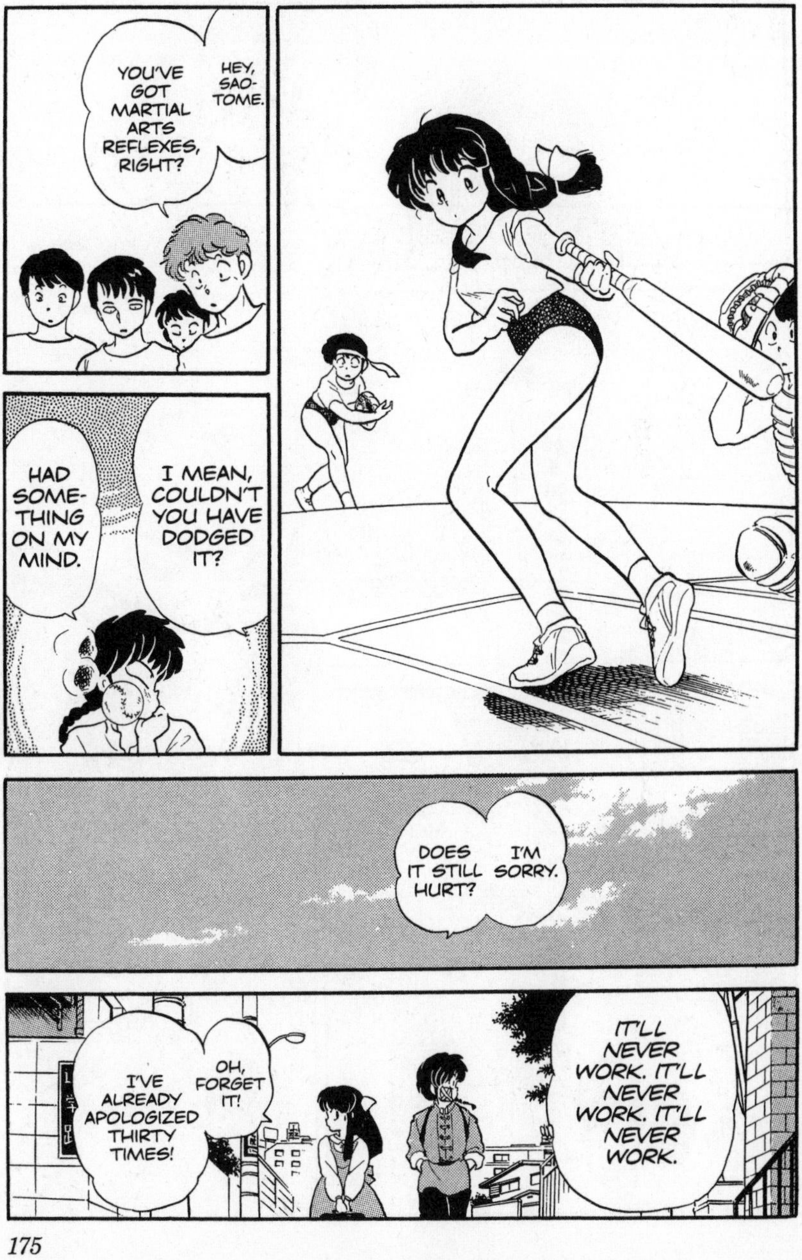
HEY, SAOTOME.
YOU'VE GOT MARTIAL ARTS REFLEXES, RIGHT?
I MEAN, COULDN'T YOU HAVE DODGED IT?
HAD SOMETHING ON MY MIND.
I'M SORRY.
DOES IT STILL HURT?
IT'LL NEVER WORK. IT'LL NEVER WORK. IT'LL NEVER WORK.
OH, FORGET IT!
I'VE ALREADY APOLOGIZED THIRTY TIMES!

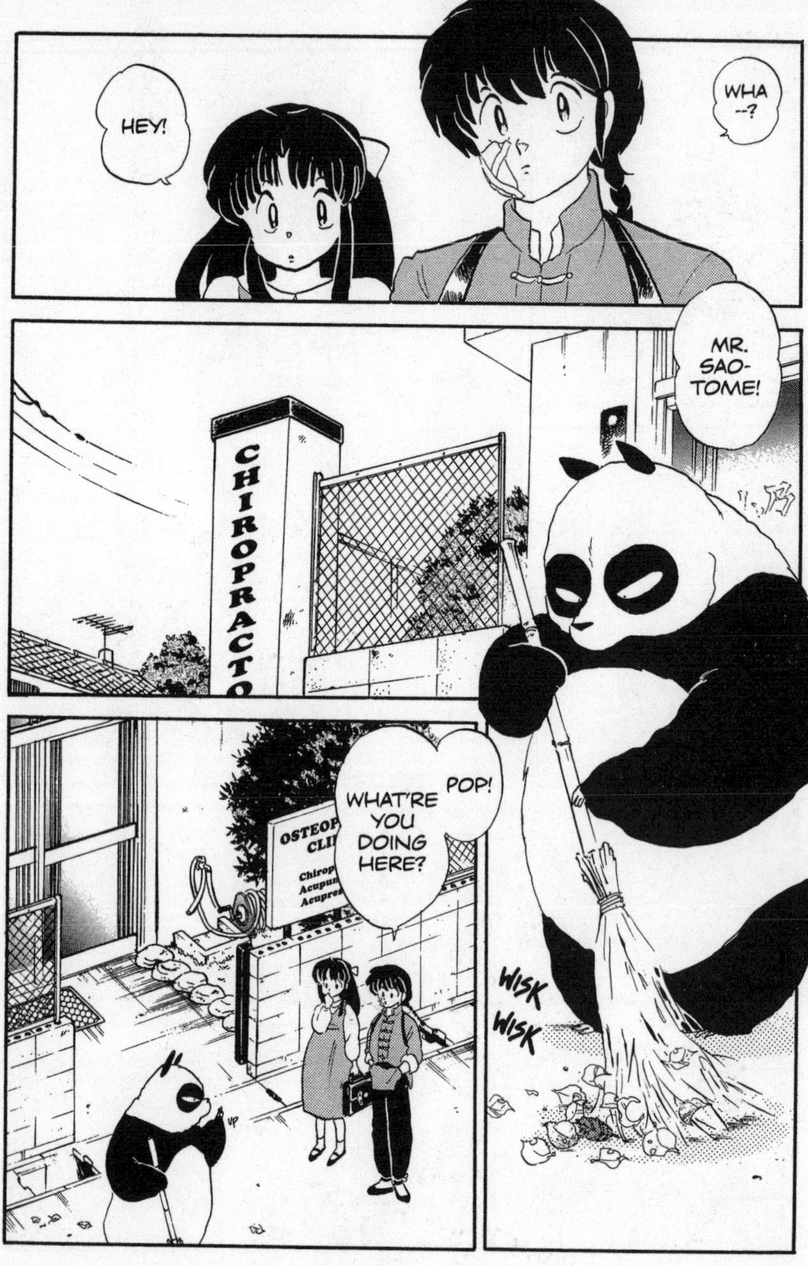
WHA --?
HEY!
MR. SAO-TOME!
WISK
WISK
POP!
WHAT'RE YOU DOING HERE?

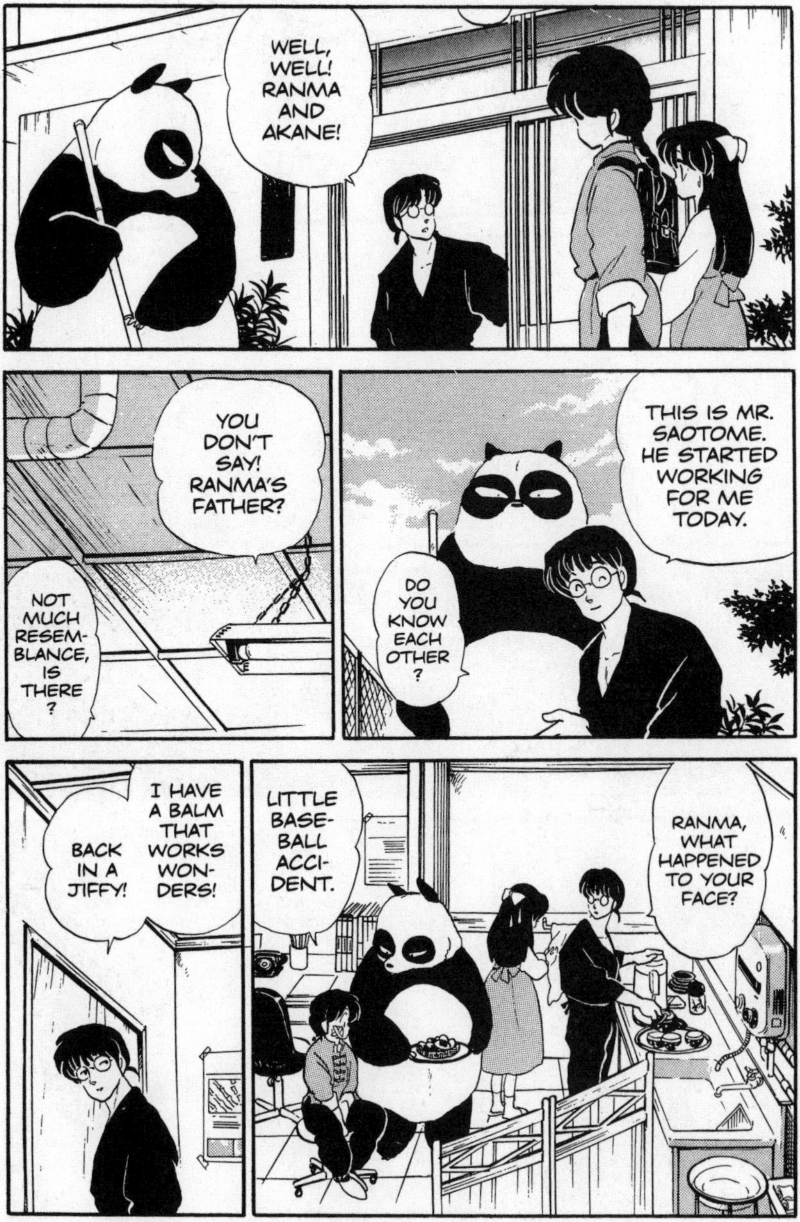
WELL, WELL! RANMA AND AKANE!
THIS IS MR. SAOTOME. HE STARTED WORKING FOR ME TODAY.
DO YOU KNOW EACH OTHER?
YOU DON'T SAY! RANMA'S FATHER?
NOT MUCH RESEMBLANCE, IS THERE?
RANMA, WHAT HAPPENED TO YOUR FACE?
LITTLE BASEBALL ACCIDENT.
I HAVE A BALM THAT WORKS WONDERS!
BACK IN A JIFFY!

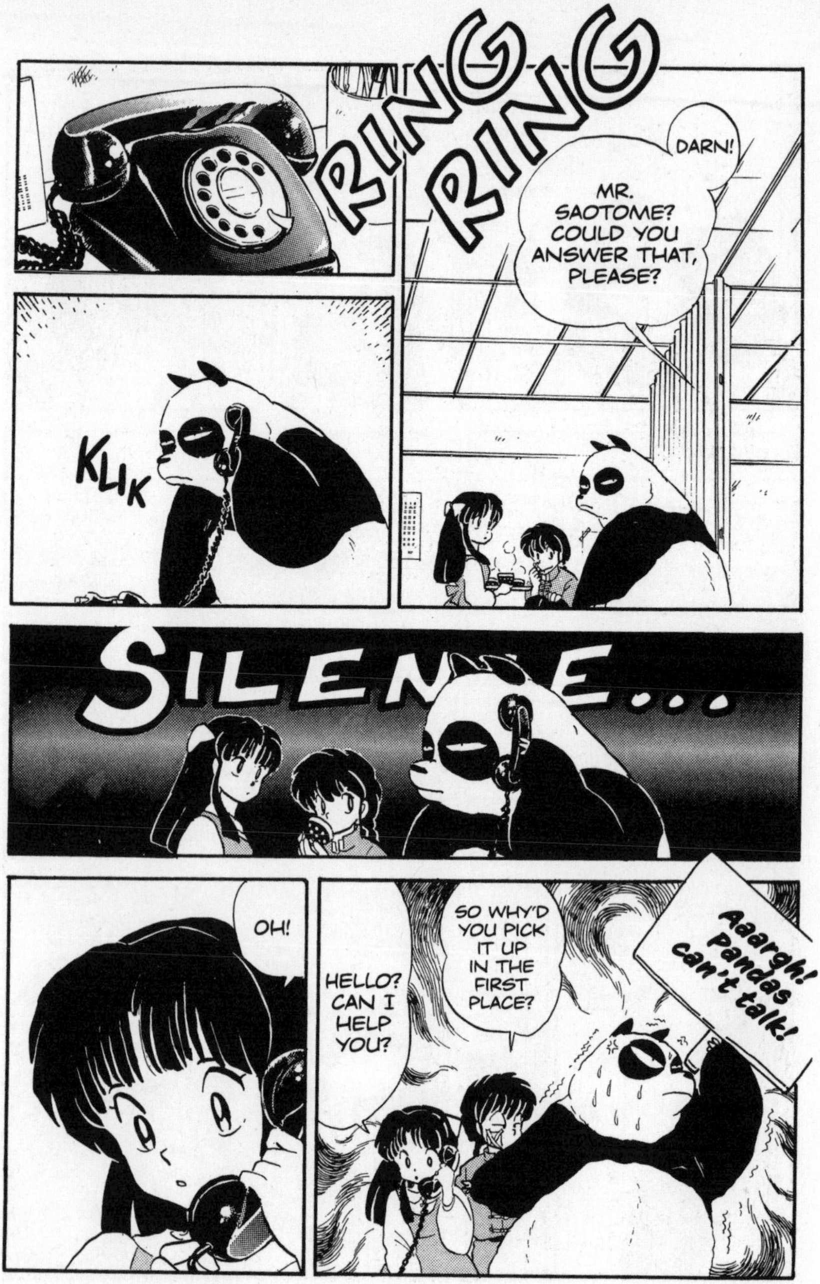
RING RING
DARN!
MR. SAOTOME? COULD YOU ANSWER THAT, PLEASE?
KLIK
SILEN E...
Aaargh! Pandas can't talk!
SO WHY'D YOU PICK IT UP IN THE FIRST PLACE?
HELLO? CAN I HELP YOU?
OH!

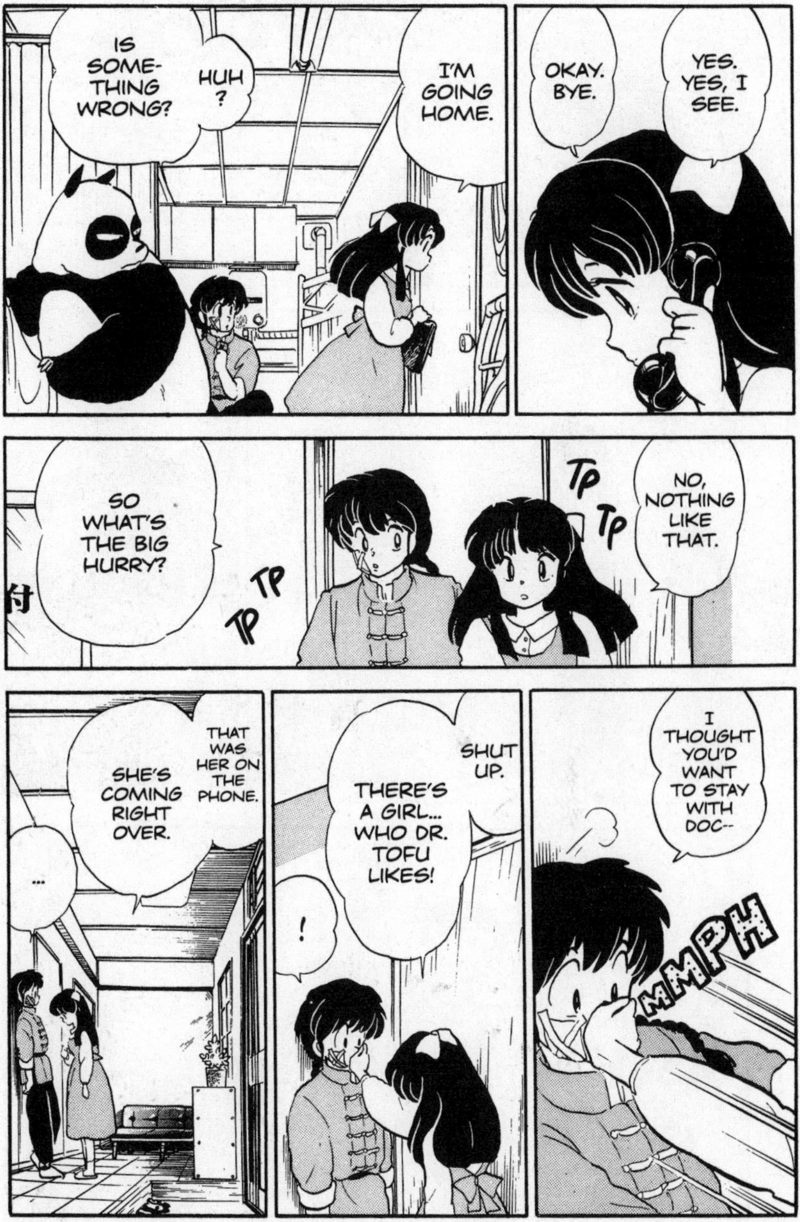
YES. YES, I SEE.
OKAY. BYE.
I'M GOING HOME.
HUH ?
IS SOMETHING WRONG?
TP
TP
NO, NOTHING LIKE THAT.
TP
TP
SO WHAT'S THE BIG HURRY?
I THOUGHT YOU'D WANT TO STAY WITH DOC--
MMPH
SHUT UP.
THERE'S A GIRL... WHO DR. TOFU LIKES!
!
THAT WAS HER ON THE PHONE.
SHE'S COMING RIGHT OVER.
...

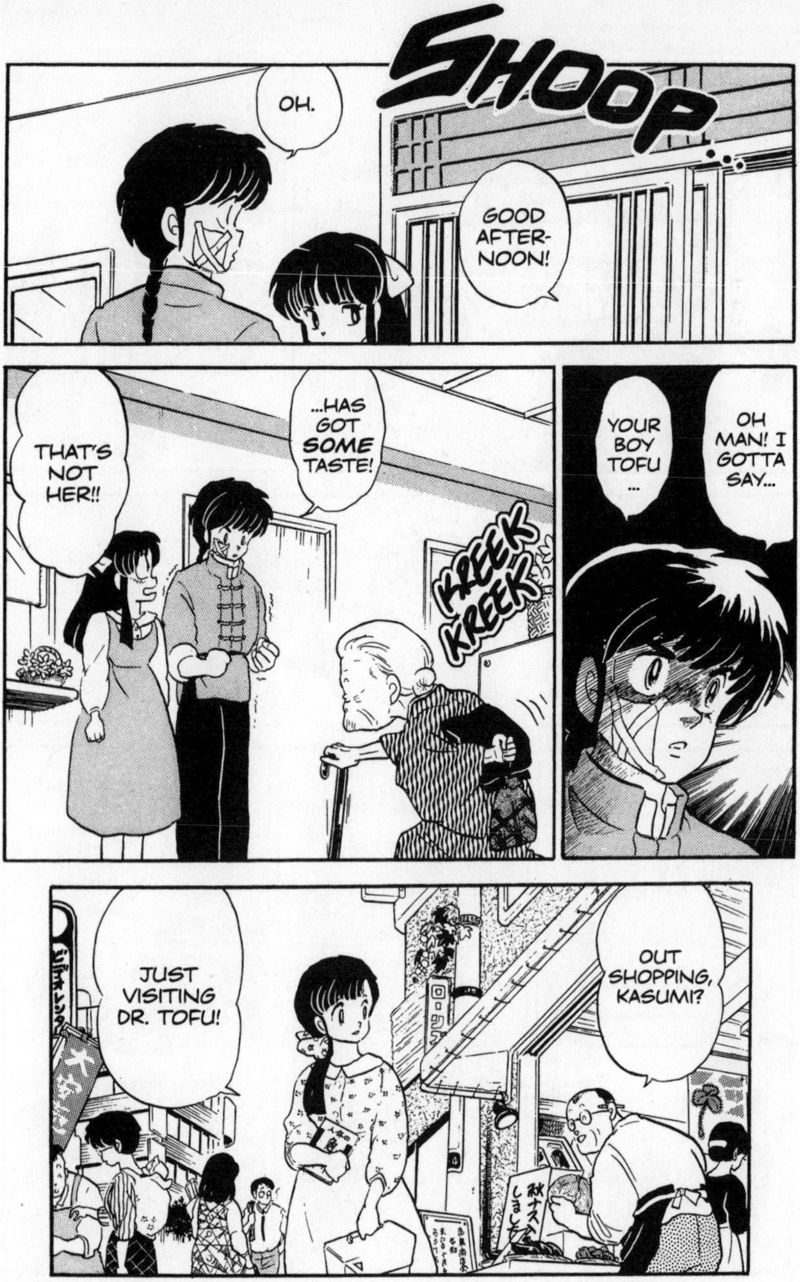
SHOOP...
GOOD AFTER-NOON!
OH.
OH MAN! I GOTTA SAY...
YOUR BOY TOFU...
...HAS GOT SOME TASTE!
KREEK KREEK
THAT'S NOT HER!!
OUT SHOPPING, KASUMI?
JUST VISITING DR. TOFU!

# PART 9
# YOU'RE CUTE WHEN YOU SMILE

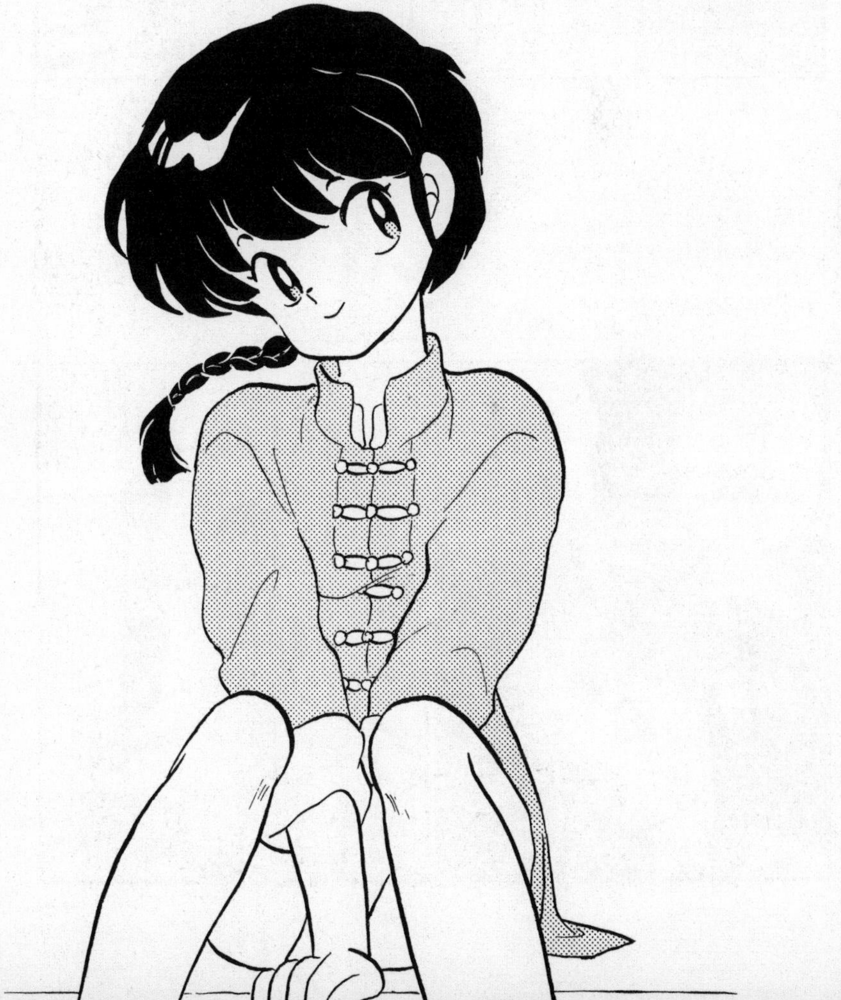

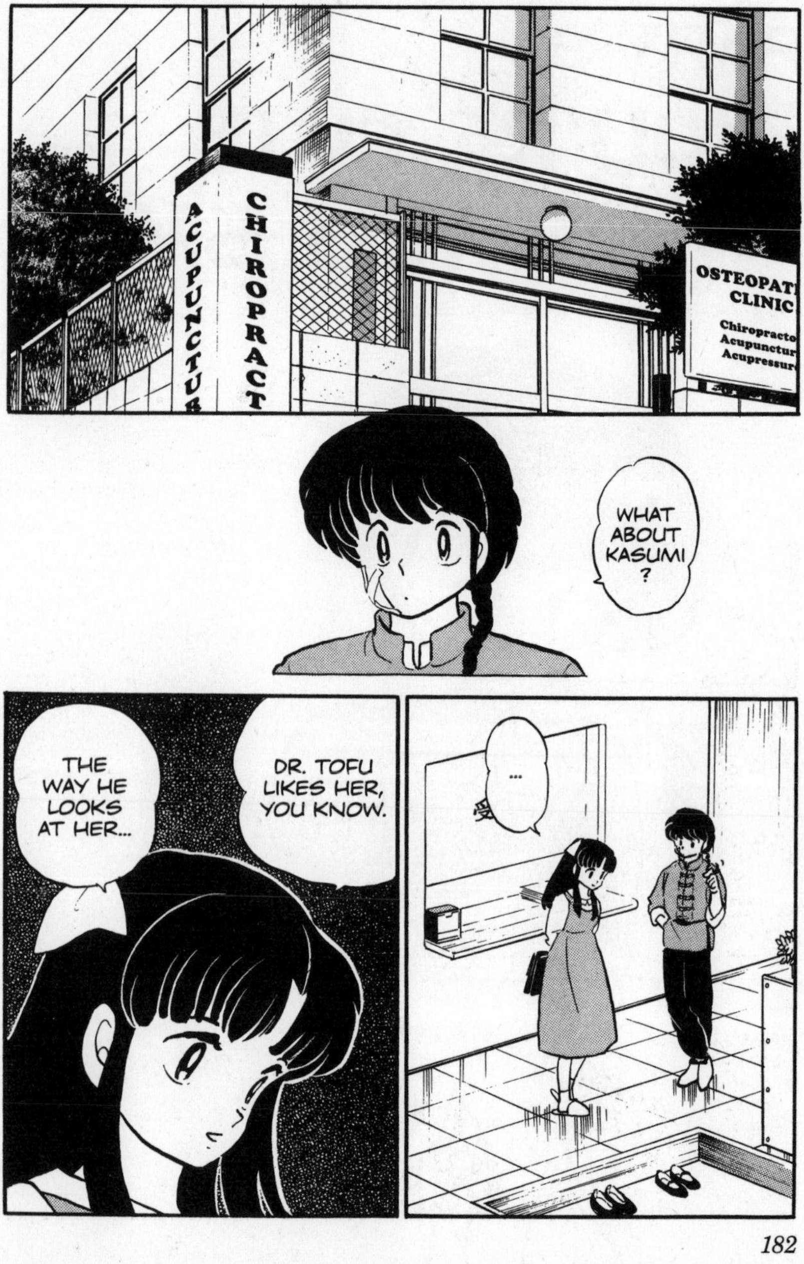
CHIROPRACT
ACUPUNCTUR
OSTEOPAT
CLINIC
Chiropracto
Acupunctur
Acupressur
WHAT ABOUT KASUMI?
...
DR. TOFU LIKES HER, YOU KNOW.
THE WAY HE LOOKS AT HER...

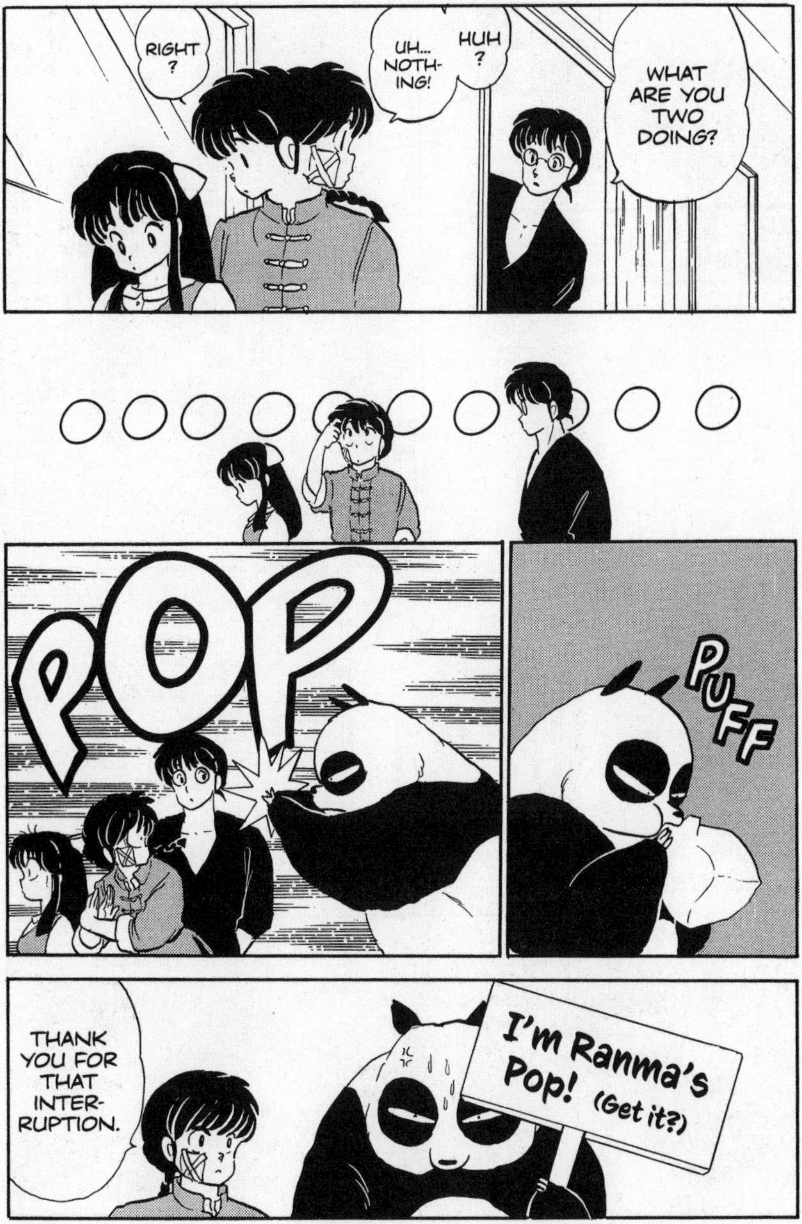
WHAT ARE YOU TWO DOING?
HUH ?
UH... NOTHING!
RIGHT ?
PUFF
POP
I'm Ranma's Pop! (Get it?)
THANK YOU FOR THAT INTERRUPTION.

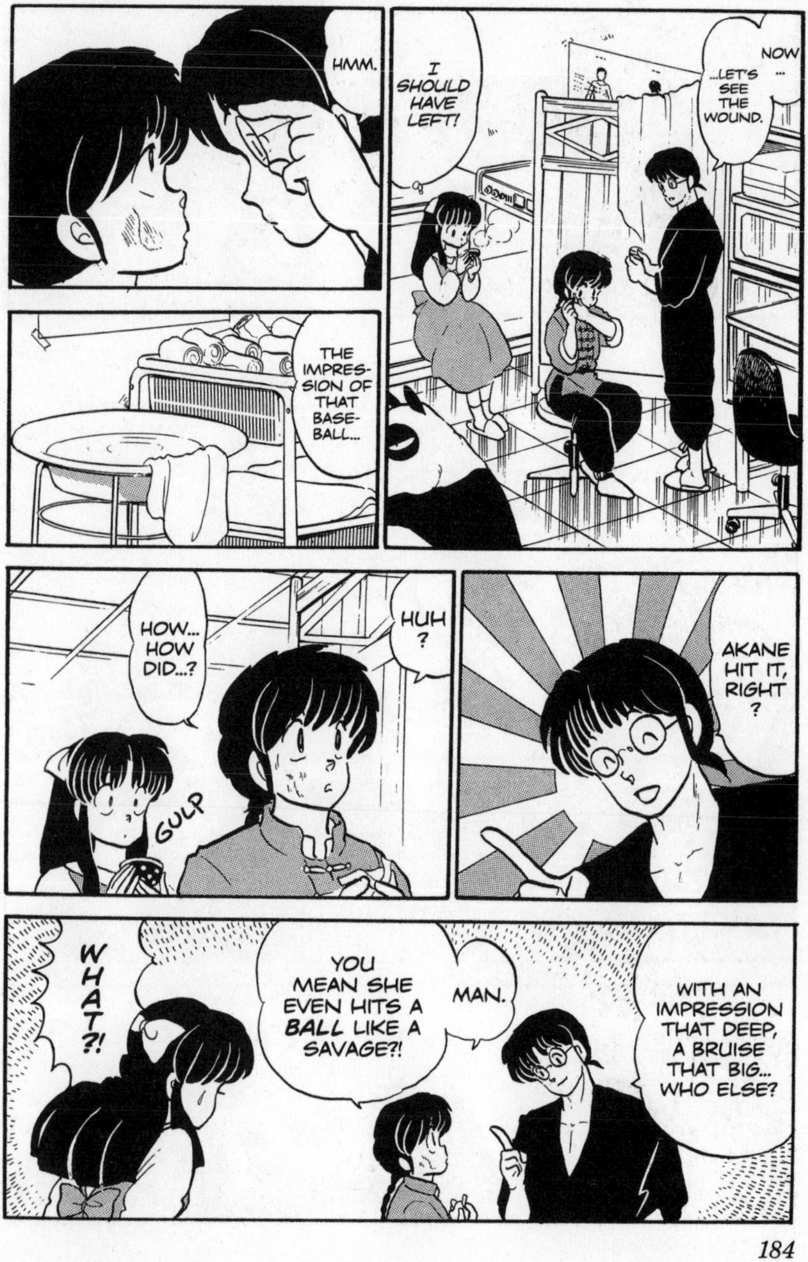
NOW ...
...LET'S SEE THE WOUND.
I SHOULD HAVE LEFT!
HMM.
THE IMPRESSION OF THAT BASEBALL...
AKANE HIT IT, RIGHT?
HUH?
HOW... HOW DID...?
GULP
WITH AN IMPRESSION THAT DEEP, A BRUISE THAT BIG... WHO ELSE?
MAN.
YOU MEAN SHE EVEN HITS A BALL LIKE A SAVAGE?!
WHAT?!

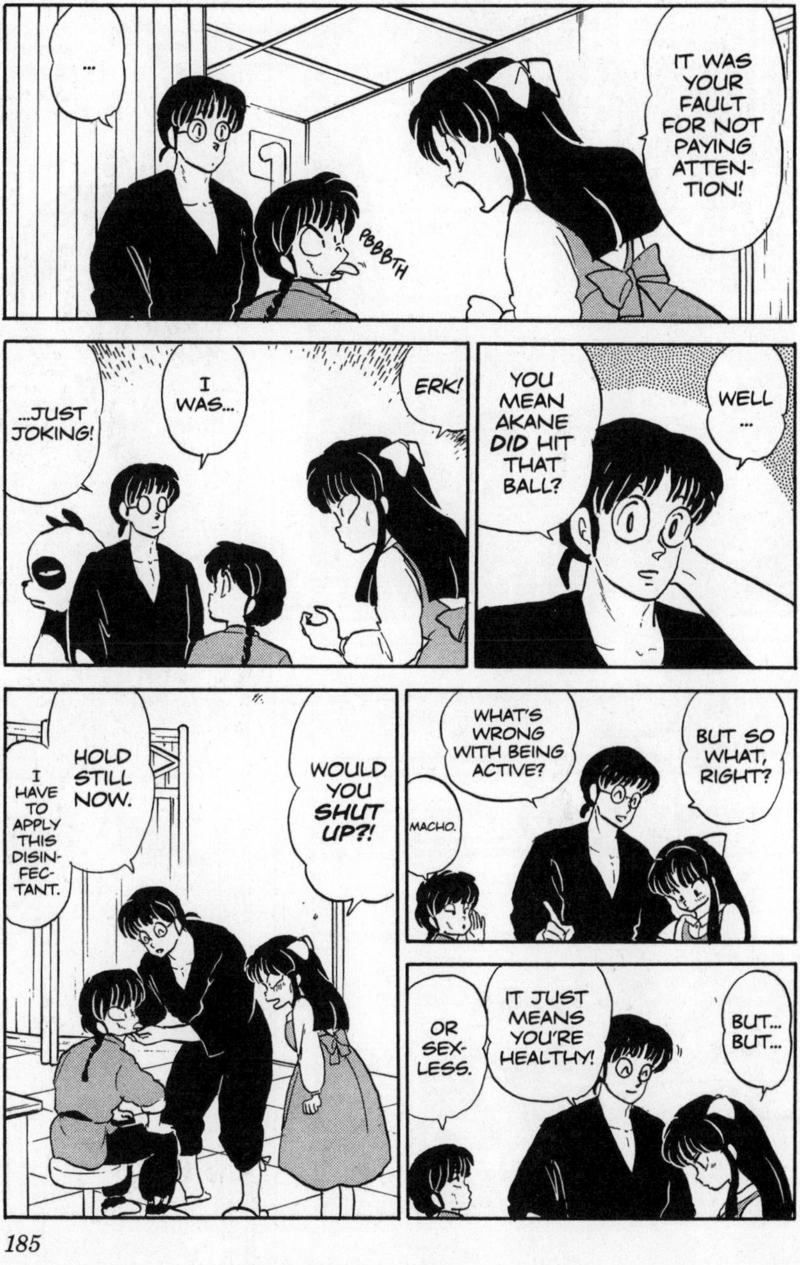
IT WAS YOUR FAULT FOR NOT PAYING ATTENTION!
...
PBBBTH
WELL ...
YOU MEAN AKANE *DID* HIT THAT BALL?
ERK!
I WAS...
...JUST JOKING!
BUT SO WHAT, RIGHT?
WHAT'S WRONG WITH BEING ACTIVE?
MACHO.
BUT... BUT...
IT JUST MEANS YOU'RE HEALTHY!
OR SEXLESS.
WOULD YOU *SHUT UP?!*
HOLD STILL NOW.
I HAVE TO APPLY THIS DISINFECTANT.

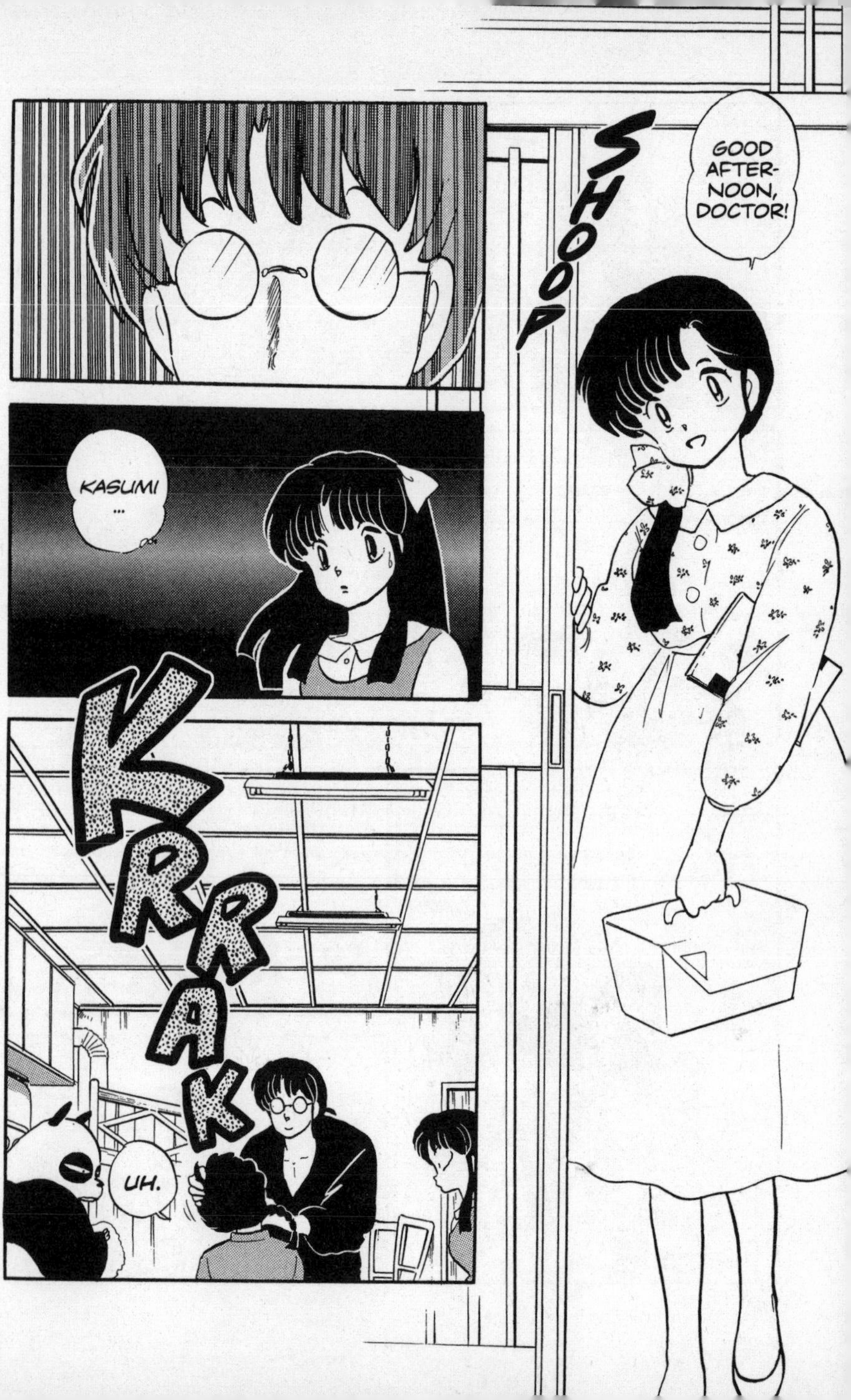
SHOOOP
GOOD AFTER-NOON, DOCTOR!
KASUMI ...
KRRAK
UH.

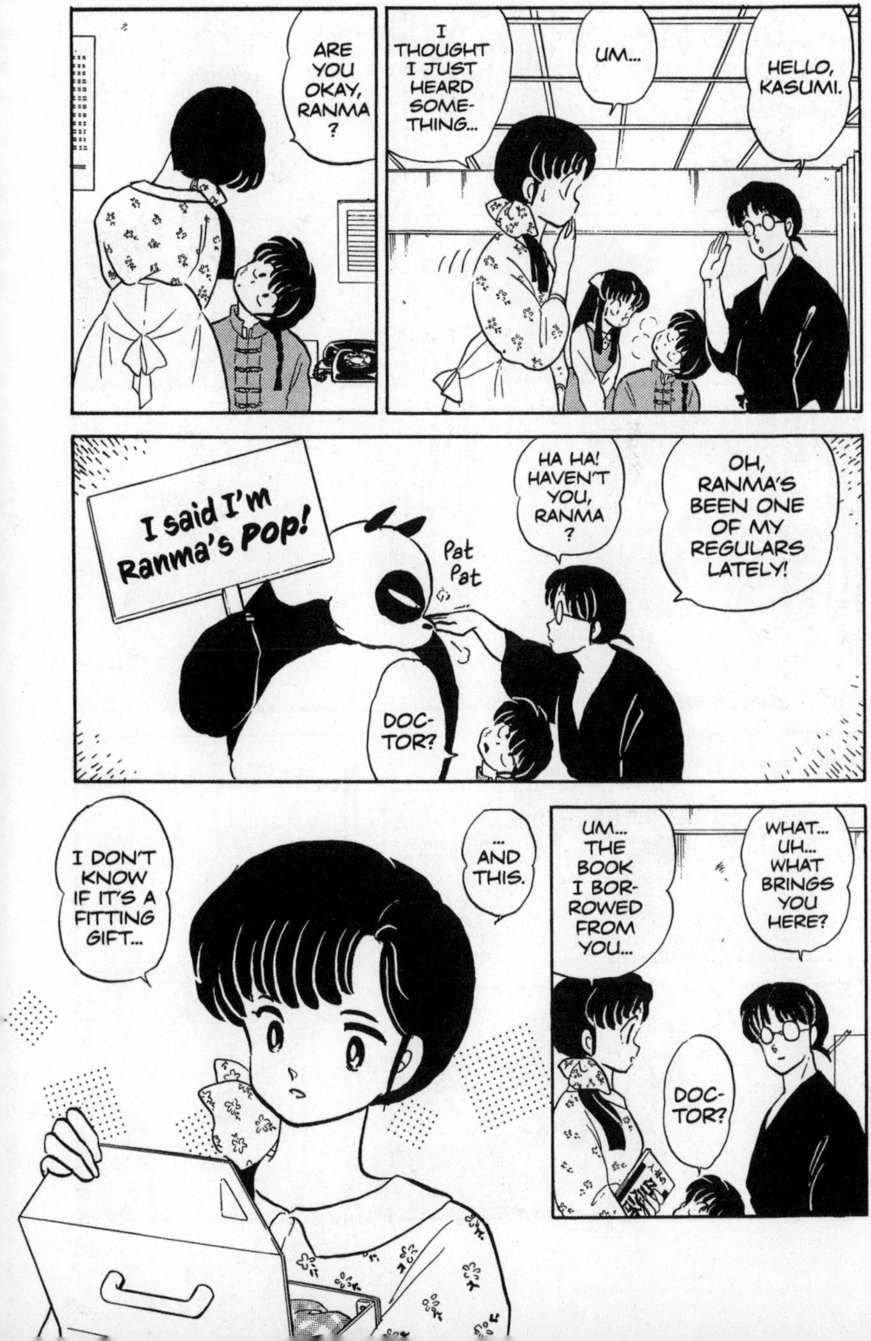
HELLO, KASUMI.
UM...
I THOUGHT I JUST HEARD SOMETHING...
ARE YOU OKAY, RANMA?
OH, RANMA'S BEEN ONE OF MY REGULARS LATELY!
HA HA! HAVEN'T YOU, RANMA?
Pat Pat
I said I'm Ranma's Pop!
DOCTOR?
WHAT... UH... WHAT BRINGS YOU HERE?
UM... THE BOOK I BORROWED FROM YOU...
DOCTOR?
... AND THIS.
I DON'T KNOW IF IT'S A FITTING GIFT...

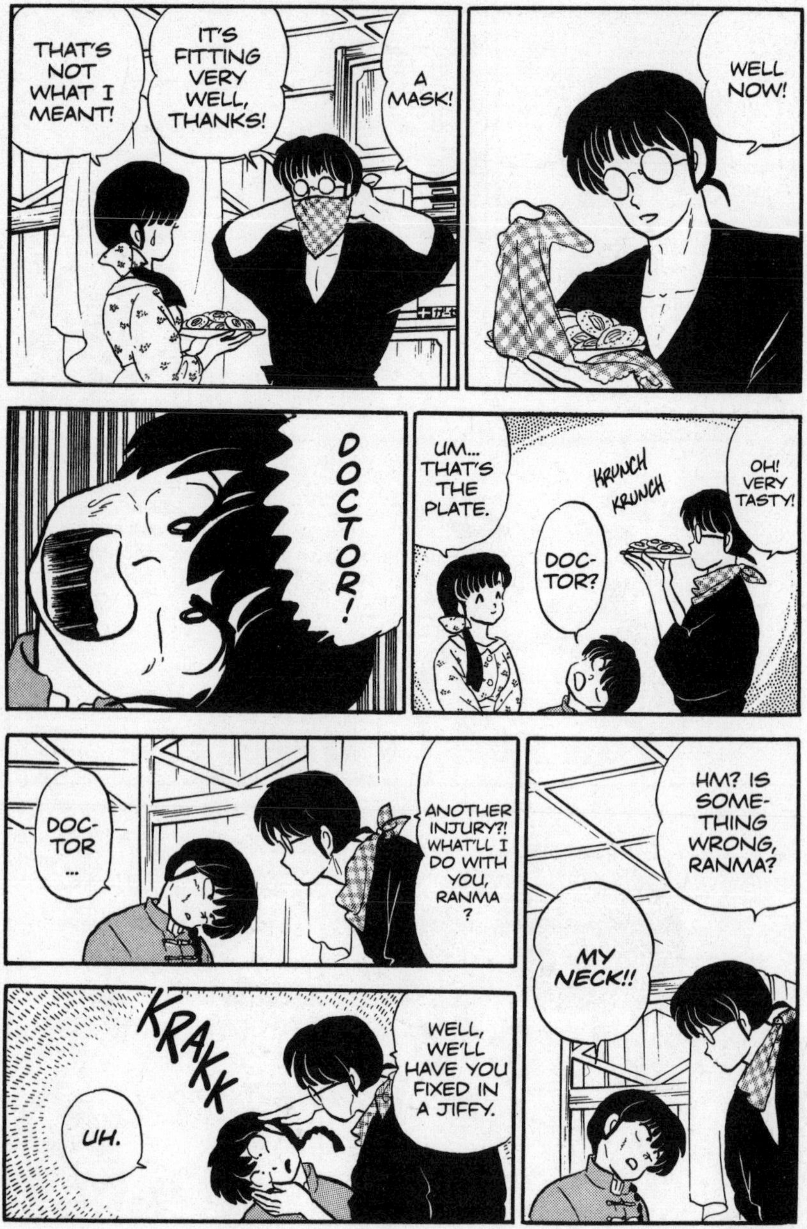
WELL NOW!
A MASK!
IT'S FITTING VERY WELL, THANKS!
THAT'S NOT WHAT I MEANT!
OH! VERY TASTY!
KRUNCH KRUNCH
UM... THAT'S THE PLATE.
DOC-TOR?
DOCTOR!
HM? IS SOME-THING WRONG, RANMA?
MY NECK!!
ANOTHER INJURY?! WHAT'LL I DO WITH YOU, RANMA ?
DOC-TOR ...
WELL, WE'LL HAVE YOU FIXED IN A JIFFY.
KRAKK
UH.

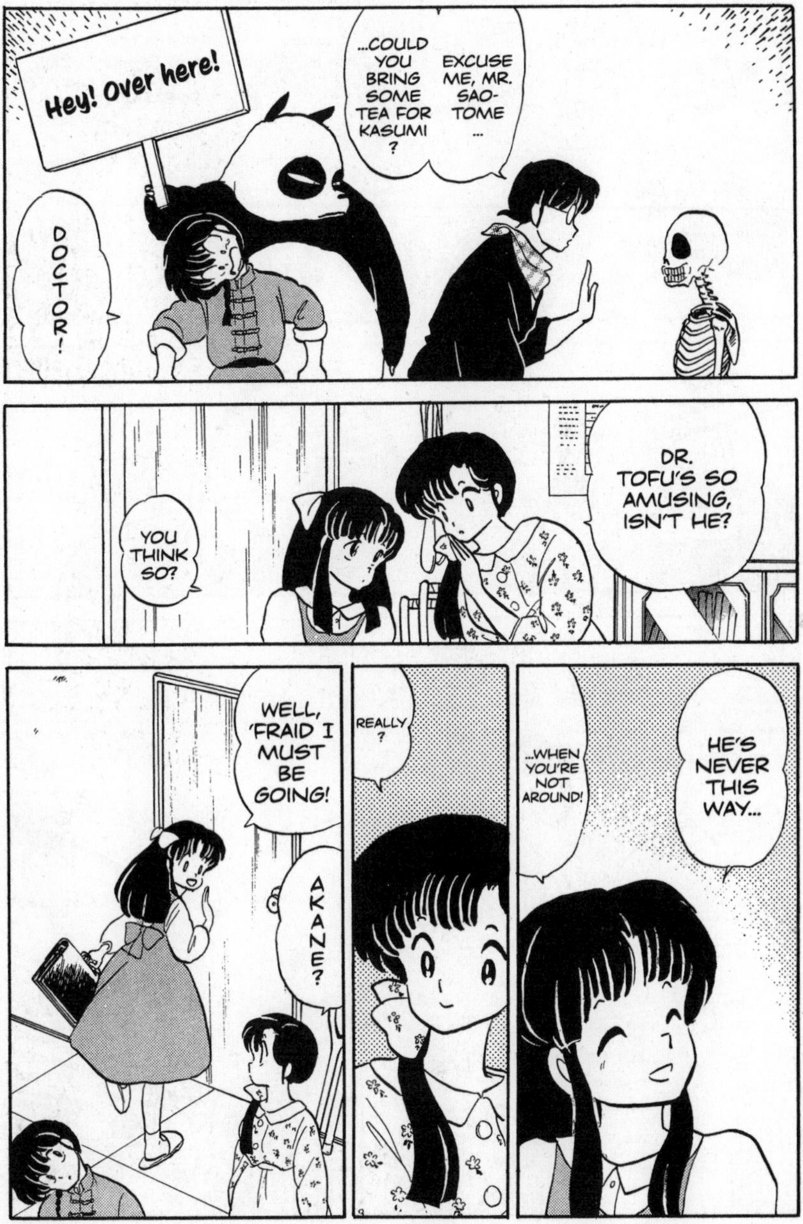
EXCUSE ME, MR. SAO-TOME...
...COULD YOU BRING SOME TEA FOR KASUMI?
Hey! Over here!
DOCTOR!
DR. TOFU'S SO AMUSING, ISN'T HE?
YOU THINK SO?
HE'S NEVER THIS WAY...
...WHEN YOU'RE NOT AROUND!
REALLY?
WELL, 'FRAID I MUST BE GOING!
AKANE?

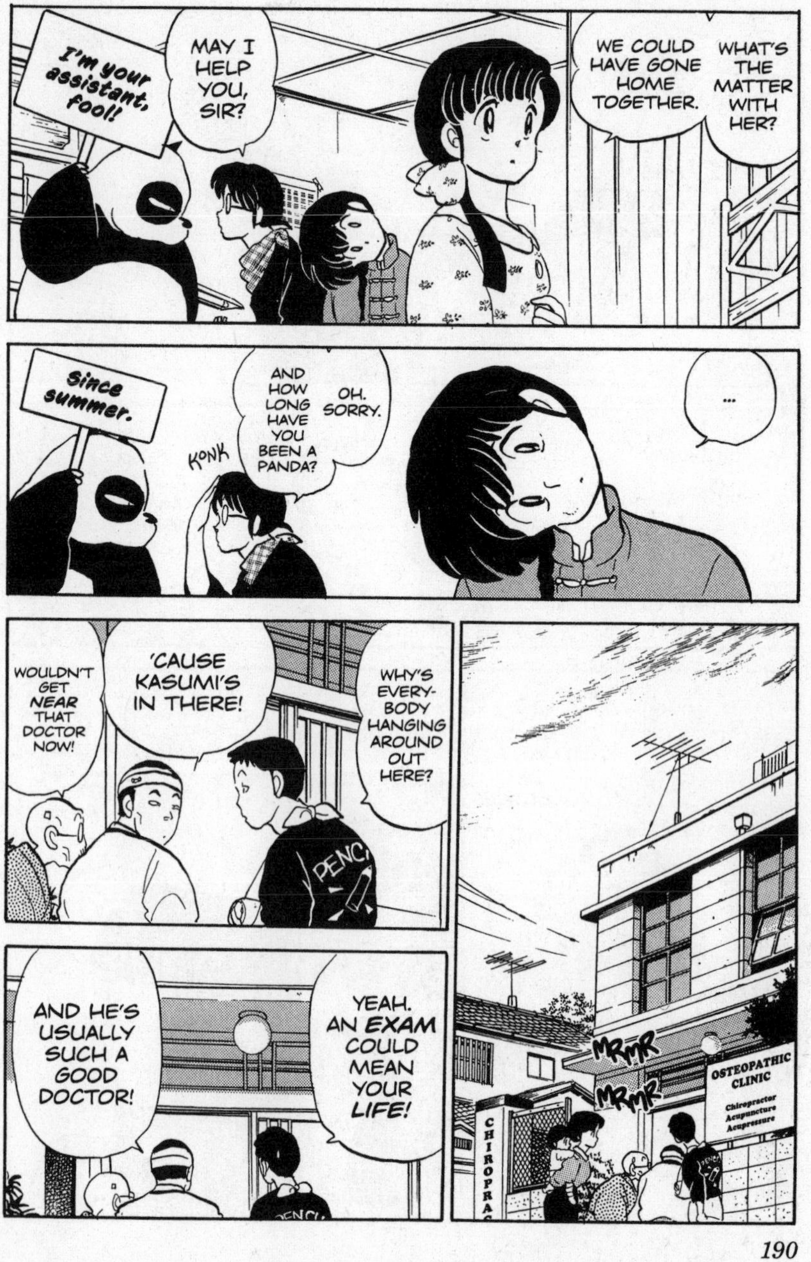
WHAT'S THE MATTER WITH HER?
WE COULD HAVE GONE HOME TOGETHER.
MAY I HELP YOU, SIR?
I'm your assistant, fool!
...
OH. SORRY.
AND HOW LONG HAVE YOU BEEN A PANDA?
KONK
Since summer.
MRMR
MRMR
OSTEOPATHIC CLINIC
Chiropractor Acupuncture Acupressure
CHIROPRAC
WHY'S EVERYBODY HANGING AROUND OUT HERE?
'CAUSE KASUMI'S IN THERE!
WOULDN'T GET NEAR THAT DOCTOR NOW!
YEAH. AN EXAM COULD MEAN YOUR LIFE!
AND HE'S USUALLY SUCH A GOOD DOCTOR!

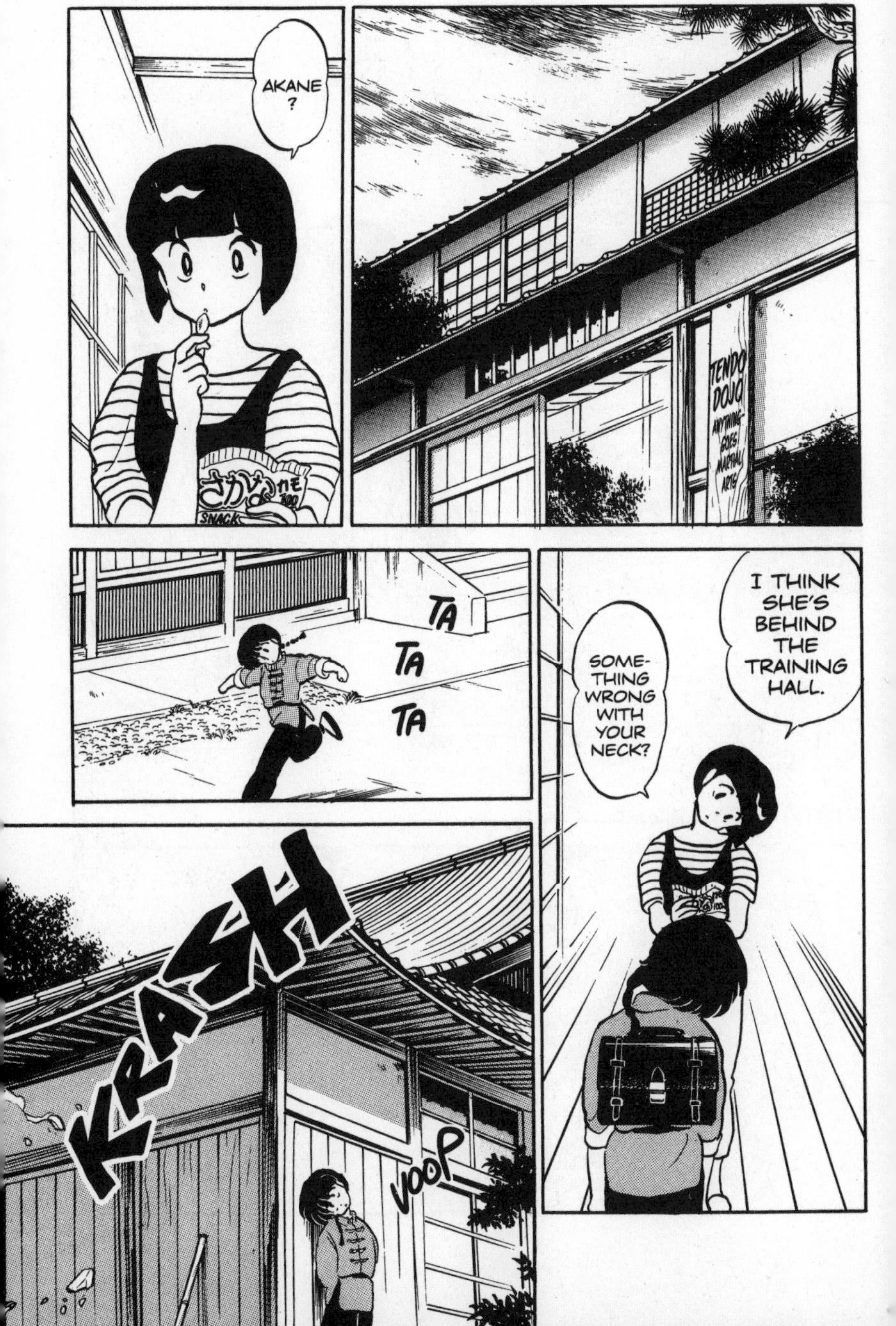
TENDO DOJO
ANYTHING-GOES MARTIAL ARTS
AKANE ?
SNACK
I THINK SHE'S BEHIND THE TRAINING HALL.
SOME-THING WRONG WITH YOUR NECK?
TA
TA
TA
KRASH
VOOP

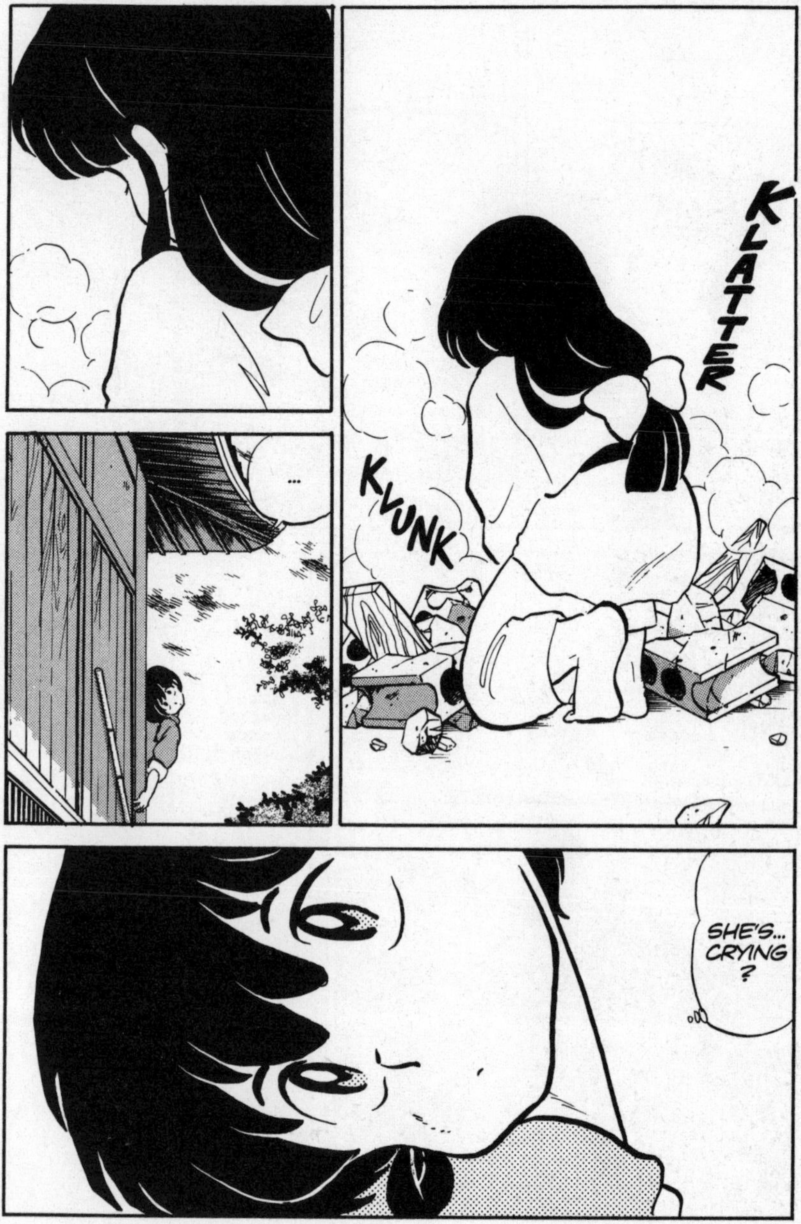
KLATTER
KVUNK
...
SHE'S... CRYING?

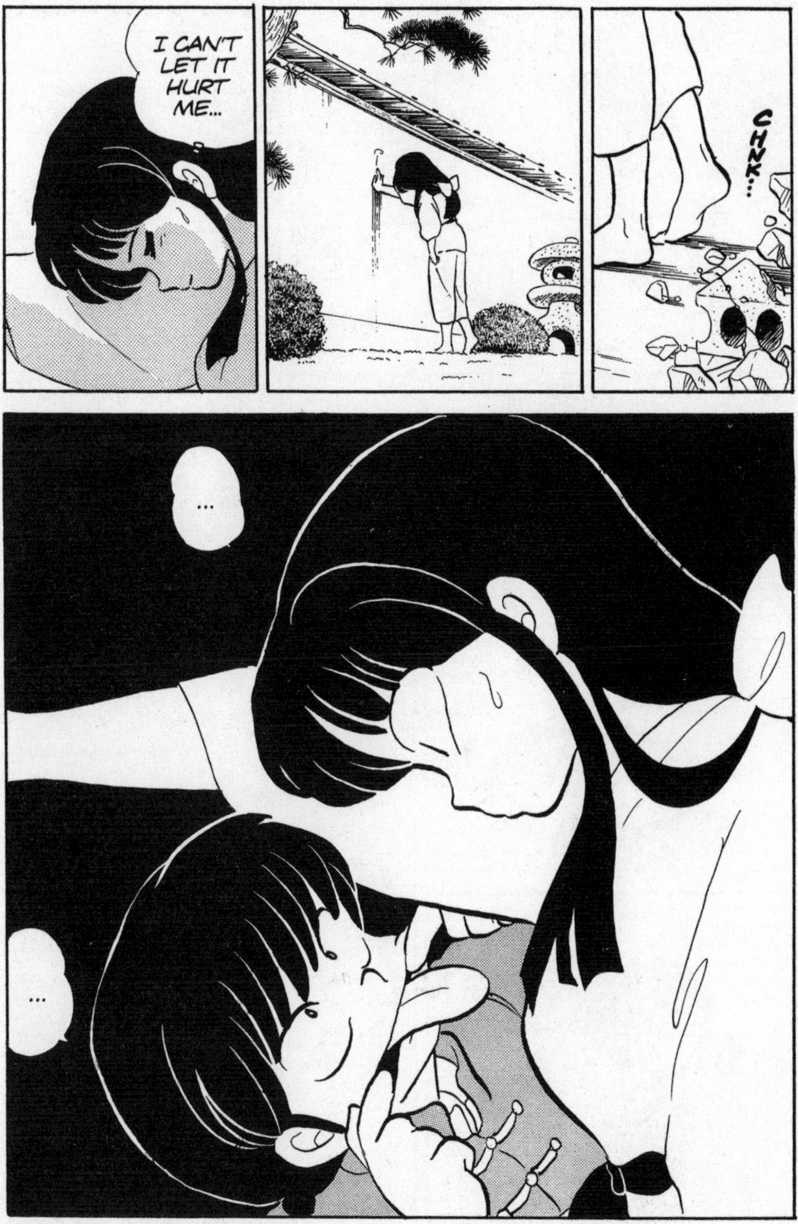
CHNK...
I CAN'T LET IT HURT ME...
...
...

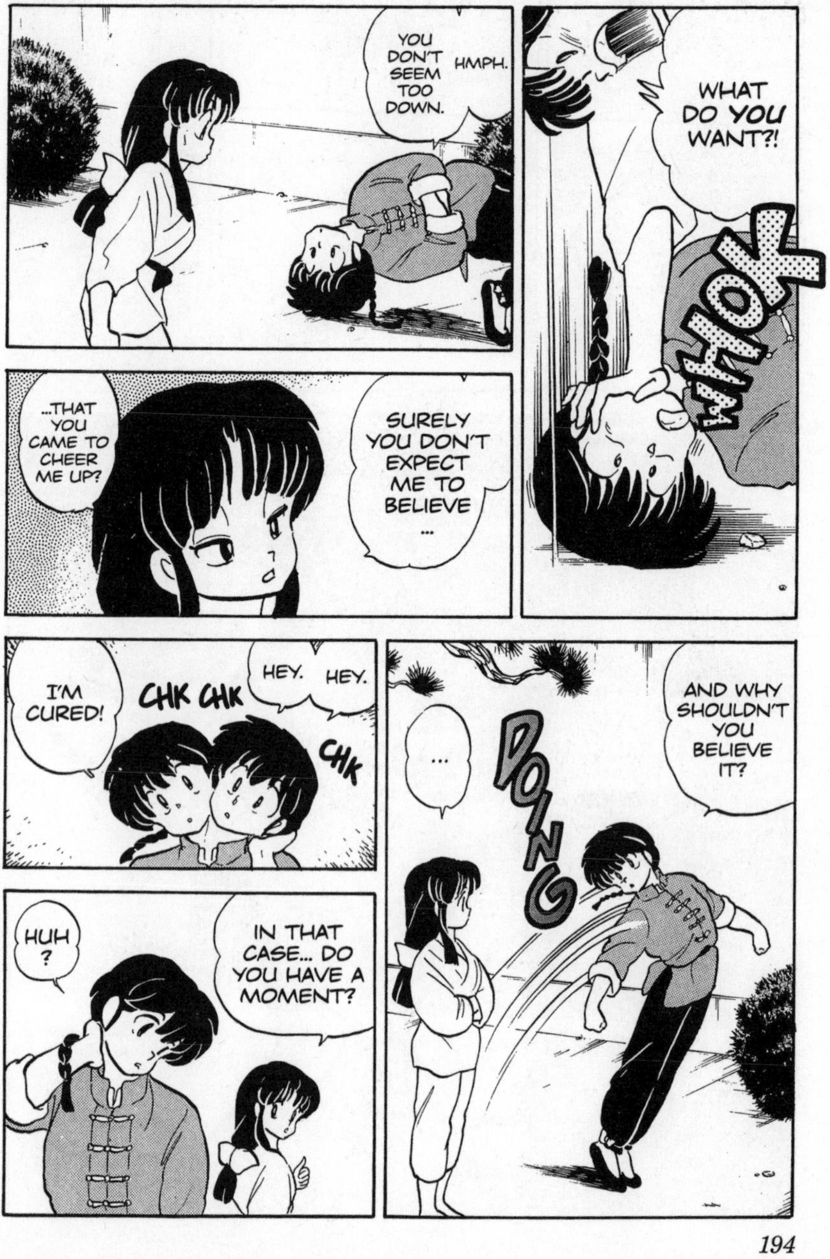
WHAT DO YOU WANT?!
WHOK
HMPH.
YOU DON'T SEEM TOO DOWN.
SURELY YOU DON'T EXPECT ME TO BELIEVE ...
...THAT YOU CAME TO CHEER ME UP?
AND WHY SHOULDN'T YOU BELIEVE IT?
DOING
...
HEY.
HEY.
CHK CHK
CHK
I'M CURED!
IN THAT CASE... DO YOU HAVE A MOMENT?
HUH?

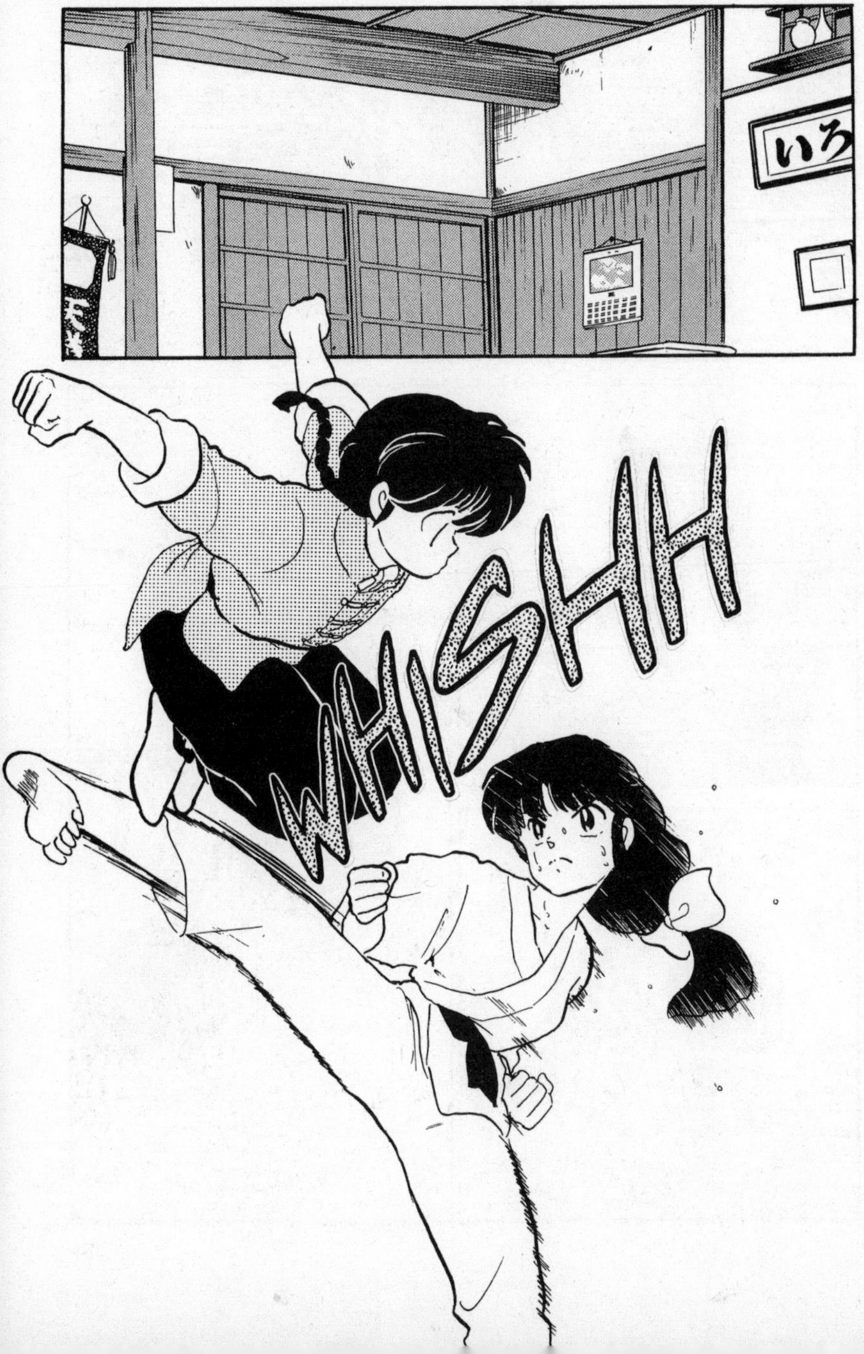
WHISHH

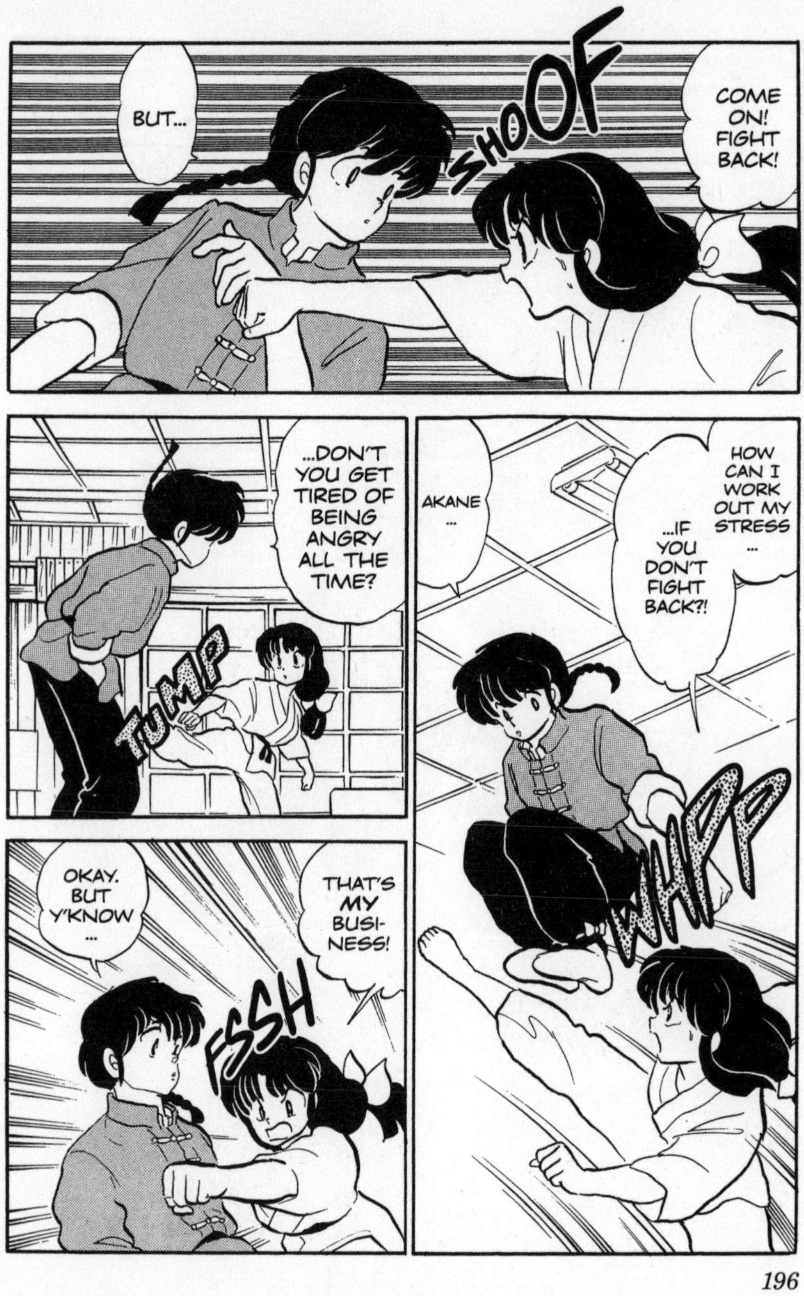
COME ON! FIGHT BACK!
SHOOF
BUT...
HOW CAN I WORK OUT MY STRESS ...
...IF YOU DON'T FIGHT BACK?!
AKANE ...
WHPP
...DON'T YOU GET TIRED OF BEING ANGRY ALL THE TIME?
TUMP
THAT'S MY BUSI-NESS!
OKAY. BUT Y'KNOW ...
FSSH

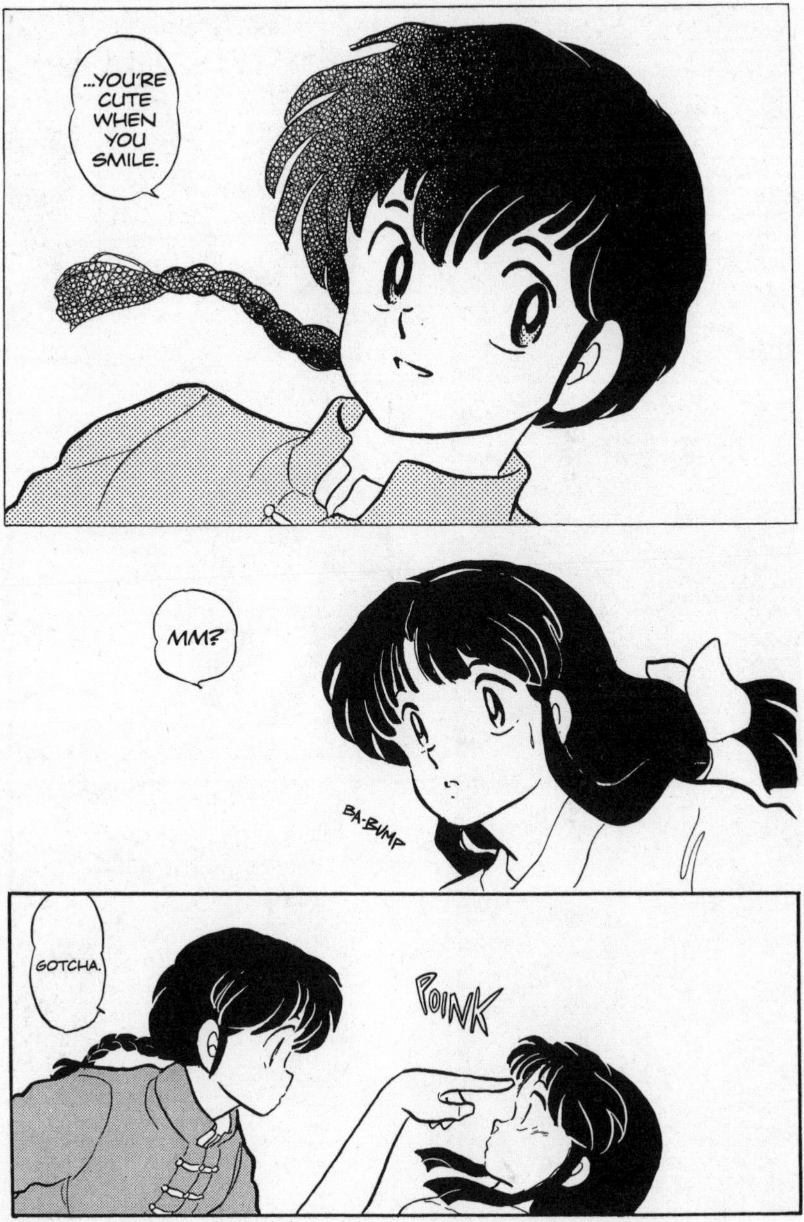
...YOU'RE CUTE WHEN YOU SMILE.
MM?
BA-BUMP
GOTCHA.
POINK

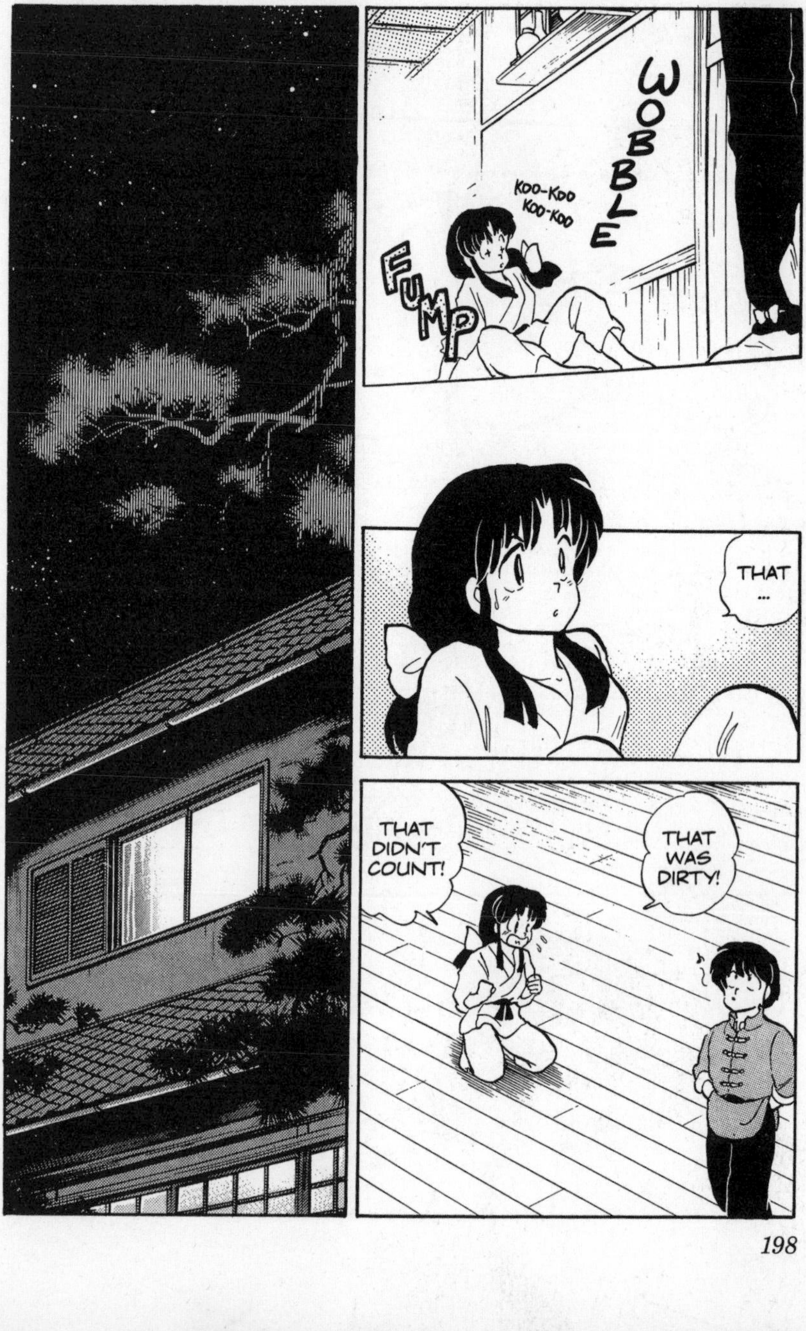
WOBBLE
KOO-KOO KOO-KOO
FUMP
THAT ...
THAT WAS DIRTY!
THAT DIDN'T COUNT!

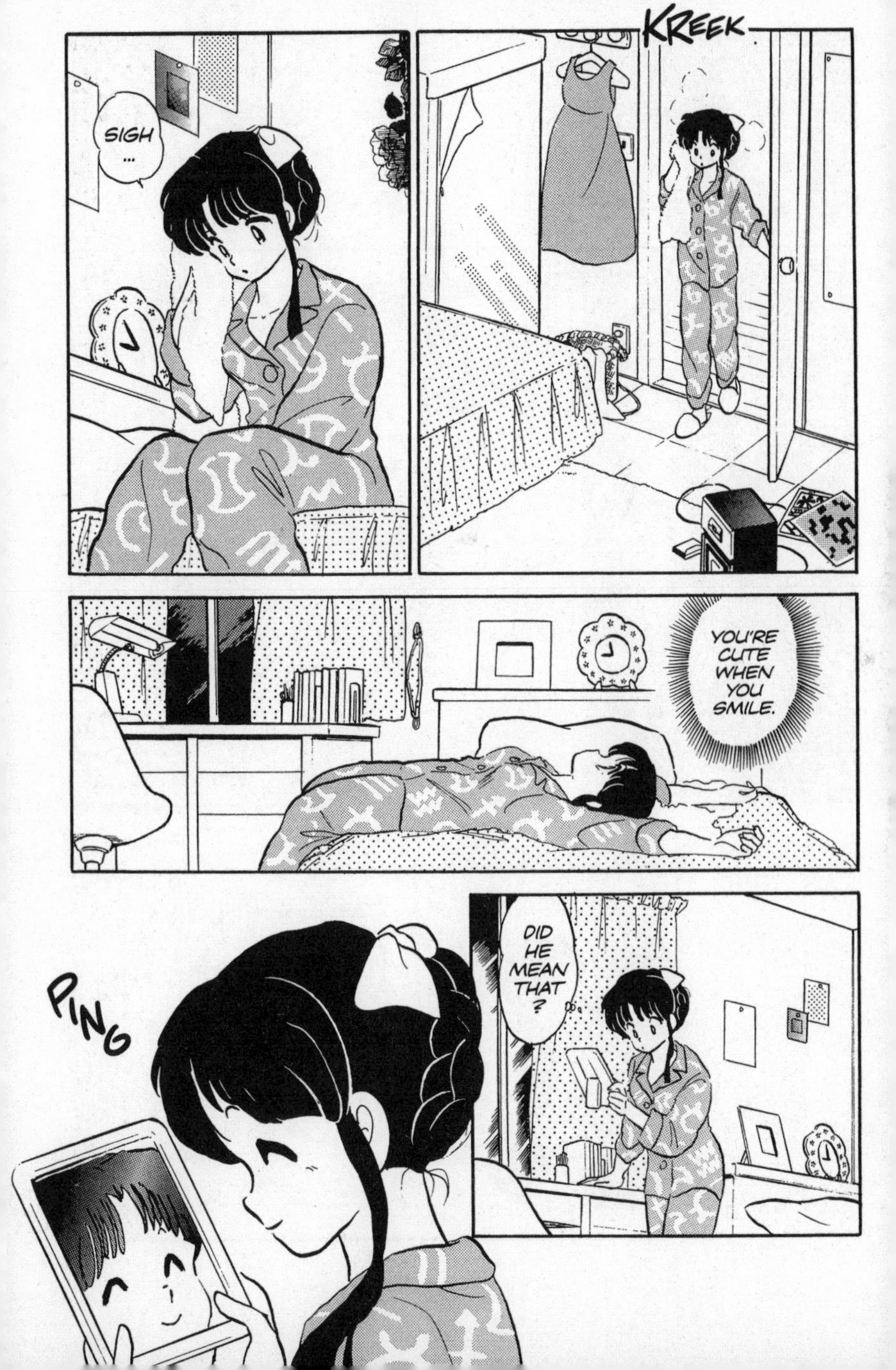
KREEK
SIGH ...
YOU'RE CUTE WHEN YOU SMILE.
DID HE MEAN THAT ?
PING

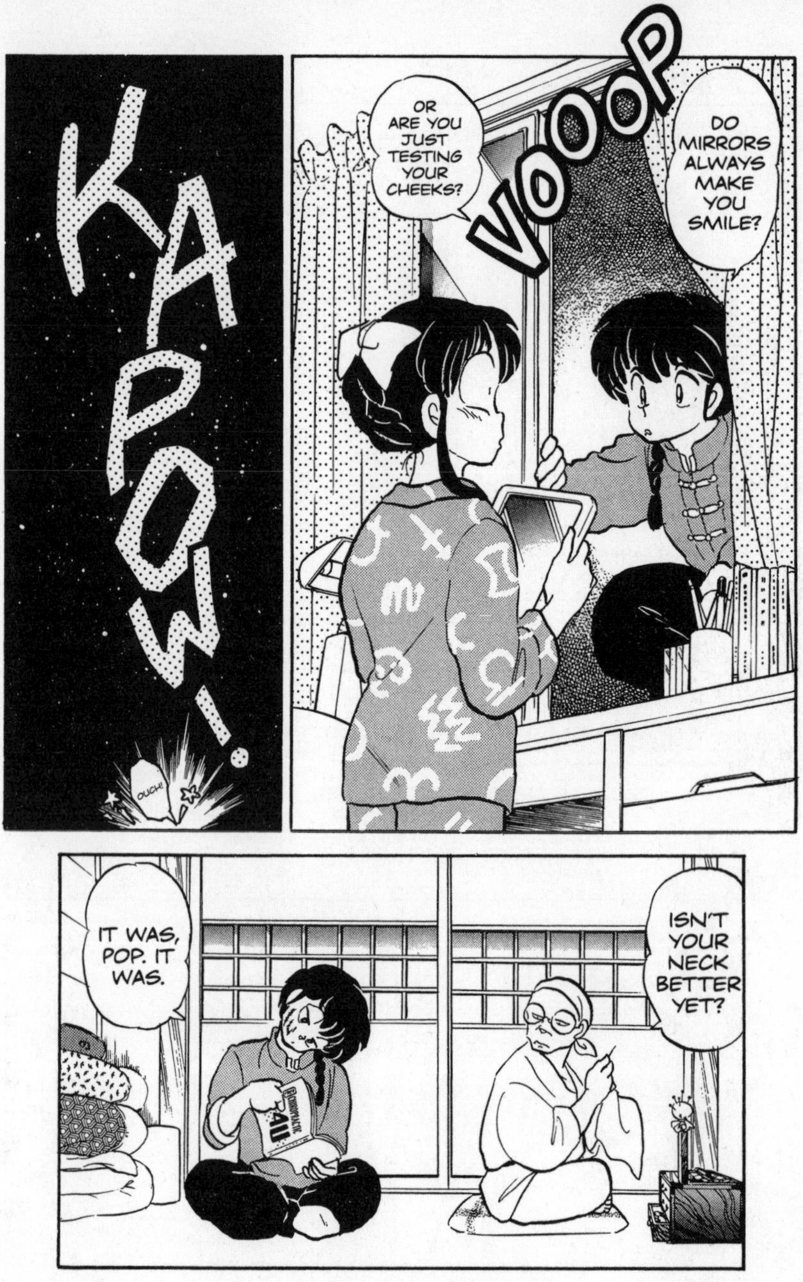
DO MIRRORS ALWAYS MAKE YOU SMILE?
VOOOP
OR ARE YOU JUST TESTING YOUR CHEEKS?
KAPOW!
OUCH!
ISN'T YOUR NECK BETTER YET?
IT WAS, POP. IT WAS.

# PART 10
# THE HUNTER

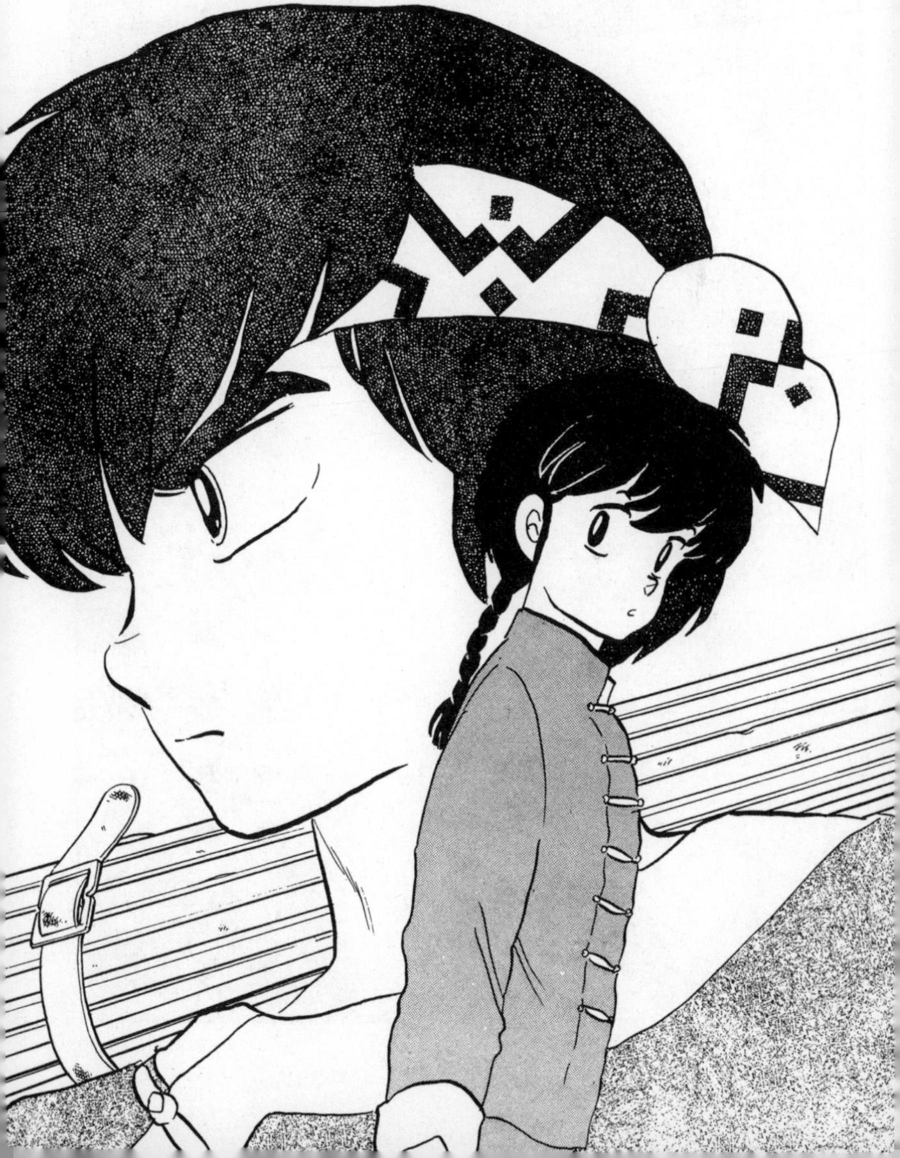

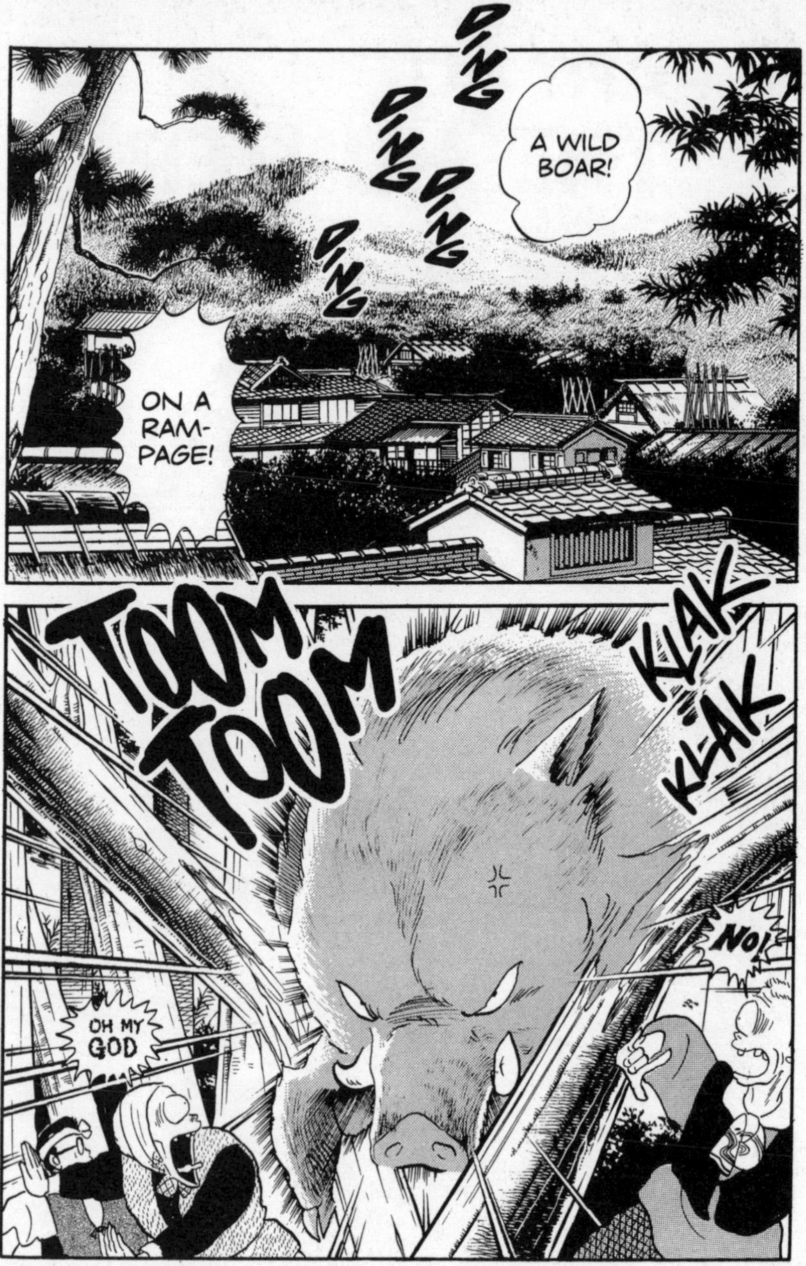
DING
DING DING
DING
A WILD BOAR!
ON A RAMPAGE!
KLAK KLAK
TOOM TOOM
NO!
OH MY GOD

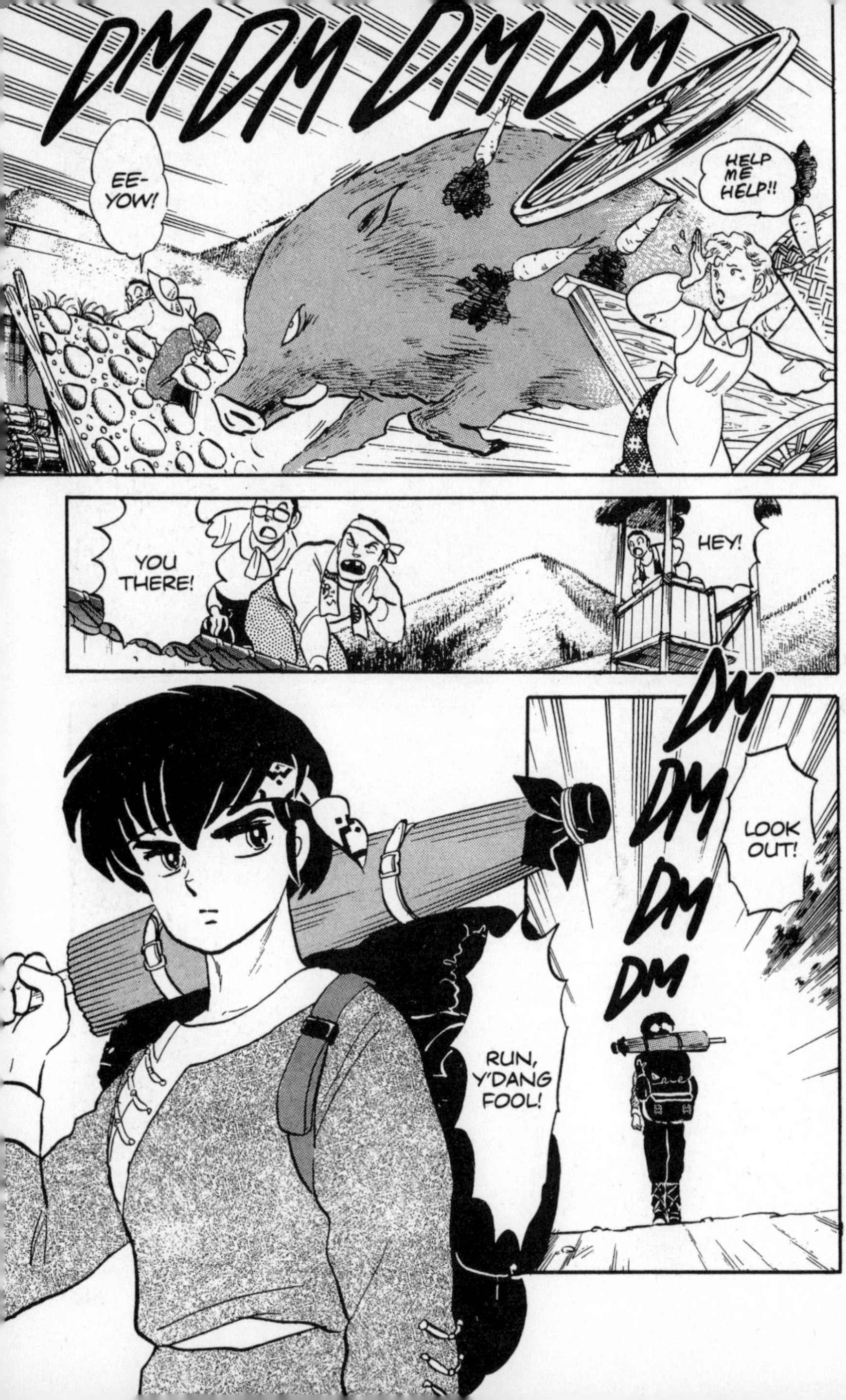
DM DM DM DM DM
HELP ME HELP!!
EE-YOW!
HEY!
YOU THERE!
DM DM DM DM DM
LOOK OUT!
RUN, Y'DANG FOOL!

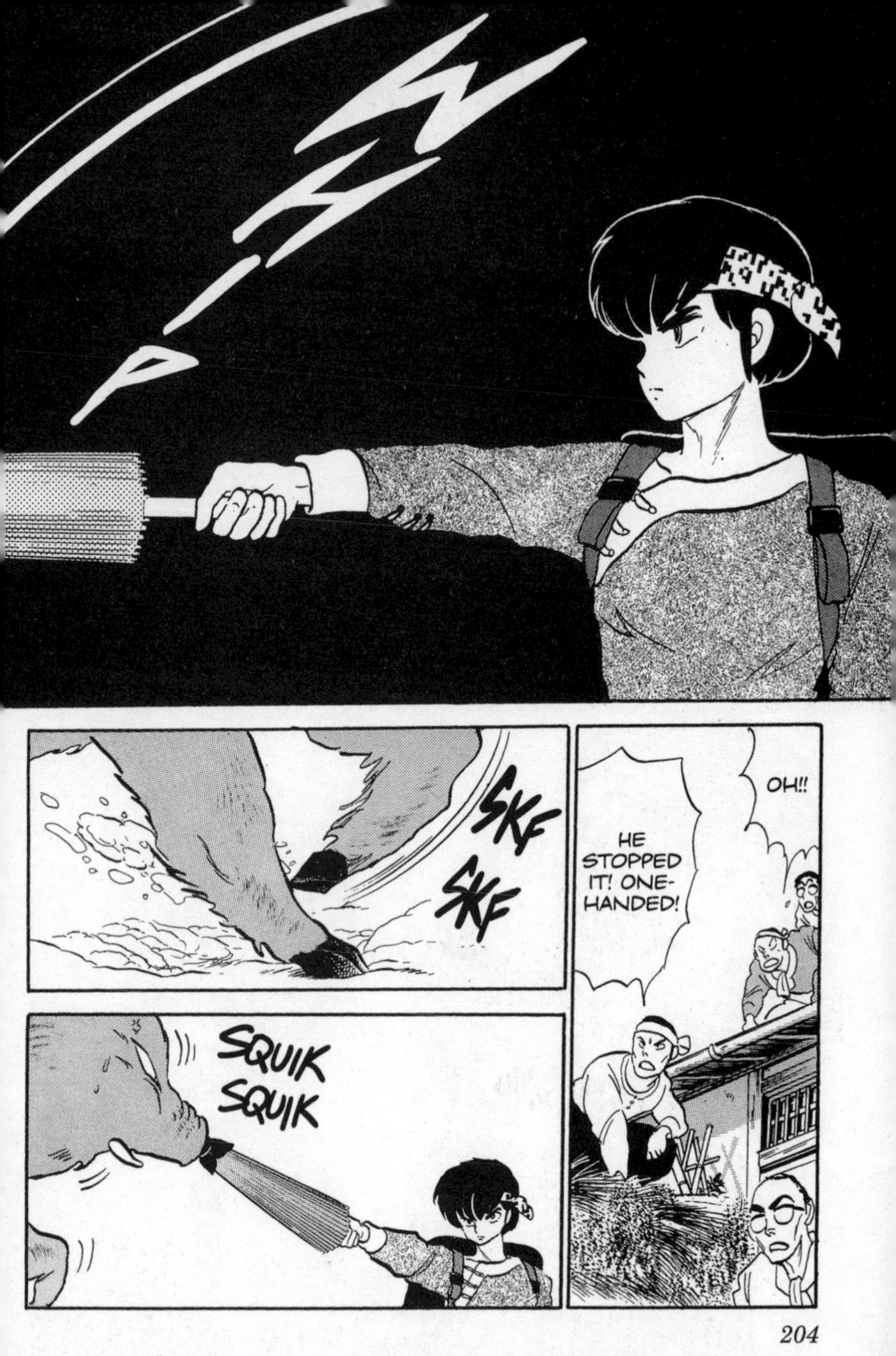
WHIP
OH!!
HE STOPPED IT! ONE-HANDED!
SKF SKF
SQUIK SQUIK

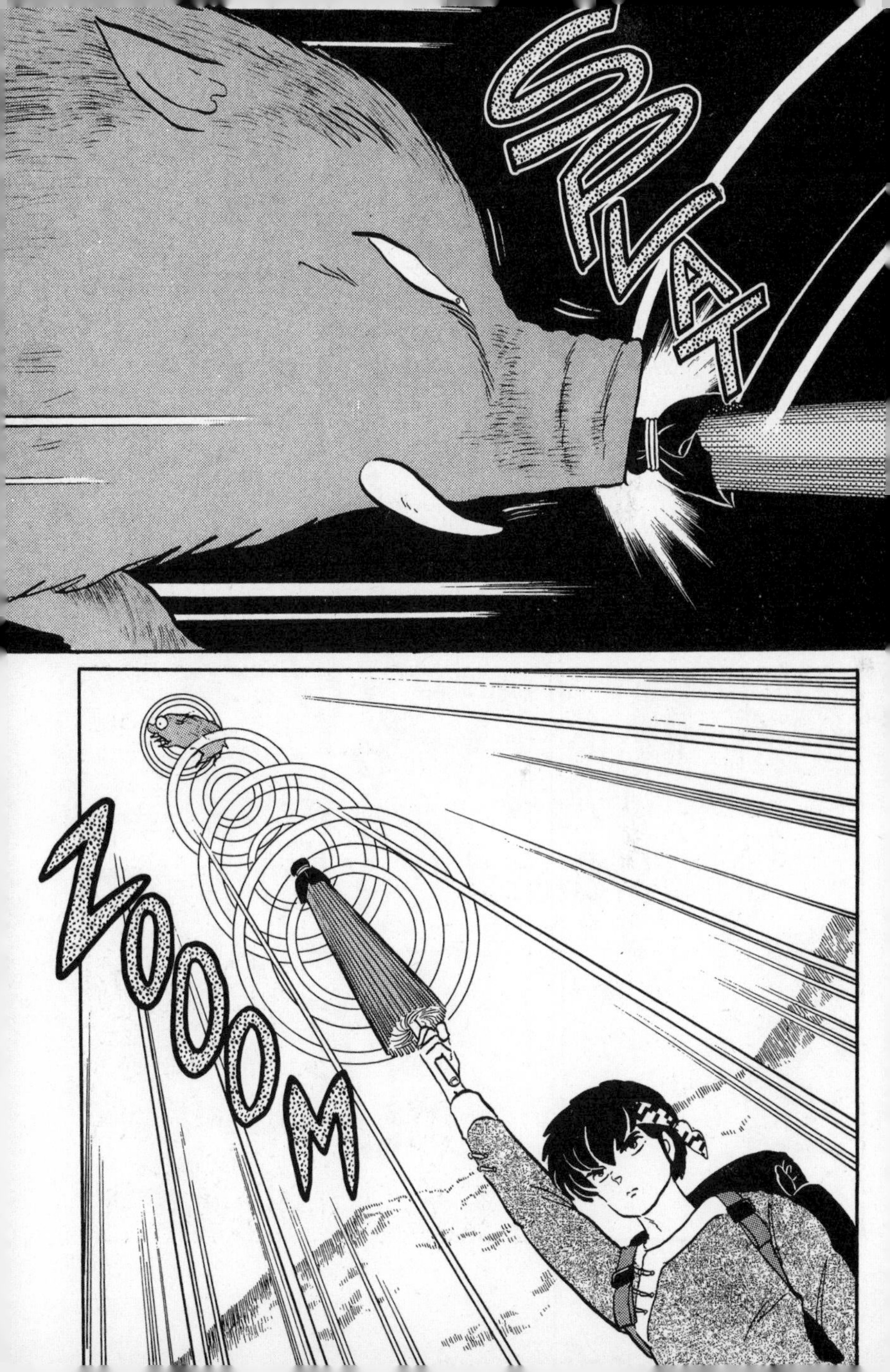
SPLAT
ZOOOM

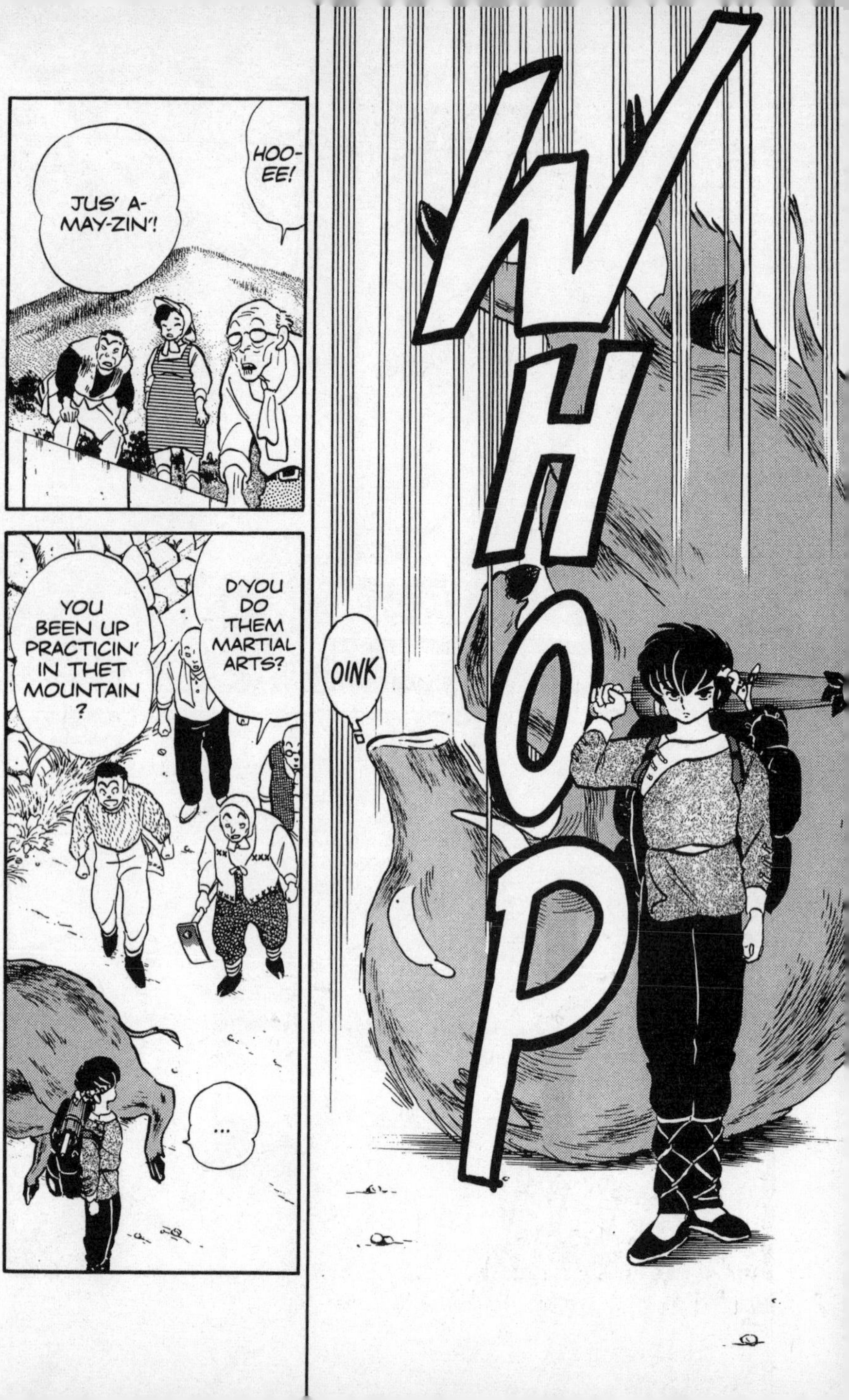
WHOP
OINK
HOO-EE!
JUS' A-MAY-ZIN'!
D'YOU DO THEM MARTIAL ARTS?
YOU BEEN UP PRACTICIN' IN THET MOUNTAIN?
...

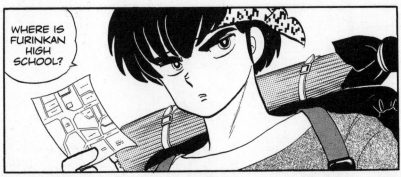

WHERE IS FURINKAN HIGH SCHOOL?
F'RIN-KAN HIGH SCHOOL?
OH-HO! A MAP, EH?
LEMME SEE 'ER.
SAY!
AIN'T THIS TOKYO?
THAT'S FIVE HUNNERT MILES NORTH O' HERE!
I SEE.
FORGIVE THE COMMOTION.
SPIN
FIGGER HE'S LOST?
HYUUUUU
SHFF SHFF
RANMA SAOTOME! PREPARE TO FACE ME!

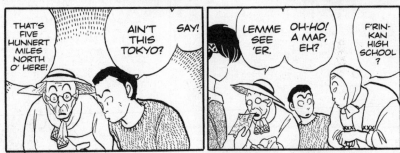

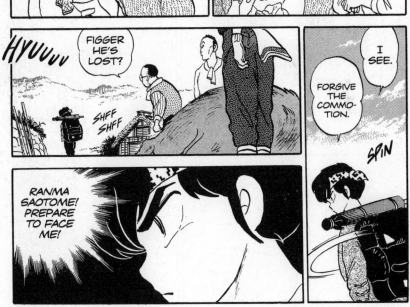

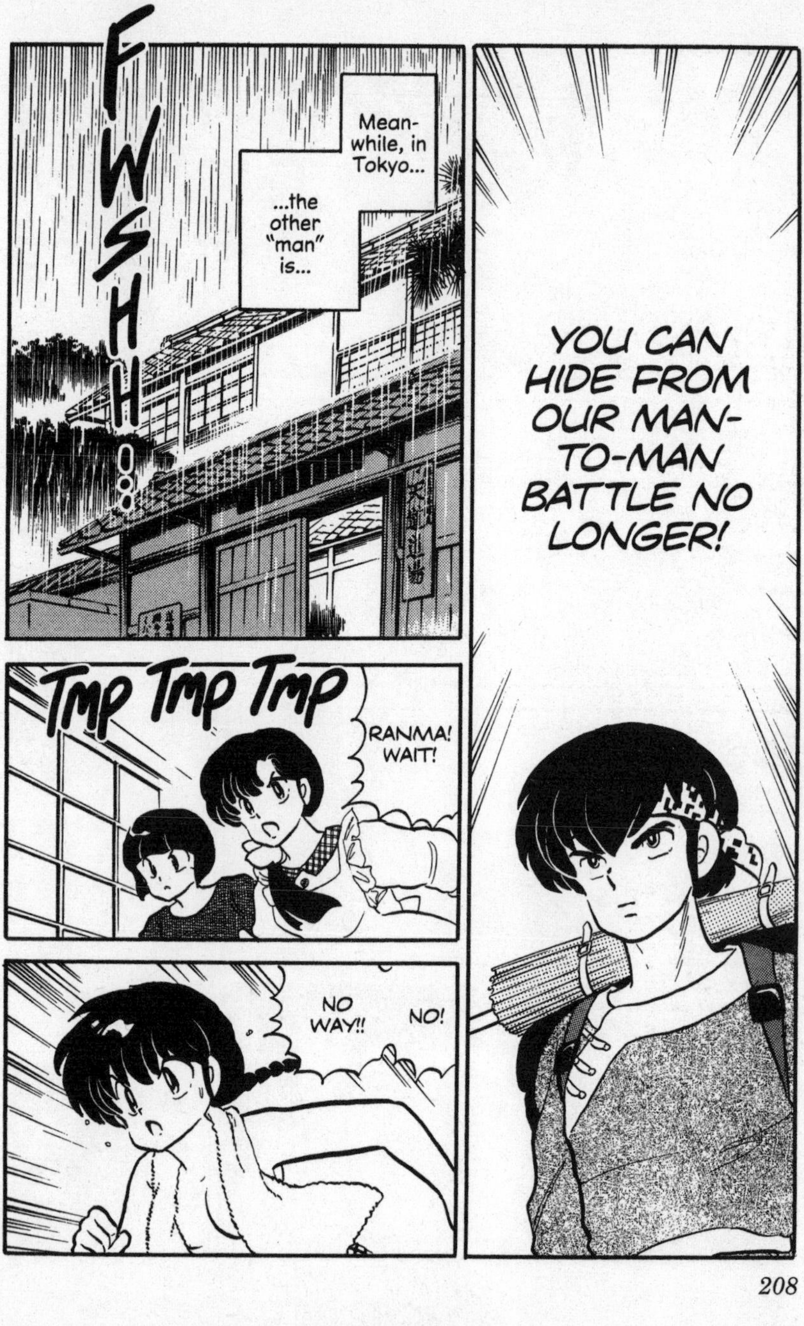
YOU CAN HIDE FROM OUR MAN-TO-MAN BATTLE NO LONGER!
Mean-while, in Tokyo...
...the other "man" is...
FWSHH...
Tmp Tmp Tmp
RANMA! WAIT!
NO!
NO WAY!!

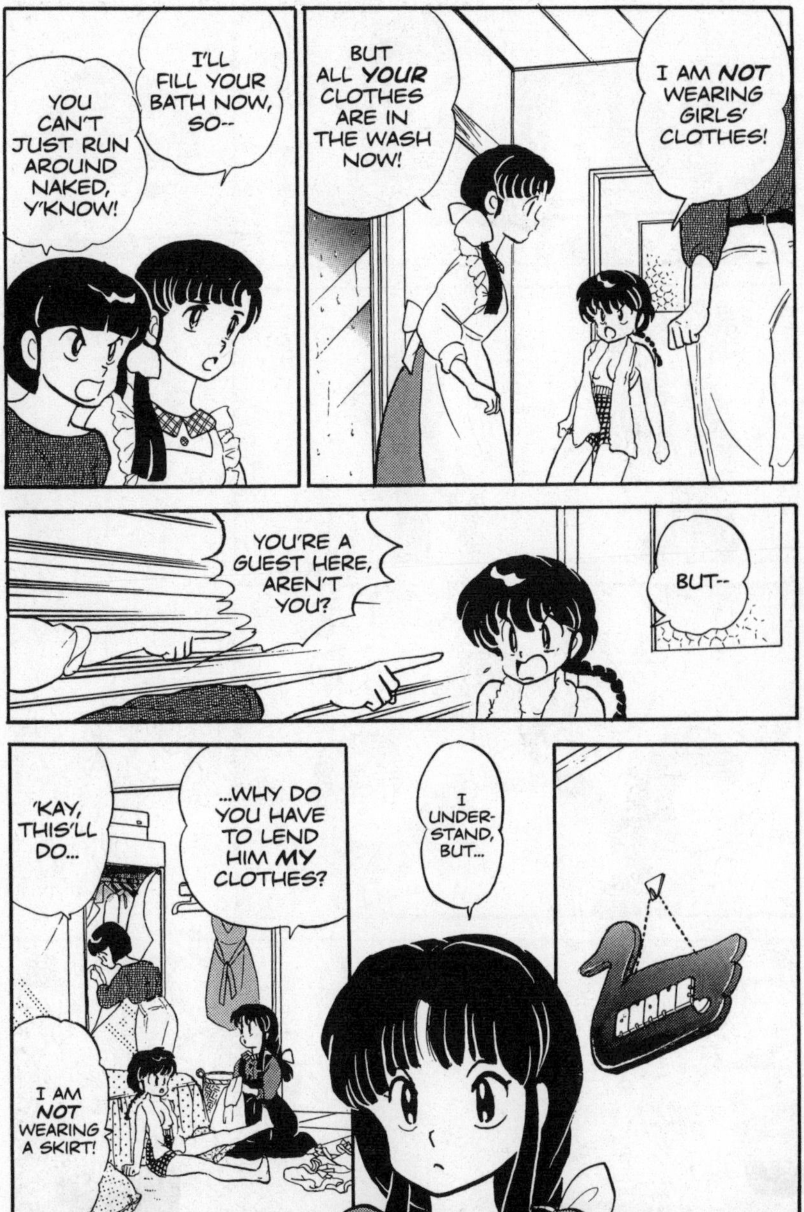
I AM NOT WEARING GIRLS' CLOTHES!
BUT ALL YOUR CLOTHES ARE IN THE WASH NOW!
I'LL FILL YOUR BATH NOW, SO--
YOU CAN'T JUST RUN AROUND NAKED, Y'KNOW!
BUT--
YOU'RE A GUEST HERE, AREN'T YOU?
I UNDERSTAND, BUT...
...WHY DO YOU HAVE TO LEND HIM MY CLOTHES?
'KAY, THIS'LL DO...
I AM NOT WEARING A SKIRT!

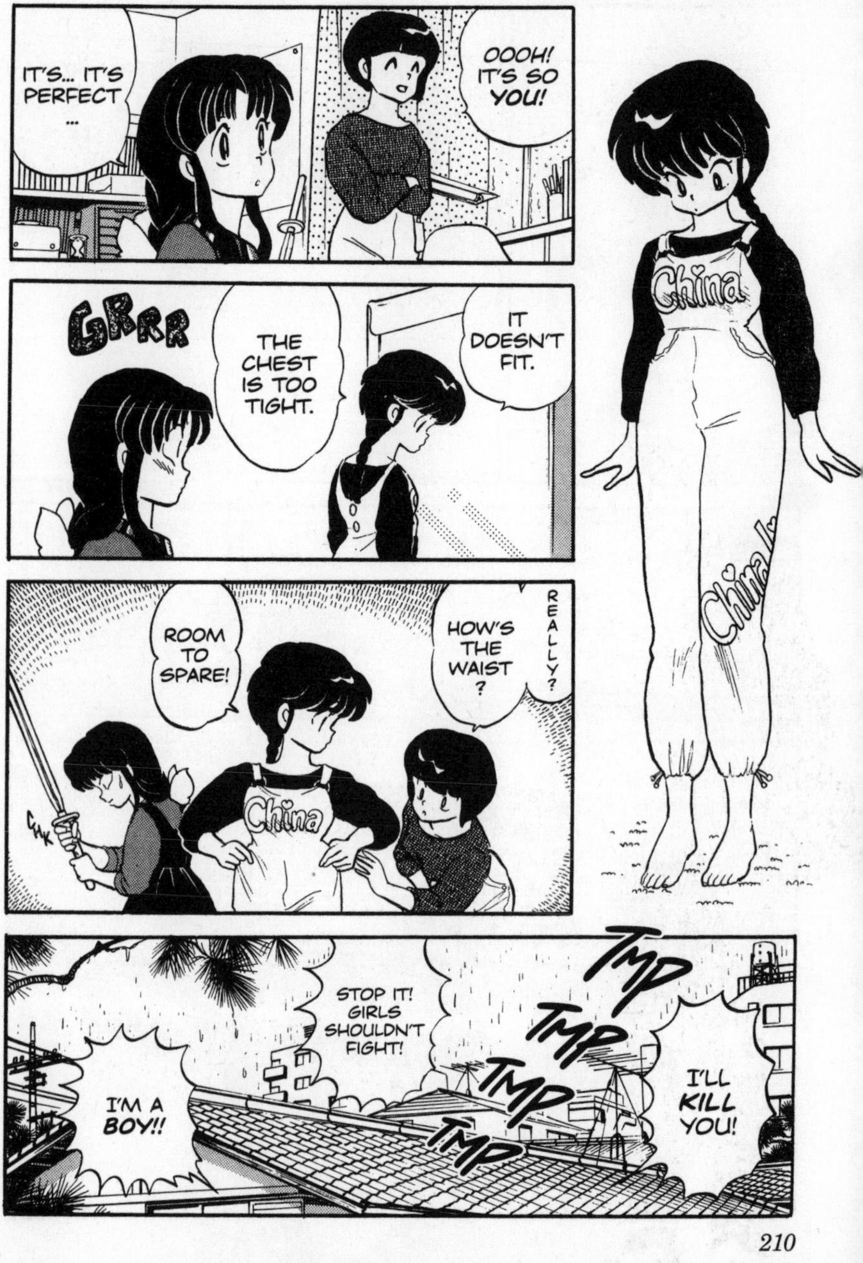
China
China
OOOH! IT'S SO YOU!
IT'S... IT'S PERFECT ...
IT DOESN'T FIT.
THE CHEST IS TOO TIGHT.
GRRR
REALLY?
HOW'S THE WAIST ?
ROOM TO SPARE!
China
CHAK
I'LL KILL YOU!
TMP TMP TMP TMP
STOP IT! GIRLS SHOULDN'T FIGHT!
I'M A BOY!!

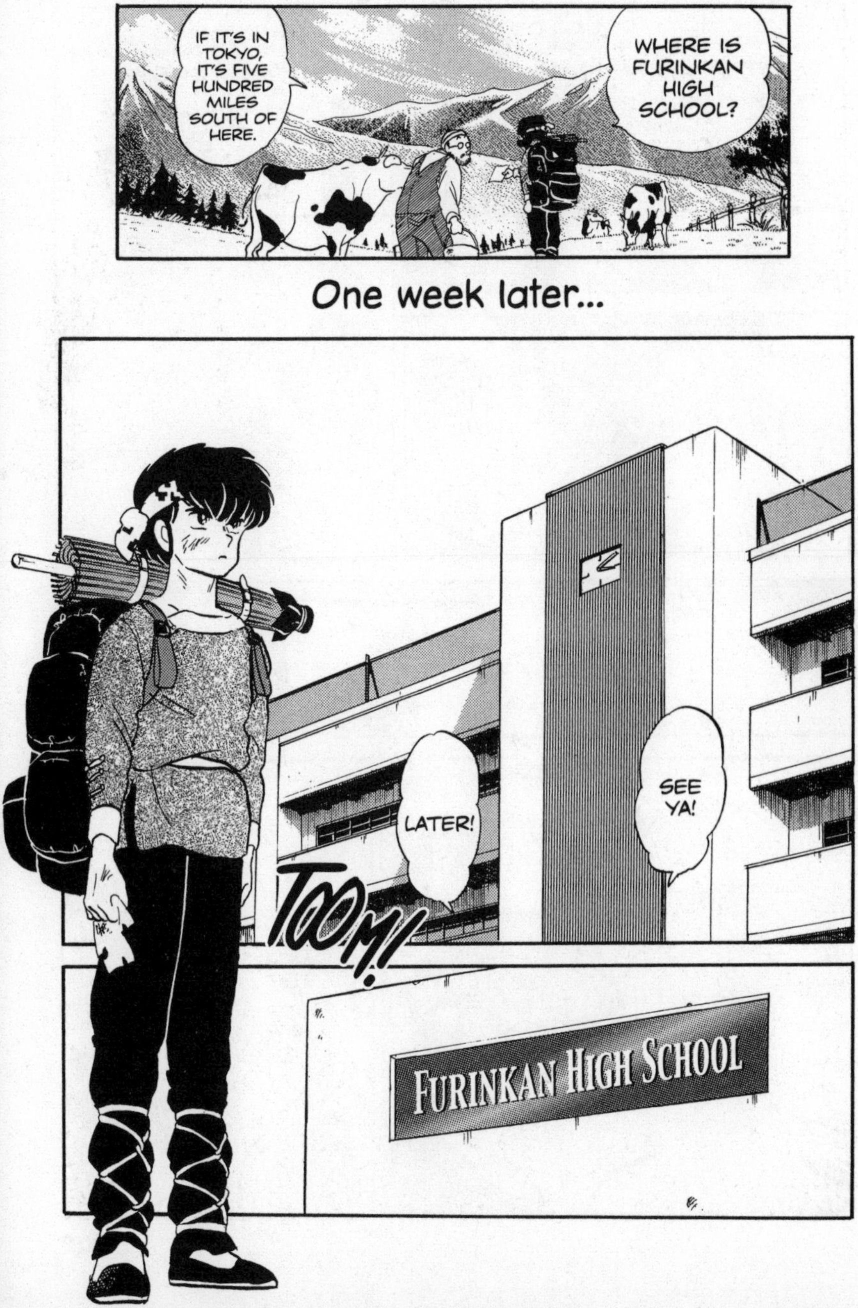
WHERE IS FURINKAN HIGH SCHOOL?
IF IT'S IN TOKYO, IT'S FIVE HUNDRED MILES SOUTH OF HERE.
One week later...
SEE YA!
LATER!
TOOM!
FURINKAN HIGH SCHOOL

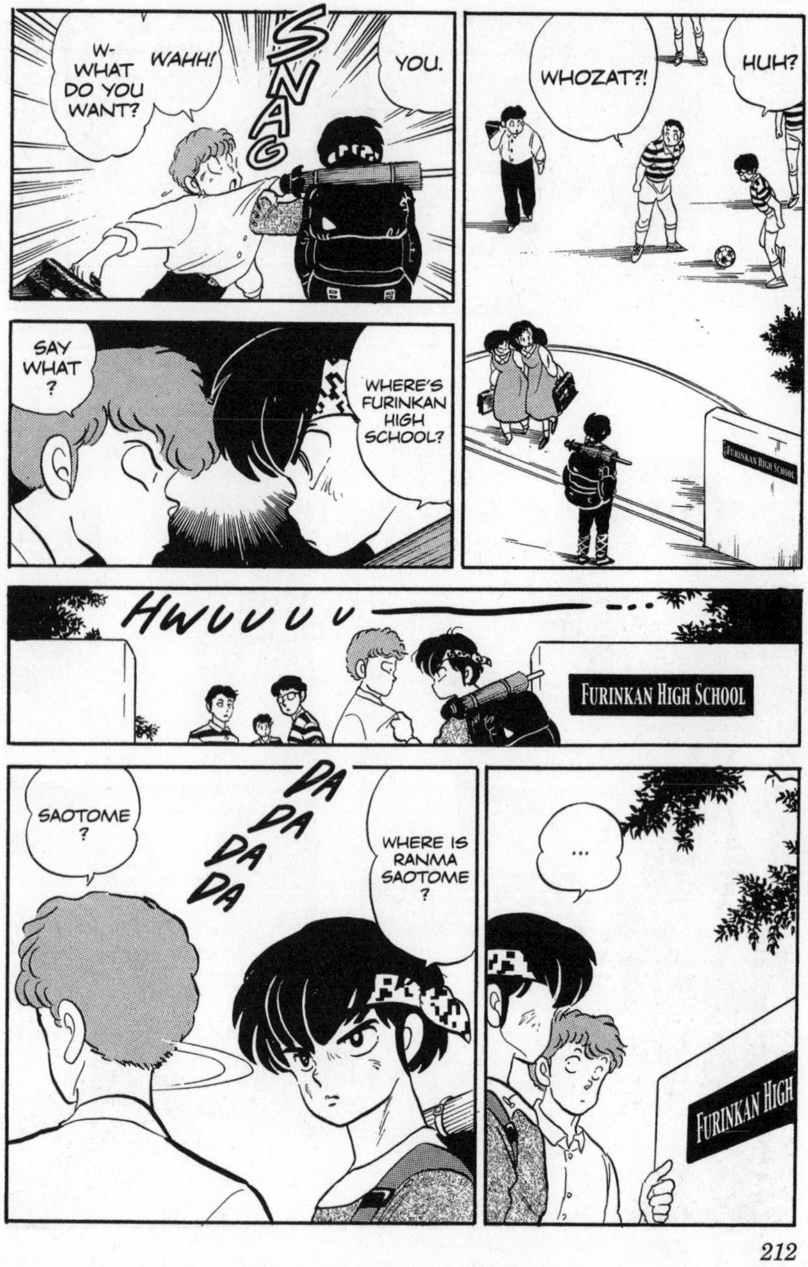
HUH?
WHOZAT?!
YOU.
SNAG
WAHH!
W- WHAT DO YOU WANT?
FURINKAN HIGH SCHOOL
WHERE'S FURINKAN HIGH SCHOOL?
SAY WHAT?
HWUUUUU
FURINKAN HIGH SCHOOL
...
FURINKAN HIGH
WHERE IS RANMA SAOTOME?
DA DA DA DA
SAOTOME?

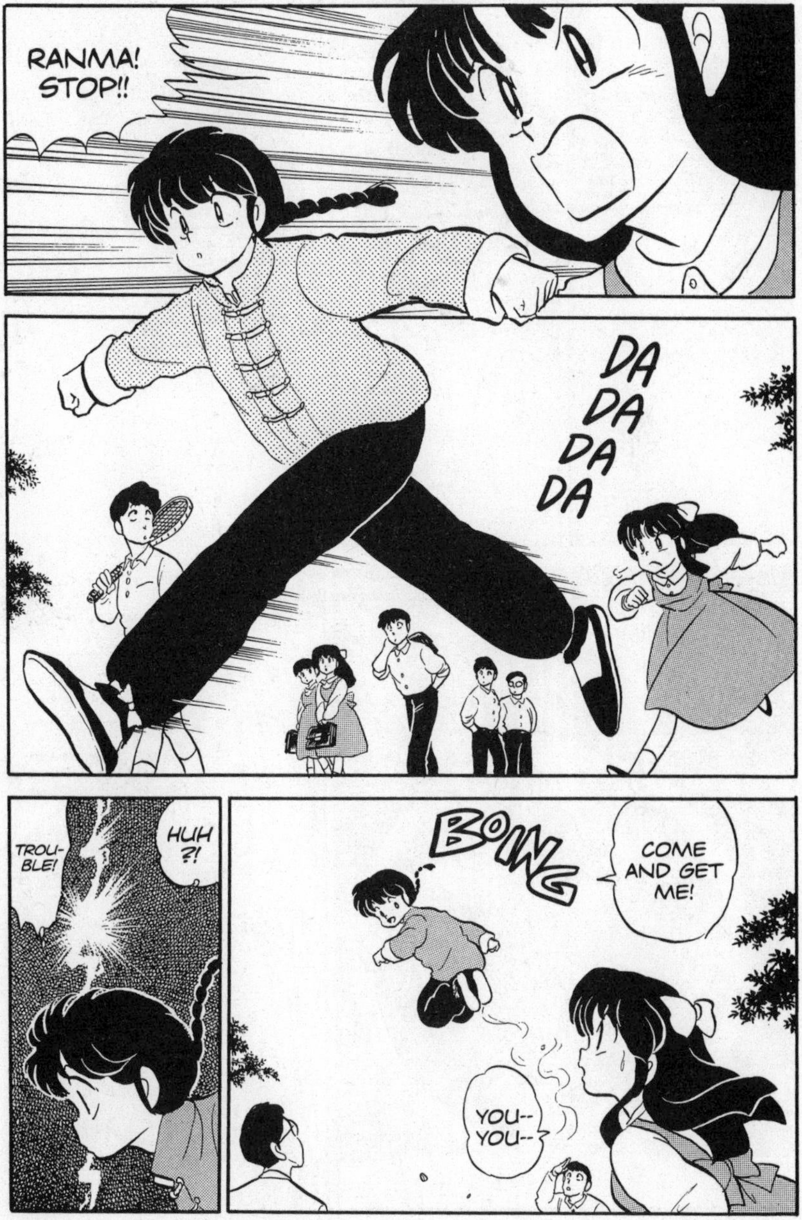
RANMA! STOP!!
DA DA DA DA
BOING
COME AND GET ME!
YOU-- YOU--
HUH ?!
TROU- BLE!

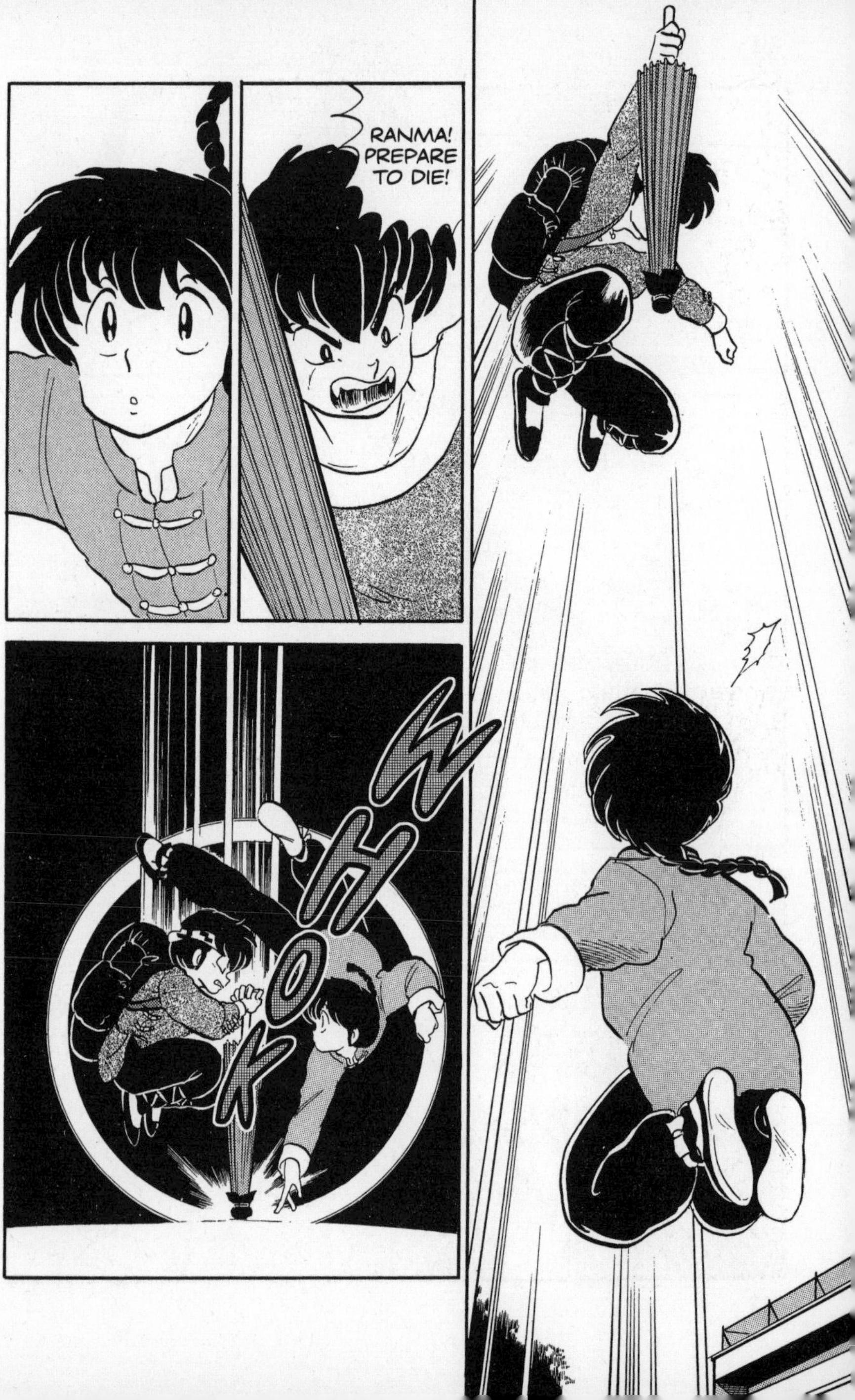
RANMA! PREPARE TO DIE!
WHOOK

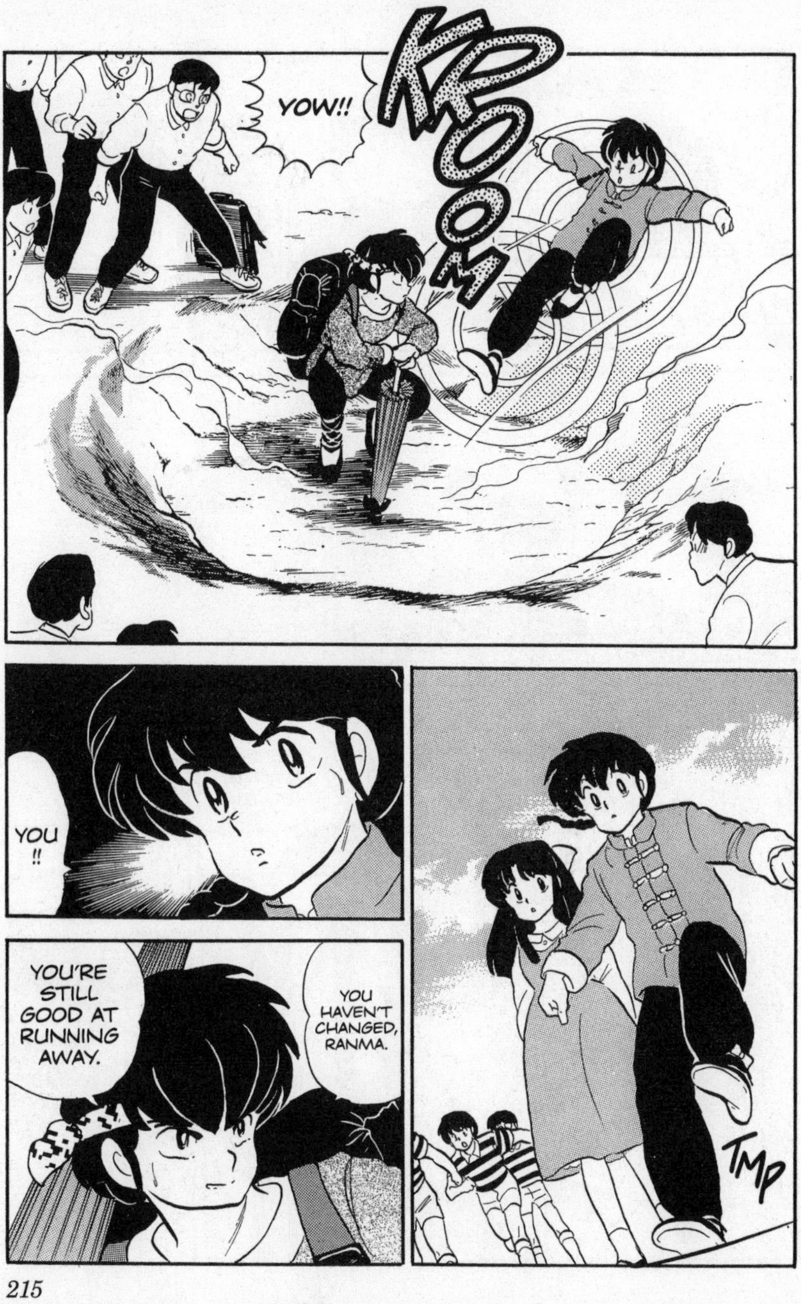
KROOM
YOW!!
TMP
YOU !!
YOU HAVEN'T CHANGED, RANMA.
YOU'RE STILL GOOD AT RUNNING AWAY.

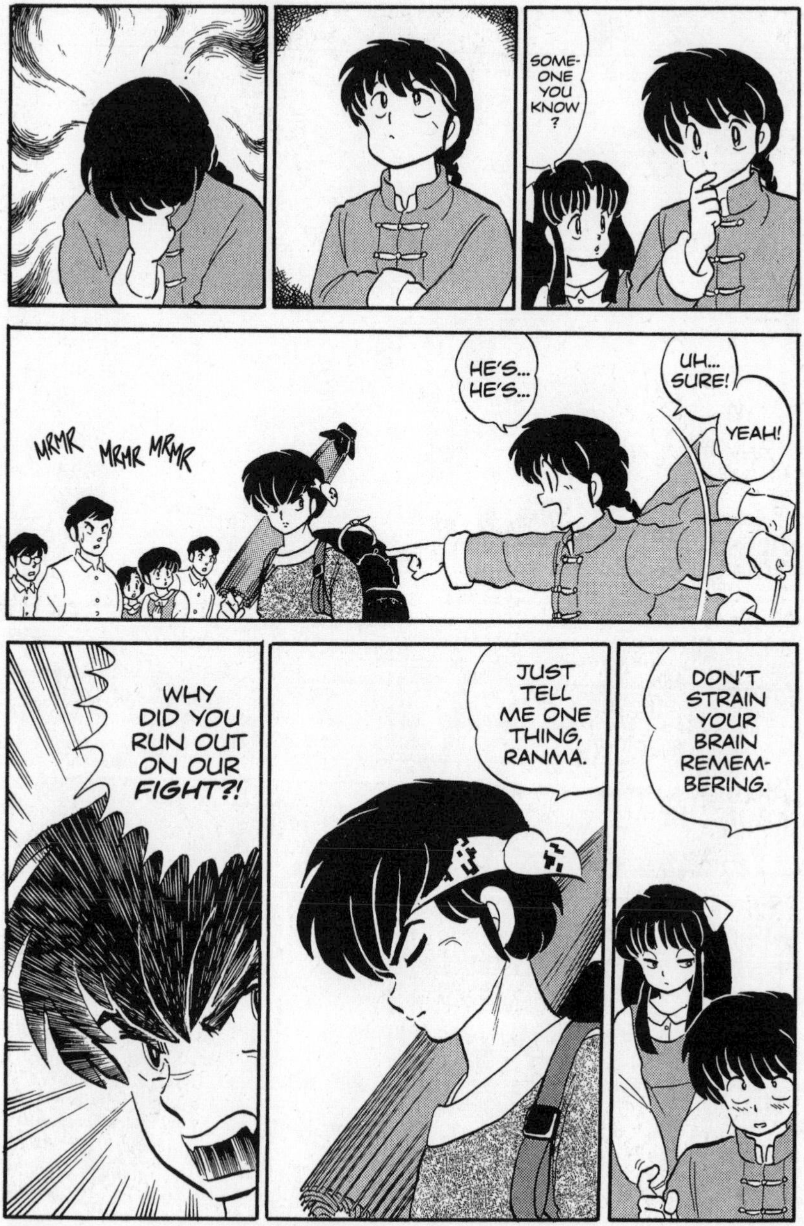
SOME-ONE YOU KNOW?
UH... SURE!
YEAH!
HE'S... HE'S...
MRMR MRMR MRMR
DON'T STRAIN YOUR BRAIN REMEM-BERING.
JUST TELL ME ONE THING, RANMA.
WHY DID YOU RUN OUT ON OUR *FIGHT*?!

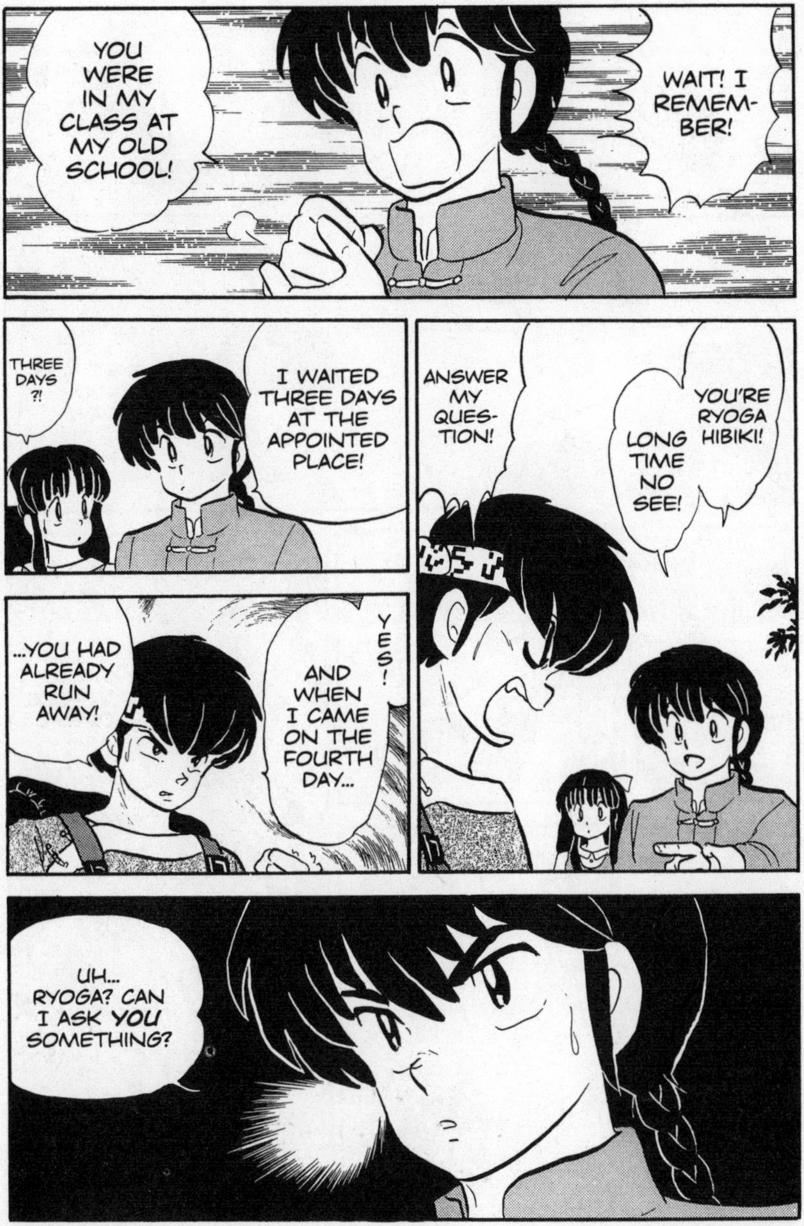
WAIT! I REMEMBER!
YOU WERE IN MY CLASS AT MY OLD SCHOOL!
YOU'RE RYOGA HIBIKI!
LONG TIME NO SEE!
ANSWER MY QUESTION!
I WAITED THREE DAYS AT THE APPOINTED PLACE!
THREE DAYS ?!
YES!
AND WHEN I CAME ON THE FOURTH DAY...
...YOU HAD ALREADY RUN AWAY!
UH... RYOGA? CAN I ASK *YOU* SOMETHING?

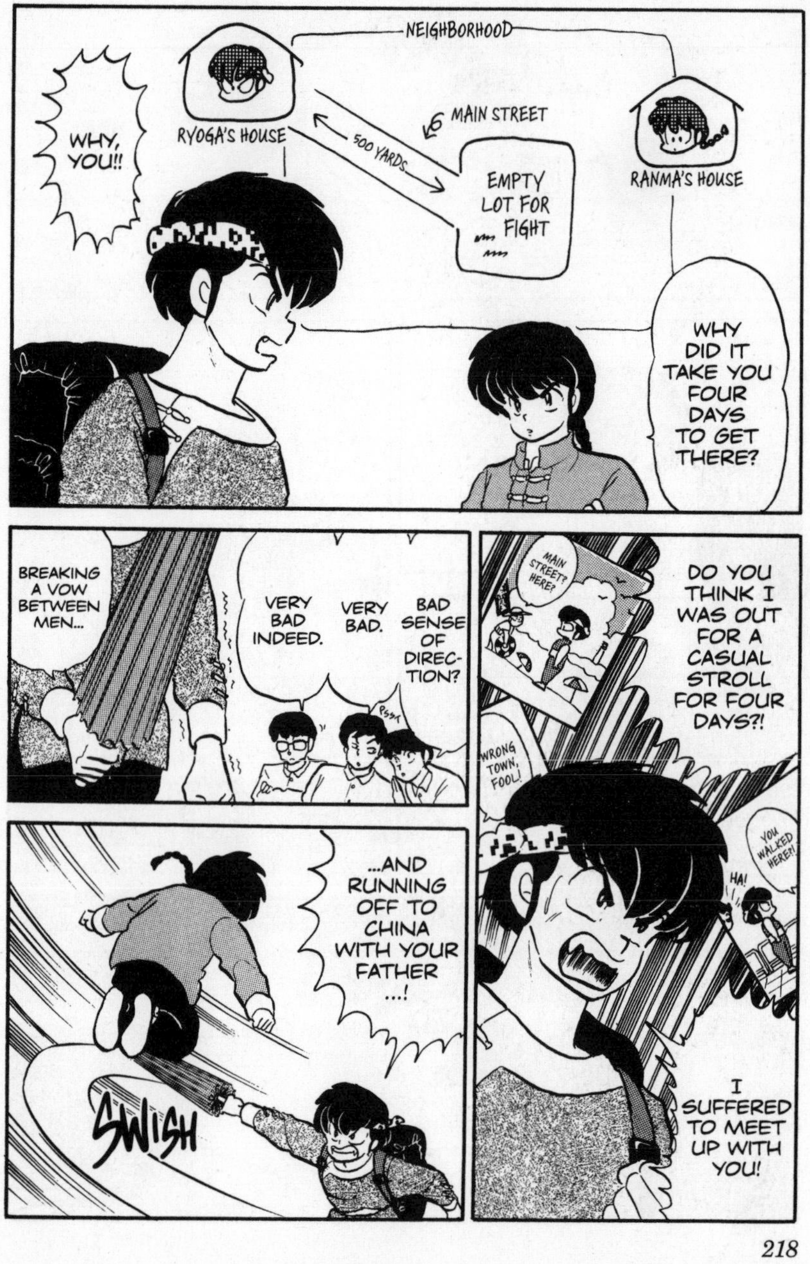
NEIGHBORHOOD
RANMA'S HOUSE
MAIN STREET
EMPTY LOT FOR FIGHT
500 YARDS
RYOGA'S HOUSE
WHY, YOU!!
WHY DID IT TAKE YOU FOUR DAYS TO GET THERE?
DO YOU THINK I WAS OUT FOR A CASUAL STROLL FOR FOUR DAYS?!
MAIN STREET? HERE?
WRONG TOWN, FOOL!
YOU WALKED HERE?!
HA!
I SUFFERED TO MEET UP WITH YOU!
BAD SENSE OF DIRECTION?
VERY BAD.
VERY BAD INDEED.
BREAKING A VOW BETWEEN MEN...
...AND RUNNING OFF TO CHINA WITH YOUR FATHER ...!
SWISH

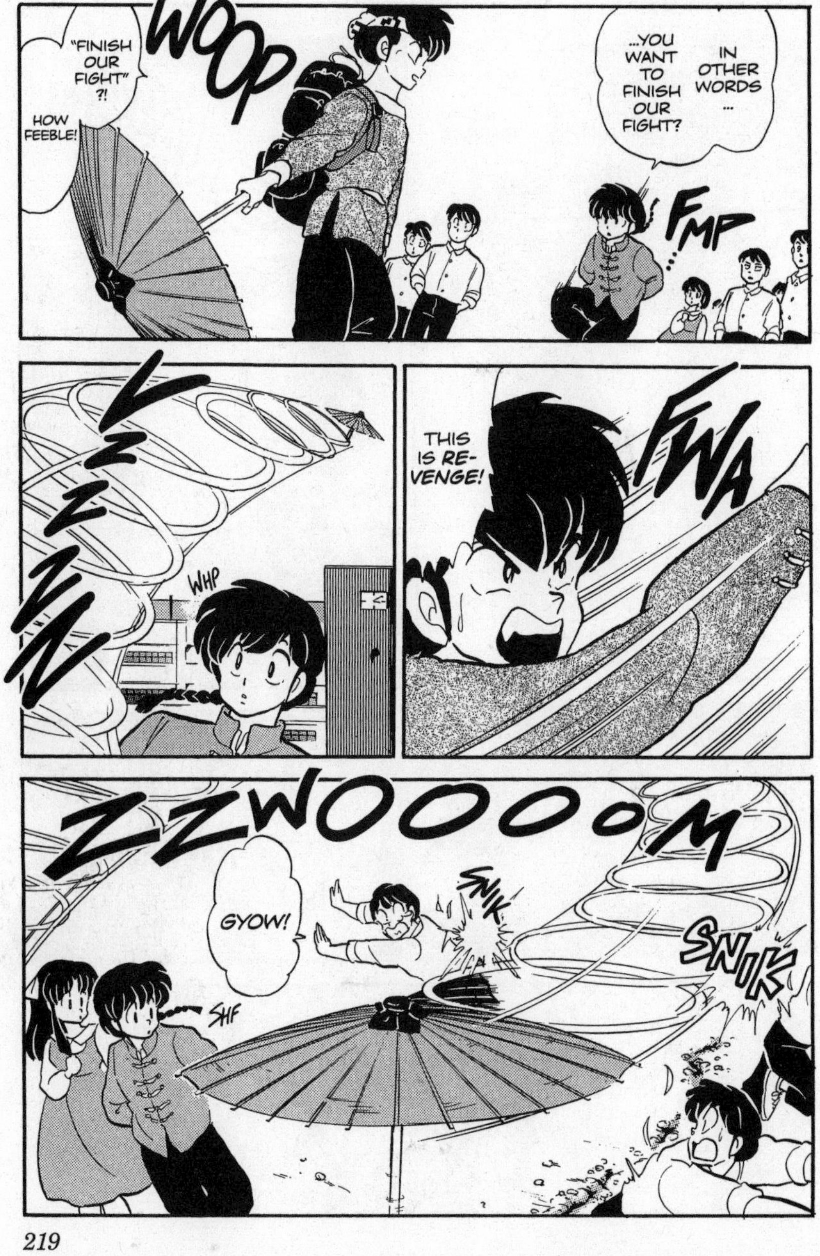
IN OTHER WORDS ...
...YOU WANT TO FINISH OUR FIGHT?
FMP
WOOP
"FINISH OUR FIGHT" ?!
HOW FEEBLE!
FWA
THIS IS RE-VENGE!
VZZNNN
WHP
ZZWOOOOOM
SNIK
SNIK
GYOW!
SHF

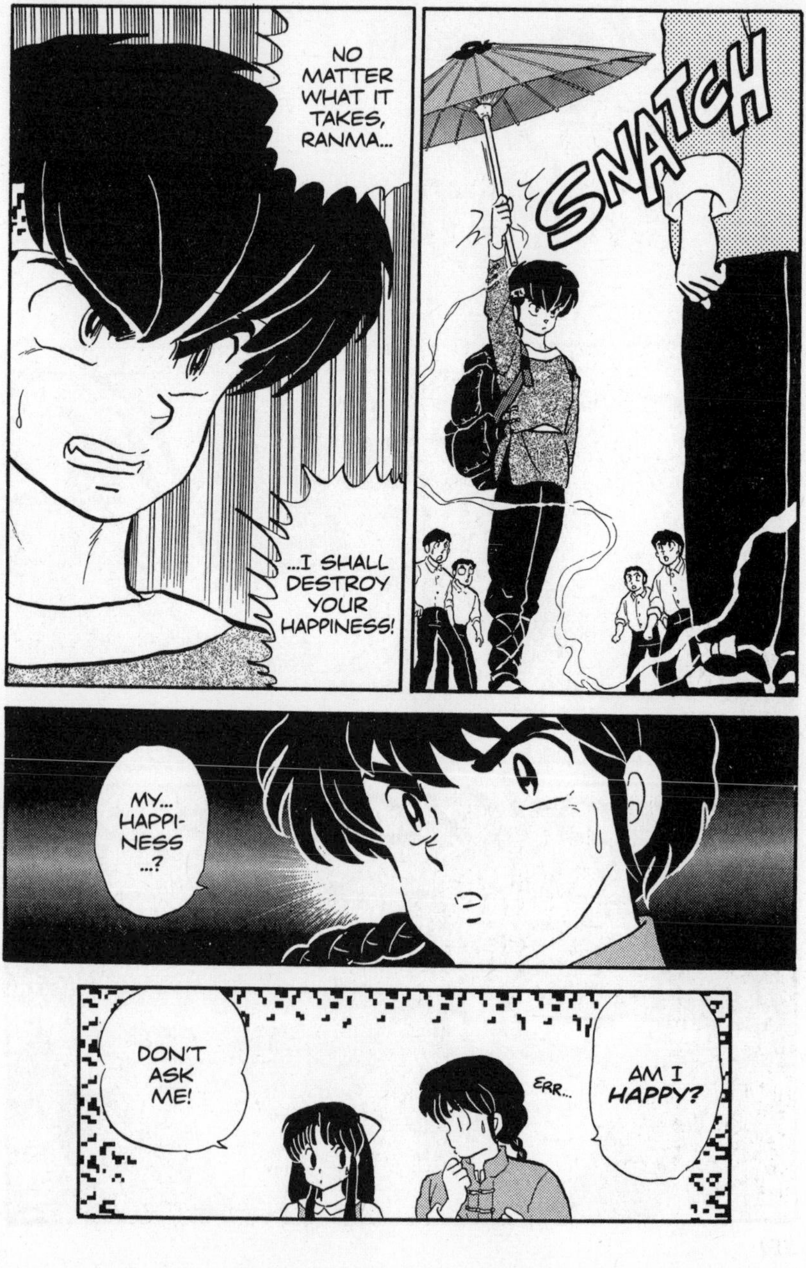
SNATCH
NO MATTER WHAT IT TAKES, RANMA...
...I SHALL DESTROY YOUR HAPPINESS!
MY... HAPPI-NESS ...?
AM I HAPPY?
ERR...
DON'T ASK ME!

# PART 11
# BREAD FEUD

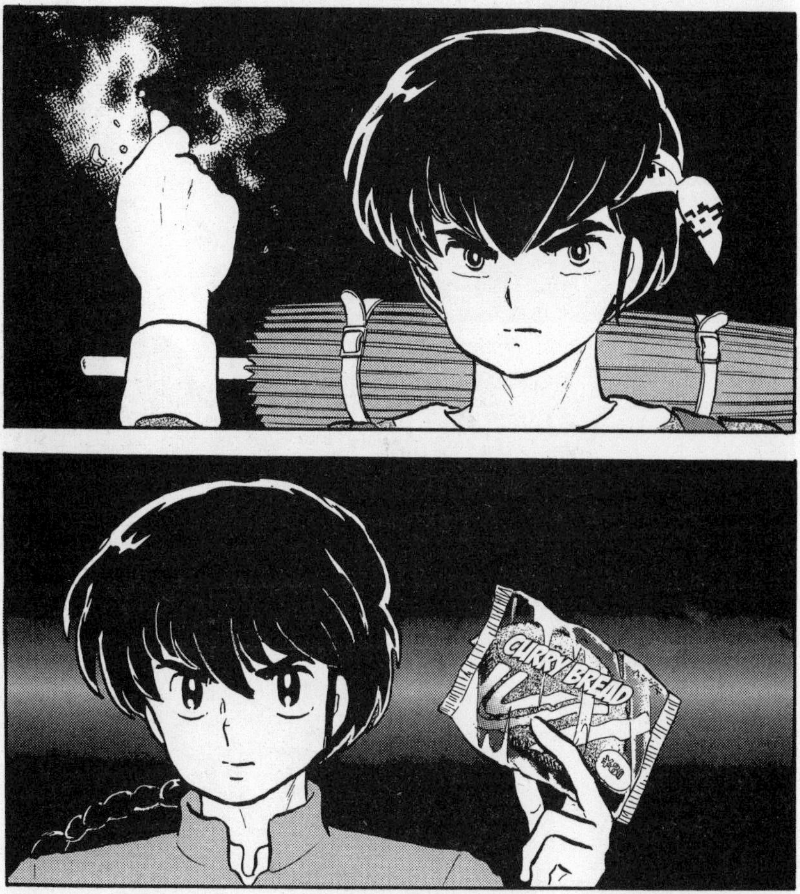
CURRY BREAD

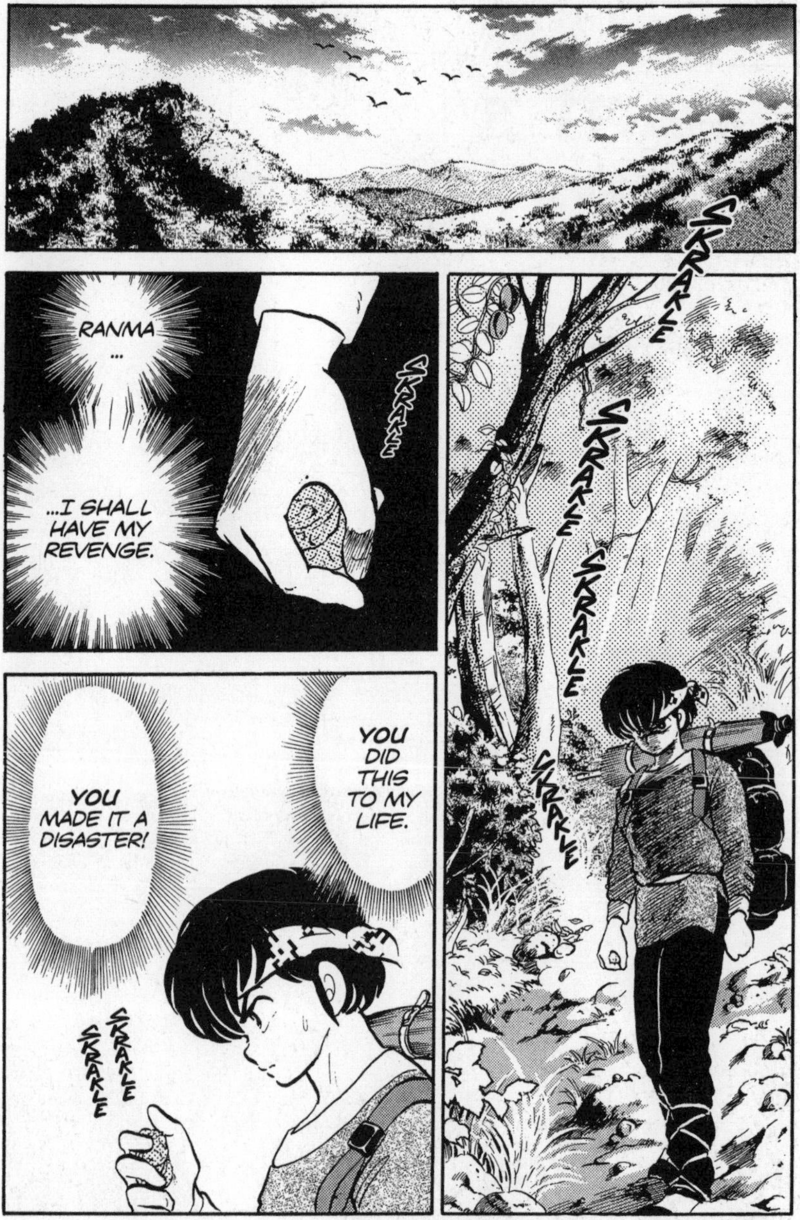
SKRAKLE
SKRAKLE
SKRAKLE
SKRAKLE
RANMA...
...I SHALL HAVE MY REVENGE.
SKRAKLE
YOU DID THIS TO MY LIFE.
YOU MADE IT A DISASTER!
SKRAKLE
SKRAKLE

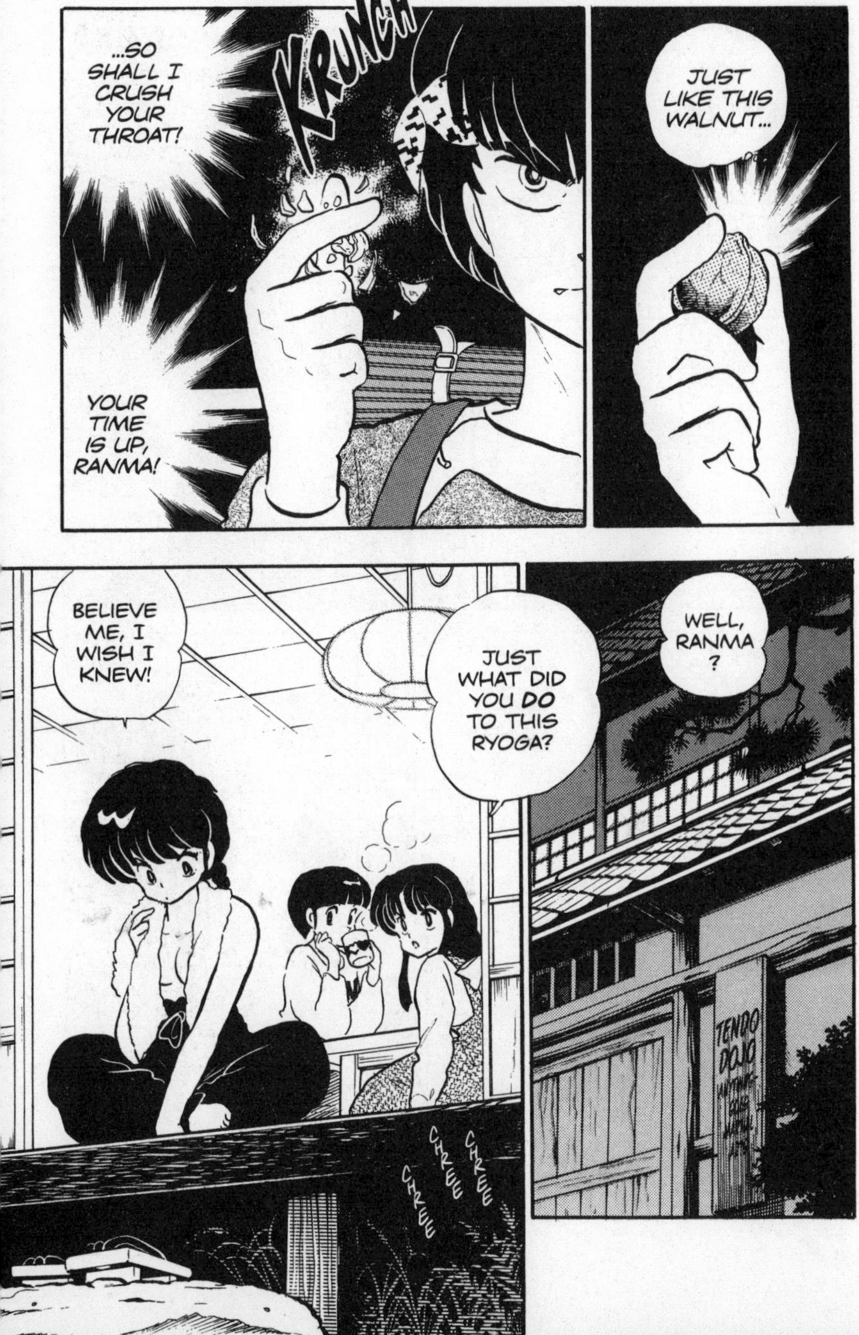
JUST LIKE THIS WALNUT...
KRUNCH
...SO SHALL I CRUSH YOUR THROAT!
YOUR TIME IS UP, RANMA!
WELL, RANMA?
TENDO DOJO
JUST WHAT DID YOU DO TO THIS RYOGA?
BELIEVE ME, I WISH I KNEW!
CHREE CHREE CHREE

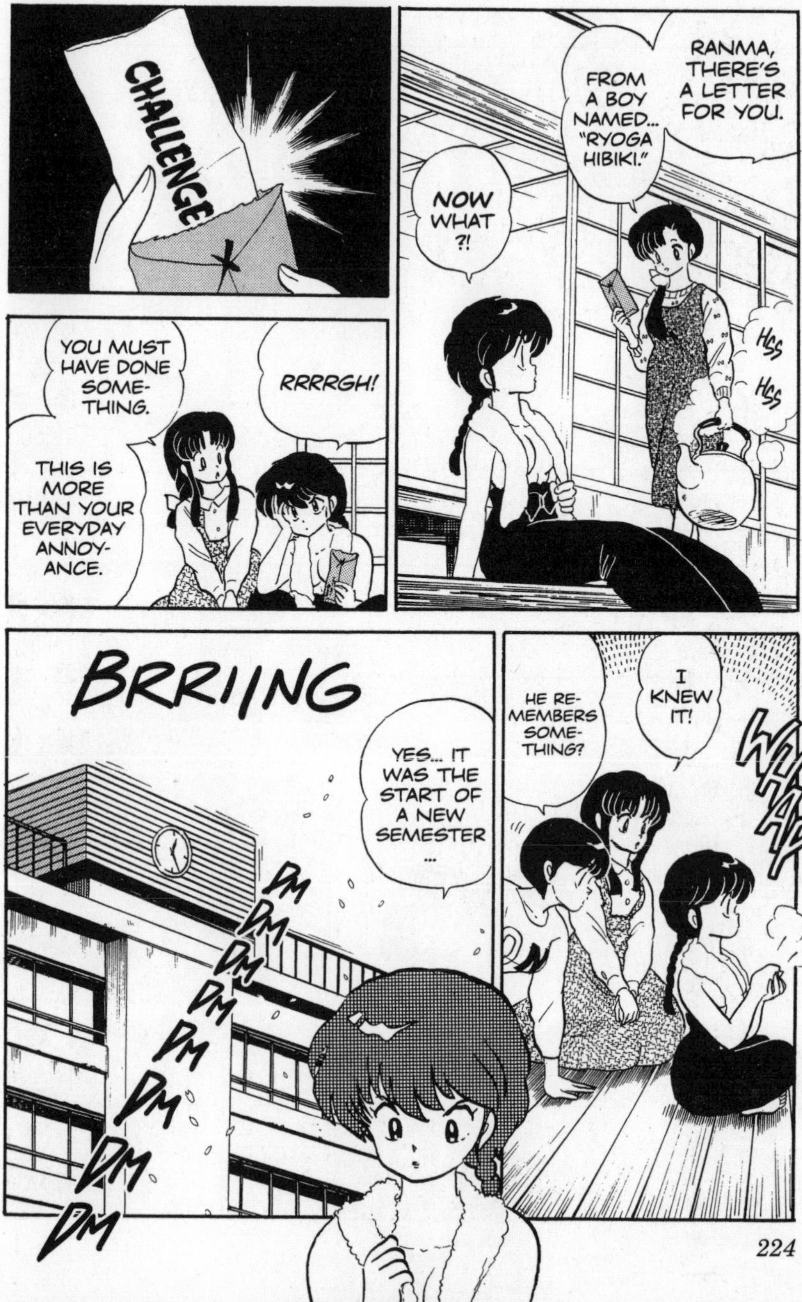
RANMA, THERE'S A LETTER FOR YOU.
FROM A BOY NAMED... "RYOGA HIBIKI."
NOW WHAT ?!
CHALLENGE
RRRRGH!
YOU MUST HAVE DONE SOME-THING.
THIS IS MORE THAN YOUR EVERYDAY ANNOY-ANCE.
WHAP
I KNEW IT!
HE RE-MEMBERS SOME-THING?
YES... IT WAS THE START OF A NEW SEMESTER ...
BRRIING
DM DM DM DM DM DM DM DM

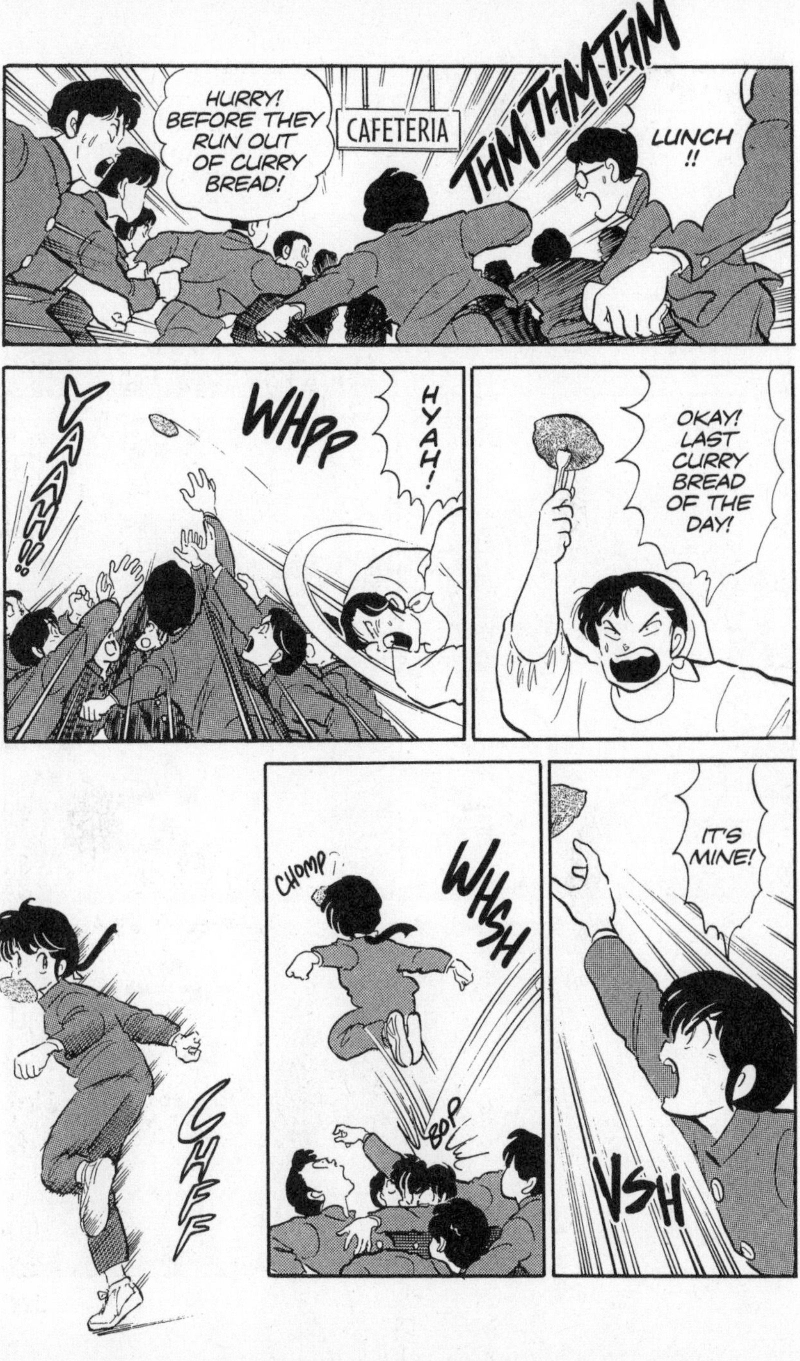
THMTHMTHM
LUNCH !!
CAFETERIA
HURRY! BEFORE THEY RUN OUT OF CURRY BREAD!
OKAY! LAST CURRY BREAD OF THE DAY!
HYAH!
WHPP
YAAAH!!
IT'S MINE!
VSH
WHSH
CHOMP
BOP
Heh
CHFF

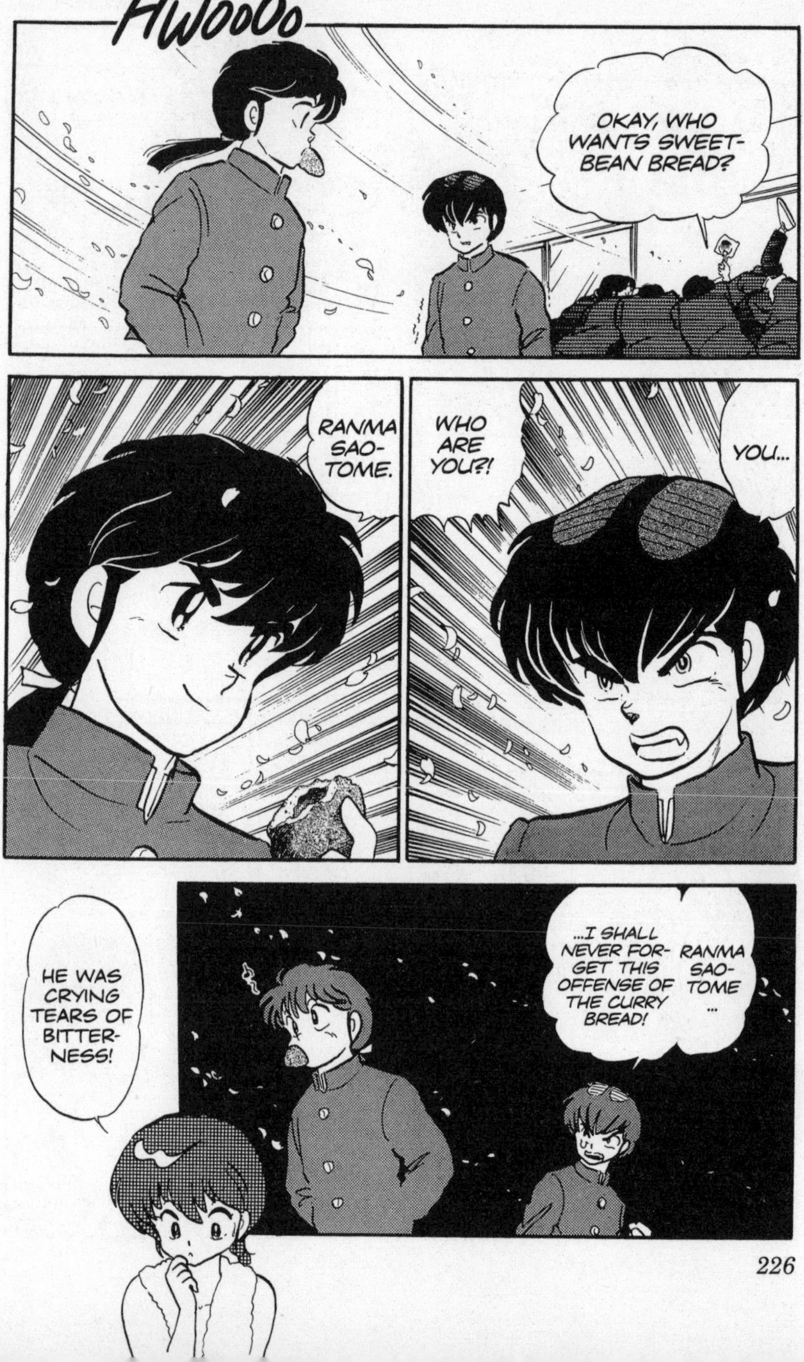
HWOOOO
OKAY, WHO WANTS SWEET-BEAN BREAD?
YOU...
WHO ARE YOU?!
RANMA SAO-TOME.
RANMA SAO-TOME ...
...I SHALL NEVER FOR-GET THIS OFFENSE OF THE CURRY BREAD!
HE WAS CRYING TEARS OF BITTER-NESS!

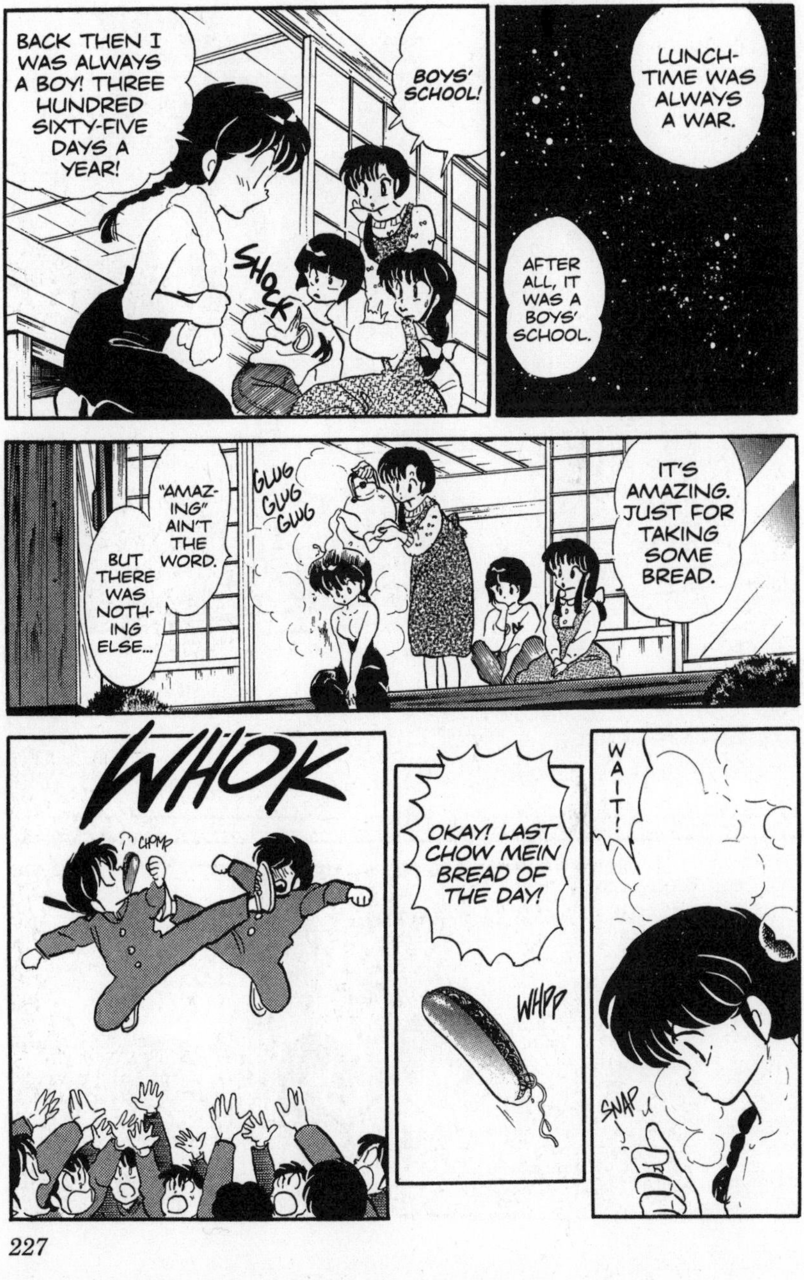
LUNCH-TIME WAS ALWAYS A WAR.
AFTER ALL, IT WAS A BOYS' SCHOOL.
BOYS' SCHOOL!
BACK THEN I WAS ALWAYS A BOY! THREE HUNDRED SIXTY-FIVE DAYS A YEAR!
SHOCK
IT'S AMAZING. JUST FOR TAKING SOME BREAD.
GLUG GLUG GLUG
"AMAZING" AIN'T THE WORD.
BUT THERE WAS NOTHING ELSE...
WAIT!
SNAP
OKAY! LAST CHOW MEIN BREAD OF THE DAY!
WHPP
WHOK

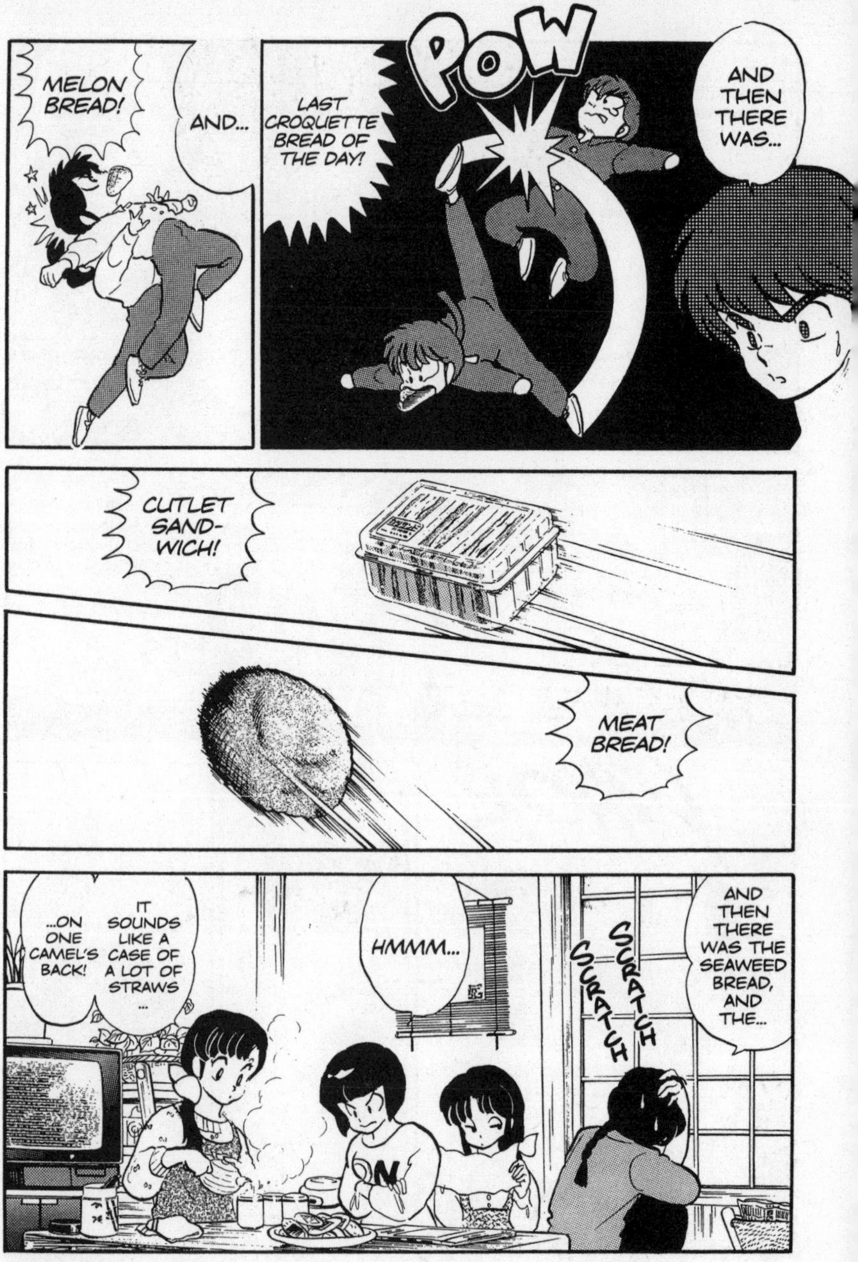
AND THEN THERE WAS...
POW
LAST CROQUETTE BREAD OF THE DAY!
AND...
MELON BREAD!
CUTLET SAND-WICH!
MEAT BREAD!
AND THEN THERE WAS THE SEAWEED BREAD, AND THE...
SCRATCH
SCRATCH
HMMM...
IT SOUNDS LIKE A CASE OF A LOT OF STRAWS ...
...ON ONE CAMEL'S BACK!

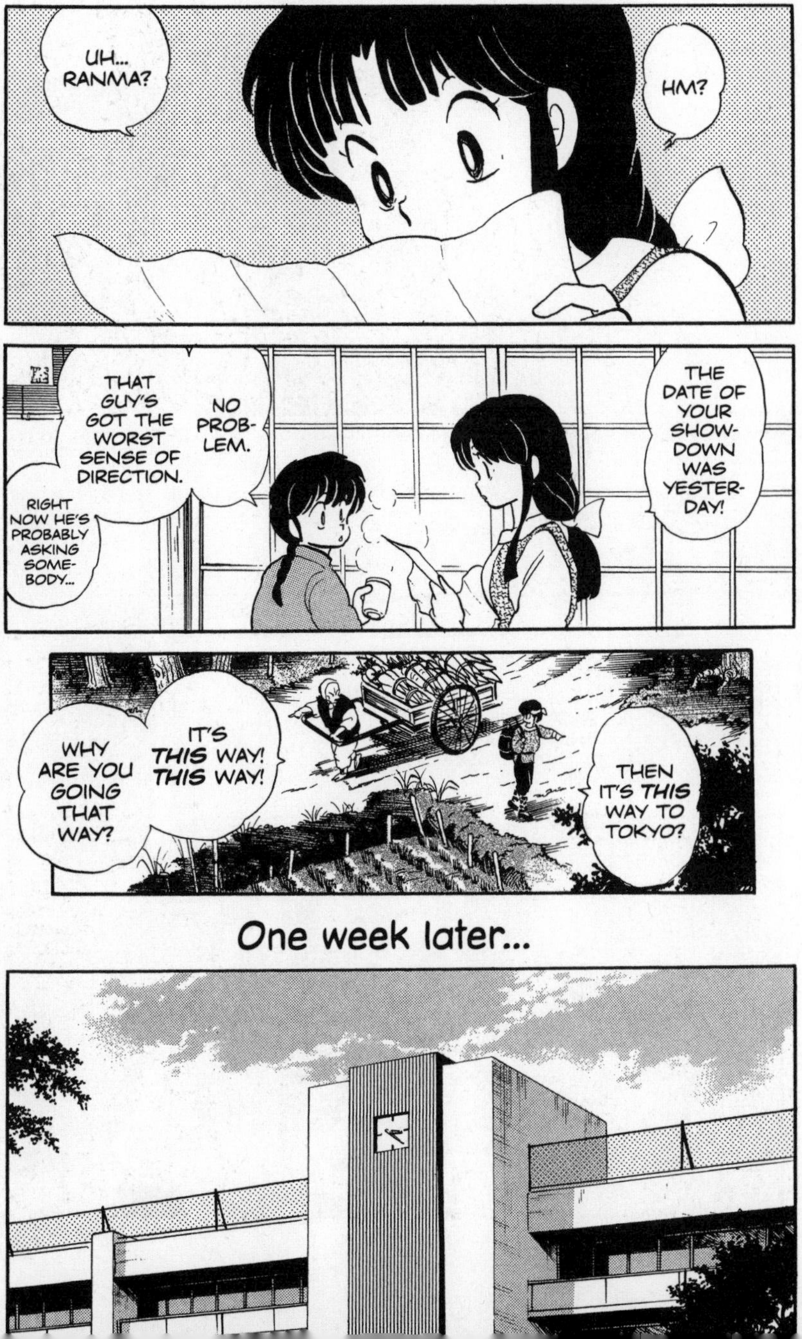
HM?
UH... RANMA?
THE DATE OF YOUR SHOW-DOWN WAS YESTER-DAY!
NO PROB-LEM.
THAT GUY'S GOT THE WORST SENSE OF DIRECTION.
RIGHT NOW HE'S PROBABLY ASKING SOME-BODY...
THEN IT'S **THIS** WAY TO TOKYO?
IT'S **THIS** WAY! **THIS** WAY!
WHY ARE YOU GOING THAT WAY?
One week later...

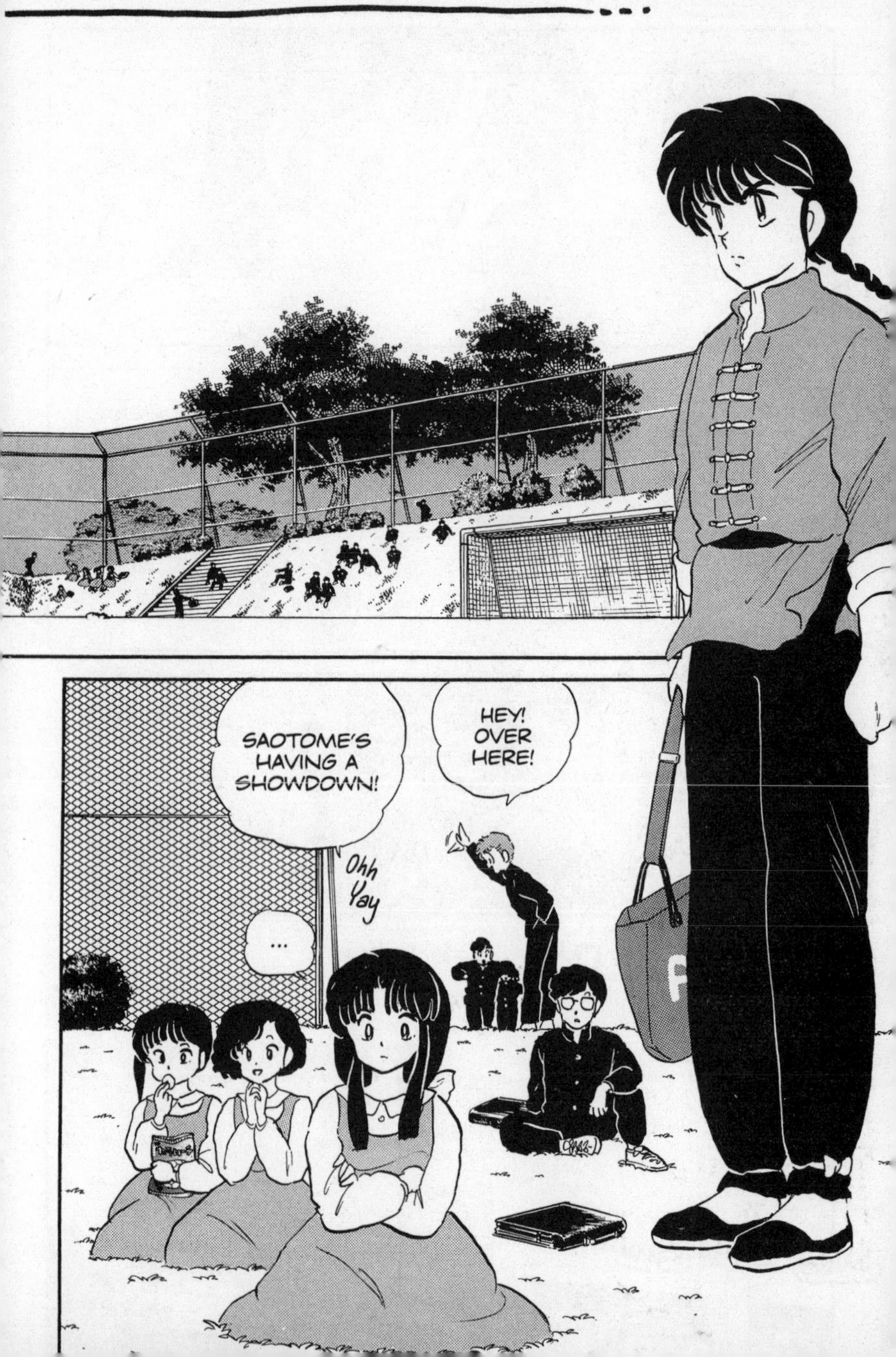
HEY! OVER HERE!
SAOTOME'S HAVING A SHOWDOWN!
Ohh Yay
...

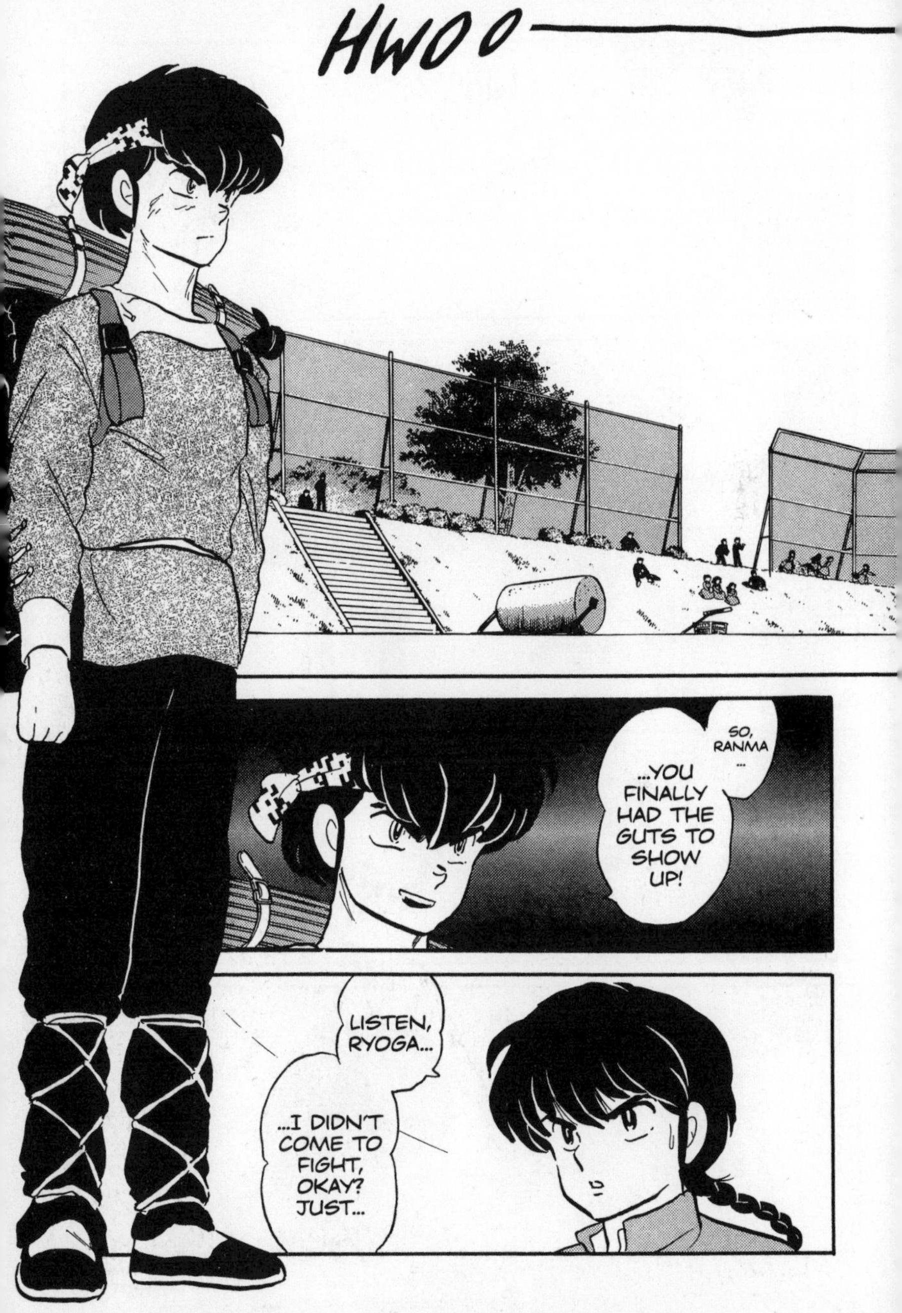
HWOO
SO, RANMA...
...YOU FINALLY HAD THE GUTS TO SHOW UP!
LISTEN, RYOGA...
...I DIDN'T COME TO FIGHT, OKAY? JUST...

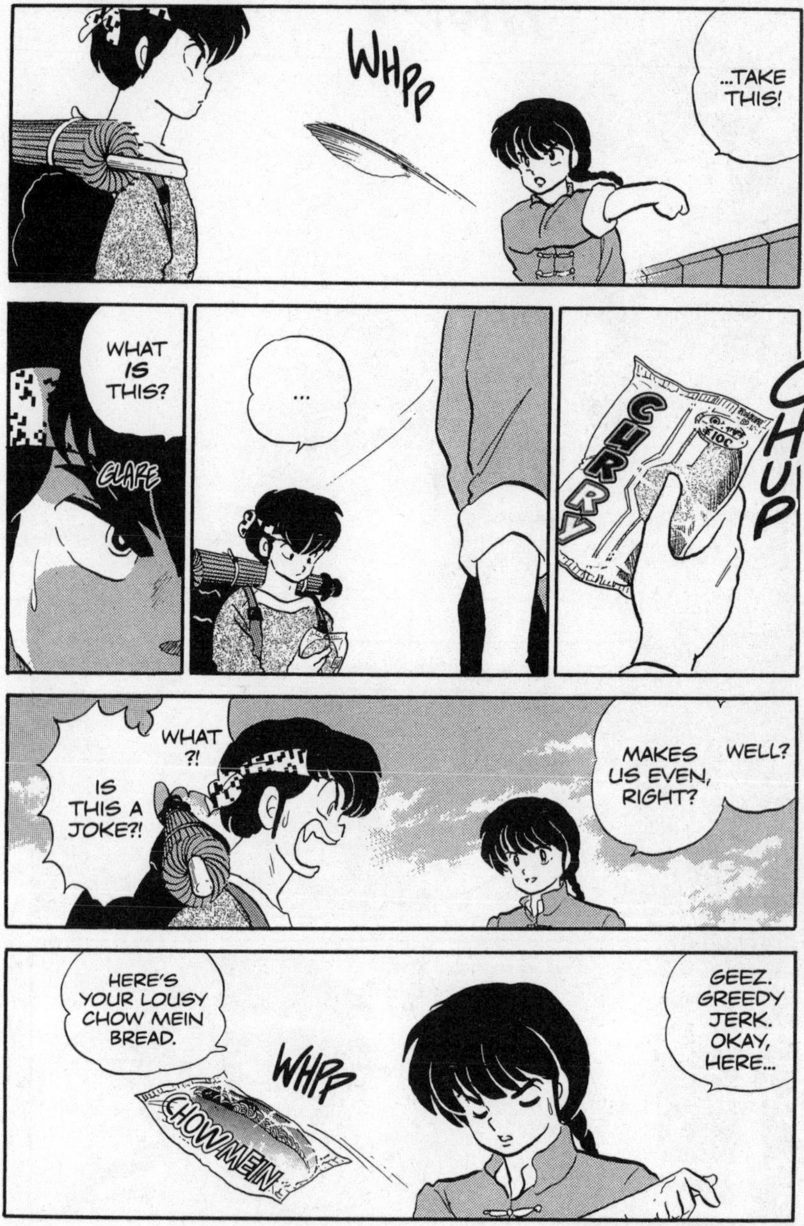

...TAKE THIS!
WHPP
CHUP
CURRY
...
WHAT IS THIS?
GLARE
WELL?
MAKES US EVEN, RIGHT?
WHAT?!
IS THIS A JOKE?!
GEEZ. GREEDY JERK. OKAY, HERE...
WHPP
HERE'S YOUR LOUSY CHOW MEIN BREAD.
CHOW MEIN

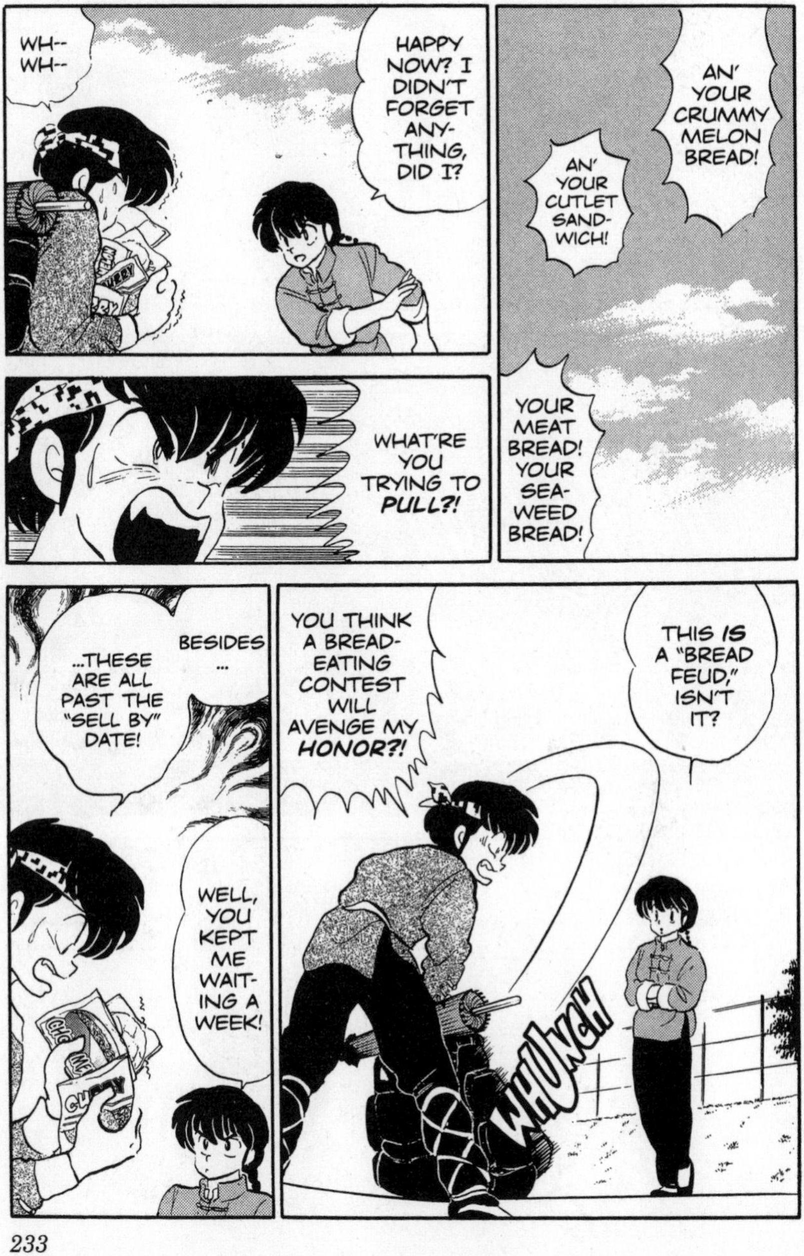
AN' YOUR CRUMMY MELON BREAD!
AN' YOUR CUTLET SANDWICH!
YOUR MEAT BREAD! YOUR SEAWEED BREAD!
HAPPY NOW? I DIDN'T FORGET ANYTHING, DID I?
WH-- WH--
WHAT'RE YOU TRYING TO PULL?!
THIS IS A "BREAD FEUD," ISN'T IT?
YOU THINK A BREAD-EATING CONTEST WILL AVENGE MY HONOR?!
WHUNCH!
BESIDES ...
...THESE ARE ALL PAST THE "SELL BY" DATE!
WELL, YOU KEPT ME WAITING A WEEK!

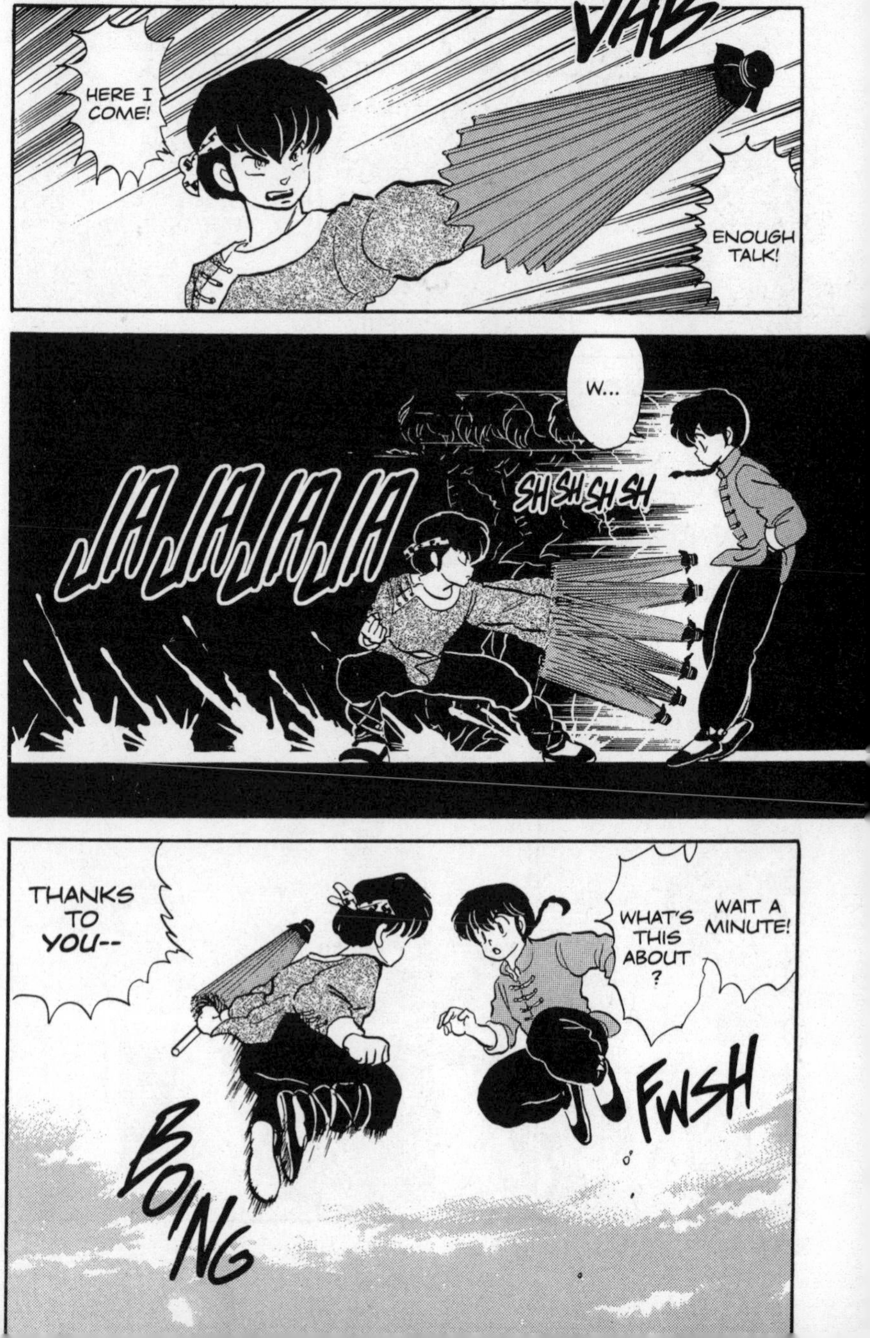
VAB
ENOUGH TALK!
HERE I COME!
W...
SH SH SH SH
JAJAJAJA
WAIT A MINUTE!
WHAT'S THIS ABOUT?
FWSH
THANKS TO YOU--
BOING

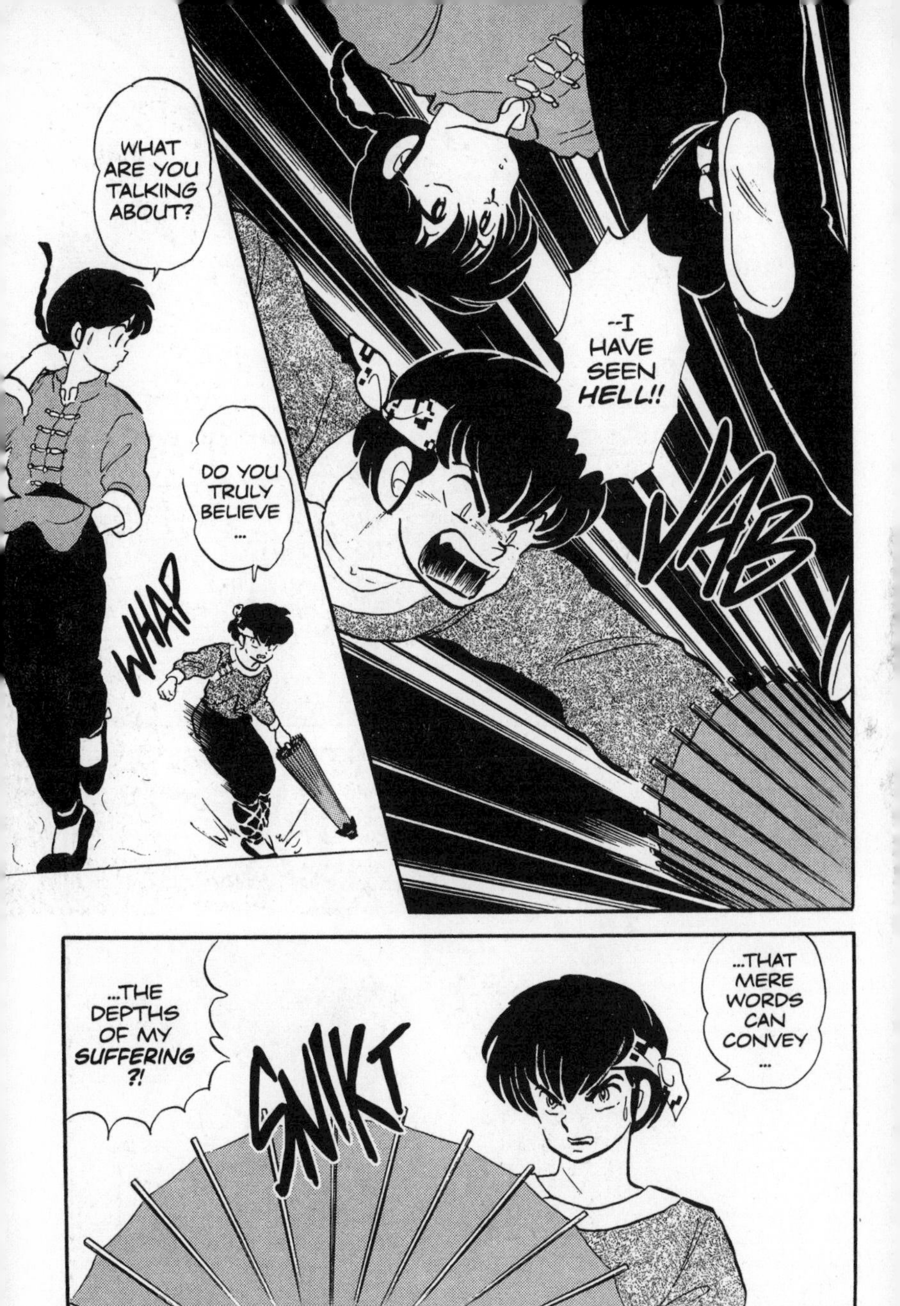
--I HAVE SEEN HELL!!
JAB
WHAT ARE YOU TALKING ABOUT?
DO YOU TRULY BELIEVE ...
WHAP
...THAT MERE WORDS CAN CONVEY ...
SNIKT
...THE DEPTHS OF MY SUFFERING ?!

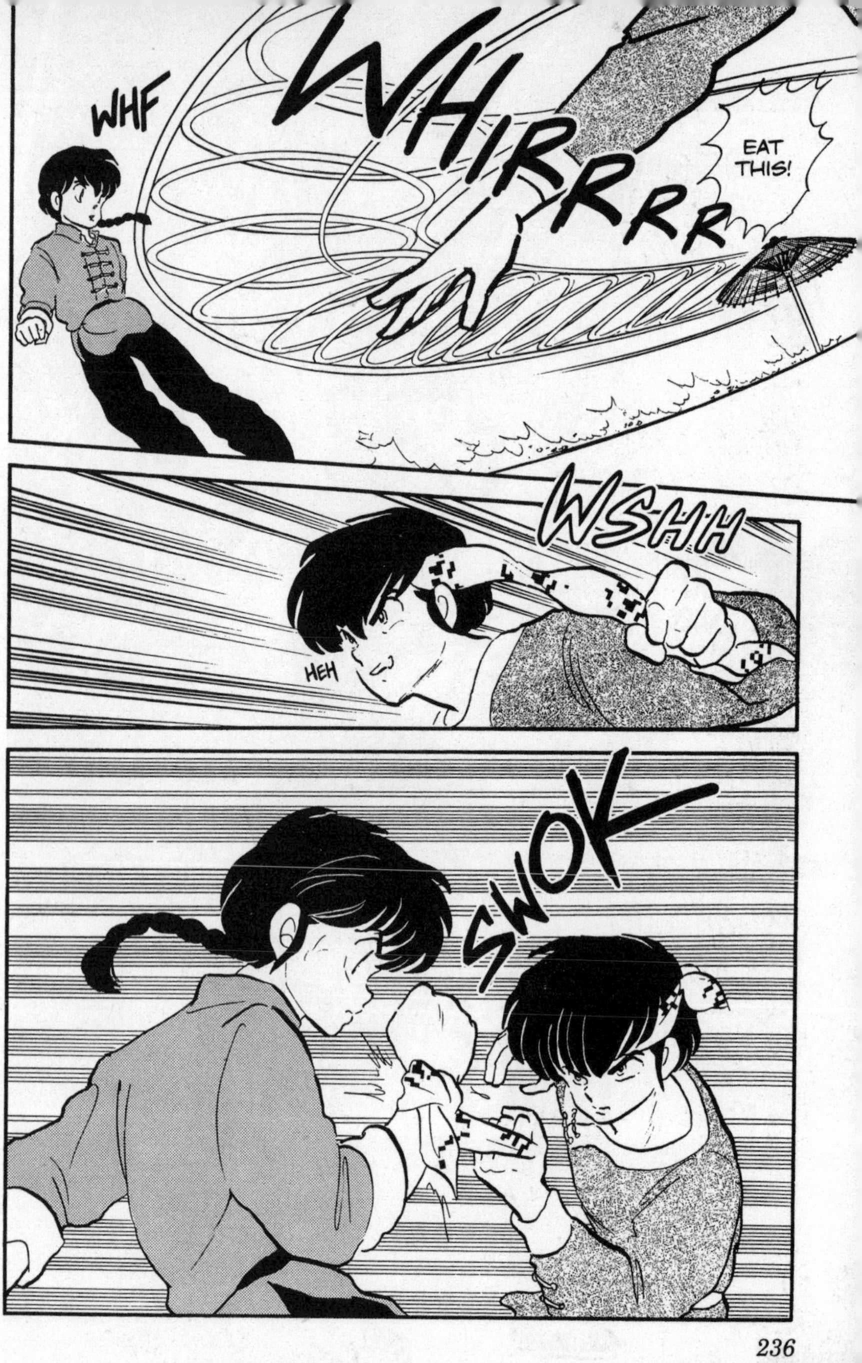
EAT THIS!
WHIRRRRR
WHF
WSHH
HEH
SWOK

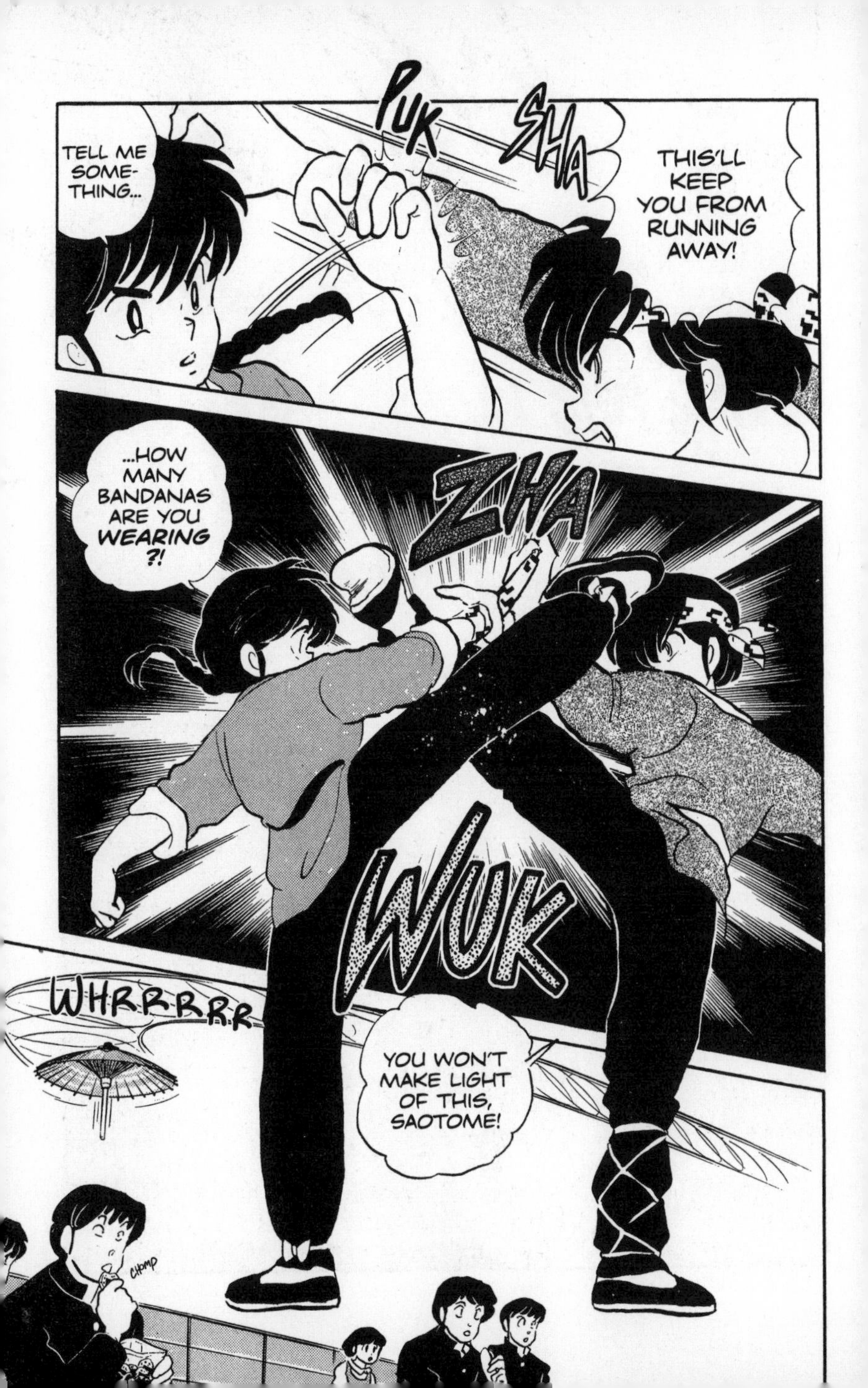
PUK
SHA
THIS'LL KEEP YOU FROM RUNNING AWAY!
TELL ME SOME-THING...
ZHA
...HOW MANY BANDANAS ARE YOU WEARING ?!
WUK
WHRRRRRR
YOU WON'T MAKE LIGHT OF THIS, SAOTOME!
CHOMP

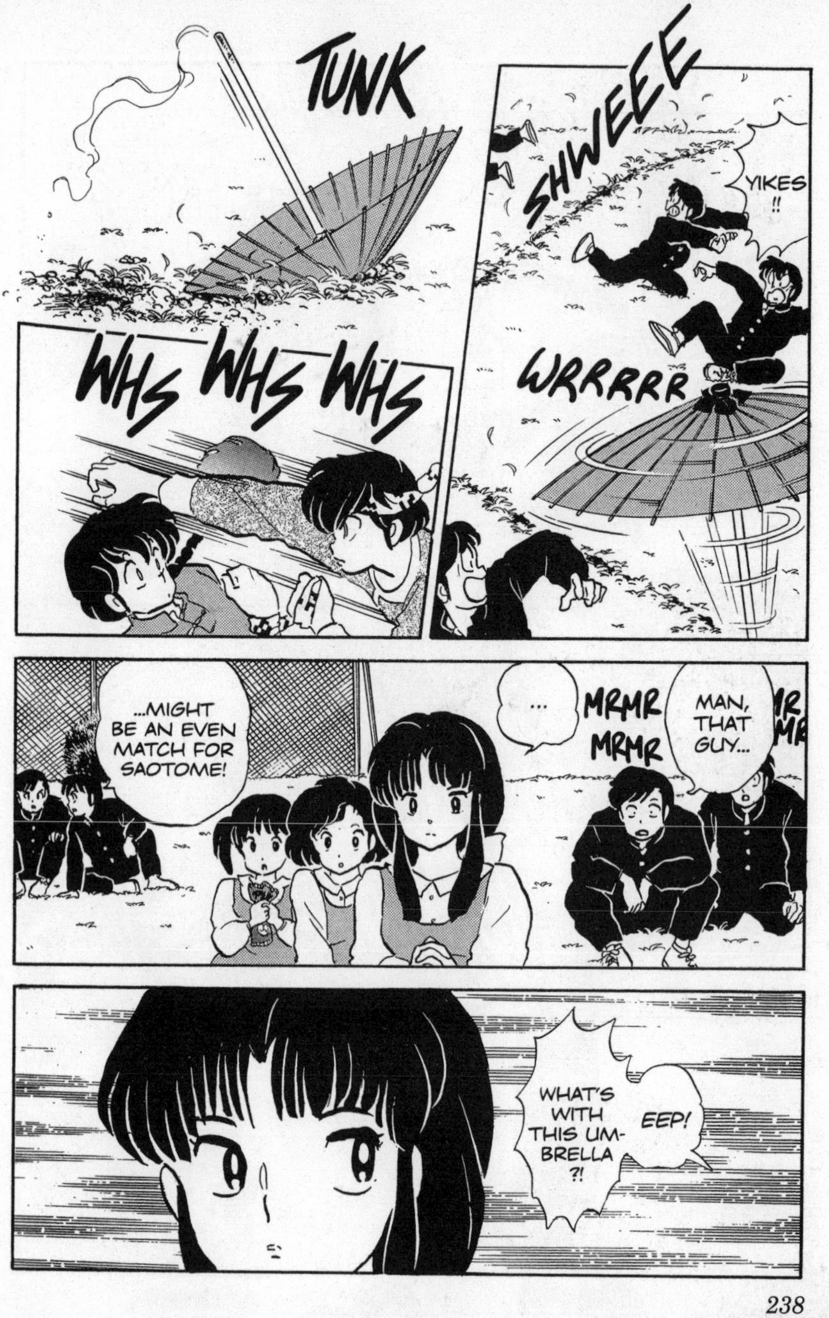
SHWEEE
YIKES!!
WRRRRR
TUNK
WHS WHS WHS
MAN, THAT GUY...
MRMR MRMR
...
...MIGHT BE AN EVEN MATCH FOR SAOTOME!
EEP!
WHAT'S WITH THIS UM-BRELLA?!

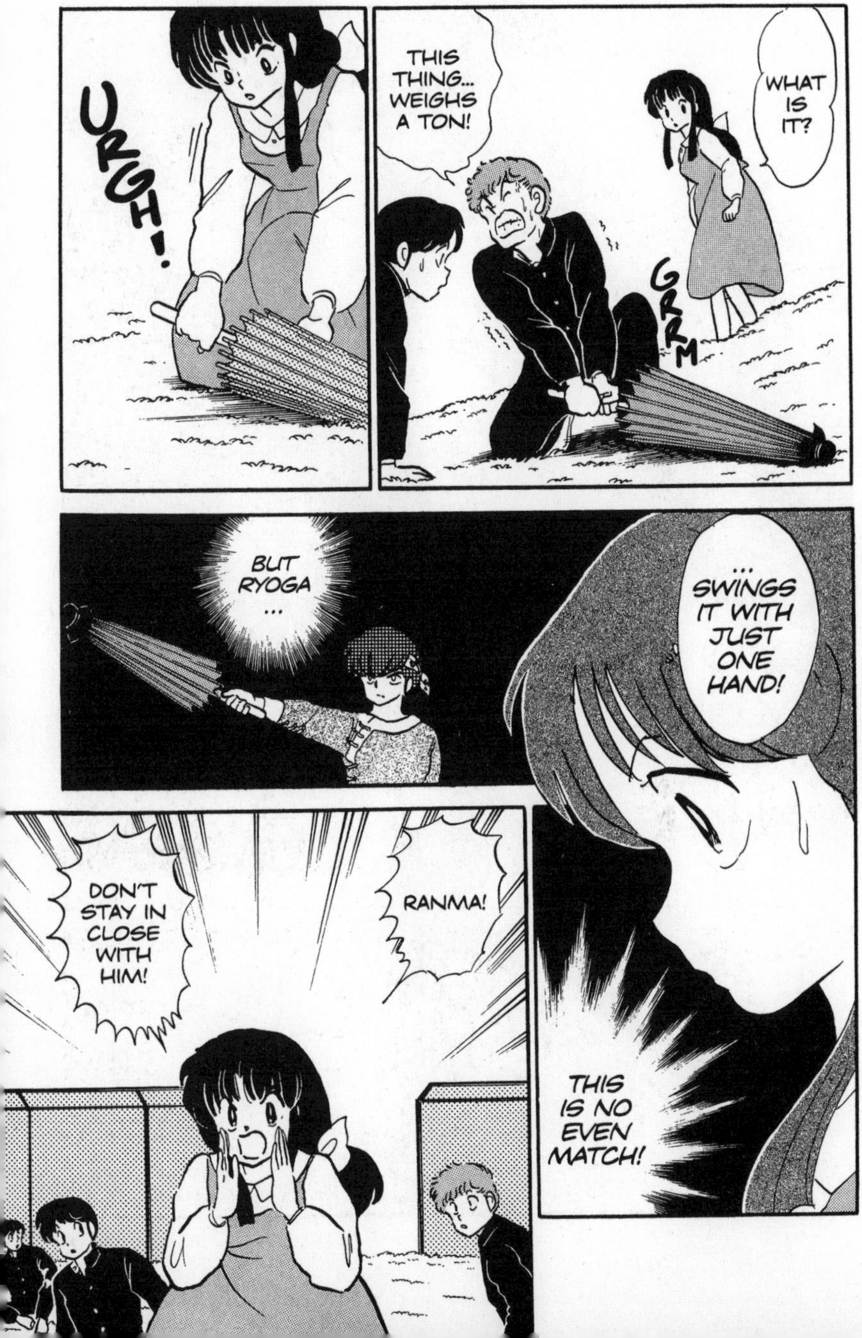
WHAT IS IT?
THIS THING... WEIGHS A TON!
GRRRM
URGH!
BUT RYOGA ...
... SWINGS IT WITH JUST ONE HAND!
THIS IS NO EVEN MATCH!
RANMA!
DON'T STAY IN CLOSE WITH HIM!

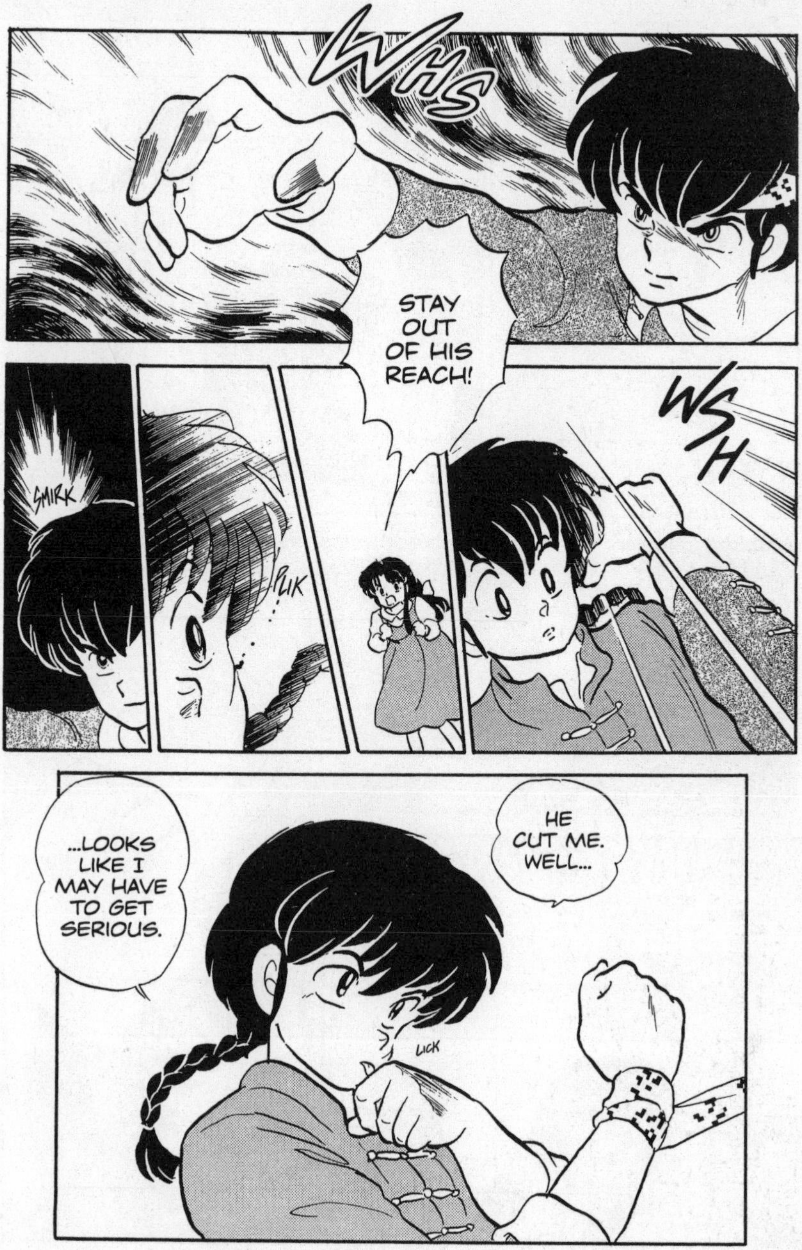
WHS
STAY OUT OF HIS REACH!
WSH
PLIK
SMIRK
HE CUT ME. WELL...
LICK
...LOOKS LIKE I MAY HAVE TO GET SERIOUS.

# PART 12
# SHOWDOWN

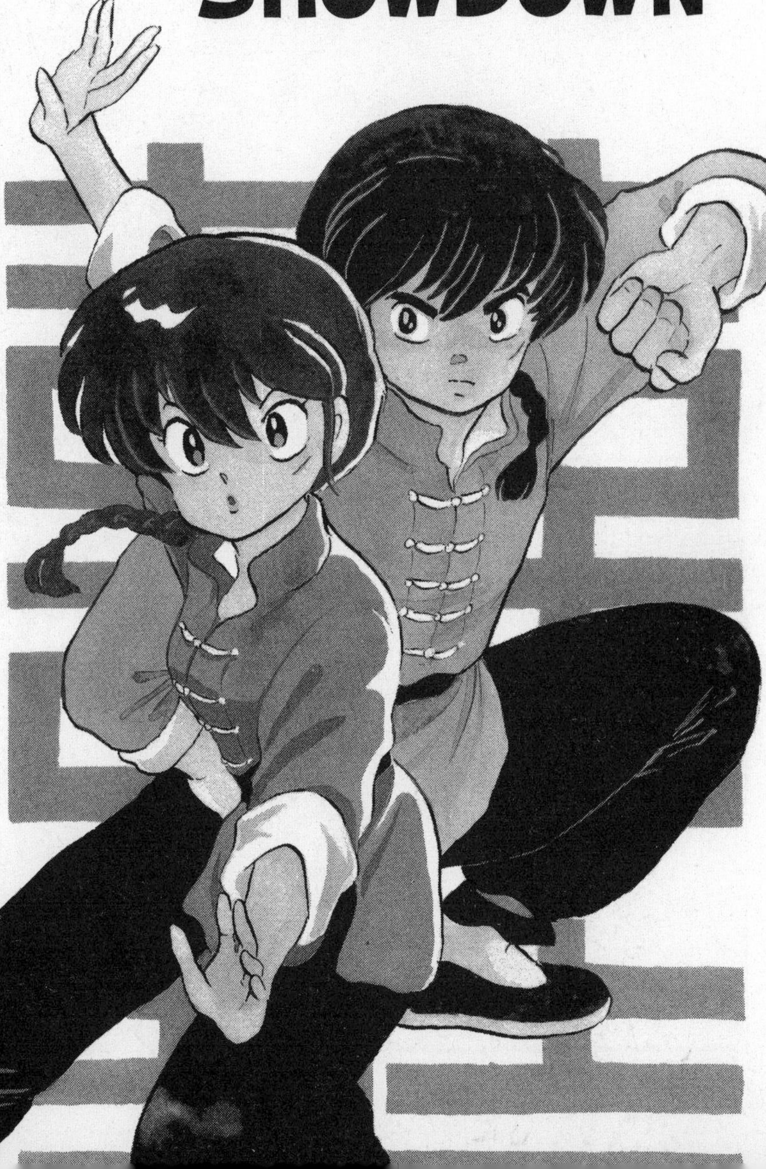

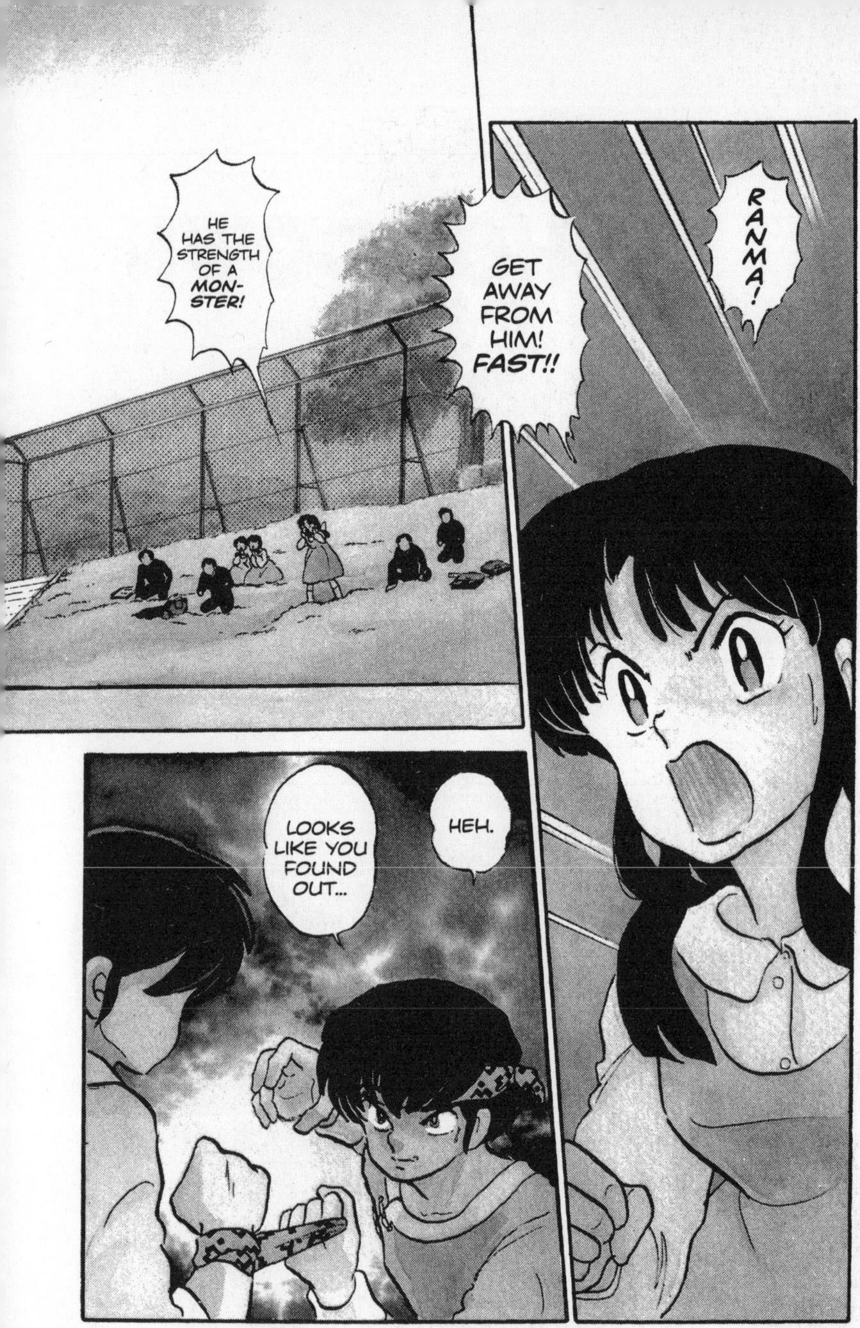
RANMA!
GET AWAY FROM HIM! FAST!!
HE HAS THE STRENGTH OF A MON-STER!
HEH.
LOOKS LIKE YOU FOUND OUT...

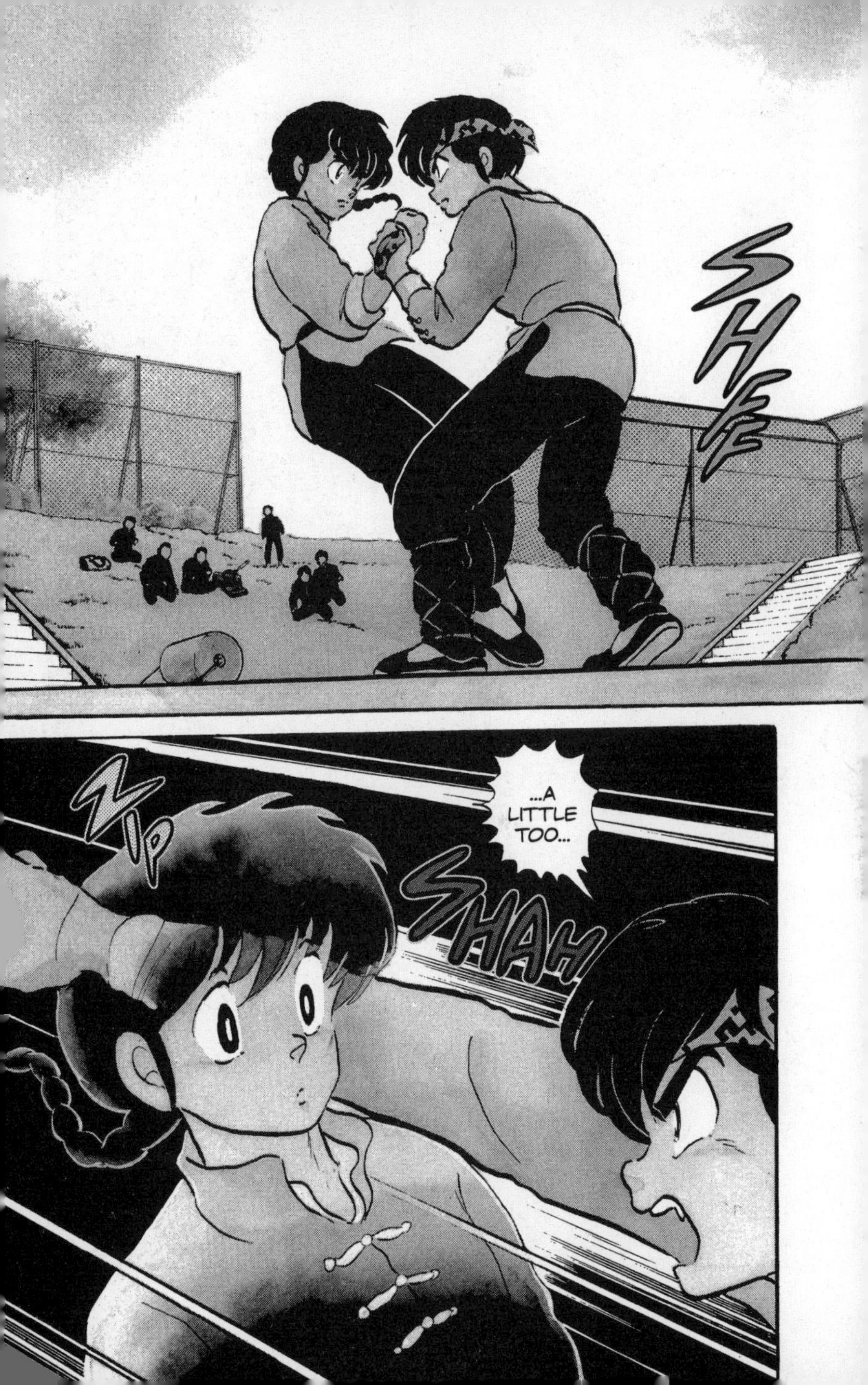
SHEE
...A LITTLE TOO...
SHAH
ZIP

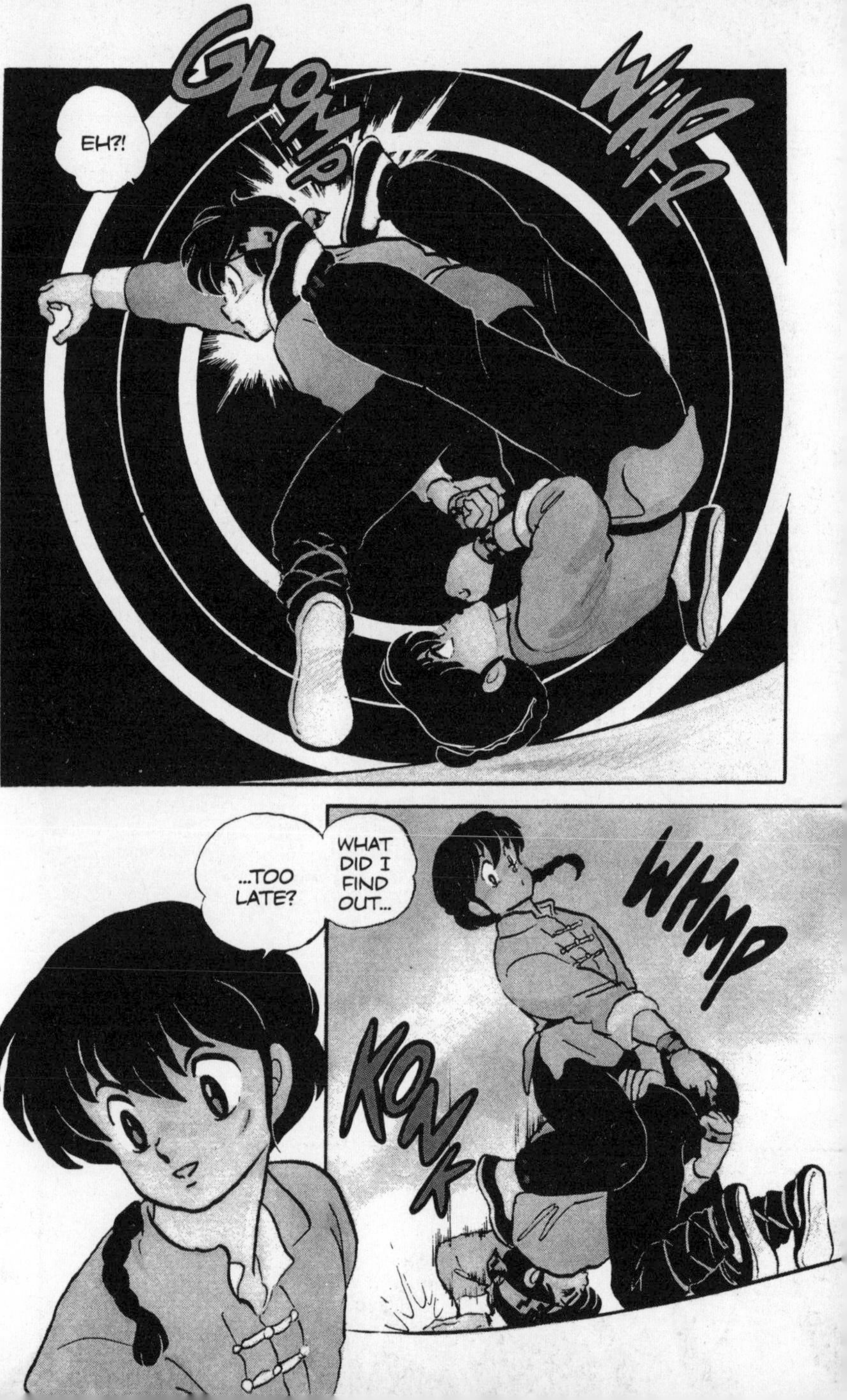
WHRR
GLOMP
EH?!
WHAT DID I FIND OUT...
WHMP
KONK
...TOO LATE?

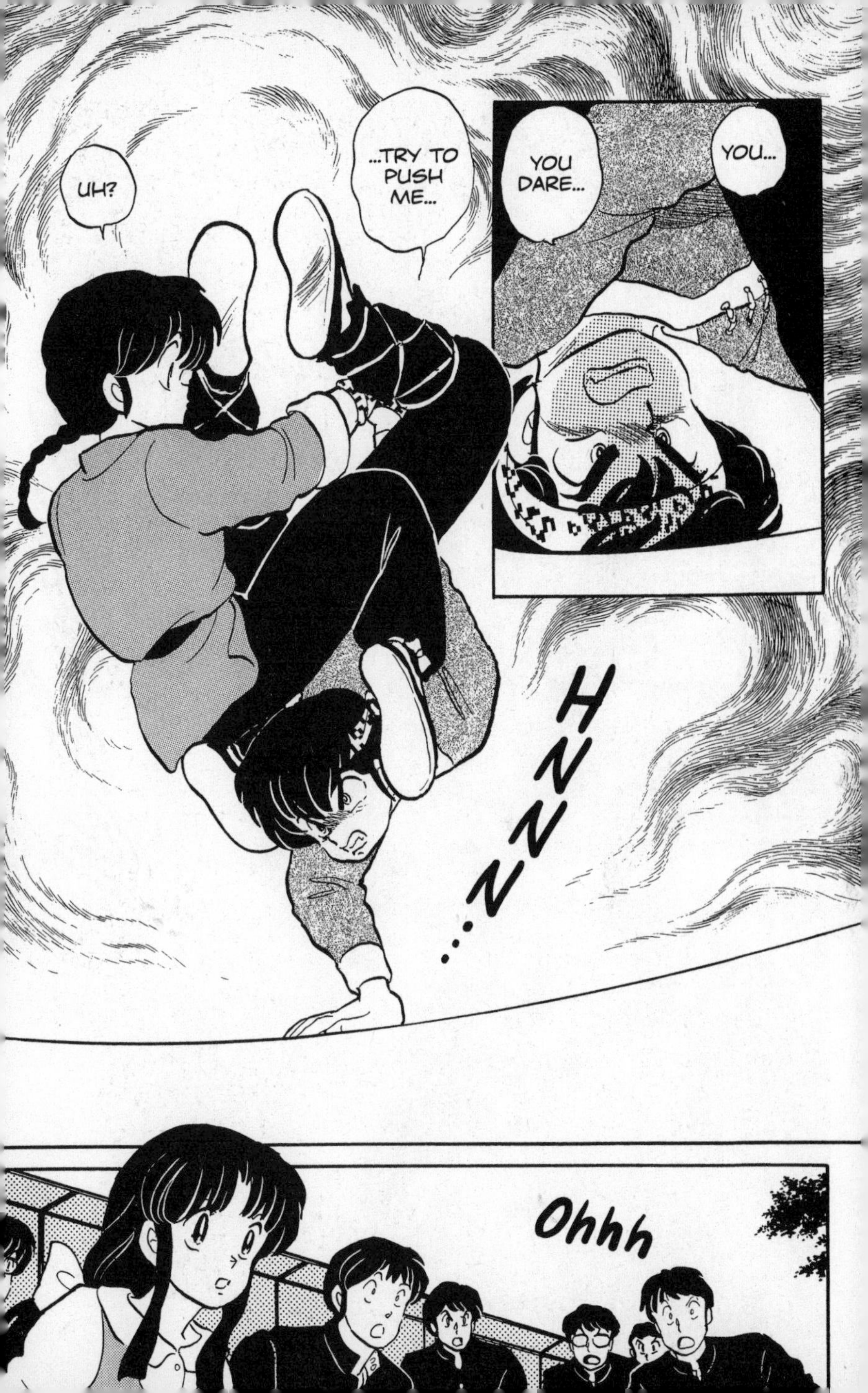
YOU...
YOU DARE...
...TRY TO PUSH ME...
UH?
HNNNN...
Ohhh

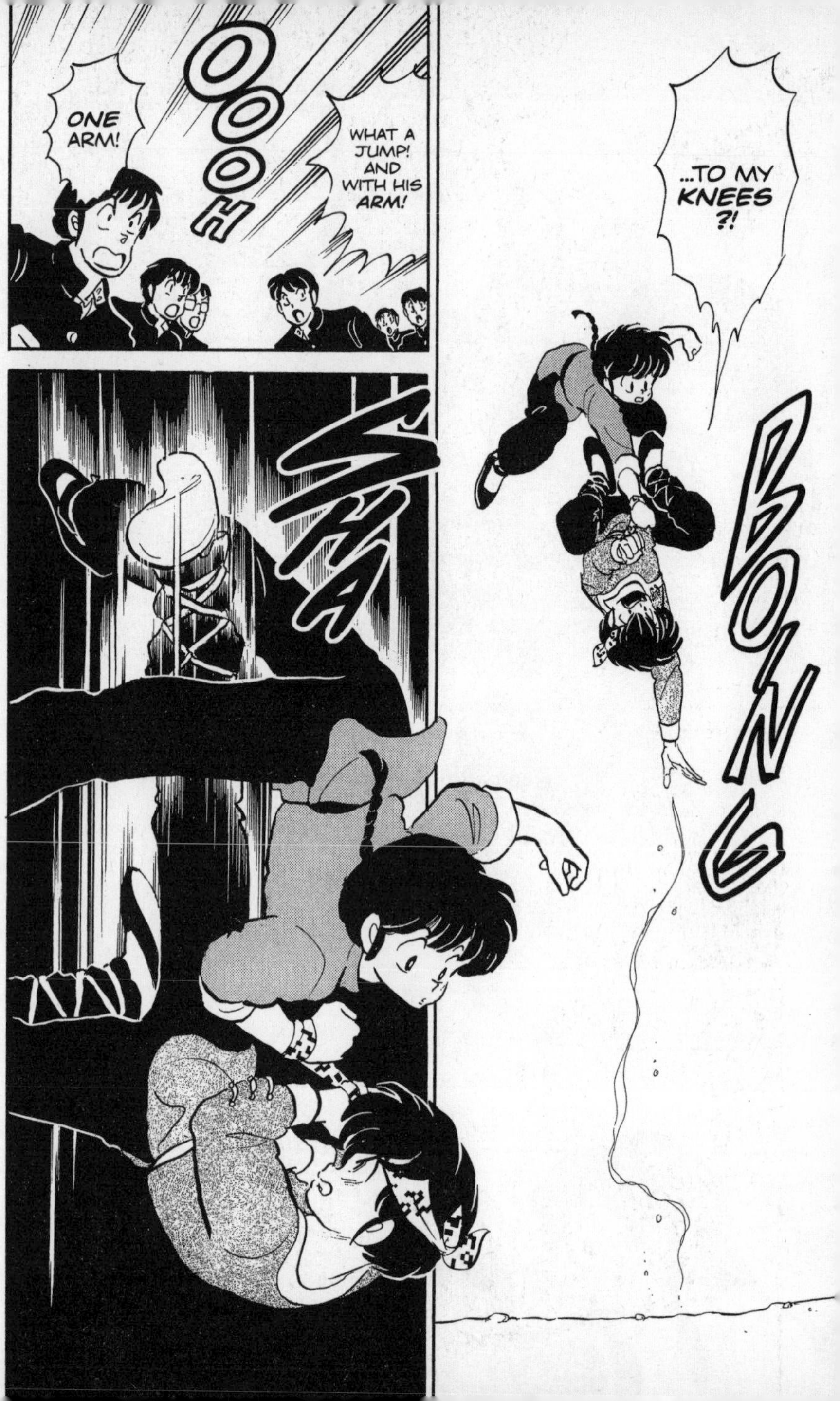
...TO MY KNEES ?!
BOING
WHAT A JUMP! AND WITH HIS ARM!
OOOOH
ONE ARM!
SWA

POW

WHP

INCOM-
ING!

WAH!

TOOM

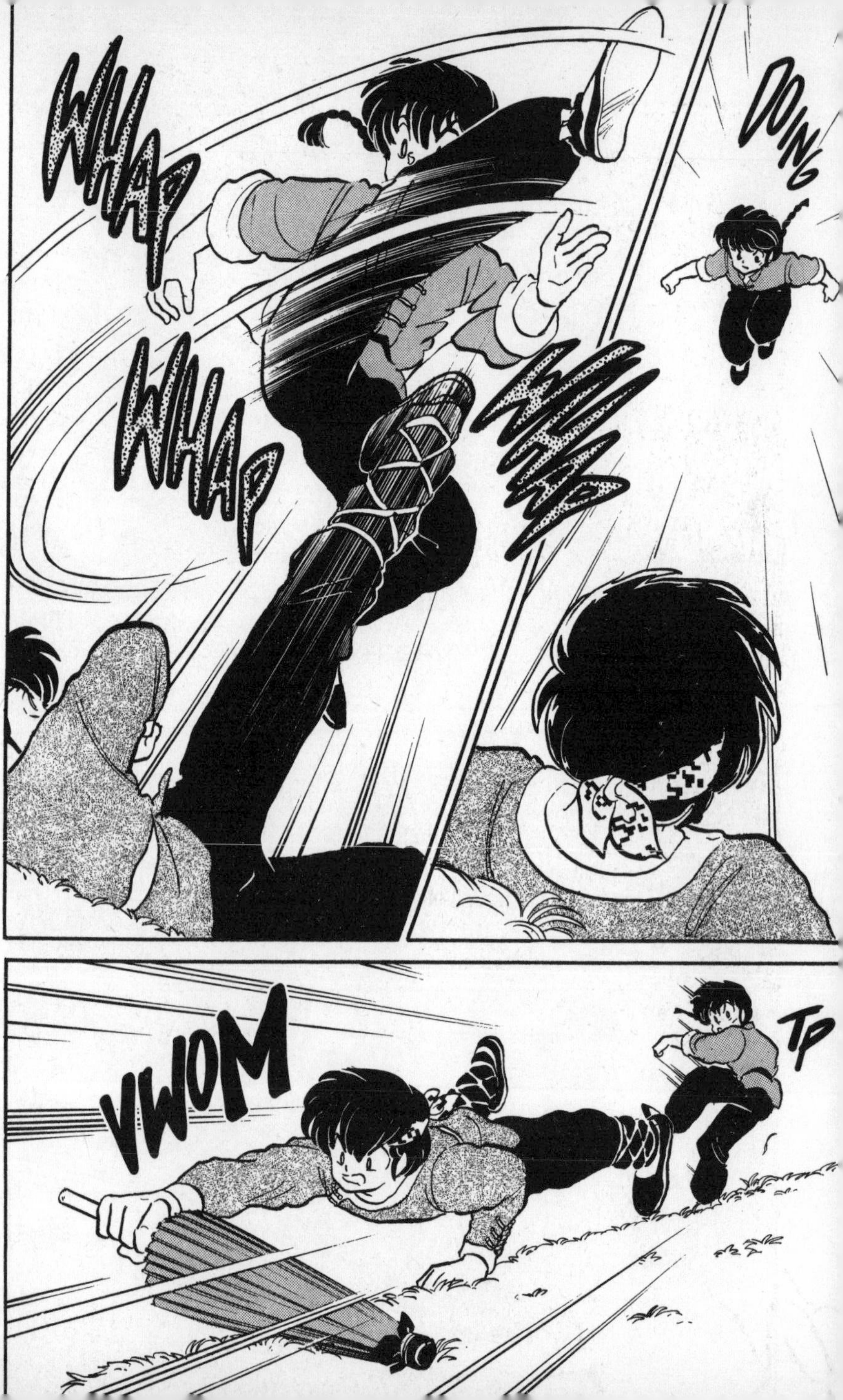

DOING
WHAP
WHAP
WHAM
TP
VWOM

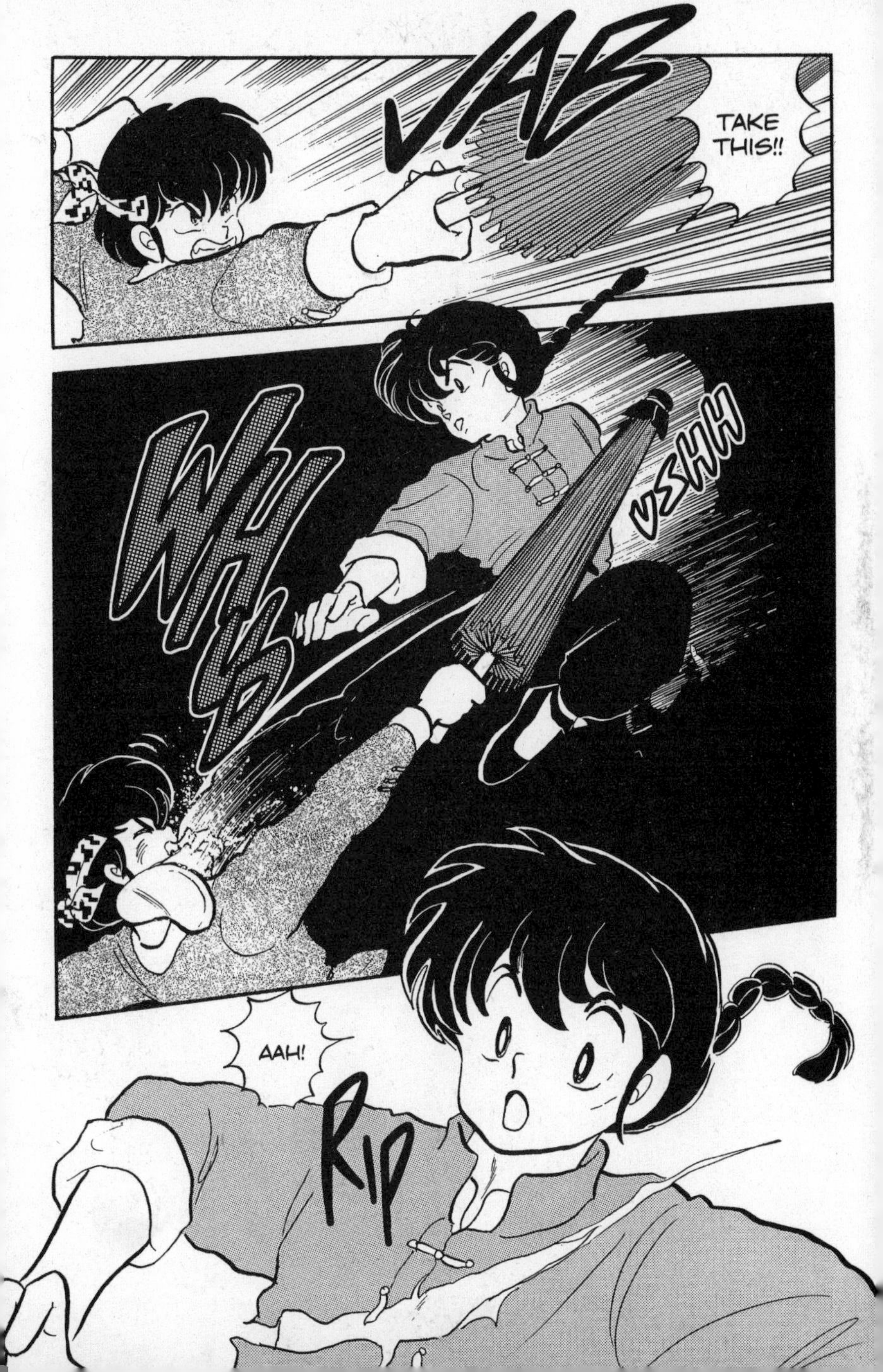
TAKE THIS!!
JAB
VSHHH
WHISH
AAH!
RIP

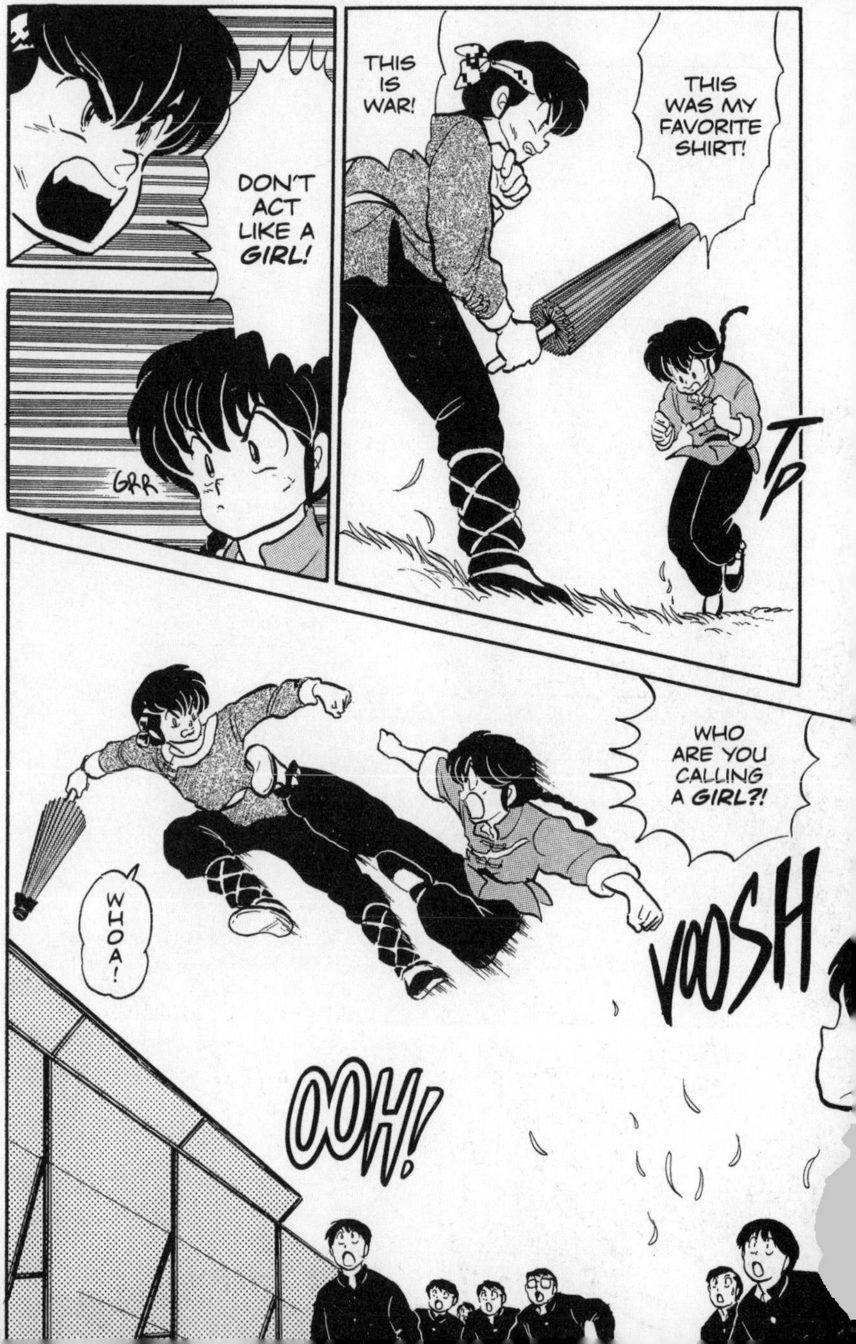
THIS WAS MY FAVORITE SHIRT!
THIS IS WAR!
TP
DON'T ACT LIKE A GIRL!
GRR
WHO ARE YOU CALLING A GIRL?!
VOOSH
WHOA!
OOH!

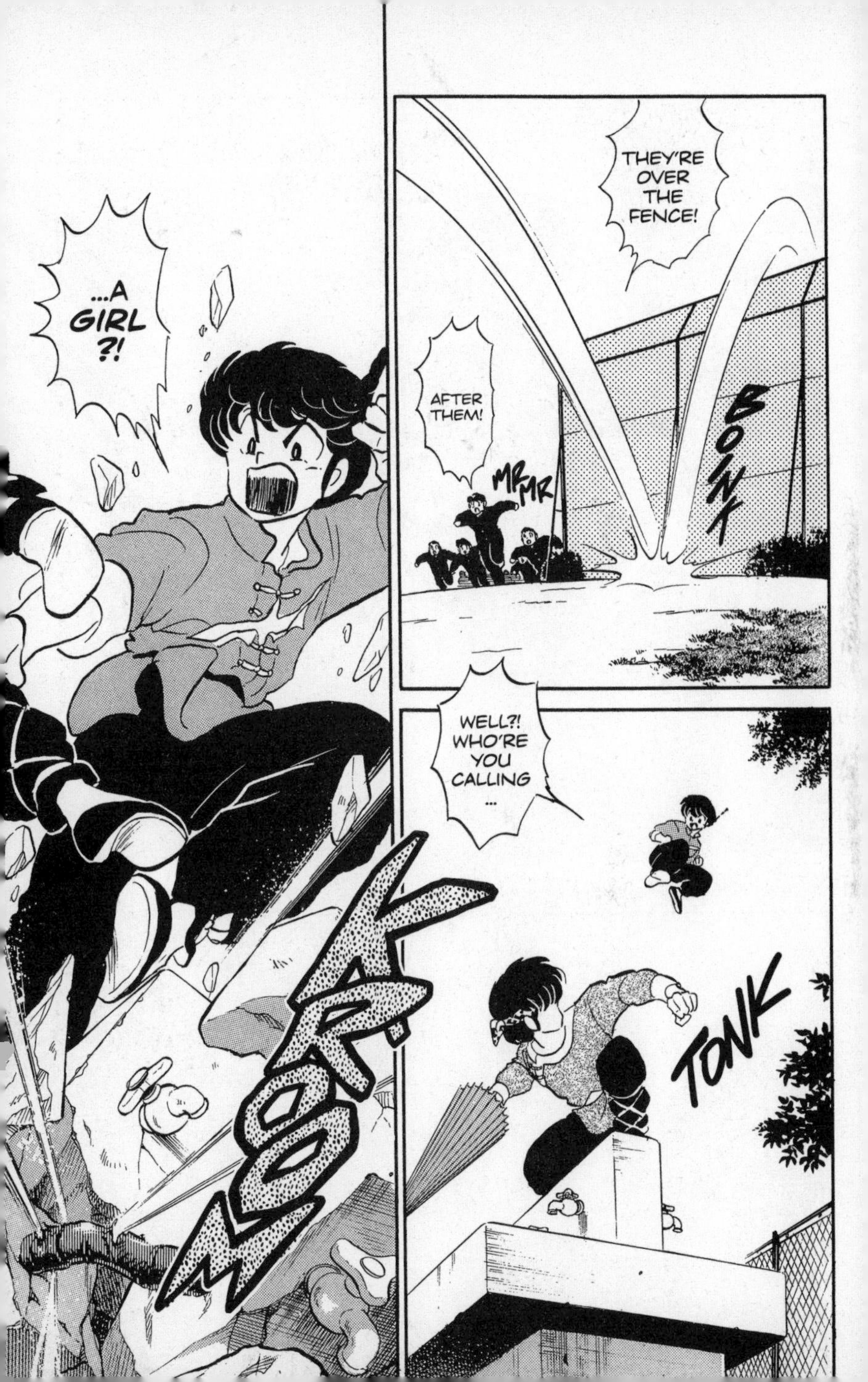
THEY'RE OVER THE FENCE!
AFTER THEM!
MR MR
BOINK
WELL?! WHO'RE YOU CALLING ...
TONK
...A GIRL ?!

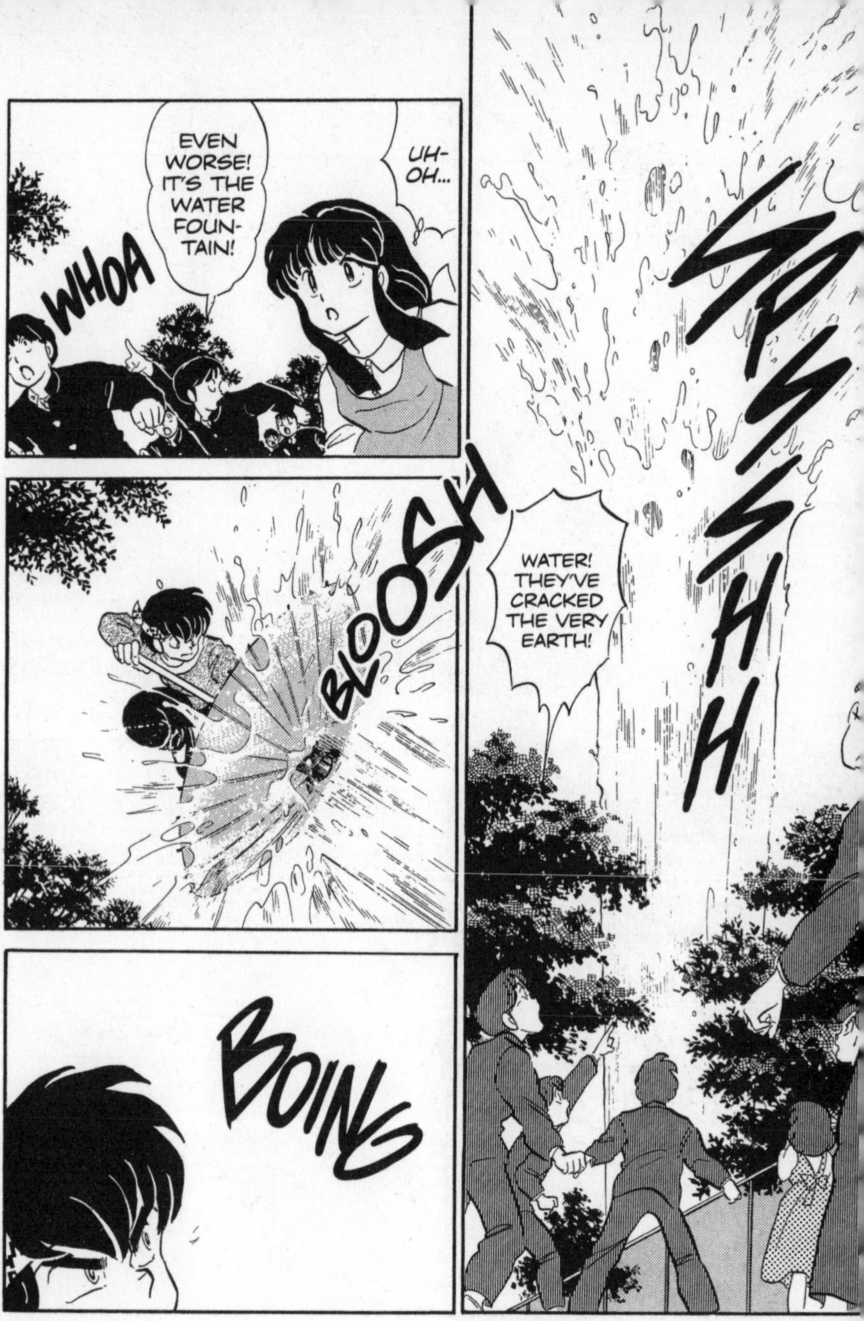

SPSSHH
WATER! THEY'VE CRACKED THE VERY EARTH!
UH-OH...
EVEN WORSE! IT'S THE WATER FOUN-TAIN!
WHOA
BLOOSH
BOING

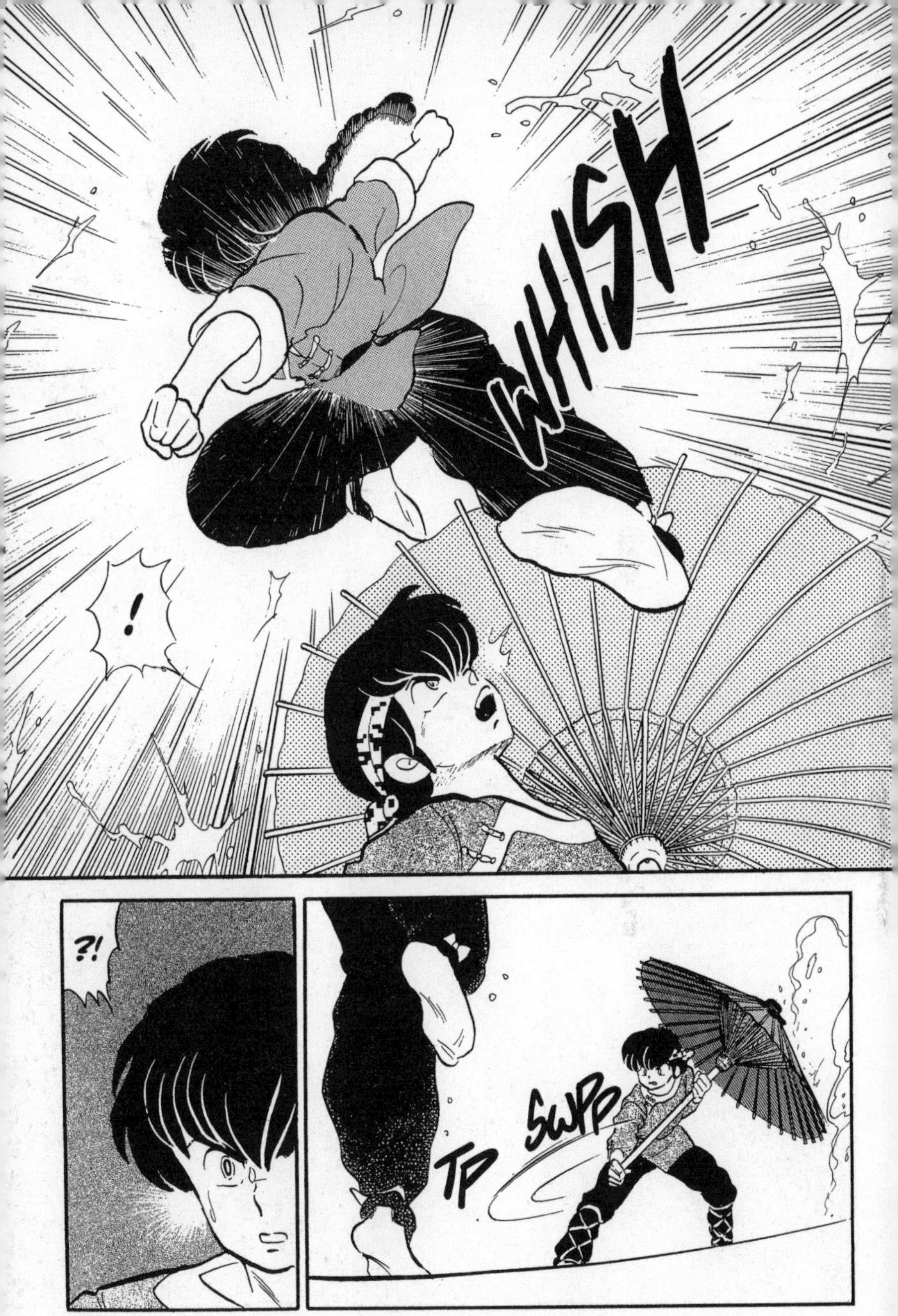
WHISH
!
SWPP
TP
?!

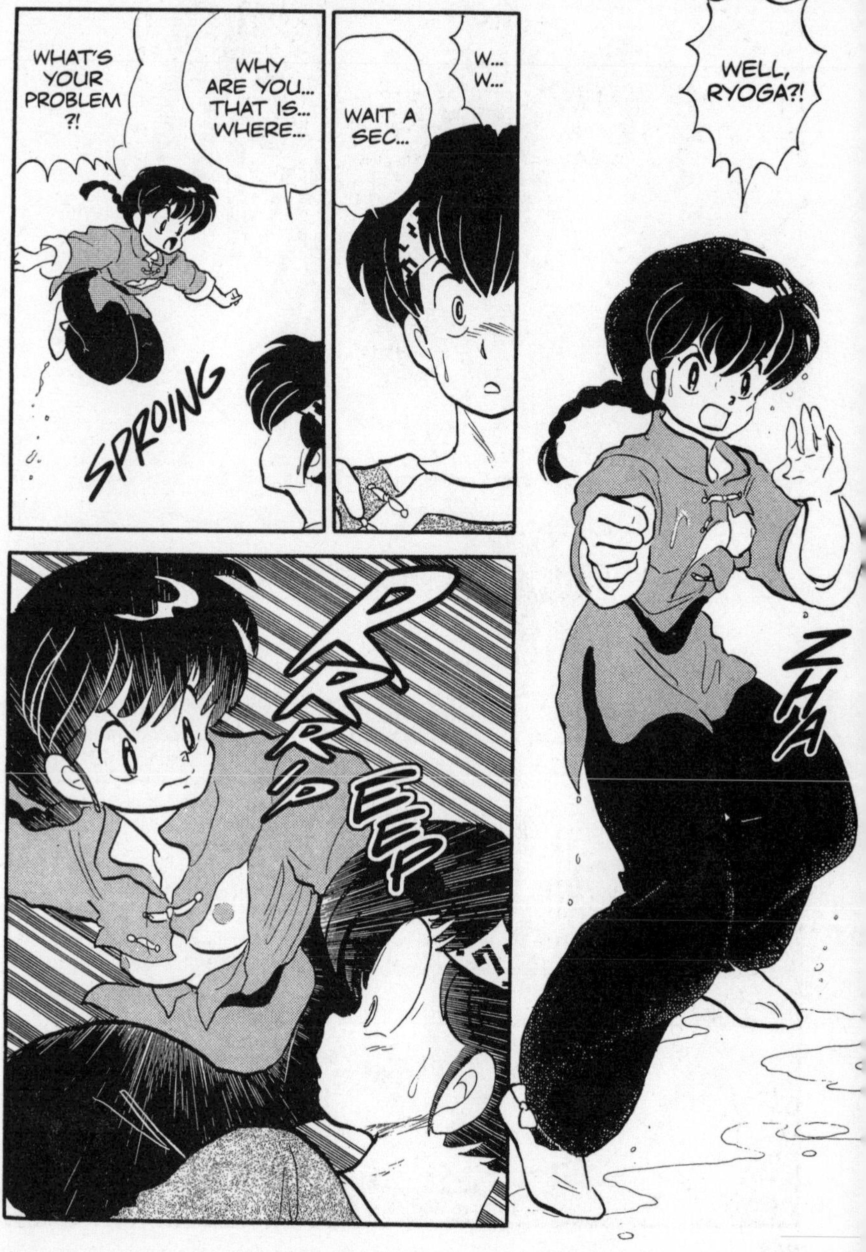
WELL, RYOGA?!
ZHA
W... W...
WAIT A SEC...
WHY ARE YOU... THAT IS... WHERE...
WHAT'S YOUR PROBLEM ?!
SPROING
PRRRIP
EEP

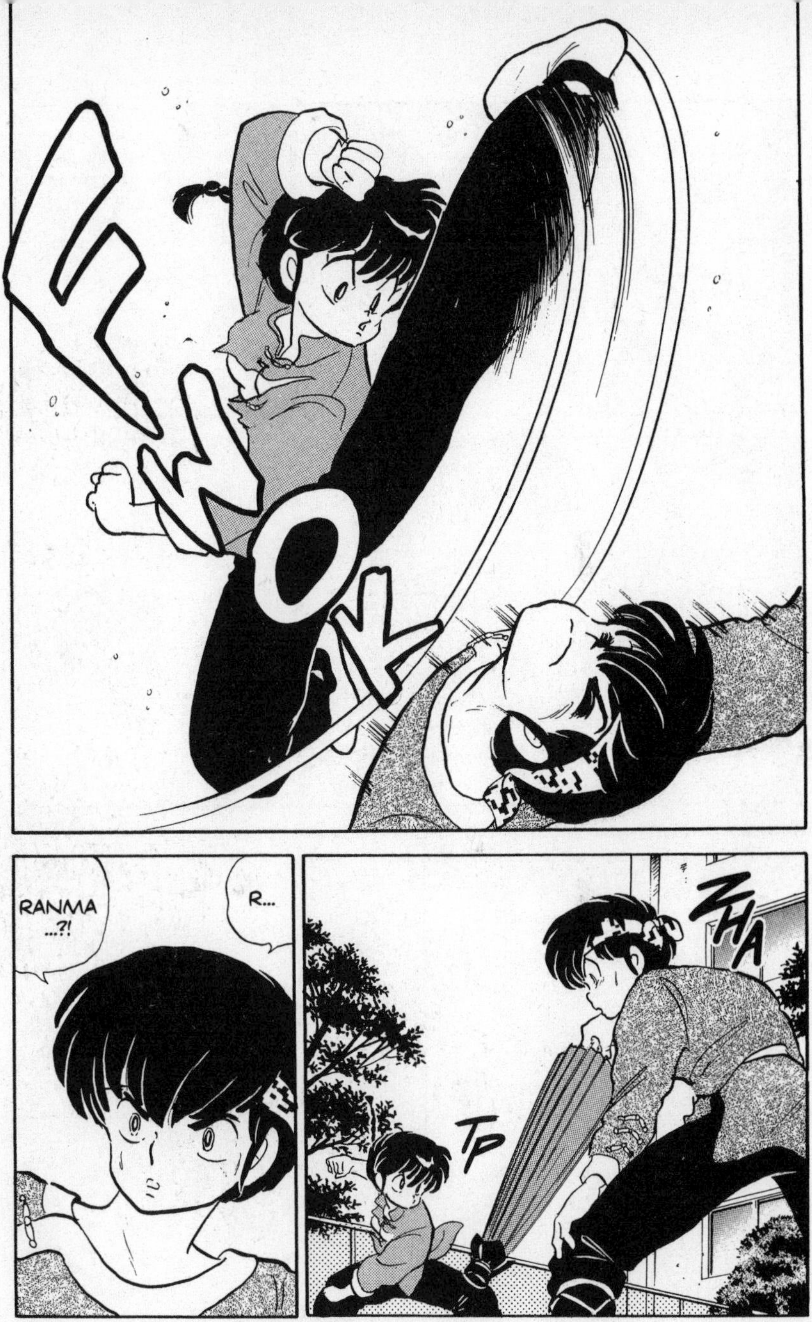
FWOK
ZHA
TP
R...
RANMA ...?!

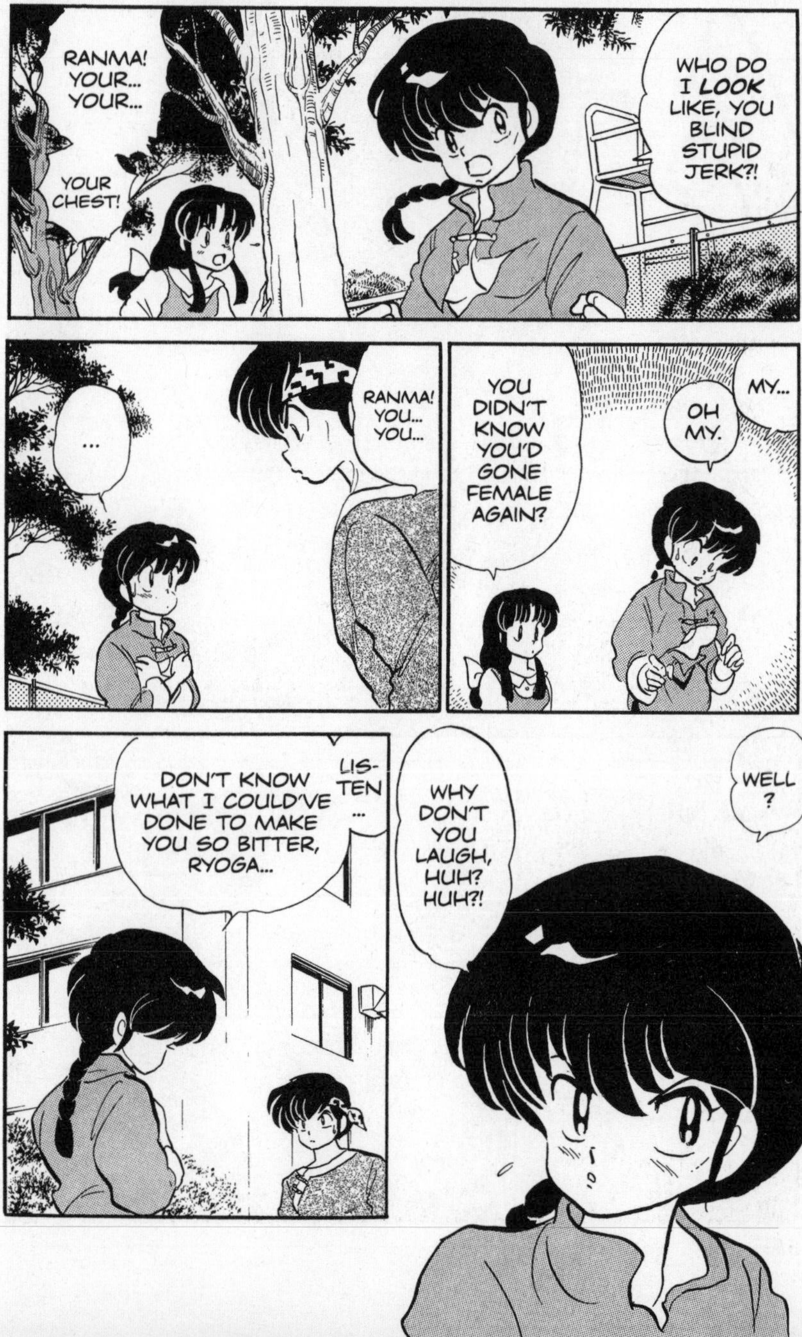
WHO DO I LOOK LIKE, YOU BLIND STUPID JERK?!
RANMA! YOUR... YOUR...
YOUR CHEST!
MY...
OH MY.
YOU DIDN'T KNOW YOU'D GONE FEMALE AGAIN?
RANMA! YOU... YOU...
...
WELL ?
WHY DON'T YOU LAUGH, HUH? HUH?!
LIS-TEN ...
DON'T KNOW WHAT I COULD'VE DONE TO MAKE YOU SO BITTER, RYOGA...

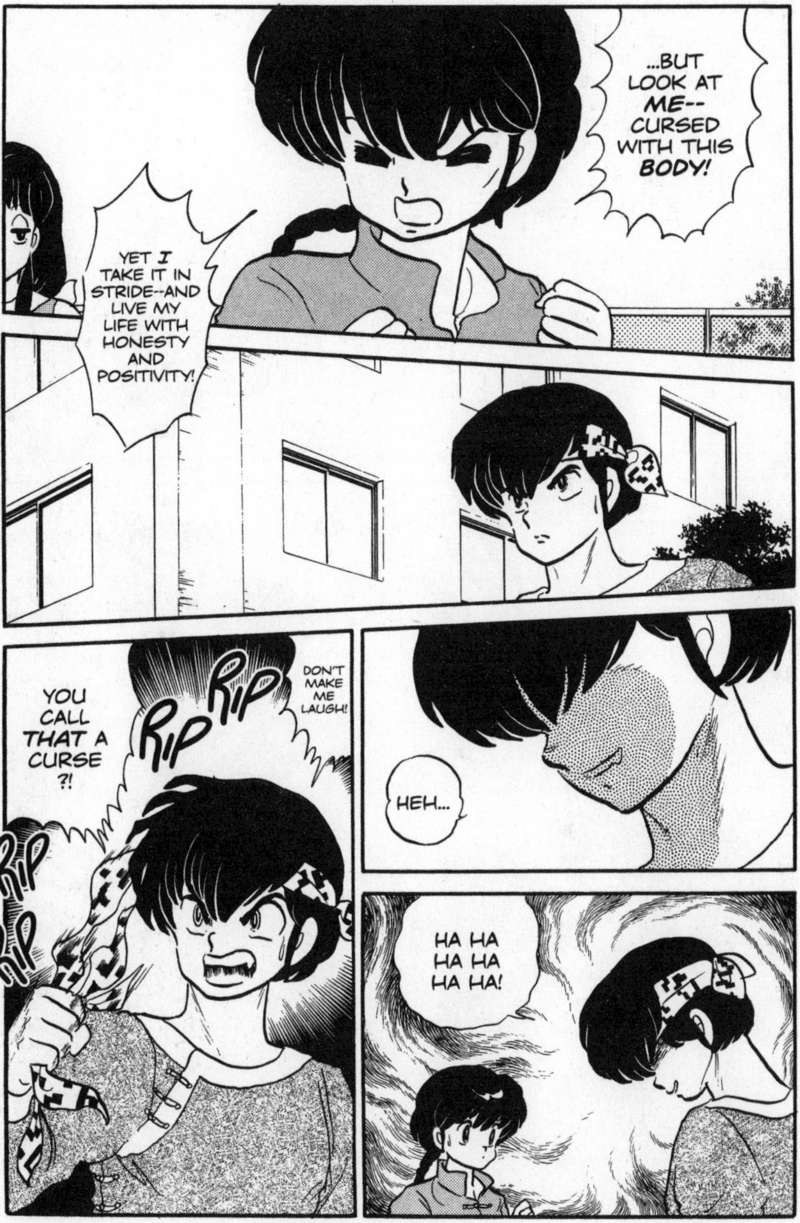
...BUT LOOK AT ME-- CURSED WITH THIS BODY!
YET I TAKE IT IN STRIDE--AND LIVE MY LIFE WITH HONESTY AND POSITIVITY!
HEH...
HA HA HA HA HA HA!
DON'T MAKE ME LAUGH!
RIP RIP
YOU CALL THAT A CURSE ?!
RIP
RIP

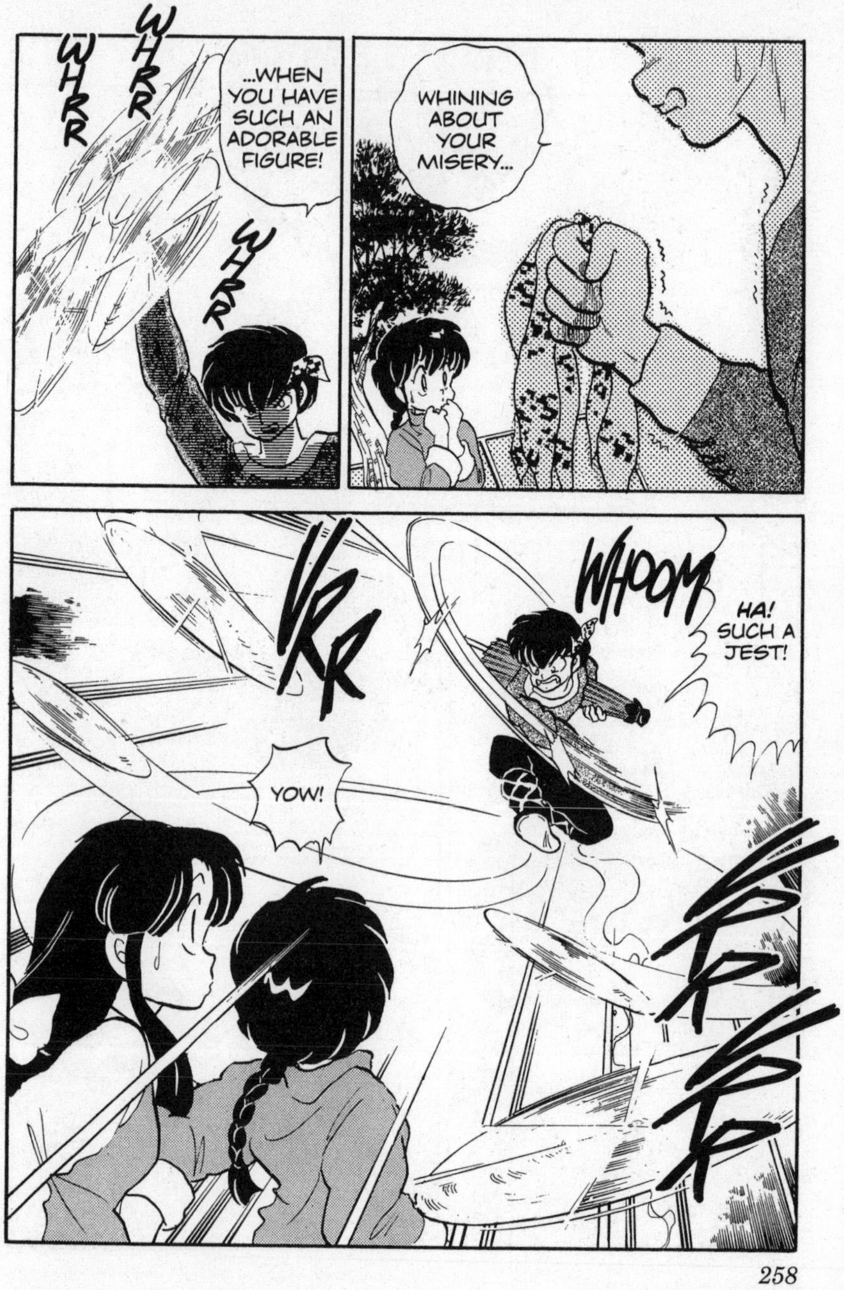
WHINING ABOUT YOUR MISERY...
WHRR WHRR
...WHEN YOU HAVE SUCH AN ADORABLE FIGURE!
WHRR
WHOOM
HA! SUCH A JEST!
VRR
YOW!
VRR VRR

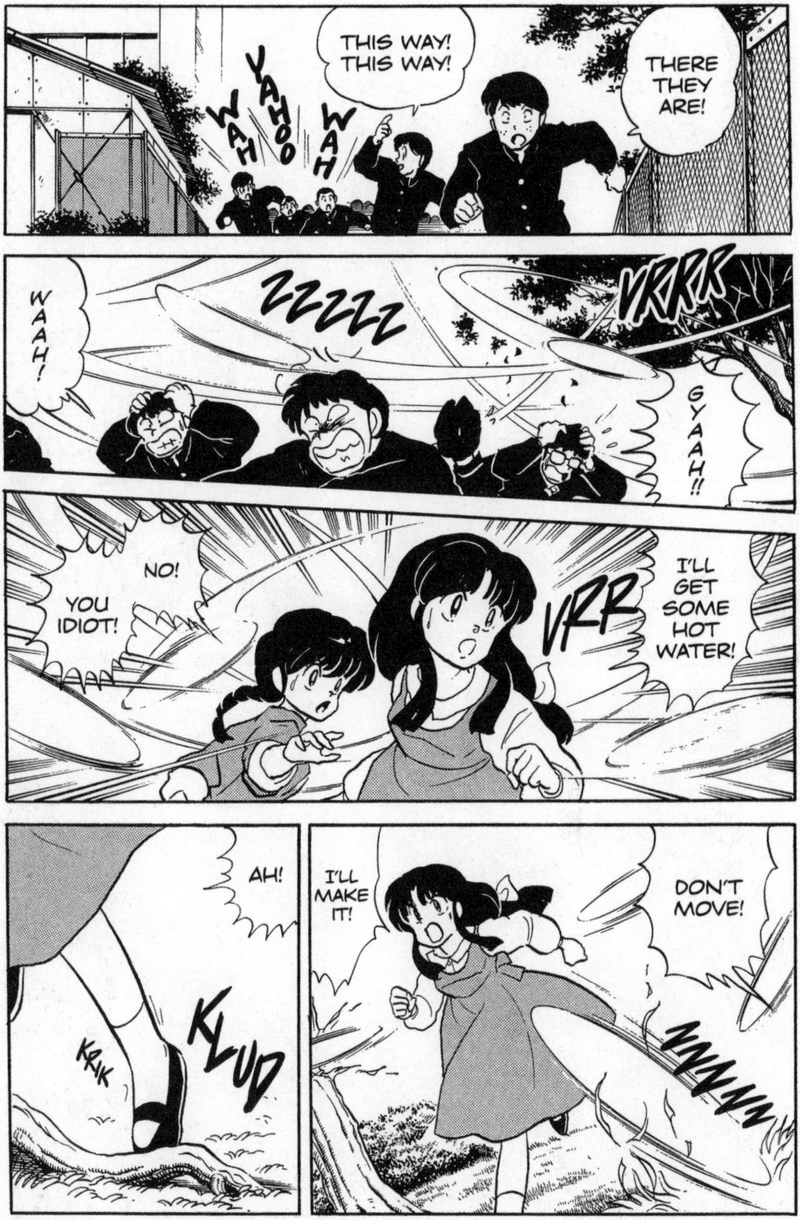
THERE THEY ARE!
THIS WAY! THIS WAY!
WAH
YAHOO
WAH
VRRRR
GYAAAH!!
ZZZZZ
WAAH!
I'LL GET SOME HOT WATER!
VRR
NO!
YOU IDIOT!
DON'T MOVE!
I'LL MAKE IT!
AH!
KLUD
KRIK

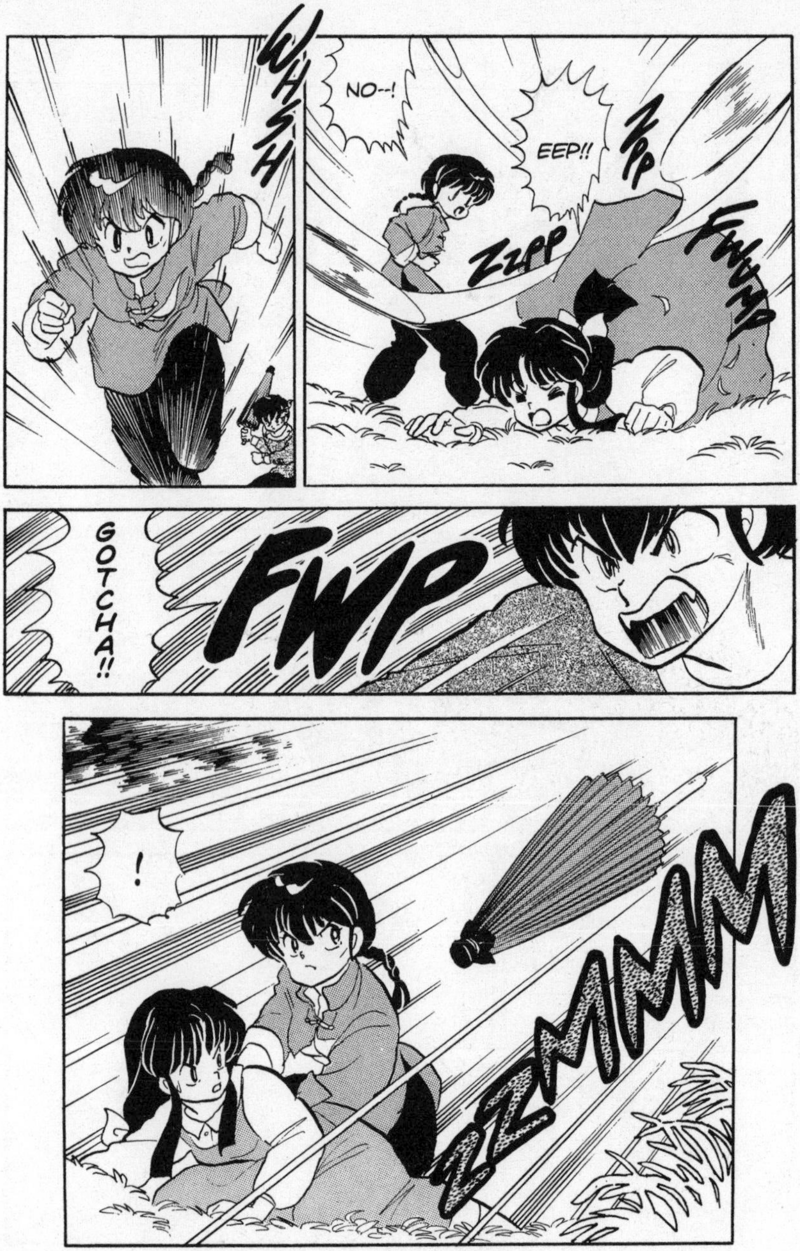
NO--!
EEP!!
ZZPP
FWUMP!
WHSH
GOTCHA!!
FWP
!
ZZMMMM

# PART 13
# A BAD CUT

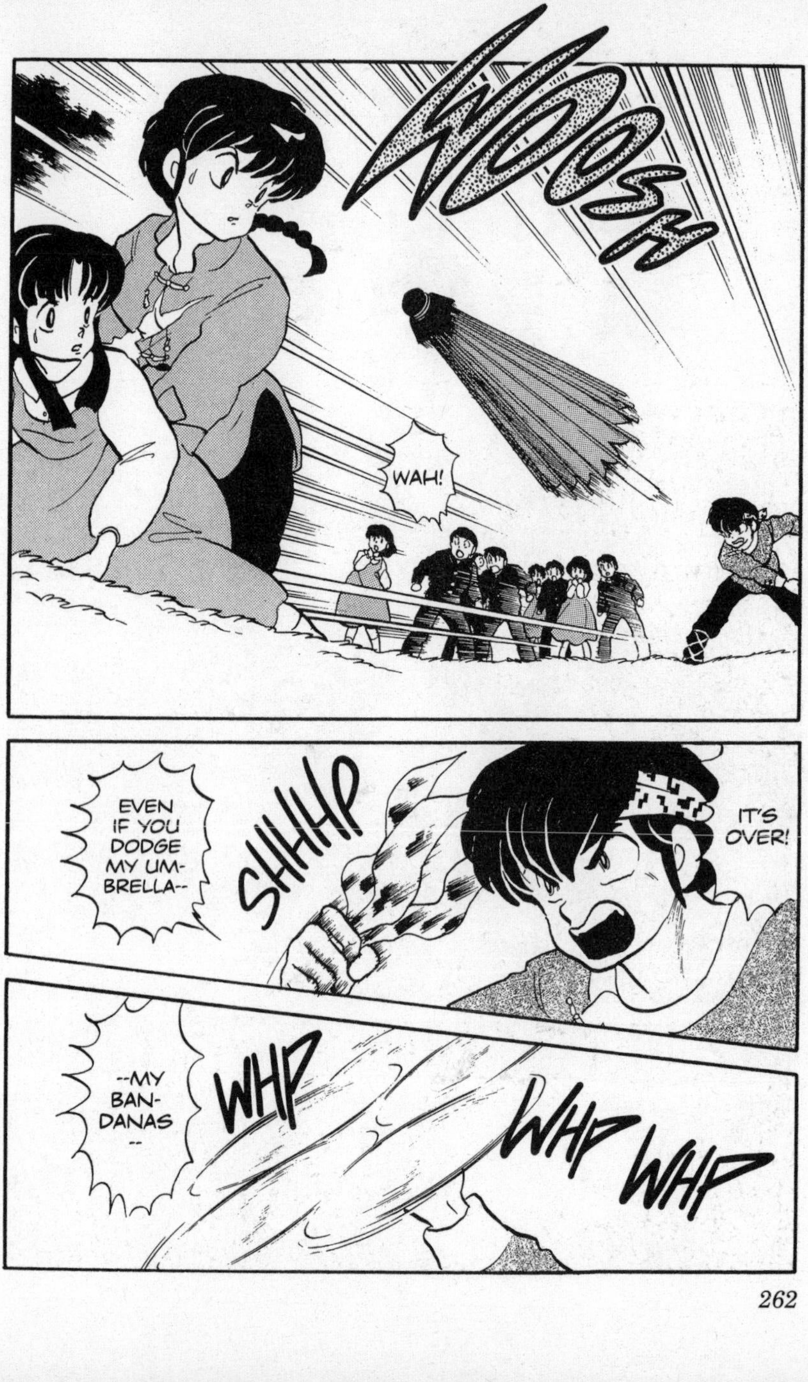
WOOSH
WAH!
IT'S OVER!
SHHHP
EVEN IF YOU DODGE MY UM-BRELLA--
WHP WHP
WHP
--MY BAN-DANAS --

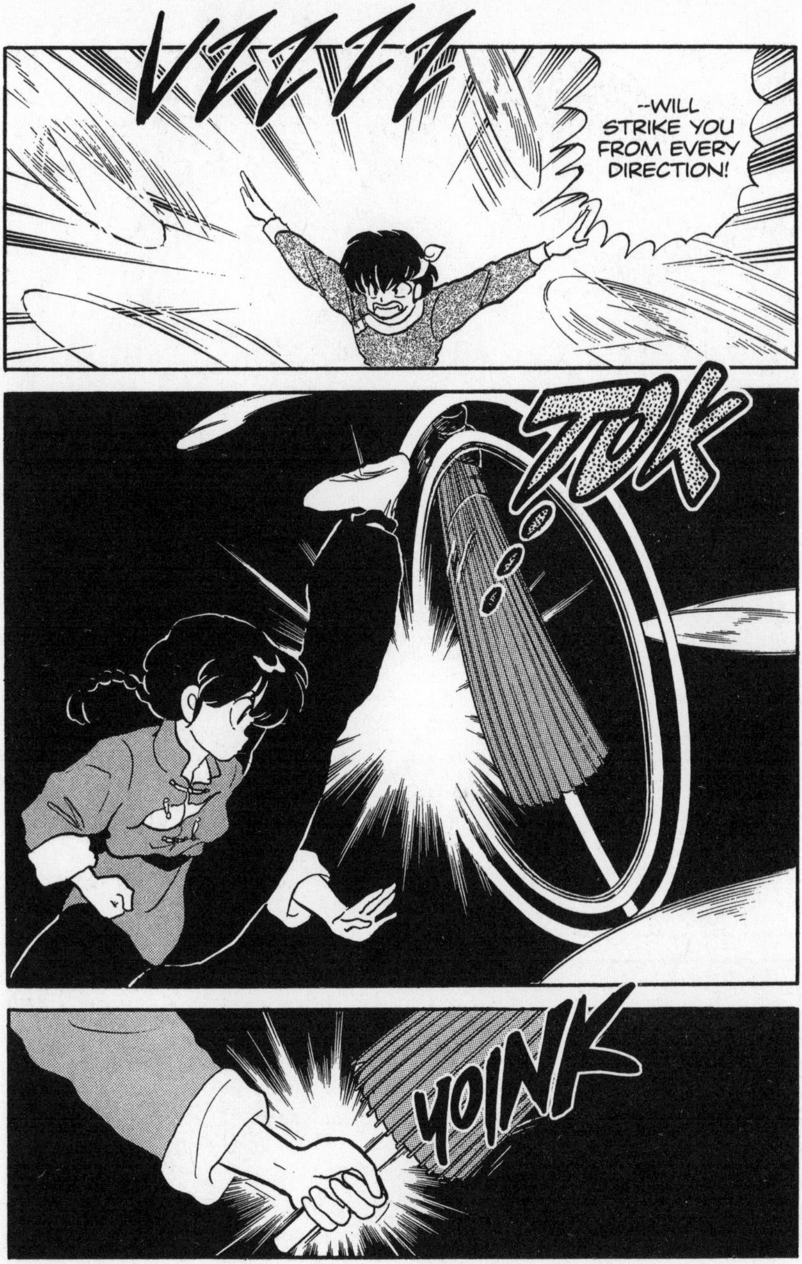
VZZZZZ
--WILL STRIKE YOU FROM EVERY DIRECTION!
TOK
YOINK

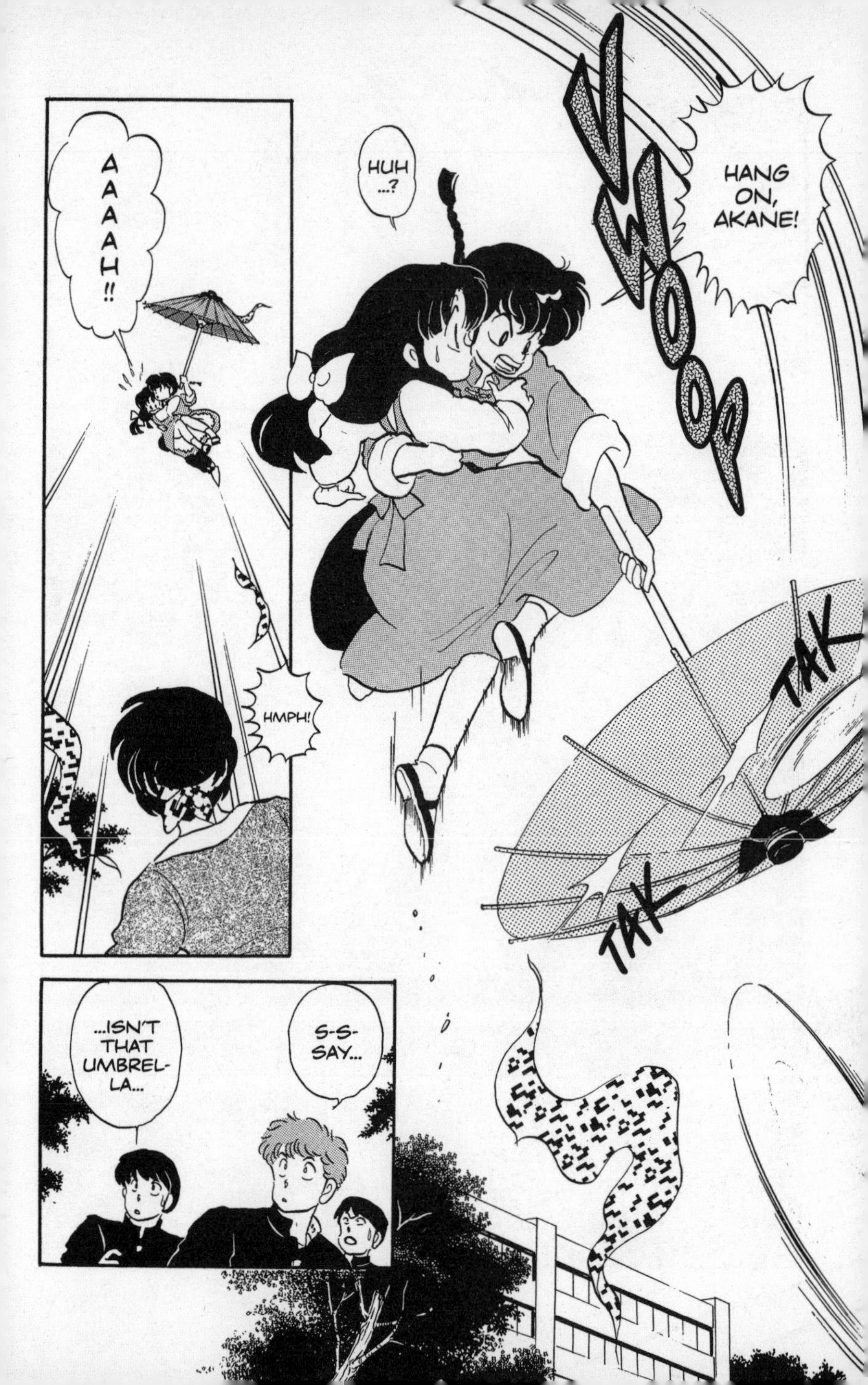
HANG ON, AKANE!
WOOOP
HUH ...?
TAK
TAK
TAK
AAAAAH!!
HMPH!
S-S-SAY...
...ISN'T THAT UMBREL-LA...

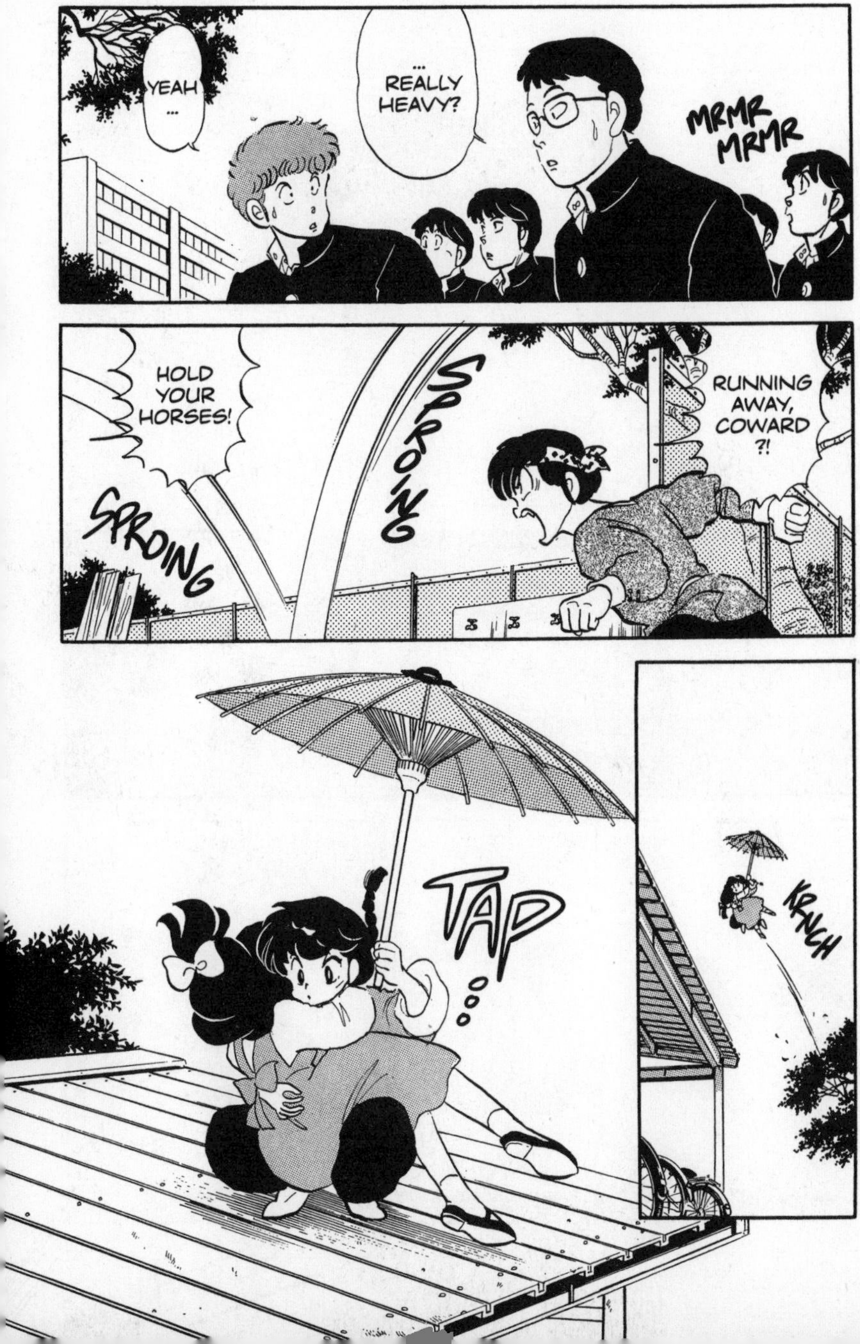
MRMR MRMR
... REALLY HEAVY?
YEAH ...
RUNNING AWAY, COWARD ?!
SPROING
SPROING
HOLD YOUR HORSES!
KRNCH
TAP

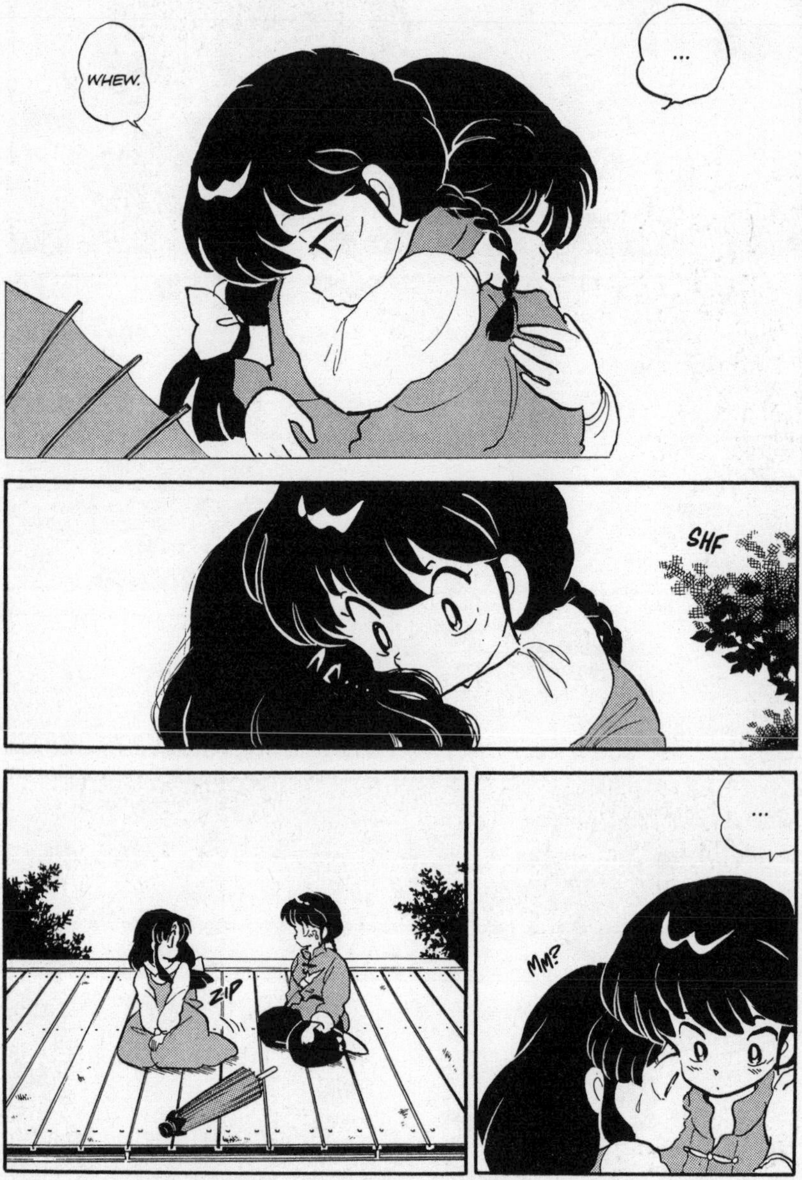
...
WHEW.
SHF
...
MM?
ZIP

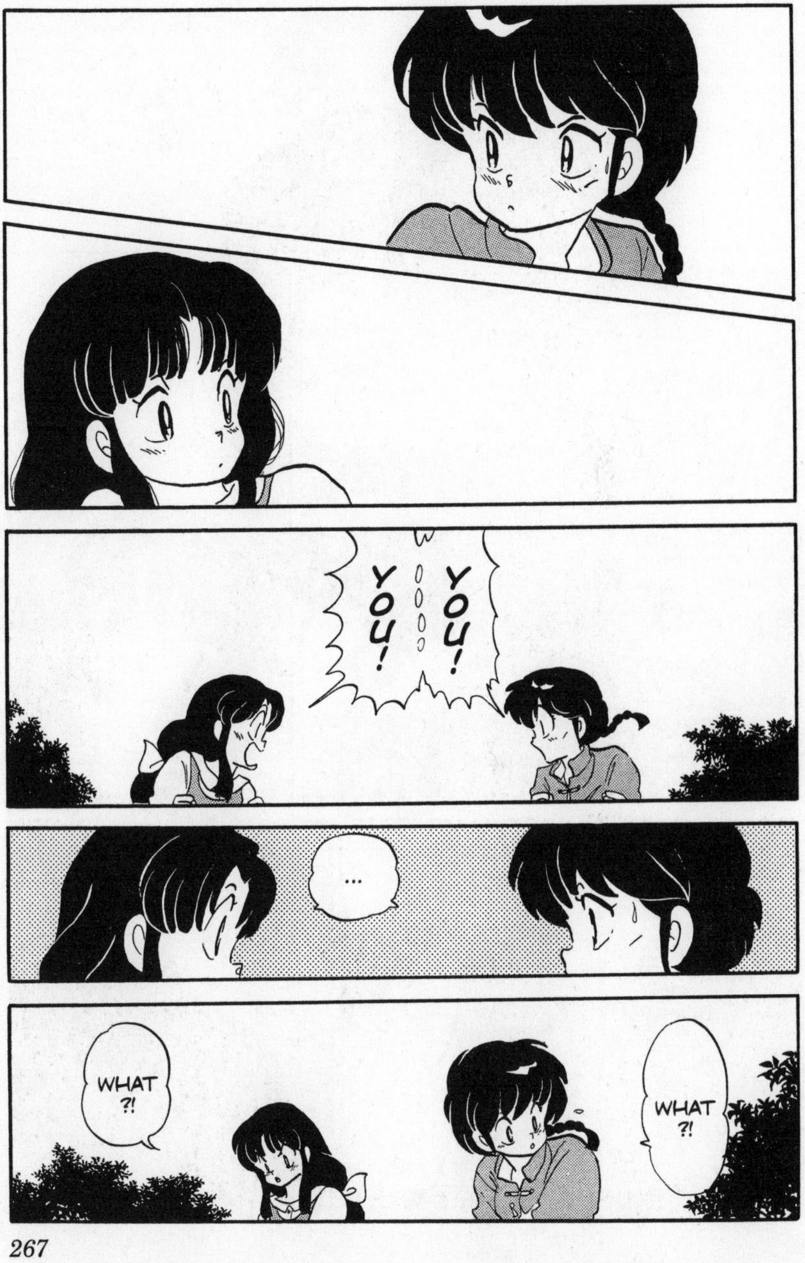
YOU!
......
YOU!
...
WHAT ?!
WHAT ?!

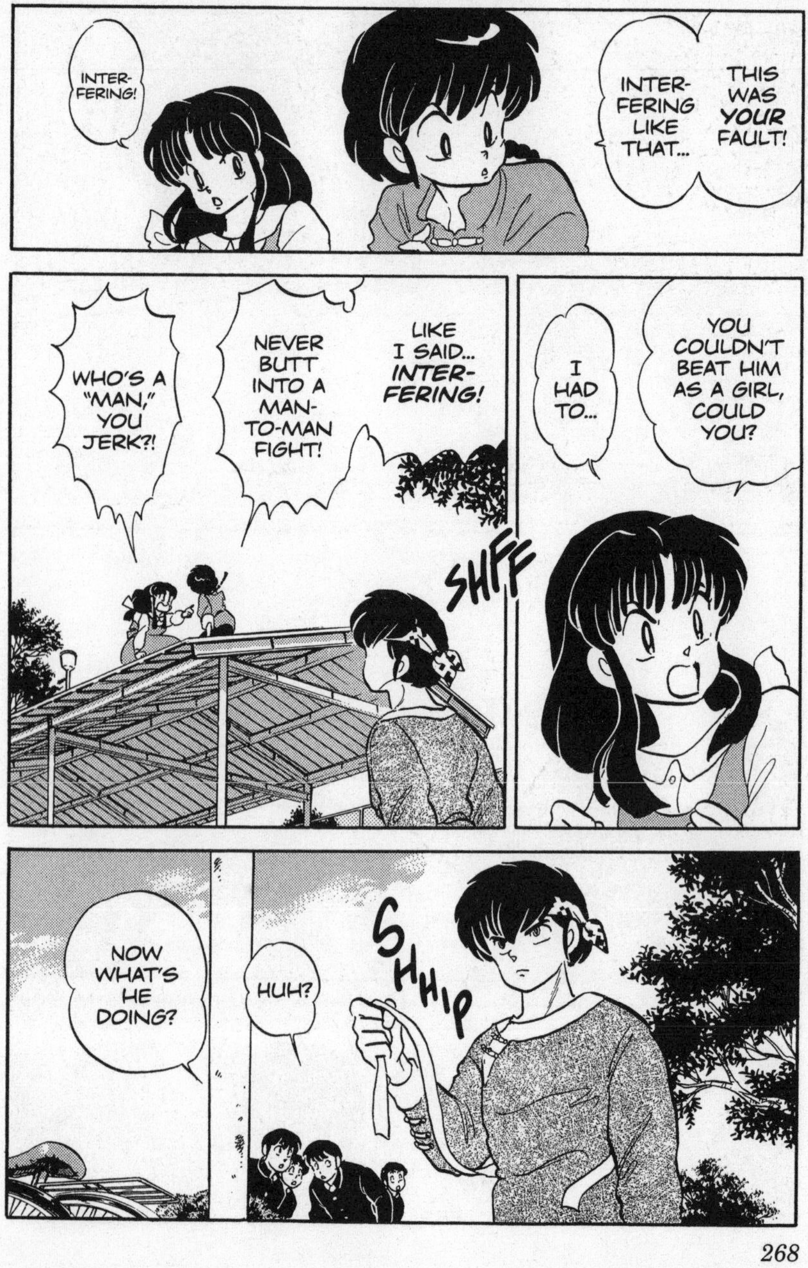
THIS WAS YOUR FAULT!
INTER-FERING LIKE THAT...
INTER-FERING!
YOU COULDN'T BEAT HIM AS A GIRL, COULD YOU?
I HAD TO...
SHFF
LIKE I SAID... INTER-FERING!
NEVER BUTT INTO A MAN-TO-MAN FIGHT!
WHO'S A "MAN," YOU JERK?!
SHHIP
HUH?
NOW WHAT'S HE DOING?

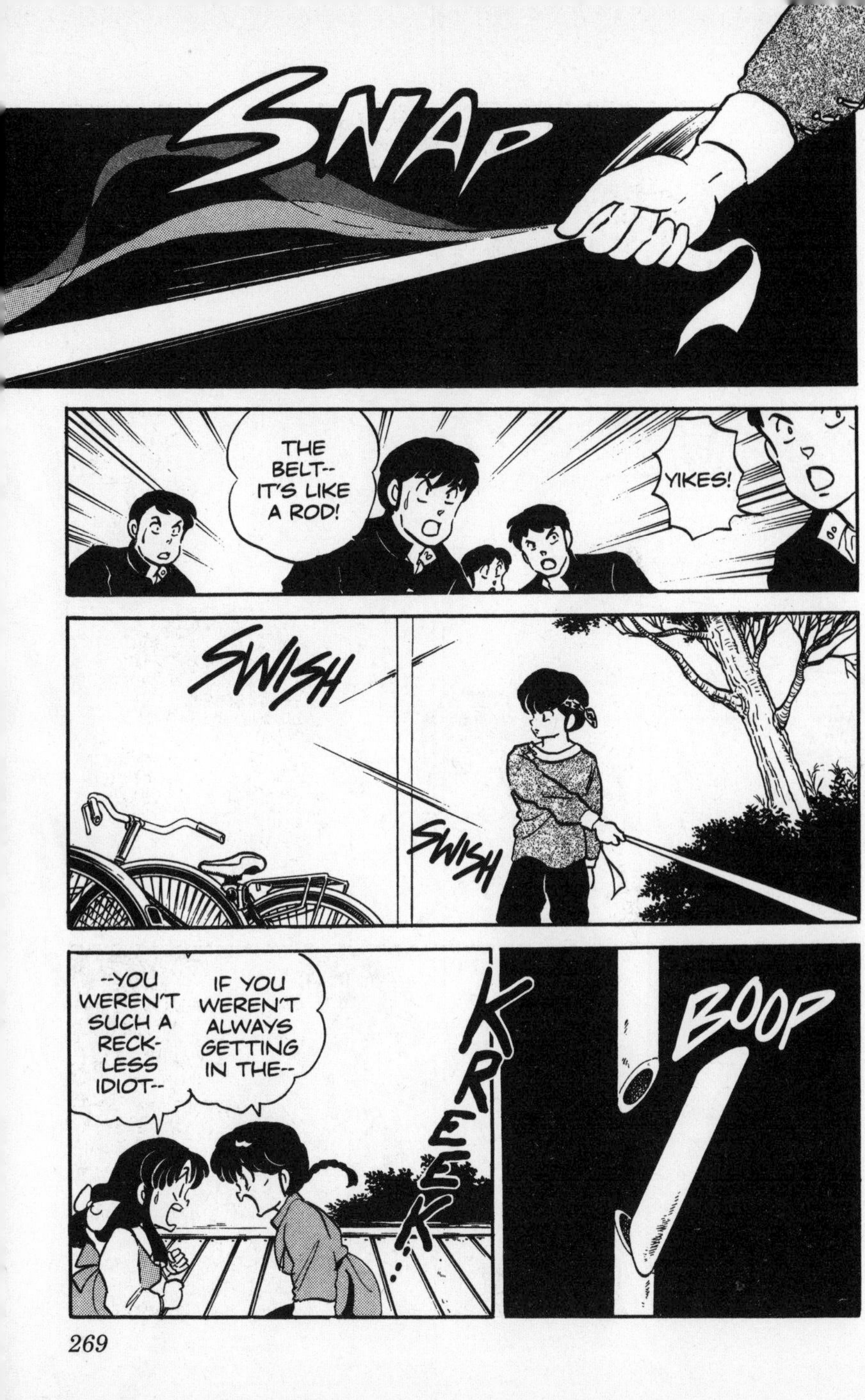
SNAP
YIKES!
THE BELT-- IT'S LIKE A ROD!
SWISH
SWISH
BOOP
KREEK...
IF YOU WEREN'T ALWAYS GETTING IN THE--
--YOU WEREN'T SUCH A RECK-LESS IDIOT--

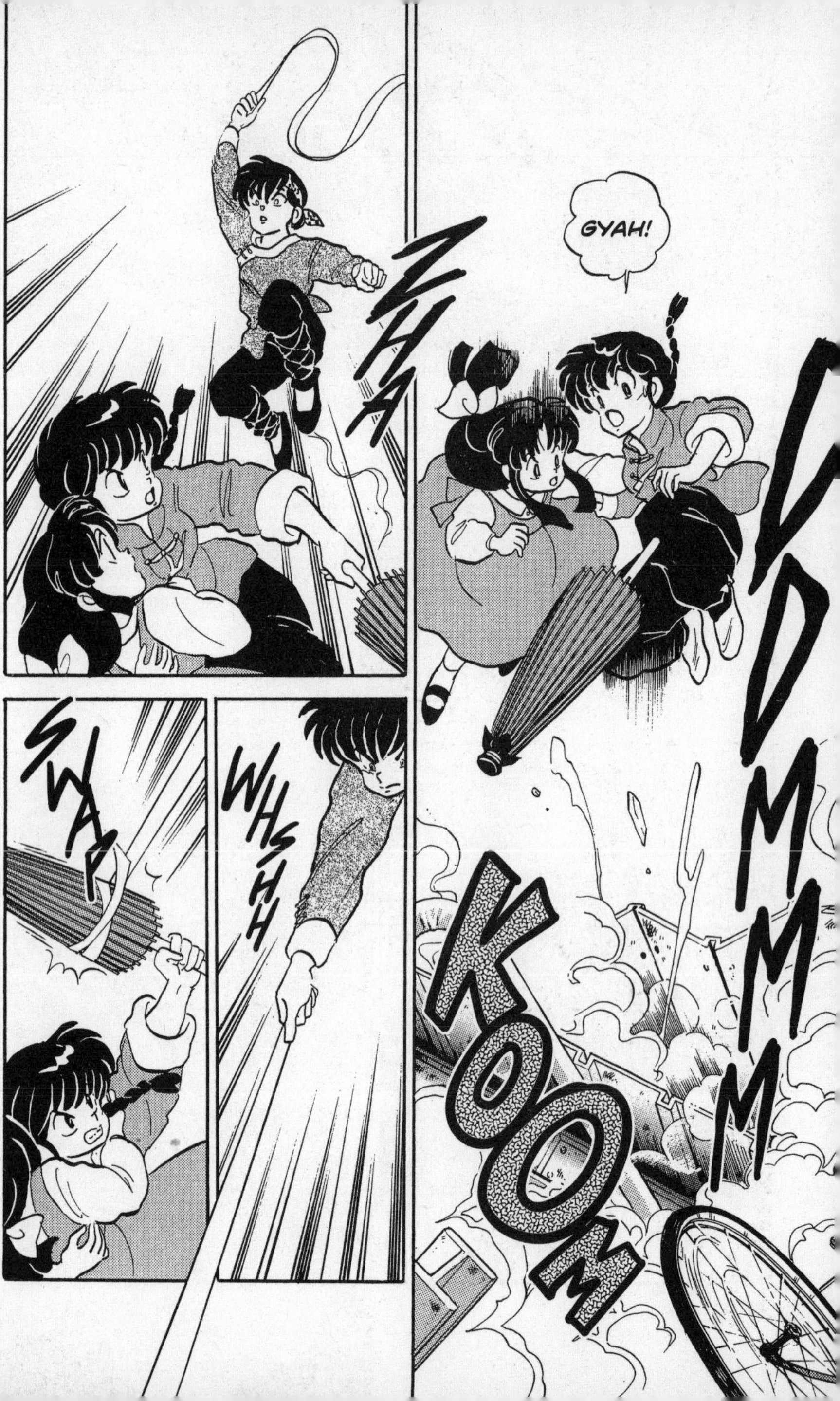
GYAH!
DMMMM
KOOOM
ZHA
WHSHHH
SWAP

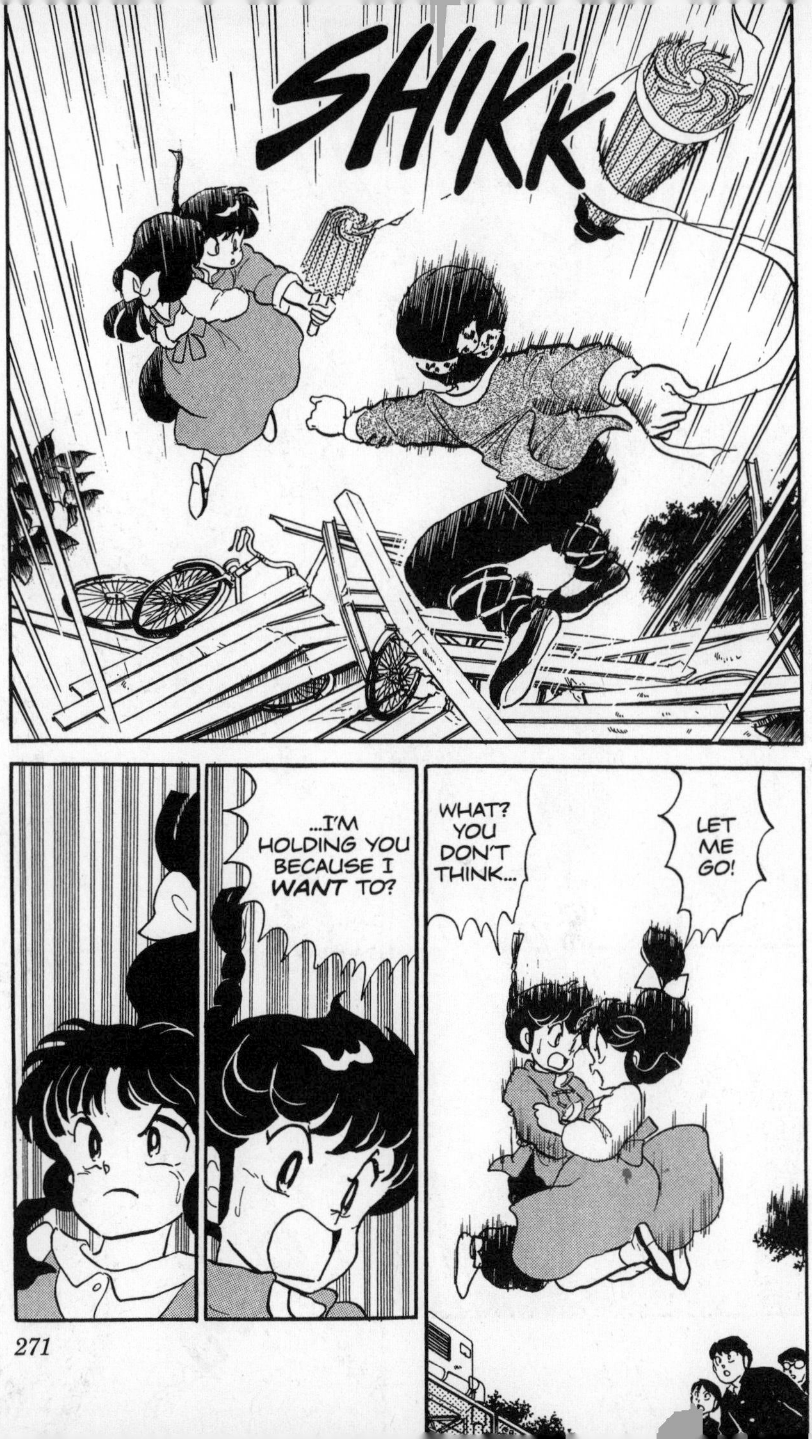
SHIKK
LET ME GO!
WHAT? YOU DON'T THINK...
...I'M HOLDING YOU BECAUSE I WANT TO?

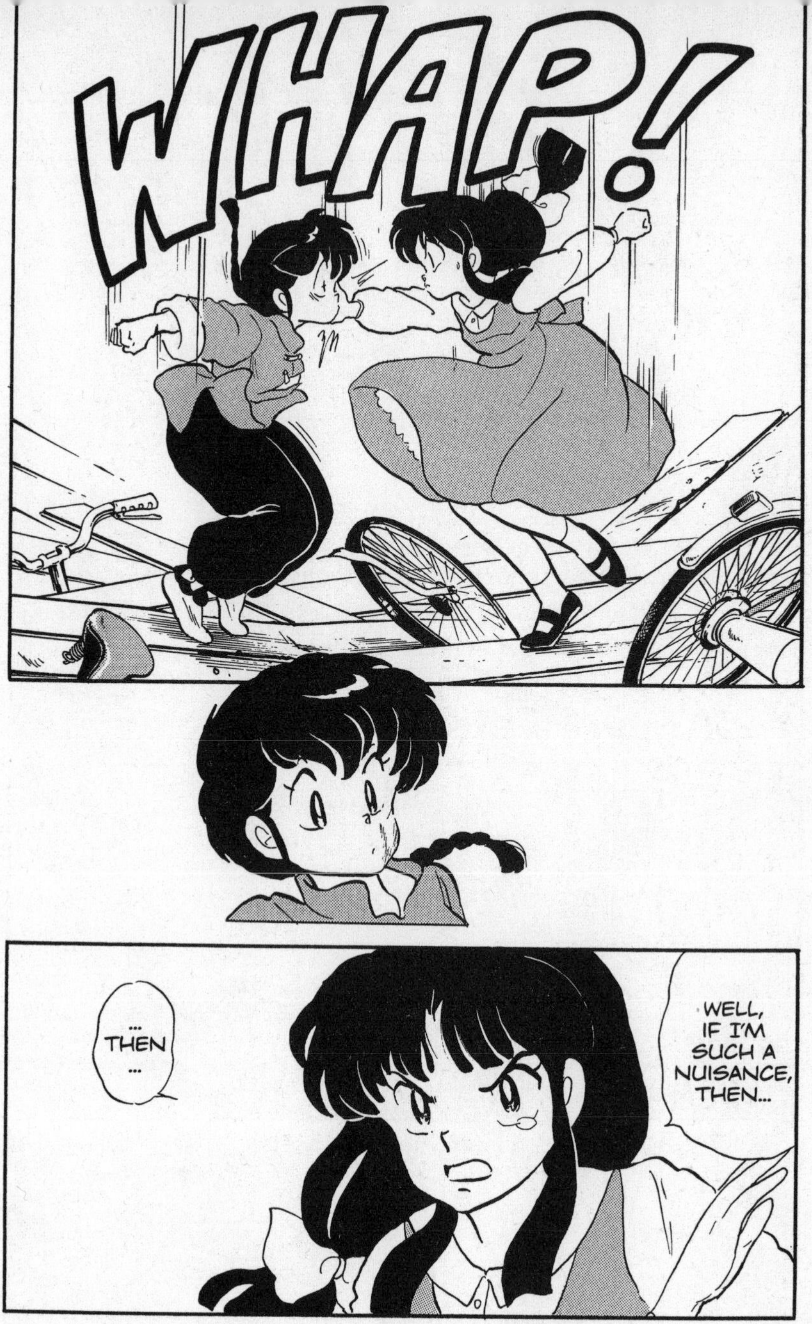
WHAP!
WELL, IF I'M SUCH A NUISANCE, THEN...
... THEN ...

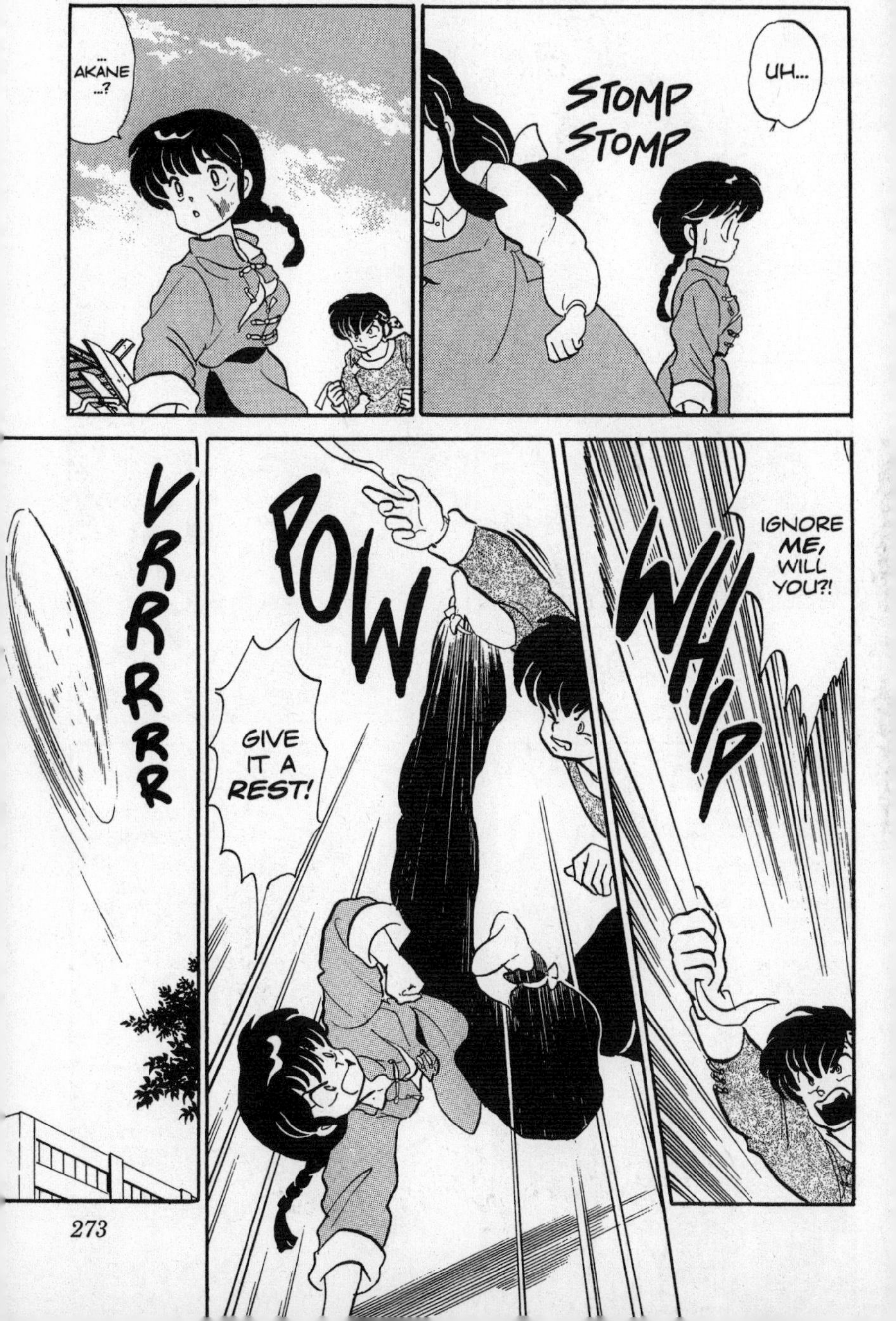
UH...
STOMP STOMP
... AKANE ...?
IGNORE ME, WILL YOU?!
WHIP
POW
GIVE IT A REST!
VRRRRR

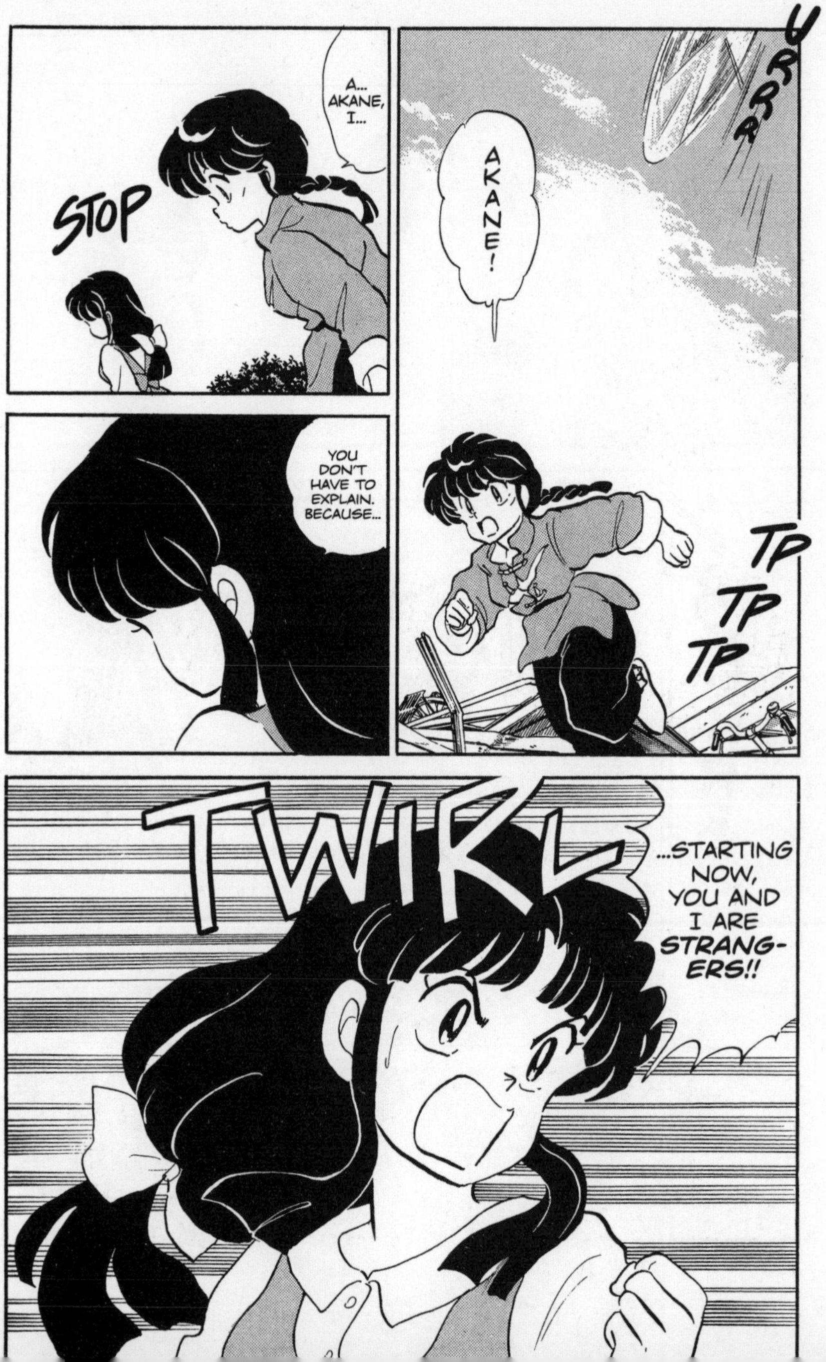
URRR
AKANE!
TP TP TP
A... AKANE, I...
STOP
YOU DON'T HAVE TO EXPLAIN. BECAUSE...
TWIRL
...STARTING NOW, YOU AND I ARE STRANG-ERS!!

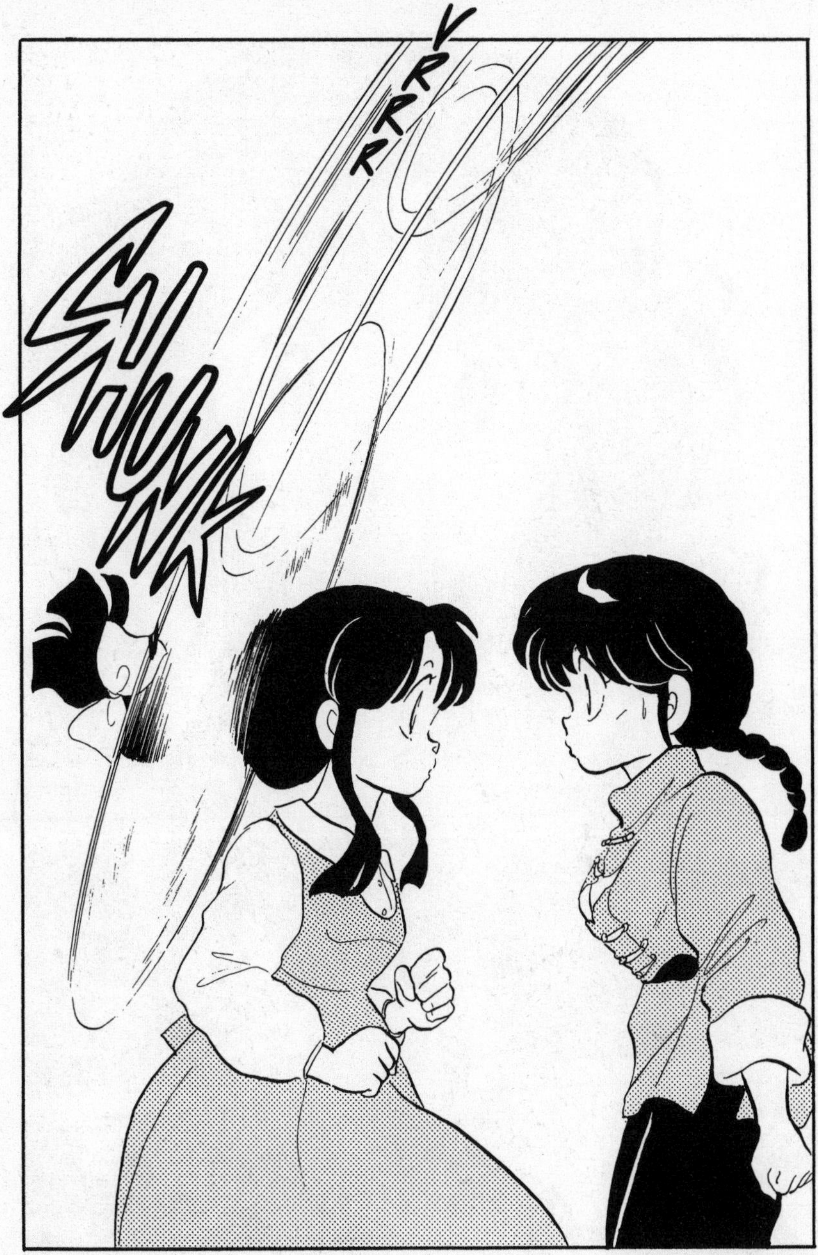
VRRRR
SHUNK

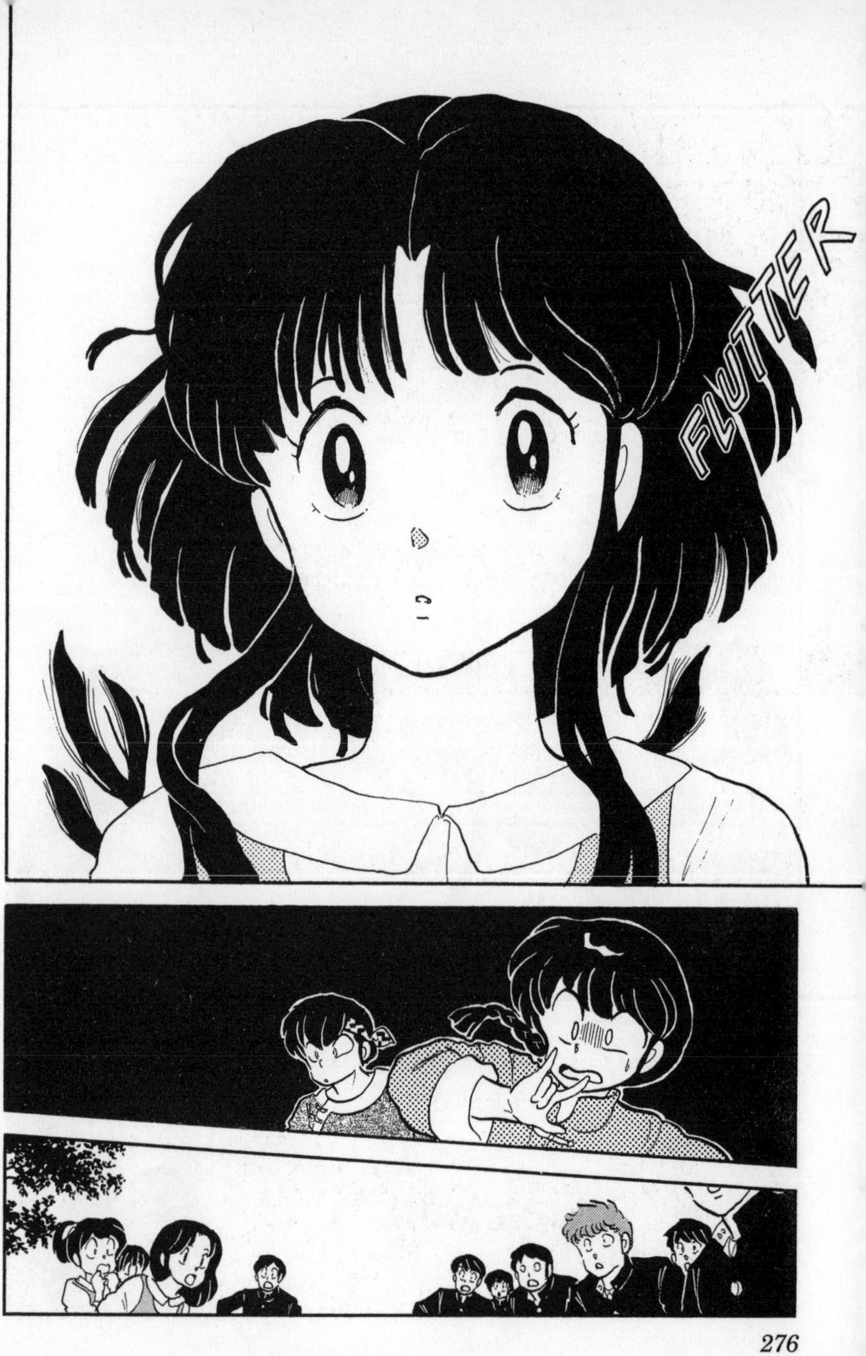
FLUTTER

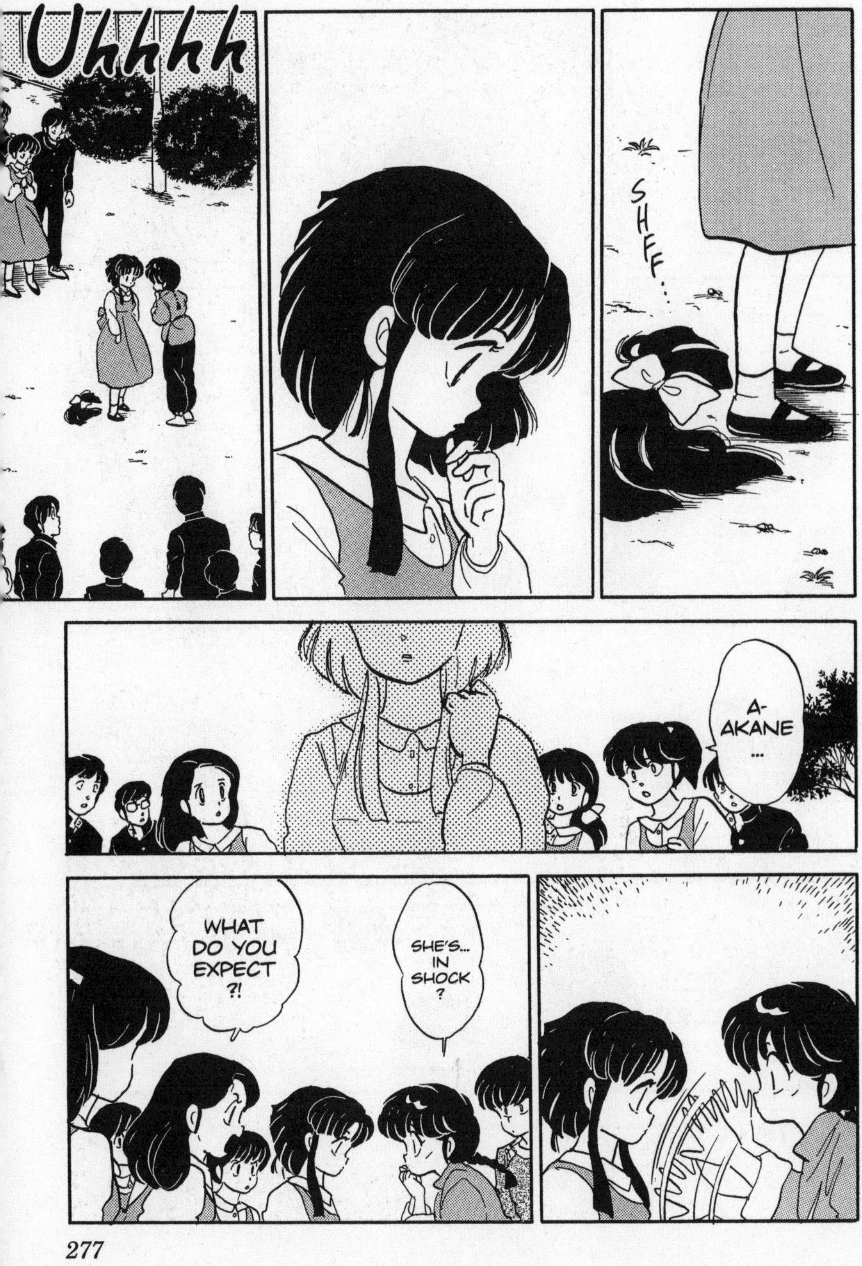
SHFF...
Uhhhh
A-AKANE...
SHE'S... IN SHOCK?
WHAT DO YOU EXPECT?!

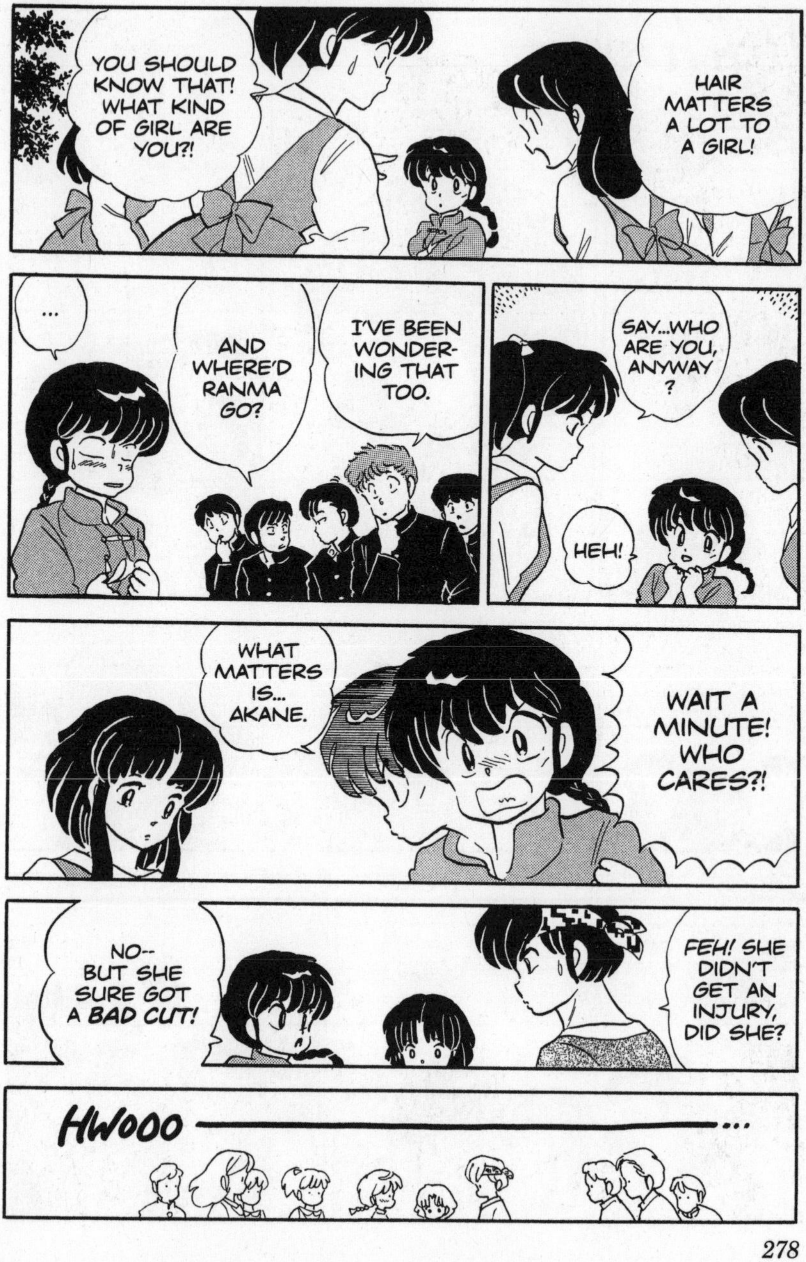
HAIR MATTERS A LOT TO A GIRL!
YOU SHOULD KNOW THAT! WHAT KIND OF GIRL ARE YOU?!
SAY...WHO ARE YOU, ANYWAY?
HEH!
I'VE BEEN WONDERING THAT TOO.
AND WHERE'D RANMA GO?
...
WAIT A MINUTE! WHO CARES?!
WHAT MATTERS IS... AKANE.
FEH! SHE DIDN'T GET AN INJURY, DID SHE?
NO-- BUT SHE SURE GOT A BAD CUT!
HWOOO ——...

HEY, AKANE.
IF IT'LL CHEER YOU UP... HIT ME!
YOU MAY HIT ME, TOO.
C'MON! SWING!
POW! LAY IT ON ME!
CAW CAW
CAW
FLAPPITY FLAP
AGREE-ABLE GIRL, ISN'T SHE?
...
SHUFFLE

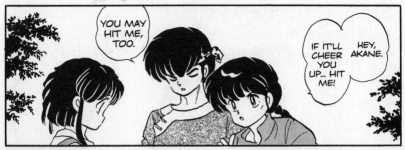

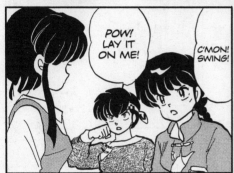

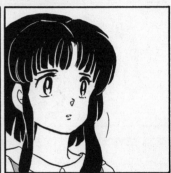

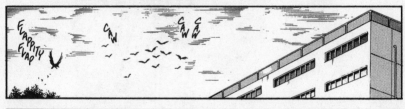

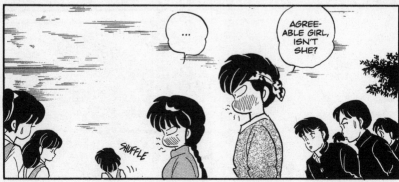

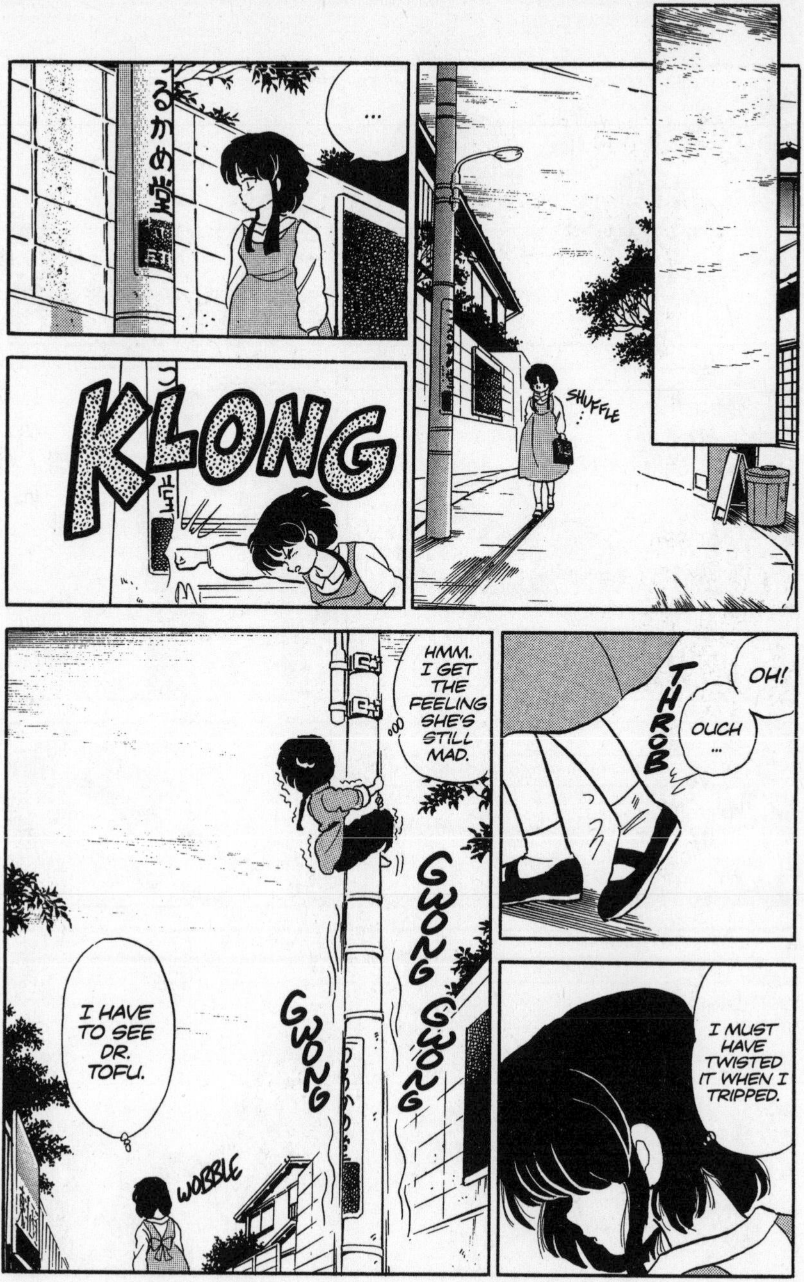
SHUFFLE
...
るかめ堂
KLONG
OH!
THROB
OUCH ...
I MUST HAVE TWISTED IT WHEN I TRIPPED.
HMM. I GET THE FEELING SHE'S STILL MAD.
GWONG
GWONG
GWONG
I HAVE TO SEE DR. TOFU.
WOBBLE

# PART 14
# WHO SAYS YOU'RE CUTE?!

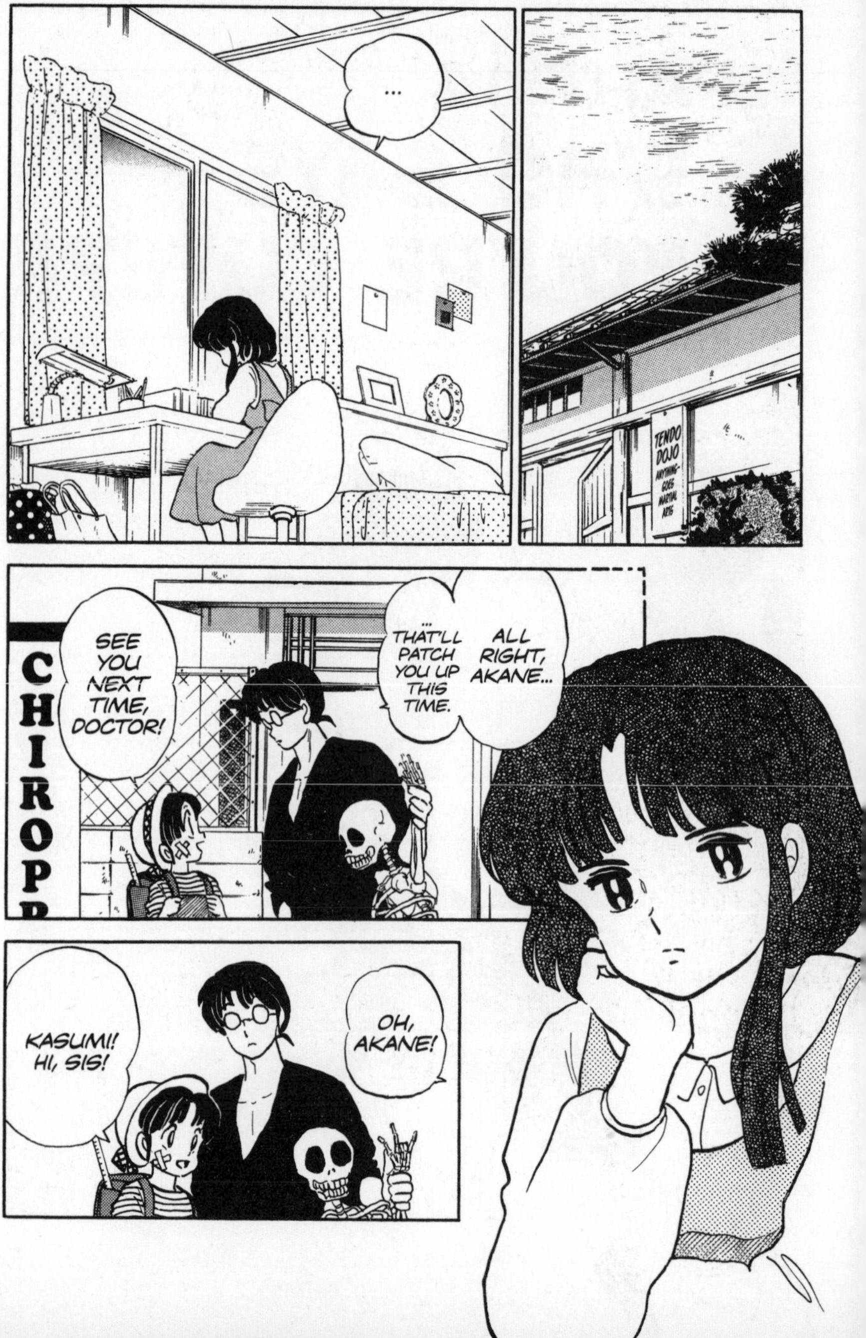
TENDO DOJO ANYTHING-GOES MARTIAL ARTS
...
ALL RIGHT, AKANE... ... THAT'LL PATCH YOU UP THIS TIME.
CHIROPR
SEE YOU NEXT TIME, DOCTOR!
OH, AKANE!
KASUMI! HI, SIS!

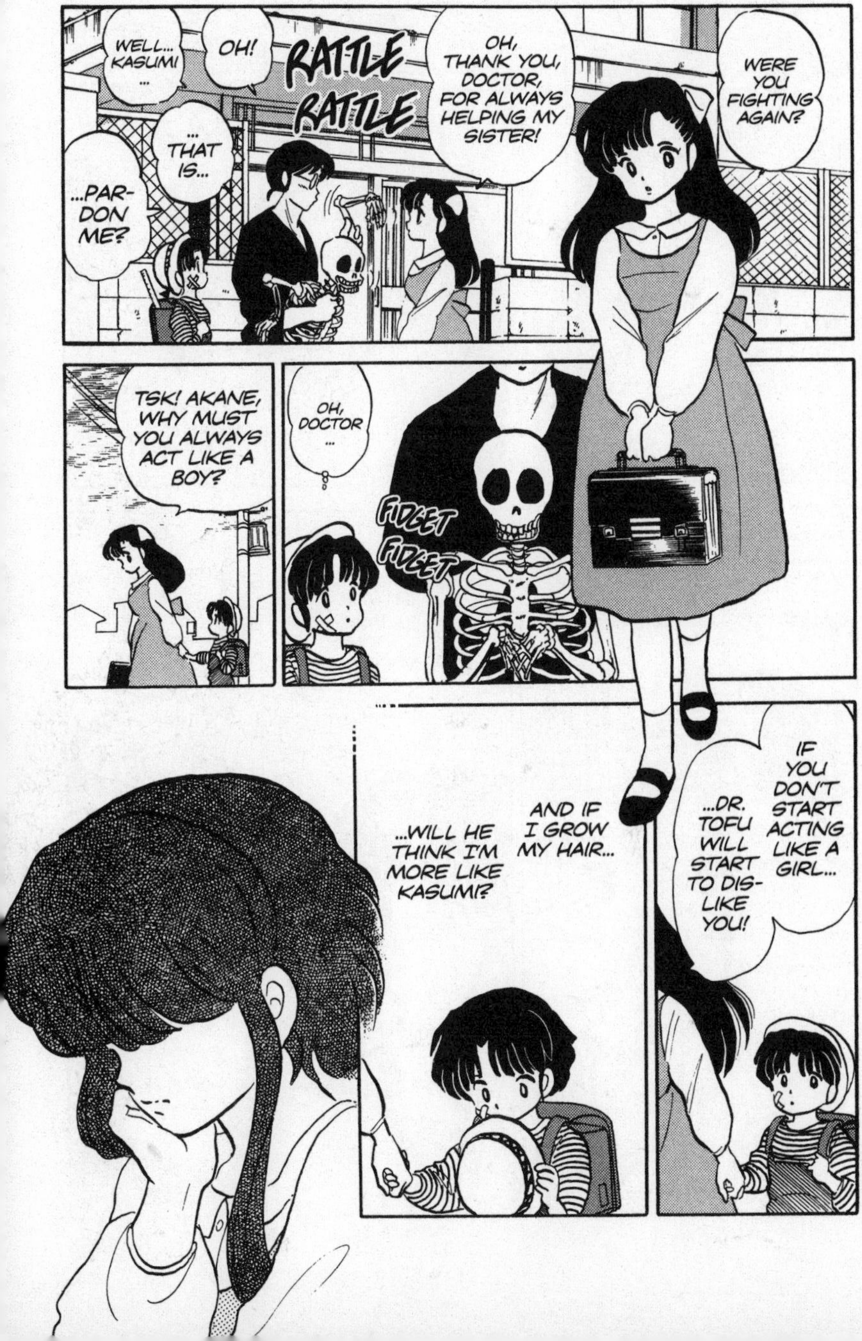
WERE YOU FIGHTING AGAIN?
OH, THANK YOU, DOCTOR, FOR ALWAYS HELPING MY SISTER!
RATTLE RATTLE
OH!
WELL... KASUMI ...
... THAT IS...
...PAR-DON ME?
OH, DOCTOR ...
FIDGET FIDGET
TSK! AKANE, WHY MUST YOU ALWAYS ACT LIKE A BOY?
IF YOU DON'T START ACTING LIKE A GIRL...
...DR. TOFU WILL START TO DIS-LIKE YOU!
AND IF I GROW MY HAIR...
...WILL HE THINK I'M MORE LIKE KASUMI?

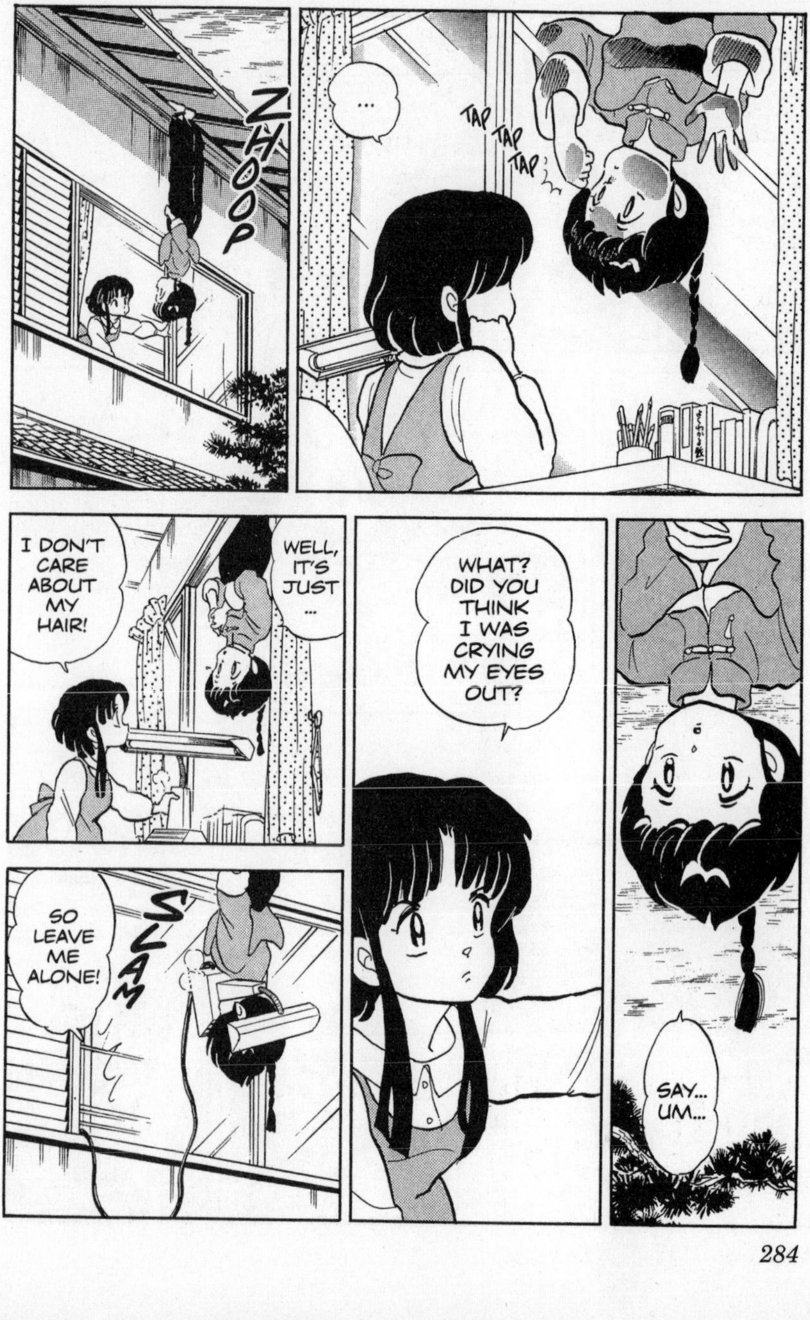
TAP TAP TAP
...
ZHOOOP
SAY... UM...
WHAT? DID YOU THINK I WAS CRYING MY EYES OUT?
WELL, IT'S JUST ...
I DON'T CARE ABOUT MY HAIR!
SO LEAVE ME ALONE!
SLAM

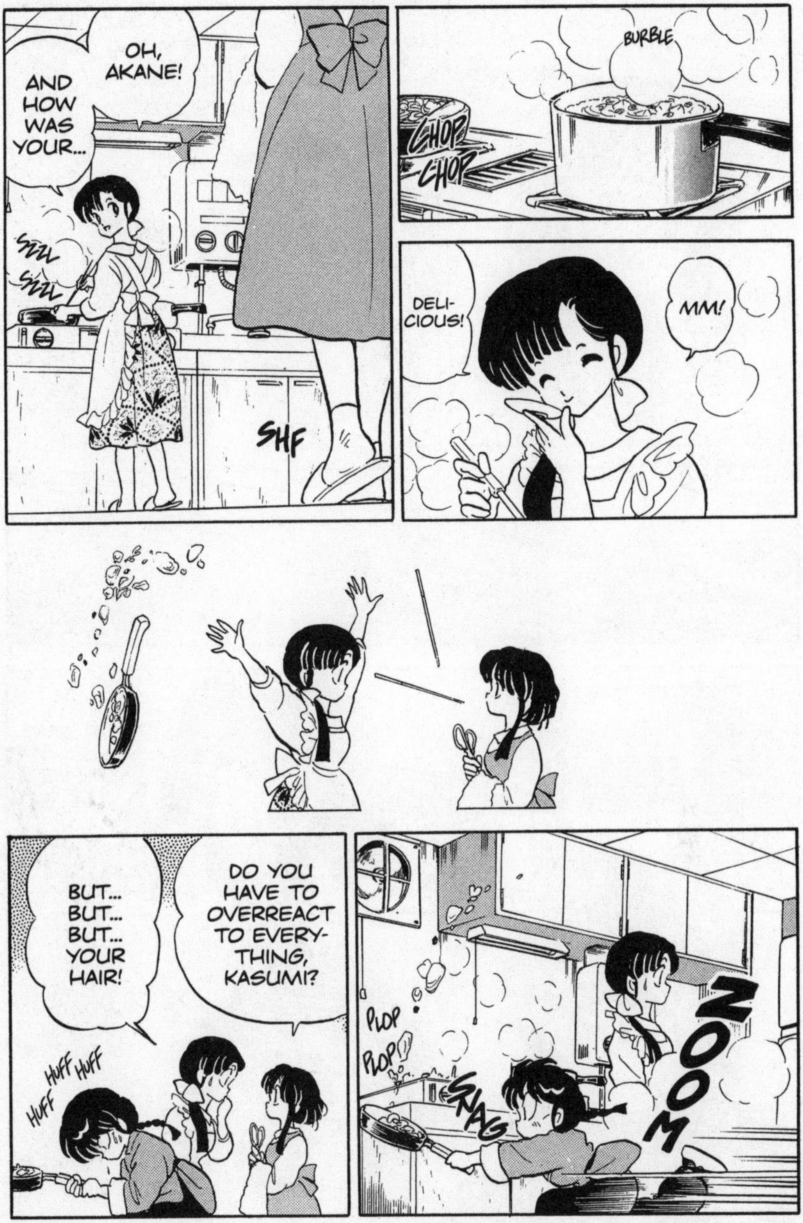
BURBLE
CHOP CHOP
MM!
DELI-CIOUS!
OH, AKANE!
AND HOW WAS YOUR...
SHF
ZOOM
SNAG
PLOP
PLOP
DO YOU HAVE TO OVERREACT TO EVERY-THING, KASUMI?
BUT... BUT... BUT... YOUR HAIR!
HUFF HUFF HUFF

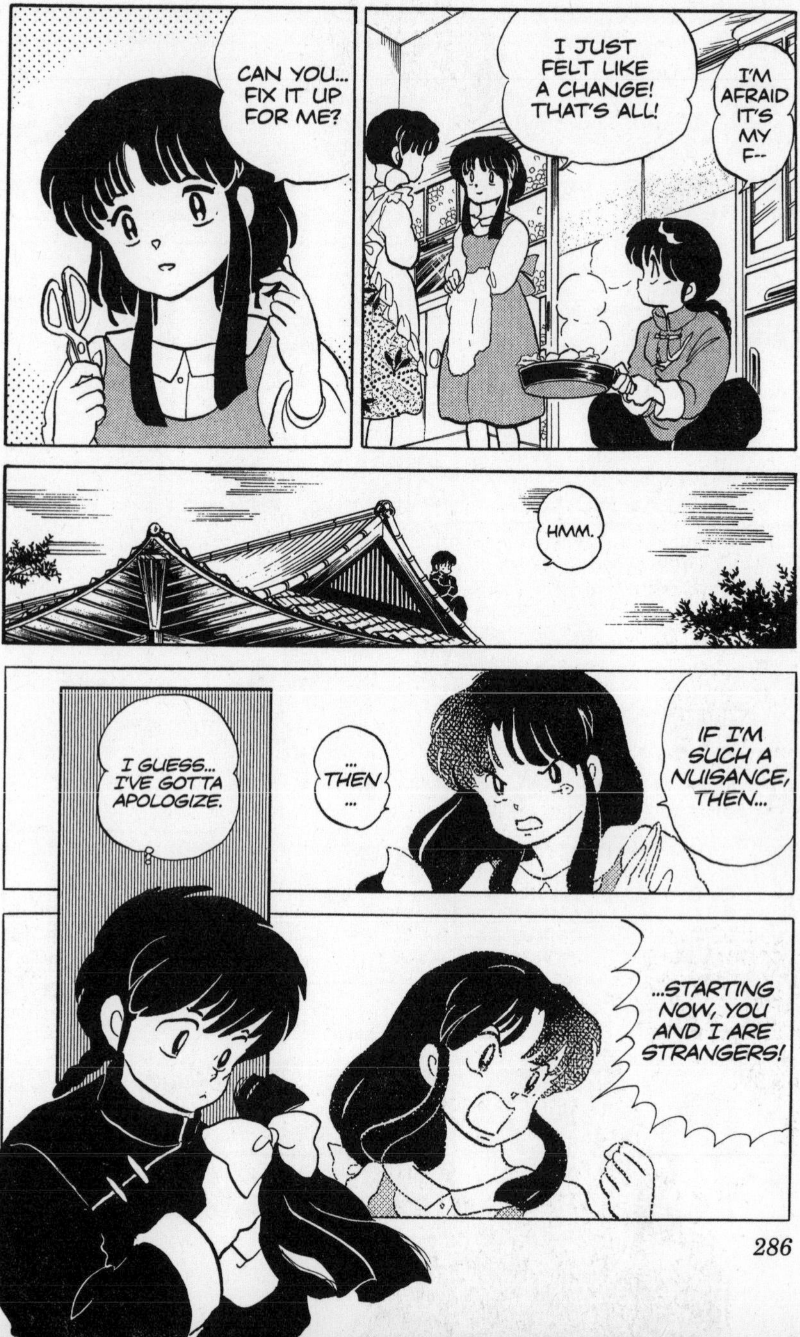
I'M AFRAID IT'S MY F--
I JUST FELT LIKE A CHANGE! THAT'S ALL!
CAN YOU... FIX IT UP FOR ME?
HMM.
IF I'M SUCH A NUISANCE, THEN...
...THEN...
I GUESS... I'VE GOTTA APOLOGIZE.
...STARTING NOW, YOU AND I ARE STRANGERS!

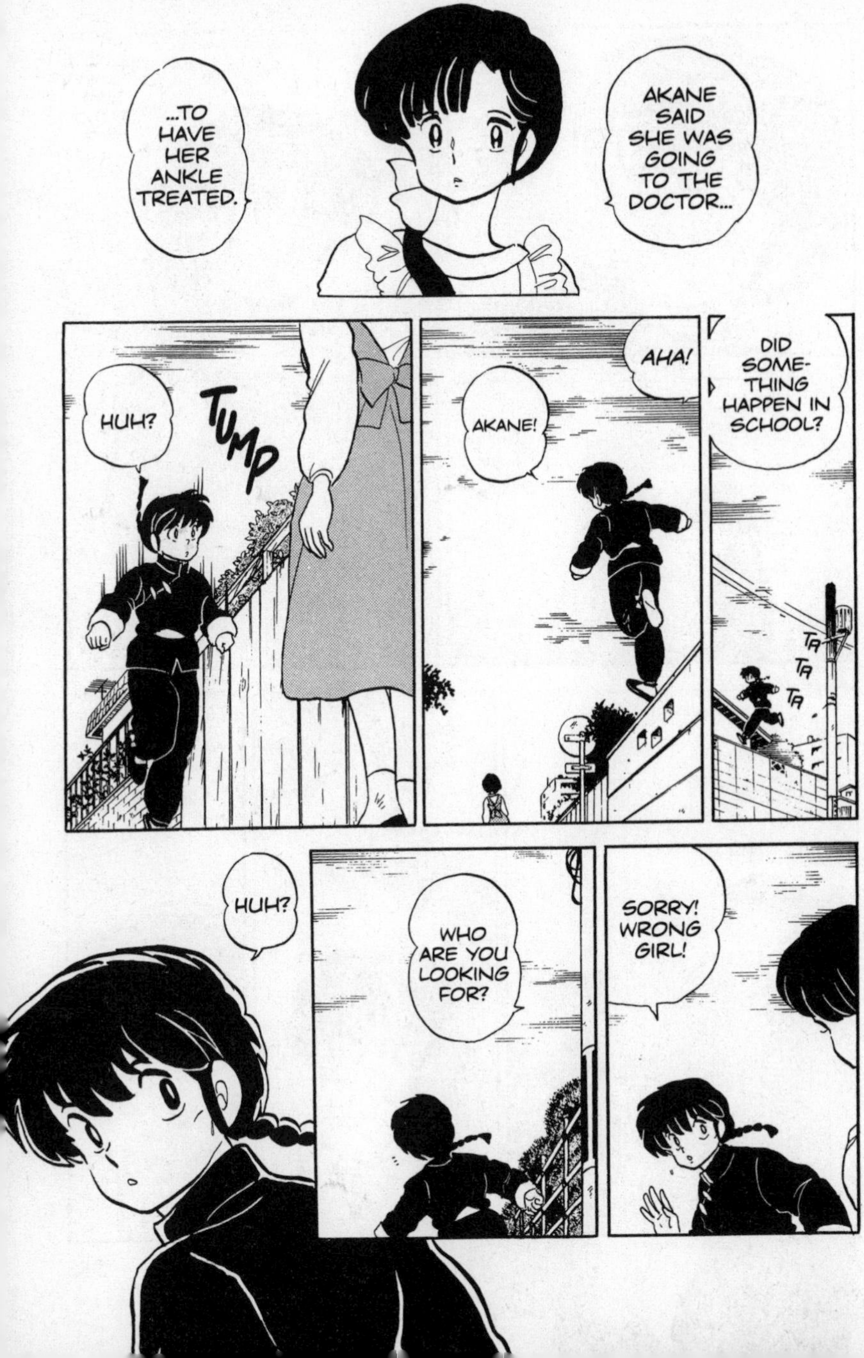
AKANE SAID SHE WAS GOING TO THE DOCTOR...
...TO HAVE HER ANKLE TREATED.
DID SOME-THING HAPPEN IN SCHOOL?
TA TA TA
AHA!
AKANE!
HUH?
TUMP
SORRY! WRONG GIRL!
WHO ARE YOU LOOKING FOR?
HUH?

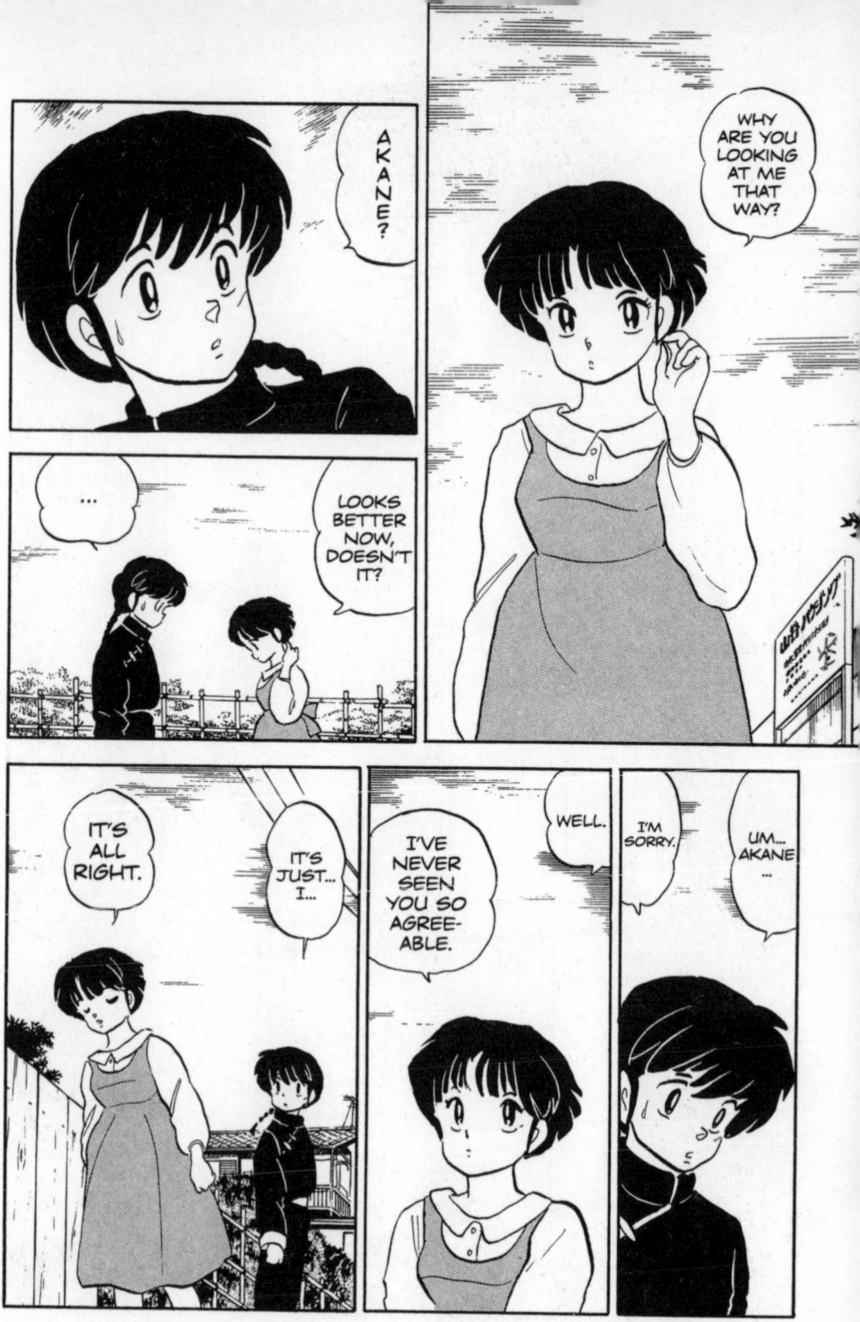
WHY ARE YOU LOOKING AT ME THAT WAY?
AKANE?
LOOKS BETTER NOW, DOESN'T IT?
...
UM... AKANE ...
I'M SORRY.
WELL.
I'VE NEVER SEEN YOU SO AGREE-ABLE.
IT'S JUST... I...
IT'S ALL RIGHT.

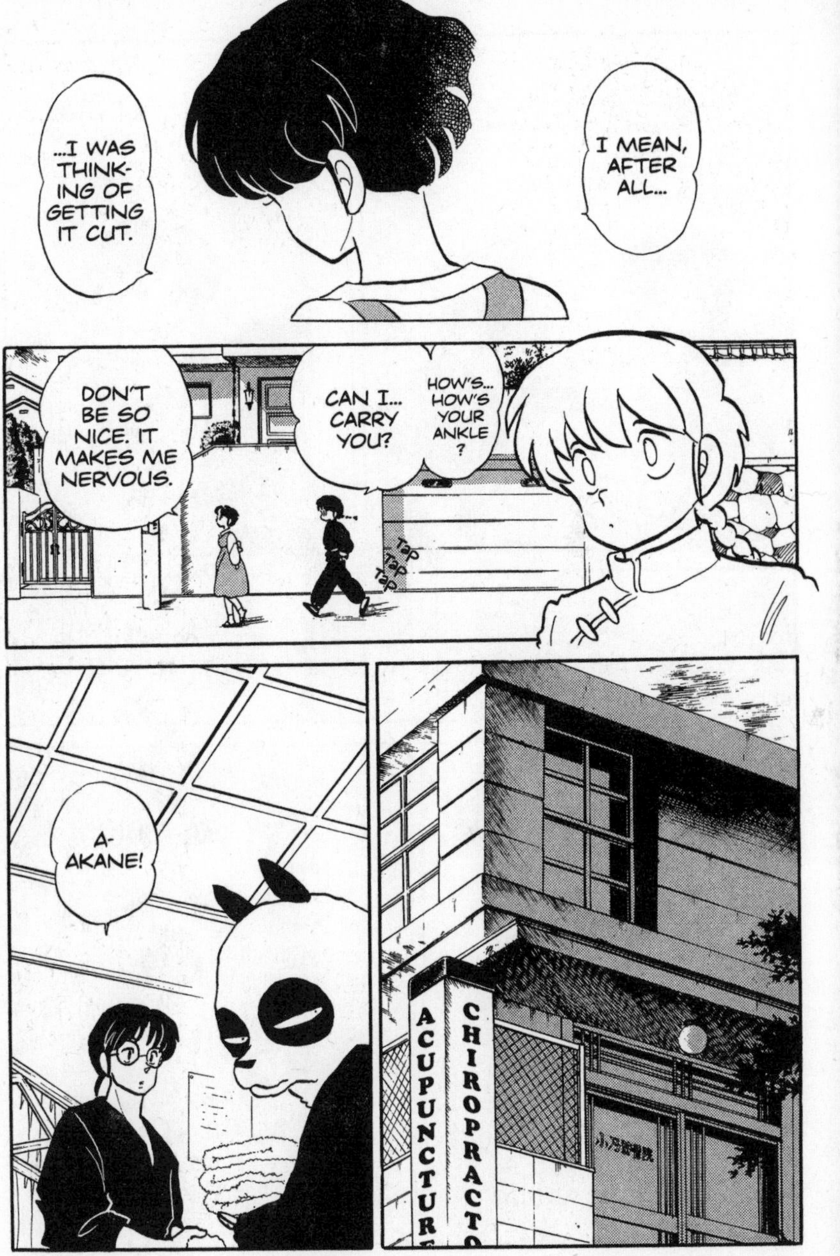
I MEAN, AFTER ALL...
...I WAS THINKING OF GETTING IT CUT.
HOW'S... HOW'S YOUR ANKLE?
CAN I... CARRY YOU?
DON'T BE SO NICE. IT MAKES ME NERVOUS.
Tap Tap Tap
CHIROPRACTO
ACUPUNCTUR
A-AKANE!

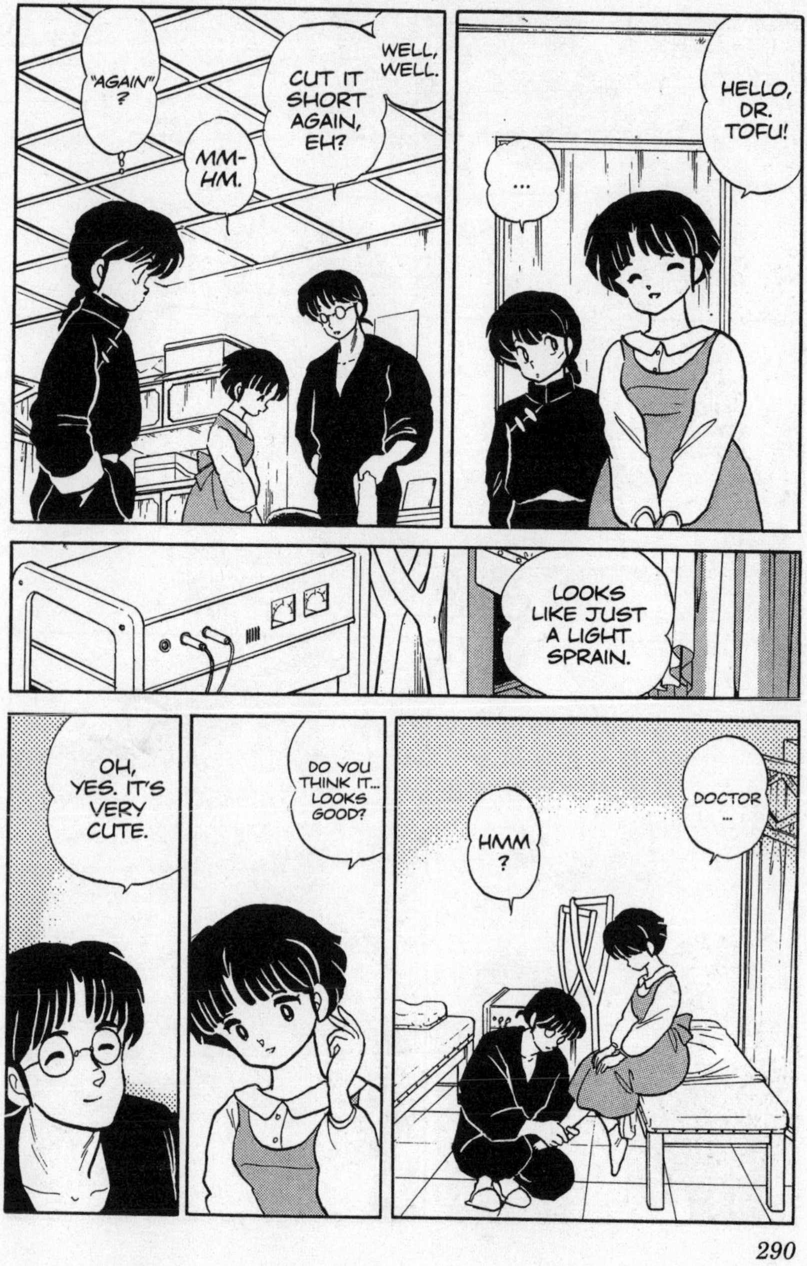
HELLO, DR. TOFU!
...
WELL, WELL.
CUT IT SHORT AGAIN, EH?
MM-HM.
"AGAIN"?
LOOKS LIKE JUST A LIGHT SPRAIN.
DOCTOR ...
HMM?
DO YOU THINK IT... LOOKS GOOD?
OH, YES. IT'S VERY CUTE.

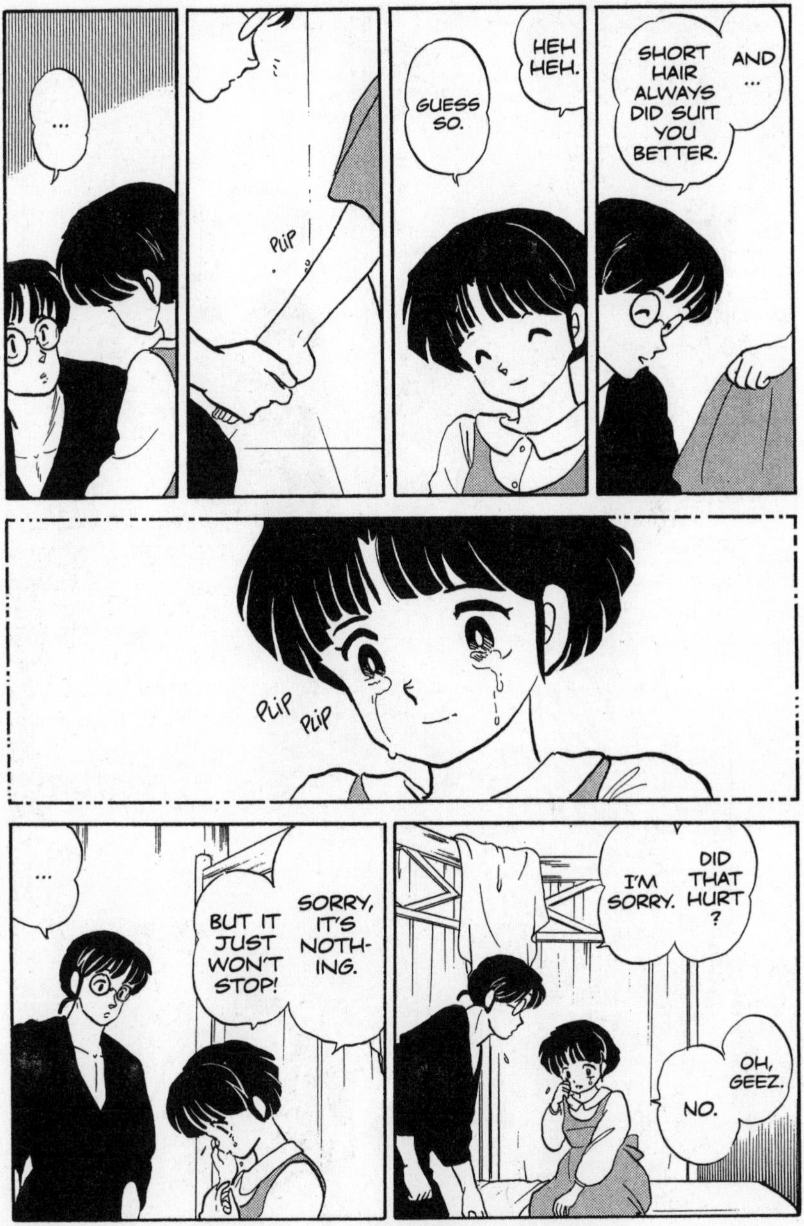
AND ...
SHORT HAIR ALWAYS DID SUIT YOU BETTER.
HEH HEH.
GUESS SO.
PLIP
...
PLIP PLIP
DID THAT HURT?
I'M SORRY.
OH, GEEZ.
NO.
SORRY, IT'S NOTHING.
BUT IT JUST WON'T STOP!
...

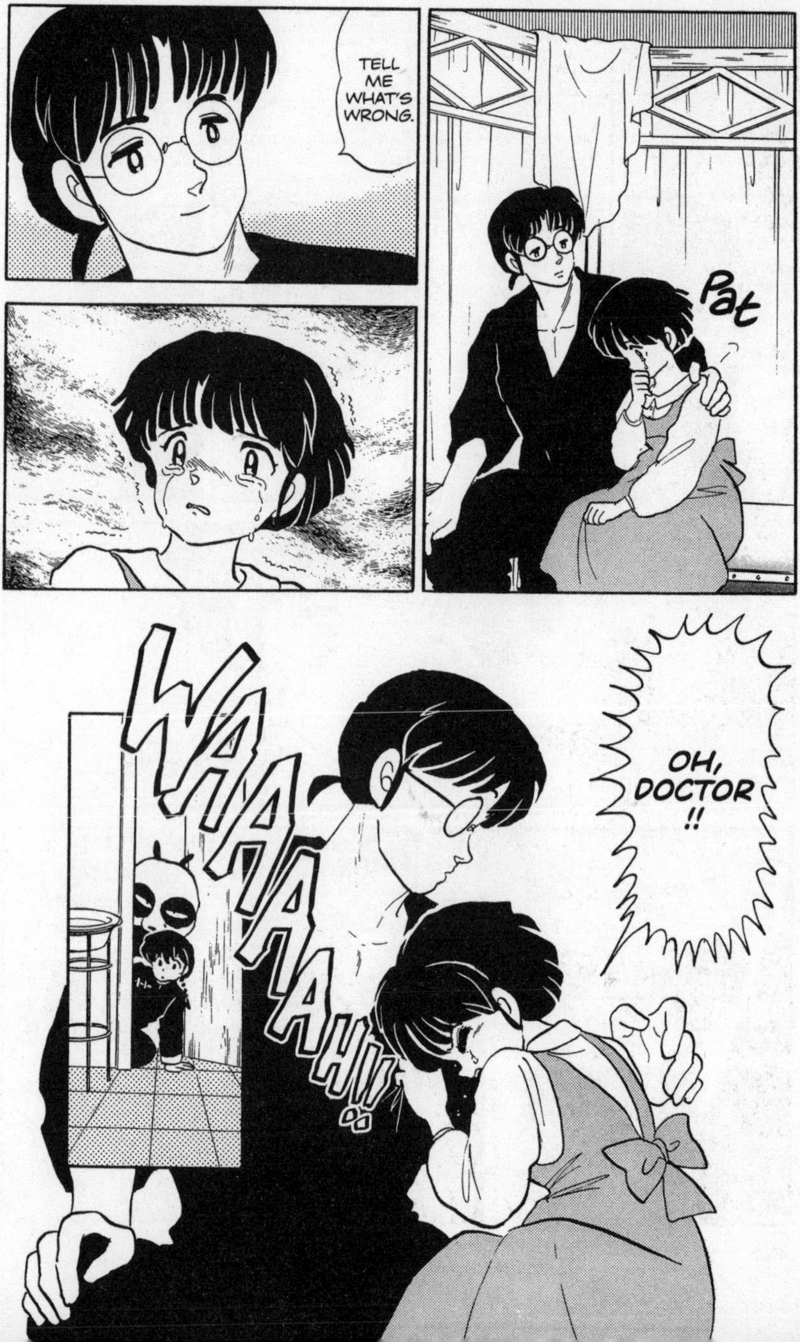
Pat
TELL ME WHAT'S WRONG.
OH, DOCTOR!!
WAAAAAH!!

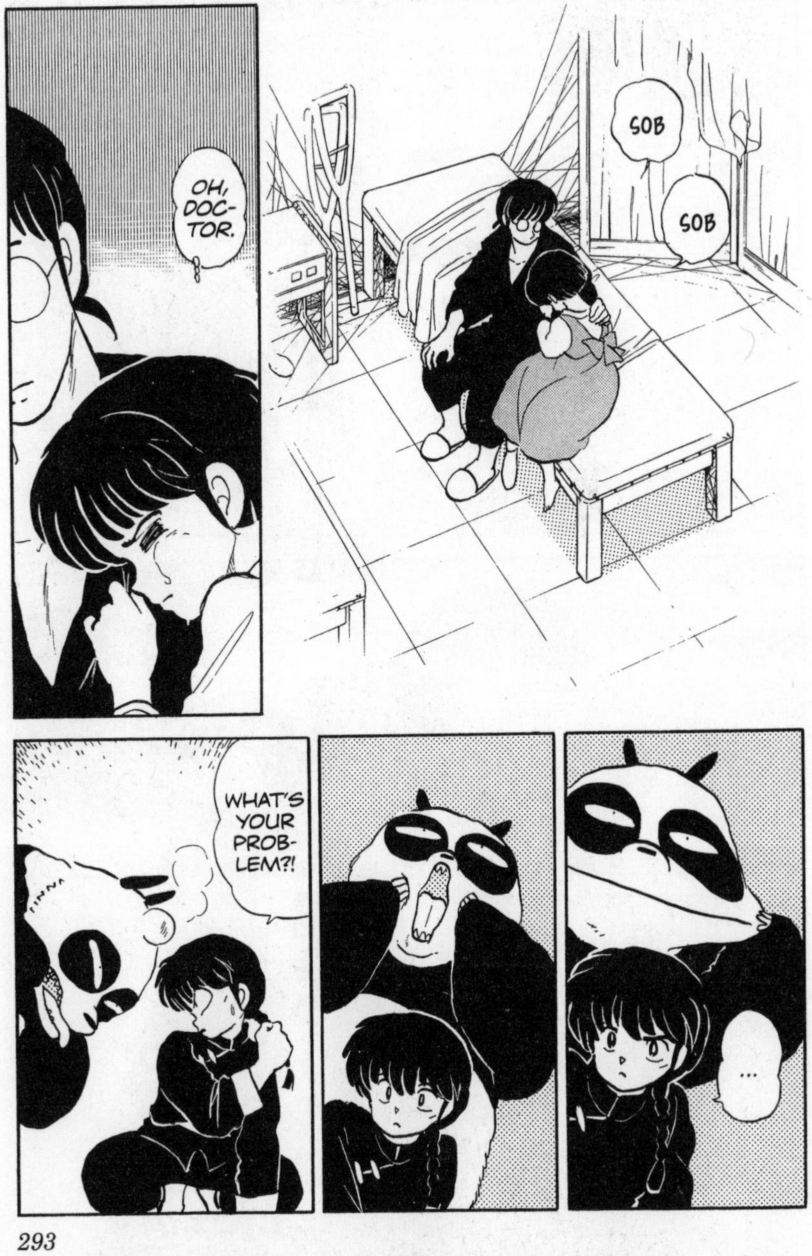
SOB
SOB
OH, DOCTOR.
...
WHAT'S YOUR PROBLEM?!

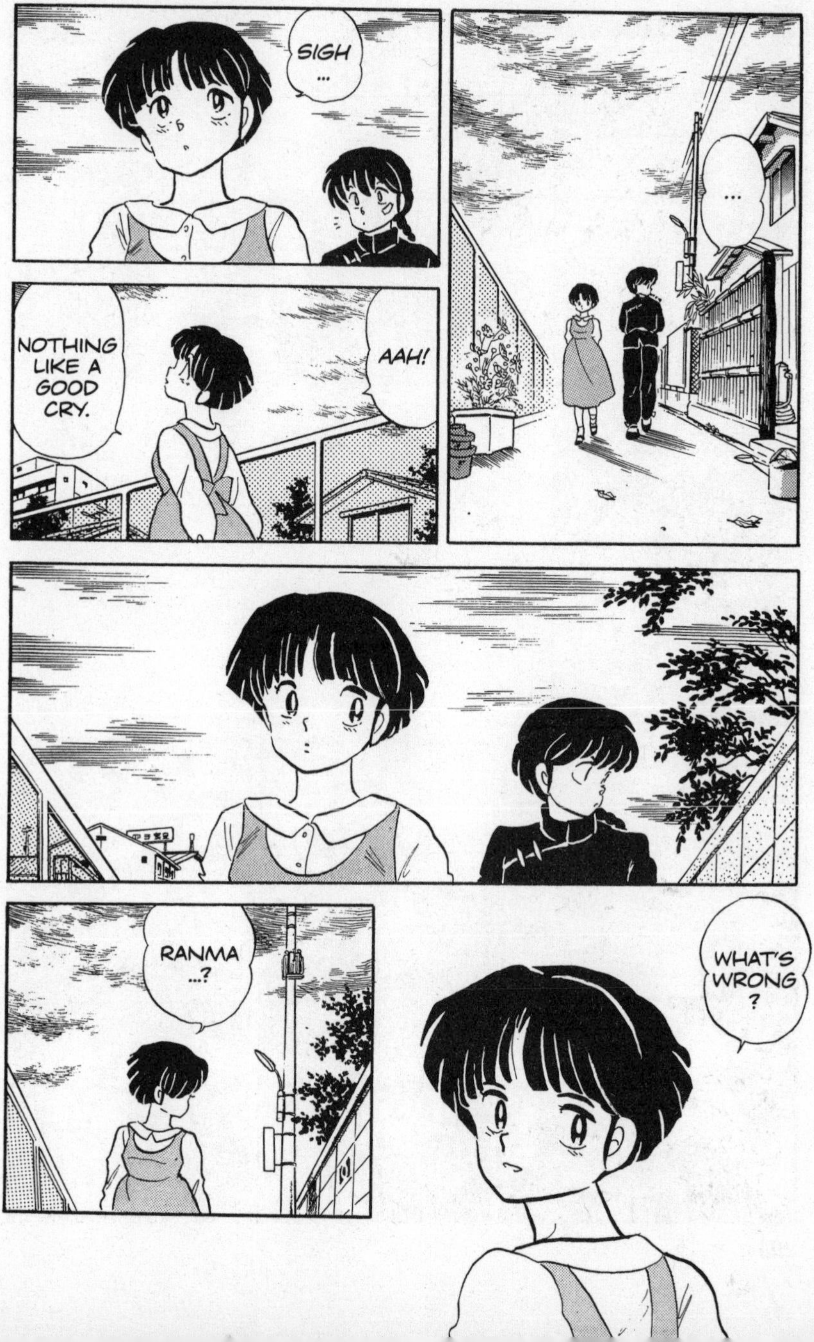
...
SIGH ...
AAH!
NOTHING LIKE A GOOD CRY.
WHAT'S WRONG ?
RANMA ...?

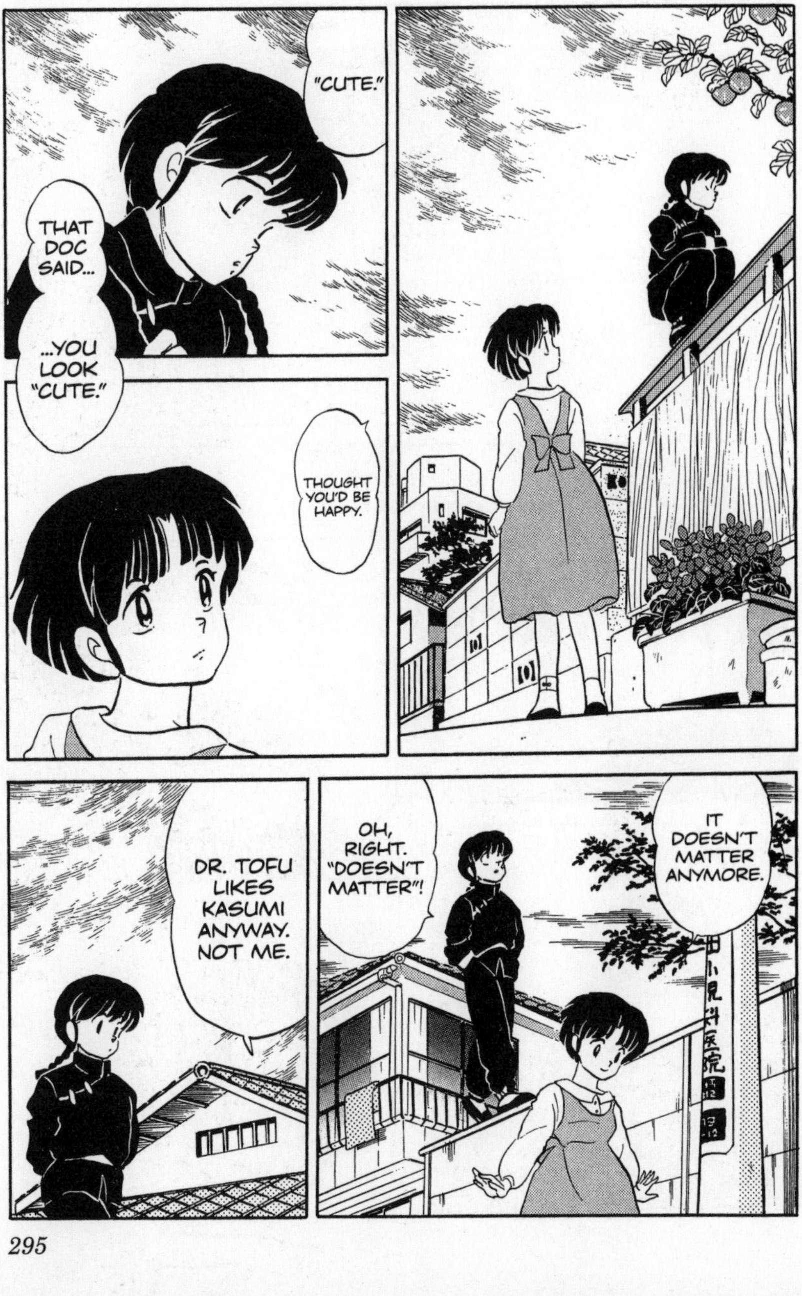
"CUTE."
THAT DOC SAID...
...YOU LOOK "CUTE."
THOUGHT YOU'D BE HAPPY.
IT DOESN'T MATTER ANYMORE.
OH, RIGHT. "DOESN'T MATTER"!
DR. TOFU LIKES KASUMI ANYWAY. NOT ME.

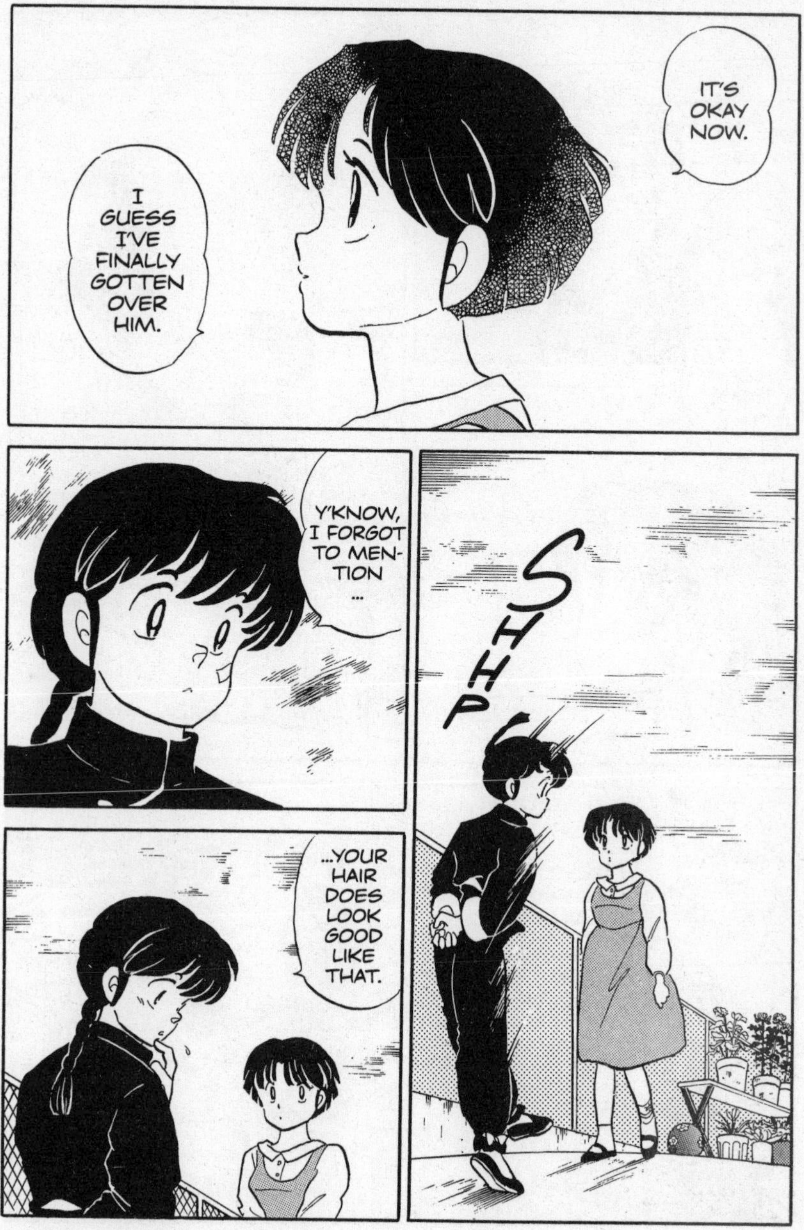
IT'S OKAY NOW.
I GUESS I'VE FINALLY GOTTEN OVER HIM.
SHHP
Y'KNOW, I FORGOT TO MEN-TION ...
...YOUR HAIR DOES LOOK GOOD LIKE THAT.

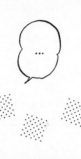

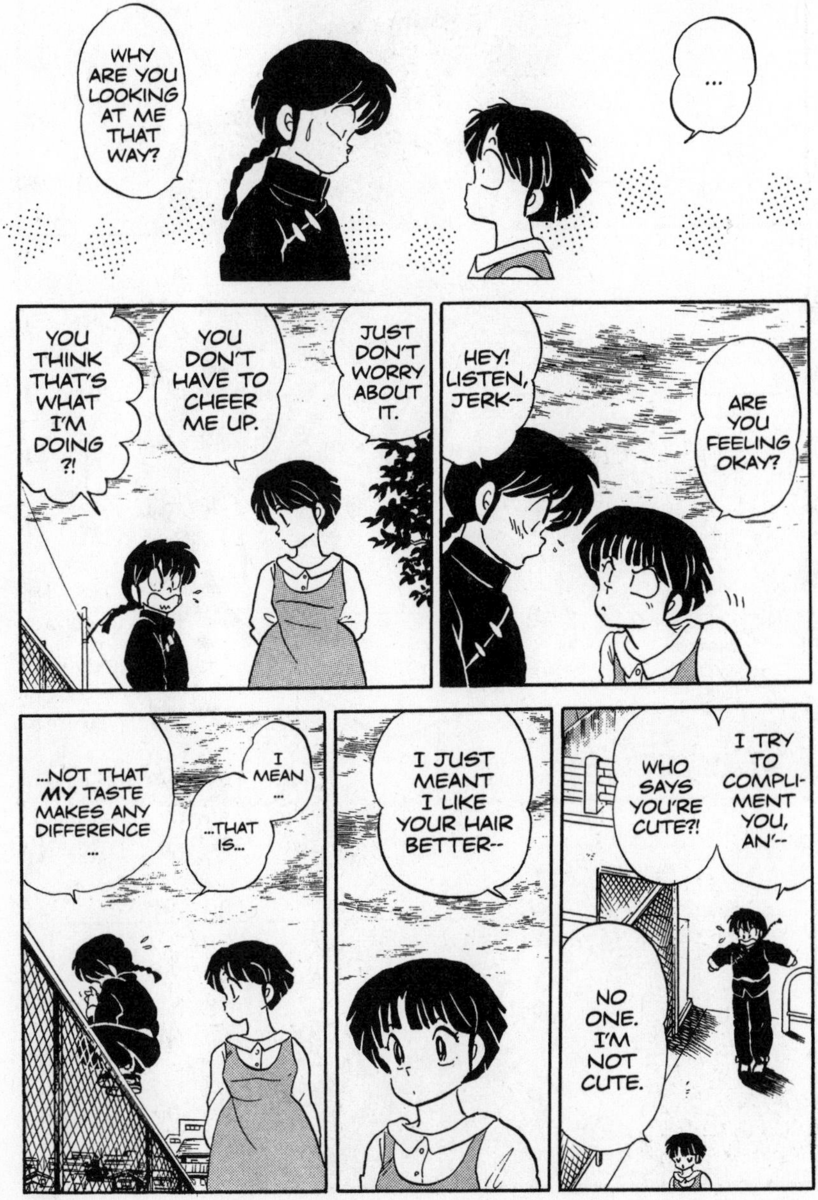
...
WHY ARE YOU LOOKING AT ME THAT WAY?
ARE YOU FEELING OKAY?
HEY! LISTEN, JERK--
JUST DON'T WORRY ABOUT IT.
YOU DON'T HAVE TO CHEER ME UP.
YOU THINK THAT'S WHAT I'M DOING ?!
I TRY TO COMPLI-MENT YOU, AN'--
WHO SAYS YOU'RE CUTE?!
NO ONE. I'M NOT CUTE.
I JUST MEANT I LIKE YOUR HAIR BETTER--
I MEAN ...
...THAT IS...
...NOT THAT MY TASTE MAKES ANY DIFFERENCE ...

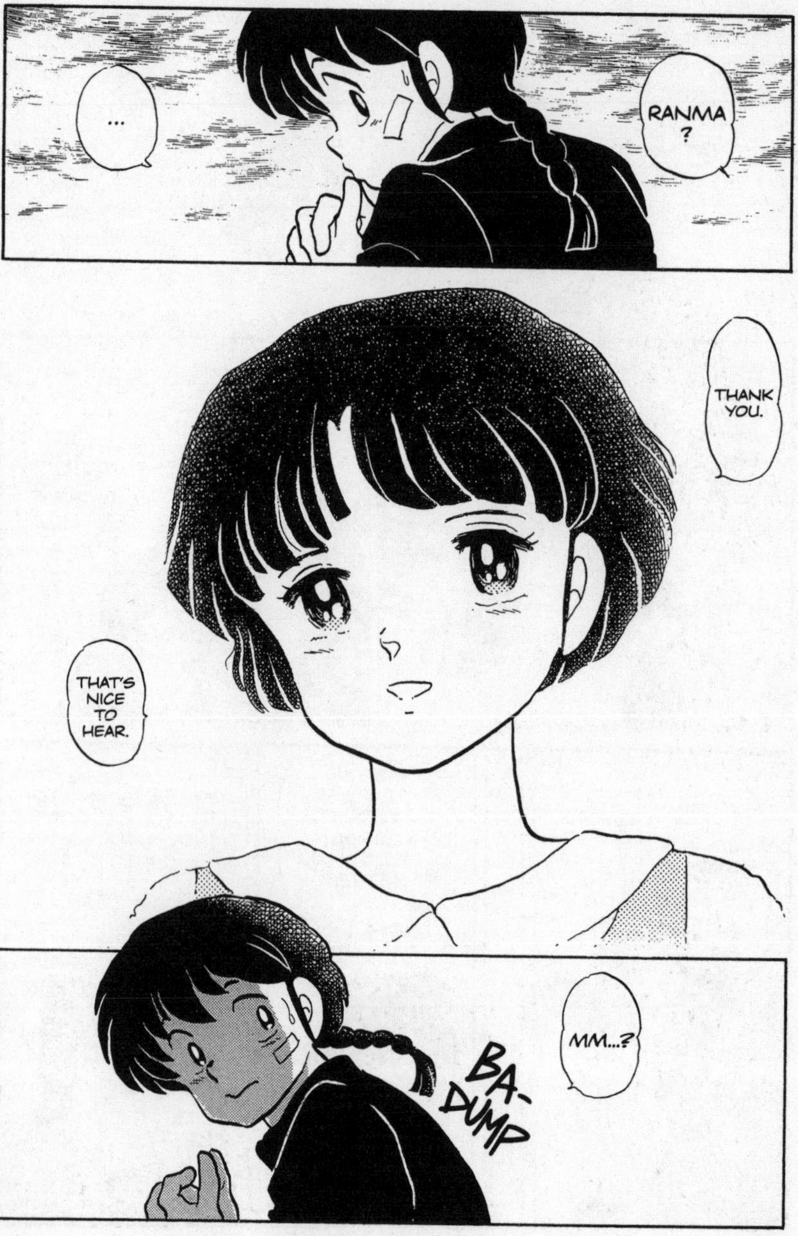
RANMA ?
...
THANK YOU.
THAT'S NICE TO HEAR.
MM...?
BA-DUMP

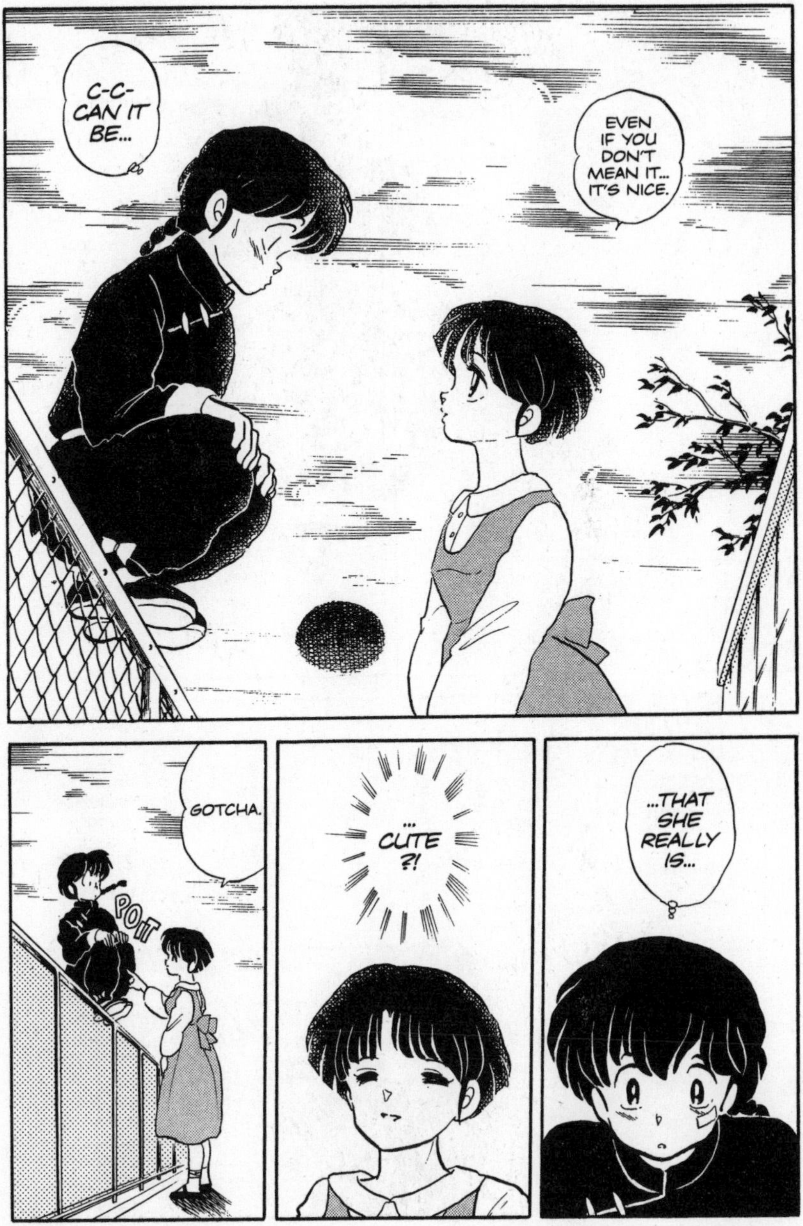
EVEN IF YOU DON'T MEAN IT... IT'S NICE.
C-C-CAN IT BE...
...THAT SHE REALLY IS...
...CUTE?!
GOTCHA.
POT

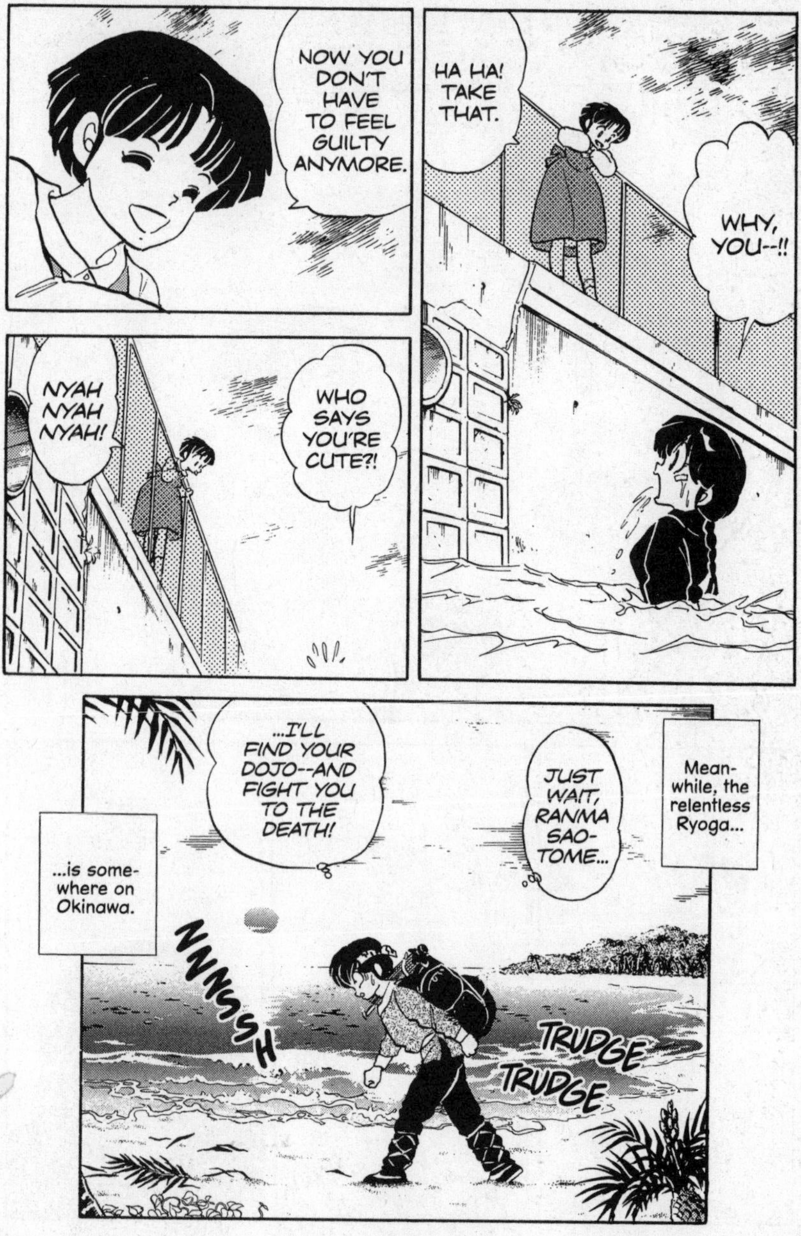
HA HA! TAKE THAT.
WHY, YOU--!!
NOW YOU DON'T HAVE TO FEEL GUILTY ANYMORE.
WHO SAYS YOU'RE CUTE?!
NYAH NYAH NYAH!
Mean-while, the relentless Ryoga...
JUST WAIT, RANMA SAO-TOME...
...I'LL FIND YOUR DOJO--AND FIGHT YOU TO THE DEATH!
...is some-where on Okinawa.
TRUDGE TRUDGE
NNNSSSH

# PART 15
# THE TRANSFORMATION OF RYOGA

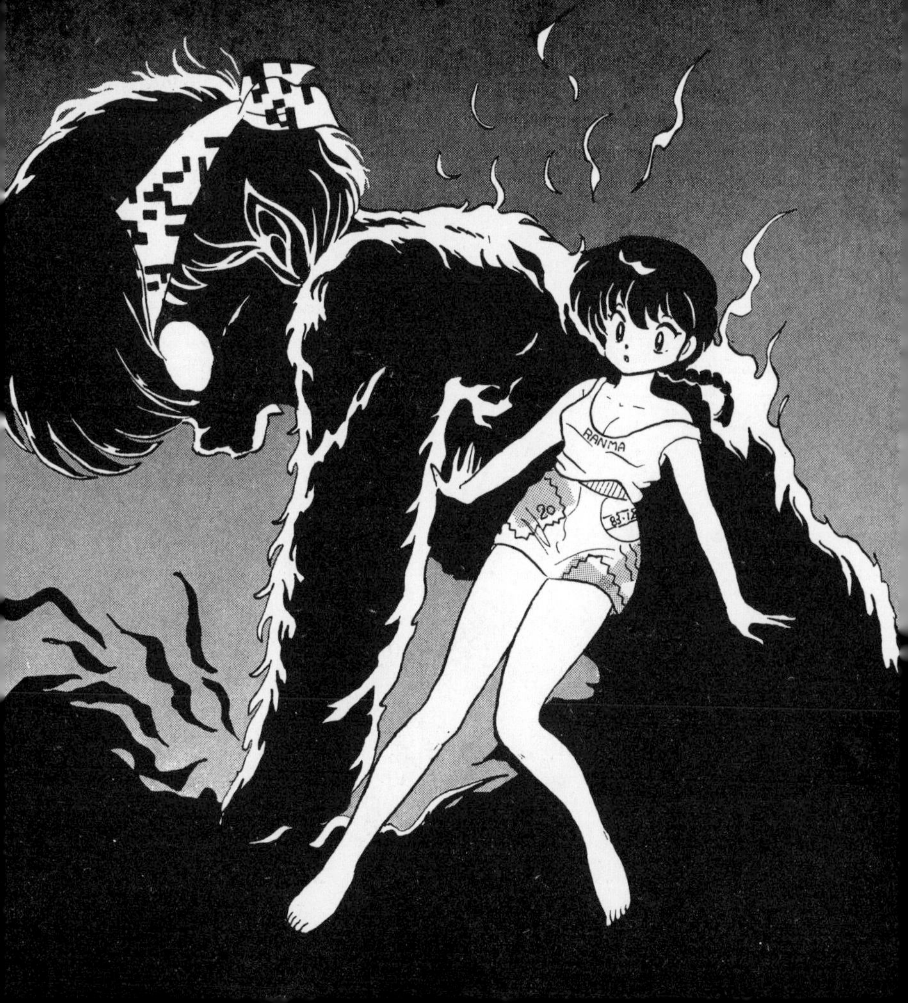
RANMA

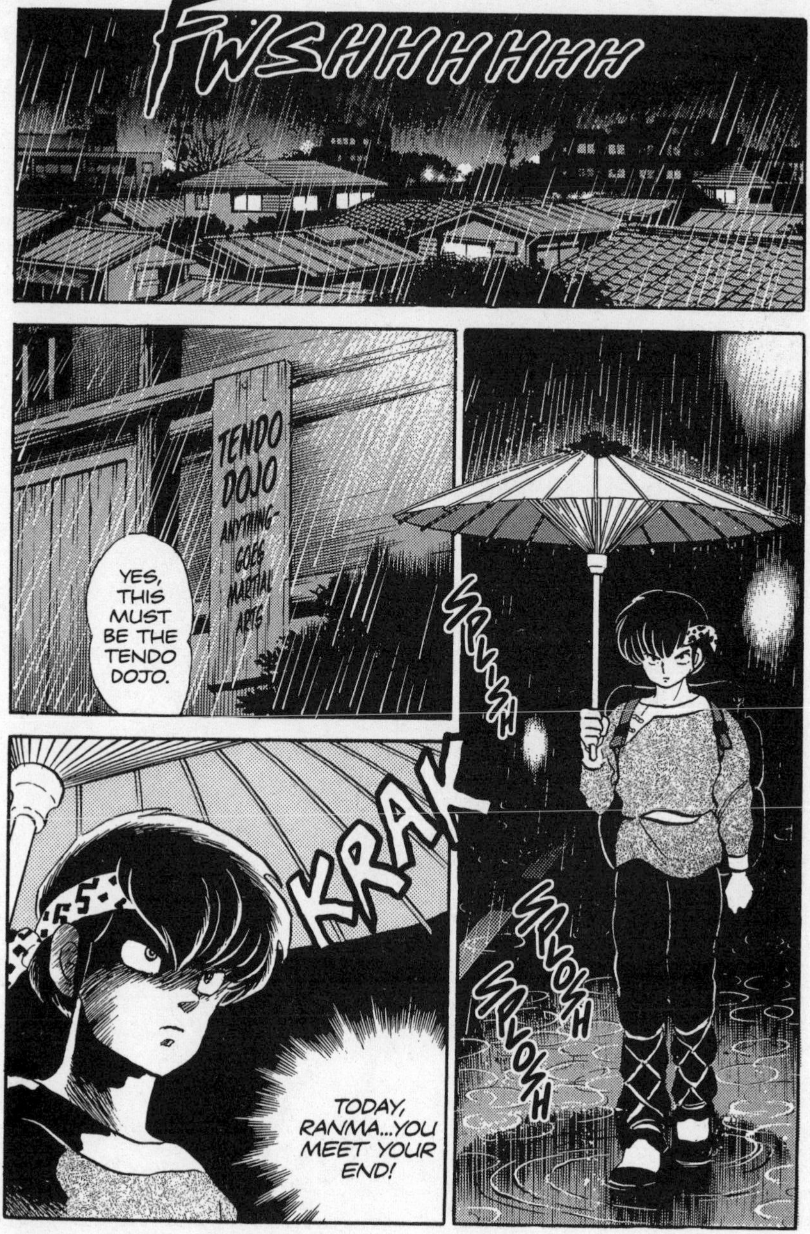
FWSHHHHHHH
SPLISH
SPLOSH
SPLOSH
TENDO DOJO ANYTHING-GOES MARTIAL ARTS
YES, THIS MUST BE THE TENDO DOJO.
KRAK
TODAY, RANMA...YOU MEET YOUR END!

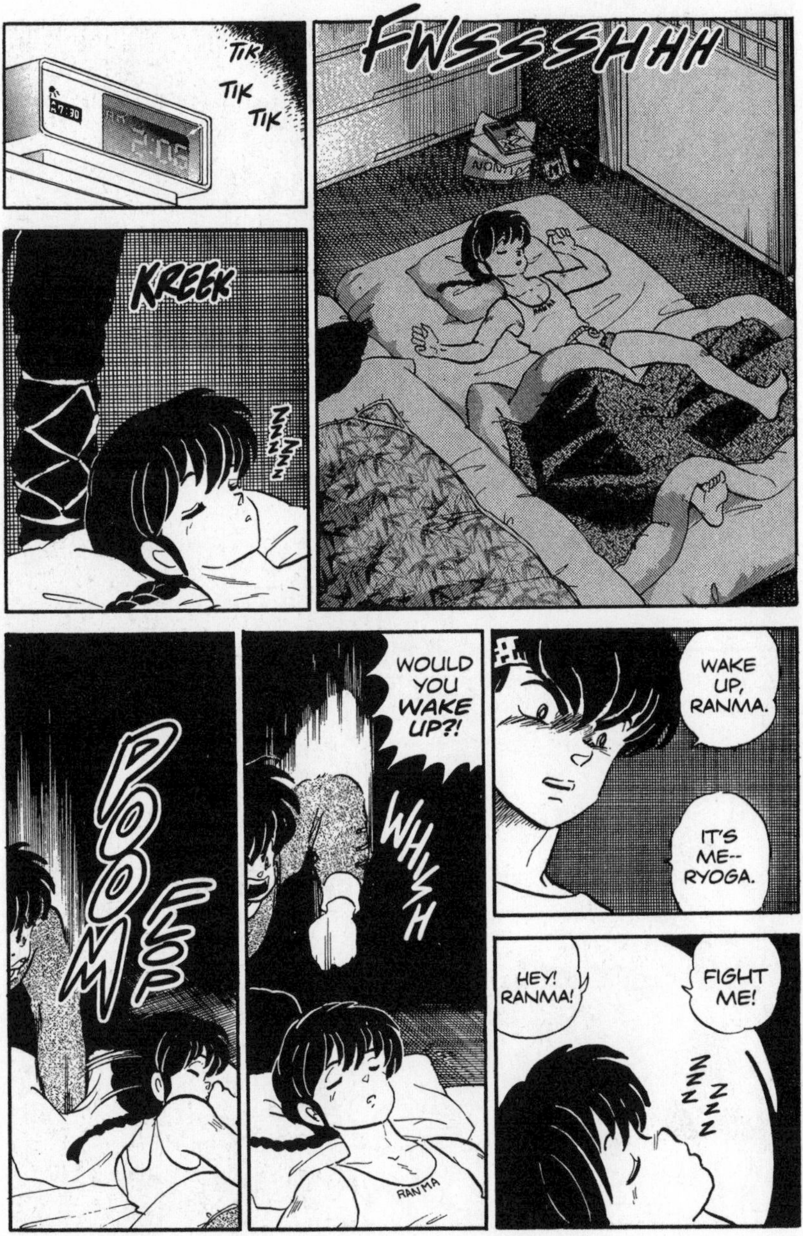
FWSSSHHH
TIK
TIK
TIK
KREEK
ZZZZZZ
WAKE UP, RANMA.
IT'S ME-- RYOGA.
FIGHT ME!
HEY! RANMA!
ZZZZZZ
WOULD YOU WAKE UP?!
WHUSH
RANMA
POOOM
FWOP

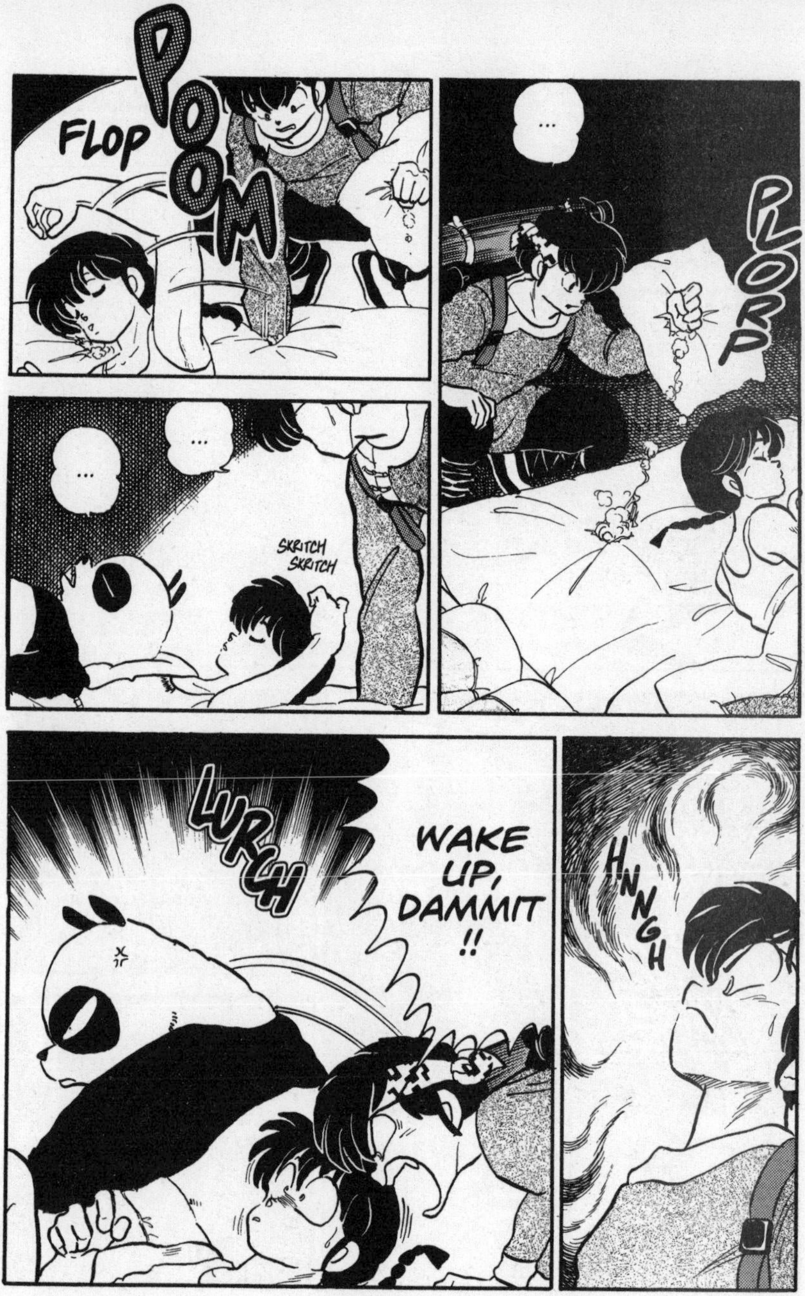
...
PLORP
FLOP
POOM
...
...
SKRITCH SKRITCH
HNNGH
LURCH
WAKE UP, DAMMIT!!

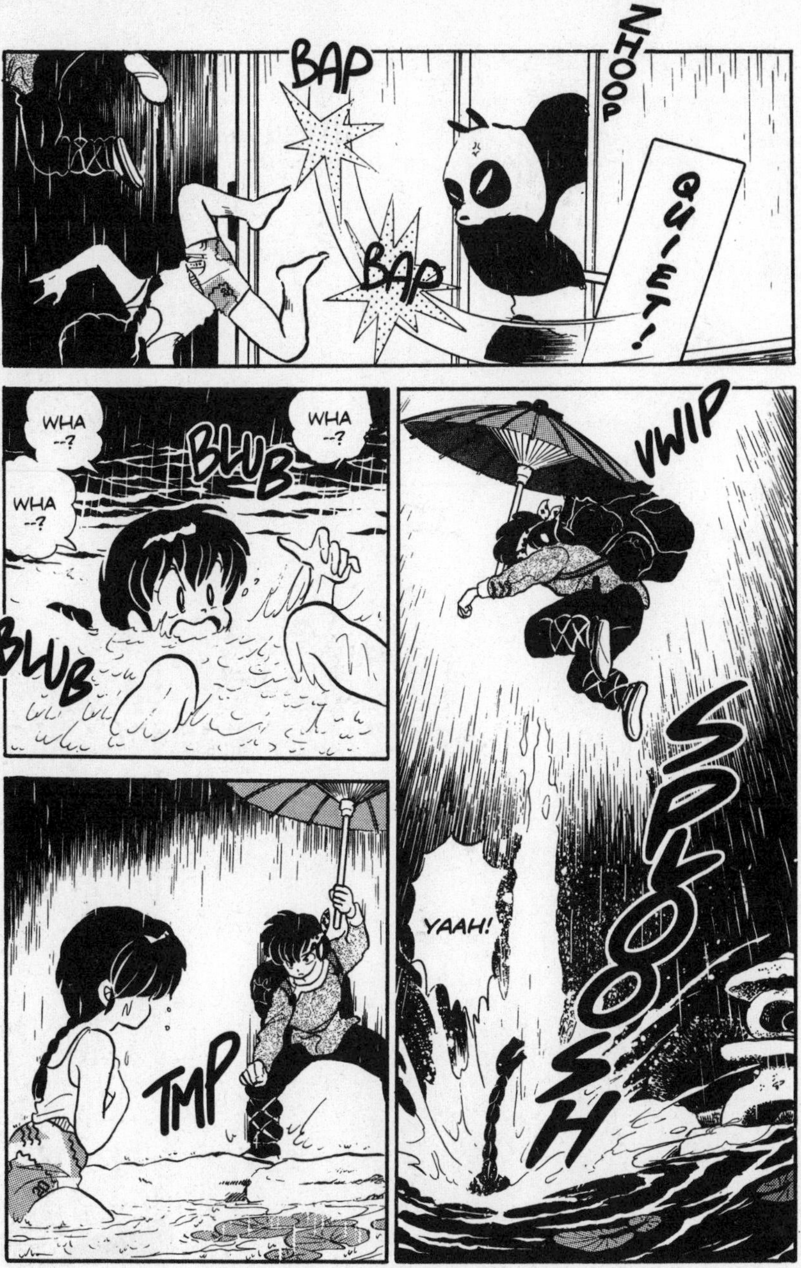
ZHOOP
QUIET!
BAP
BAP
VWIP
SPLOOSH
YAAH!
WHA --?
BLUB
WHA --?
WHA --?
BLUB
TMP

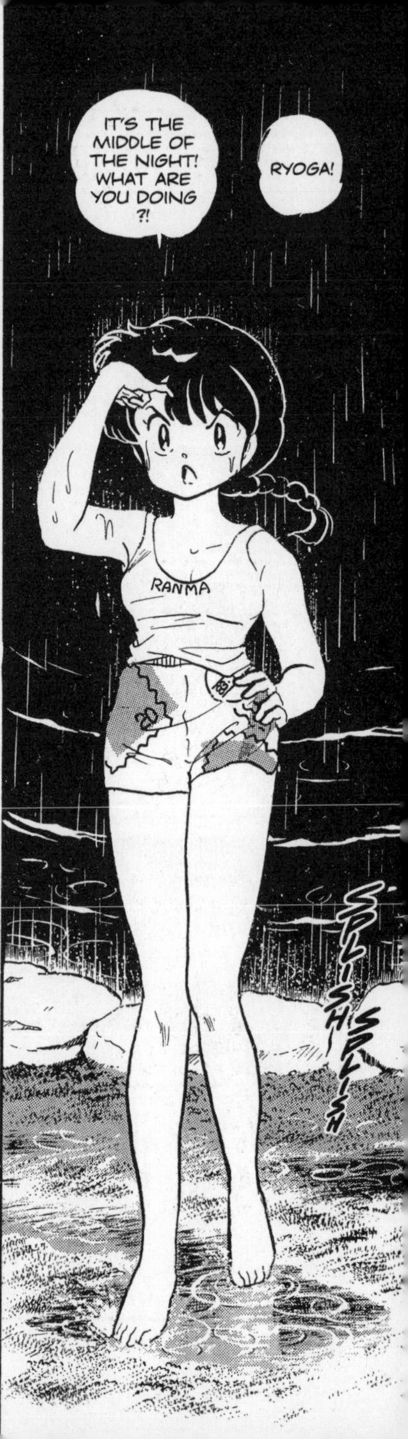
RYOGA!
IT'S THE MIDDLE OF THE NIGHT! WHAT ARE YOU DOING ?!
SPLISH SPLISH
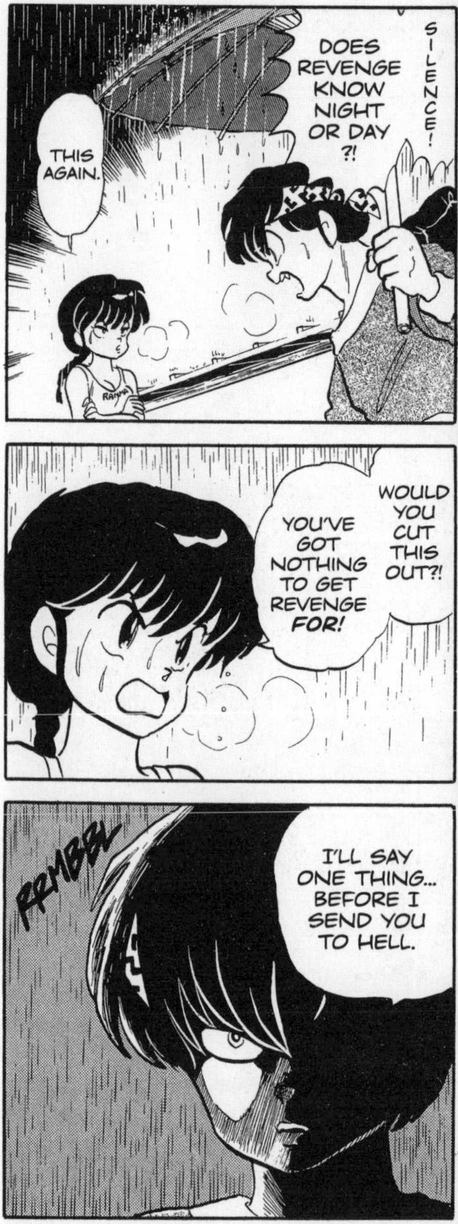
SILENCE!
DOES REVENGE KNOW NIGHT OR DAY ?!
THIS AGAIN.
WOULD YOU CUT THIS OUT?!
YOU'VE GOT NOTHING TO GET REVENGE FOR!
I'LL SAY ONE THING... BEFORE I SEND YOU TO HELL.
RRMBBL

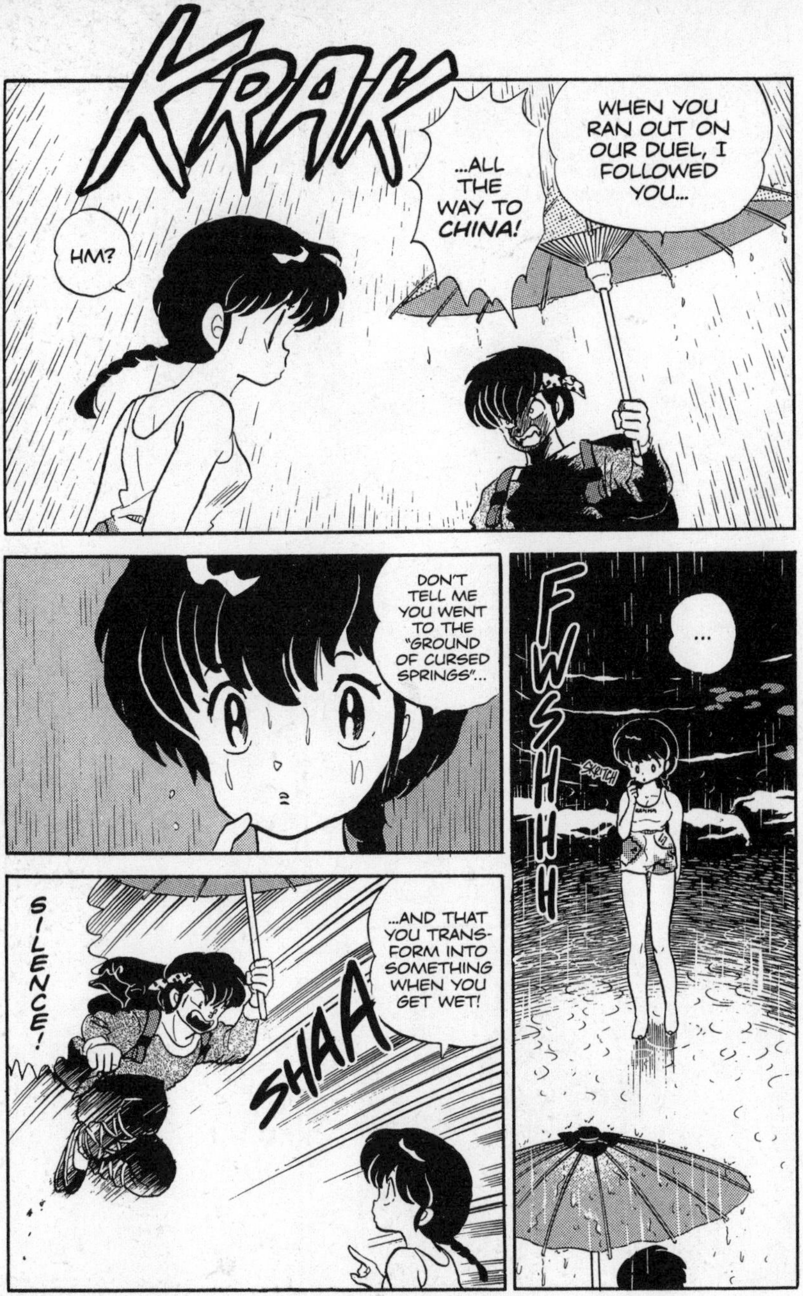

WHEN YOU RAN OUT ON OUR DUEL, I FOLLOWED YOU...
...ALL THE WAY TO CHINA!
KRAK
HM?
FWSHHHH
...
SKRITCH
DON'T TELL ME YOU WENT TO THE "GROUND OF CURSED SPRINGS"...
...AND THAT YOU TRANS-FORM INTO SOMETHING WHEN YOU GET WET!
SHAA
SILENCE!

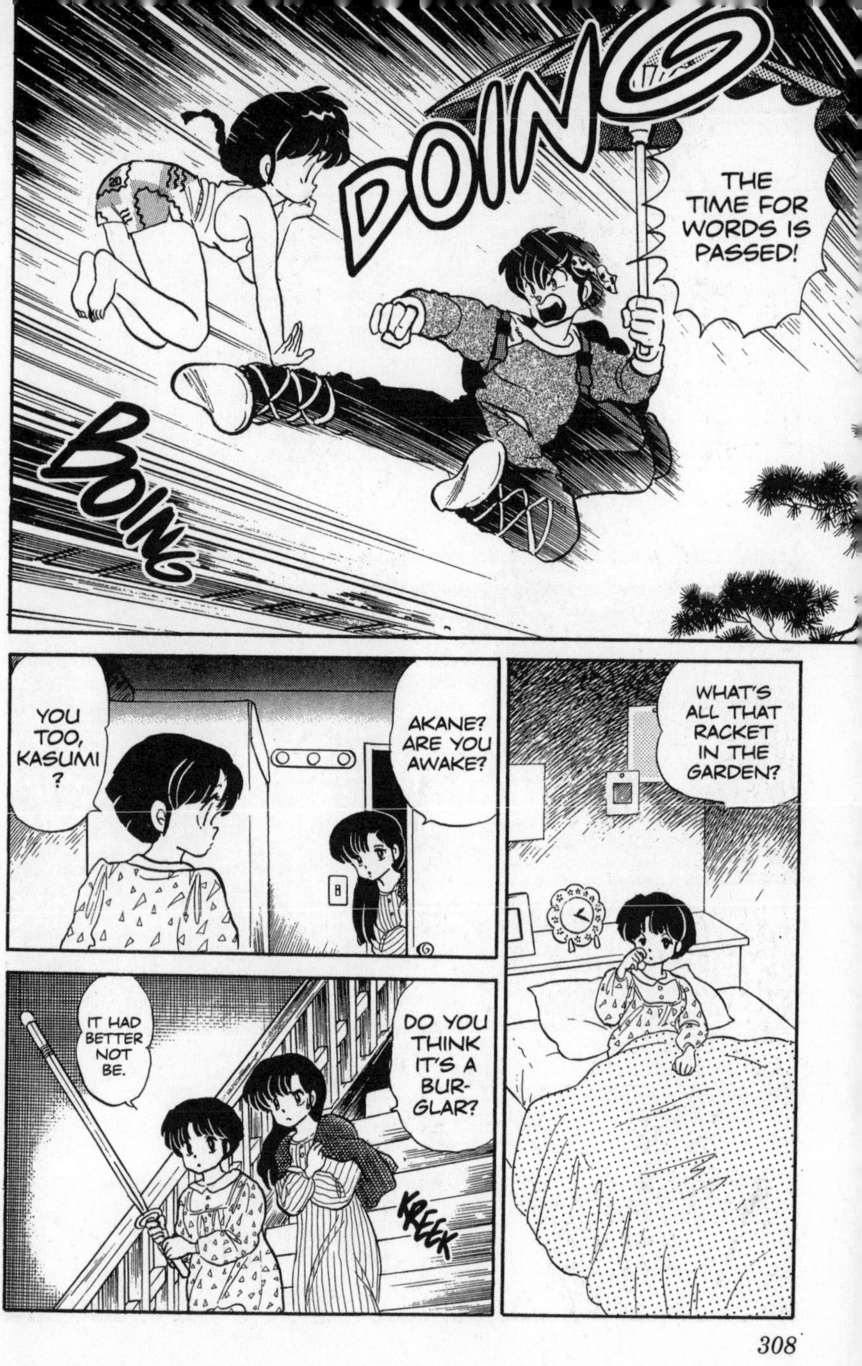
THE TIME FOR WORDS IS PASSED!
DOING
BOING
WHAT'S ALL THAT RACKET IN THE GARDEN?
AKANE? ARE YOU AWAKE?
YOU TOO, KASUMI?
DO YOU THINK IT'S A BUR-GLAR?
IT HAD BETTER NOT BE.
KREEEK

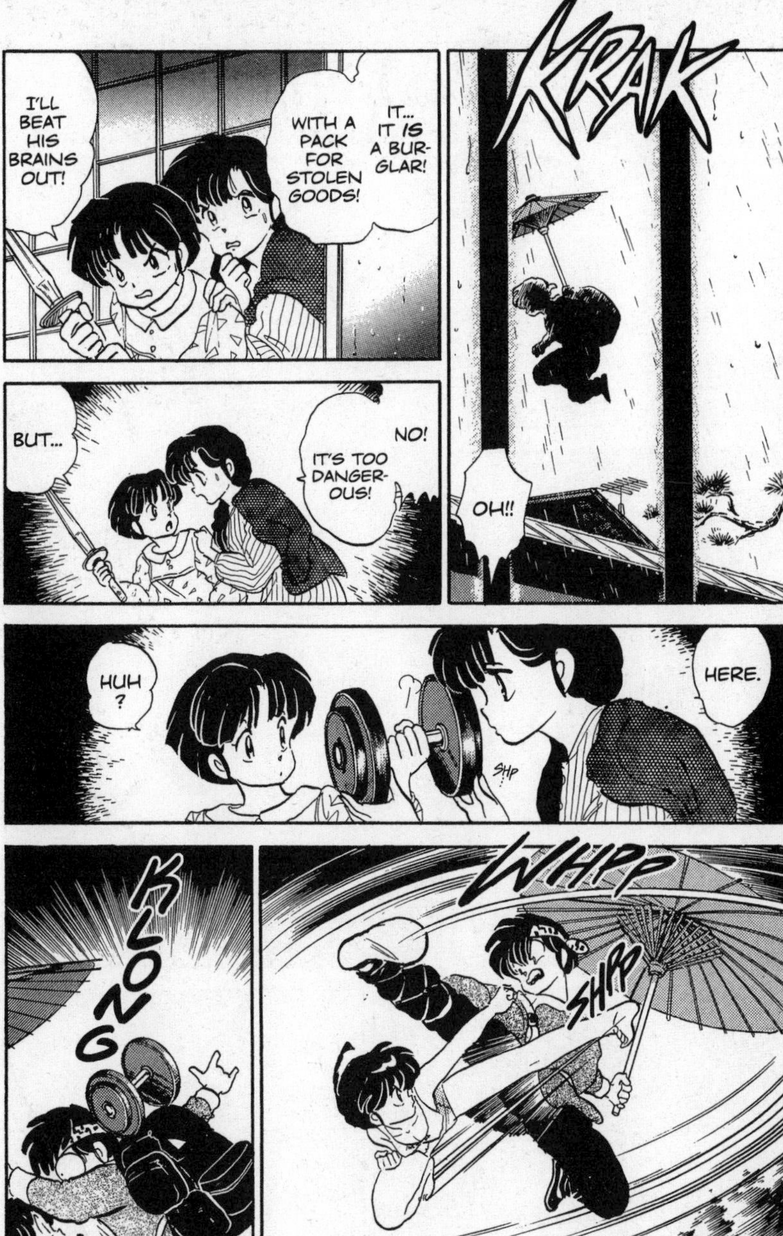
KRAK
OH!!
IT... IT IS A BURGLAR!
WITH A PACK FOR STOLEN GOODS!
I'LL BEAT HIS BRAINS OUT!
NO! IT'S TOO DANGEROUS!
BUT...
HERE.
SHP
HUH ?
WHPP
SHPP
KLONG

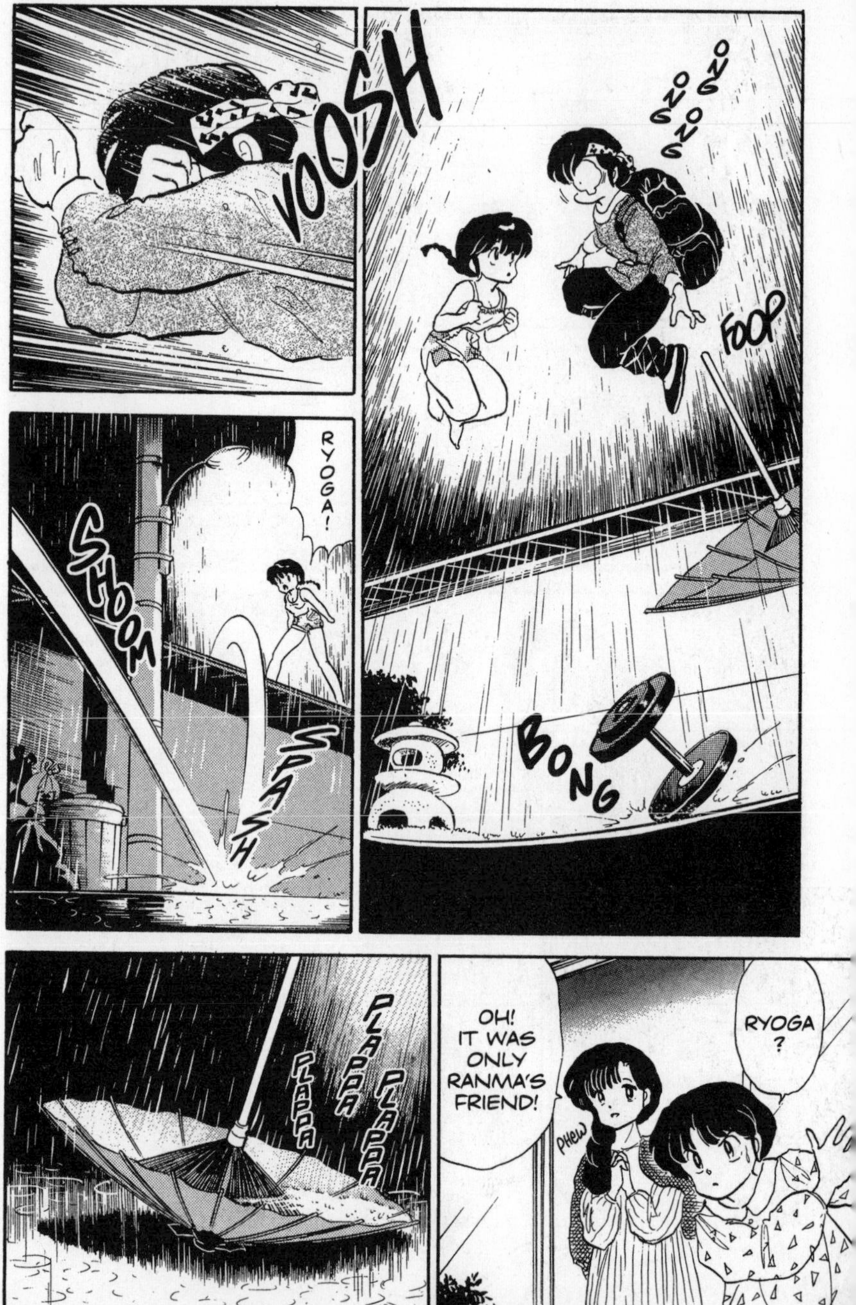
ONG ONG
ONG ONG
FOOP
BONG
VOOSH
RYOGA!
SHOOM
SPLASH
RYOGA?
OH! IT WAS ONLY RANMA'S FRIEND!
PHEW
PLAPPA PLAPPA
PLAPPA PLAPPA
PLAPPA

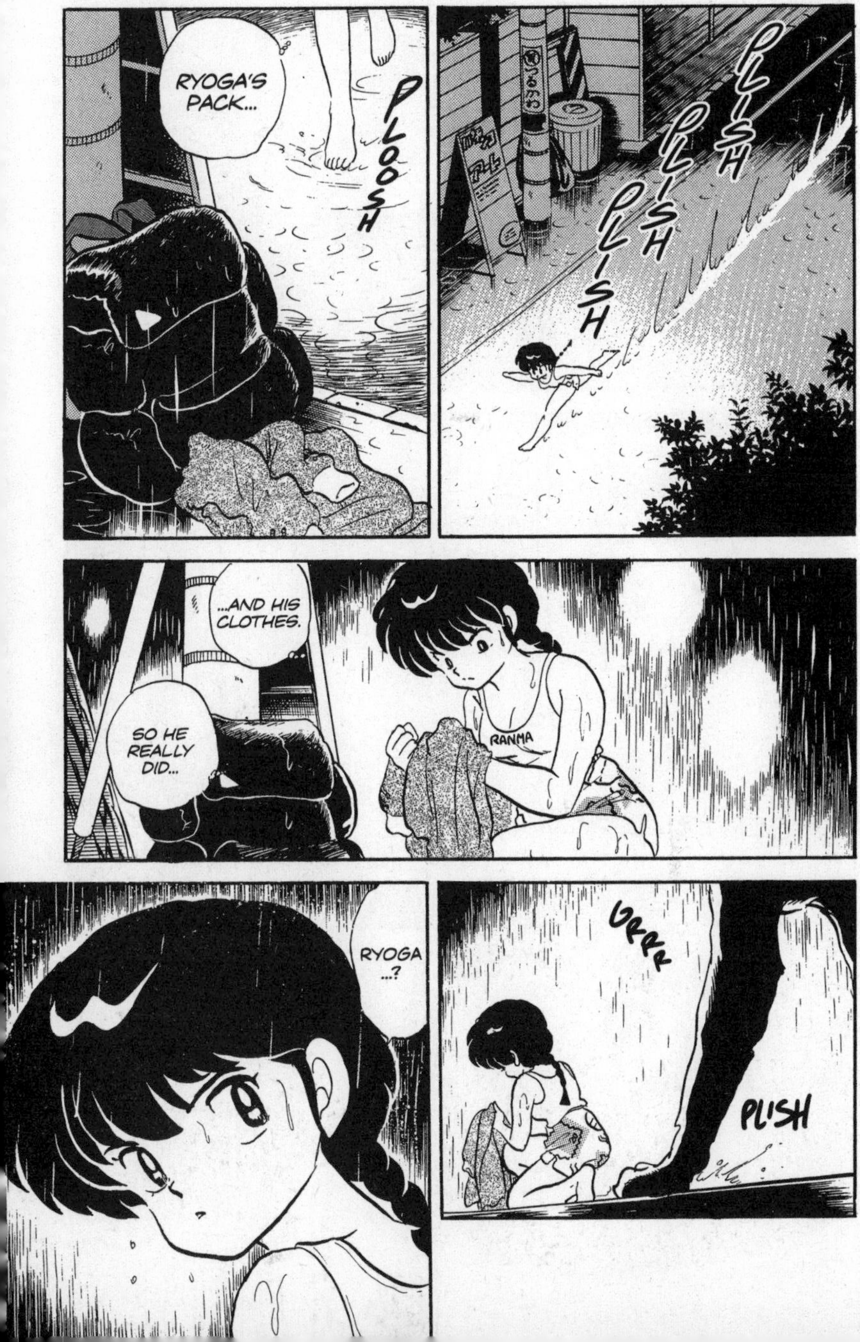
PLISH
PLISH
PLISH
PLISH
RYOGA'S PACK...
PLOOSH
...AND HIS CLOTHES.
SO HE REALLY DID...
URRR
PLISH
RYOGA ...?

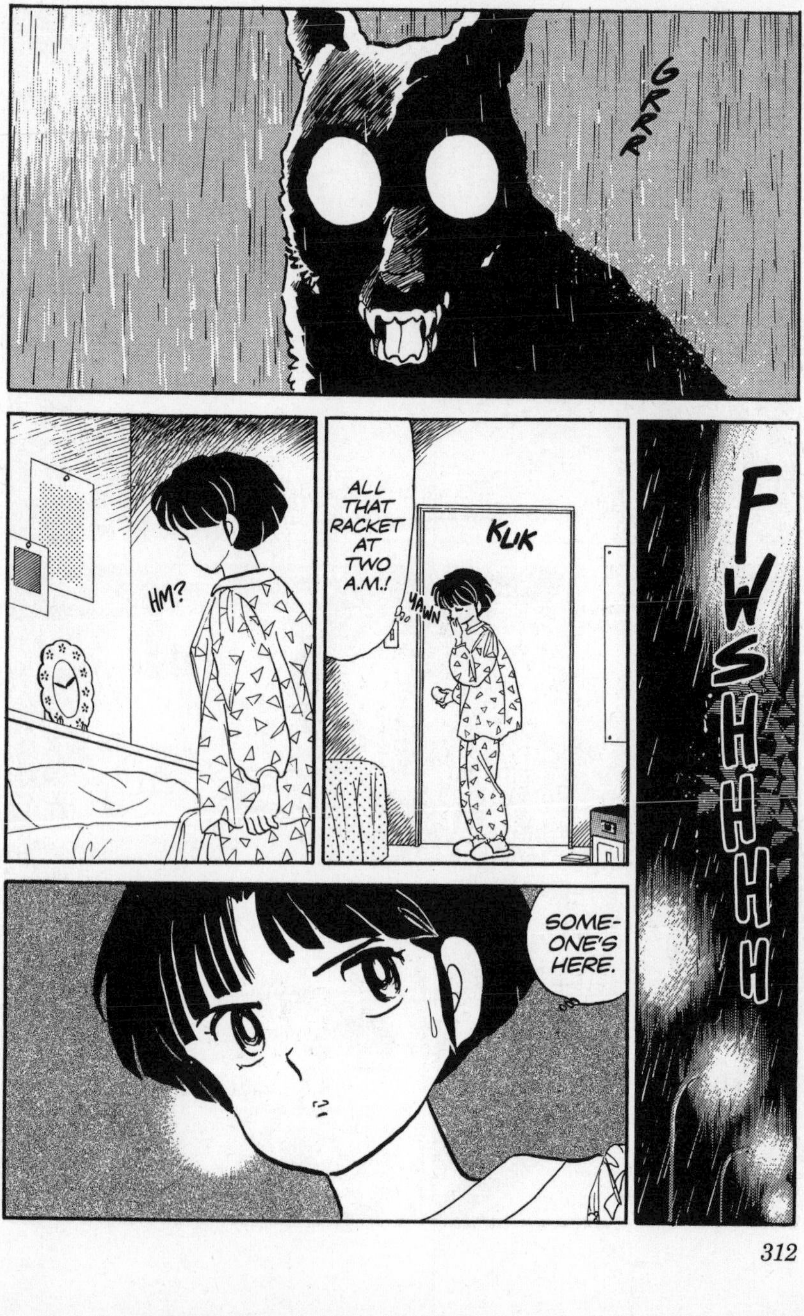
GRRR
FWSHHHHH
ALL THAT RACKET AT TWO A.M.!
KLIK
YAWN
HM?
SOME-ONE'S HERE.

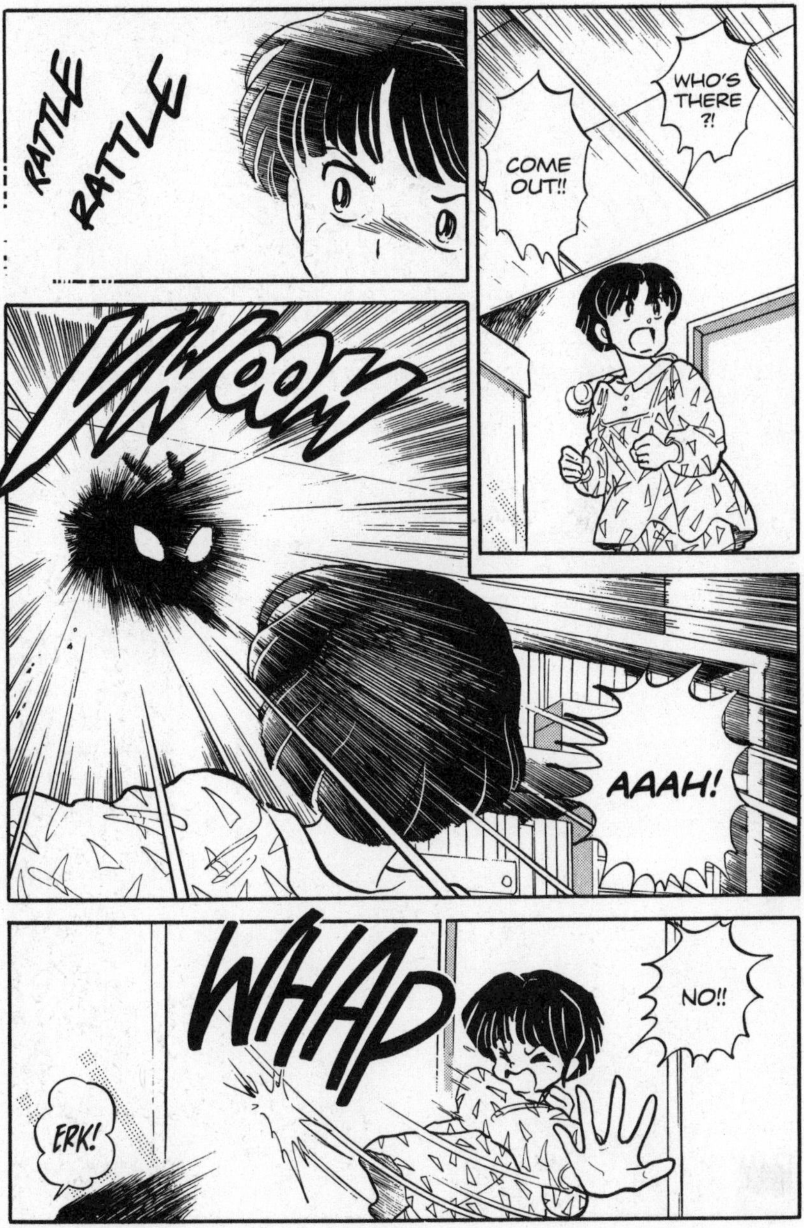
WHO'S THERE ?!
COME OUT!!
RATTLE RATTLE
WHOOM
AAAH!
NO!!
WHAP
ERK!

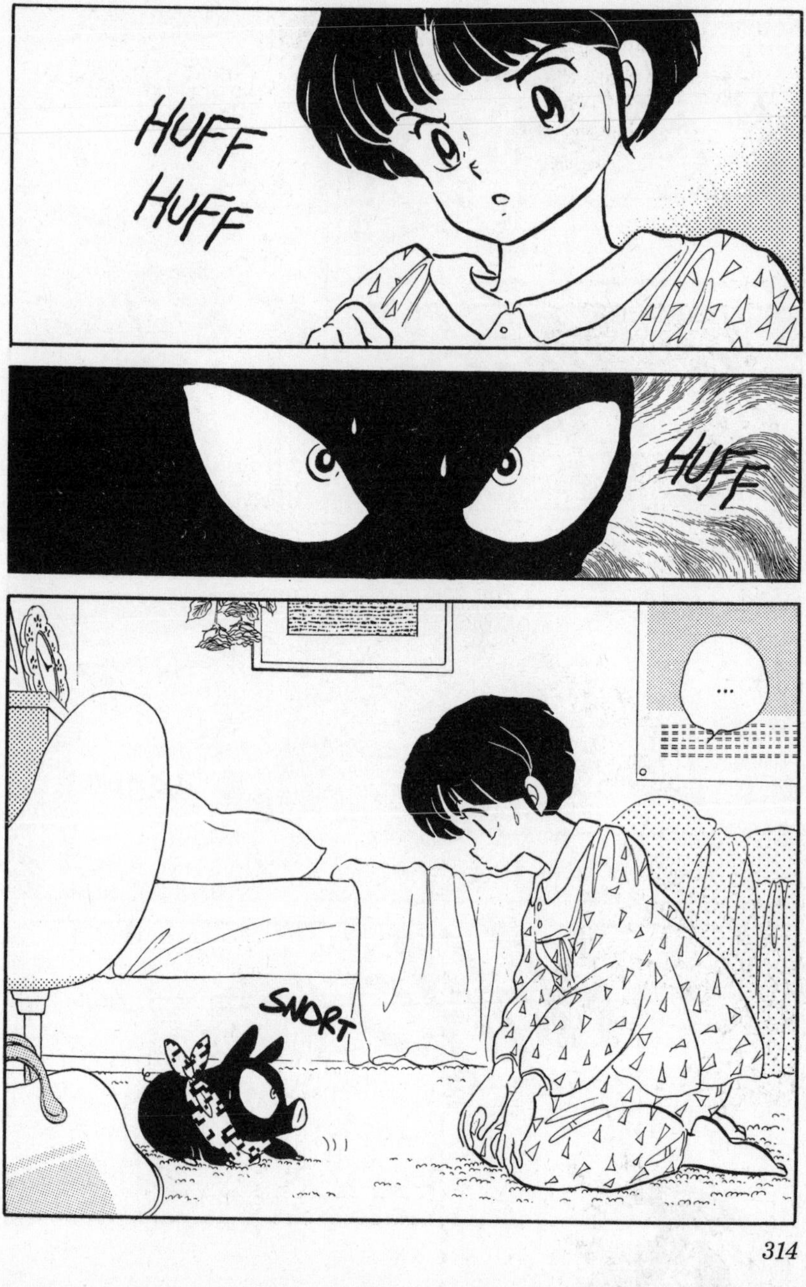
HUFF
HUFF
HUFF
...
SNORT

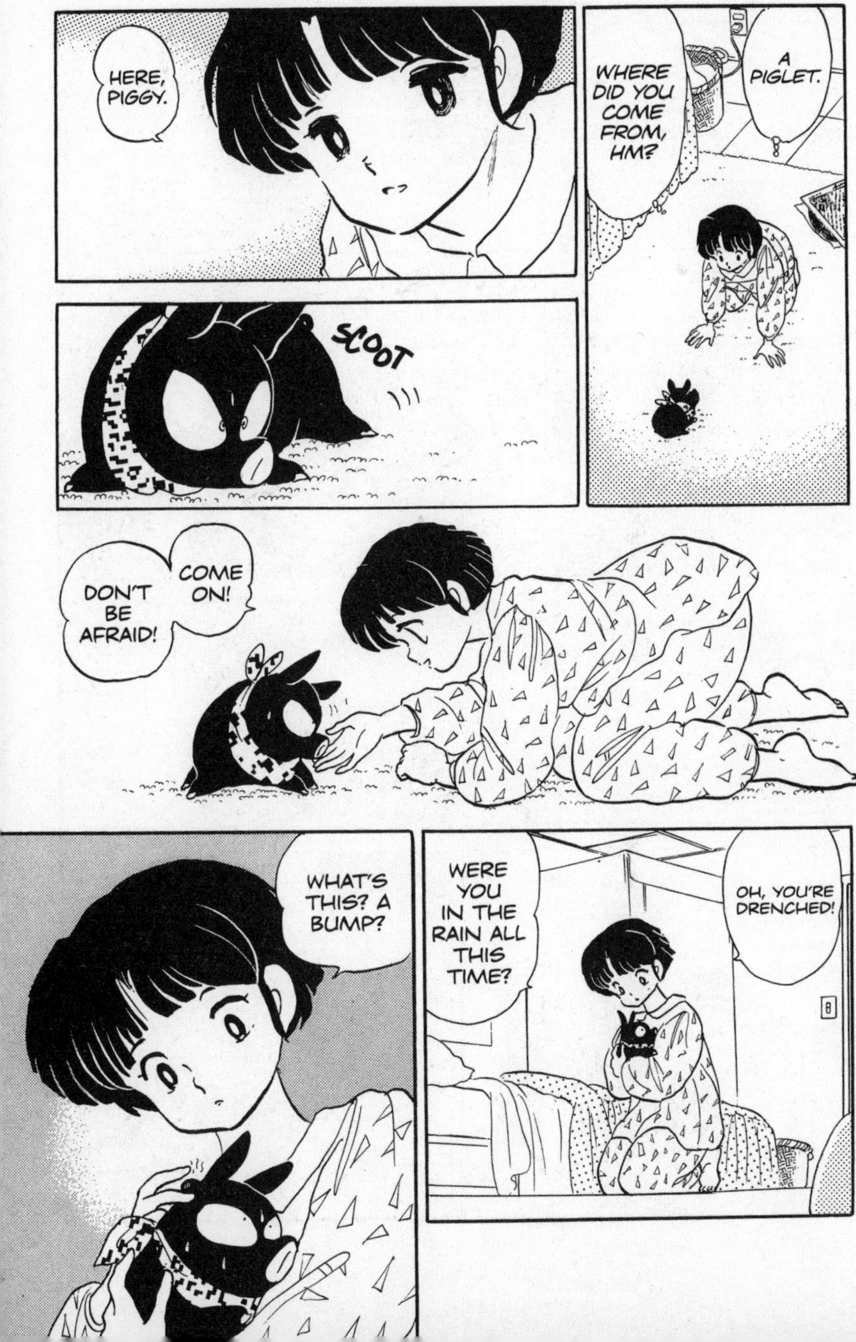
A PIGLET.
WHERE DID YOU COME FROM, HM?
HERE, PIGGY.
SCOOT
COME ON!
DON'T BE AFRAID!
OH, YOU'RE DRENCHED!
WERE YOU IN THE RAIN ALL THIS TIME?
WHAT'S THIS? A BUMP?

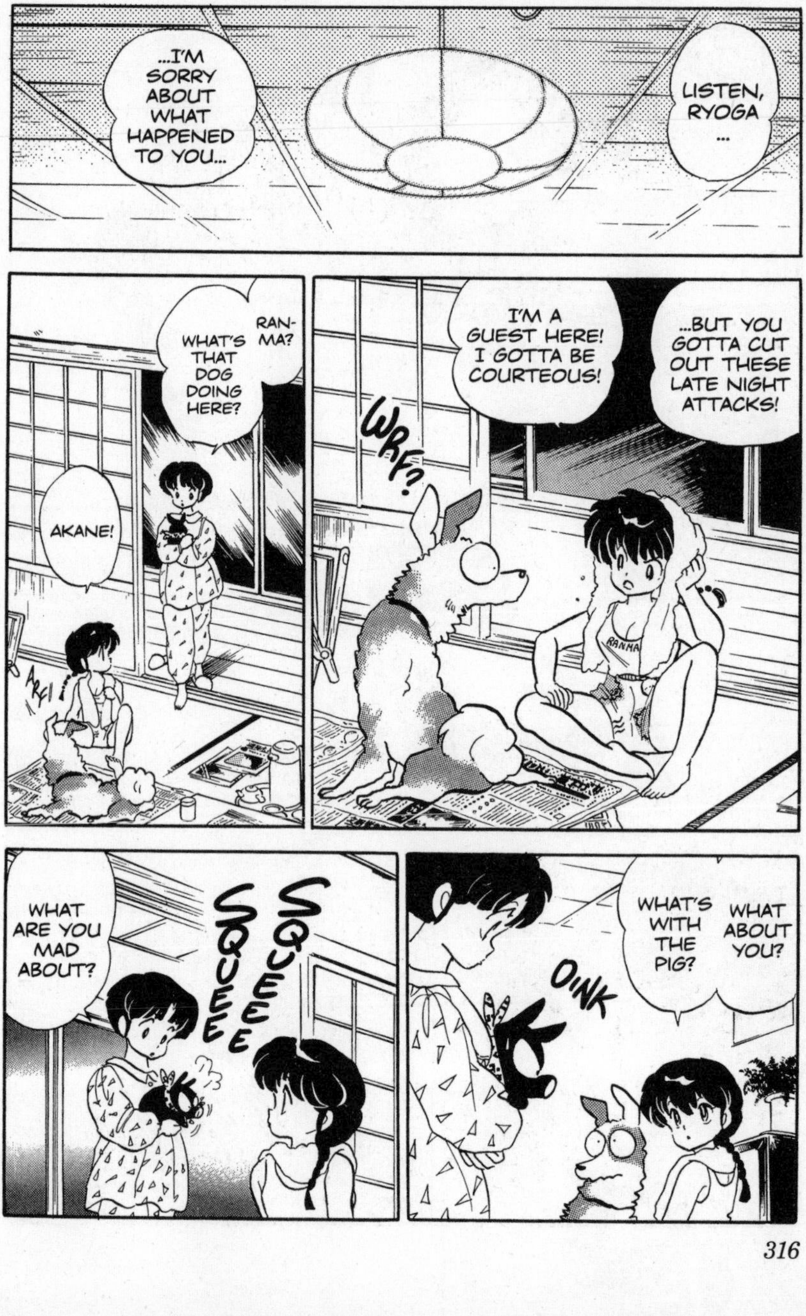
LISTEN, RYOGA ...
...I'M SORRY ABOUT WHAT HAPPENED TO YOU...
...BUT YOU GOTTA CUT OUT THESE LATE NIGHT ATTACKS!
I'M A GUEST HERE! I GOTTA BE COURTEOUS!
WRF?
RAN-MA?
WHAT'S THAT DOG DOING HERE?
AKANE!
ARF!
WHAT ABOUT YOU?
WHAT'S WITH THE PIG?
OINK
SQUEEE
SQUEEE
WHAT ARE YOU MAD ABOUT?

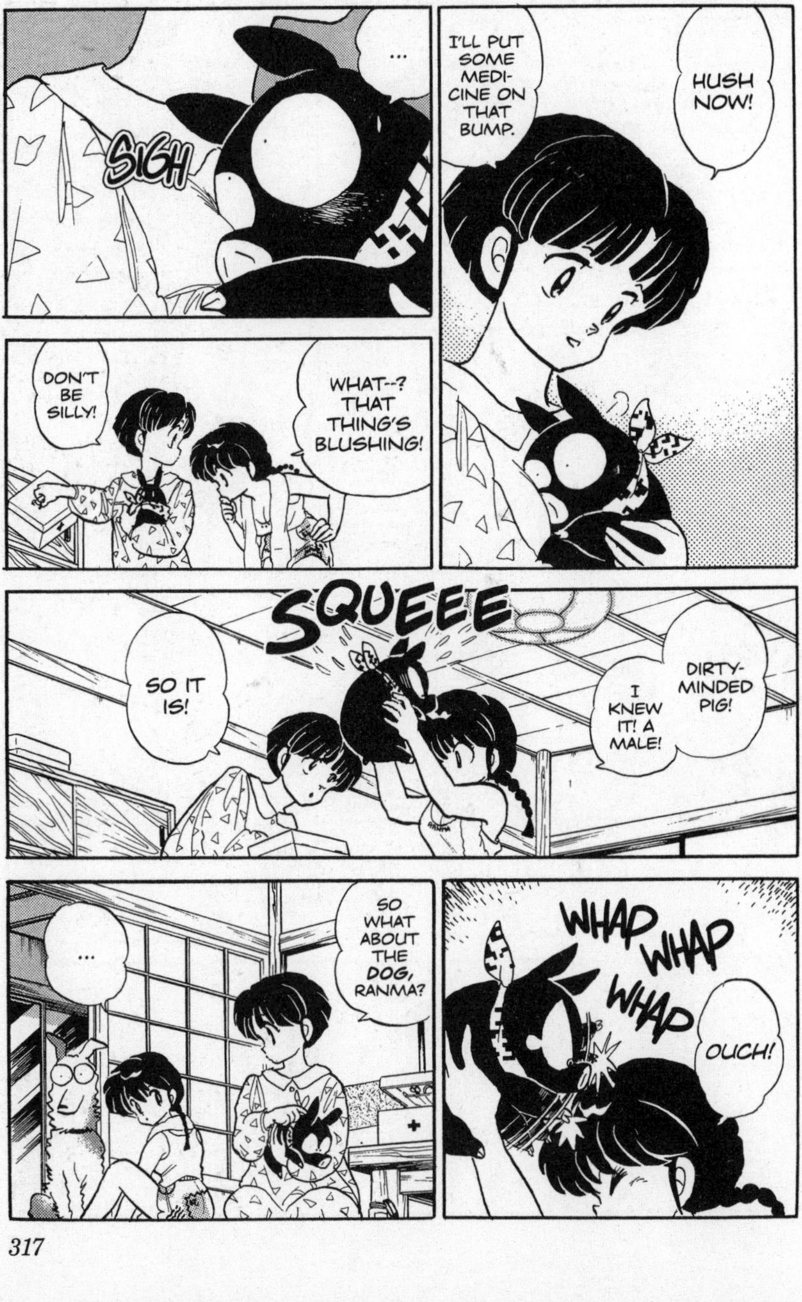
HUSH NOW!
I'LL PUT SOME MEDICINE ON THAT BUMP.
...
SIGH
WHAT--? THAT THING'S BLUSHING!
DON'T BE SILLY!
SQUEEE
DIRTY-MINDED PIG!
I KNEW IT! A MALE!
SO IT IS!
WHAP WHAP WHAP
OUCH!
SO WHAT ABOUT THE *DOG*, RANMA?
...

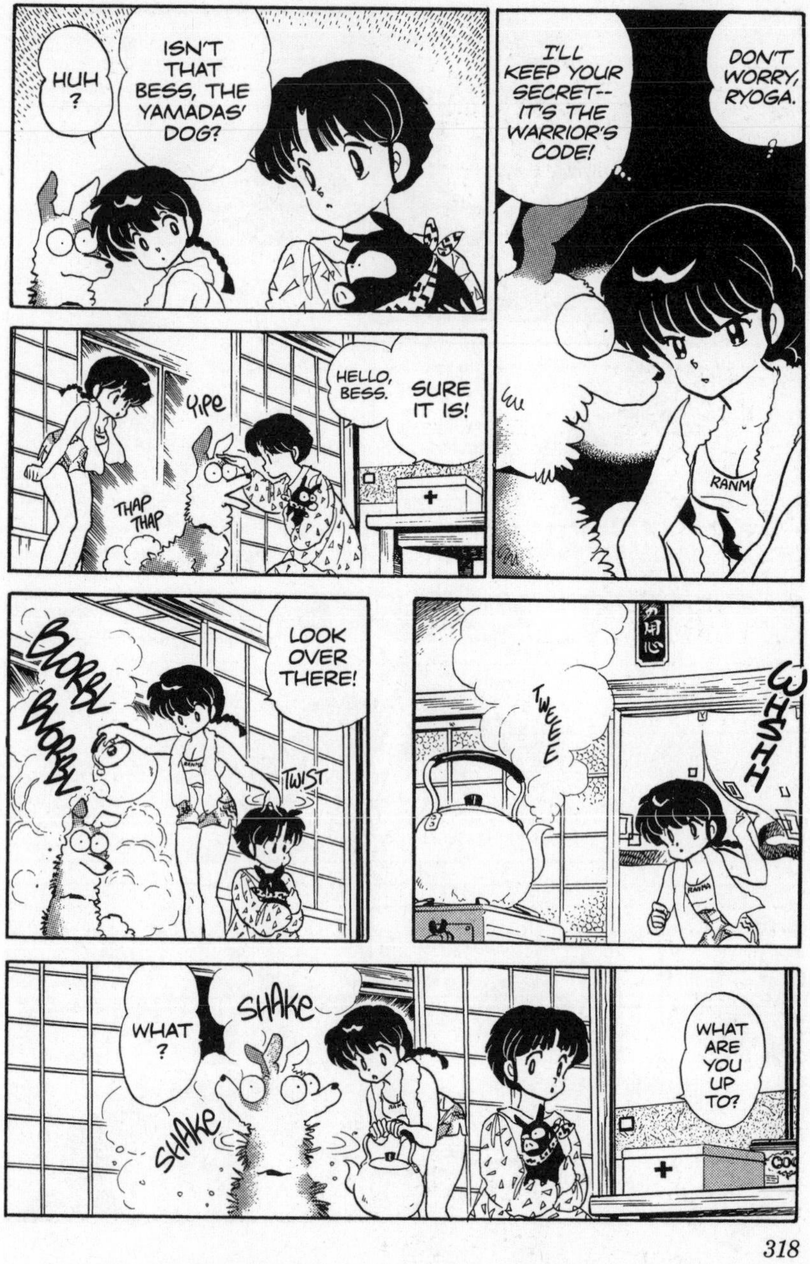
DON'T WORRY, RYOGA.
I'LL KEEP YOUR SECRET-- IT'S THE WARRIOR'S CODE!
ISN'T THAT BESS, THE YAMADAS' DOG?
HUH ?
SURE IT IS!
HELLO, BESS.
YIPE
THAP THAP
WHSHH
TWEEE
LOOK OVER THERE!
TWIST
BLORBL BLORBL
WHAT ARE YOU UP TO?
SHAKE
WHAT ?
SHAKE

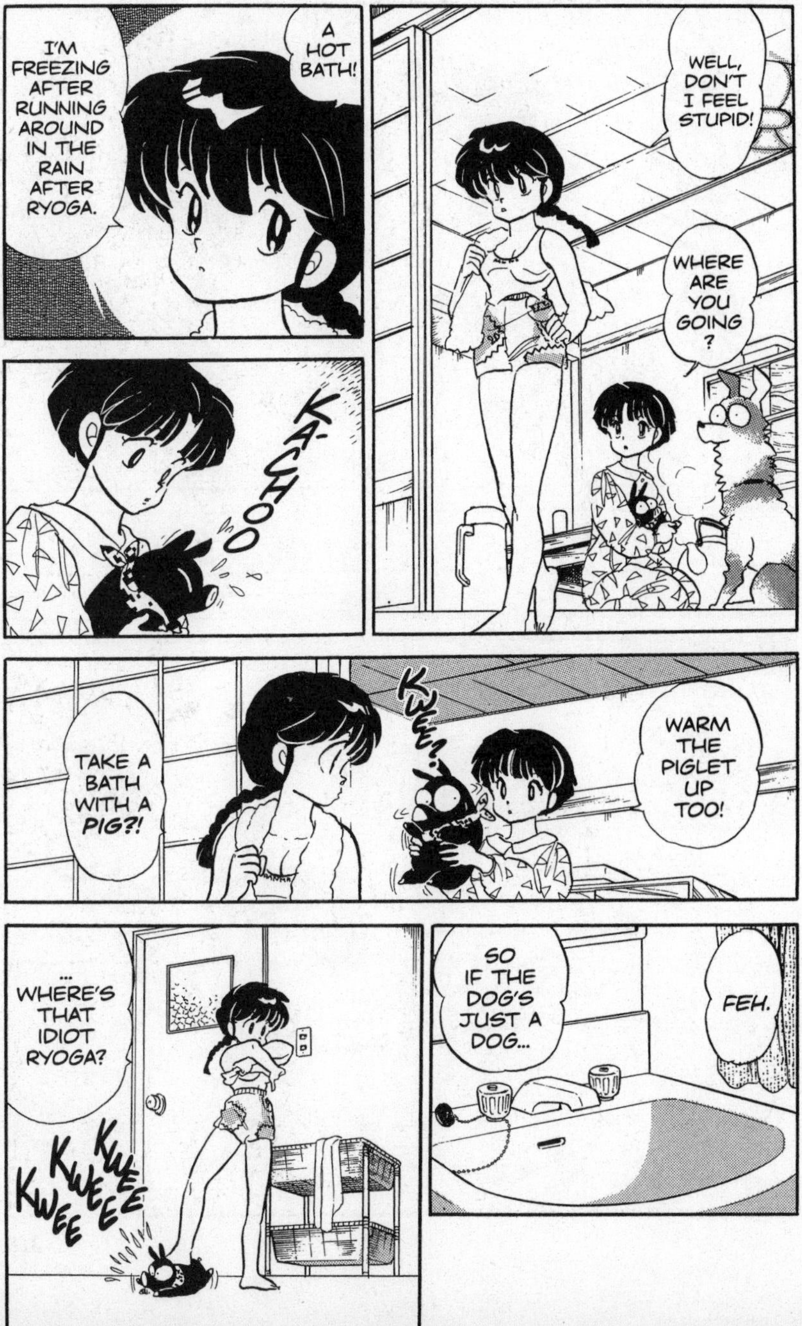
WELL, DON'T I FEEL STUPID!
WHERE ARE YOU GOING?
A HOT BATH!
I'M FREEZING AFTER RUNNING AROUND IN THE RAIN AFTER RYOGA.
KA-CHOO
WARM THE PIGLET UP TOO!
KWEE?
TAKE A BATH WITH A *PIG?!*
FEH.
SO IF THE DOG'S JUST A DOG...
...WHERE'S THAT IDIOT RYOGA?
KWEE KWEEE KWEEE

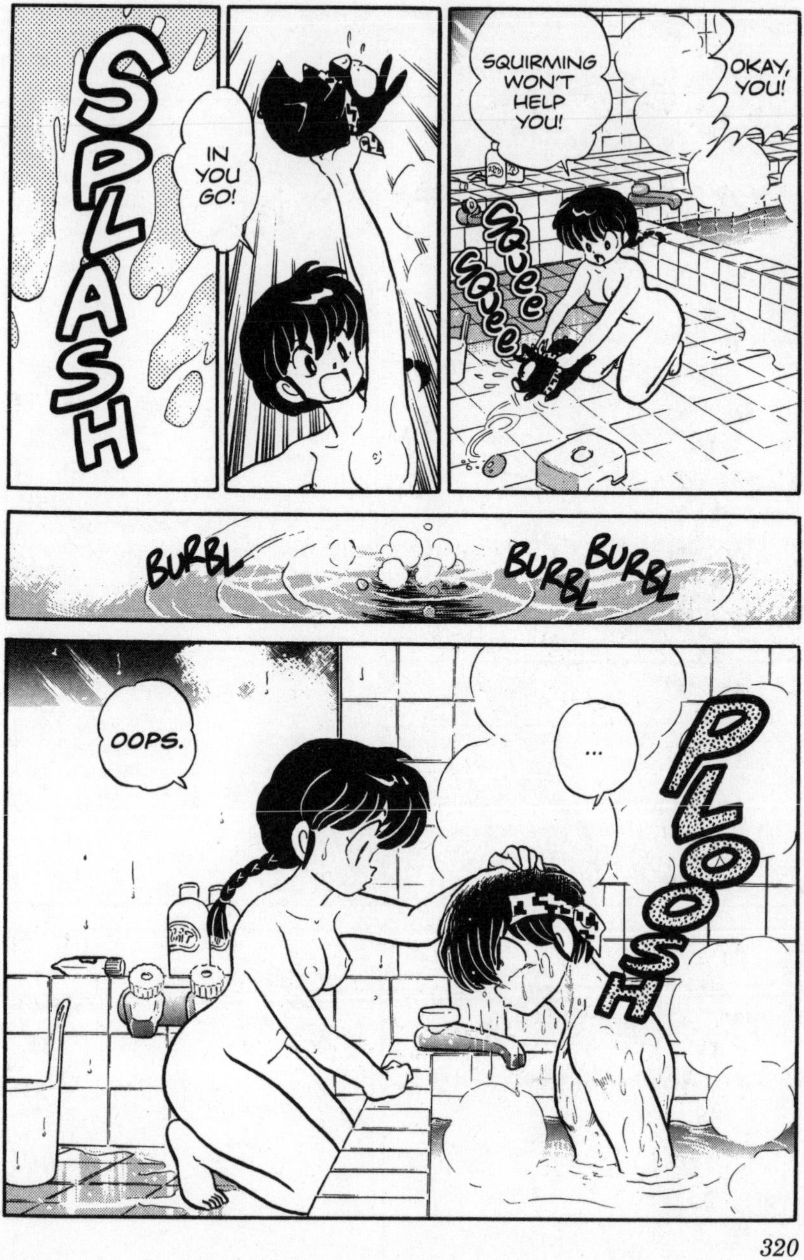
OKAY, YOU!
SQUIRMING WON'T HELP YOU!
SQUEE SQUEE
IN YOU GO!
SPLASH
BURBL BURBL
BURBL
...
PLOOSH
OOPS.

# PART 16
# HE'S GOT A BEEF

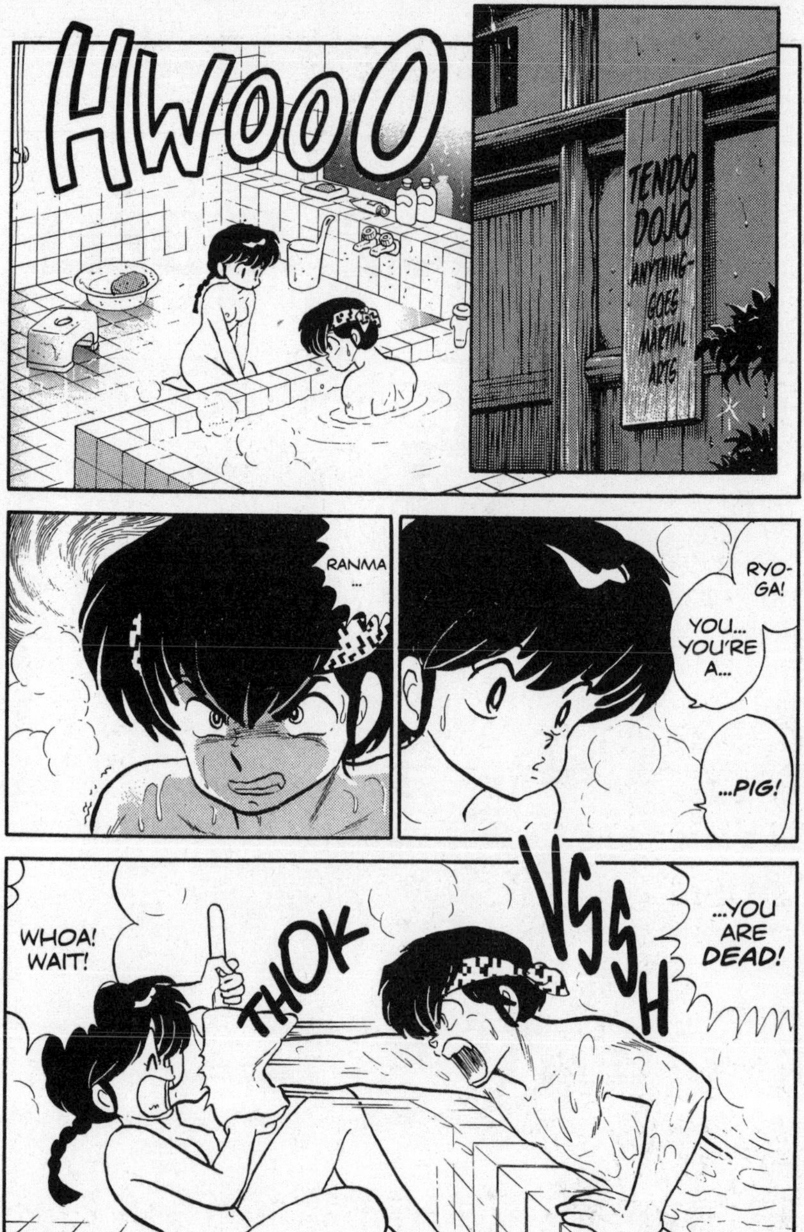
TENDO DOJO ANYTHING-GOES MARTIAL ARTS
HWOOO
RYO-GA!
YOU... YOU'RE A...
...PIG!
RANMA ...
...YOU ARE DEAD!
VSSH
THOK
WHOA! WAIT!

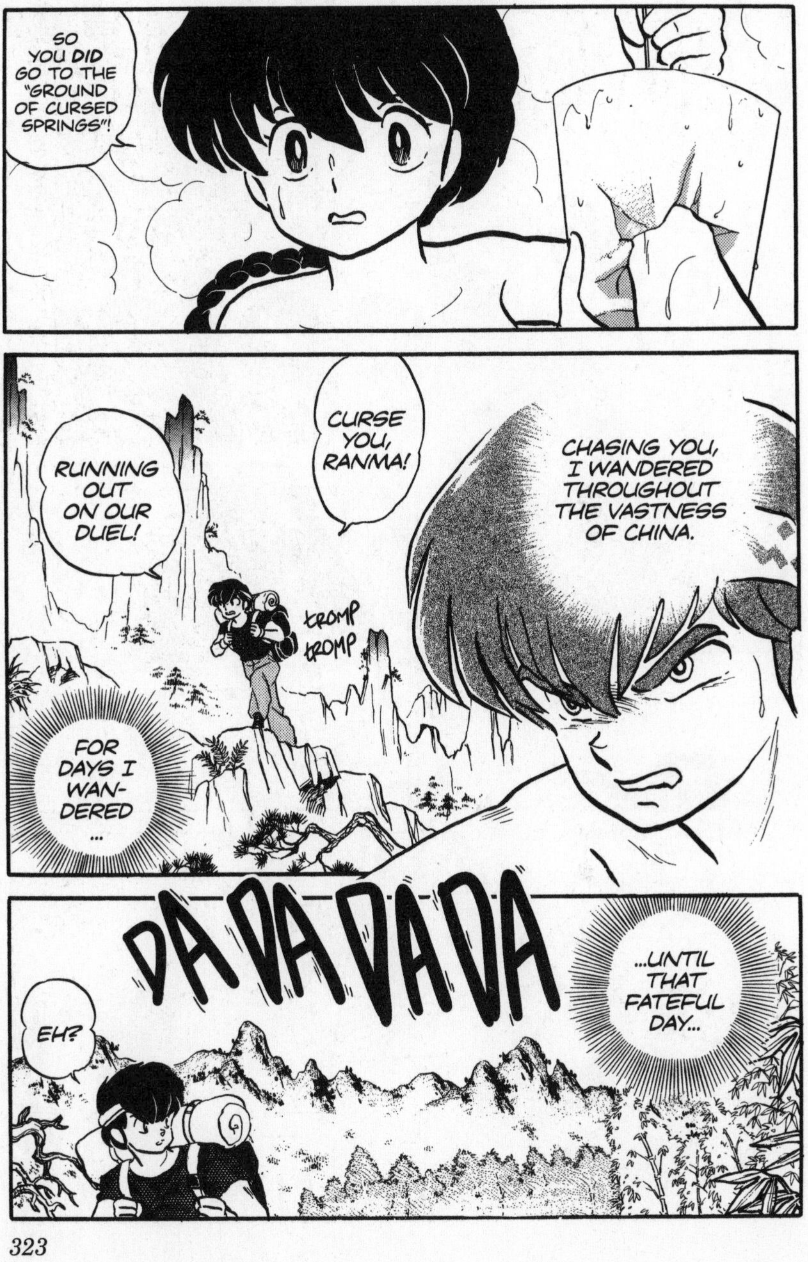
SO YOU **DID** GO TO THE "GROUND OF CURSED SPRINGS"!
CHASING YOU, I WANDERED THROUGHOUT THE VASTNESS OF CHINA.
CURSE YOU, RANMA!
RUNNING OUT ON OUR DUEL!
TROMP TROMP
FOR DAYS I WAN-DERED ...
...UNTIL THAT FATEFUL DAY...
DA DA DA DA DA
EH?

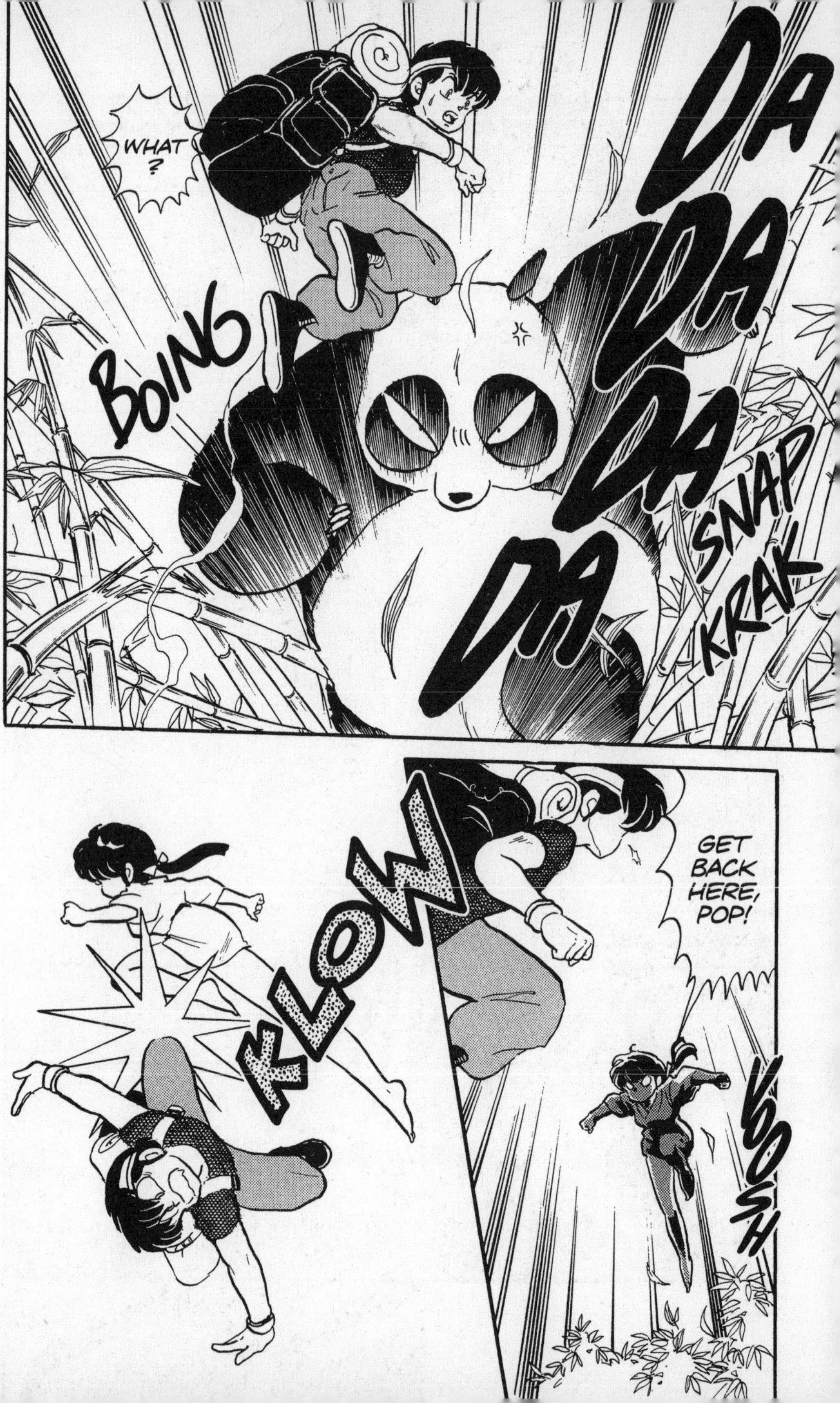
DA DA DA DA
SNAP
KRAK
WHAT?
BOING
GET BACK HERE, POP!
WOOSH
KLOW

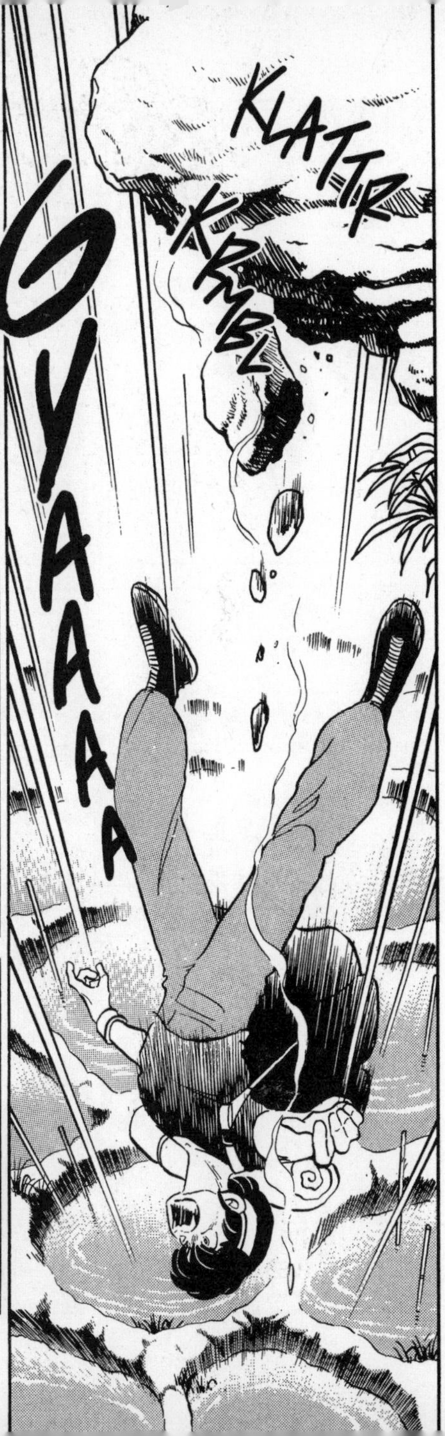
KLATTR
KRMBL
GYAAAAA

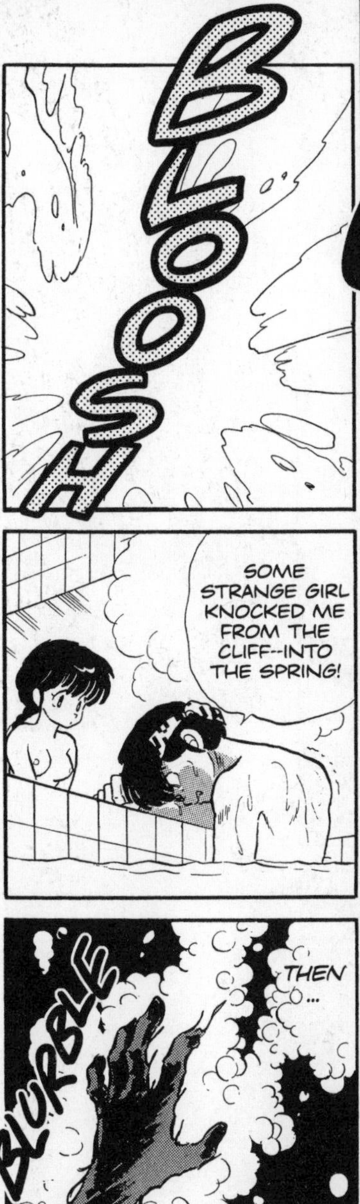
BLOOSH
SOME STRANGE GIRL KNOCKED ME FROM THE CLIFF--INTO THE SPRING!
THEN ...
BLURBLE

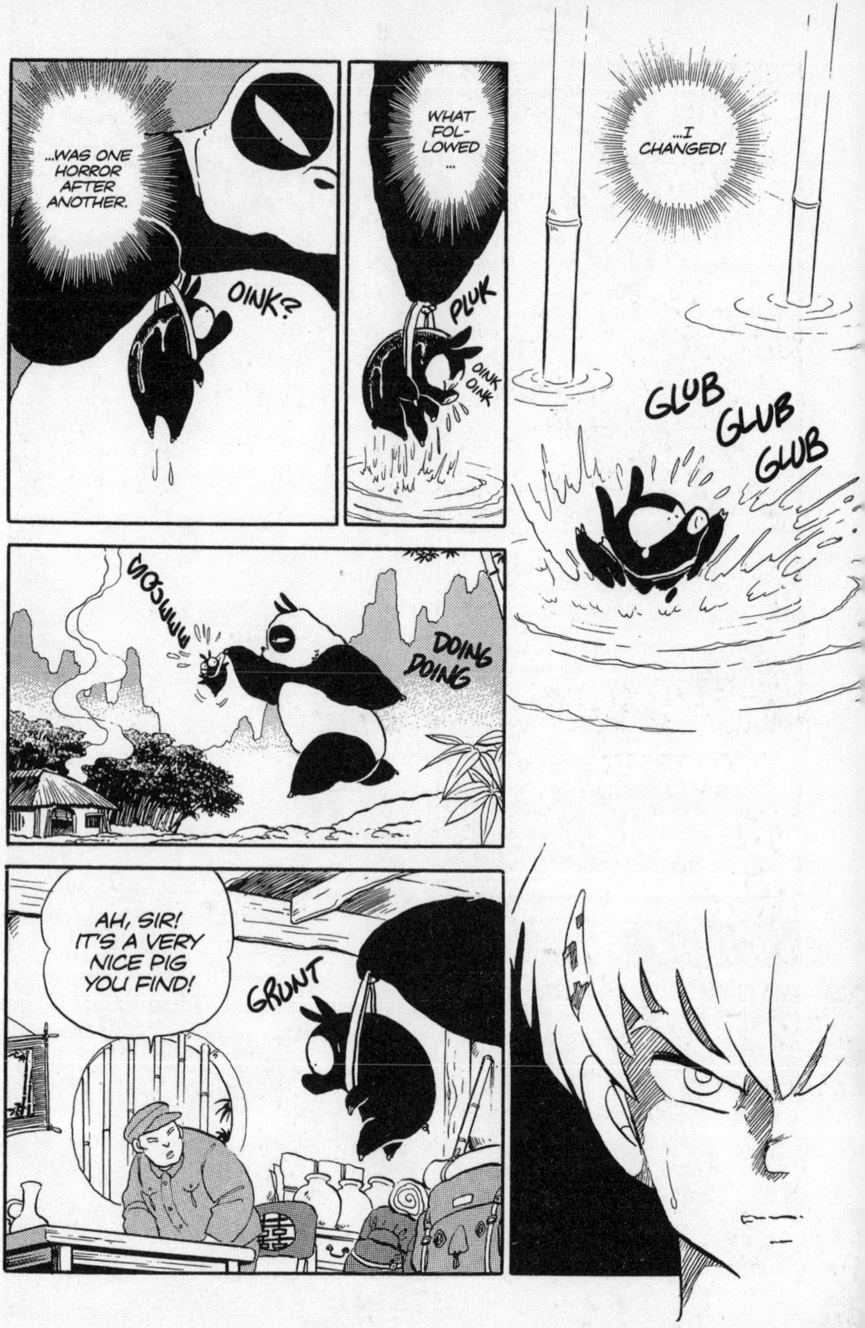
...I CHANGED!
GLUB
GLUB
GLUB
WHAT FOL-LOWED ...
PLUK
OINK OINK
...WAS ONE HORROR AFTER ANOTHER.
OINK?
DOING DOING
AH, SIR! IT'S A VERY NICE PIG YOU FIND!
GRUNT

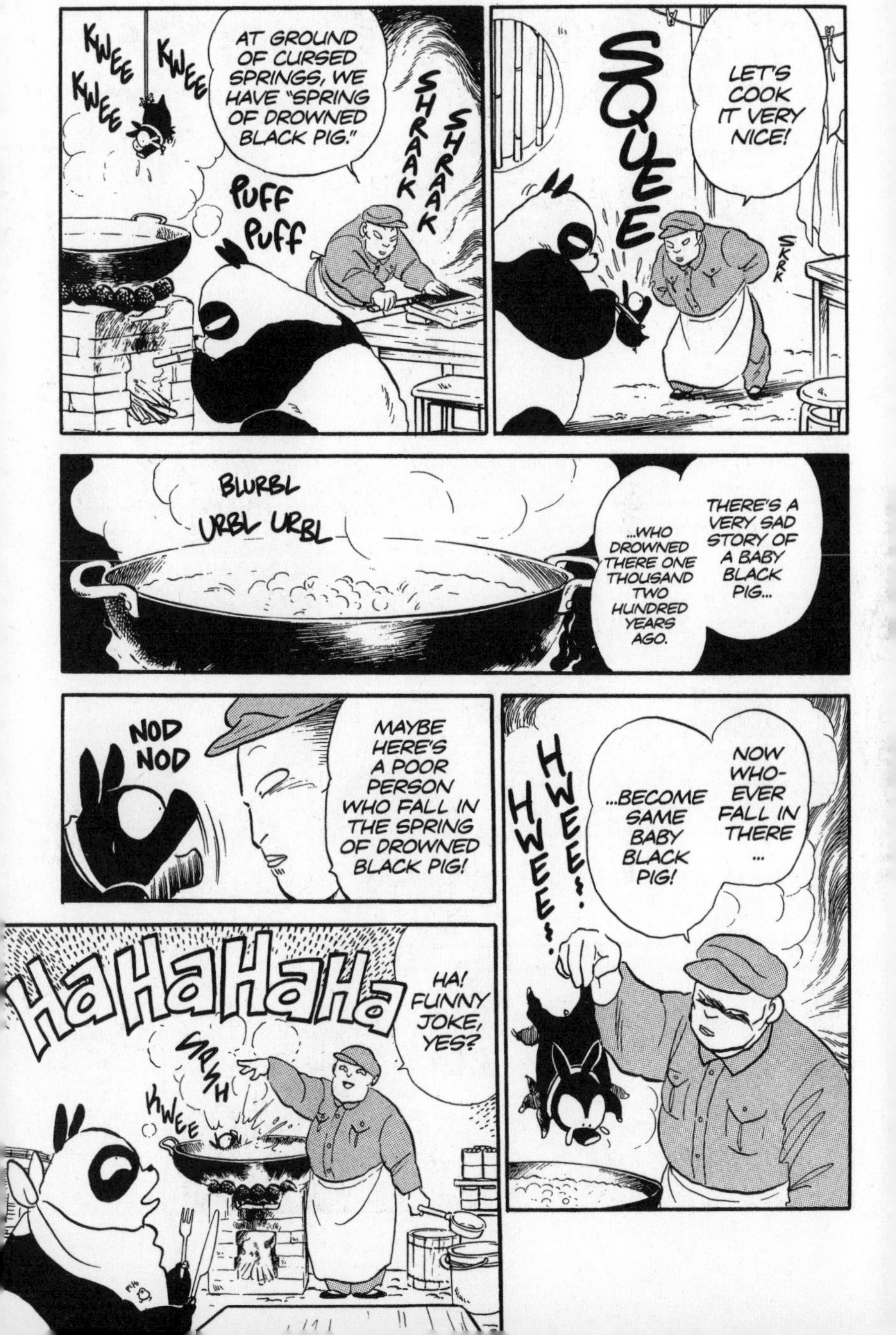
SQUEE
LET'S COOK IT VERY NICE!
SKRK
AT GROUND OF CURSED SPRINGS, WE HAVE "SPRING OF DROWNED BLACK PIG."
SHRAAK SHRAAK
PUFF PUFF
KWEE KWEE KWEE
THERE'S A VERY SAD STORY OF A BABY BLACK PIG...
...WHO DROWNED THERE ONE THOUSAND TWO HUNDRED YEARS AGO.
BLURBL URBL URBL
NOW WHOEVER FALL IN THERE...
...BECOME SAME BABY BLACK PIG!
HWEE HWEE
MAYBE HERE'S A POOR PERSON WHO FALL IN THE SPRING OF DROWNED BLACK PIG!
NOD NOD
HA! FUNNY JOKE, YES?
HAHAHAHA
KWEE

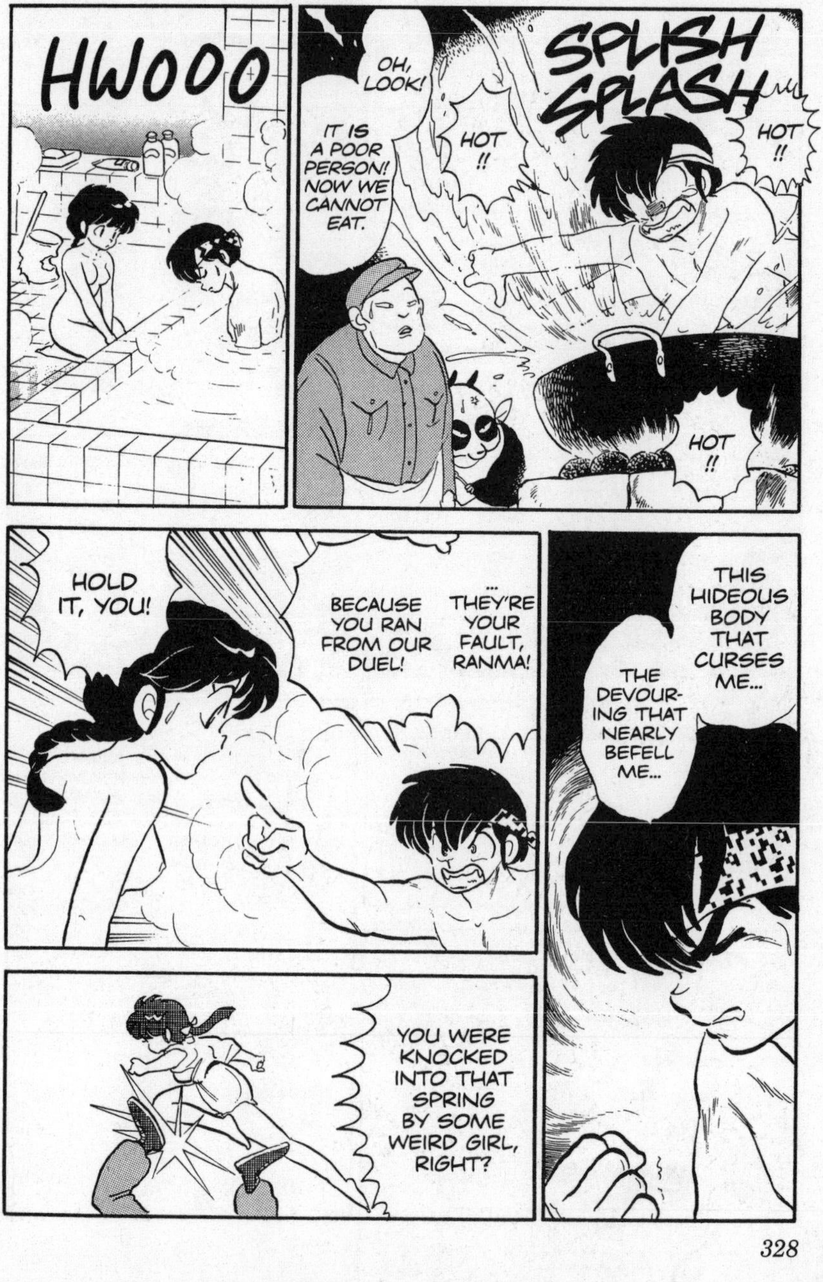
SPLISH SPLASH
HOT !!
OH, LOOK!
HOT !!
IT IS A POOR PERSON! NOW WE CANNOT EAT.
HOT !!
HWOOO
THIS HIDEOUS BODY THAT CURSES ME...
THE DEVOURING THAT NEARLY BEFELL ME...
... THEY'RE YOUR FAULT, RANMA!
BECAUSE YOU RAN FROM OUR DUEL!
HOLD IT, YOU!
YOU WERE KNOCKED INTO THAT SPRING BY SOME WEIRD GIRL, RIGHT?

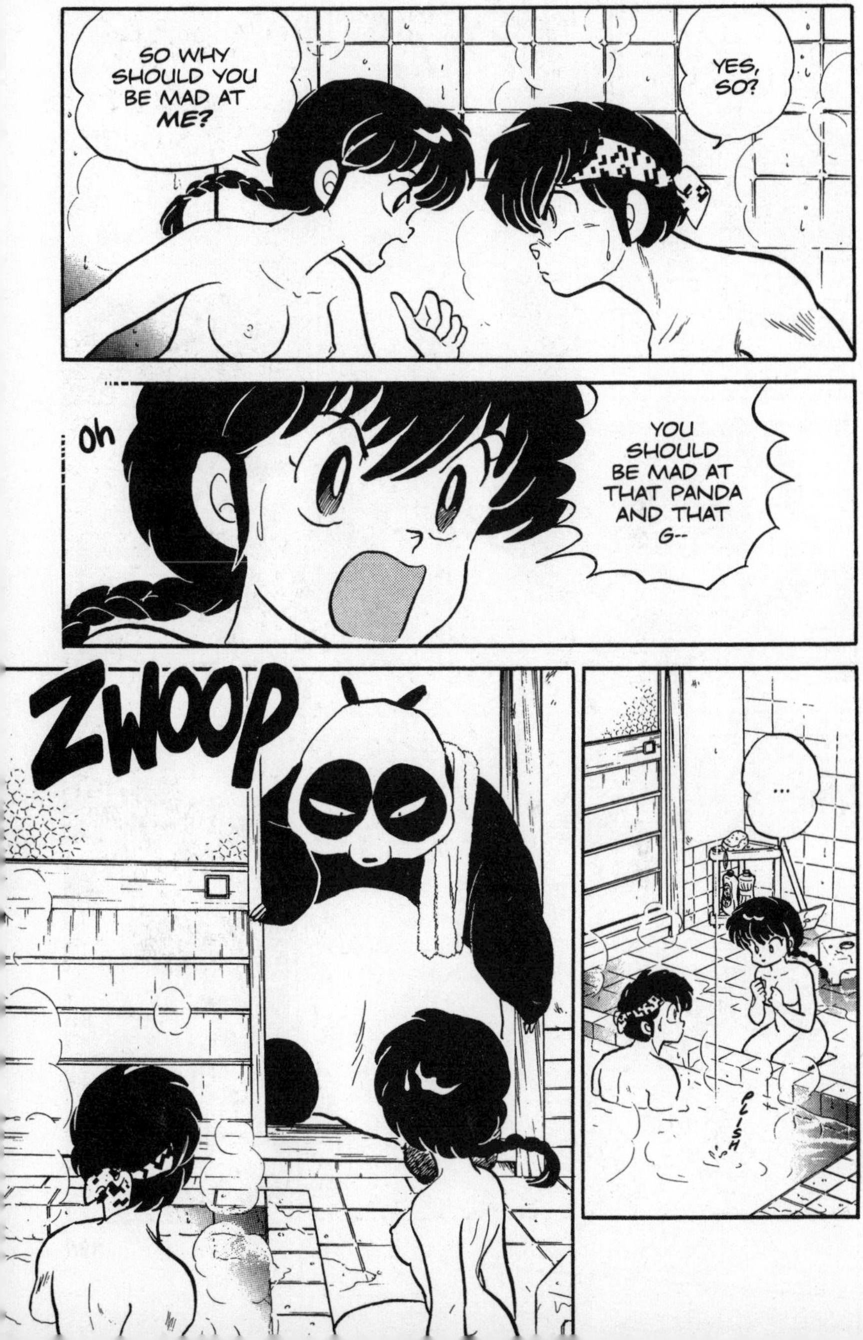
YES, SO?
SO WHY SHOULD YOU BE MAD AT ME?
YOU SHOULD BE MAD AT THAT PANDA AND THAT G--
Oh
...
PLISH
ZWOOP

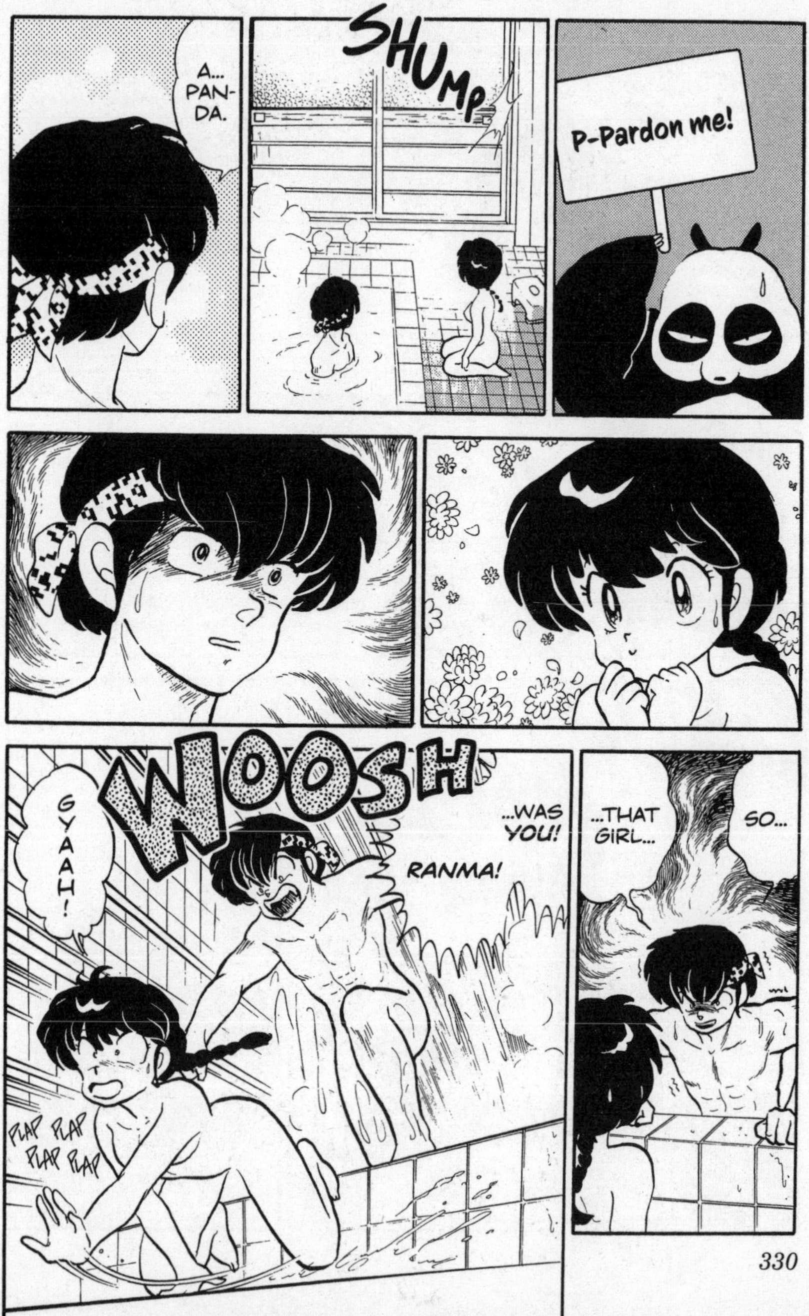
P-Pardon me!
SHUMP
A... PAN-DA.
SO...
...THAT GIRL...
...WAS YOU!
RANMA!
WOOSH
GYAAH!
PLAP PLAP PLAP PLAP

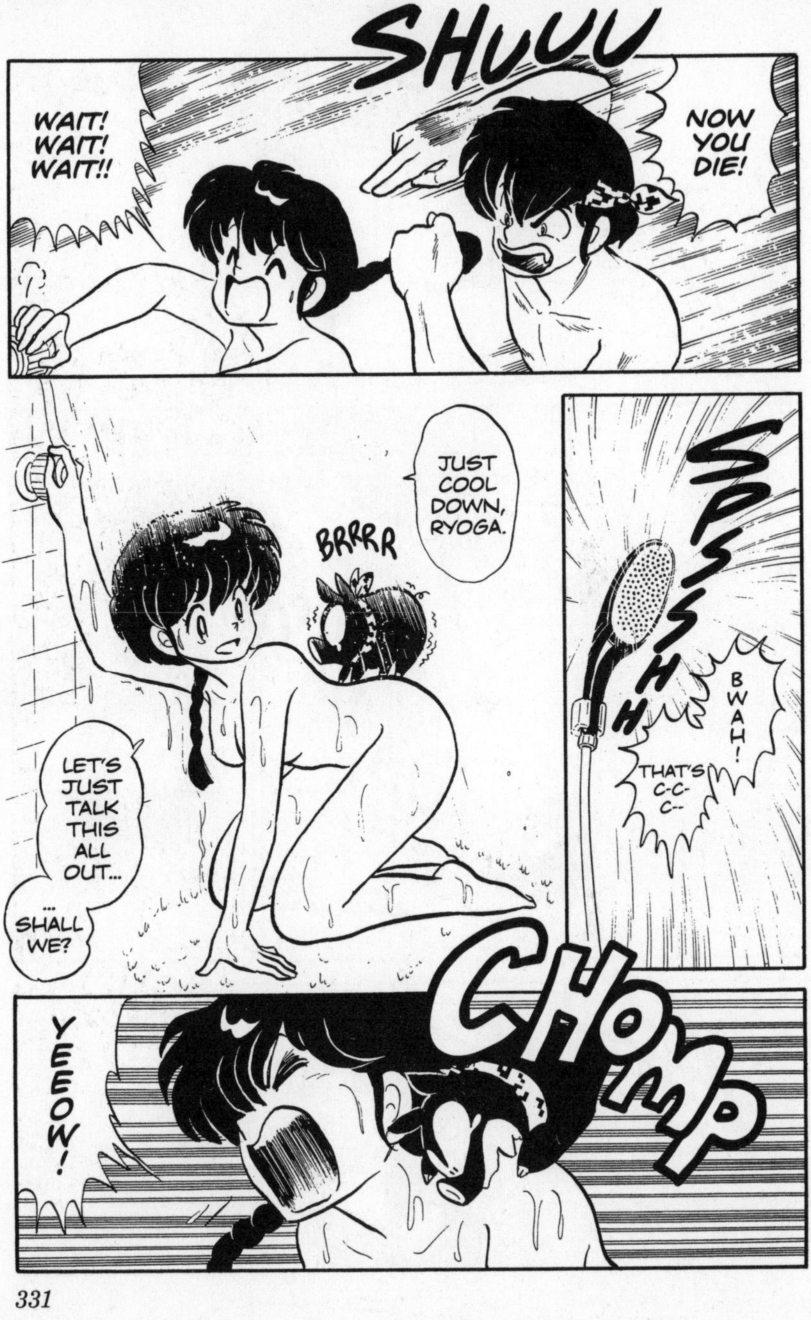
SHUUU
NOW YOU DIE!
WAIT! WAIT! WAIT!!
SPSSHHH
BWAH!
THAT'S C-C-C--
JUST COOL DOWN, RYOGA.
BRRRR
LET'S JUST TALK THIS ALL OUT...
... SHALL WE?
CHOMP
YEEOW!

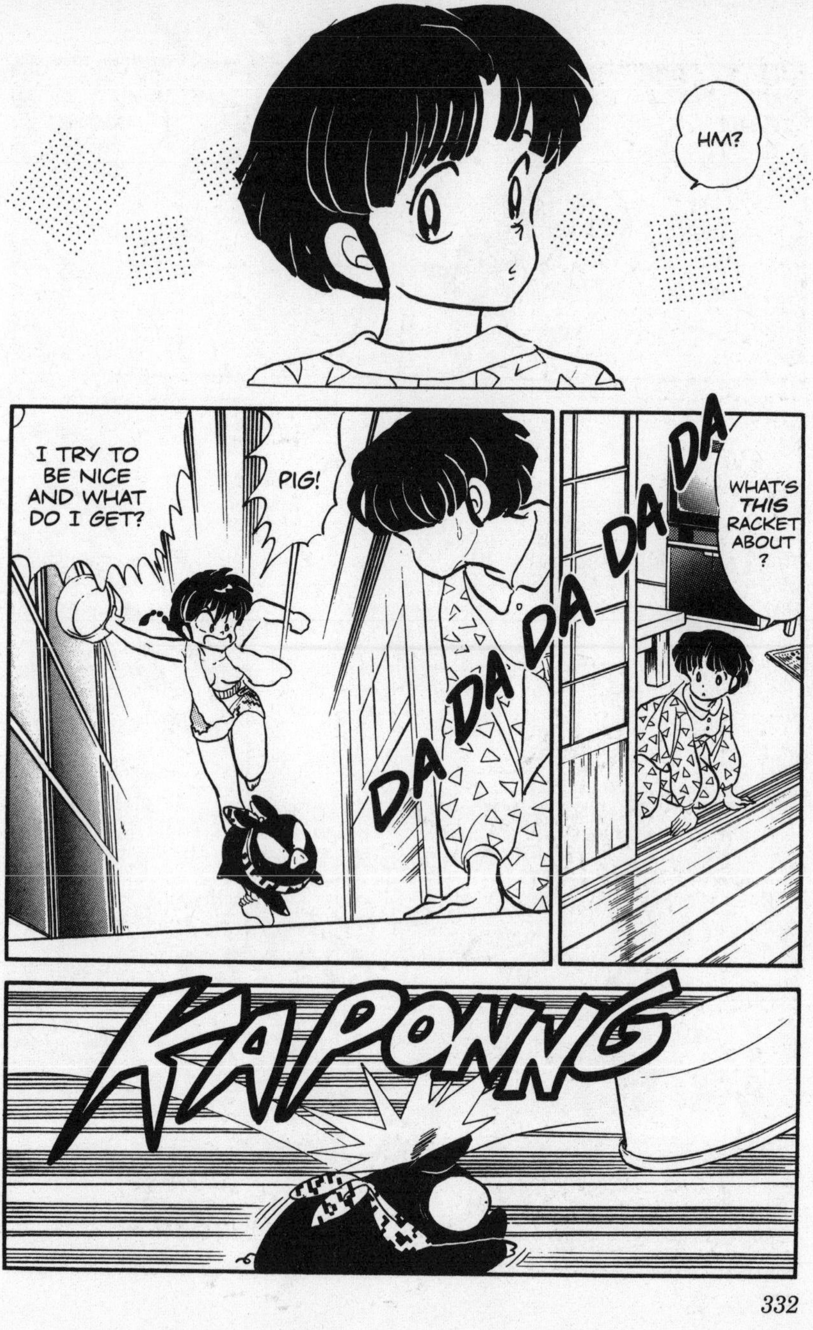
HM?
WHAT'S THIS RACKET ABOUT ?
DA DA DA DA DA DA
PIG!
I TRY TO BE NICE AND WHAT DO I GET?
KAPONNG

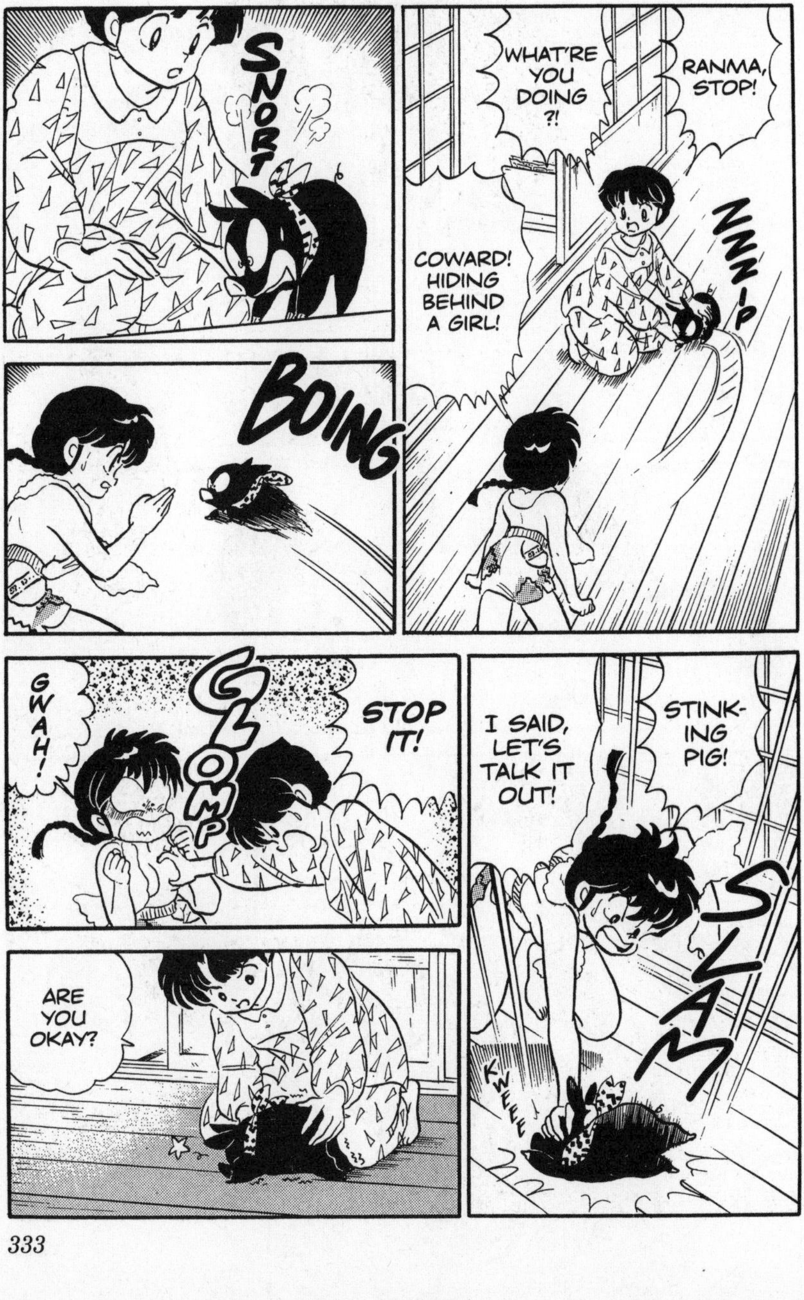
RANMA, STOP!
WHAT'RE YOU DOING ?!
ZZZIP
COWARD! HIDING BEHIND A GIRL!
SNORT
BOING
STINK-ING PIG!
I SAID, LET'S TALK IT OUT!
SLAM
KWEEE
STOP IT!
GLOMP
GWAH!
ARE YOU OKAY?

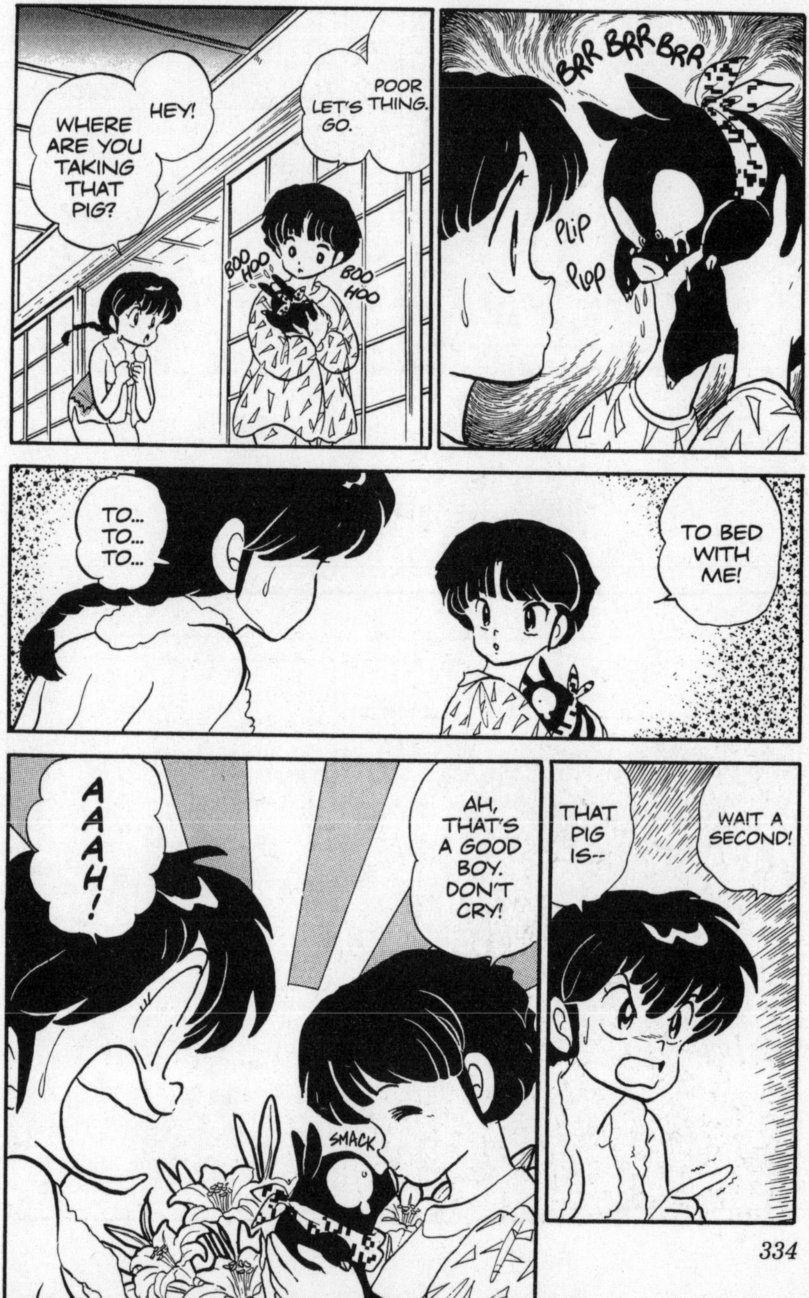
BRR BRR BRR
PLIP
PLOP
POOR THING. LET'S GO.
HEY!
WHERE ARE YOU TAKING THAT PIG?
BOO HOO
BOO HOO
TO BED WITH ME!
TO... TO... TO...
WAIT A SECOND!
THAT PIG IS--
AH, THAT'S A GOOD BOY. DON'T CRY!
AAAAH!
SMACK

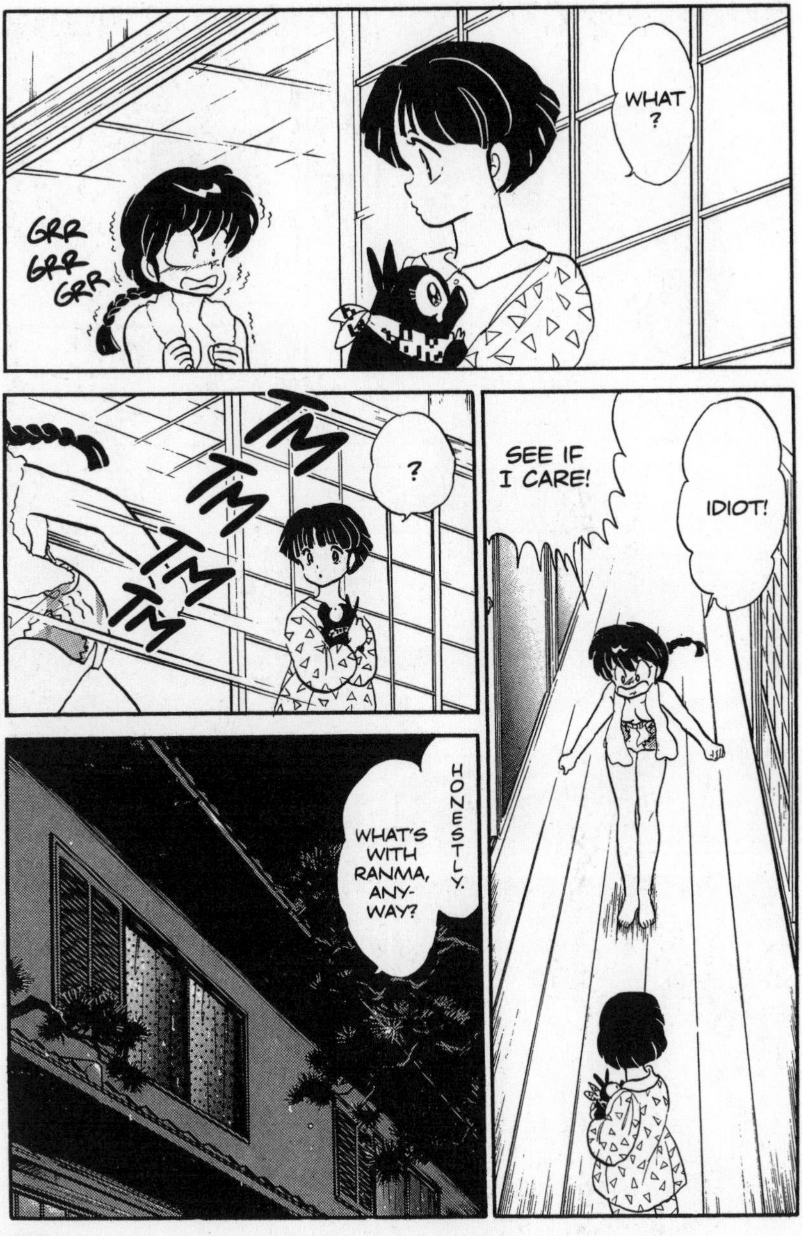
WHAT?
GRR GRR GRR
IDIOT!
SEE IF I CARE!
?
TM TM TM TM
HONESTLY.
WHAT'S WITH RANMA, ANY-WAY?

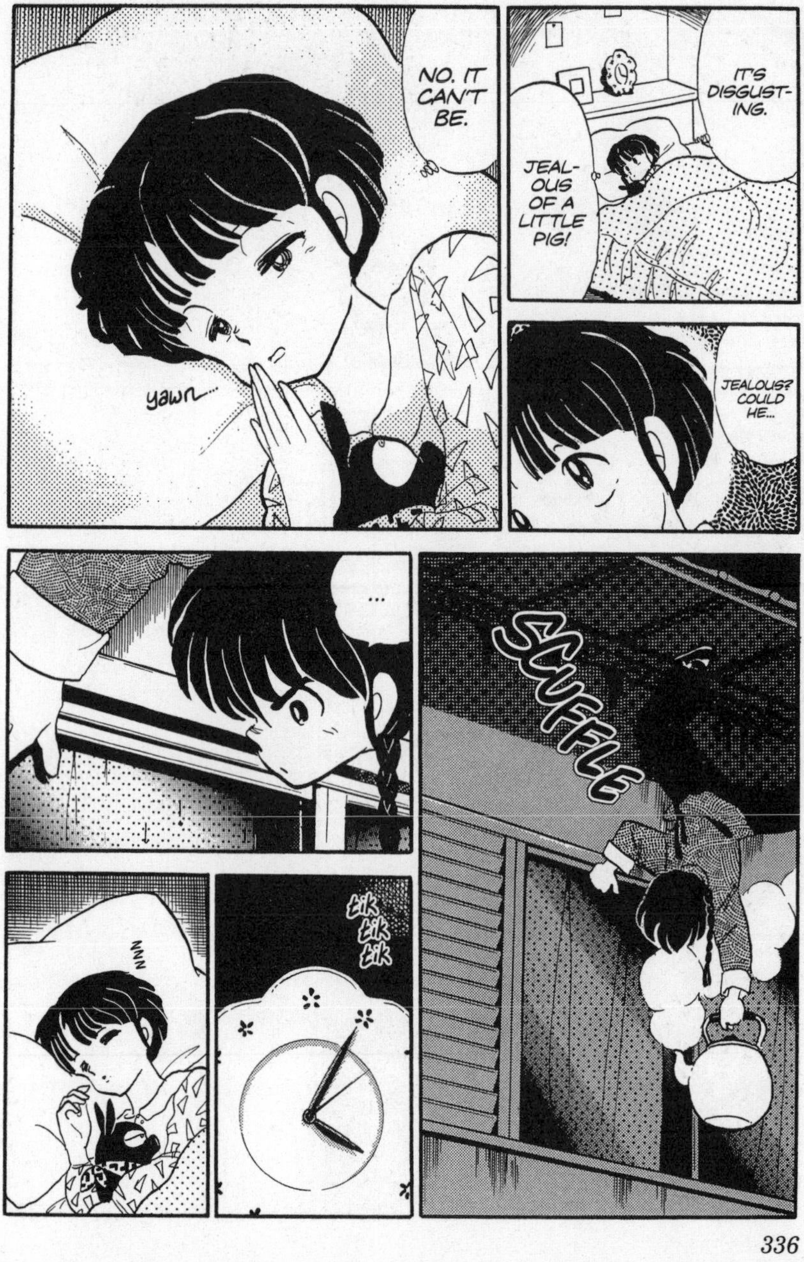
IT'S DISGUST-ING.
JEAL-OUS OF A LITTLE PIG!
JEALOUS? COULD HE...
NO. IT CAN'T BE.
yawn...
SCUFFLE
...
tik tik tik
zzz

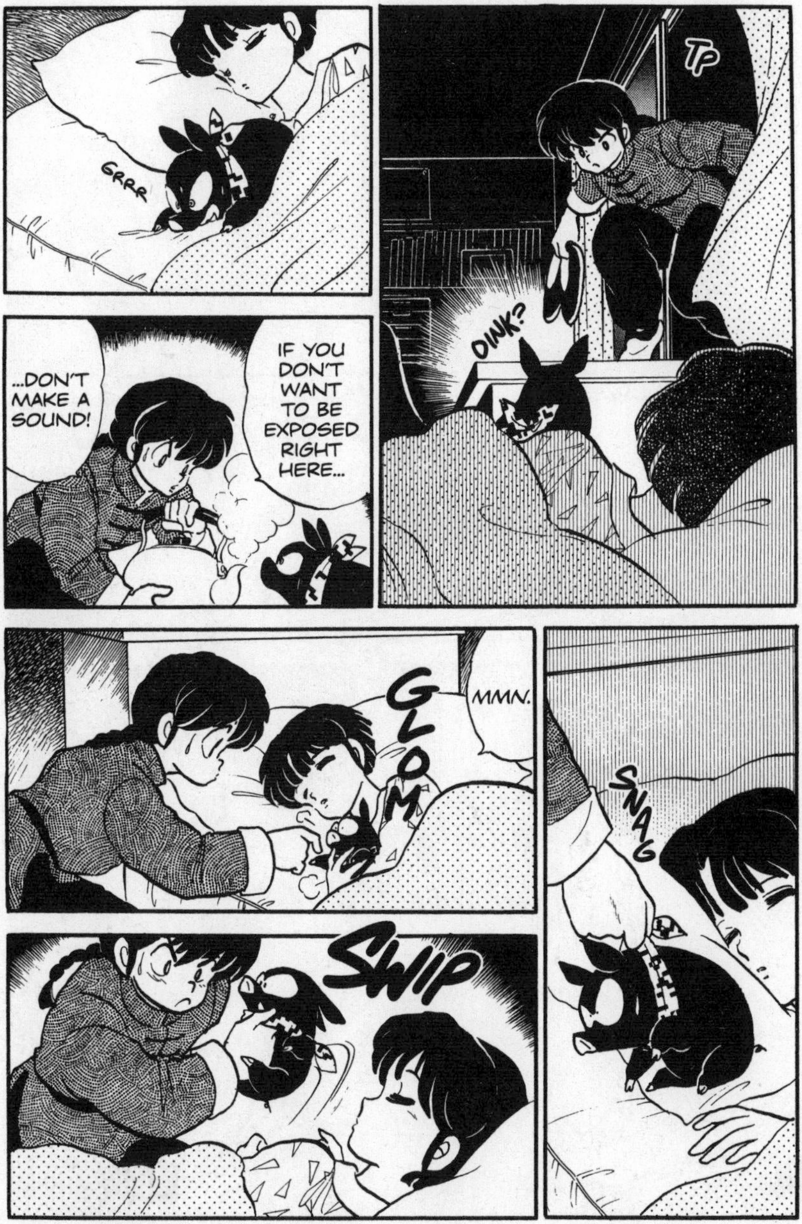
TP
DINK?
GRRR
IF YOU DON'T WANT TO BE EXPOSED RIGHT HERE...
...DON'T MAKE A SOUND!
SNAG
MMN.
GLOM
SWIP

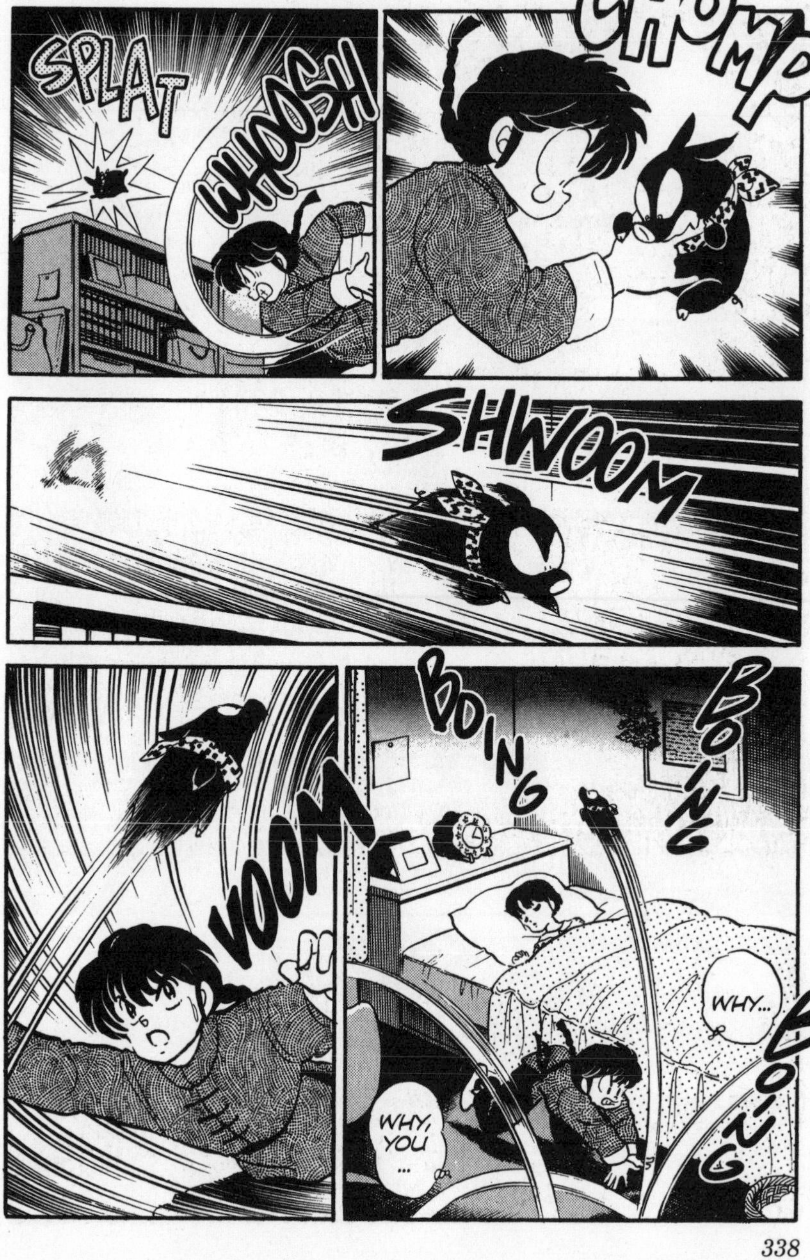
CHOMP
WHOOSH
SPLAT
SHWOOM
BOING
BOING
WHY...
BOING
WHY, YOU ...
VOOM

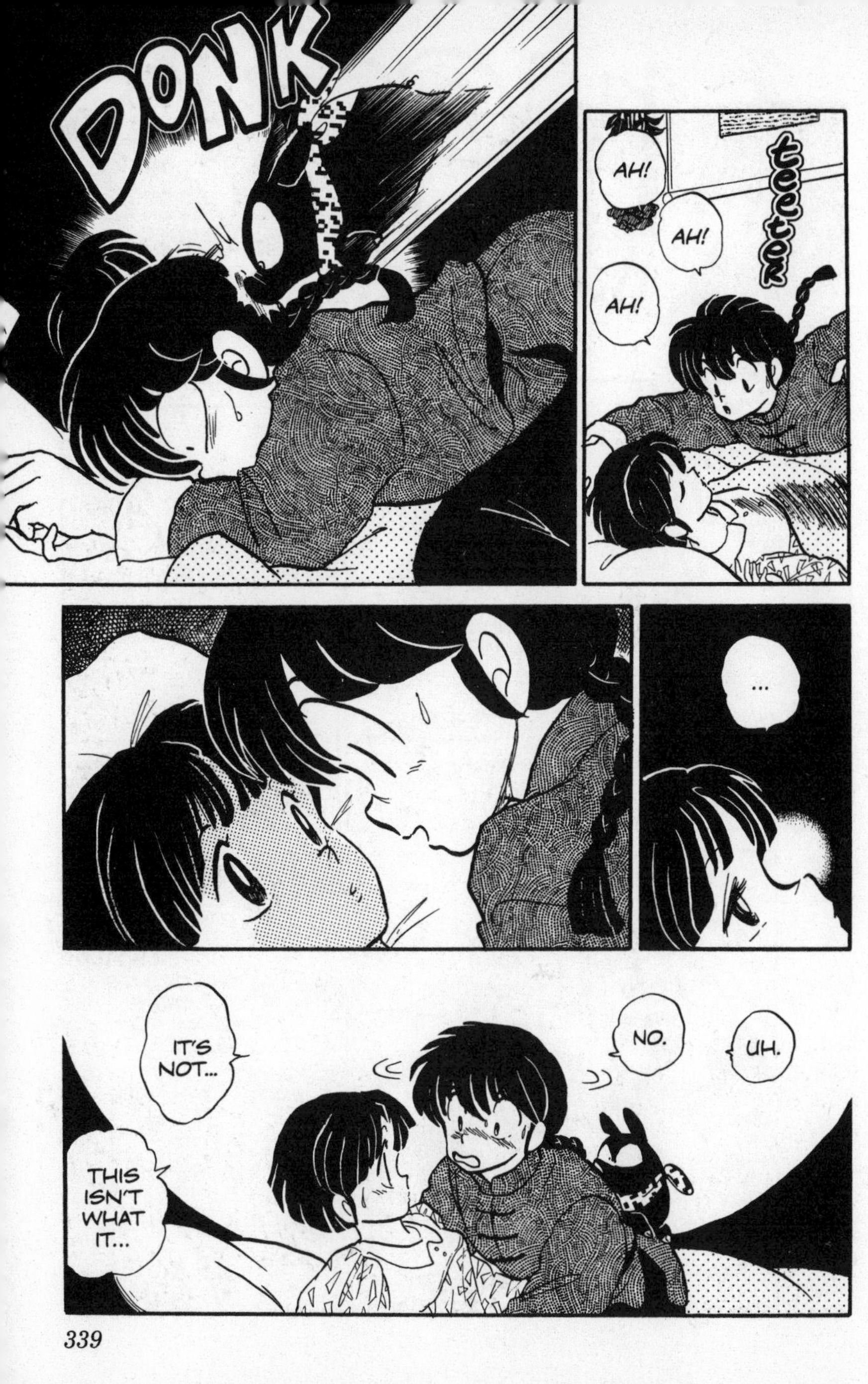
AH!
AH!
AH!
teeter
DONK
...
UH.
NO.
IT'S NOT...
THIS ISN'T WHAT IT...

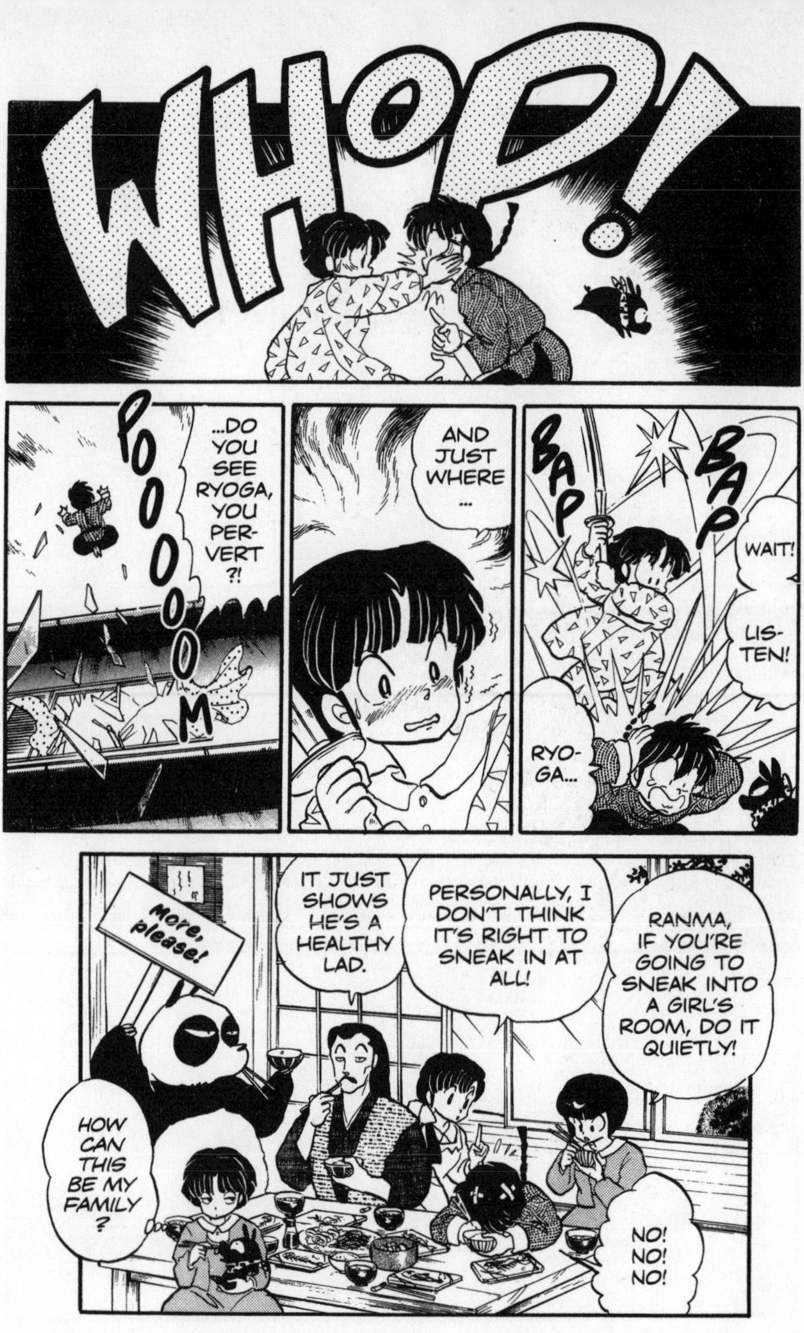
WHOP!
BAP
BAP
WAIT!
LIS-TEN!
RYOGA...
AND JUST WHERE ...
...DO YOU SEE RYOGA, YOU PER-VERT ?!
POOOOOOOM
RANMA, IF YOU'RE GOING TO SNEAK INTO A GIRL'S ROOM, DO IT QUIETLY!
PERSONALLY, I DON'T THINK IT'S RIGHT TO SNEAK IN AT ALL!
IT JUST SHOWS HE'S A HEALTHY LAD.
More, please!
NO! NO! NO!
HOW CAN THIS BE MY FAMILY ?

# PART 17
# KODACHI, THE BLACK ROSE

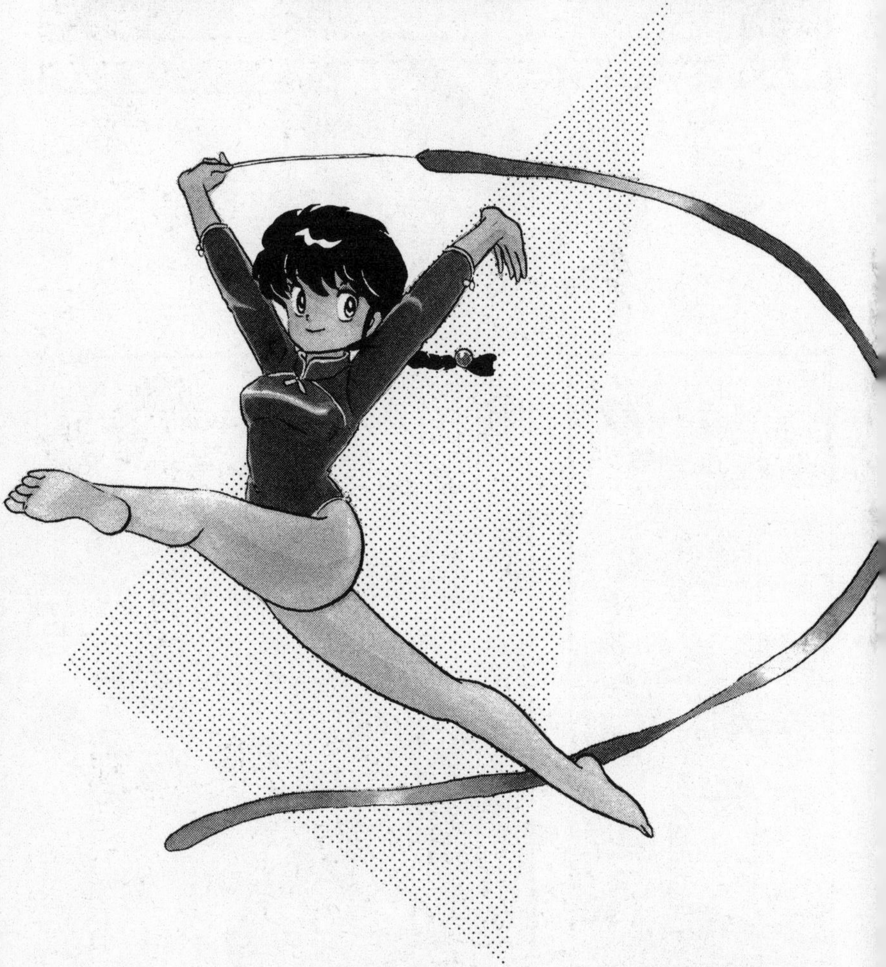

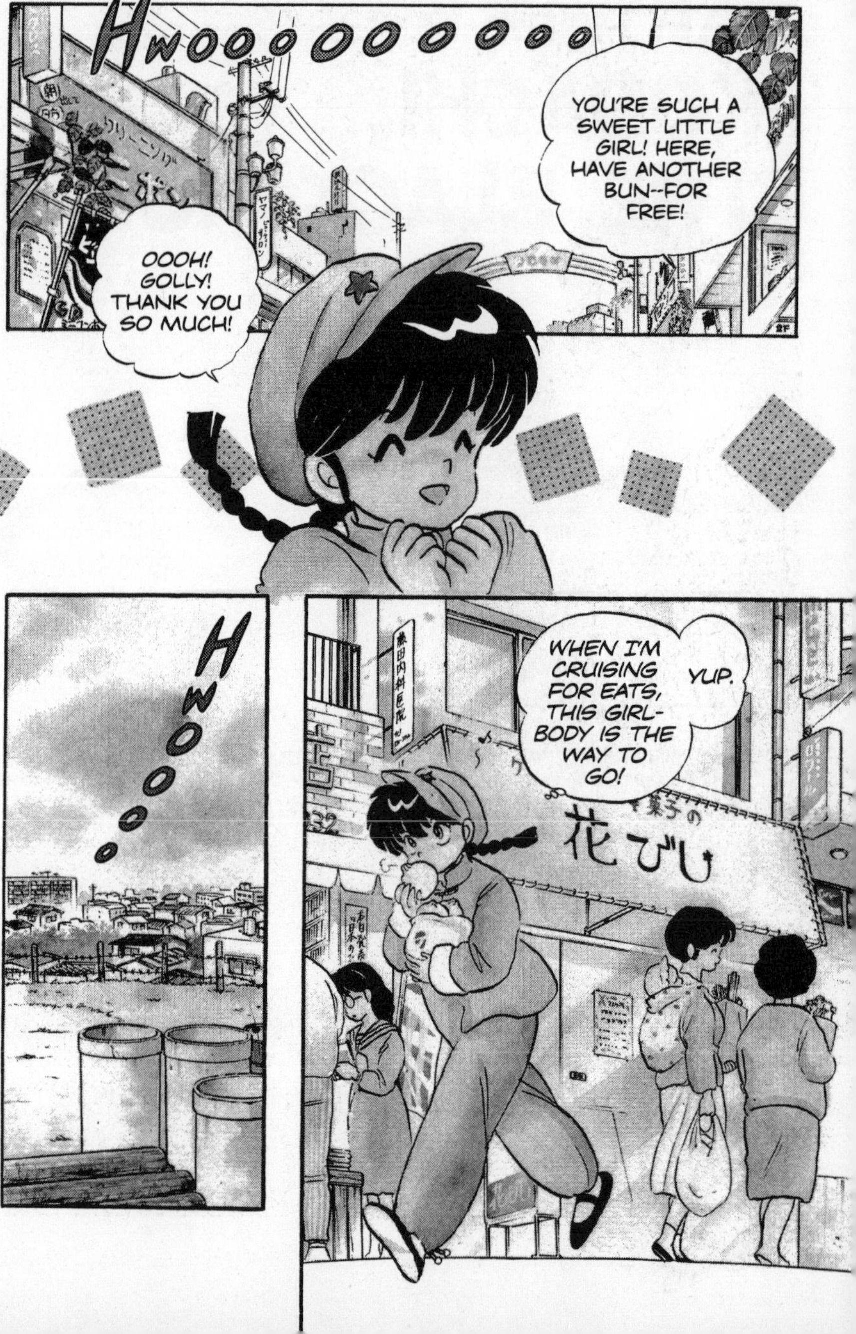
HWOOOOOOOOOOO
YOU'RE SUCH A SWEET LITTLE GIRL! HERE, HAVE ANOTHER BUN--FOR FREE!
OOOH! GOLLY! THANK YOU SO MUCH!
YUP.
WHEN I'M CRUISING FOR EATS, THIS GIRL-BODY IS THE WAY TO GO!
HWOOOOOOO

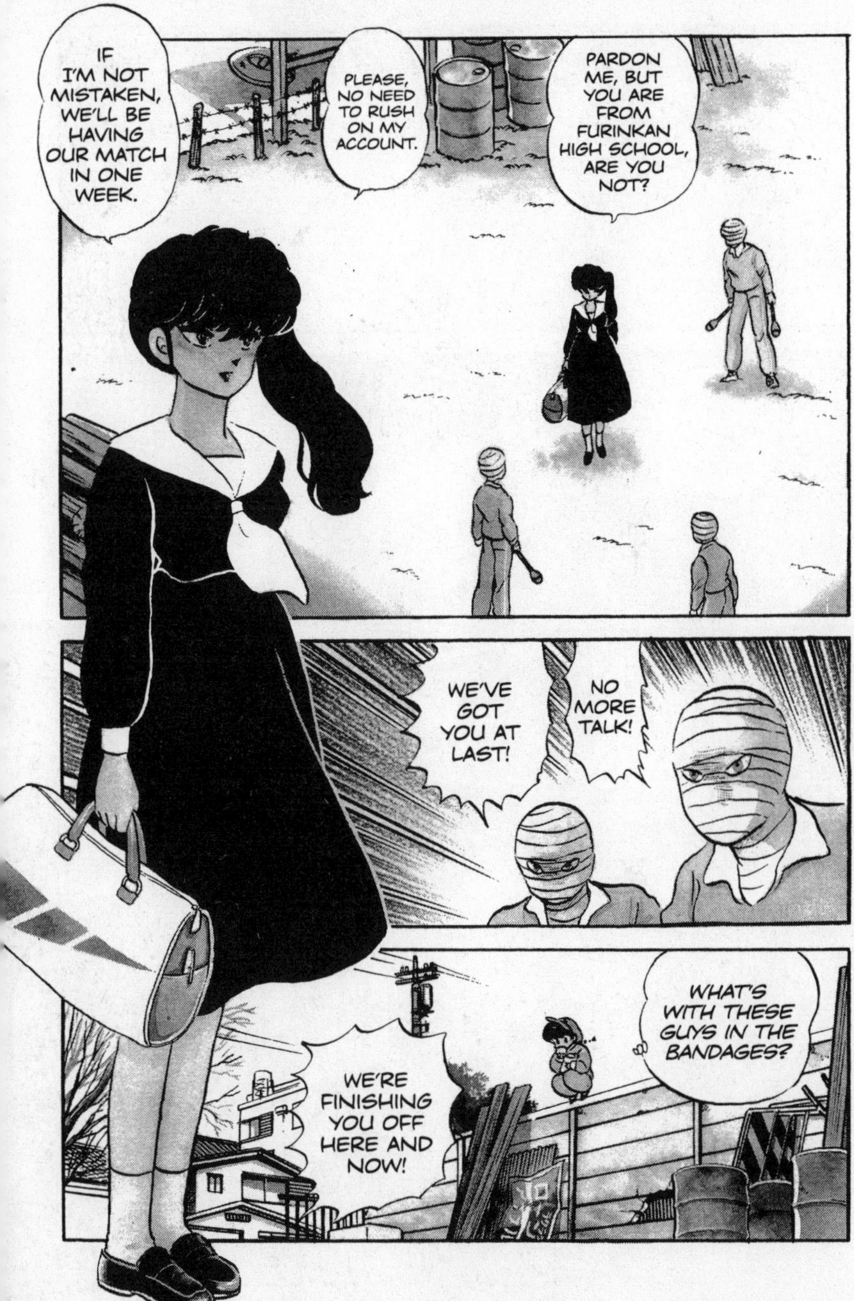
PARDON ME, BUT YOU ARE FROM FURINKAN HIGH SCHOOL, ARE YOU NOT?
PLEASE, NO NEED TO RUSH ON MY ACCOUNT.
IF I'M NOT MISTAKEN, WE'LL BE HAVING OUR MATCH IN ONE WEEK.
NO MORE TALK!
WE'VE GOT YOU AT LAST!
WHAT'S WITH THESE GUYS IN THE BANDAGES?
WE'RE FINISHING YOU OFF HERE AND NOW!

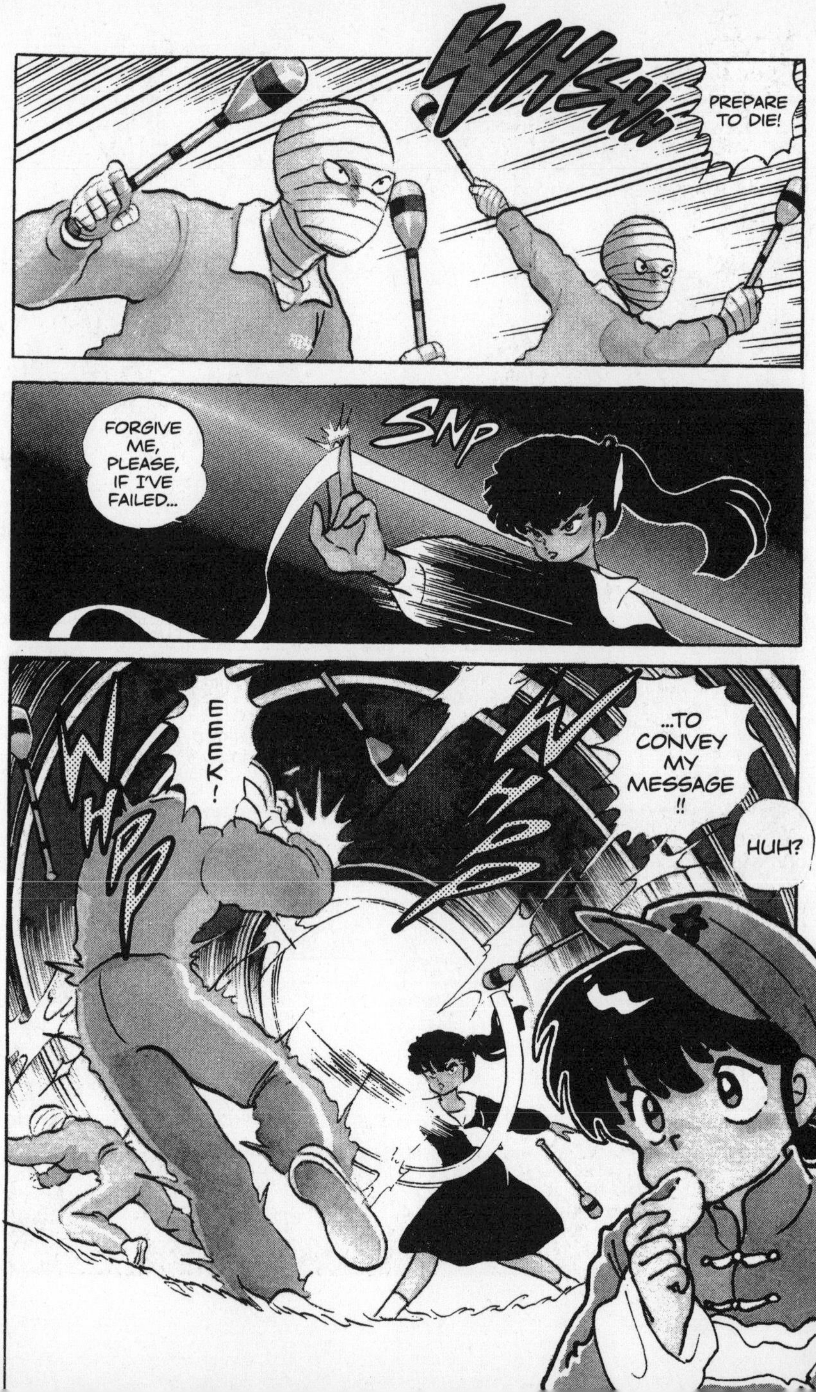
WHSHH
PREPARE TO DIE!
SNP
FORGIVE ME, PLEASE, IF I'VE FAILED...
...TO CONVEY MY MESSAGE!!
HUH?
WHAP
EEEK!
WHAP

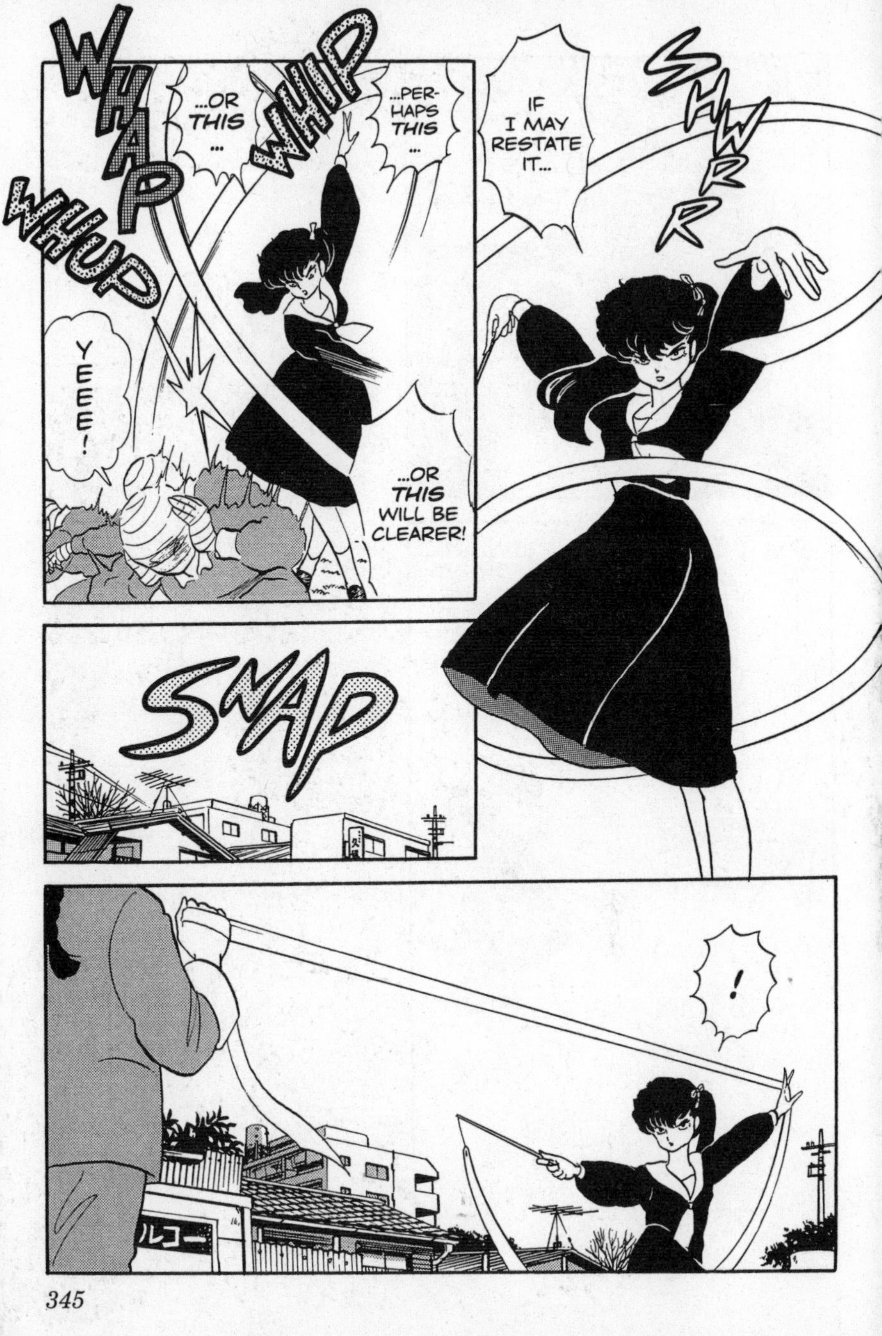
SHWRRR
IF I MAY RESTATE IT...
...PER-HAPS THIS ...
WHIP
...OR THIS ...
WHAP
WHUP
YEEE!
...OR THIS WILL BE CLEARER!
SNAP
!
ルコー

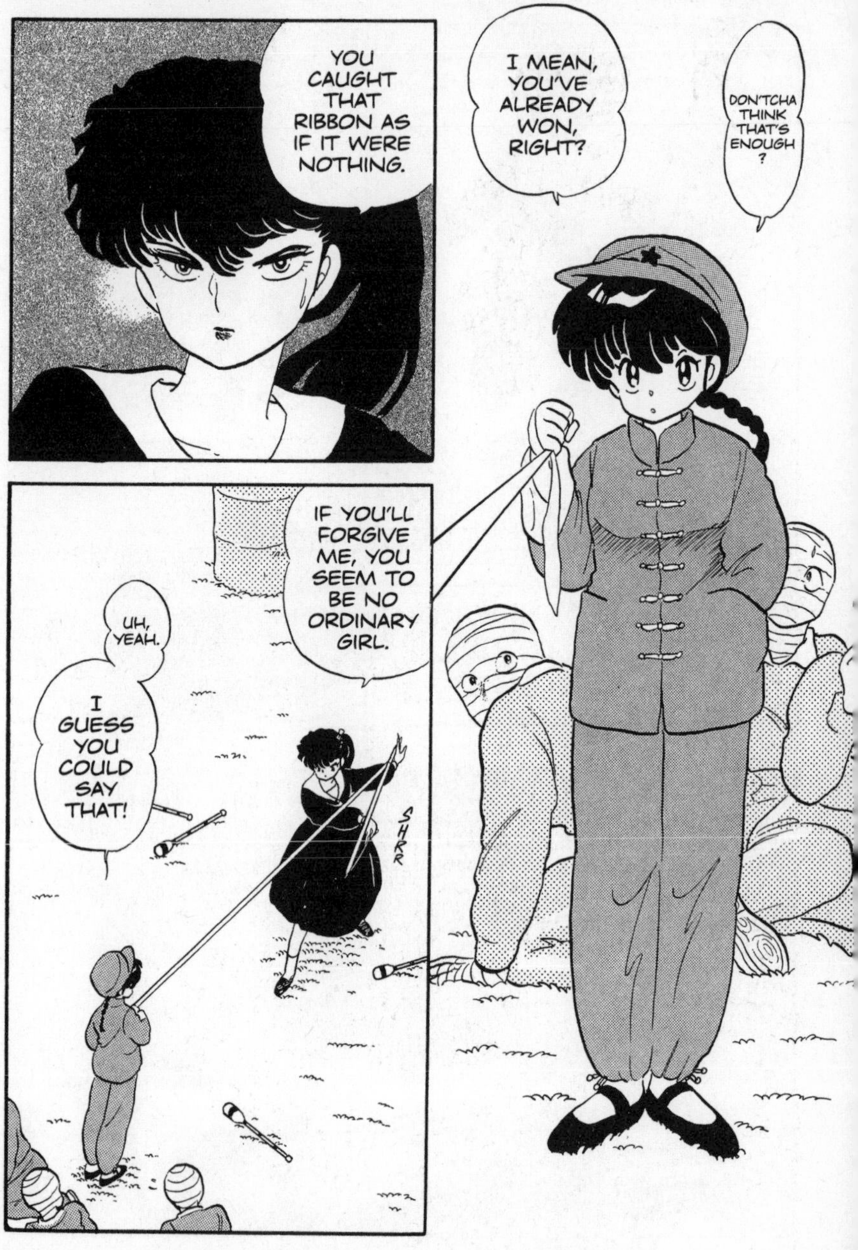
I MEAN, YOU'VE ALREADY WON, RIGHT?
DON'TCHA THINK THAT'S ENOUGH?
YOU CAUGHT THAT RIBBON AS IF IT WERE NOTHING.
IF YOU'LL FORGIVE ME, YOU SEEM TO BE NO ORDINARY GIRL.
SHRR
UH, YEAH.
I GUESS YOU COULD SAY THAT!

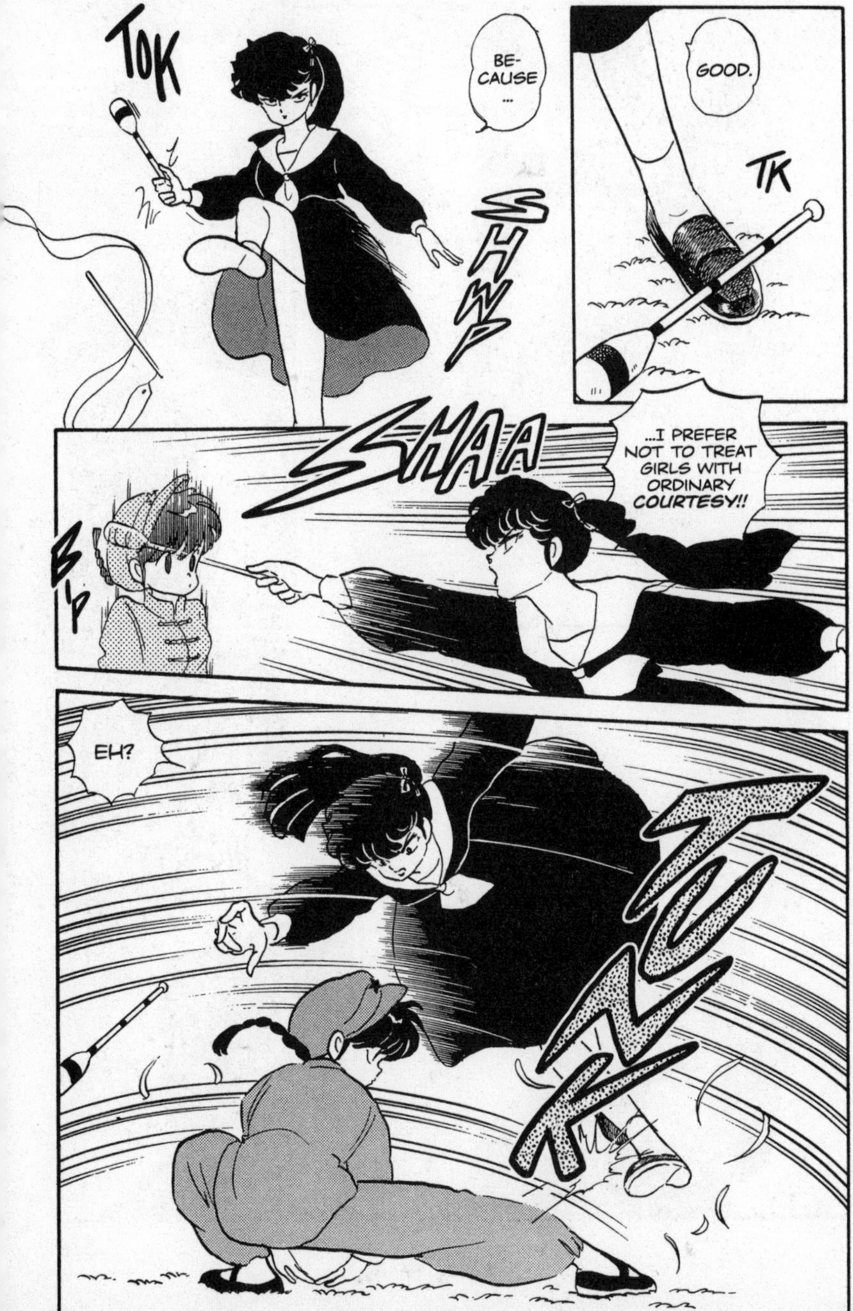
GOOD.
TK
BE-CAUSE ...
TOK
SHWIP
...I PREFER NOT TO TREAT GIRLS WITH ORDINARY **COURTESY!!**
SHAA
BLIP
EH?

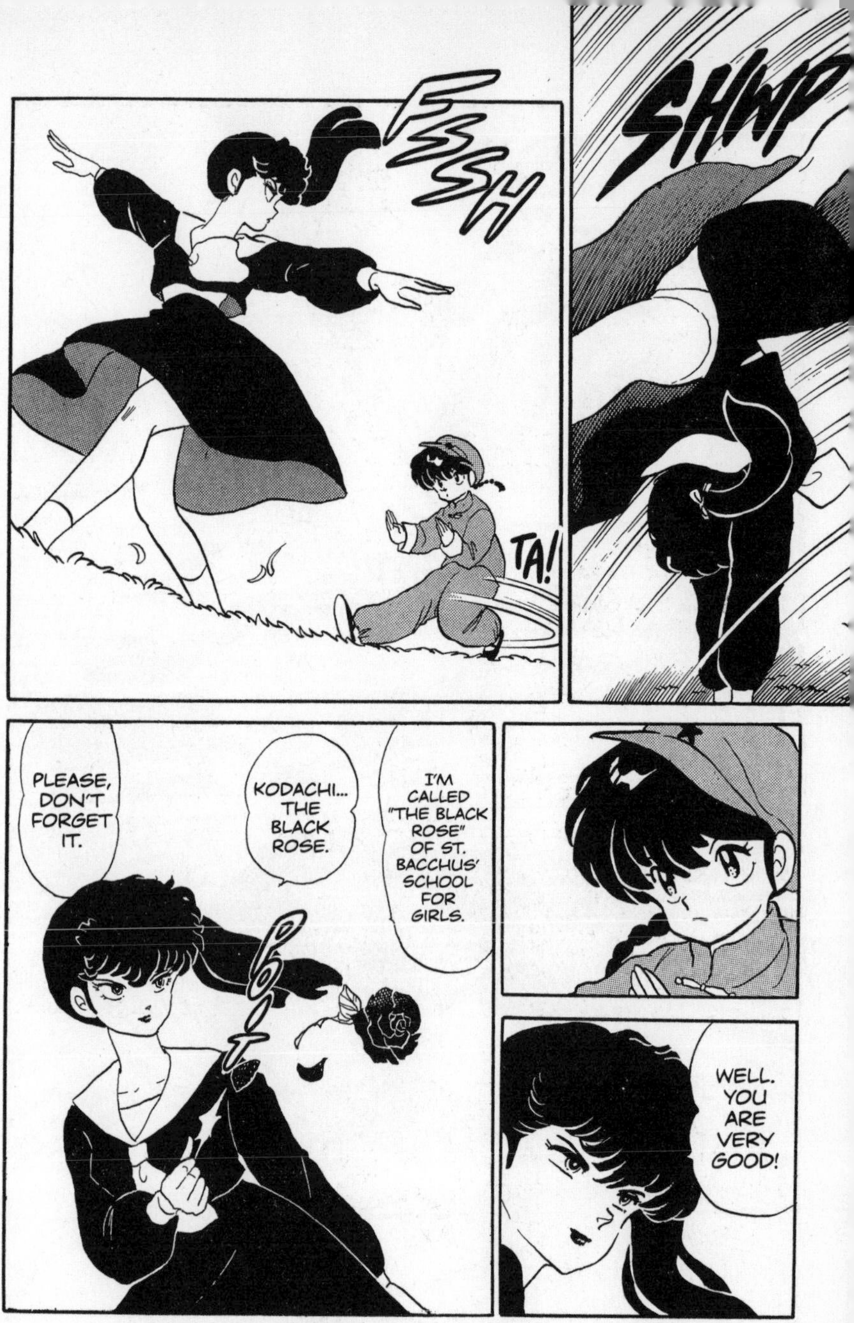

SHWP
FSSH
TA!
WELL. YOU ARE VERY GOOD!
I'M CALLED "THE BLACK ROSE" OF ST. BACCHUS' SCHOOL FOR GIRLS.
KODACHI... THE BLACK ROSE.
PLEASE, DON'T FORGET IT.

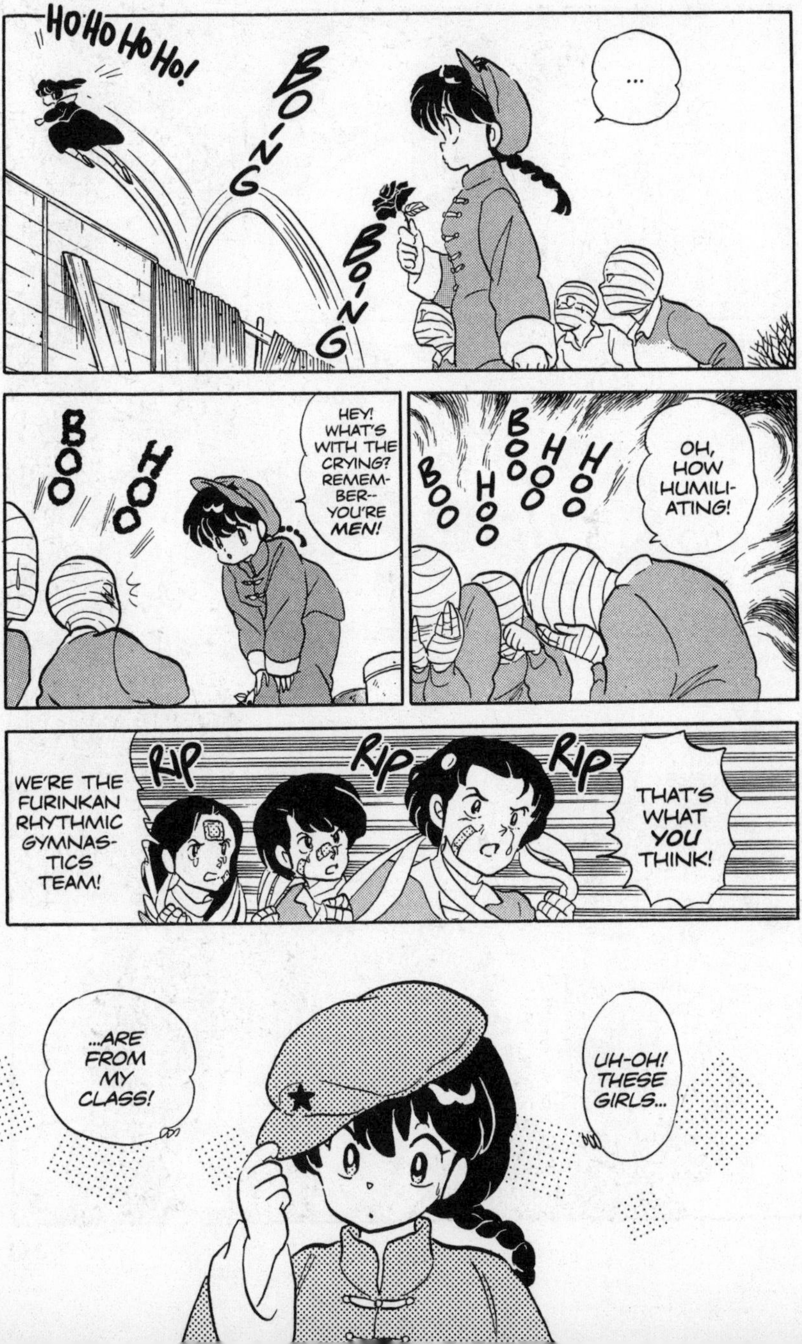
...
BOING BOING
HO HO HO HO HO!
OH, HOW HUMILIATING!
BOO HOO BOO HOO BOO HOO
HEY! WHAT'S WITH THE CRYING? REMEMBER-- YOU'RE MEN!
BOO HOO
THAT'S WHAT YOU THINK!
RIP RIP RIP
WE'RE THE FURINKAN RHYTHMIC GYMNASTICS TEAM!
UH-OH! THESE GIRLS...
...ARE FROM MY CLASS!

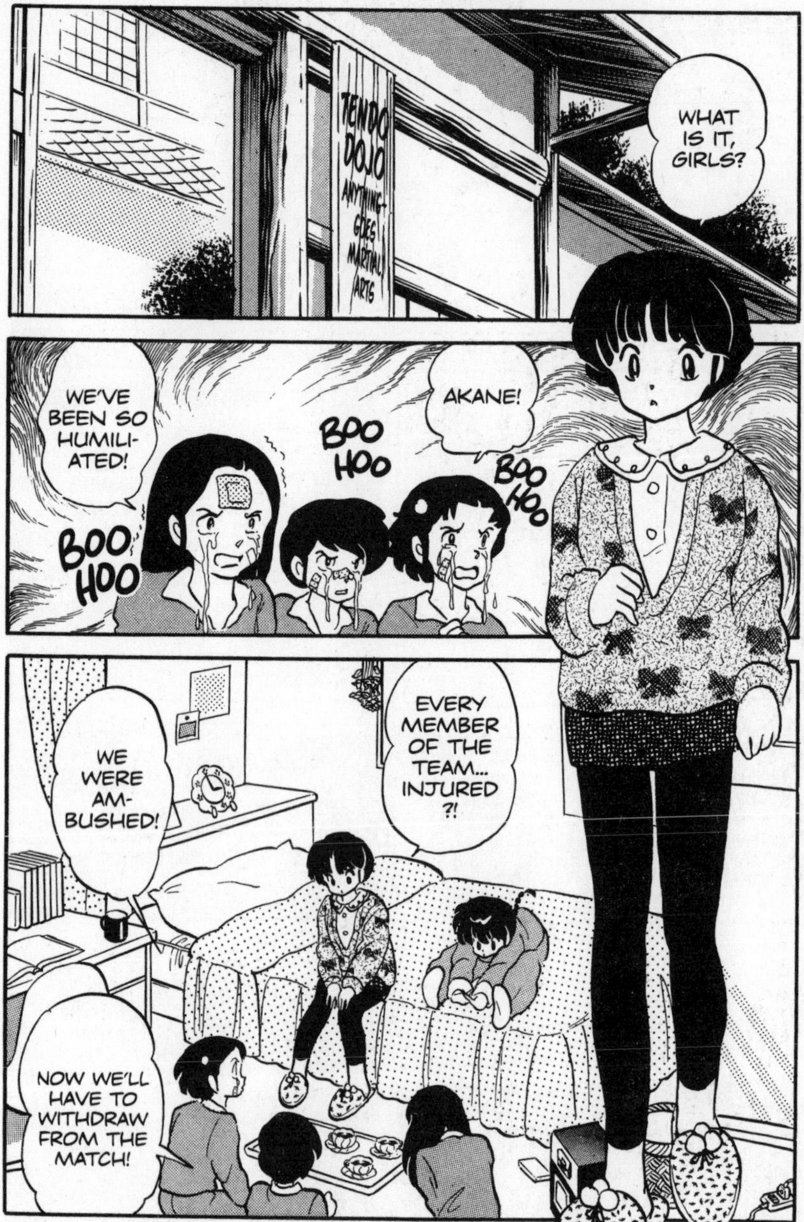
WHAT IS IT, GIRLS?
TENDO DOJO ANYTHING-GOES MARTIAL ARTS
BOO HOO
AKANE!
BOO HOO
WE'VE BEEN SO HUMILI-ATED!
BOO HOO
EVERY MEMBER OF THE TEAM... INJURED ?!
WE WERE AM-BUSHED!
NOW WE'LL HAVE TO WITHDRAW FROM THE MATCH!

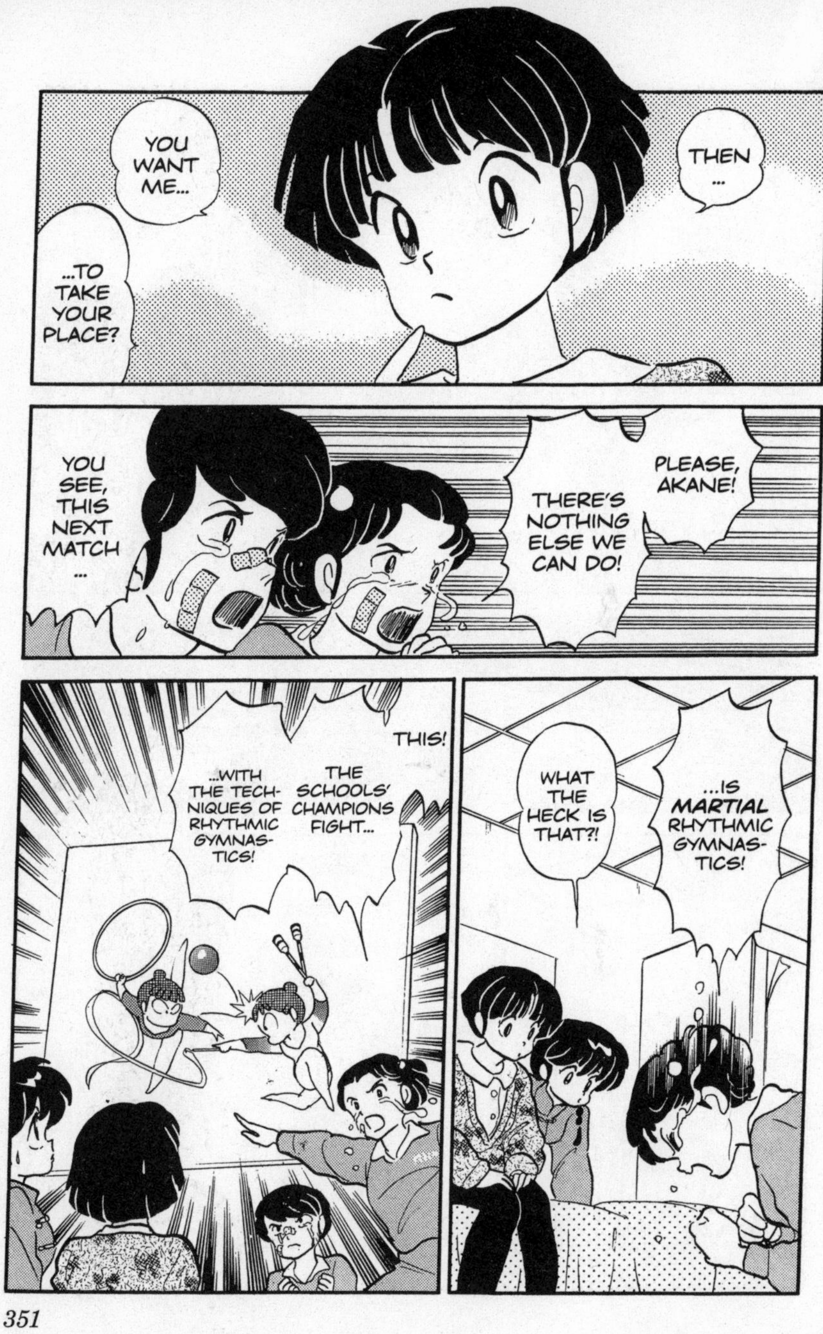
THEN ...
YOU WANT ME...
...TO TAKE YOUR PLACE?
PLEASE, AKANE!
THERE'S NOTHING ELSE WE CAN DO!
YOU SEE, THIS NEXT MATCH ...
...IS MARTIAL RHYTHMIC GYMNASTICS!
WHAT THE HECK IS THAT?!
THIS!
THE SCHOOLS' CHAMPIONS FIGHT...
...WITH THE TECHNIQUES OF RHYTHMIC GYMNASTICS!

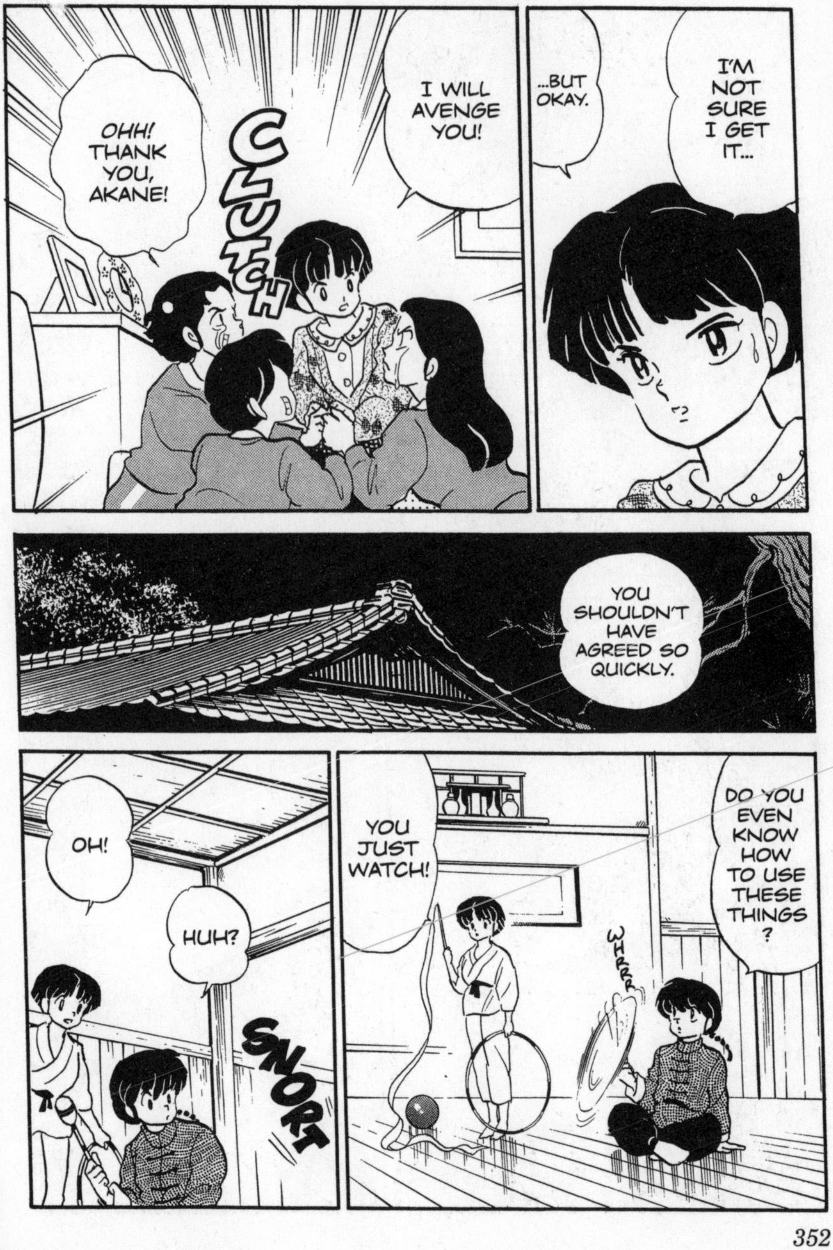
I'M NOT SURE I GET IT...
...BUT OKAY.
I WILL AVENGE YOU!
CLUTCH
OHH! THANK YOU, AKANE!
YOU SHOULDN'T HAVE AGREED SO QUICKLY.
DO YOU EVEN KNOW HOW TO USE THESE THINGS?
WHRRR
YOU JUST WATCH!
OH!
HUH?
SNORT

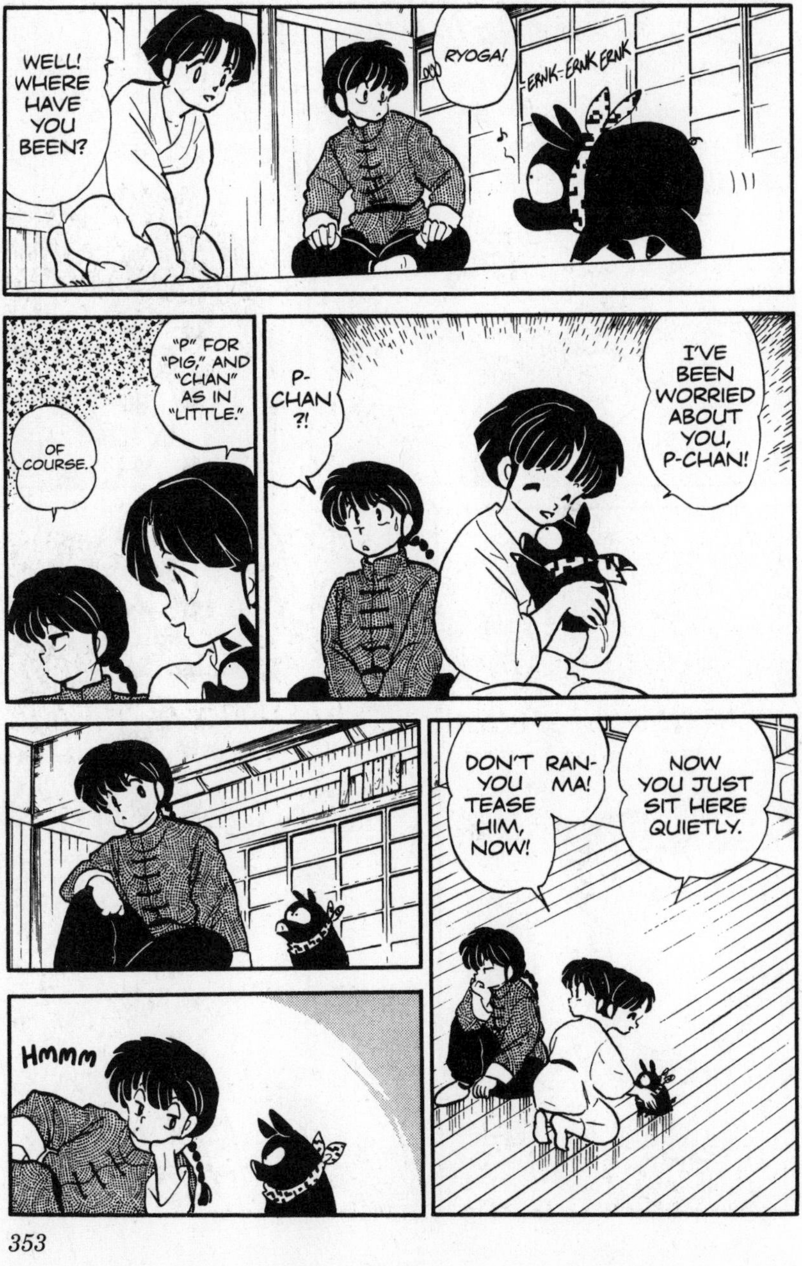
RYOGA!
ERNK-ERNK ERNK
WELL! WHERE HAVE YOU BEEN?
I'VE BEEN WORRIED ABOUT YOU, P-CHAN!
P-CHAN?!
"P" FOR "PIG," AND "CHAN" AS IN "LITTLE."
OF COURSE.
NOW YOU JUST SIT HERE QUIETLY.
RANMA! DON'T YOU TEASE HIM, NOW!
HMMM

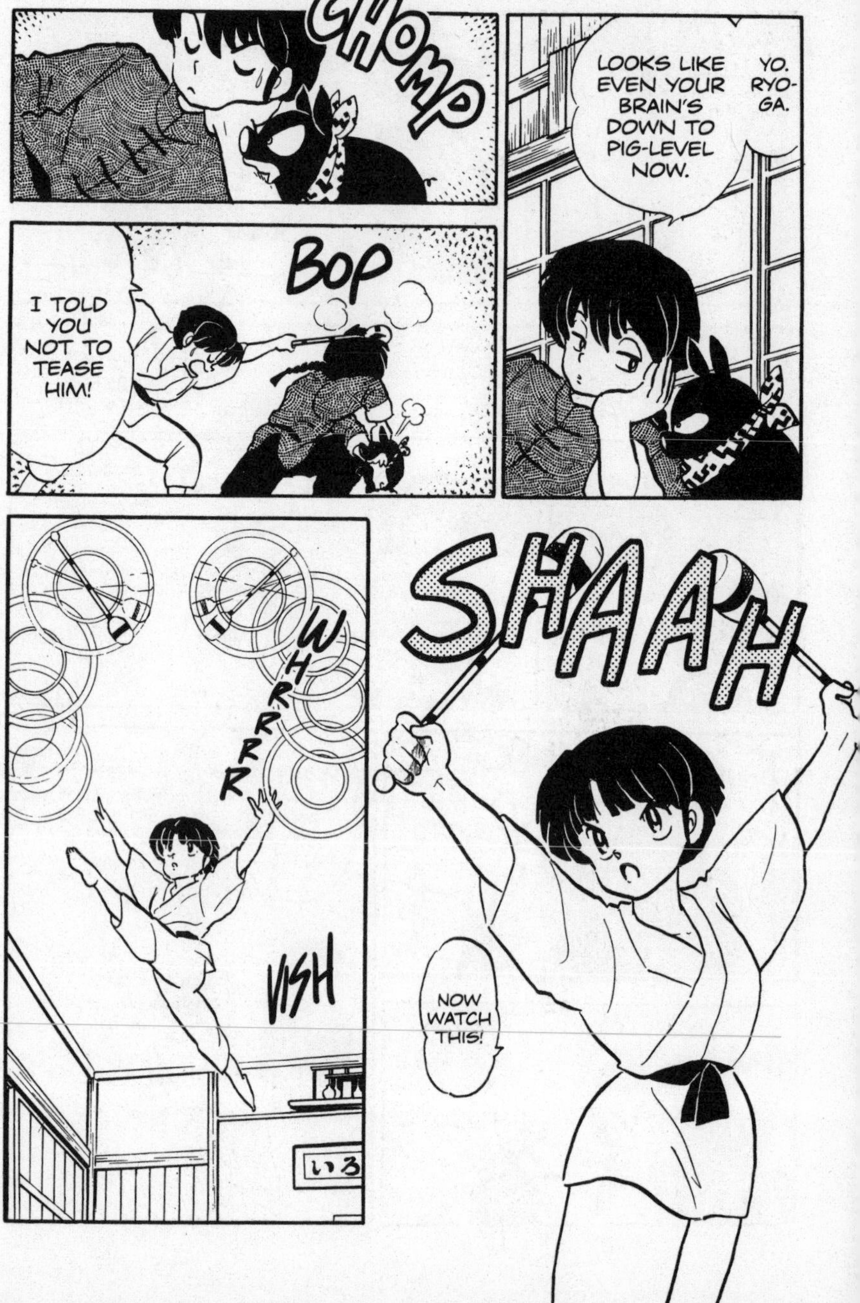
YO. RYOGA.
LOOKS LIKE EVEN YOUR BRAIN'S DOWN TO PIG-LEVEL NOW.
CHOMP
BOP
I TOLD YOU NOT TO TEASE HIM!
SHAAAH
NOW WATCH THIS!
WHRRRRR
VISH
いろ

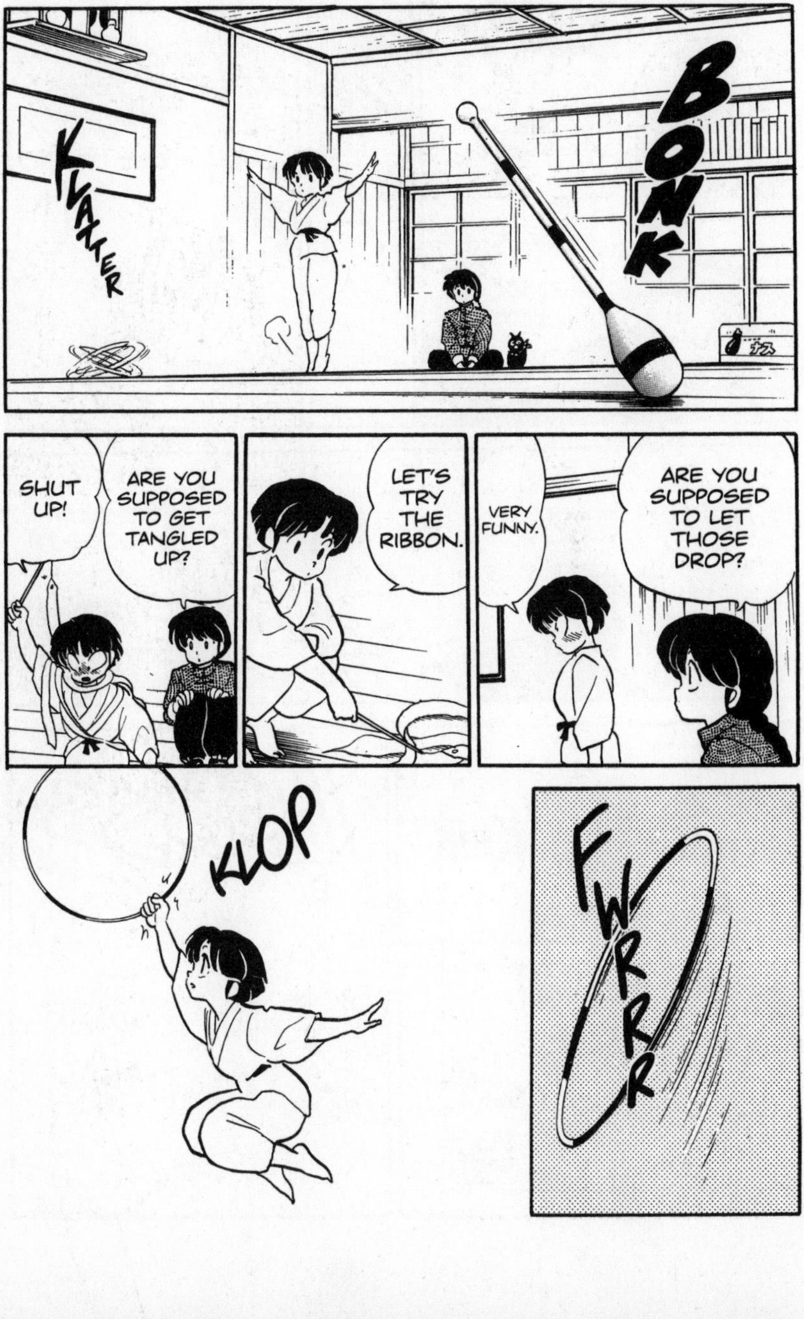
BONK
KLATTER
ARE YOU SUPPOSED TO LET THOSE DROP?
VERY FUNNY.
LET'S TRY THE RIBBON.
ARE YOU SUPPOSED TO GET TANGLED UP?
SHUT UP!
FWRRRR
KLOP

FLIP
KRAK
ARE YOU SUPPOSED TO BREAK THE HOOP?
THAT DOES IT!
STOMP STOMP
AREN'T YOU SUPPOSED TO HAVE...
...JUST A LITTLE BIT OF GRACE?
HSSSS
AAH!
KLIK
ERNK ERNK ERNK

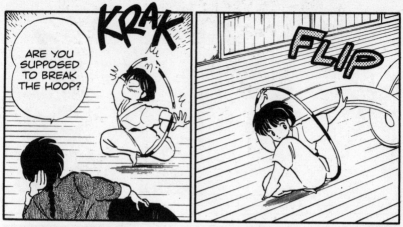

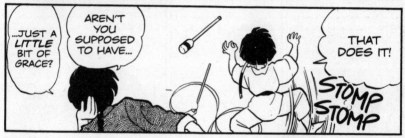

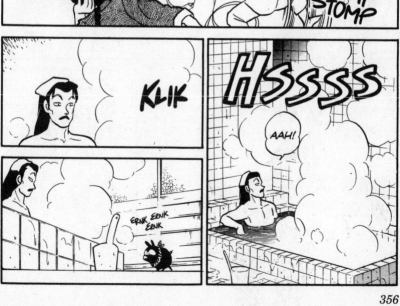

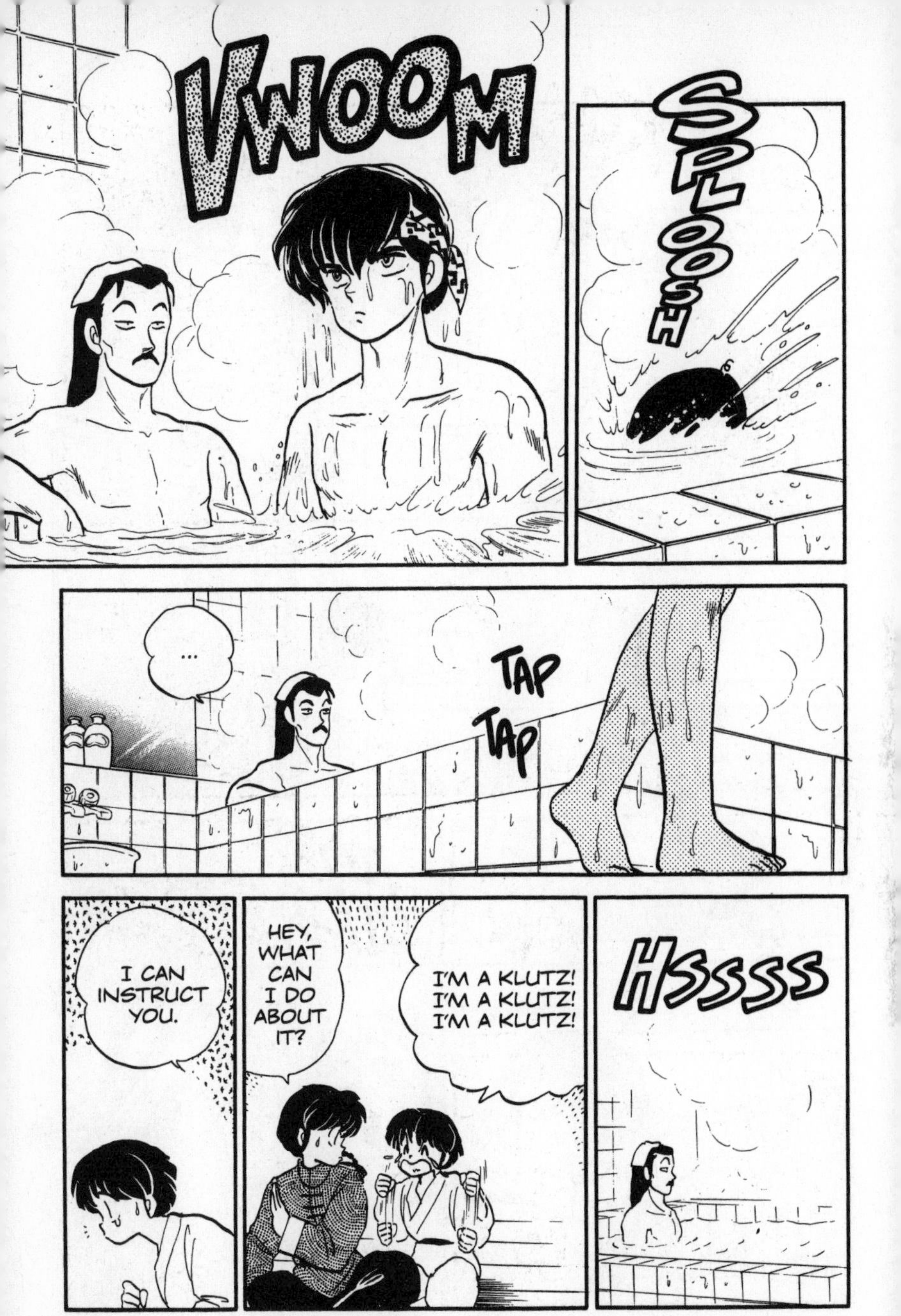
SPLOOSH
VWOOM
...
TAP TAP
HSSSS
I'M A KLUTZ! I'M A KLUTZ! I'M A KLUTZ!
HEY, WHAT CAN I DO ABOUT IT?
I CAN INSTRUCT YOU.

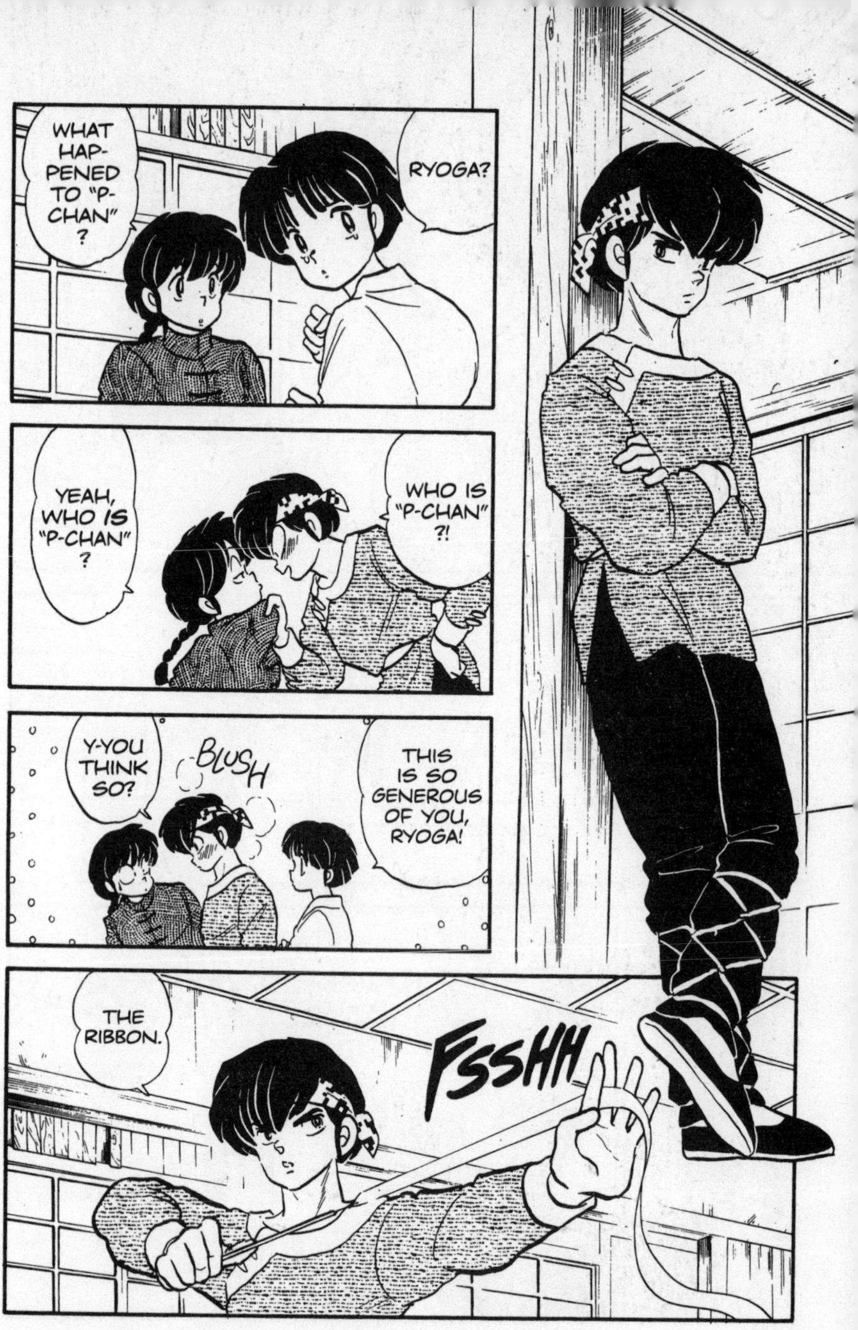
RYOGA?
WHAT HAP-PENED TO "P-CHAN"?
WHO IS "P-CHAN"?!
YEAH, WHO *IS* "P-CHAN"?
THIS IS SO GENEROUS OF YOU, RYOGA!
BLUSH
Y-YOU THINK SO?
FSSHH
THE RIBBON.

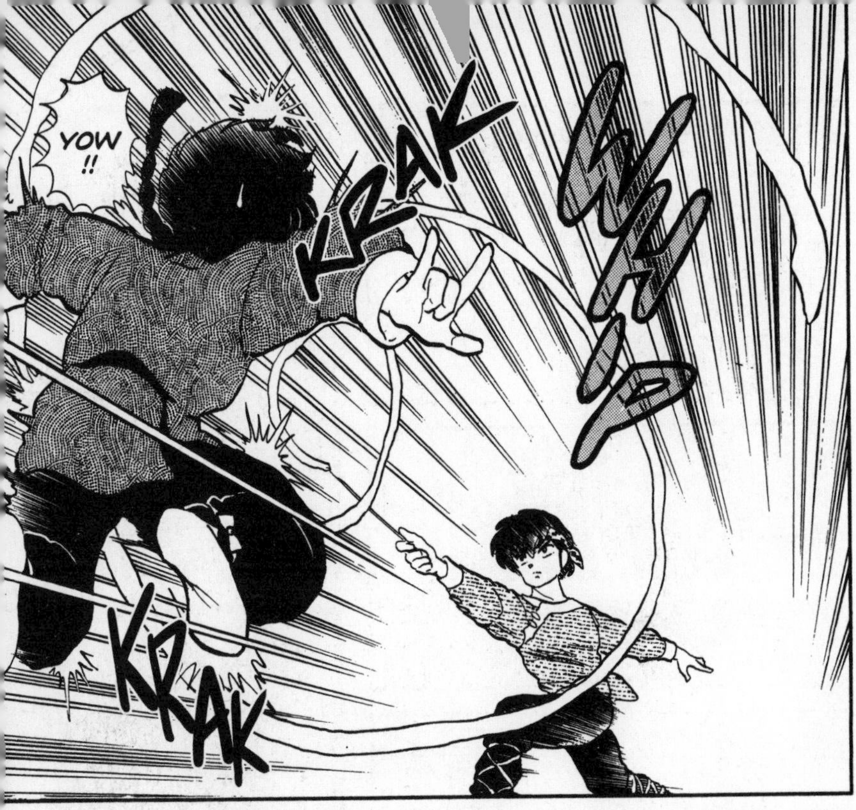
WHIP
KRAK
YOW!!
KRAK

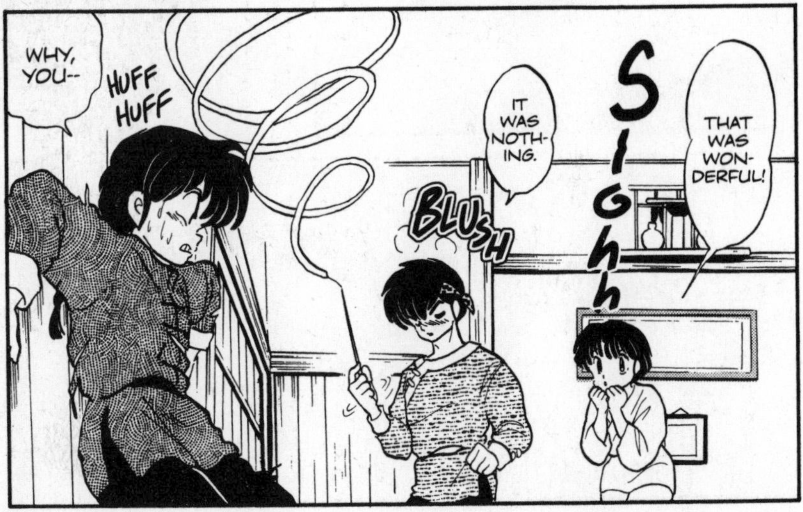
THAT WAS WONDERFUL!
SIGhh
IT WAS NOTHING.
BLUSH
HUFF HUFF
WHY, YOU--

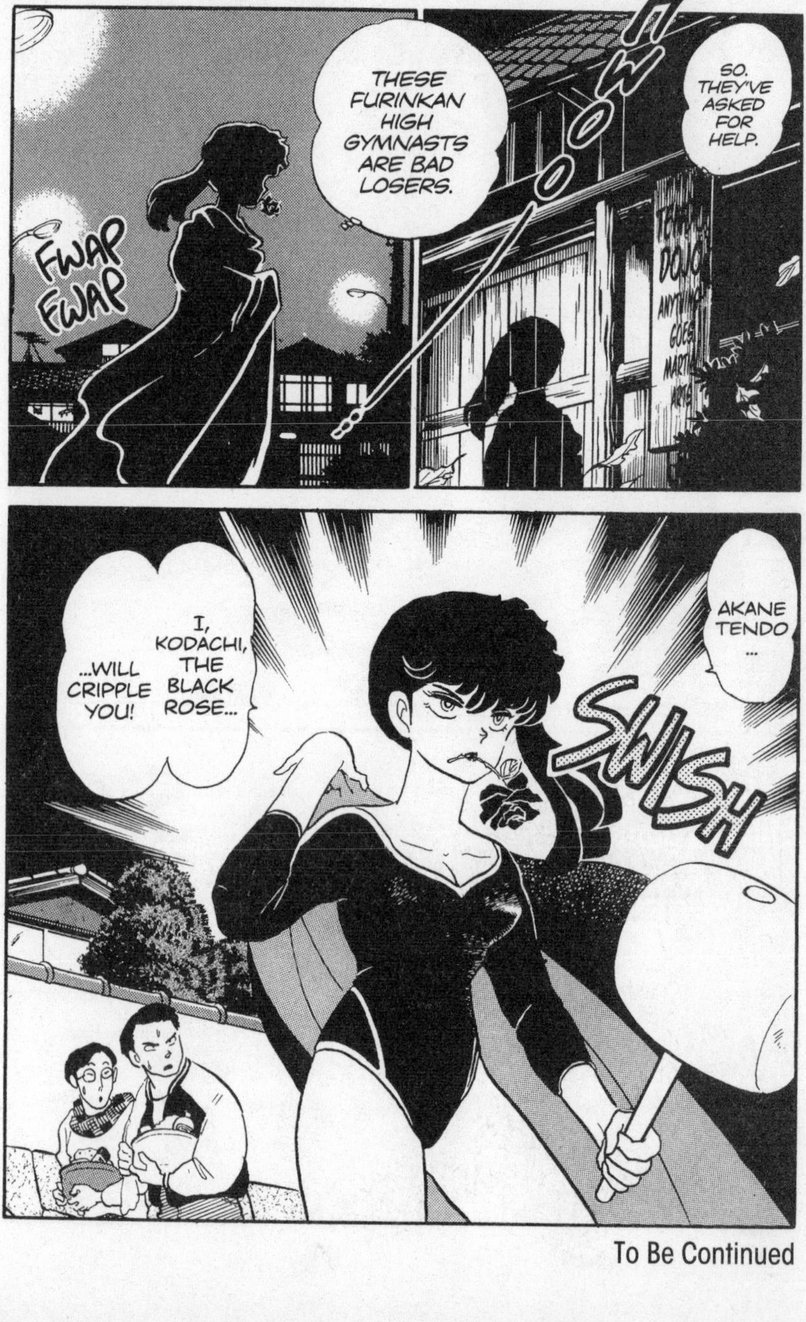
SO. THEY'VE ASKED FOR HELP.
THESE FURINKAN HIGH GYMNASTS ARE BAD LOSERS.
FWAP FWAP
AKANE TENDO ...
SWISH
I, KODACHI, THE BLACK ROSE...
...WILL CRIPPLE YOU!

To Be Continued

# Rumiko Takahashi

The spotlight on Rumiko Takahashi's career began in 1978 when she won an honorable mention in Shogakukan's annual New Comic Artist Contest for *Those Selfish Aliens*. Later that same year, her boy-meets-alien comedy series, *Urusei Yatsura*, was serialized in *Weekly Shonen Sunday*. This phenomenally successful manga series was adapted into anime format and spawned a TV series and half a dozen theatrical-release movies, all incredibly popular in their own right. Takahashi followed up the success of her debut series with one blockbuster hit after another—*Maison Ikkoku* ran from 1980 to 1987, *Ranma ½* from 1987 to 1996, and *Inuyasha* from 1996 to 2008. Other notable works include *Mermaid Saga*, *Rumic Theater*, and *One-Pound Gospel*.

Takahashi won the prestigious Shogakukan Manga Award twice in her career, once for *Urusei Yatsura* in 1981 and the second time for *Inuyasha* in 2002. A majority of the Takahashi canon has been adapted into other media such as anime, live-action TV series, and film. Takahashi's manga, as well as the other formats her work has been adapted into, have continued to delight generations of fans around the world. Distinguished by her wonderfully endearing characters, Takahashi's work adeptly incorporates a wide variety of elements such as comedy, romance, fantasy, and martial arts. While her series are difficult to pin down into one simple genre, the signature style she has created has come to be known as the "Rumic World." Rumiko Takahashi is an artist who truly represents the very best from the world of manga.

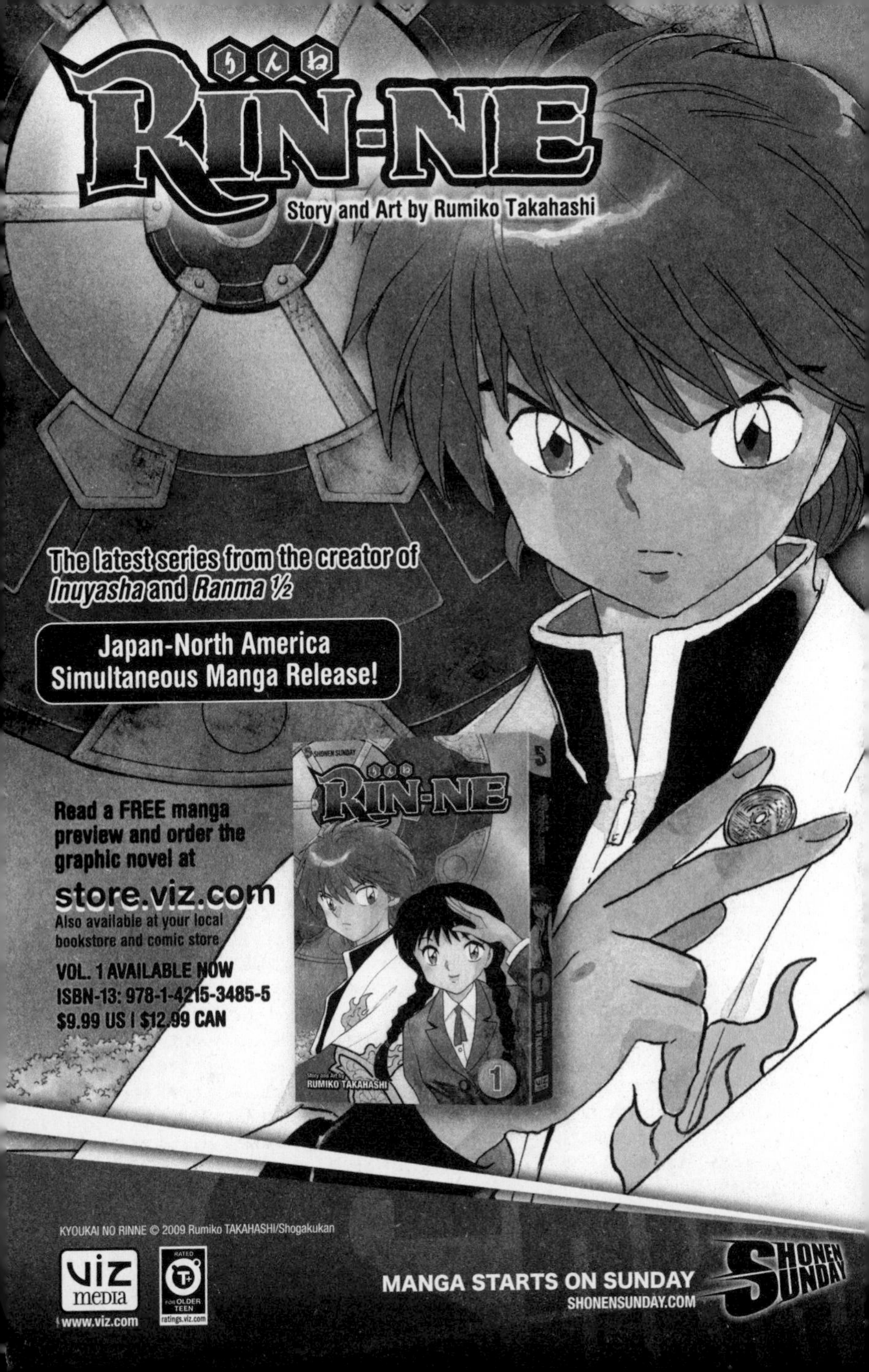